Staying Off the Beaten Track was founded 17 years ago by Elizabeth Gundrey. As it grew in size and coverage – the first edition contained only about a hundred entries, this one about 600 – Elizabeth's brother, Walter Gundrey, became increasingly involved and is now taking the major part in running the book. Elizabeth remains actively involved as a consultant.

Staying Off the Beaten Track is regularly the best-seller among Britain's b & b guides. It is a book for all seasons.

VOUCHERS WORTH £18

(by courtesy of the houses concerned)

OFFER OF NEXT EDITION

Using an out-of-date edition can lead to costly disappointments. A new edition appears every November, updated, with fresh entries added, some deleted and all revised, and with vouchers worth £18 valid for the next year. Make sure you are not using an out-of-date edition by sending a stamped self-addressed envelope to Explore Britain, Alston, Cumbria, CA9 3SL, for an order form on which you can apply for the 1999 edition even before it reaches the shops. No need for a letter: just put SOTBT 1999 on top left corner of the envelope you send.

Complaints about matters which could not have been settled on the spot will be forwarded to proprietors for comment. Please enclose a stamped addressed envelope if you want the authors to acknowledge receipt of your complaint.

STAYING OFF THE BEATEN TRACK

IN ENGLAND & WALES 1998

ELIZABETH GUNDREY
and WALTER GUNDREY

*A personal selection of moderately priced
guest-houses, small hotels, farms and country houses*

17th EDITION
1998

Edited by Jacqueline Krendel

ARROW

TO ANDREW, WITH LOVE

Published by Arrow Books Limited in 1997

1   3   5   7   9   10   8   6   4   2

First published in Great Britain 1982   Eleventh edition 1991
by Hamlyn Paperbacks   Twelfth edition 1992
Arrow edition (Sixth edition) first published 1986   Thirteenth edition 1993
Seventh edition 1987   Fourteenth edition 1994
Eighth edition 1988   Fifteenth edition 1995
Ninth edition 1989   Sixteenth edition 1996
Tenth edition 1990   Seventeenth edition 1997

Copyright © 1982, 1983, 1984, 1985, 1986, 1987, 1988, 1989, 1990, 1991, 1992, 1993, 1994,
1995, 1996, 1997 by Elizabeth Gundrey

Elizabeth Gundrey has asserted her right to be identified as the author of this work in
accordance with the Copyright, Designs and Patents Act, 1988

Arrow Books Limited
20 Vauxhall Bridge Road, London, SW1V 2SA

Random House Australia (Pty) Limited
20 Alfred Street, Milsons Point, Sydney,
New South Wales 2061, Australia

Random House New Zealand Limited
18 Poland Road, Glenfield
Auckland 10, New Zealand

Random House South Africa (Pty) Limited
Endulini, 5a Jubilee Road, Parktown 2193, South Africa

Random House UK Limited Reg. No. 954009

Designed by Bob Vickers
Maps by David Perrott

Printed and bound in Great Britain by
The Guernsey Press Co. Limited, Guernsey, C.I.

Front cover picture: **Bettman's Oast**, Kent
Back cover pictures: **Cobblers Cottage**, Cornwall (left);
Milton Farm, Wiltshire (right)

A CIP catalogue record for this book is available from the British Library

ISBN 0-09-979641-4

The author and publishers would like to thank all those owners who allowed us to use
their drawings. Additional line drawings by Rhona Garvin, Alison Brown, Leslie Dean and others.

Although every care has been taken to ensure that all the information in this book is
correct and up to date, neither the author nor the publishers can accept responsibility
for details which may have changed since the book went to press.

Acknowledgments

We acknowledge with much appreciation the assistance of the rest of the
SOTBT team (Jan Bowmer, Jennifer Christie, Andrew Cockburn, Pat
Gundrey, Jonathan May, Kate McCarney and Nancy Webber) as well as
of all the proprietors of houses.

Elizabeth and Walter Gundrey

CONTENTS

INTRODUCTION

18 FEET OF SHELVES . . .

. . . are occupied by brochures of houses, many recommended to us by readers (thank you all). There the brochures stay until we need to top up a particular area, when we have a full inspection done of any likely houses.

We do not, unlike some guides, publicize any house on the basis of an unknown correspondent's say-so. We reject houses, however highly commended, when not up to our own criteria. (Recently one place was warmly praised by – apparently – two correspondents: both, we spotted, had remarkably similar handwriting to the proprietor's.)

A guide based on readers' letters would be easier and cheaper to produce (think of the savings in time and expense of travelling – nationwide – plus cost of food and accommodation, even before inspectors are paid). That way is not ours.

Inspections, and reinspections, may be either thorough or perfunctory. Among other guides are a few whose inspections are rigorous and frequent (the AA and Tourist Boards particularly). Their criteria, however, differ from ours.

We do not give merit marks for hair-dryers, radio-alarms and direct-dial phones in bedrooms; rating more highly a discriminating taste in such things as furnishings, pictures and books ('ambience') and, above all, a caring host.

No guide is comprehensive and this is not the biggest. The houses in it are, however, our choice and ours alone: in many books the houses (even when well inspected) are self-selected because they are limited to those willing to pay to get in. Commonly, a proprietor may have to pay a substantial sum merely to be inspected, another amount just to be registered or listed; and hundreds of pounds for even a quarter-page advertisement – with no certainty of recovering this outlay from resultant trade. As a consequence, proprietors of some of the smallest, and best, houses do not choose to go in. But you *will* find a selection of these in our pages, for no one has to pay to get into *Staying Off the Beaten Track*.

Instead, we invite a voluntary contribution from proprietors, but only after the year's results from inclusion are apparent to them; and this the majority are glad to send. This unconventional approach seems to make everyone happy: readers (the book, now in its 17th year, regularly tops its category in the bestseller lists), proprietors, our team, and the charities to which any surplus goes after all fees and expenses have been paid. The system works entirely on a basis of trust.

The pages of the book speak for themselves. The subjective judgment of each place is expressed in a written style intended to bring out its character clearly so that the reader can with confidence say 'This one is for me!' (or not, as the case may be).

Note

Readers of past editions will see a difference in presentation this year. Houses in England are grouped in counties, which are in alphabetical sequence. Within each county, entries, which now have equal space, are in alphabetical order. In some cases, counties (or the new unitary authorities which have replaced them) have been amalgamated. If you cannot find the county in which you are interested, you need only refer to the detailed contents pages (pp.v–vi). Welsh houses are grouped regionally, also with entries in alphabetical order within each region. The object of these changes was to make the book more 'user-friendly' – we hope you find it so.

HOW TO HAVE A GOOD TIME

As the readership of this book grows so does the diversity of readers' tastes. The detailed descriptions are meant to help each one pick out the places that suit him or her best; but there are still readers who write to complain about bar or carpark noise at inns (so why pick an inn rather than a house without a bar?), and the presence of dogs (why go to a house with the code letter **D**, meaning dogs accepted, or to a farm where dogs are almost certainly kept?). Light sleepers should avoid rooms overlooking, for instance, a market square: not all houses in this book are rural.

Some people have very particular requirements; and it is up to them to discuss these when telephoning to book. Many hosts in this book are more flexible than big hotels, and all are eager to help if they can. The sort of things to bear in mind are: a bad back, needing a very *firm mattress*; special *dietary* requirements, and *allergies* to feather pillows or animals; a strong preference for *separate tables* rather than a shared dining-table – or vice versa; *fewer courses* than on the fixed menu; *twin beds* rather than double beds – or vice versa; freedom to *smoke* – or freedom from it; a particular wish for *electric blanket, hot water-bottle,* etc. or a dislike of *duvets;* the need to arrive, depart or eat at *extra-early* or *extra-late* hours; an intention to pay by *credit card* (this should not be taken for granted, particularly at small guest-houses).

The code letters that appear after the name of each house will help you identify houses suitable for children, dogs, people with mobility problems, users of public transport, etc.: for full explanation, see inside front cover. Please also use the 'how to book' checklist on page ix when telephoning.

It's best to stay at least 2–3 days: you cannot possibly appreciate an area if you only stay overnight (prices per night are often less, too, if you stay on). The vouchers on page ii are usable for 3-night stays. At some houses, 1-night bookings may be refused.

When to go? Seaside resorts or other places suitable for children will be at their busiest (and dearest) in July–August and during half-term holidays (especially, in late May, which is also a bank holiday period). Houses which do *not* take children tend to have vacancies in July and August – even in the popular Cotswolds, for instance. Other peak periods are, of course, Easter, Christmas, New Year and the bank holiday in late August. There are local peaks, too (the Gold Cup races at Cheltenham or the regatta at Henley, for instance, are apt to fill hotels for miles around), and local troughs (Brighton, a conference centre, is least busy in high summer). In holiday areas, travel on any day other than a summer Saturday if you can. Make travel reservations well in advance.

One final tip on ensuring that you get all that you hope for: at the end of each season, throw away this year's copy of the book and get next year's edition before it sells out in the bookshops later in the year (you can soon recoup its cost by using the fresh set of accommodation vouchers it contains). Here's why this is so important. A reader wrote as follows: 'The house was dirty; room smelt damp; toilet-seat wobbly and stained; under-pillows had no cases; grubby carpets . . . (etc.)'. The house had changed hands years ago, and been dropped from this book as a consequence; but the reader was using an out-of-date edition. Prices change, so do telephone numbers and much else. Change of owner or inflated prices are the two most common reasons why houses are dropped; a third is that we find somewhere better – or of better value – nearby.

Houses which accept the discount vouchers on page ii are marked with a
V symbol next to the relevant entries.

TELEPHONING TO BOOK: A CHECKLIST

Book well ahead: many of these houses have few rooms. Further, at some houses, rooms (even if similarly priced) vary in size or amenities: early applicants get the cheapest and/or best ones. Mention that you are a reader of this book: sometimes there are discounts on offer exclusively for readers. Telephoning is preferable to writing to enquire about vacancies, and, in many cases, the best time is early evening.

1. Ask for the owner by the *name* given in this edition. (If there has been a change, standards and prices may differ.)
2. Specify *your precise needs* (such as en suite bathroom, if available), see previous page. (Do not turn up with children, dogs or disabilities if you have not checked that these are accepted or provided for.) Elderly people may wish to ensure that their room is not above the first floor.
3. Check *prices* – these, too, can change (particularly after spring). Ask whether there are any bargain breaks. Are credit cards accepted?
4. Ask what *deposit* to send (or quote a credit card number). Overseas visitors may be asked to pay up to 50 per cent.
5. State your intended *time of arrival,* what meals are wanted and at what times. (If you should then be late, telephone a warning – otherwise your room may be let to someone else. It is inconsiderate to arrive late for home-cooked meals prepared especially for you.) Most proprietors expect visitors to arrive about 5pm. In country lanes, finding your way after dark can be difficult.
6. Ask for precise instructions for *locating the house:* many are remote. Better still, ask for a brochure with map to be posted to you. Check where to park.
7. Few proprietors expect visitors to stay out of the house in the daytime; but if you want to stay in, check this when booking.

At houses where dinner is not served, a light supper can often be obtained (if ordered in advance), ranging from sandwiches to family 'pot luck'. (Packed lunches too.)

PRICES

This book came into being to provide a guide to good accommodation at prices suited to people of moderate means. That remains its policy.

In the current edition are houses at which it is possible to stay, at the time of publication, for as little as £13–£20 (London excepted) for b & b – that is, per person sharing a double room. However, for the best rooms in the house, or later in the year, you may well be asked for more. **Check when booking.** High-season prices start at different times. For instance, in the Isle of Wight few proprietors raise prices until summer (if then), while in the Lake District and Yorkshire Dales many put them up in spring.

The prices are as quoted to us when the book was in preparation during 1997. But sometimes unexpected costs force proprietors to increase their prices subsequently: becoming liable for VAT or business rates, for instance.

Inclusive terms for dinner, bed-and-breakfast (particularly for a week) can be much lower than those quoted here for these items taken separately. Most houses in this book have bargain breaks or other discounts on offer, some exclusive to readers. A 'bargain break' is usually a 2- or 3-day booking including dinners, at a discount; usually at low season only.

YOU AND THE LAW

Once your booking has been confirmed – orally or in writing – a contract exists between you and the proprietor. He is legally bound to provide accommodation as booked; and you are legally bound to pay for this accommodation. If unable to take up the booking – even because of sickness – you still remain liable for a very substantial proportion of the charges (in addition to losing your deposit).

If you have to cancel, let the proprietor know as soon as possible; then he may be able to re-let the accommodation (in which case you would be liable to pay only a re-letting cost or forfeit your deposit). Phone if you are going to arrive late.

(**A note to overseas readers.** It may be an acceptable practice elsewhere to make bookings at several houses for the same date, choosing only later which one to patronize; but this way of doing things is not the British practice and you are legally liable to compensate any proprietors whom you let down in this way.)

THANK YOU . . . to those who send details of their own finds, for possible future inclusion in the book. Do not be disappointed if your candidate does not appear in the very next edition. We never publish recommendations from unknown members of the public without verification, and it takes time to get round each part of England and Wales in turn. Please, however, do not send details of houses already featured in many other guides, nor any that are more expensive than those in this book (see page ix).

COMPLAINTS: If anything was not of reasonable standard (e.g. chilly bedroom or badly cooked food) you are entitled to claim a reduction on your bill, but *only if* you had previously told the proprietor and given him or her a chance to put matters right. In a recent court case involving a restaurant meal, it was ruled that, because a customer had not made a specific complaint at the time, he had no right subsequently to withhold payment (he had cancelled his cheque). The moral is obvious: if dissatisfied, you are expected to say so at once and not later. We regularly inspect; and also will forward complaints to proprietors for their comments. Write to: Walter Gundrey (SOTBT), % Arrow Books, 20 Vauxhall Bridge Road, London SW1V 2SA. Please enclose a stamped addressed envelope if you want him to acknowledge receipt of your complaint.

Readers' comments quoted in the book are from letters sent to us: they are not supplied via the proprietors.

COUNTY DIRECTORY OF
HOUSES AND HOTELS IN

ENGLAND

Prices are per person sharing a double room, at the beginning of the year. You may be quoted more later or for single occupancy.

Prices and other facts quoted at the head of each entry are as supplied by the proprietors.

Paradise House, Bath & North-East Somerset (see page 236)

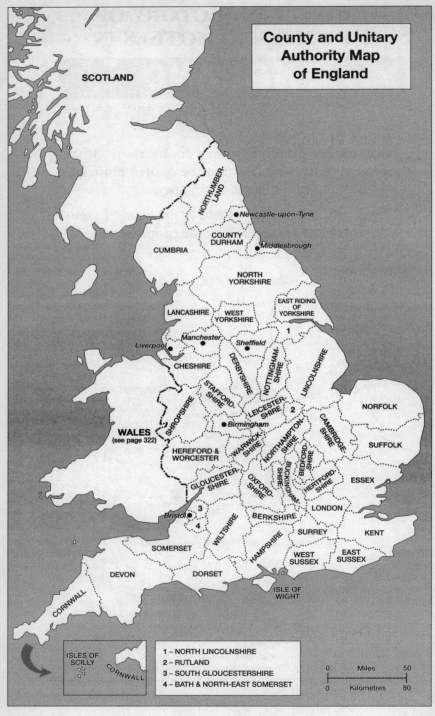

County and Unitary Authority Map of England

SCOTLAND

NORTHUMBERLAND

Newcastle-upon-Tyne

CUMBRIA

COUNTY DURHAM

Middlesbrough

NORTH YORKSHIRE

EAST RIDING OF YORKSHIRE

LANCASHIRE

WEST YORKSHIRE

Liverpool

Manchester

Sheffield

1

CHESHIRE

DERBYSHIRE

NOTTINGHAMSHIRE

LINCOLNSHIRE

STAFFORDSHIRE

LEICESTERSHIRE

2

NORFOLK

SHROPSHIRE

WALES
(see page 322)

Birmingham

WARWICKSHIRE

NORTHAMPTONSHIRE

CAMBRIDGESHIRE

SUFFOLK

HEREFORD & WORCESTER

BEDFORDSHIRE

BUCKINGHAMSHIRE

HERTFORDSHIRE

ESSEX

GLOUCESTERSHIRE

OXFORDSHIRE

LONDON

3

Bristol

BERKSHIRE

SURREY

KENT

4

WILTSHIRE

HAMPSHIRE

WEST SUSSEX

EAST SUSSEX

SOMERSET

DORSET

ISLE OF WIGHT

DEVON

CORNWALL

ISLES OF SCILLY

CORNWALL

1 – NORTH LINCOLNSHIRE
2 – RUTLAND
3 – SOUTH GLOUCESTERSHIRE
4 – BATH & NORTH-EAST SOMERSET

| 0 | Miles | 50 |
| 0 | Kilometres | 80 |

BEDFORDSHIRE

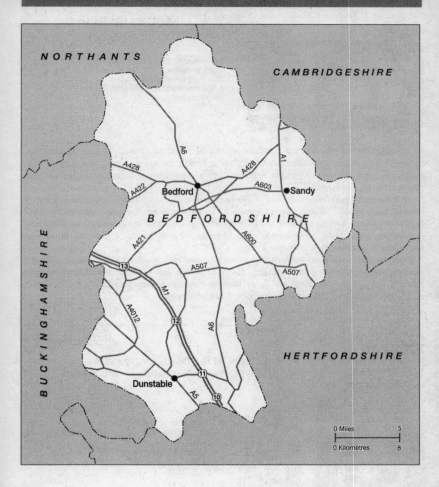

Addresses shown are to enable you to locate a house on a map. They are not necessarily complete postal addresses (though the essential post-code is included), and detailed directions for finding a house should be obtained from the owner.

CHURCH FARM

CDPTSX

High Street, Roxton, Bedfordshire, MR44 3EB   Tel: 01234 870234
(Fax: 01234 871574)
North-east of Bedford. Nearest main road: A1 from Sandy to St Neots.

2 Bedrooms. £19–£21. No smoking.
Light suppers if ordered. Vegetarian or other special diets if ordered. No smoking.
1 Sitting-room. With open fire, TV. No smoking.
Large garden

It is a surprise to find such a peaceful village (a thatched church as well as thatched cottages) only a mile from the busy Great North Road (the A1) and in it this house – part 17th- and part 18th-century. One bedroom has a royal coat-of-arms carved in the wall, dating from Stuart times.

A beautiful breakfast-room has a Chippendale-style table and a sideboard with its original brass rails. Bedrooms are in a guest wing; all rooms are furnished with an informal mixture of family antiques. There is a pleasant sitting-room with a log fire and oil paintings. For dinner, Janet Must recommends restaurants in either St Neots or Bedford, but guests are welcome to bring their own snack suppers in.

Visitors who stay here are often surprised to discover Bedfordshire's little-publicized charms, particularly its pretty villages, many of which are sited on wandering streams. Popular outings include Bedford (John Bunyan museum), Sandy (RSPB's headquarters and bird reserve) and Huntingdon (Cromwell associations).

V

FIRS FARM

CD

Stagsden West End, Bedfordshire, MK43 8TB   Tel/Fax: 01234 822344
West of Bedford. Nearest main road: A422 from Milton Keynes towards Bedford (and M1, junction 14).

3 Bedrooms. £16–£20 (less for 3 nights or more). Bargain breaks. One has own shower/toilet. No smoking.
Light suppers if ordered. No smoking.
1 Sitting-room. With open fire, TV.
Large garden

Until 1922, this quiet arable farm and all of Stagsden was Crown property, which is why the village inn (good pub food) is called the Royal George. The Hutcheons have farmed here for generations. In autumn, the firs contrast with chestnuts turning golden, the crimson of Virginia creeper with the ochre walls of the old house itself.

There's a homely sitting-room with log fire; and Pam's bedrooms are roomy as well as pretty – two overlook the swimming-pool and lawn (where chickens roam), one the farm buildings. The stone-walled dinning-room has rural bygones.

Southward you can motor the 35-mile 'Mid-Beds Scenic Route' which goes through some of the county's most scenic moorlands and heaths, over streams and hills, and with a score of interesting sights at which to stop – such as Woburn Abbey and safari park. Picturesque villages like Aspley Guise and Millbrook abound, so do mediaeval inns. It is worth getting the leaflet that details this route (as well as others about walks, numerous nature reserves, etc.) from any Tourist Information Centre in the area.

V

GOWER COTTAGE

C M S

5 Brightwell Avenue, Totternhoe, Bedfordshire, LU6 1QT Tel: 01582 601287
West of Dunstable. Nearest main road: A5 from Dunstable to Milton Keynes (and M1, junction 11).

3 Bedrooms. £18–£20. Bargain breaks. TV (in two). No smoking.
Light suppers if ordered. Vegetarian or other special diets if ordered.
1 Sitting-room. With TV. No smoking.
Small garden

At the foot of Dunstable Downs, on the borders of three counties, is the village of Totternhoe and Gower Cottage, well built in the 1920s in vernacular style. Views are of Ivinghoe Beacon in one direction, Adele Mardell's exceptionally pretty garden in the other. Everything is pristine inside, and Adele is a most kindly hostess. There is one ground-floor bedroom.

On Totternhoe Knolls wild orchids grow. Nearby Doolittle Mill is almost unique – wind and water combined. There are numerous old inns, you can have a balloon ride, pop into north London to shop at Ikea or the excellent Brent Cross shopping centre, go to old Ampthill for its antique shops. Scenic walks, Whipsnade drive-through zoo, Dunstable Downs (hang-gliding and kite-flyers), canal boats, the natural history museum at Tring, and historic Dunstable Priory are other attractions of this area.

V

---

1 THE GRANGE

C(5) D S X

Sunderland Hill, Ravensden, Bedfordshire, MK44 2SH Tel: 01234 771771
North of Bedford. Nearest main road: A428 from Bedford towards St Neots (and M1, junction 14).

rear view

3 Bedrooms. £18 (less for 4 nights or more). Some have all of the following: own bath/shower/toilet; TV. No smoking.
Dinner. £15 for 3 courses, sherry and coffee, from 6pm. Vegetarian or other special diets if ordered. No smoking. **Light suppers** if ordered.
1 Sitting-room. With stove, TV. No smoking.
Large garden

This large manor house has been divided into three dwellings, of which No. 1 is the handsome home of Patricia Roberts, with views downhill of terraced lawns and great cedars. Patricia has furnished the rooms in keeping with the architectural style, with chandeliers in each room. Good paintings (some by her daughter) hang on silky coral walls; silver, big velvet armchairs and Chippendale furniture are in one room; another has damask curtains and a Victorian sofa. Even the bathrooms are carpeted and have flowery wallpaper.

Dinner is very attractively presented. Salmon and pheasant often appear on the menu but guests can have whatever they like if it is ordered in advance. (Sunday lunch also available.)

Readers' comments: Nothing too much trouble. Food delicious. Charming hostess. Wished we could have stayed longer. Dinners imaginatively prepared. Elegantly furnished, and every comfort. Kind welcome, we felt at home. Excellent.

V

HIGHFIELD FARM

C D M

Sandy, Bedfordshire, SG19 2AQ   Tel: 01767 682332 (Fax: 01767 692503)
North of Sandy. Off the A1 from Biggleswade to Peterborough.

6 Bedrooms. £19–£22.50 (less for 7 nights or more). All have some or all of the following: own bath/shower/toilet; TV. No smoking.
Light suppers (by arrangement).
1 Sitting-room. With open fire, TV. No smoking.
Garden

Set well back from the A1, Highfield Farm is surrounded by fields of peas or wheat. Two single cottages a century ago, the house is now enlarged and painted sparkling white outside, with a trim lawn and colourful flowerbeds. The interior is equally immaculate, the six bedrooms (two on the ground floor in former stables) having such features as bedheads matching the yew furniture hand-made locally. The L-shaped sitting-room has soft colours and comfortable armchairs. Every room is elegantly furnished by Margaret Codd.

This is an area with many NT properties: Cardinal Wolsey's imposing dovecote and stables at Willington, the palatial mansions (and gardens) of Ascott and Waddesdon, Bernard Shaw's house, Pitstone windmill, even a NT inn (the mediaeval King's Head at Aylesbury). There are Bunyan sights in and around Bedford (and in the town is a notable art gallery, the delightful Cecil Higgins Museum by the swan-frequented river). You can walk the Greensand Ridge path or wander in Maulden Wood, and look at Shuttleworth's historic aircraft collection or the 140 kinds of bird in the RSPB's headquarters reserve.

V

ORCHARD COTTAGE

C M PT S

1, High Street, Wrestlingworth, Bedfordshire, SG19 2EW   Tel: 01767 631355
East of Bedford. Nearest main road: A1 from Baldock to Biggleswade.

3 Bedrooms. £18–£19. No smoking.
1 Sitting-room. With open fire, TV. No smoking.
Large garden

A talented lady lives at thatched Orchard Cottage, once the village bakery and now a tea-room. Joan Strong makes delicate bobbin-lace – an old craft for which the area was once famous – while some of the furniture in the house was made by her husband, Owen. The pleasant rooms have views of fields, or of the garden enclosed by high cupressus hedges. From the large sitting-room (with log fire) glass doors open onto a paved terrace. For dinner, sample food at the many inns in this area.

Much Bedfordshire scenery is lovely (some of it in the care of the National Trust). Wide open spaces alternate with wooded hills, there are thatched cottages, old mills and winding streams – many of them tributaries of the very beautiful Great Ouse. Stately homes include Luton Hoo and Hinwick; gardens – Wrest Park and Old Warden's Swiss Garden. There are half-a-dozen bird or wildlife centres.

Readers' comments: Very good value; spotless and comfortable.

BERKSHIRE

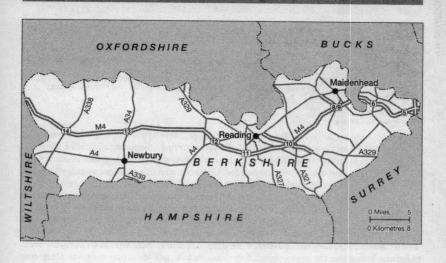

APPLYING FOR INCLUSION IN SOTBT   Many proprietors ask for their houses to be included in this book, and – although few can be accepted – such applications are welcomed, particularly from areas not already well covered; *provided that* the b & b price is within the book's limits (see page ix). Ideally, either dinner or light snacks should be available in the evening. There is no charge for an entry but, compiling the book being expensive, nearly all proprietors make a contribution at the end of each year (no bills are issued). Every house has to be visited first and it may be some time before this takes place. Brochures, prices, menus, etc. should be posted to: Walter Gundrey (SOTBT), c/o Arrow Books, 20 Vauxhall Bridge Road, London SW1V 2SA. No phone calls please.

BEEHIVE MANOR

C(12) **PT**

Cox Green Lane, Maidenhead, Berkshire, SL6 3ET Tel: 01628 20980
(Fax: 01628 21840)
South of Maidenhead. Nearest main road: A4 from Maidenhead to Reading (and M4, junction 8/9).

3 Bedrooms. £19–£29. Bargain breaks. All have own bath/shower/toilet. No smoking.
1 Sitting-room. With TV. No smoking.
Small garden

An exceptional mediaeval building – from the strange, carved heads at the front door to the beautiful stone roses around the fireplace of the long sitting-room, from linenfold panelling to stained-glass panels (dated 1560) of ships and coats-of-arms. Low ceilings have chamfered beams, lattice-paned windows open onto a garden where paths wind among camellias, ceanothus, wisteria and a multitude of other flowers.

More linenfold woodwork and a fireplace of carved stone are in the dining-room (where breakfasts are served at a great refectory table); while upstairs every bedroom door has a different wrought-iron latch. One has 'ropework' ceiling-beams; another, pine panelling. All have been attractively furnished. Bathrooms are marble-floored.

The Manor is run by sisters Barbara Barbour and Sue Lemin, who not only are a mine of information about the many sights in the vicinity but may also take visitors to Heathrow Airport (15 minutes away) or the railway (which runs between London and Bath).

Cox Green is very close to Windsor (with castle, and Legoland theme and amusement park for families), Eton, lovely Savill Gardens, and Runnymede (the Kennedy memorial).

CHAMBERHOUSE MILL

PT S

Thatcham, Berkshire, RG19 4NU Tel: 01635 865930
East of Newbury. Nearest main road: A4 from Newbury to Reading (and M4, junction 13).

1 Bedroom. £19.50. Has own bath/toilet; TV; views of river. No smoking.
Dinner (by arrangement). £13 for 3 courses and coffee, at 8pm. Vegetarian or other special diets if ordered. No smoking. **Light suppers** if ordered.
1 Sitting-room. With TV. No smoking.
Large garden
Closed in winter sometimes.

The huge watermill, where from at least 1086 to 1969 grain used to be ground into flour, has been skilfully converted into a number of modern houses. Betty de Wit, her husband and six cats live at no. 2, right over one of the two great wooden wheels – the sound of rushing water is always present. One crosses footbridges and a big sluice to reach their hidden garden, enclosed by box hedges. Here there is a summer-house on the riverbank from which to watch the grebes and swans.

The second-floor guest-room is neat as a ship's cabin but more spacious, with a room-divider of louvred fitments. Here and elsewhere are Betty's landscape photographs: she is a Fellow of the Royal Photographic Society. Both she and Gerry enjoy cooking the meals which they serve in their own dining-kitchen. Dinners have a Provençal influence.

Readers' comments: Felt very much at home. Cosy and comfortable. A real delight. Room was great, snug. Mrs de Wit extremely pleasant. Setting very beautiful, accommodation most comfortable.

CHERRY COURT

C(7) **PT S**

Hollybush Lane, Burghfield Common, Berkshire, RG7 3JS Tel/Fax: 01734 832404
South-west of Reading. Nearest main road: A4 from Reading to Newbury (and M4, junction 12).

3 Bedrooms. £19–£22.50. All have own bath/shower/toilet; TV. No smoking.
Dinner. £15 for 4 courses and coffee, at 7.30pm. Vegetarian or other special diets if ordered. Wine available. No smoking. **Light suppers** if ordered.
2 Sitting-rooms. With open fire, TV. No smoking.
Large garden

Typical of its county and its period (turn-of-the-century), this is a spacious, solid and dignified house. Rooms are well carpeted and furnished, mostly in pinks and greens. A log fire crackles on chilly days, and for sunny ones there is a heated swimming-pool in the grounds. A sunken garden is full of roses – when not eaten by deer. Fruit and eggs are home-produced.

Jacqueline Levey serves such meals as pâté, salmon hollandaise, and fresh fruit salad, after which one can relax in a small sun-room with a grapevine overhead.

Heathrow is a half-hour taxi ride, and you can park your car at Cherry Court while you are abroad. To the west lies picturesque Hungerford, famous for its scores of antique shops (many open even on Sundays). Nearby are the windswept heights of the Berkshire Downs where racehorses train, and you can walk along the prehistoric Ridgeway Path.

Readers' comments: Remarkably hospitable and friendly. Very pretty. Ideally located. The nicest people – exceptional. Lovely house, first rate.

MARSHGATE COTTAGE HOTEL

C D M P T X

Marsh Lane, Hungerford, Berkshire, RG17 0QN Tel: 01488 682307
(Fax: 01488 685475)
West of Newbury. Nearest main road: A338 from Hungerford to Salisbury (and M4, junction 14).

6 Bedrooms. £19–£24.25. All have own shower/toilet; TV; views of canal (most). Some no-smoking rooms.
Light suppers by arrangement.
1 Sitting-room. With open fire. No smoking. Bar.
Large garden

The marshes which give this cottage its name stretch down to the 18th-century Kennet & Avon Canal, a haven for birds and wildflowers. Marshgate is even older than the canal, its thatched roof descending almost to ground level; but it is an extension which provides guest-rooms, in keeping with the house's original character. Most rooms overlook the marshes.

Mike Walker, once a journalist, did much of the conversion himself, re-using old handmade bricks and laying floors of beautiful chestnut boards. The breakfast-room is in white and pine with brick walls. All bedrooms are on the ground floor, furnished with a pleasing simplicity – modern pine and various shades of pastel predominate. A patio with garden benches allows guests to enjoy the view of canal life including passing narrow-boats.

In addition to many eating-places, there is a plethora of antique shops in Hungerford.

This is a good walking and cycling area. Barge trips also available.

Readers' comments: Agreeably cosy. Delightful river setting. Friendly atmosphere. One of the most delightful places. Accommodation first-rate, good hosts, smashing breakfast.

WOODPECKER COTTAGE

C(8) **M S**

Star Lane, Warren Row, Berkshire, RG10 8QS   Tel: 01628 822772
(Fax: 01628 822125).

West of Maidenhead. Nearest main road: A4 from Maidenhead to Reading (also M4, junction 8/9; and M40, junction 4).

rear view

3 Bedrooms. £20–£25 (less for 4 nights or more). All have some or all of the following: own bath/shower/toilet; TV. No smoking.
Light suppers if ordered. Vegetarian or other special diets if ordered. Wine available. No smoking.
1 Sitting-room. With open fire, TV. No smoking.
Large garden

There really are woodpeckers here – three kinds – for the cottage is deep in bluebell woods, their many old tracks frequented by birdwatchers. A pretty garden (with breakfast on the terrace a possibility) and croquet lawn add to the attractions, and all this within a half-hour of Heathrow Airport and Windsor, Oxford and Henley.

Flint-walled cowsheds were converted and extensions added to create this attractive home. One ground-floor bedroom overlooks fish-pools, sundial and rock garden; another (with leather sofa and television) has a woodland view. There's an en suite single room, a small 'snug', and a dining-room where Chippendale-style chairs surround a Paisley-clothed table. Here, by arrangement, Joanna Power may serve a light meal such as onion tart and gooseberry fool.

Readers' comments: Excellent. Attentive and very welcoming. Fantastic breakfast. Will stay again. Totally uncontrived atmosphere.

For explanation of code letters and **V** symbol, see inside front cover.

Private bathrooms are not necessarily en suite.

'Bargain breaks' are usually out-of-season reductions for half-board stays of several nights.

Some proprietors stipulate a minimum stay of two nights at weekends or peak seasons; or they will accept one-nighters only at short notice (that is, only if no lengthier booking has yet been made).

BUCKINGHAMSHIRE

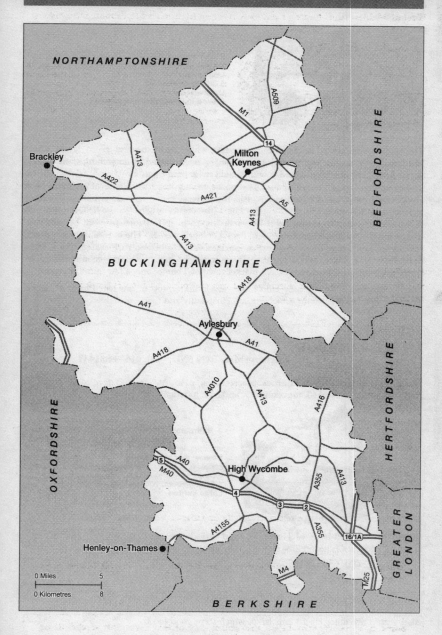

NORTHAMPTONSHIRE

BEDFORDSHIRE

Brackley

Milton Keynes

BUCKINGHAMSHIRE

Aylesbury

OXFORDSHIRE

HERTFORDSHIRE

High Wycombe

Henley-on-Thames

GREATER LONDON

0 Miles   5
0 Kilometres   8

BERKSHIRE

Prices are per person sharing a room at the beginning of the year.

FOXHILL

C(5) S

Kingsey, Aylesbury, Buckinghamshire, HP17 8LZ   Tel:.01844 291650
South-west of Aylesbury. On A4129 from Princes Risborough to Thame (and near M40, junctions 7/8).

3 Bedrooms. £18–£22. Some have the following: own shower; TV. No smoking.
Light suppers if ordered.
2 Sitting-rooms. With TV. No smoking.
Large garden
Closed in December and January.

The instant impression is delightful: sparkling white house beyond green lawns where Muscovy ducks waddle with their young towards a pool crossed by an arching stone bridge. At the back of the house is a garden with heated swimming-pool.

The interior is just as attractive. The house having been the home of architect Nick Hooper and his family for many years, it is not surprising that its modernization was done with imagination and with care to respect its 17th-century origins. In the hall, floored with polished red quarry-tiles, a wrought-iron staircase leads up to bedrooms with beamed ceilings, attractive wallpapers and rugs, and restful colour schemes. The breakfast-room (which also serves as a sitting-room) has brown gingham tablecloths and rush-seated chairs. Here Mary-Joyce – a warm, gentle hostess – usually serves only breakfast, recommending for other meals restaurants in the ancient market town of Thame, only a few minutes away.

Readers' comments: Wonderfully kind hosts, lovely home, top of our list! Beautiful house. The Hoopers and their home are charming. Hospitality and food excellent.

LITTLE PARMOOR

C S X

Parmoor Lane, Frieth, Buckinghamshire, RG9 6NL   Tel: 01494 881447
(Fax: 01494 883012)
North-east of Henley-on-Thames. Nearest main road: A40 from Oxford to High Wycombe (also M40, junctions 4/5; and M4, junctions 8/9).

3 Bedrooms. £20–£25 (less for 2 nights or more). Some have some or all of the following: own bath/shower/toilet; TV. No smoking.
Dinner (by arrangement). £14 for 3 courses and coffee, at 7.30pm. Vegetarian or other special diets if ordered. No smoking. **Light suppers** if ordered.
1 Sitting-room. With open fire. No smoking.
Large garden

Within a mere half-hour of Heathrow (and little longer to London) is a peaceful spot among the lovely Chiltern Hills, and in it this attractive house built in 1724.

Inside are green and white panelling, a log fire and watercolours painted by Wynyard Wallace's grandfather. An elegant pine staircase leads to two large panelled bedrooms and another, smaller but also very good single. Julia Wallace provides breakfast (sometimes taken under the vine outside) and dinners which may include such dishes as home-made vegetable or fish soup, Chiltern game pie with locally grown vegetables, and lemon mousse. Also, within five miles are 10 inns, all of which serve good food.

Readers' comments: Made us feel part of the family. Lovely. Most impressed by the warmth of welcome, the comfort and the outstanding quality of the meals. Excellent. Charming people. Thoughtful, caring hospitality. Kindness itself. Brilliant hospitality.

12

MILL FARMHOUSE

CDS

Westbury, Buckinghamshire, NN13 5JS   Tel/Fax: 01280 704843
East of Brackley. Nearest main road: A422 from Brackley to Buckingham.

3 Bedrooms. £18–£22 (less for 3 nights or more). Bargain breaks. Some have all of the following: own bath/shower/toilet; TV. No smoking.
Dinner (by arrangement). £12 for 3 courses and coffee, till 9pm. Vegetarian or other special diets if ordered. **Light suppers** if ordered.
1 Sitting-room. With open fire, TV.
Large garden

The mill itself is now used as workshops, and the miller's stone house (built in the 18th century) is the heart of a 1000-acre farm with sheep, cattle and horses. The building has been immaculately restored and furnished by the Owens. Although the old, deep-set casements and shutters remain, as do panelled oak doors and other traditional features, Jacqueline has used pretty fabrics and colours to give a light and attractive look to the bedrooms – a wisteria frieze, figured cotton spreads and velvet bedheads in one, for instance; while another has a rosy frieze and bamboo furniture. These rooms are reached by a stair rising from the sitting/dining-room which has a big refectory table at one end, hunting-prints on cream walls and chairs and a sofa at the other. Carved oak furniture recalls the past while sliding glass doors to the garden are wholly of today (as is the covered, heated swimming-pool).

For dinner, you may be treated to home-made pâté followed by plaice in mushroom and prawn sauce under a topping of courgettes and cheese, and hot chocolate pudding.

The garden has stone-walled terraces and shrubs with foliage and berries selected to be colourful even in winter. There is stabling for horses and ponies – this is good riding country.

V

OLD VICARAGE

PT

Leighton Road, Wingrave, Buckinghamshire, HP22 4PA   Tel: 01296 681235
North-east of Aylesbury. Nearest main road: A418 from Aylesbury to Leighton Buzzard.

2 Bedrooms. £19 (less for 3 nights or more). Both have own bath/shower/toilet. No smoking.
Dinner. £12 for 3 courses and coffee, at times to suit guests. Vegetarian or other special diets if ordered. No smoking. **Light suppers** if ordered.
1 Sitting-room. With open fire, TV, piano. No smoking.
Small garden

Mallards and moorhens nest on the village pond in front of this 1840s house, a view enjoyed by one of the pleasant bedrooms; other rooms overlook the old-fashioned garden of lupins and roses at the back. Throughout, there are such handsome features as arched doorways and tall bay windows, which language teacher Jean Keighley has complemented with strong plain colours for the walls.

One passes through a large hall to the pink sitting-room with its marble fireplace and grand piano. On the other side of the hall is a dining-room that has handsome mahogany furniture in period with the house; and here Jean serves such meals as home-made pâté, French classics like coq au vin (she lived in France for many years), English puddings (crumbles, tarts, etc.) and then cheeses.

Quite near London yet truly rural, Wingrave is surrounded by places of interest such as high Dunstable Downs (NT), Whipsnade, the Chiltern Hills, canals with boat trips near Tring, Saxon or Norman churches (the one at Dunstable is of considerable splendour), the gardens at Stowe and at Wrest Park, Woburn Abbey and Mentmore Towers.

V

POLETREES FARM

C(10) M S X

Ludgershall Road, Brill, Buckinghamshire, HP18 9TZ Tel/Fax: 01844 238276
West of Aylesbury. Nearest main road: A41 from Aylesbury to Bicester (and M40, junction 9).

4 Bedrooms. £19–£25 (less for 4 nights or more). Some have some or all of the following: own bath/shower/toilet; TV. No smoking.
Dinner (by arrangement). £12 for 4 courses and coffee, at 6.30pm. Vegetarian or other special diets if ordered. **Light suppers** if ordered.
1 Sitting-room. With TV. No smoking.
Large garden

There is clematis round the porch, baskets brimming with begonias and lobelias hang on the walls, and all around are roses, apple-trees and views of fields. Inside, stone walls, oak beams and an inglenook with a rare window beside it have survived five centuries. The water for the house still comes from a spring.

Anita Cooper has furnished her ancient home well and has collections of old railway keys and of earthenware boots. Bedrooms are pleasantly decorated too, with handsome walnut furniture. She caned the bedheads herself.

Dinner may comprise such dishes as home-made soup, roast pork, chocolate mousse, and cheese with fruit. The nearby village of Ludgershall is where Wycliffe started his great work of translating the Bible into English.

Readers' comments: Fantastic weekend! Very friendly; felt totally at home. Comfortable, and lovely breakfasts. Would recommend Poletrees time and time again.

V

RICHMOND LODGE

C(6) S

Mursley, Buckinghamshire, MK17 0LE Tel: 01296 720275
South of Milton Keynes. Nearest main road: A421 from Buckingham to Milton Keynes (and M1, junction 13).

3 Bedrooms. £19–£21.50. One has own bath/shower/toilet; TV (in all). No smoking.
Dinner (by arrangement). £12.50 for 4 courses and coffee, at 7pm. Vegetarian or other special diets if ordered. No smoking.
1 Sitting-room. With open fire, TV. No smoking.
Large garden

Just before the First World War this house was built as a hunting-lodge for a wealthy London butcher who decided to make his weekend retreat in this high, windswept spot. Sedate, solid comfort still prevails: even the garden is formal, with immaculate lawn, stately blue cedar, croquet, lawn tennis and far views. Chris Abbey, once a hotel manager, sets high standards in all her rooms (one, in jade and strawberry, overlooks a lily-pool) and in the preparation of such meals as salmon mousse, pork chops with celery-and-pineapple sauce, and summer pudding. Breakfast may be served among the fuchsias and clematis of a sunny patio.

Waddesdon Manor, recently refurbished by the National Trust, is close.

Readers' comments: Most luxurious and comfortable. Charming, perfect room. Warm hospitality and care. Wonderful dinners. Strongly recommended.

V

WHITES' FARMHOUSE

Town End Road, Radnage, Buckinghamshire, HP14 4DY   Tel: 01494 482333
(Fax: 01494 484677)

North-west of High Wycombe. Nearest main road: A40 from High Wycombe to Oxford
(and M40, junction 5).

1 Bedroom. £20 **to readers of this book** (less for 3 nights or more). Has own bath/toilet. No smoking.
Light suppers if ordered.
1 Sitting-room. With open fire, TV, piano.
Large garden

Claudia Wilcox's husband having been chairman of the Contemporary Applied Arts gallery, it
is hardly surprising that their home, all mellow brick and rambling roses outside, is filled with
the best in modern, craftsman-made furniture (designed by Makepeace, La Trobe Bateman
and others), ceramics and textiles – to all of which the 17th-century house is an admirable
background. Even the two baby-chairs are craftsman-made.

Guests have a bedroom with views over the Radnage valley to beech woods and a Saxon
church, a private sitting-room and their own entrance.

Claudia can provide light suppers (such as soup and sandwiches), after which guests are
welcome to enjoy a stroll in the garden with its collection of rare flowering shrubs and trees, or
just sit with a drink and watch the tame white doves fly across the unspoilt valley. The more
energetic walk the many well-signed paths, or even the long-distance Ridgeway footpath.

Readers' comments: Couldn't praise more highly; really peaceful; thoughtful and caring hostess.

WHITEWEBBS

26 Lower Road, Chalfont St Peter, Buckinghamshire, SL9 9AQ   Tel: 01753 884105
South-east of High Wycombe. Nearest main road: A413 from Amersham to Denham
(also M40, junction 1a; and M25, junction 16).

2 Bedrooms. £18–£20 (less for 4 nights). Both have
own bath/shower/toilet; TV. No smoking.
Dinner (by arrangement). £10 for 2 courses and
coffee, at 7pm. Vegetarian or other special diets if
ordered. No smoking. **Light suppers.**
Small garden

This house, secluded by tall oaks and pines, was built in 1928 on ground belonging to the
nearby Grange, once the home of William Penn's father-in-law (who sailed with him on the
Mayflower). Now it is the home of artist Maureen Marsh, who specializes in portraits of
houses and country views: visitors are welcome to see her studio and little printing-press.

Often tea (with home-produced raspberry jam and cakes) is served in the pretty garden –
or visitors can use the kitchen to make their own at any hour. A typical dinner: courgette
and cheese gratin followed by pecan pie into which go sherry-soaked raisins.

Upstairs are trim, cottagey bedrooms, and everywhere Maureen's delightful watercolours.

Readers' comments: Warm hospitality. Large, airy and comfortable rooms. One feels like a
family guest. Delicious breakfasts. Extremely pretty. Food and ambience perfect.
Comfortable and charming. Welcoming, caring; lovely room, excellent breakfast.

V

CAMBRIDGESHIRE

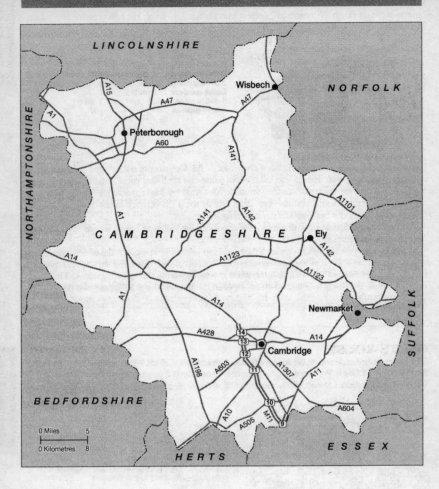

Major tourist attractions, such as Stratford-upon-Avon and Cambridge, can often be easily reached from houses in adjacent counties.

BRAMLEY COTTAGE

MSX

Sutton Road, Wisbech, Cambridgeshire, PE13 5DU   Tel: 01945 463132
North of Wisbech. On the A1101 from Wisbech towards Boston.

rear view

2 Bedrooms. £15. Both have own bath/shower/toilet; TV. No smoking.
Light suppers if ordered (in summer).
1 Sitting-room
Large garden

Just outside Wisbech, on the main road into Lincolnshire, stands little Bramley Cottage (and Bramley apples do still grow in its garden). Small rooms, homely in style as befits a Victorian farm cottage (one is on the ground floor), are kept immaculate by Audrey O'Donnell – a very caring hostess, who also runs an antique shop in Wisbech. The big attraction of staying here is the colourful garden, created from an overgrown jungle, which is beautifully laid out around a pool with cascade. It provides fresh salads for the light suppers occasionally available, and an attractive view from the conservatory sitting-room. There's a barbecue in the garden, and the long Nene Way footpath is close by.

Wisbech is worth a lingering visit for its historic buildings, which include handsome Peckover House (NT) and, facing it across the river, the birthplace museum of Octavia Hill – not only co-founder of the National Trust but pioneer of the first movement to replace city slums with good housing. There is a superb rose festival every June.

This is a great area for painting and photography (because of the light); and for gardeners, likely to return home laden with lavender bushes, African violets and much else grown here.

GLEBE HOUSE

C PT

Park Lane, Longstowe, Cambridgeshire, CB3 7UJ   Tel: 01954 719509
(Fax: 01954 718033)
West of Cambridge. Nearest main road: A1198 from Huntingdon to Royston (and M11, junction 12).

2 Bedrooms. £19.50–£20 (less for 7 nights or more). Both have own bath/shower/toilet; TV. No smoking.
Dinner. £16 for 3 courses and coffee, at 6–8pm. Less for 2 courses. Vegetarian or other special diets if ordered. No smoking. **Light suppers** if ordered.
Small garden

Scalloped white bargeboards round the roof are like a demure lace collar on the pink walls of this secluded 16th-century house. In summer, poppies, clematis and peonies contribute colourful touches. The house was (as 'glebe' indicates) church property.

Charlotte Murray has decorated all the rooms attractively, using soft pinks and greens in the bedrooms (one is a family room) and deep mulberry for the dining-room where she serves either simple meals or dinners cooked to professional standard – for Charlotte, after training at the Cordon Bleu Cookery School in London, used to cook for City directors' dining-rooms. She chooses dishes to suit her guests' tastes, one popular menu being carrot-and-coriander soup, pork tenderloin stuffed with mushrooms, and almond applecake. When children stay, she can do a separate and early meal with simpler food.

Readers' comments: Absolutely lovely. Beautiful house, warm and comfortable. Very comfortable, warm and tasteful. Lovely supper. Nice hostess. Delightful bedroom. Very friendly. Memorable cordon bleu cooking. Cosy, well kept and lovingly decorated.

V

THE GROVE

C

Sutton Gault, Cambridgeshire, CB6 2BD   Tel/Fax: 01353 777196
West of Ely. Nearest main road: A142 from Ely to Chatteris.

2 Bedrooms. £20–£25. Both have some or all of the following: own bath/shower/toilet; views of river. No smoking.
1 Sitting-room. With open fire, TV, piano.
Large garden

The Grove, surrounded by lime trees (unusual in the Fens), was built for a Dutch drainage engineer around 1700, and later 'Victorianized'. It stands almost alone before a bridge which crosses the New Bedford River. This is an idyllic place for birdwatchers, especially to view waders.

Stella Anderson, an amiable hostess, serves breakfast in the highly polished oak dining-room, or in the kitchen, with large baskets and bunches of dried flowers seemingly growing out from the beams, blue-and-white gingham curtains, plates on the wall and a royal blue Aga. French doors lead onto a terrace and garden with snowdrops, aconites and daffodils under tall trees bedecked with bird-boxes. Beyond is a field with sheep and geese (goose-egg omelettes for breakfast!), and an all-weather tennis court.

There is an excellent pub next door.

The twin room is spacious and has William Morris curtains. The double room, light and airy, enjoys the garden views. Three heavy oak beams in the ceiling date from the original construction; dark green and white tiles make its bathroom sparkle.

HILL HOUSE FARM

C(12)

9 Main Street, Coveney, Cambridgeshire, CB6 2DJ   Tel: 01353 778369
West of Ely. Nearest main road: A142 from Ely to Chatteris.

3 Bedrooms. £19–£20 (less for 2 nights or more). All have some or all of the following: own shower/toilet; TV. No smoking.
1 Sitting-room. No smoking.
Small garden

The Nix family have been farmers in Coveney since 1640, when they arrived from Holland to work on the Fens drainage scheme. At that time Coveney was an 'island in the bay' from which one travelled by boat to Ely, three miles away. From the guests' lounge is a panoramic view of the Fens, with Ely Cathedral a focal point in the distance.

Mrs Nix is a very attentive and welcoming hostess. Her breakfasts include kippers and croissants as well as a full farmhouse option.

There are three purpose-built bedrooms, one on the ground floor (with its own entrance). Double and twin rooms are approached via an outdoor staircase. Everything is immaculate. Outside there are a terrace and small garden where guests may sit.

The house is very well placed to visit not only Ely, Cambridge, Peterborough (another fine cathedral) and Newmarket but also the scenic parts of Norfolk and Suffolk too. For those who love wildlife, Welney's bird reserve and Wicken Fen are near.

Readers' comments: Very comfortable and attractive. Delicious breakfast. Made most welcome.

OLD EGREMONT HOUSE

31 Egremont Street, Ely, Cambridgeshire, CB6 1AE   Tel: 01353 663118
Nearest main road: A10 from Cambridge to King's Lynn.

2 Bedrooms. £20–£21 (less for 3 nights or more). Bargain breaks. Both have some or all of the following: own bath/toilet; TV. No smoking.
Large garden
Closed in late December.

rear view

The 300-year-old house has been filled by Sheila Friend-Smith with attractive furnishings, the garden is lovely and there is a cathedral view.

One bed/sitting-room has a cream carpet and beribboned duvet, sprigged wallpaper and stripped pine furniture. There are armchairs from which to enjoy a view of the winding flower garden and its herbaceous bed; from the other bedroom one sees the neat vegetable garden where Victorian hedges of box flank the symmetrical paths, and the tennis lawn. The house is full of interesting things to look at: Jeremy's collection of clocks (one is silent, being gravity-operated), pretty Portuguese tiles in bathrooms (and some depicting old military costumes), embroideries from Jordan and stone-rubbings from Thailand. Breakfast is served at a big mahogany table surrounded by Chippendale-style chairs, with antique china, numerous books and prints around.

Reader's comments: Character, comfort and good food.

OLD RECTORY

Swaffham Bulbeck, Cambridgeshire, CB5 0LX   Tel/Fax: 01223 811986
North-east of Cambridge. Nearest main road: A14 from Cambridge to Newmarket (and M11, junction13).

3 Bedrooms. £20–£25 (less for 3 nights or more). All have some or all of the following: own bath/shower/toilet; TV. No smoking.
2 Sitting-rooms. With open fire/stove, TV. No smoking in one.
Large garden

Well sited to explore most of the East Anglian region, the Old Rectory was built in 1818 for the Rev. Leonard Jenyns, a distinguished naturalist who was offered but declined a place on the *Beagle* expedition, recommending instead his pupil Charles Darwin – who was a frequent visitor to the rectory.

Jenny Few-Mackay frequents sale-rooms to seek out all the Victoriana which furnishes the house in the style of Jenyns's time: one room has a handsome brass bed from which, through big windows, to enjoy the view of fields. There is a garden and swimming-pool; plus billiards in a converted barn. The best place for dinner is the Hole in the Wall at Little Wilbraham (or the Red Lion in Swaffham Prior).

Cambridge itself takes days to explore, and then there is a lot to see in the vicinity. Anglesey Abbey, for instance, which was really a priory only, founded in 1135. This century, a wealthy connoisseur filled it with art treasures and around it created one of the really great gardens of England. Also within easy reach are Newmarket (horseracing) and Ely, with its celebrated cathedral.

QUEENSBURY
196 Carter Street, Fordham, Cambridgeshire, CB7 5JU Tel: 01638 720916
(Fax: 01638 720233)
North of Newmarket. Nearest main road: A142 from Newmarket to Ely.

C D PT

3 Bedrooms. £20–£25. One has own shower/toilet; TV (in all). No smoking.
Dinner (by arrangement). £10 for 2 courses or £15 for 3 courses and coffee, at times to suit guests. Vegetarian or other special diets if ordered. No smoking. **Light suppers** if ordered.
1 Sitting-room. With open fire, piano. No smoking.
Small garden

A little gem of a place, especially for those interested in horse-racing. Jan, ebullient and welcoming, and Malcolm Roper, a former amateur jockey, are keen to show you maps and information about training yards, race meetings and horse sales in the area.

Their house is full of interesting furniture, prints (15 by Spy in the dining-room) and china – including a Japanese tea service. Silver-framed family portraits adorn the piano and there is an abundance of silk flowers.

Malcolm makes fresh orange juice to serve with breakfast at the mahogany dining-table. A traditional Coles wallpaper gives warmth to this room, where there are also fruit pot-pourris and displays of china in cabinets. Guests may order haddock, kippers, traditional farmhouse food and croissants. Jams are home-made.

Jan loves making sponges for tea when guests arrive. She uses fresh local produce for her soups; smoked salmon and fresh salmon are often served; and the puddings are a treat (with mulberry pie a speciality – the fruit from their own tree).

Bedrooms are delightfully furnished; swirls in the lace duvet-cover complement the wallpaper pattern in one.

SPINNEY ABBEY
Wicken, Cambridgeshire, CB7 5XQ Tel: 01353 720971
South of Ely. Nearest main road: A10 from Cambridge to Ely (and M11, junction 14).

C(5)

3 Bedrooms. £20. All have some or all of the following: own bath/shower/toilet; TV. No smoking.
1 Sitting-room. With TV, piano.
Large garden

The original Spinney Abbey was closed by Henry VIII, became a private house (where Cromwell's son lived after the Stuarts were restored to the throne) and was later pulled down. Its stones were used to build a new house in 1775. This is now the home of Valerie Fuller (and of her inherited collection of Victorian stuffed birds), who has three roomy and comfortable bedrooms with private bathrooms and, from the farm lands, views into ancient Wicken Fen, a National Trust nature reserve. There is a tennis court.

Ely has one of Europe's most glorious cathedrals, a multiplicity of pinnacles and spires outside, lofty vista within. The city still has an 18th-century air.

Readers' comments: Excellent hostess, capable and friendly. Very comfortable. Accommodation, service and food exceptionally good. Lovely hostess. Very welcoming, very comfortable rooms.

SPRINGFIELD

C PT S X

16 Horn Lane, Linton, Cambridgeshire, CB1 6HT Tel: 01223 891383
South-east of Cambridge. Nearest main road: A1307 from Haverhill towards
Cambridge. (and M11, junctions 9/10).

2 Bedrooms. £17.50–£19 (less for 5 nights or more).
Both have own bath/toilet; TV; views of river. No
smoking.
1 Sitting-room. With open fire, TV, piano. No
smoking.
Large garden

The spring which gives this 19th-century house its name rises in a carp pond at the far end
of the garden – or, rather, gardens; for there is a succession of hedge-enclosed areas. One of
these (almost islanded by a twist of the River Granta) is equipped for children.

The house is of gracious design, its gables decorated with fretted bargeboards and at its
side a spacious conservatory where breakfast is often served (or you can eat in your bedroom, provided with table and chairs for the purpose). Judith Rossiter has filled the conservatory with white flowering plants. Adjoining it is a comfortable sitting-room. Bedrooms are
on the second floor, furnished with antiques including old maps of America and other
Americana (Fred is descended from George Washington's aide-de-camp).

Readers' comments: Very comfortable, and a really splendid breakfast. Charming and very
comfortable. Warm welcome. Strongly recommended.

V

THE WATERMILL

C PT

Hildersham, Cambridgeshire, CB1 6BS Tel: 01223 891520
South-east of Cambridge. Nearest main road: A1307 from Haverhill towards Cambridge
(and M11, junctions 9/10).

1 Bedroom. £20. Bargain breaks. Has own bath/toilet;
views of river. No smoking.
Light suppers if ordered. No smoking.
Large garden
Closed weekdays during school term time.

The Watermill, a melange of clapboard and brick, is hidden at the end of a long track, with
black-faced Suffolk sheep on the left and a wooden bridge opposite.

Lynne Hartland, a teacher, relates the history of the present mill, which was built in
1830, though the Domesday Book records a mill on this site. The guest-room, originally
occupied by the mill boy, is up a winding staircase. Breakfast is served here, beside a window overlooking an orchard and wild garden with alder and yew trees, where herons and
kingfishers can be seen. In summer, breakfast can be taken in the courtyard among scented
herbs and climbing roses.

The double bed has a carved oak headboard, and holes along the sides of the bed where
ropes were tied to support the original straw mattress. (An additional single bed is also
available.)

Evening meals are not usually provided, but guests can walk to nearby pubs. Lynne
accepts visitors at weekends, half-terms and school holidays *only*.

Readers' comments: Superb – a lovely weekend. Enjoyed very much. Warm welcome.
Comfortable room. Most welcoming.

CHESHIRE

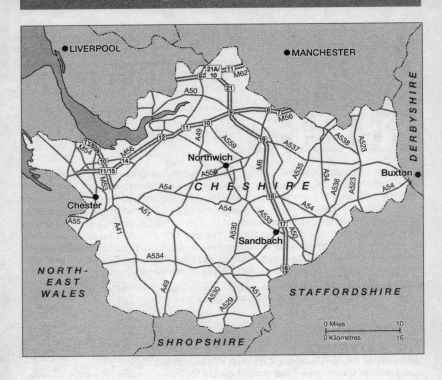

BARRATWICH

PT S X

Cuddington Lane, Cuddington, Cheshire, CW8 2SZ   Tel: 01606 882412
South-west of Northwich. Nearest main road: A49 from Whitchurch to Warrington.

3 Bedrooms. £18. All have TV. No smoking.
Light suppers if ordered.
1 Sitting-room. With open fire. No smoking.
Large garden

Just beyond the Delamere Forest is Cuddington village and this Victorian cottage with a large garden from which to enjoy the fine views of open countryside. These include a valley trout lake that, like many other Cheshire meres (old marl diggings), attracts unusual birds – and birdwatchers.

Visitors enter a white and celadon hall with galleried staircase leading to fresh, cottagey bedrooms – one with white boarded wall, another with stencilled decoration. There is a pink sitting-room opening onto a prettily tiled conservatory, many antiques, and a wall with five generations of family photos.

Mary Riley prides herself on her good breakfasts, with fresh fruit and farm eggs. While she will usually provide a light supper, the nearest pub which serves food is only a mile away, and there are more restaurants in Northwich.

Readers' comments: A warm welcome. Warmth and hospitality; setting peaceful. Delightful. Charming; hosts most helpful and friendly. How welcome I was made.

CANAL CENTRE

C D M PT S X

Hassall Green, Cheshire, CW11 4YB   Tel: 01270 762266
East of Sandbach. Nearest main road: A533 from Kidsgrove to Middlewich. (and M6, junction 17).

6 Bedrooms. £18–£20. Bargain breaks. Some have some or all of the following: own bath/shower/toilet; TV; views of canal.
Dinner (by arrangement). £11 for 3 courses and coffee, from 7pm. Vegetarian or other special diets if ordered. Wine available.
1 Sitting-room. With open fire, TV.
Small garden

Along the Trent & Mersey Canal there is an immense flight of 30 locks, known as 'Heartbreak Hill'; halfway lies pretty little Hassall Green and a complex of 18th-century buildings which once served the boatmen.

Today the former stables and bakery are a shop catering for holiday boats calling in at the marina (it also sells traditionally painted canalware); and adjoining it Ray and Sue Paine have created very attractive bedrooms for visitors, using Laura Ashley fabrics and thick carpets (the ground-floor bedroom is particularly spacious and elegant). Picture-windows in some rooms make the most of canal views beyond a lawn with sunshades where people take tea in summer (in winter, there is a log stove ablaze in the sitting-room). Evening meals are available in the tea-room; or in an à la carte restaurant by a lock, where such dishes as salmon terrine, and chicken in a creamy sauce are freshly prepared.

V

CASTLE HOUSE

CDPTSX

23 Castle Street, Chester, Cheshire, CH1 2DS   Tel/Fax: 01244 350354

Nearest main road: A483 from Wrexham to Chester (and M56, junction 16).

5 Bedrooms. £20 **to readers of this book only.**
Sunday half-price if part of 3-night booking, November
to March. Bargain breaks. Some have some or all of
the following: own bath/shower/toilet; TV.
1 Sitting-room. With open fire. No smoking.
Small garden

Right in the middle of the city but in a quiet by-road, this interesting house has a breakfast-room which dates from 1540 behind an 18th-century frontage and staircase. The arms of Elizabeth I (with English lion and Welsh dragon) are over the fireplace. It is both the Marls' own home and a guest-house with modern bedrooms that are exceptionally well furnished and equipped. Bed-and-breakfast only, for Chester has so many good restaurants; but visitors are welcome to use the kitchen. Newspapers and local phone calls are free. Coyle Marl, a local businessman, is an enthusiast for Chester and loves to tell visitors about its lesser-known charms.

Chester's cathedral of red stone dates back to the 14th century and the city's zoo is outstanding.

Readers' comments: Breakfasts absolutely first class. Excellent room and hospitality. Delightful hosts. So welcoming and friendly. Breakfast a delight. Liked it immensely. Very atmospheric. Superb position, comfortable, excellent food. A week well spent.

V

HARDINGLAND FARMHOUSE

Macclesfield Forest, Cheshire, SK11 0ND   Tel: 01625 425759

West of Buxton. Nearest main road: A537 from Macclesfield towards Buxton.

3 Bedrooms. £19–£22. All have own bath/shower/
toilet. No smoking.
Dinner. £13 for 3 courses and coffee, at 7pm (not
Sundays). Vegetarian or special diets if ordered. Wine
available. No smoking.
1 Sitting-room. With open fire. No smoking.
Large garden
Closed from December to February.

It is exceptional to find at one house outstanding surroundings, food and furnishings: Hardingland is just such a place. The secluded house is perched high up on the fringe of the Peak District National Park, on a hillside with stupendous panoramic views.

Anne used to be a professional caterer, winning an award at Buxton's Salon Culinaire in 1989. She uses a great many of John Tovey's Miller Howe recipes when she prepares for her visitors such meals as tarragon apples with Boursin cheese; lamb cutlets in ginger and orange sauce; an array of imaginative vegetables; and chocolate pots. The Reads' own smallholding provides beef and lamb; venison comes from forest deer.

The large sitting-room has comfortable sofas covered in a William Morris satin. The beamed dining-room is furnished in Regency style, and one of the bedrooms has an attractive apricot and pale turquoise colour scheme. Bathrooms are excellent.

Readers' comments: Food excellent. Went to so much trouble. Whole atmosphere very good, will go again. Beautifully furnished. Very comfortable, excellent dinner, friendly atmosphere, elegant. Super.

V

MITCHELL'S

Green Gables House, 28 Hough Green, Chester, Cheshire, CH4 8JQ
Tel: 01244 679004
On A5104 from Chester to Saltney.

4 Bedrooms. £20–£25 (less for 3 nights or more). Bargain breaks. All have own shower/toilet; TV. No smoking.
2 Sitting-rooms. With open fires, TV, piano. No smoking in one.
Small garden

On the south side of the city, this handsome house, built in 1856, has large windows and fine, high-ceilinged rooms with moulded cornices which Helen Mitchell has furnished in period: buttoned velvet chairs, old clocks, even a Victorian baby-chair and sewing-machine. Some rooms have a leafy outlook and there is a lily-pool cascade that is lit up at night. There is parking space (an asset in Chester), with buses to the centre passing outside.

The city is, of course, of outstanding interest – second only to Bath and York in what there is to see. It is surrounded by ancient walls of red sandstone, just outside which is a large Roman amphitheatre. The most unusual feature, however, is the Rows: here, steps from street level lead up to balustraded galleries overhanging the pavements, serving a second level of small shops above the ones below.

Reader's comments: Welcome friendly, help and advice forthcoming.

NEWTON HALL

Tattenhall, Cheshire, CH3 9AY Tel: 01829 770153 (Fax: 01829 770655)
South-east of Chester. Nearest main road: A41 from Whitchurch to Chester.

3 Bedrooms. £18.50–£21. One has own bath/shower/toilet; TV. No smoking.
1 Sitting-room. With TV. No smoking.
Large garden

The centre of a big dairy-farm, Newton Hall is a 300-year-old house surrounded by gardens and with fine views of both Beeston and Peckforton castles. Anne Arden's rooms have an air of solid comfort (the blue bedroom is particularly beautiful, with handsome Victorian mahogany furniture and an en suite bathroom). In the breakfast-room are wheelback chairs, oak table and dresser, the original quarry-tiles, a brick fireplace, huge beams and oak doors with great iron hinges. Like those in the sitting-room, its casements open onto sweeping lawns.

The walled city of Chester is famous for its cathedral, castle and Rows, an outstanding zoo as well, and the River Dee for salmon. At nearby Bunbury, alabaster monuments are a feature of the church; and from Brown Knowl you can go up Bickerton Hill to get stunning views across Wales. Except for the hills in this part of the county, Cheshire consists mostly of level pastureland which supports the cows whose milk has made Cheshire cheese into a classic variety.

Readers' comments: Exceptionally charming. Hostess of great care. Most warmly received. Outstanding. Very pleasant. Exceeded our expectations. Lovely room and gracious hostess.

ROUGHLOW FARMHOUSE

C(6) **X**

Chapel Lane, Willington, Cheshire, CW6 0PG   Tel/Fax: 01829 751199

East of Chester. Nearest main road: A54 from Congleton towards Chester (and M6, junction 18).

3 Bedrooms. £20–£30 (less for 3 nights or more in January and February). All have own bath/shower/toilet. No smoking.
Dinner. £15 for 3 courses and coffee, at 7.30pm. Vegetarian or other special diets if ordered. No smoking. **Light suppers** if ordered.
3 Sitting-rooms. With open fire/stove, TV, piano. No smoking.
Large garden

Warm sandstone was used to build this 200-year-old farmhouse, well sited 450 feet up for superb views towards Shropshire in one direction and Wales in the other.

From a graceful sitting-room in shades of pink and grey, stairs wind up to the bedrooms. There is an enormous suite above the barn with beamed sitting-room and pretty quilts contrasting with bedheads of white bamboo; beyond it is a luxurious, outsize shower. Sally Sutcliffe used to be an interior decorator and this shows in her choice of colours, antiques, and pictures by a local artist. The terracotta single room is well up to standard.

A typical dinner (provided there are at least four people dining) might be soup made from freshly picked field mushrooms; chicken in a sauce of cream, lemon and tarragon; local strawberries with shortbread; and cheeses.

Readers' comments: Superb bedrooms. Meals delightfully served and overwhelming in abundance. Quite enchanting. Beautifully appointed, peaceful, elegant. Absolutely delighted with the reception we received. Delightfully secluded. Breathtaking views. Delicious dinner.

TILSTON LODGE

C S X

Tilston, Malpas, Cheshire, SY14 7DR   Tel/Fax: 01829 250223

South of Chester. Nearest main road: A41 from Chester to Whitchurch.

3 Bedrooms. £19–£30 (less for 3 nights or more). Bargain breaks. All have own bath/shower/toilet; TV. No smoking.
Dinner (by arrangement). From £15 for 3 courses and coffee, at times to suit guests. Vegetarian or other special diets if ordered. No smoking.
1 Sitting-room. With open fire, TV, piano. No smoking.
Large garden

Handy for North Wales as well as historic Chester, the pretty village of Tilston is surrounded by the Peckforton and Bickerton hills. Tilston Lodge, set in 16 acres of grounds which include award-winning gardens and two big ponds to attract wildfowl, is now home to Kathie Ritchie and her collection of rare breeds. The original Victorian features include a handsomely tiled hall with pretty marble fireplace and galleried mahogany staircase. Kathie has made patchwork bedspreads; stencilled woodbines on walls; draped a four-poster with lace; and collected an array of Victorian jugs. In the raspberry-walled dining-room – with William-and-Mary style chairs, good linen and silver – she serves imaginative meals using home-grown produce, local lamb, Cheshire and other local cheeses, but many guests opt to dine at the excellent village pub. You might be offered duck eggs for breakfast; jams and marmalade are home-made.

Readers' comments: Excellent in every way. Fine bedroom and bathroom. Very good, quiet setting.

V

CORNWALL

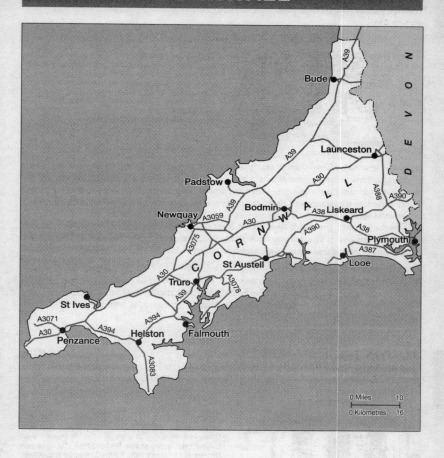

Facts (prices, etc.) at the top of entries are supplied by the proprietors themselves. While every effort is made to ensure that these are correct at the time of going to press, they may alter thereafter: please check when you book.

BOSWEDDEN HOUSE HOTEL

C D S

Cape Cornwall, St Just, Cornwall, TR19 7NJ   Tel: 01736 788733
West of Penzance. Nearest main road: A3071 from Penzance to St Just.

8 Bedrooms. £19 (less for 7 nights or more). Bargain breaks. Some have some or all of the following: own bath/shower/toilet; views of sea.
Light suppers. Vegetarian or other diets if ordered. Wine available.
1 Sitting-room. With open fire, TV. Piano. **Bar.**
Large garden
Closed in December and January.

Once the mansion of an 18th-century mine-owner, this house is kept immaculate by Mary Stokes and Sheila Bond, from the bedrooms (some overlooking the distant sea) to the sitting-room and dining-room, both with big windows to make the most of the sunny views. There is double-glazing as well as a log fire for winter comfort. An indoor swimming-pool is available at certain hours.

This far part of Cornwall is so different from the rest of England that it feels like another country (it has much in common with Brittany): wild, ancient, beautiful and mysterious. Land's End is only a few miles away, also the cliffside Minack Theatre, coastal beauty-spots between fishing villages like Mousehole and such coves as Lamorna on the south side of the peninsula.

Readers' comments: Very high standard. Nothing too much trouble. Perfect hotel and surroundings. Excellent accommodation. Like being with friends at home.

BOSWEDNACK MANOR

C PT S

Zennor, Cornwall, TR26 3DD   Tel: 01736 794183
West of St Ives. Nearest main road: A3074 from St Ives to Hayle.

5 Bedrooms. £16–£19 (less for 2 nights or more). Some have some or all of the following: own shower/toilet; views of sea. No smoking.
Dinner (by arrangement). £9 for 3 courses and coffee, at 7pm. No smoking.
1 Sitting-room. With stove, piano. No smoking.
Large garden

Overlooking a magnificent headland, Boswednack Manor is run in slightly Bohemian style by Graham and Elizabeth Gynn, former wardens of Skokholm Island nature reserve. Inside are Turkish hangings, bamboo furniture, stuffed birds, dragons painted on the dining-room's blue ceiling (conservatory beyond). Outside are three acres of grounds, a studio, a games room, open-air chess and a meditation room for visitors' use. Organic produce goes into the vegetarian evening meals. Visitors in the self-catering cottage may eat in. The Gynns offer birdwatching and archaeology holidays, and guided walks.

Pretty St Ives suffers from summer crowds, but its long-time popularity as an artists' haven can be explored at (among many other galleries) the Tate's outpost which specializes in Cornish art. Southward one passes Botallack and an area peppered with disused mines ('Poldark' country) and prehistoric remains.

V

Readers' comments: A truly wonderful spot, quiet and comfortable. Extremely well fed.

CLIFF HOUSE

PT S X

Devonport Hill, Kingsand, Cornwall, PL10 1NJ Tel: 01752 823110
South-west of Plymouth. Nearest main road: A374 from Plymouth towards Looe.

3 Bedrooms. £18–£25 (less for 3 nights or more). All have some or all of the following: own bath/shower/toilet; views of sea. No smoking.
Dinner (by arrangement). £20 for aperitif, 4 courses and coffee, at times to suit guests. Vegetarian or other special diets if ordered. Wine available. No smoking.
Light suppers if ordered.
2 Sitting-rooms. With stove, TV, balcony, piano. No smoking.
Small garden

In a fishing village on the Rame peninsula, an Area of Outstanding Natural Beauty, is 17th-century Cliff House – perched high above the sea and within a few yards of the south Cornwall coastal path.

From its hexagonal bay windows or the verandah, one can watch naval ships passing in and out of Plymouth Sound or children playing on the sands of Cawsand Bay. To make the most of these views, the sitting-room is on the first floor. On the walls of the house are paintings by local artists that are for sale. Some bedrooms, too, enjoy the fine views – the largest having armchairs in the bay window. Some visitors have found parking awkward.

Ann Heasman is an enthusiastic wholefood cook of such meals as lentil pâté with spiced fruit salad, carbonnade of beef, and chocolate roulade. She bakes her own bread.

Readers' comments: Lovely, friendly welcome, dinners delicious, beautiful landscape, would go again time after time. Wonderful six days. Made us feel instantly at home; house so friendly, comfortable and stylish; cooking absolutely superb. Enjoyed every moment.

V

COBBLERS COTTAGE

PT

Nantithet, Cury, Cornwall, TR12 7RB Tel: 01326 241342
South-east of Helston. Nearest main road: A3083 from Helston to the Lizard.

3 Bedrooms. £20 (less for 7 nights or more). All have own bath/shower/toilet. Restricted smoking.
Dinner. £10 for 3 courses and coffee, at 6.30pm. Vegetarian or other special diets if ordered. No smoking. **Light suppers** if ordered.
1 Sitting-room. With open fire, TV. Restricted smoking.
Large garden

The history of David and Hilary Lugg's attractive pink-painted stone cottage is waiting to be explored; the house certainly dates from the 17th century and has been, in turn, a school and a cobbler's shop: the local shoemaker used to keep the tools of his trade in one of the upstairs rooms. Today no traces of chalk-dust or leather linger in the pretty bedrooms (one pink, another palest celadon) with their sloping ceilings, deep-set windows and good bathrooms, nor downstairs in the cosy beamed sitting-room where brass and copper gleam round the stove in the big stone fireplace. Lace tablecloths add an elegant touch to the dining-room *(see back cover)*, where Hilary might serve, for example, pork in apple and onion sauce (accompanied by generous quantities of vegetables), a delectable trifle, and cheeses.

Lugg is a Cornish name meaning 'rearer of cattle'. The family has farmed the same land in Cury (now run by David and Hilary's son and daughter-in-law – see **Tregaddra Farm** entry) for five generations. From here, in the centre of the Lizard peninsula, most of Cornwall is within easy reach; the Goonhilly Earth Satellite Station is well worth a visit.

V

COOMBE FARMHOUSE

C(5) M S

Widegates, Cornwall, PL13 1QN Tel: 01503 240223 (Fax: 01503 240895)
North-east of Looe. On B3253 from Looe to Widegates.

10 Bedrooms. £20–£23 (less for 2 nights or more if dinner is taken). Bargain breaks. All have own shower/toilet; TV; views of sea. No smoking.
Dinner. £15 for 4 courses and coffee, usually about 7pm. Vegetarian or other special diets if ordered. Wine available. No smoking. **Light suppers** if ordered.
1 Sitting-room. With open fire, TV. Bar. No smoking.
Large garden
Closed from November to February.

At this spacious and comfortable guest-house, built on a marvellous site with a distant sea view, Alex and Sally Low provide many extras such as a swimming-pool, croquet and a stone-walled games room for snooker and table tennis. Antiques, paintings and interesting objects fill the house.

From a glassed-in verandah are views of terraced lawns where peacocks roam, and of a pond (one of several) frequented by coots. Elsewhere, ponies graze, there are rhododendron woods, and camellias grow wild. One bedroom opens onto this garden; others upstairs have armchairs from which to enjoy the view. Visitors can picnic in the garden.

A typical dinner may comprise something like home-made soup, roast duck, a fruit sponge with Cornish clotted cream, and cheeses (including local yarg). Visitors help themselves to drinks, writing down in a book what they have had.

Readers' comments: Excellent! A wonderful experience. Place superb, hospitality gracious. A haven of peace. Excellent food. Wonderful spot; very professionally run.

CRANTOCK PLAINS FARMHOUSE

C PT S

Cubert, Cornwall, TR8 5PH Tel: 01637 830253
South-west of Newquay. Nearest main road: A3075 from Newquay towards Redruth.

5 Bedrooms. £16–£22 (less for 7 nights or more). Bargain breaks. Some have some or all of the following: own bath/shower/toilet. No smoking.
Dinner. £9 for 3 courses and coffee, at 6.30pm (not Tuesdays or Fridays). Vegetarian or other special diets if ordered. Wine available. No smoking.
1 Sitting-room. With open fire, TV, organ.
Garden

Jackie Rowlands is justly proud of the lovely gardens she and Buzz have created at Crantock Plains: out of five annual entries to the Newquay in Bloom competition, they have won four firsts and a third. And the pleasure is not merely aesthetic: vegetables are organically grown for the table, too. Upstairs bedrooms look out onto the old well which is a central feature of the grounds; there are two pretty bedrooms on the ground floor as well, and an abundance of bath- and shower-rooms for guests. The sitting-room, in the older part of the house (it dates back to the 18th century), has original beams and window-seats, and comfortable, chintzy sofas; the dining-room is spectacularly furnished with an old wooden altar serving as a refectory-style table, an impressive pair of Belgian carvers, and a set of unusual barleytwist-and-cane dining chairs. Here Jackie serves such meals as soup, fillet of beef Stroganoff, and fresh fruit pavlova.

The farmhouse is near the attractive village of Crantock, with thatched pub and interesting church; Newquay and splendid beaches are close.

Reader's comments: Lovely house and garden, good food.

CRASKEN

Falmouth Road, Helston, Cornwall, TR13 0PF   Tel: 01326 572670
Off A394 from Helston to Falmouth.

3 Bedrooms. £18.50–£20.50 **(less to readers of this book staying 5 or more nights).**
Dinner (by arrangement). £17.50 for 3 courses and coffee, at 7–9pm. Vegetarian or other special diets if ordered. **Light suppers** if ordered.
1 Sitting-room. With TV.
Large garden
Closed from mid-December to January.

Down a very long drive is a rare survival – a 17th-century farmhouse built courtyard-style, rather French, with its granary and old carpentry-shop adjoining it. The ancient midden (for dung), a 'listed' structure, is now a pretty, low-walled garden. And in the grounds a prehistoric site has been discovered – the name 'Crasken' is Celtic for 'settlement'. The rooms are full of 'unconsidered trifles', from rag dolls to an array of willow-pattern plates, nosegays of wildflowers to log-cabin patchwork, Victorian crochet and jugs, rag rugs, pots of begonias. Additional rooms in outbuildings have their own baths, etc.

Jenny Ingram may serve such good home-made meals (if ordered in advance) as crab and broccoli au gratin, chicken in lemon sauce, and meringues with gooseberry cream. There are ducks, goats and donkeys as well as, in spring, a wonderful variety of wildflowers.

Readers' comments: Best I have visited. Picturesque and very welcoming. Uniquely decorated, secluded and peaceful. Most friendly, kind and thoughtful. Splendid place. Excellent value.

V

CREED HOUSE

Grampound, Cornwall, TR2 4SL   Tel: 01872 530372
South-west of St Austell. Nearest main road: A390 from St Austell to Truro.

rear view

3 Bedrooms. £20. All have own bath/shower/toilet. No smoking preferred.
Light suppers if ordered. No smoking preferred.
1 Sitting-room. With log stove, TV. No smoking preferred.
Large garden

Virtually in the centre of Cornwall, and within easy reach of many of its most famous gardens, lie five less well-known but no less beautiful acres of spectacular landscaping: the grounds of Creed House, a Georgian rectory dating from about 1730, whose sweeping lawns, walled herbaceous garden and stream-fed ponds provide an entrancing outlook for Lally Croggon's guests. These gardens are occasionally open to the public. Lally serves lavish breakfasts round the Georgian mahogany table in the elegant dining-room, often with an open fire in the grate. The blue-and-yellow sitting-room is furnished with deep, comfortable armchairs and a leather sofa. Bedrooms are light and airy, with pastel walls and Colefax & Fowler fabrics.

Despite – or perhaps because of – the fact that she grew up in India and lived in Malaya for 10 years, Lally's speciality is the creation of an English country house-party atmosphere, in some of the most gracious surroundings in this book.

Readers' comments: Excellent; the best of 'old world' b & b. Marvellous hostess, outstanding value. A highlight. Delightful; delicious breakfast, magnificent garden.

THE CROFT

D PT

Coverack, Cornwall, TR12 6TF   Tel: 01326 280387
South-east of Helston. Nearest main road: A3083 from Helston to the Lizard.

3 Bedrooms. £16.50–£22.50 (less for 5 nights or more). All have some or all of the following: own bath/shower/toilet; views of sea; balcony (one). No smoking.
Dinner. £9 for 3 courses and coffee, at 7–7.30pm. Vegetarian or other special diets only. No smoking.
1 Sitting-room. With TV. No smoking.
Garden. No smoking.

The charm of the Croft lies not in any elegance of exterior or entrance, though it is a handsome house (with ample parking space), but rather in the empathetic character of its host, a photographer who came here from London in 1993, and in its quite outstanding position within a stone's throw of the sea. Views from two of the bedrooms are truly spectacular. One has an enclosed balcony from which to relish these to the full, and the lie of the land is such that the prospect from both the dining-room and the sitting-room downstairs is just as mesmerizing. Peter Chèze-Brown's terraced gardens end at the drop to the beach and are probably the only no-smoking grounds in the book, because plants have been chosen for their scent. Indoors, walls are hung with memorable paintings and prints.

Meals are strictly vegetarian, so guests are surprised by the 'bacon' and 'sausages' supplied for meat-eating breakfasters; at dinner, Peter's soups are gaining an international reputation.

Readers' comments: Extremely friendly, you feel totally relaxed, and the best breakfast I've ever had; superb view.

DEGEMBRIS FARM

C S

St Newlyn East, Cornwall, TR8 5HY   Tel: 01872 510555 (Fax: 01872 510230)
South-east of Newquay. Nearest main road: A3058 from St Austell to Newquay.

5 Bedrooms. £18–£20. Bargain breaks. Some have some or all of the following: own bath/shower/toilet; TV.
Dinner. £10 for 4 courses and coffee, at 6.30pm. Vegetarian or other special diets if ordered. **Light suppers** if ordered.
1 Sitting-room. With open fire, TV, piano.
Garden

A survey published in the 1830s recorded the name as the much more Cornish-sounding Tregembris. From the parking area a few steep steps lead up to the pretty sloping front garden (wonderful views over the wooded valley) and the unusual slate-clad house, over 200 years old. It is now the hub of a busy working farm which has been in Roger Woodley's family since his great-uncle bought it from the Trerice estate in 1915. Kathy is happy to let guests wander into the traditional farmhouse kitchen but meals are served in the low-beamed dining-room, originally the farm's dairy. A typical dinner: soup, a roast or casserole, blackberry-and-apple pie, and cheese. The attractive, individually furnished bedrooms vary in size from a small, flowery single to a spacious family room.

In spring the surrounding woodland walks are carpeted with bluebells. Newquay is close, Truro not far in the other direction, and the magnificent beaches of Cornwall's west coast are within easy reach.

Readers' comments: Delightful farmhouse; charming hostess; quiet and comfortable. Highly recommended. Portions generous. Cooking of highest standard.

V

EDNOVEAN FARM

Perranuthnoe, Cornwall, TR20 9LZ   Tel: 01736 711883
East of Penzance. Nearest main road: A394 from Helston towards Penzance.

C(10) **D PT S**

3 Bedrooms. £17–£25 (less for 3 nights or more). Bargain breaks. Some have some or all of the following: own bath/toilet; TV; views of sea. No smoking. **Light suppers** if ordered.
1 Sitting-room. With TV. No smoking.
Small garden

Everything is upside-down at Ednovean: bedrooms on the ground floor, open-plan living area upstairs; breakfast by candlelight in this immaculate conversion of a 17th-century barn set in 22 acres of farmland where Christine and Charles Taylor train horses for shows and eventing. The dividing slabs from old pigpens form the hall floor; and the other materials used in the rebuilding were all recycled too – one wooden window-sill bears the unmistakable signs of ship's beetle.

There is much use of stripped beams and white paint, Liberty fabrics and Sanderson prints; wooden floors are strewn with colourful rugs; and bathrooms are outstanding. The bedrooms vary to suit every taste: one with bow-fronted mahogany bed, free-standing bath in the luxurious en suite bathroom, and magnificent views of St Michael's Mount; a delightful smaller, simpler room with white-painted stone walls and pretty fabrics; and a cottage-style room across the courtyard, with a sea view from its sunny yellow bathroom. From the patio you can see four harbours.

Readers's comments: Superb rooms, excellent food.

V

ENNYS FARM

Trewhella Lane, St Hilary, Cornwall, TR20 9BZ   Tel/Fax: 01736 740262
East of Penzance. Nearest main road: A30 from Camborne to Penzance.

C S

5 Bedrooms. £20–£30 (less for 7 nights or more). Bargain breaks. All have some or all of the following: own bath/shower/toilet; TV; views of river. No smoking. **Dinner** (by arrangement). £17.50 for 4 courses and coffee, at 7pm. Vegetarian or other special diets if ordered. No smoking. **Light suppers** if ordered.
1 Sitting-room. With open fire, TV. No smoking.
Large garden

A former mine-owner's house of silvery granite, 17th-century Ennys Farm is ideal for gourmets in particular. Sue White is a dedicated cook, who prepares such candlelit meals as avocado mousseline with smoked salmon, chicken in green peppercorn sauce, and iced nut-cake with Kirsch (even more elaborate menus in winter). Bread is home-baked. There are a barbecue, a grass tennis court, a patio for breakfast and a swimming-pool.

Indoors one finds alcoves, deep-set sash windows, pretty plasterwork and a shapely staircase. Rooms have handsome beds (two are four-posters), lacy pillows, leather and velvet armchairs and flower pictures by a local artist. Family suites and a laundry-room have been created in the stables.

Readers' comments: Wonderful hostess. Beautifully situated. Super food. Happy, caring atmosphere. Food exquisite. Highest commendation. The perfect place to unwind. Total peace and quiet. Made very welcome. Very welcoming, comfortable.

FLEARDON FARM

Lezant, Cornwall, PL15 9NW   Tel: 01579 370364 (Fax: 01579 370760)
South of Launceston. On A388 from Launceston to Plymouth.

2 Bedrooms. £19–£20. Both have own bath/shower/toilet; TV. No smoking.
Light suppers only. Vegetarian or other special diets if ordered. No smoking.
1 Sitting-room. With open fire, TV. No smoking.
Large garden
Closed from November to February.

Tolkien devotees should head for Lezant because here, in the newly modernized barns of Fleardon Farm, is an art gallery displaying the work of Roger Garland, creator of those brilliant and intricate covers to the Hobbit books.

The farmhouse itself belongs to his parents and here Doreen Garland welcomes bed-and-breakfast guests (for dinner, they usually go to the Springer Spaniel inn, or the White Hart in Launceston). The 250-year-old house has a surprising interior after one enters through a conventional porch (filled with geraniums), for there is a big open-plan kitchen/dining-area with mahogany staircase to the floor above. The large sitting-room with windows on three sides has a log stove, sofas and a profusion of pot-plants. A handsome feature is the polished hardwood floors throughout. The bedrooms have pleasant views (and excellent bathrooms).

The grounds are full of interest: in addition to a lawn with flowerbeds and shrubs, there is a decorative folly with weathervane and a lake frequented by Canada geese.

Readers' comments: Welcomed warmly, gardens beautiful, a place we would return to. Lovely place, pleasant and friendly hostess.

HARESCOMBE LODGE

Watergate, Cornwall, PL13 2NE   Tel: 01503 263158
North-west of Looe. Nearest main road: A387 from Looe to Polperro.

3 Bedrooms. £18–£20 (less for 3 nights or more). All have some of the following: own bath/shower/toilet; views of river.
1 Sitting-room. With open fire.
Large garden

Of all the idyllic settings in this book, Harescombe Lodge's situation at the bottom of a winding, wooded, one-track road must be one of those closest to perfect. The house, built in 1760 and once the shooting-lodge of the Trelawne estate, is cosily furnished with some fine antiques, including an enchanting Victorian high chair. The two cottagey bedrooms upstairs have excellent bathrooms, and a third room in adjoining Fig Tree Cottage (its namesake is right beside the door) is just as attractive.

True to its traditions, Harescombe Lodge still offers the best of hospitality; Jane Wynn's breakfasts include home-baked bread and rolls.

Pretty Looe is a half-hour walk along the river path.

Readers' comments: Wonderful welcome; made to feel completely at home. First class; very comfortable. The house has real charm; beautifully furnished.

HURDON FARM

Hurdon, Cornwall, PL15 9LS   Tel: 01566 772955

South of Launceston. Nearest main road: A30 from Launceston to Bodmin.

6 Bedrooms. £16–£19 (less for 4 nights or more). Some have some of the following: own bath/toilet; TV. No smoking.
Dinner. £11 for 4 courses and coffee, at 6.30pm (not Sundays). Vegetarian or other special diets if ordered. No smoking. **Light suppers** if ordered.
1 Sitting-room. With woodstove, TV. No smoking.
Large garden
Closed from November to mid-April.

The 18th-century stone house is in a picturesque area, not far from Dartmoor and Bodmin Moor (both the north and south coasts are within reach, too). It has large sash windows with the original panelled shutters and built-in dressers in the dining-room. The sitting-room has large and comfortable chairs and a great log stove.

Upstairs, all is spick-and-span with fresh paintwork and light, bright colour schemes in the bedrooms. There is also a family suite on the ground floor.

Meals, often prepared by Margaret Smith's daughter Nicola, are above average 'farm-house fare'. Soups are accompanied by home-made rolls; lamb by such vegetables as cour-gettes au gratin; puddings include pavlovas and home-made ice creams. She uses the farm's own produce and clotted cream.

Readers' comments: Superb atmosphere. Idyllic – we were spoilt! Excellent meals, very comfortable, very reasonable. Enjoyable and relaxing. We return year after year. Well above average farm cooking. Food of the highest standard. Everything immaculate.

MANUELS FARM

Quintrell Downs, Cornwall, TR8 4NY   Tel: 01637 873577

South-east of Newquay. Off A392 from Indian Queens to Newquay.

3 Bedrooms. £18.50. One has own shower/toilet. No smoking.
Dinner. £12 for 4 courses and coffee, at 6.30pm. Vegetarian or other special diets if ordered. No smoking. Late **light suppers** if ordered.
1 Sitting-room. With TV. No smoking.
Large garden

There has been a dwelling on this spot since 1284, and much of the present farmhouse dates from the 17th century or earlier, but there's nothing primitive about the warmth and comfort of Manuels Farm although it retains all its old-fashioned charm (working shutters in the sitting-room, and huge inglenook fireplace – with log fires – in the beamed dining-room). The name means 'place of stone': local churches and nearby Elizabethan Trerice Manor are built of granite taken from the old quarry at the back of the house. It's a working farm, and Jean Wilson's dinners might well include the farm's home-bred, grass-fed beef between, say, lettuce-and-cucumber soup and bread-and-butter pudding. The hall is floored with Cornish Delabole slate, and bedrooms are pretty with flowery fabrics and papers. There's a comfortable bathroom, complete with sloping ceiling and rocking chair.

There's lots to keep children happy on the farm, with calves to be bottle-fed and eggs to be collected, as well as pigs, goats, ducks and rabbits to make friends with; the attractions of Newquay are close, too.

Reader's comments: Very comfortable, lovely breakfast.

V

MARINA HOTEL

D PT X

The Esplanade, Fowey, Cornwall, PL23 1HY Tel: 01726 833315
(Fax: 01726 832779)
East of St Austell. Nearest main road: A390 from Lostwithiel to St Austell.

rear view

11 Bedrooms. Normally £27–£45 **but for readers of this book only there are 2 rooms at a dinner-inclusive price of £72 for 2 days; also half-price b & b for 2 nights, November to mid-December and in March.** Bargain breaks. All have some or all of the following: own bath/shower/toilet; TV; views of sea; balcony.
Dinner. £16 for 3 courses and coffee, at 7–8.30pm. Vegetarian or other special diets if ordered. Wine available. No smoking. **Light suppers.**
3 Sitting-rooms. With TV. **Bar.**
Small garden
Closed in January and February.

Built in 1830 as a seaside retreat for the Bishop of Truro, this fine house has been furnished with the elegance it deserves. The handsome mouldings, arches and panelling of the hall and octagonal landing are now decorated in green and cream; and each bedroom is different – a pale colour scheme in one; sprigged covers and pine in another; four with covered verandahs of lacy ironwork facing the tiny walled garden and waterfront beyond it. The dining-room has spacious views from the big picture-windows; the bar, rosy armchairs and a thick pale carpet. Eight-foot marble pillars were uncovered in one bedroom.

Carol and John Roberts give equal attention to the standard of the food. At dinner, you might choose your main dish from a selection that includes (for instance) boned chicken in a sauce of mushrooms and cider, beef Wellington, rack of lamb and local fish in a variety of ways.

MEVAGISSEY HOUSE

C(7) PT

Vicarage Hill, Mevagissey, Cornwall, PL26 6SZ Tel: 01726 842427
(Fax: 01726 844327)
South of St Austell. Nearest main road: A390 from Truro to St Austell.

4 Bedrooms. £19–£22 (less for 7 nights or more). Some have some or all of the following: own bath/shower/toilet; TV; views of sea. No smoking.
Light suppers if ordered.
2 Sitting-rooms. With open fire, TV. No smoking (in one). **Bar.**
Large garden
Closed from November to March.

Perched high on a hill above Mevagissey, and looking south towards the sea, is this handsome 18th-century house (once it was a vicarage and one of the bedrooms is in the old Sunday school). A great picture-window in the sitting-room makes the most of the view. The cupboards and chests of drawers have been attractively drag-rolled in pastel shades. A huge carpeted bathroom belongs to bedroom no. 2. Brass beds upstairs, enormous red sofas in the sitting-room and handsome dining-chairs round the big old table in the breakfast-room add individual touches.

For evening meals, Gill and John Westmacott recommend the School House restaurant in Pentewan, or one of the local pubs.

Four acres of garden surround the house, which is approached down a long tree-lined drive: spectacular in spring, when the rhododendrons and azaleas are in bloom, and lovely in autumn. The Lost Gardens of Heligan are a few minutes' drive away.

OLD BOROUGH HOUSE

Bossiney, Tintagel, Cornwall, PL34 0AY   Tel: 01840 770475
South of Bude. Nearest main road: A39 from Bude to Camelford.

6 Bedrooms. £17–£20. Bargain breaks. Some have some or all of the following: own bath/shower/toilet; views of sea.
Dinner. £12 for 4 courses and coffee, at 7pm. Vegetarian diets if ordered. Wine available. No smoking. **Light suppers** if ordered.
2 Sitting-rooms. With open fire/stove, TV. **Bar.**
Small garden

1683 is carved on one wall of slate that came from England's largest quarry (at Delabole, near Camelford), a spectacular sight, which has been getting bigger and bigger since Tudor times. You are unlikely ever to see a bigger hole.

Once the house was the residence of the mayors of Bossiney (later, of J.B. Priestley). It has small windows set in thick walls, low beams, steps up and down, twisting corridors, a log stove in the sitting-room which has crimson velvet armchairs, and a bar in the roomy entrance hall. From the garden there is a sea view.

Christina Rayner serves such meals as tomato soup with cream, carbonnade of beef, crème brûlée, and cheeses.

All along this coast are picturesque fishing villages such as Boscastle, Tintagel and Port Isaac, but the scenery inland deserves to be explored too. An interesting day's drive might start at Tintagel with a visit to the ruined seashore castle.

Readers' comments: Charming and friendly. Lovely old house. Food of consistently high standard – sweets delectable! Could not fault the house.

V

OLD MILL

Little Petherick, Cornwall, PL27 7QT   Tel: 01841 540388
South of Padstow. On A389 from Padstow to Bodmin.

6 Bedrooms. £19–£27.50 **to readers with a current edition of this book.** Bargain breaks. All have some or all of the following: own bath/shower/toilet; views of river. No smoking.
Light suppers if ordered. Wine available. No smoking.
3 Sitting-rooms. With TV. No smoking in one.
Small garden
Closed from November to February.

This picturesque 16th-century watermill (with a working waterwheel) is beside a stream that winds its way into the Camel estuary – an Area of Outstanding Natural Beauty, along a coastline celebrated for its many beautiful beaches (a number protected by the National Trust).

Michael and Pat Walker have furnished the Mill very attractively. The beamy sitting-room has white stone walls, one with a mural of ploughing. William Morris fabric and Berber carpet contrast with the green slate of the floor. All around are unusual 'finds': an ancient typewriter and sewing-machines, clocks, and old tools such as planes and picks. The paved terrace by the stream is enclosed by sun-trapping walls, and there is a waterside seating-area at the bottom of the garden. Bedrooms are homely (very nice bathrooms); quieter ones are at the back.

Little Petherick is a pretty village, close to Padstow which is still agreeably antiquated.

Readers' comments: Beautifully furnished. Could not be more pleasant and helpful. Lovely setting. Very hospitable. Excellent in every way. Greatly enjoyed our stay.

V

OLD RECTORY HOTEL

C(12) **D M PT S**

Duloe Road, St Keyne, Cornwall, PL14 4RL   Tel: 01579 342617
South of Liskeard. Nearest main road: A38 from Liskeard to Saltash.

8 Bedrooms. £20–£27 (less for 7 nights or more). Bargain breaks. All have some or all of the following: own bath/shower/toilet; TV.
Dinner. £16 for 3 courses and coffee, at 7pm. Vegetarian or other special diets if ordered. Wine available. No smoking. **Light suppers** if ordered.
2 Sitting-rooms. With open fires, TV, piano. **Bar.**
Large garden

An early 19th-century building, the Old Rectory has very handsome architectural features, and fine furniture in keeping with this.

In the sitting-room (with glass doors to the garden) are capacious velvet sofas and, through an arch, a green and red bar. Two bedrooms have lacy, modern four-posters; one bedroom is on the ground floor.

Pat and John Minifie either offer snacks or such dishes as soup, a roast or locally caught fish (with garden vegetables), and meringues or bread-and-butter pudding.

St Keyne, being fairly high up, has panoramic views and is surrounded by varied scenery: moors, beaches, cliffs and woodland paths are all at hand.

Readers' comments: Excellent cooking with quality ingredients; warm and welcoming. Charming atmosphere of true repose and Victorian elegance. Food exceptional. Very good; nice people. Very well furnished; food beautifully cooked. Quite exceptional.

OLD VICARAGE

C

Morwenstow, Cornwall, EX23 9SR   Tel: 01288 331369 (Fax: 01288 356077)
North of Bude. Nearest main road: A39 from Bude to Bideford.

3 Bedrooms. £20. Bargain breaks. All have some or all of the following: own bath/shower/toilet; views of sea. No smoking.
Dinner. £16 for aperitif, 4 courses, wine and coffee, at 7.30pm. Vegetarian or other special diets if ordered. No smoking. **Light suppers** if ordered.
2 Sitting-rooms. With open fire/stove, TV. No smoking (in one). **Bar.**
Large garden
Closed from December to mid-January.

Find Morwenstow church and you are within calling distance of the Old Vicarage, although you might think you are never coming to it as you descend the winding, wooded drive. Then you will see the extraordinary chimneys of this splendid Victorian pile, each reputedly modelled on the tower of a church with which its first incumbent had been associated.

Jill and Richard Wellby have created an elegant and comfortable ambience for their visitors, while retaining such original features as the handsome slate-and-tile hall floor and the marble fireplace in the dining-room. The sitting-room is pink and grey, with claret velvet curtains and a carved stone fireplace. Up the shallow staircase, all the bedrooms have arched windows and an individual style. There is a billiard-room up here, too, with a bar.

A typical dinner might comprise crab bisque, chicken in herbs, and summer pudding with Cornish cream, followed by cheese and biscuits.

Readers' comments: Delightful, a mouthwatering place, a gastronomic feast.

OLD VICARAGE

Treneglos, Cornwall, PL15 8UQ   Tel: 01566 781351

North-west of Launceston. Nearest main road: A395 from Launceston towards Camelford.

C(2)

2 Bedrooms. £20–£24. Both have some or all of the following: own bath/shower/toilet. No smoking.
Dinner (by arrangement). £15 for 3 courses and coffee, at 7pm. Vegetarian or other special diets if ordered. No smoking.
1 Sitting-room. With TV, piano. No smoking.
Large garden
Closed from November to February.

At the idyllically situated, 18th-century Old Vicarage, Maggie Fancourt grows old-fashioned, fragrant sweetpeas and shrub roses for her guests, as well as organically produced fruit and vegetables. Dinners, such as goat's cheese soufflé, Normandy pork (local meat with apples and cream), and home-made ice cream or orange and lemon mousse, are served in the elegant blue and cream dining-room with its lovely Chinese-style curtains. Cream teas with home-made jam are irresistible. In the bedrooms, Maggie's attention to detail extends even to the coathangers, which are covered in fabric to match the pretty flowered wallpaper.

From Launceston you can visit the majestic and romantic north Cornish coast, or head inland to wild Bodmin Moor to discover hidden, unspoilt villages. The coast has stark cliffs, waterfalls and wide sands; the moor, high tors that can be reached only on foot or horse-back. Don't miss the elaborately carved church (St Mary's) in Launceston itself, an old-world market town. The area is full of Arthurian legends; Daphne du Maurier's Jamaica Inn is on the moor.

OLD VICARAGE HOTEL

Parc-an-Creet, St Ives, Cornwall, TR26 2ET   Tel/Fax: 01736 796124

Nearest main road: A30 from Redruth to Penzance.

C D PT

8 Bedrooms. £18–£24 (less for 3 nights or more). All have some or all of the following: own bath/shower/toilet; TV.
Light suppers by arrangement.
1 Sitting-room. With TV. **Bar.** Piano, etc.
Large garden
Closed from November to Easter.

Built of silvery granite in the 1850s, this hotel (among houses on the outskirts of St Ives) is entered via a small conservatory and a great iron-hinged door of ecclesiastical shape, which opens into a hall with red-and-black tiled floor. Mr and Mrs Sykes have done their best to pre-serve this period ambience, furnishing the bar with crimson-and-gold flock wallpaper and all kinds of Victoriana. In addition, there are a sitting-room and a blue-and-gold dining-room. Big windows and handsome fireplaces feature throughout; and the Sykeses have put in excellent carpets, along with good, solid furniture – a 'thirties walnut suite in one bedroom, and velvet-upholstered bedheads. The Anna French fabrics and wallpapers were designed by the Sykeses' talented daughter, and many of the paintings in the house are hers too. There is a refurbished Victorian loo, preserved in all its glory of blue lilies and rushes.

Readers' comments: Excellent in every way. Attention to detail outstanding. Cannot praise highly enough. So good, beautifully kept, warm welcome. Thoroughly recommended. Atmosphere most civilized, attention to detail impeccable.

V

PENROSE HOUSE

C D P T

Nancherrow, St Just, Cornwall, TR19 7PP   Tel: 01736 787218
West of Penzance. Nearest main road: A3071 from Penzance to St Just.

3 Bedrooms. £18–£23. Bargain breaks. One has own bath/shower/toilet; TV (in all). No smoking preferred.
Dinner (by arrangement). £12 for 3 courses and coffee, at times to suit guests. Vegetarian or other special diets if ordered. No smoking. **Light suppers** if ordered.
1 Sitting-room. With open fire. No smoking.
Large garden

There were tin mines operating in this area right up until the market collapsed in the 1980s. In 1854, however, the industry was buoyant enough to enable Stephen Harvey James, a mine captain from nearby Botallack, to build this substantial granite house on a commanding site high above the road outside St Just. Both Anthony Holman and Beth are steeped in Cornish lore, and can suggest local walks and trips to sacred sites, stone circles, etc.

Bedrooms are big, light and airy, with solid old furniture; the bathroom shared by two of them is positively luxurious. Downstairs, the pink-and-peppermint dining-room (where Beth serves, by arrangement, such meals as egg mayonnaise, a casserole or fish, and fruit with clotted cream) is hung, like the rest of the house, with her mother's paintings; Beth herself is an artist and a potter, and runs healing and meditation sessions for those who want them. Relaxation is the order of the day, whether in the sitting-room, in the book-filled hall, or on the south-facing terrace in front of the house.

Reader's comments: Excellent rooms, a most welcoming lady.

PENVITH BARNS

C D M S X

St Martin by Looe, Cornwall, PL13 1NZ   Tel: 01503 240772
East of Looe. Nearest main road: A387 from Looe to Torpoint.

3 Bedrooms. £15–£20 (less for 3 nights or more). Bargain breaks. All have own shower/toilet; TV. No smoking.
Dinner. £13 for 3 courses and coffee, at 7pm. Vegetarian or other special diets if ordered. Wine available. No smoking. **Light suppers** if ordered.
1 Sitting-room. With open fire, TV. No smoking.
Large garden

Across the river above East Looe, the imaginative conversion of Anne McQueen's Penvith Barns unearthed an underground tunnel whose original purpose is still obscure; Anne has gathered a file of historical notes for her own and her guests' interest. What is known is that parts of the barn are 500 years old (you enter the kitchen under an original beam), and a millwheel found in the tunnel now forms the hearth of the back-to-back sitting- and dining-room fires. Bedrooms are immaculate, with roomy showers; dinner might comprise home-made soup, fresh local trout, and Bakewell tart.

It is easy to find secluded beaches and coves westward, or scenic walks along clifftops. Easily reached from here are Lanhydrock House and gardens, Restormel Castle, Charlestown and Wheal Martin China Clay Museum. Cornwall has a spring gardens festival with a leaflet about the 55 gardens that participate. One, famous for camellias in an 18th-century setting, is perched on the clifftop at Trewithen; another, with superb sea views, is Trelissick; and Polruan is a spectacular headland garden.

V   *Readers' comments:* Highly recommended; extremely good meal.

ROSEVEAR BRIDGE COTTAGE
Mawgan, Cornwall, TR12 6AZ Tel: 01326 221672
South-east of Helston. Nearest main road: A3083 from Helston to the Lizard.

3 Bedrooms. £16–£22 (less for 4 nights or more). One has own shower/toilet. No smoking.
Dinner. £9.50 for 2 courses and coffee, at 7pm. Vegetarian diets if ordered. No smoking. **Light suppers** if ordered.
1 Sitting-room. With TV. No smoking.
Small garden
Closed from October to Easter.

Near the centre of the lovely Lizard peninsula is Rosevear Bridge Cottage, on a little tributary of the Helford River. A white house with neat brown shutters, it began life as a cowman's cottage centuries ago. Everything, including the sloping garden, is trim, the windows are low and deep-set, and an open-tread staircase rises through the sitting-room to immaculate bedrooms, varying in size. Hazel Howard uses garden produce for such homely meals as chicken pie and trifle.

The Lizard (Cornish for 'high place') is England's southernmost point, stunningly beautiful but with a craggy coast infamous for shipwrecks. It is less frequented than most of Cornwall despite its many charms. There are thatched cottages by the beaches at Coverack and Cadgwith where crabs are landed. Ruan Minor has a church built of the local serpentine stone (with snakelike markings).

Readers' comments: Absolutely loved it. Extremely friendly and helpful. A most happy and comfortable stay.

V

SUNDAY SCHOOL
C S X
Copthorne, North Petherwin, Cornwall, PL15 8NB Tel: 01566 785723 or 781552
North-west of Launceston. Nearest main road: A30 from Launceston to Bodmin.

2 Bedrooms. £18–£20. Both have own shower/toilet; TV. No smoking.
Dinner. £14 for 3 courses and coffee, from 7pm. Vegetarian or other special diets if ordered. No smoking. **Light suppers** if ordered.
1 Sitting-room. With stove. No smoking.
Large garden

In a tiny hamlet deep in the Cornish countryside, Sharon Seal has succeeded in creating something quite out of the ordinary. A century ago, farmers stabled their horses in what is now a comfortable sitting-room, with its original roughcast stone walls, while their children trooped up the wide, shallow stairs to the huge room above to learn their Bible stories. That space has now been beautifully converted into two immaculate, unfussy bedrooms bright with fresh flowers, patchwork and pine furniture; in one, a ladder leads to a gallery bed above. On Thursdays to Saturdays, the pretty blue-and-green dining-room is open to non-residents and the choice of dishes is wide; on other nights, the choice is more limited but the quality just as good – for Sharon is a professional cook. One might start with smoked mackerel and horseradish pâté served with oatcakes, followed by beef cooked in stout with herb and cheese dumplings. Puddings are equally delicious.

The house is within easy reach of spectacular walking country.

Reader's comment: Renovated in a most attractive way.

V

TREGADDRA FARM

C X

Cury, Cornwall, TR12 7BB   Tel/Fax: 01326 240235
South of Helston. Nearest main road: A3083 from Helston to the Lizard.

5 Bedrooms. £18.50–£22. Bargain breaks. All have some or all of the following: own bath/shower/toilet; views of sea; balcony. No smoking.
Dinner. £10 for 3 courses and coffee, at 6.30pm. Vegetarian or other special diets if ordered. No smoking.
2 Sitting-rooms. With open fire (in one), TV. No smoking.
Large garden

A beautifully kept garden of winding flowerbeds, tennis court and spacious swimming-pool (heated) is the setting for this immaculate house, built in the 18th century but much modernized since. Two upstairs bedrooms have balconies. All around are distant views, especially fine when the sun is setting over the sea. In the other direction, Goonhilly's satellite station on the moors is quite spectacular too.

Rooms are well furnished, with plenty of space and comfort. When evenings are chilly, logs blaze in a granite inglenook, and there is a glass sun-room to make the most of the mild climate in this very southerly part of England.

For dinners, June Lugg uses the produce of the farm (vegetables, beef) whenever she can. With the beef comes something different from the usual Yorkshire pudding: Cornish cobblers. This might be followed by blackberry and apple crumble – one for each family – with clotted cream.

The Lizard peninsula is a particularly beautiful area. There are sandy beaches and coves, fishing villages, old inns, coastal walks and all the creeks of the Helford River to explore.

TREGOLLS FARM

C S

St Wenn, Cornwall, PL30 5PG   Tel: 01208 812154
West of Bodmin. Nearest main road: A30 from Exeter to Penzance and A39 from Wadebridge to Truro.

4 Bedrooms. £14.50–£16 (less for 3 nights or more). One has own shower. No smoking.
Dinner. £7.50 for 3 courses and coffee, at 7pm. Vegetarian or other special diets if ordered. No smoking. **Light suppers** if ordered.
1 Sitting-room. With stove, TV. No smoking.
Garden

Tregolls is more or less bang in the middle of Cornwall, making it an ideal centre from which to explore the whole beautiful and endlessly varying county. The old stone-built farmhouse is the hub of a 107-acre mixed farm, rearing cattle and sheep (with some arable crops); it has been in the Hawkey family for over 50 years, and Marilyn's husband was born here. Bedrooms – with handsome stripped pine doors – are prettily furnished and comfortable; the family room has its own shower and coronet drapes over the bedhead, and there's a single room too. Those at the front share the lovely view to be had from both the sitting- and the dining-rooms downstairs: across the sloping garden to the rolling countryside beyond, as far as the eye can see.

The farm's own beef and lamb may appear in the dining-room (whose walls are hung with Marilyn's collection of attractive china plates), followed by, perhaps, blackberry and apple pie (with custard *and* Cornish cream), or queen of puddings.

Reader's comments: Beautiful views, beautifully decorated bedrooms, excellent home-cooked food.

TREGONGON HOUSE

Ruan High Lanes, Cornwall, TR2 5LD   Tel: 01872 501708
South-east of Truro. Nearest main road: A3078 from Tregony to St Mawes.

2 Bedrooms. £19 (less for 6 nights or more). Both have own bath/shower/toilet; TV. No smoking.
Dinner. £12 for 3 courses and coffee, at 7pm. Vegetarian or other special diets if ordered. No smoking.
1 Sitting-room. With woodstove, piano. No smoking.
9 acres including gardens
Closed from December to February.

The present house, built on classic Georgian lines, replaced a much older farmhouse; today, Tregongon, with its remaining nine acres of land (including lovely gardens and paddocks for two horses), is the home of Joan and Terry Scullion, who moved down here from Cheshire in 1987.

Bedrooms are charming, bright with chintz and pine; both command magnificent country views, and one has its own small sitting-room from which to enjoy them, as well as a pretty pink-and-green bathroom. A baby grand piano takes pride of place in the downstairs sitting-room, where the exposed stone of the original timber-frame walls is white-painted. Through an alcove, the book-filled dining-room is the setting for such meals as seafood Mornay pancakes; roast duckling with orange, caramel and brandy sauce; and brown bread ice cream.

Set in the heart of the popular Roseland peninsula, Tregongon is within easy reach of gardens (Trelissick), beaches (Pendower, Carne) and, for walkers, the South-West Coast Path.

TREGONY HOUSE

Tregony, Cornwall, TR2 5RN   Tel: 01872 530671
East of Truro. Nearest main road: A3078 from St Mawes towards St Austell.

rear view

5 Bedrooms. £18.75–£22.50 (less for 7 nights or more). Bargain breaks. Some have some or all of the following: own bath/shower/toilet. No smoking.
Dinner. £11 for 4 courses and coffee, at 7pm. Vegetarian or other special diets if ordered. Wine available. No smoking. **Light suppers** if ordered.
1 Sitting-room. With open fire, TV. **Bar.**
Garden
Closed from December to mid-February.

Behind a cream façade is a house partly dating from the 17th century; later, additions were made – so the slate-flagged dining-room, for instance, is low-beamed and thick-walled while the hall and sitting-room have great elegance. All the bedrooms have their own individual character and comfortable style.

In the dining-room (furnished with oriental rugs, oak tables and Windsor chairs) Cathy and Andy Webb serve such meals as home-made soup, Spanish pork (cooked with olives and tomatoes), and lemon pudding (plus local cheeses). Herbs etc. are from the garden.

Readers' comments: Extremely comfortable. Dinners excellent and varied. A very happy stay. Well looked after, kindness itself. Friendly and obliging hosts, dinners particularly enjoyable. Exceptional value, comfort and attention to detail. Food excellent; most helpful.

V

TREMEARNE

C D PT

Bone Valley, Heamoor, Cornwall, TR20 8UJ   Tel: 01736 364576 (Fax: 01736 350957)
West of Penzance. Nearest main road: A30 from Penzance to Land's End.

5 Bedrooms. £20–£27.50 (less for 3 nights or more). All have some or all of the following: own bath/ shower/toilet. No smoking.
Dinner. £12.50 for 2 courses and coffee, at 7pm. Vegetarian or other special diets if ordered. No smoking. **Light suppers if ordered.**
1 Sitting-room. With open fire, TV.
Large garden
Closed in December and January.

The granite house was neglected and the walled grounds completely overgrown with brambles, a Sleeping Beauty scene, when Sally Adams and her family came here. They restored the 'Jubilee' rose garden (planted in the year of Queen Victoria's diamond jubilee), and found many old-fashioned varieties still surviving – such as the lovely Albertine rambler rose, the scent of which greets you as you arrive.

One enters through a tiled conservatory, decorated with garlands of dried flowers. This is where Sally serves such dinners as chicken in saffron and tomato sauce, and plum crumble.

In the Victorian-style sitting-room, there are carpets and armchairs of deep turquoise contrasting with cream walls, and an open fire. Bedrooms have artistic touches and features such as a crochet bedspread in one, old toys in another. There are two family suites.

Readers' comments: Thoroughly recommended. It was home from home, with very friendly attention when needed. Warm welcome, delicious meals. High spot of our holiday.

TRENARTH

S

High Cross, Constantine, Cornwall, TR11 5JN   Tel: 01326 340444
South-west of Falmouth. Nearest main road: A39/A394 from Falmouth to Helston.

2 Bedrooms. £20–£25. Both have own bath/shower/ toilet; TV (in one). No smoking.
Light suppers if ordered.
1 Sitting-room. With open fire, TV.
Large garden

One of those houses which has taken 400 years to grow to its present size, Trenarth is an immediately pleasing combination of the old (the slate-flagged kitchen, through which guests enter the house, dates from the 16th century) and the luxuriously modern: both bathrooms, reached via a few steps from their respective twin bedrooms, are excellent, and one is positively decadent, with a raised Jacuzzi complete with appropriate mural, and a roomy shower. The bedrooms themselves are light and elegant; one has warm red Welsh tapestry spreads, the other particularly fine views of the surrounding countryside and Trenarth's spacious grounds, which include a listed 18th-century walled garden as well as rosebeds, orchard and rhododendron copse.

Breakfast, with home-made marmalade and local honey, is taken in the slate-floored dining room, which has an enormous open fireplace and mullioned windows. Lucie Nottingham offers light suppers only, but there are several eating-places within a few miles' radius.

Magnolia grandiflora, jasmine and plumbago flourish in the splendid Edwardian conservatory – there is table tennis too.

Readers' comments: Utterly quiet; beautiful garden and incomparable views, super breakfasts and a delightful lady.

TRENESTRALL FARM

C D M S

Ruan High Lanes, Cornwall, TR2 5LX   Tel: 01872 501259
South-east of Truro. Nearest main road: A3078 from Tregony to St Mawes.

3 Bedrooms. £15. No smoking.
Dinner (by arrangement). £11 for 3 courses and coffee, at times to suit guests. Vegetarian or other special diets if ordered. No smoking. **Light suppers** if ordered.
1 Sitting-room. With TV. No smoking.
Garden
Closed from November to February.

A farm holiday for walkers, a beach holiday, or just a country holiday for townies: Trenestrall offers all of these, situated as it is within easy reach of the South-West Coast Path, a choice of fine beaches (south-facing Pendower is the closest) and the cathedral city of Truro. Accommodation is homely and comfortable: there are books and games in the sitting-room (with far views over the surrounding farmland and countryside; guests take breakfast here, too, in high-backed, cane-seated chairs round the communal table). The family room looks out over a 200-year-old stone barn on one side and has a circular window set into the roughcast stone wall on another. It's a mixed farm – beef, sheep and cereals – and the Palmers rear pedigree Charolais cattle which they sometimes show. Ann's farmhouse meals might feature Trenestrall's own produce; alternatively, visitors dine at the pleasant Roseland Inn a mile away in Philleigh, which welcomes children and provides good-value food.

Cornwall's famous rhododendrons are at their best in April and May, and several gardens can be easily visited from Trenestrall.

V

TREROSEWILL FARM

C M PT S

Paradise, Boscastle, Cornwall, PL35 0DL   Tel/Fax: 01840 250545
South-west of Bude. Nearest main road: A39 from Wadebridge to Bude.

7 Bedrooms. £16–£30 (less for 3 nights or more). Bargain breaks. All have some or all of the following: own bath/shower/toilet; TV; views of sea. No smoking.
Dinner (by arrangement). £16 for 4 courses and coffee, at 6.30pm. Vegetarian or other special diets if ordered. Wine available. No smoking. **Light suppers** if ordered.
1 Sitting-room. With log stove, TV. No smoking. **Bar. Large garden**

Perched high above the picturesque fishing village of Boscastle is this modern farmhouse built by Steve and Cheryl Nicholls, whose families have farmed and fished in this area for generations. In each bedroom is a copy of an old newspaper photograph of Steve's great-grandfather, who was rescued and brought home by a Welsh fishing vessel after his own boat had foundered and he had been given up for lost. In the photograph, he is wearing a Guernsey sweater knitted in the traditional Boscastle style: each fishing village had its own distinctive pattern so that bodies salvaged after accidents at sea could be brought home to their own communities for identification and burial.

Bedrooms – named after areas of Boscastle – are delightful, varying considerably in size but all prettily decorated in pastel shades and flowered fabrics; several have sea views. One has a brass bed, another a four-poster. Downstairs in the cheerful peppermint-green dining-room, Cheryl serves such farmhouse fare as home-made soup, a roast (the farm produces its own pork and lamb) or a dish like steak-and-kidney pudding, and apple pie.

V

TREVIADES BARTON

D S

High Cross, near Constantine, Cornwall, TR11 5RG   Tel/Fax: 01326 340524
South-west of Falmouth. Nearest main road: A39 from Truro to Falmouth.

3 Bedrooms. £19–£25. All have some or all of the following: own bath/shower/toilet; TV; views of river. No smoking.
Dinner (by arrangement). £17 for 4 courses, wine and coffee, at 8pm. Vegetarian or other special diets if ordered. No smoking. **Light suppers** if ordered.
1 Sitting-room. With open fire. Piano, TV room.
Large garden

This most unusual, U-shaped, 16th-century house is approached through a narrow and picturesque courtyard (paved with slate and full of daisies). Some parts of the present building may be as old as the 13th century, and successive owners have discovered old wells, fish tanks, disused fireplaces and windows, ancient steps and alcoves.

The long sitting-room is 18th-century, with an Adam fireplace at one end, flanked by alcoves of china. Elegant tapestry and patchwork cushions (Judy Ford's skilled work) are on the armchairs and sofas, marine watercolours on the walls.

An example of Judy's dinners: pâté with green mayonnaise, salmon trout, French apple flan with elderflower sorbet, and cheeses (wine included).

Readers' comments: A unique experience. Charming and welcoming hosts. Exceptionally attractive gardens. Excellent dinner, comfortable room. Best place we have stayed in. Helpful, pleasant and friendly. Wonderful food. Sheer delight.

TREWERRY MILL

C(7) PT S

St Newlyn East, Cornwall, TR8 5HS   Tel: 01872 510345
South-east of Newquay. Nearest main road: A3058 from Newquay to St Austell.

6 Bedrooms. £16–£21 (less for 7 nights or more). Some have some or all of the following: own shower/toilet; views of river. No smoking.
Light suppers if ordered. Vegetarian or other special diets if ordered. Wine available. No smoking.
1 Sitting-room. With open fire, TV. No smoking.
Large garden
Closed from November to February.

Trewerry Mill was built in 1639 to provide flour for the household of the nearby Elizabethan manor, Trerice (now a National Trust property), and corn continued to be milled here until after the Second World War.

One passes through a stone-flagged hall to a sitting-room with log fire and a window through which there is a view inside the old waterwheel. Bedrooms are not large, but neat and comfortable. Extensive, tranquil gardens lead down to a pond and the River Gannel, and include a length of the old Newquay to Perranporth railway line, with its arched bridge over the river.

Light suppers only, but morning coffee, lunches and cream teas are served in the garden on warm summer days (your table may be made from an old millstone). David and Terri Clark can recommend local walks and a variety of nearby eating-places to guests.

Readers' comments: Nothing too much trouble. Gloriously quiet and peaceful, wonderful care and attention. Marvellous garden.

TREWORGIE BARTON

Crackington Haven, Cornwall, EX23 0NL   Tel/Fax: 01840 230233
South-west of Bude. Nearest main road: A39 from Bude to Camelford.

4 Bedrooms. £18–£23 (less for 7 nights or more). Bargain breaks. All have some of the following: own bath/shower/toilet; TV; views of sea. No smoking.
Dinner. £15 for 4 courses and coffee, at 7pm. Vegetarian or other special diets if ordered. No smoking.
1 Sitting-room. With open fire. No smoking.
Large garden
Closed in October, December and January.

Although the name of this 16th-century house means 'homestead above the water, capable of growing corn', the farmland is now confined to grazing for cattle, with 30 acres of ancient woodland (there are marked trails for walkers). Annexed to the Duchy of Cornwall by Henry VIII, illegally sold by Elizabeth I and then repossessed by James I, the manor was previously held by the Prior of Launceston; the inglenook in the dining-room has been dated back to that period. Its recent history, however, has been less turbulent; before Pam and Tony Mount came here, the house had been in the same family for 120 years.

Stairs lead up from the slate-floored hall to a small landing sitting-area and two attractive bedrooms (one with far sea view), with pine furniture and pretty floral fabrics. Some guests prefer the privacy of the family suite, immaculately converted, in a former tractor shed.

Pam, an accomplished cook, serves such dinners as leek and bacon soup with freshly baked rolls, lamb cooked with fresh rosemary, and whisky-and-coffee pudding with hazelnut macaroons and Cornish clotted cream.

WHEATLEY FARM

Maxworthy, Cornwall, PL15 8LY   Tel/Fax: 01566 781232
North-west of Launceston. Nearest main road: A39 from Wadebridge to Bude.

4 Bedrooms. £20–£22 (less for 3 nights or more). Bargain breaks. All have some or all of the following: own bath/shower/toilet; TV. No smoking.
Dinner (by arrangement). From £13 for 4 courses and coffee, at about 7pm. Vegetarian or other special diets if ordered. No smoking. **Light suppers** if ordered.
1 Sitting-room. With woodstove, TV. No smoking.
Large garden
Closed from November to February.

Wheatley has been in the same family for generations; Raymond and Valerie Griffin's son will be the fifth in succession to work this substantial dairy and sheep farm deep in the rolling Cornish countryside. The handsome farmhouse was built in 1871 by the Duke of Bedford; when the Griffins repaired an ageing window, they discovered the ducal seal stamped in the original oak lintel.

One enters the house through the imposing hall. It is beautifully decorated in shades of green, with floral curtains and frieze. The sitting-room, too, is sumptuous and welcoming, and there is a granite inglenook with cloam (bread) oven in the dining-room, which also has a magnificent antique mahogany table and matching sideboard.

Upstairs, the bedrooms are attractively furnished with country-style pine; one has a fourposter and en suite corner bath.

A typical dinner might be home-made soup or pâté, home-produced or local beef or lamb, rhubarb-and-blackcurrant crumble topped with Cornish clotted cream, and English cheeses.

WOODLANDS

CMPTS

Trewollock, Goran Haven, Cornwall, PL26 6NS   Tel: 01726 843821
South of St Austell. Nearest main road: A390 from St Austell to Truro.

6 Bedrooms. £20–£22. All have some or all of the following: own shower/toilet; views of sea. No smoking.
Dinner (by arrangement). £16.50 for 3 courses and coffee, at 7pm. Vegetarian or other special diets if ordered. No smoking.
1 Sitting-room. With open fire, TV. No smoking.
Large garden
Closed in December and January.

Near the one-time fishing village of Gorran Haven is Woodlands, a homely 1930s house on a lovely site with sea views and a 10-minute path leading down to the sands and rocks. In the garden is a pair of wild ponds – the top one has fish and waterlilies, and by the secluded bottom one are seats from which to enjoy the sight of the sea below. There's a verandah to sit on, too, and a barbecue for visitors' use. Four bedrooms have sea views; one is on the ground floor.

Lynn Shelton makes all her own scones, cakes and jams and cooks such evening meals as celery chowder, roast beef with organic local vegetables, and apple strudel – served in a sun-trapping dining-room.

The coastline is rightly called 'the English Riviera': subtropical flowers abound between sandy coves, steep headlands like Dodman Point (of the novel *Dead Man's Rock*), quaint fishing villages and secretive creeks.

Readers' comments: Impressed with the decor of the bedrooms and the wonderful views. Entertained us with imagination and generosity. More than hospitable, excellent meals.

V

For explanation of code letters and **V** symbol, see inside front cover.

Prices are per person sharing a room at the beginning of the year.

Where wine is not available (meaning it is on sale or can be fetched for you), you are nearly always welcome to bring in your own drinks.

THANK YOU . . . to those who send details of their own finds, for possible future inclusion in the book. Do not be disappointed if your candidate does not appear in the very next edition. We never publish recommendations from unknown members of the public without verification, and it takes time to get round each part of England and Wales in turn. Please, however, do not send details of houses already featured in many other guides, nor any that are more expensive than those in this book (see page ix).

CUMBRIA

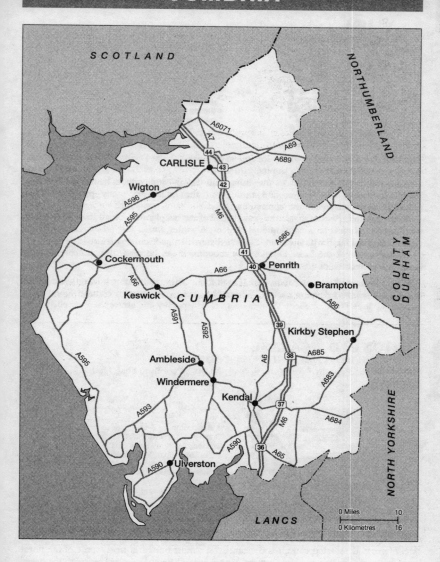

'Bargain breaks' are usually out-of-season reductions for half-board stays of several nights.

THE ARCHWAY

College Road, Windermere, Cumbria, LA23 1BY   Tel: 015394 45613
Nearest main road: A591 from Kendal to Ambleside.

4 Bedrooms. £20–£22 (less for 3 nights or more). Bargain breaks. All have some or all of the following: own bath/shower/toilet; TV. No smoking.
Dinner. £12.50 for 2 courses and coffee, at 6.45pm (not Sundays). 3 courses in winter. Vegetarian or other special diets if ordered. Wine available. No smoking.
Light suppers if ordered.
1 Sitting-room. With open fire. No smoking.
Small garden

The Archway is in a Victorian terrace typical of those in Lake District towns, built of green slate above road level behind a sloping garden.

A big semicircular arch divides the sitting-cum-dining-room with its handsome fireplace. There are books everywhere; and throughout the house are many pictures. (Tony Greenhalgh has a degree in the history of art).

Anthony and Aurea share the cooking, baking wholemeal bread every morning. Breakfast could include unconventional choices. A winter dinner might be cream of watercress soup; roast lamb with home-made rowanberry jelly; and frangipani tart.

In the centre of the Lake District (the mountains can be seen from the rooms), the house is within reach of many 'sights'.

Readers' comments: Pleasant atmosphere. Good food. They really know how to make guests happy. Attention to detail is perfect. Where else could you get such comfort, good food, good company? Truly excellent. A fabulous time. Hospitality and atmosphere excellent.

V

BARTON OLD VICARAGE

Tirril, Cumbria, CA10 2LR   Tel: 017684 86307
South-west of Penrith. Nearest main road: A6 from Penrith to Shap (and M6, junction 40).

3 Bedrooms. £17–£19.50 (less for 3 nights or more). One has own shower/toilet; TV. No smoking.
Dinner (by arrangement). £14 for 4 courses and coffee, at 6–8pm. Vegetarian or other special diets if ordered. Wine available. No smoking. **Light suppers.**
2 Sitting-rooms. With open fire. TV, piano.
Large garden
Closed from December to February.

A mediaeval church and a Victorian vicarage make a familiar pair in the English countryside. Here, both isolated church and vicarage lie almost buried in trees, some of the finest being in the wooded part of the Walkers' big garden. The rooms too are big, with the heavy pitch-pine joinery of the period. Folding doors lead from the sitting-room, with its view of Helvellyn, to the music room – which lives up to its name, as it contains a Bechstein grand, music stands and a music centre.

Scottish Sherie Walker is not only a linguist but a trained cook (who enjoys company in the kitchen). A typical meal: watercress soup, pork en croûte, and a fruit pie.

Bedrooms are large, with fine views towards the mountains of the Lake District.

Readers' comments: We received a warm welcome, comfort, an excellent dinner. The house stands in a lovely situation and is well furnished. Relaxed and welcoming atmosphere.

V

BIRSLACK GRANGE

Hutton Lane, Levens, Cumbria, LA8 8PA   Tel: 015395 60989
South-west of Kendal. Nearest main road: A590 from Kendal towards Ulverston (and M6, junction 36).

4 Bedrooms. £19 (less for 4 nights or more). Bargain breaks. All have own bath/shower/toilet. No smoking.
Dinner (by arrangement). £12 for 3 courses and coffee, at 7pm. Vegetarian or other special diets if ordered. No smoking. **Light suppers** if ordered.
1 Sitting-room. With open fire, TV. No smoking.
Large garden

In a converted barn, John and Jean Carrington-Birch offers comfortable accommodation overlooking the Lyth Valley, famous for damsons. Evening meals (such as home-made vegetable soup, chicken breast in tarragon sauce, and queen of puddings) can be provided. The house is close to two mansions: Levens Hall and Sizergh Castle.

Levens Hall, still in family hands, is Elizabethan, with Jacobean plasterwork and woodwork and contemporary furniture. It contains, as well as much else of interest, the earliest English patchwork. In an outhouse is a collection of steam engines showing the development of steam power in model form. Full-size traction engines are sometimes in steam too. The gardens have been maintained to their original late 17th-century design, including the famous topiary. Nearby Sizergh Castle (NT) has a 14th-century peel tower at its heart. The gardens were among the favourites of the late Dr Alan Gemmell of 'Gardeners' Question Time' fame.

Readers' comments: Good fortune to stay. Delicious breakfast.

CAUSA GRANGE

Rosley, Caldbeck, Cumbria, CA7 8DD   Tel/Fax: 016973 45358
South-east of Wigton. Nearest main road: A595 from Carlisle to Cockermouth (and M6, junction 41).

2 Bedrooms. £19–£25 (less for 3 nights or more). Both have some or all of the following: own bath/shower/toilet; TV. No smoking.
Dinner (by arrangement). £13 for 4 courses and coffee, at 7pm. Vegetarian or other special diets if ordered. No smoking. **Light suppers** if ordered.
2 Sitting-rooms. With open fire, TV. No smoking.
Large garden

Once a farmhouse, Causa Grange was built in 1856 as one of the first works of what is now the giant contracting firm of John Laing. It has luckily escaped subsequent interference, so marble fireplaces, tiled floors, pine joinery, and so on are still intact, and the painted and gilded cornice in the sitting-room has never been defaced with whitewash. (A second sitting-room is available to those who want to avoid television.)

Ann Falck has decorated and furnished the house in keeping while adding such amenities as an extra-large cast-iron bath and bidet to serve one of the bedrooms, which are particularly well equipped. Colours are harmonious, with discreet use of paint and paper on dadoes and ceilings.

One of Ann's dinners (available, like packed lunches, by arrangement) might comprise smoked salmon pâté, braised beef, apple-and-blackberry crumble, cheese, and fruit.

Outside the well-tended garden (Ken Falck's enthusiasm) is beautiful countryside, with the Lake District, the Scottish border, and the west Cumbrian coast not far beyond.

Cumbria

CRACROP FARM

D S

Kirkcambeck, Cumbria, CA8 2BW Tel: 016977 48245 (Fax: 016977 48333)
North of Brampton. Nearest main road: A6071 from Brampton to Longtown.

3 Bedrooms. £20 **to readers of this book.** All have some or all of the following: own shower/toilet; TV. No smoking.
Dinner (by arrangement). £15 for 3 courses and coffee, at 7pm. Vegetarian or other special diets if ordered. No smoking. **Light suppers** if ordered.
1 Sitting-room. With open fire, TV. No smoking.
Large garden

Agriculture and forestry still predominate in the Border hills, truly unspoiled countryside. Typically for the area, Cracrop is principally a stock farm, where the friendly Stobarts are pleased if visitors take an interest in the work. Semi-finalists in a local conservation competition, they have produced an excellent farm trail leaflet which gives an insight into the holding and its interesting past, and also leaflets for walks of a few miles from the house. Sturdier walkers have plenty of routes to follow, too.

If walking is not exertion enough, in the Victorian house are an exercise bike and a rowing-machine (and a snooker table), and to recuperate in, a sauna (for an extra charge) and a spa bath. Then you can relax in the garden to the sound of the ornamental stream.

Bedrooms are sizeable, two giving views of the northern Pennines and the Lake District hills, the other of the farmyard. Each has its own character, with colour-co-ordinated furnishings. The downstairs rooms are comfortably furnished in conventional style.

A typical meal: salmon mousse, a traditional roast, rhubarb crumble and cream. Alternatively, there is a choice of pubs for dinner, including the Abbey Bridge Inn by the river at Lanercost.

Reader's comment: Superior accommodation.

FELL EDGE

C(10) S

High Ireby, Cumbria, CA5 1HF Tel: 016973 71397
North-west of Keswick. Nearest main road: A591 from Keswick towards Carlisle.

2 Bedrooms. £15 (less for 7 nights or more). Both have some or all of the following: own bath/shower/toilet; TV. No smoking.
Dinner. £10 for 4 courses and coffee, at 6.30pm. Vegetarian or other special diets if ordered. No smoking.
1 Sitting-room. With open fire, piano.
Small garden

In the tiny, remote hamlet of High Ireby, Fell Edge, which was built in the 18th century as a chapel, is the home of the highly musical Allison family. This is a place for people who appreciate quietness and views – of the northern fells in one direction and, across the garden which Arthur Allison is landscaping, as far as Dumfries in the other. The garden contributes to such dinner menus as tomato and basil soup, pork in raisin sauce, and meringue glacé. The Allisons have produced a leaflet of walks of various standards. Apart from the northern Lake District, the area is worth exploring for its own sake. People who resist the lure of the Lake District can visit Holm Cultram Abbey, the saltmarshes of the Solway Firth (where salmon are still netted in the old way) and the site of the very end of Hadrian's Wall.

Readers' comments: Stayed there twice and been very satisfied. Wonderful hospitality. Very interesting people. Each meal well cooked and well presented.

V

FOLDGATE FARM

near Bootle Village, Cumbria, LA19 5TN   Tel: 01229 718660
North-west of Ulverston. Nearest main road: A595 from Whitehaven towards Millom.

3 Bedrooms. £14–£15. No smoking.
Dinner (by arrangement). £9 for 4 courses and coffee, at 6pm. Vegetarian or other special diets if ordered. Wine available. No smoking. **Light suppers** if ordered.
1 Sitting-room. With open fire, TV. No smoking.
Small garden
Closed in December.

A real Cumbrian farm near Millom, and well outside the main tourist areas, it covers 170 acres on which are kept sheep as well as some cattle. The approach to the farm is through a cobbled yard, with a great stone byre and stables at one side, Muscovy ducks perching on a dry-stone wall, and pots filled with stonecrop, London pride or primroses.

Guests sometimes eat with the family, by a dresser where mugs hang, the clothes airer suspended overhead and a grandfather clock ticking in one corner. There are bacon-hooks in the ceiling, shepherds' crooks stacked in the hall, and a bright coal fire in the evenings.

Mary Hogg serves real country fare here: Cumberland sausage, 'tatie pot', plum pudding with rum sauce, farm duckling, Herdwick lamb or mutton, rum butter on bread, currant cake with tea on arrival and at bedtime, and jams made from local produce.

Readers' comments: Excellent food, good company. Good food. Lovely welcome. A great success. Never a dull moment! Food, atmosphere and welcome couldn't be faulted. Delighted with our welcome, the food and all the local attractions.

V

Private bathrooms are not necessarily en suite.

Book well ahead: many of these houses have few rooms. Do not expect dinner if you have not booked it or if you arrive late.

Houses which accept the discount vouchers on page ii are marked with a **V** symbol next to the relevant entries.

Facts (prices, etc.) at the top of entries are supplied by the proprietors themselves. While every effort is made to ensure that these are correct at the time of going to press, they may alter thereafter: please check when you book.

THE HERMITAGE

Shap, Cumbria, CA10 3LX Tel: 01931 716671
South of Penrith. On A6 from Kendal to Penrith (and near M6, junction 39).

3 Bedrooms. £16–£20 (less for 4 nights or more). Bargain breaks. All have some or all of the following: own bath/shower/toilet; TV. No smoking.
Dinner. £10.50 for 3 courses and coffee, from 7pm. Vegetarian or other special diets if ordered. No smoking. **Light suppers** if ordered.
2 Sitting-rooms. With open fire, TV, piano. No smoking.
Small garden

This house is perhaps so called because it was built, at least three centuries ago, of stone from Shap Abbey (whose ruins can still be visited). It is a rambling house of beams and low ceilings, with a big old grate glistening with blacking in one guests' sitting-room and a piano in another. A previous owner added a stained-glass window and carved panelling from Lowther Castle a few miles away, now only a shell (of which Jean Jackson has collected a number of old pictures), and in a recent extension, Jean has used window-frames from a demolished cottage at the back of the house. A bedroom in the old part, with lavishly flowery decoration, has a particularly spacious bathroom complete with bidet.

Though the house stands on a main road, there is now little through traffic.

For evening meals, there is a choice of half a dozen simple dishes at each course, including local ingredients and garden produce – robust fare much appreciated by the Coast-to-Coast walkers and cyclists with whom the house is popular.

Readers' comments: Beautifully decorated and furnished; a most welcoming hostess. An exceptionally good find.

HILL TOP HOUSE

C(7) **S**

Morland, Cumbria, CA10 3AX   Tel: 01931 714561
South-east of Penrith. Nearest main road: A6 from Shap to Penrith (and M6, junction 40).

3 Bedrooms. £19. All have some or all of the following: own bath/shower/toilet; TV.
Dinner (by arrangement). £12 for 4 courses and coffee, at 7pm. Vegetarian or other special diets if ordered. Wine available.
1 Sitting-room. With open fire.
Large garden

The Eden Valley is scattered with pleasant villages, their houses built of red sandstone. Hill Top House overlooks the centre of what is probably the oldest, with a Saxon church tower, through which runs a stream with ducks on it. It was built in the 18th century as a farmhouse and is now comfortably furnished with reproduction pieces. It is run by May Smith, one of whose specialities is a 'taste of Cumbria' dinner: Penrith peppered lamb, followed by hot gingerbread and rum butter, and preceded by grilled grapefruit with port. When guests do not dine in the house, they can have generous portions of steak and the like at the village inn.

Visitors are attracted to the area by its peace and quiet – it is very different from the Lake District in summer – and the opportunities for walking (Morland is on the Cumbrian Way long-distance footpath). The nearest town is Appleby, where there is a Norman castle and an old church with a fine organ.

Readers' comments: Professional, friendly, always helpful; food excellent.

HOLMFIELD

41 Kendal Green, Kendal, Cumbria, LA9 5PP   Tel/Fax: 01539 720790
Nearest main road: A591 from Kendal to Windermere.

C(12) **PT S**

3 Bedrooms. £20–£22 (less for 4 nights or more). No smoking.
2 Sitting-rooms. With open fire, TV. No smoking.
Large garden

In a little cul-de-sac at one end of a grassy, open space is this large house, built in the reign of Edward VII and showing the influence of the progressive architecture of the time.

Inside, the rooms are light and airy, and Eileen Kettle has appropriately decorated and furnished them in harmonizing pastel colours. Though the house is close to the town centre, the views from this elevated spot are wide, from Kendal Castle's ruins on the other side of the town to the hills of the Lake District. In the foreground is a large and well tended garden, with a croquet lawn, swimming-pool and summer-house.

The garden is overlooked by a big sitting/dining-room with a characteristically Edwardian inglenook at one end. Here guests help themselves to a big choice of fresh and stewed fruit and breakfast cereals while Eileen cooks – she has become particularly adept at providing for people with special requirements, such as coeliacs.

HULLERBANK

Talkin, Cumbria, CA8 1LB   Tel: 016977 46668
South of Brampton. Nearest main road: A69 from Carlisle to Brampton (and M6, junction 43).

C(12)

3 Bedrooms. £20 (less for 7 nights or more). Bargain breaks. All have some or all of the following: own bath/shower/toilet. No smoking.
Dinner (by arrangement). £12 for 3 courses and coffee, at 7pm. Vegetarian or other special diets if ordered. Wine available. No smoking. **Light suppers** if ordered.
1 Sitting-room. With open fire, TV. No smoking.
Small garden
Closed from mid-December to mid-January.

Little Talkin village is in an interesting part of the country, surrounded by fells that are popular with walkers and near a country park and tarn with various watersports. Hullerbank is in a secluded spot only half a mile from the village, and offers farmhouse accommodation at its most comfortable. Though this is only a 14-acre smallholding, Brian and Sheila Stobbart are local farming people. The sheep they raise provide the chops and joints which guests greatly appreciate. Lamb (or other straightforward farmhouse dishes, all entirely home-made) might be preceded by soup, or grapefruit or prawn-and-mushroom parcels, and followed by apple pie, for example, to which the orchard and garden have contributed.

Readers' comments: Very friendly. I can definitely recommend Hullerbank. Very comfortable and spotlessly clean. Delightful house. Dinners and breakfasts exceptionally good. Hosts extremely considerate, excellent accommodation, first-class food. Good value.

ING HILL LODGE

Mallerstang Dale, Cumbria, CA17 4JT   Tel/Fax: 017683 71153
South of Kirkby Stephen. Nearest main road: A685 from Tebay to Brough.

D X

4 Bedrooms. £20–£25 (less for 7 nights or more). Bargain breaks. All have some or all of the following: own shower/toilet; TV; views of river. No smoking.
Dinners (by arrangement). £12.50 for 3 courses and coffee, at 7.30pm. Vegetarian or other special diets if ordered. Wine available. No smoking. **Light suppers** if ordered.
1 Sitting-room. With open fire.
Large garden

Mallerstang must be the Cumbrian valley least known to tourists. Yet it is rich in associations, real or legendary: King Arthur, Dick Turpin, the Romans and the Vikings, Thomas à Becket, Michael Faraday. Ing Hill – built probably as a hunting-lodge in 1820 – stands above the valley floor, and the views are splendid, especially from the bedrooms. The latter have neatly co-ordinated fabrics and ingenious bedheads-cum-backrests designed by Tony Sawyer. A retired surveyor, he has done all the design and conversion.

Sheelagh Sawyer provides menus to suit the appetites of the walkers who stay here: typically, mushroom soup, steak pie, and blackberry crumble with cream.

Readers' comments: Standard of a top hotel. Food delicious. Thrilled by standard of accommodation. Marvellous hospitality. Delightful furnishings and location. Food excellent, accommodation outstanding. Made us so very welcome. Standard exceptional.

KNIPE GROUND

Coniston, Cumbria, LA21 8AE   Tel: 015394 41221
West of Windermere. Nearest main road: A593 from Ambleside towards Broughton-in-Furness.

C(6) S X

4 Bedrooms. £14–£18 (less for 2 nights or more). No smoking.
1 Sitting-room. With open fire, piano. No smoking.
Small garden

When Mary Dutton and her late husband bought Knipe Ground, it was almost a ruin, and they laboured for years to bring it to its present condition, farming and living almost self-sufficiently the while. It sits in a pretty garden where there is still a rare old rose planted by the previous owner. Like most farmhouse cottages in the Lake District, it is stone-built and stone-roofed, tucked into the hillside above Coniston Water (the access is steep).

Inside, it is full of beams and old woodwork, with bedrooms (including two singles) reached by a staircase with open treads of slate. There are books and pictures all over the place. Breakfast (the only meal available, apart from packed lunches to order) is eaten in what was the dairy, with a good view. The bathroom is on the ground floor.

This is the place for people to whom it is more important that a house should have character than that it should be spick and span. Character it has in abundance, as has its owner, who has been in her time physiotherapist, art teacher and carriage-driving enthusiast.

Readers' comments: Idyllic setting; caring, friendly host. Beautiful and intriguing place.

LINK HOUSE
Bassenthwaite Lake, Cumbria, CA13 9YD Tel: 017687 76291 (Fax: 017687 76670)
East of Cockermouth. Nearest main road: A66 from Keswick to Cockermouth.

C(7) **M PT S**

9 Bedrooms. £20 **to readers of this book.** Bargain breaks. All have some or all of the following: own bath/shower/toilet; TV.
Dinner. £13 for 4 courses and coffee, at 7pm. Vegetarian or other special diets if ordered. Wine available.
2 Sitting-rooms. With open fire. **Bar.**
Small garden
Closed in December and January.

Victorian Link House has, as well as a sitting-room with a log fire, a conservatory bar with tiled floor and cane seats. The single bedrooms are of a high standard.

The house is run by Michael and Marilyn Tuppen, who offer such dinners as pâté, cauliflower soup, lemon chicken, and a choice of sweets or cheeses.

Guests can use the leisure club at the nearby Castle Inn Hotel (swimming-pool, solarium, sauna, tennis court, etc.).

On one side of Bassenthwaite Lake is the great peak of Skiddaw and on the other Thornthwaite Forest, with a visitor centre provided by the Forestry Commission. By the lake is Mirehouse, one of the least intimidating of mansions. Westward is Cockermouth, Wordsworth's birthplace.

Readers' comments: Lovely setting. Comfort super. Food and accommodation remain very good.

V

THE MILL
Mungrisdale, Cumbria, CA11 0XR Tel: 017687 79659
West of Penrith. Nearest main road: A66 from Keswick to Penrith (and M6, junction 40).

C D S

9 Bedrooms. £39.50–£49 **including dinner, to readers of this book.** Less for 5 nights or more. Most have some or all of the following: own bath/shower/toilet; TV; views of river.
Dinner. 5 courses and coffee, at 7pm. Vegetarian or other special diets if ordered. Wine available. No smoking. **Light suppers** if ordered.
2 Sitting-rooms. With open fire, TV. No smoking in one.
Large garden
Closed from November to February.

In a peaceful spot, with little more than the sound of the River Glendermackin rushing down its rocky bed, The Mill (adjoining, but not connected with, the Mill Inn) is a simple white house with moss on the slate roof. A small conservatory faces a stone terrace and a lawn with seats by the water's edge.

Eleanor and Richard Quinlan believe that dinner is the high point of a stay. A typical menu might include a tartlet of wild mushrooms; green bean and apple soup with freshly baked soda bread; quail with orange, brandy and thyme. There is always a vegetarian option.

The main sitting-room is pretty and there is a small TV room with well-filled bookshelves. In the dining-room each oak table has willow-pattern china, candles and a nosegay. Bedrooms are trim and simple. On the walls are pictures from Richard's collection of Victorian paintings.

Readers' comments: Beautiful, quiet, excellent food. Service attentive and friendly. Food is superb. Outstanding. Interesting dinner with Mozart background. Food good. Charming. Hospitality exceptional, food absolutely delicious.

V

MILTON HOUSE BARN

C(10) **D**

Crooklands, Cumbria, LA7 7NL Tel: 015395 67628
South of Kendal. Nearest main road: A65 from Kirkby Lonsdale towards Kendal (and M6, junction 36).

2 Bedrooms. £19 (less for 3 nights or more). Bargain breaks. Both have own bath/toilet. No smoking.
Dinner. £11 for 3 courses and coffee, at 7pm. Vegetarian or other special diets if ordered. No smoking. **Light suppers** if ordered.
1 Sitting-room. With TV. No smoking.
Small garden
Closed in December.

On what was once a busy coaching road but is now only a backwater close to the M6, Milton House Barn has been ingeniously converted to give lots of nooks and crannies. Guests use a characterful sitting-room at the top of the building, and they have their breakfast by a double-height window where the wide barn doors used to be.

The house was a 'bank barn' – typical of Westmorland – built into the hillside to house cattle below and hay above. There is a self-catering flat sometimes available to b & b visitors.

Pauline Jones serves such dinners as home-made soup, beef cooked in ale with puff-pastry crust, and sticky-toffee pudding. Otherwise, many visitors eat at Crooklands or else at one of the numerous restaurants in the nearby town of Kirkby Lonsdale. The town also has a number of antique shops (and 3-day auctions); signs point to Ruskin's View (over the River Lune, which gave Lancashire its name).

Readers' comments: Lovely house; made very welcome; excellent dinner and breakfast; very good value.

OLD RECTORY

Crosby Garrett, Cumbria, CA17 4PW Tel: 017683 72074
West of Kirkby Stephen. Nearest main road: A685 from Tebay to Brough.

3 Bedrooms. £18–£21 (less for 4 nights or more). Some have some or all of the following: own bath/shower/toilet. No smoking.
Dinner (by arrangement). £11 for 3 courses and coffee, at times to suit guests. Vegetarian or other special diets if ordered. No smoking.
1 Sitting-room. With open fire, TV, piano. No smoking.
Large garden

This remote village, reached only by narow lanes, seems to have changed little since this house was the home of its rectors. But it was in bad shape when it came into the possession of Alex McCrickard, an architect, and his locally-born wife Anne, a solicitor. Fortunately, the modernization carried out in the early 18th century was intact: there is an oak staircase with burr-inlaid handrail, and fine panelling in the downstairs rooms – dark with age in the dining-room, painted duck-egg blue in the sitting-room – which are furnished largely with contemporary antiques. There is a playable square piano and good pictures all over the walls – modern paintings, Japanese prints, old engravings.

The bedrooms – very pleasantly furnished, one with a four-poster bed – have the original window-seats and shutters and even much crown glass.

One of Anne's dinners, served at a big mahogany table with Chippendale-style chairs around it under a modern wrought-iron chandelier, might be roasted red peppers, honeyed lamb with gratin dauphinois, and sticky-toffee pudding.

OWL BROOK

High Lorton, Cumbria, CA13 9TX   Tel: 01900 85333
South-east of Cockermouth. Nearest main road: A66 from Keswick to Cockermouth.

CDMSX

3 Bedrooms. £16.50–£17.50. Bargain breaks. TV. No smoking.
Dinner (by arrangement). £12.50 for 4 courses and coffee, at 7pm. Vegetarian or other special diets if ordered. No smoking. **Light suppers** if ordered.
1 Sitting-room. With open stove, TV. No smoking.
Small garden

At the western end of spectacular Whinlatter Pass, Ann Roberts provides dinner, bed-and-breakfast at Owl Brook all the year round. This architect-designed and attractive bungalow of green lakeland slate with pine ceilings was built a few years ago, and all the airy bedrooms have fine views. Dinner might comprise soup, risotto, and fresh fruit salad, using wholefood ingredients.

Whinlatter Pass, running from the direction of Keswick and beautiful Derwent Water, rises through woodland to give magnificent views, but it is not too alarming for cautious motorists. The Vale of Lorton is less popular than the central Lake District but no less beautiful. Loweswater, Buttermere and Crummock Water are quiet lakes nearby. Much of the woodland in this area is owned by the National Trust, which was founded in the Lake District.

Booklovers staying here could take the opportunity to visit Whitehaven (a Georgian port, once among England's busiest) for its enormous secondhand bookshop.

Readers' comments: Beautiful views and utter tranquillity. Breakfasts were superb. Very friendly family atmosphere.

V

RIGGS COTTAGE

Routenbeck, Bassenthwaite Lake, Cumbria, CA13 9YN   Tel/Fax: 017687 76580
East of Cockermouth. Nearest main road: A66 from Keswick to Cockermouth.

C(5) D PT X

3 Bedrooms. £19–£25. Some have some or all of the following: own bath/shower/toilet; TV. No smoking.
Dinner. £12.50 for 4 courses and coffee, at 6.30pm. Vegetarian or other special diets if ordered. Wine available. No smoking.
1 Sitting-room. With open fire, TV. No smoking.
Large garden

Hidden at the foot of a (rather steep) private lane is a little group of dwellings of which 16th-century Riggs Cottage is one. It is a low-beamed place, literally with roses round the door, where a big L-shaped settee faces a dog-grate under an iron canopy.

Hazel and Fred Wilkinson share the cooking, offering unusual choices for breakfast: a variety of sausages, wild mushrooms in season, or kedgeree. Bread is home-made, herbs and many vegetables are home-grown, going into a dinner menu such as lettuce and coriander soup, gravadlax (using local wild salmon), and a traditional pudding – hot or cold according to season – and local cheese. If you feel like a change (or a drink), the excellent Pheasant Inn is close.

Hazel's watercolours of owls and hawks decorate the staircase; elsewhere there are examples of her china-painting (which, as well as decoupage, she teaches). In one bedroom is a collection of the drawings of Arthur Wainwright, the famous author of hand-written Lake District walkers' guides.

Nearby Bassenthwaite Lake is the most northerly of the lakes and the only one with the word 'lake' in its name (the others being 'meres' or 'waters').

V

SILVERHOLME

C D S X

Graythwaite, near Hawkshead, Cumbria, LA12 8AZ   Tel/Fax: 015395 31332
North-east of Ulverston. Nearest main road: A590 from Ulverston towards Windermere.

3 Bedrooms. £20 **to readers of this book**–£23 (less for 3 nights or more). Bargain breaks. All have some or all of the following: own bath/shower/toilet; TV; views of lake. No smoking.
Dinner. £13.50 for 4 courses and coffee, at 7pm. Vegetarian or other special diets if ordered. No smoking. **Light suppers** if ordered.
1 Sitting-room. With open fire, TV. No smoking.
Large garden

Buried in dense woodland on the unspoilt side of Windermere, Silverholme is a mansion built in the early years of Victoria's reign. It has very large rooms with high windows, all of which look eastward across the waters of the lake. From them you may watch deer grazing – even from one of the private bathrooms. Each bedroom has an impressive mahogany bedstead from the period of the house. In the Venetian-red dining-room, its walls hung with engravings, George Walker might serve prawn cocktail, lamb cutlets, and peach flan.

Moorings and lakeside walks are available.

Enthusiasts for industrial archaeology will love Stott Park bobbin mill, with its magnificent steam engine and ingenious old machinery. In the other direction is Grizedale Forest, where there are well laid-out walks and an assortment of specially commissioned sculptures here and there. The forest's visitor centre contains the expected souvenir shop and café, and an informative tree nursery, but more unusual are an exhibition gallery and an adjoining workshop for craft 'residencies', and a theatre for live performances by touring companies.

SUMMERLANDS TOWER

Endmoor, Cumbria, LA8 0ED   Tel: 015395 61081
South of Kendal. Nearest main road: A65 from Kirkby Lonsdale to Kendal (and M6, junction 36).

2 Bedrooms. £19.50–£24.50 (less for 3 nights or more). Both have some or all of the following: own bath/shower/toilet; TV. No smoking.
Light suppers if ordered. Vegetarian or other special diets if ordered. No smoking.
1 Sitting-room. With piano. No smoking.
Large garden
Closed from December to March.

A mansion built for an ironmaster in 1846 is now three dwellings, of which this is one. A fraction of the Jacobethan house it may be, but its scale is still huge, with large, high-ceilinged rooms and vast windows looking out onto three acres of lawns and shrubberies. From the hall which is one of the guests' sitting-rooms – with a carved stone fireplace inscribed 'Where friends meet hearts warm' – a massive oak staircase leads to large bedrooms with lavish bathrooms. In the twin room is an unusual pair of symmetrically matching brass bedsteads. As well as antiques, the house contains some interesting souvenirs of Michael and Hazel Green's trips abroad, such as a small carpet loom from Pakistan. Hazel (who used to be craft teacher to the blind) makes her own muesli and uses free-range eggs and local sausage for breakfasts. The house is a few miles outside the enjoyable town of Kendal and close not only to the Lake District but to the westernmost Yorkshire Dales as well.

V

SWALEDALE WATCH

Whelpo, Caldbeck, Cumbria, CA7 8HQ   Tel: 016974 78409

South-east of Wigton. Nearest main road: A595 from Carlisle to Cockermouth (and M6, junction 41).

4 Bedrooms. £16–£19. All have some or all of the following: own bath/shower/toilet; TV; views of river. No smoking.
Dinner (by arrangement). £10 for 3 courses and coffee, at 7pm. Vegetarian or other special diets if ordered. No smoking. **Light suppers** if ordered.
2 Sitting-rooms. With open fire/stove, TV. No smoking.
Large garden

At Whelpo ('Wolf's lair'), Swaledale Watch is a sheep farm, named after the breed kept here. There are rooms in the modern farmhouse and also two in a converted byre which share a sitting-room and a kitchenette. Guests eat in a big dining-room in the house, which is set in fine scenery and good walking country just inside the Lake District National Park. Cookery enthusiast Nan Savage serves, for instance, Highland prawns, chicken baked with honey, and chocolate roll; bread rolls are home-baked.

Caldbeck is one of the Lake District's prettiest villages, with an old inn (handy for lunch), a churchyard where lie John Peel and the real-life heroine of Melvyn Bragg's *Maid of Buttermere*, and a restored watermill for craft shops and a good vegetarian restaurant. Near Caldbeck are Carrock Fell, known for the variety of minerals that can be found there, and Hesket New Market's village inn, where they brew their own beer.

Reader's comments: Delightful place, food of remarkably high quality and value.

V

TARN HOUSE FARM

Ravenstonedale, Cumbria, CA17 4LJ   Tel: 015396 23646

South-west of Kirkby Stephen. On A683 from Kirkby Stephen to Sedbergh.

2 Bedrooms. £15–£18 (less for 3 nights or more). Bargain breaks. One has views of lake. No smoking.
Dinner. £12 for 4 courses and coffee, at 7pm. Vegetarian or other special diets if ordered. No smoking. **Light suppers** if ordered.
1 Sitting-room. With open fire, TV. No smoking.
Garden

On a switchback road across breezy fells which joins two picturesque towns is the farm where Michael Metcalfe-Gibson, who was in banking until he took over this family property a decade ago, keeps sheep and dairy cows. Sally offers such dinners as sardine terrine, pork chops provençale, and chocolate brandy pudding (with some choices), using as much local and farm produce as she can. (Sunday lunch and packed lunches too.) She serves dinner in a room where there are still stone shelves (it was once a dairy): much of the stone and woodwork of the 17th-century house is unchanged. There is a prettily furnished twin bedroom and a plainer double room with a good view of the tarn (small lake).

Southwards are Cautley Spout, the highest single-drop waterfall in England, and Sedbergh, with an antiquarian bookshop and a tweed mill. Beyond, via a beautiful but demanding drive, are cobbled Dent, with a pub where they brew their own beer, and the Yorkshire Dales. In the other direction, you can visit Kirkby Stephen for its antique shops and interesting mediaeval church with Crusader monuments.

Readers' comments: Very strongly recommended. Truly warm welcome, very homely. Excellent cooking. Lovely walks on the fells and around the tarn.

V

VIOLET BANK
Hawkshead, Cumbria, LA22 0PL   Tel: 015394 36222
South-west of Ambleside. Nearest main road: A591 from Windermere to Keswick.

2 Bedrooms. £19. No smoking.
1 Sitting-room. With open fire/stove, TV. No smoking.
Large garden

Tucked up a lane half a mile from Hawkshead, Violet Bank is an 18th-century farmhouse with Victorian improvements, including a striking fireplace of coloured marble in the dining-room, which Nancy Penrice has furnished with mostly 19th-century antiques. Around the house are pictures and relics of shooting and fishing – prints and paintings, old gunsmiths' equipment, an aggressive-looking stuffed pike. Chris has a collection of country bygones which he keeps in the slate-shelved dairy and will show to fellow enthusiasts.

The Penrices' main interest is pigs – rare breeds such as Gloucester Old Spots and Berkshires – which Chris takes to shows all over the country. Some live in old sties built of big slate slabs or graze with their litters in the paddock. There are also ducks and geese (the latter of the Toulouse breed, which are friendlier than most).

Hawkshead, picturesque and pedestrianized, is handy for a choice of good evening meals.

Prices are per person sharing a room at the beginning of the year.

Months when houses are shown as closed are inclusive.

Complaints about matters which could not have been settled on the spot will be forwarded to proprietors. Please enclose a stamped addressed envelope if you want the authors to acknowledge receipt of your complaint.

Addresses shown are to enable you to locate a house on a map. They are not necessarily complete postal addresses (though the essential postcode is included), and detailed directions for finding a house should be obtained from the owner.

WILLOW COTTAGE

Bassenthwaite, Cumbria, CA12 4QP   Tel: 017687 76440
North-west of Keswick. Nearest main road: A591 from Keswick towards Carlisle.

2 Bedrooms. £19 (less for 2 nights or more). Both have own bath/toilet. No smoking.
Light suppers sometimes on Sundays. Vegetarian or other special diets if ordered. No smoking.
1 Sitting-room. With stove. No smoking.
Small garden

You will sleep under gnarled rafters at Willow Cottage, which Chris Beaty and her husband have carefully converted from an ancient barn (together with self-catering accommodation next door). One bedroom has views of Skiddaw, the other the use of a big cast-iron bath. At the foot of the staircase (on which hangs Chris's collection of antique baby-linen) is a beamed sitting-cum-breakfast-room, with comfortable seats facing an iron stove in a nook. A smaller room has French windows opening onto a paved area by the vegetable and herb garden, where guests often sit to watch the sun set behind the mountains. The cottage is attractively decorated, with unobtrusive stencilling and furniture-painting by Chris. She offers some choice at breakfast, and she sometimes provides snack suppers, though most guests eat well at the Sun Inn a few hundred yards away in the village.

Bassenthwaite Lake, to which the village has given its name, is popular with small-boat sailors, but this, the most northerly part of the Lake District National Park, is never as crowded as the more popular centre, and Cockermouth is one of the least spoiled of the towns. For good pub lunches, Ireby and Caldbeck are not far, and Isel Hall and the nearby Norman church are well worth visiting.

V

YEW TREE COTTAGE

35 Loftus Hill, Sedbergh, Cumbria, LA10 5SQ   Tel: 01539 621600
East of Kendal. On A684 from Kendal to Hawes (and M6, junction 37).

2 Bedrooms. £17 (less for 2 nights or more). No smoking.
Light suppers if ordered. Vegetarian or other special diets if ordered. Wine available.
1 Sitting-room. With TV.
Small garden

Anne Jones has lovingly restored this tiny cottage, keeping intact such details as pine panelling and cast-iron grates, using plain colours for the walls and carpets, and furnishing it in simple country style. On the walls are flower pictures, Anne's own samplers, and drawings by her daughter (including the animal portraits in which she specializes).

One of a row on the edge of Sedbergh – a small and characterful town where one can dine – the cottage is at the start of a rewarding drive for the motorist who can cope with steep, winding and narrow roads: past a good craft gallery, through cobbled Dent, by a spectacular Victorian railway viaduct, alongside a little river running over limestone pavements, and to the highest inn in England. Outside the town, at Brigflatts, is one of the oldest Quaker meeting-houses in the country – a tranquil and historic place.

Readers' comments: Lovely, elegant, warm, welcoming and comfortable. Delightful welcome, charming hospitality.

V

DERBYSHIRE

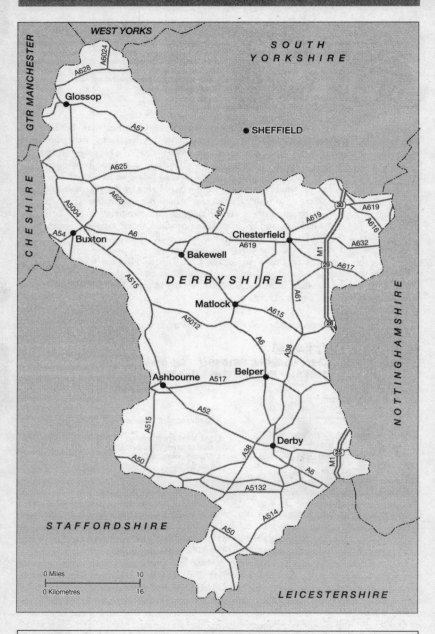

For explanation of code letters and **V** symbol, see inside front cover.

BARMS FARM
Fairfield, Derbyshire, SK17 7HW   Tel: 01298 77723 (Fax: 01298 78692)
North of Buxton. On A6 from Buxton to Stockport.

rear view

3 Bedrooms. £20–£22. Bargain breaks. All have some or all of the following: own bath/shower/toilet; TV. No smoking.
Light suppers if ordered. Vegetarian or other special diets if ordered. No smoking.
1 Sitting-room. With TV. No smoking.
Small garden

One mile out of the Georgian spa town of Buxton and overlooking the High Peak golf course is this working dairy-farm. When John Naden's grandfather bought the farm in the 1930s, it was three separate dwellings. Now, Lorraine and John Naden have refurbished the farmhouse to provide comfortable accommodation of a high standard.

You can be as independent as you choose here, since guests have a separate entrance and their own key. Upstairs, well-equipped bedrooms (located at one end of the farmhouse, away from the family) have oak beams and sloping ceilings. Lorraine has chosen pretty floral fabrics, and pinks and blues predominate. The bathrooms are excellent (the double rooms also have separate shower cubicles), with satin-edged towels and gold-plated taps.

Off the dining-room is an oak-beamed sitting-room containing plenty of literature on what to see and do in the area. As Lorraine has two young children, she does not provide evening meals, but a short drive away are several pubs with good food, or you could eat in nearby Buxton.

V

BEECHENHILL FARM   C
Ilam Moor Lane, Ilam, Derbyshire, DE6 2BD   Tel: 01335 310274
North-west of Ashbourne. Nearest main road: A515 from Ashbourne to Buxton.

2 Bedrooms. £19–£25 (less for 2 nights or more). Both have own shower/toilet. No smoking.
1 Sitting-room. With open fire/stove, TV. No smoking.
Large garden
Closed from December to February.

Perched on a south-facing hillside between the beauty-spots of Dovedale and the Manifold Valley, Beechenhill Farm is a long, low house built from limestone two centuries ago. It overlooks grazing sheep and cows, and picturesque Ilam village. Sue Prince has stencilled flowers and stars on the walls. Her breakfasts have won an award (there is always plenty of fruit and, in winter, porridge). No dinners, but there are local inns. There's a pretty garden and a goat wanders in the paddock. One of the two pleasant bedrooms is a light and spacious family room.

Author William Horwood stays here; and you'll find the farm described as 'the best place in the world' by one of the moles in his *Duncton Quest*. The farm is ideally placed for walking in the beautiful park of Ilam Hall (NT), and for exploring Dovedale – a scenic route known as Little Switzerland.

V

BOWER LODGE

D

Well Lane, Repton, Derbyshire, DE65 6EY Tel: 01283 702245 (Fax: 01283 704361)
South-west of Derby. Nearest main road: A38 from Derby to Burton-upon-Trent (and M1, junction 23a).

6 Bedrooms. £20–£30. All have some or all of the following: own bath/shower/toilet; TV.
Dinner. £17 for 4 courses and coffee, at 7.45pm. Vegetarian or other special diets if ordered. Wine available. **Light suppers** if ordered.
2 Sitting-rooms. With open fires, TV. No smoking in one.
Large garden

Mercian kings made Repton their capital over a thousand years ago. All down the High Street are scores of historic stone buildings, many now used by Repton's public school; and at the end is this lane of large houses in wooded grounds (one by Lutyens).

Rooms here are spacious and handsome, elegantly furnished by Elizabeth Plant. In one pretty sitting-room with Corinthian pillars she has used chinoiserie fabrics and festoon blinds, with old china and good paintings around; in another, leafy fabrics contrast with apricot-coloured walls, French doors opening onto a terrace. The dining-room has pretty china and placemats (the separate breakfast-room can be used by any visitors who prefer to eat on their own). Here Elizabeth – who does outside catering too – serves such meals as melon, coq-au-vin, brandy ice cream, and cheese (vegetables come from the garden).

Bedrooms are well furnished and, in some cases, have views of fine trees and the lily-pond. For overseas visitors, two airports are conveniently near.

BROADLOW ASH FARM

Thorpe, Derbyshire, DE6 2AW Tel: 01335 350259
North of Ashbourne. Nearest main road: A515 from Ashbourne to Buxton.

2 Bedrooms. £15–£16. No smoking.
Dinner (by arrangement). £10 for 3 courses and coffee, at 7pm. Wine available. No smoking. **Light suppers** if ordered.
1 Sitting-room. With open fire, TV. No smoking.
Small garden

On the site of a former manor house, this working dairy-farm is 200 years old and spreads over 216 acres. To reach the farmhouse, which is hidden from the main road, you travel down a long, well-maintained track and right through the farmyard where black-and-white Muscovy ducks nestle contentedly.

Elizabeth and Roger Round have been here for 25 years. The beauty of this house, in its peaceful setting, is that almost every room (including the bedrooms) has windows on two sides, offering panoramic views over Dovedale, towards Thorpe village and beyond. The sitting-room has a green velvet sofa with contrasting red cushions, and blue-and-white china on the walls. Upstairs, the bright and spacious bedrooms are simply but comfortably furnished.

Elizabeth prides herself on her traditional home-cooking using fresh local produce. Dinner might comprise home-made asparagus soup, a roast and vegetables, with pavlova to finish. In warm weather you can sit in the garden and sip a cup of tea while enjoying the fine views.

CRESSBROOK HALL

Cressbrook, Derbyshire, SK17 8SY Tel: 0500 121248 (free) (Fax: 01298 871845)
East of Buxton. Nearest main road: A6 from Buxton to Bakewell.

C D M

3 Bedrooms (plus 5 in cottages). £18.50–£37.50 (less for 3 nights or more). Bargain breaks. All have some or all of the following: own bath/shower/toilet; TV; views of river. No smoking.
Dinner (by arrangement). £16.50 for 3 courses and coffee, at 7pm. Vegetarian or other special diets if ordered. Wine available. No smoking. **Light suppers** if ordered.
1 Sitting-room. With open fire, TV, piano. No smoking preferred.
Large garden

A spectacular mansion in a spectacular setting, looking over a deep limestone gorge. The gorge is almost alpine; the extensive gardens were laid out by an assistant to Paxton (of Chatsworth and Crystal Palace fame), and the rooms are of exceptional splendour.

Some bedrooms are on two floors of the main house: one has a remarkable domed ceiling and a bay window from which to enjoy the superb view. Others are in lodges mostly for self-catering (with optional meals in the Hall).

Bobby Hull-Bailey and her husband added a conservatory, where meals are sometimes served instead of in the big dining-room. A typical dinner: melon, stuffed lamb parcels, and oranges in Cointreau (breakfasts are equally ample).

The Hull-Baileys have provided a beauty therapy room, sunbed, sauna, and games room (fee for the first three) as well as a children's play area. (Carriage drives available.)

Readers' comments: Idyllic. Welcomed with warmth and sincerity. Strongly recommended.

V

DELF VIEW HOUSE

Church Street, Eyam, Derbyshire, S32 1QH   Tel: 01433 631533
(Fax: 01433 631972)
North of Bakewell. Nearest main road: A623 from Chapel-en-le-Frith towards Chesterfield.

2 Bedrooms. £20–£28 (less for 3 nights or more). Both have some or all of the following: own bath/shower/toilet; TV. No smoking.
Light suppers if ordered.
1 Sitting-room. With open fire, piano. No smoking.
Large garden

In 1665, infection from the Great Plague travelled from London to Eyam in a roll of cloth. Heroically, the villagers cut themselves off lest they should infect others in the county. They held their church services outdoors in a hollow called the Cucklet Delf, above which was this gritstone house (much enlarged in 1830).

Today, Delf View is one of the most elegant houses in this book, lovingly restored by architect David Lewis and his wife. They have furnished it with such outstanding antiques as silver-legged beds from France painted with romantic pastoral scenes, a Sheraton four-poster, an inlaid fortepiano of 1820 and a ship made by Napoleonic prisoners-of-war. Sometimes candles are lit in the crystal chandelier of the blue sitting-room. There are a sunken bath in a brown-and-gold bathroom, embroidered towels, Augustus John drawings . . . and to complement all this you may be offered at breakfast a soufflé omelette or apples poached in Calvados, as well as local bacon and so forth. Outside is a garden with croquet lawn which overlooks the Delf.

Reader's comment: Very pleasing room and excellent breakfast.

V

THE HALL

C(5) **D M PT S**

Great Hucklow, Derbyshire, SK17 8RG   Tel: 01298 871175 (Fax: 01298 873801)
North-east of Buxton. Nearest main road: A623 from Chapel-en-le-Frith towards
Chesterfield.

4 Bedrooms. £18.50–£20 (less for 4 nights or more). Some have some or all of the following: own bath/shower/toilet. No smoking.
Dinner. £15 for 3 courses and coffee, at 7pm. Vegetarian or other special diets if ordered. No smoking. **Light suppers** if ordered.
1 Sitting-room. With woodstove. No smoking.
Large garden
Closed in December and January.

Rows of small, mullioned windows give the 17th-century Hall particular charm, and in the former kitchen (now a dining-room) the original fireplace, which would have housed a great spit, has been exposed. John Whatley has restored an unusual, very narrow, cellar-to-attic window which lights the staircase. In one of the very big family rooms there is a huge cockerel he carved, as well as stools and bedside tables made by him. A twin room in the converted barn has its own sitting-area. Guests greatly enjoy the large garden.

Angela is a discriminating cook, using fresh garden produce. A typical dinner: her own pâté; chicken pie with ratatouille and boulangère potatoes; then unusual water-ices.

Readers' comments: Most friendly welcome. Most enjoyable. Very comfortable. Excellent food. In a beautiful setting. Charming people. We couldn't have been better fed and looked after if we had been staying at the Ritz. Beautiful house being lovingly restored.

V

THE HOLLOW

C S

Little Longstone, Derbyshire, DE45 1NN   Tel: 01629 640746
North-west of Bakewell. Nearest main road: A6 from Bakewell to Buxton.

2 Bedrooms. £20. Both have some or all of the following: own bath/shower/toilet; TV. No smoking.
Light suppers if ordered. Vegetarian breakfasts if ordered. No smoking.
Small garden

As you enter this handsome stone house, part of which dates back 300 years, the over-whelming impression is one of sheer elegance. For Elizabeth Chadwick has filled it with stylish antiques and imaginative furnishings. You step straight onto the beech-panelled floor of the dining-room. Cherrywood chairs with gold-coloured damask seats surround an imposing mahogany table, and deep red velvet drapes hang at the windows. Up a gracious wooden staircase are impressive, south-facing bedrooms with stone fireplaces, Victorian-style dressing-tables and such touches as frosted green candles in one, Somerset patchwork cushions in another.

Outside is a glorious landscaped garden, beyond which lies the Monsal Trail. The majestic scenery of Monsal Dale is a short stroll away. Although Elizabeth does not provide full evening meals, there are several good pubs and restaurants in the area, the nearest being the Packhorse pub across the road.

Readers' comments: What a find! The situation is idyllic, the accommodation exquisite, the breakfast a sheer extravagance. Delightful hosts. We couldn't have found a more perfect place.

HOLLY COTTAGE

Rowland, Derbyshire, DE45 1NR   Tel: 01629 640624
North of Bakewell. Nearest main road: A6 from Buxton to Bakewell.

2 Bedrooms. £20–£24 (less for 4 nights or more). No smoking.
Dinner. £11 for 3 courses and coffee, at 7pm. Vegetarian or other special diets if ordered. No smoking. **Light suppers** if ordered.
2 Sitting-rooms. With open fire/stove, TV, piano. No smoking.
Small garden
Closed in November and December.

As one of England's golf champions (1972), Mary Everard used to travel the world but eventually chose the quiet hamlet of Rowland in which to settle down. Here, at 18th-century Holly Cottage, she welcomes guests to her elegant sitting-room, a raspberry-and-white dining-room furnished with old maple chairs from America, and pretty bedrooms with white board doors. A typical dinner menu: home-made mushroom soup; sweet-and-sour pork or fish pie, with vegetables from the garden; Bakewell tart and crème fraîche. For breakfast, bread, rolls and muffins are home-baked; jams and marmalade home-made.

If you want more than just the hill scenery, there are stately homes to visit, the market town of Bakewell, and Sheffield for its many and varied attractions: excellent art gallery, cathedral, industrial heritage museum with steel craftsmen ('the little mesters') at work, and an industrial hamlet (bellows and waterwheel still active).

Readers' comments: Excellent in every way. Lovely house, warm welcome, good food and wonderful setting.

V

HORSLEYGATE HALL

Horsleygate Lane, Holmesfield, Derbyshire, S18 5WD   Tel: 0114 2890333
North-west of Chesterfield. Nearest main road: A621 from Baslow to Sheffield.

3 Bedrooms. £19–£22 (less for 4 nights or more). One has own bath/shower/toilet. No smoking.
Light suppers if ordered.
1 Sitting-room. With open fire, TV. No smoking.
Large garden

Garden enthusiasts, in particular, will enjoy staying here to see the transformation wrought by Margaret Ford on a sloping site which was an overgrown wilderness when she took over. The house too (part early Victorian, part Georgian) had hardly been touched for generations: its original features were intact and have now been carefully restored.

The Fords painted the panelling in the sitting-room apricot and grey, with fabrics to match. What was once the children's schoolroom is now a breakfast-room. Here and elsewhere are Margaret's 'flea market' finds which add to the character of the house.

There are spacious bedrooms, some with armchairs from which to enjoy the superb Peak District scenery. Stripped pine doors and baths set in alcoves are features of the house.

In just a few years, Margaret has created a fascinating terraced garden of hidden patios, woodland paths, rock garden, herbaceous beds and brimming stone troughs.

Readers' comments: Very impressed. Picturesque and quiet location, with good views. Friendly and helpful. Enjoyed our stay tremendously.

LANE END HOUSE

C D M P T

Green Lane, Tansley, Derbyshire, DE4 5FJ   Tel/Fax: 01629 583981

East of Matlock. Nearest main road: A615 from Matlock to Alfreton (and M1, junction 28).

4 Bedrooms. £18–£25 (less for 3 nights or more). Bargain breaks. All have some of the following: own bath/shower/toilet; TV. No smoking.
Dinner. £14.95 **to readers of this book only** for 4 courses and coffee, at 7.30pm. Vegetarian or other special diets if ordered. Wine available. No smoking.
1 Sitting-room. With TV. No smoking. **Bar.**
Small garden
Closed from late December to early January.

To this old house a new wing has been added, in which there is a big picture-window opening onto a stone terrace with lawn and flowers beyond. Antiques and ample sofas encourage one to linger indoors, but croquet awaits in the landscaped garden from which there is a spectacular view of gaunt Riber Castle looming over the horizon.

One bedroom is on the ground floor, while from the dining-room a staircase rises to others which have fine views of the wonderful scenery all around. One particularly pleasant room has a rather splendid Victorian bathtub and cistern in its bathroom.

Marion Smith and her husband, who used to run a large hotel, apply professional standards to everything they do – particularly the meals (including a very varied breakfast). A typical dinner might be: chicken vol-au-vent; sorbet; trout with honey, orange and raisin sauce; individual sticky-toffee puddings. Vegetarian options are numerous; yogurt and muesli are home-made, and there is much emphasis on low-fat foods. The wine list is lengthy.

Readers' comments: Attentive and friendly proprietors. Delightful surroundings. Most peaceful, and so many personal touches. Meticulous care and attention. Home cooking at its very best. Exceptional in every way. Food beautifully cooked and served.

V

MOUNT TABOR HOUSE

C PT S

Crich, Derbyshire, DE4 5DG   Tel: 01773 857008

South-east of Matlock. Nearest main road: A6 from Matlock to Derby (and M1, junction 28).

2 Bedrooms. £20. Bargain breaks. Both have some or all of the following: own bath/shower/toilet; TV. No smoking.
Dinner (by arrangement). £9.75 for 3 courses and coffee, from 7pm. Vegetarian or other special diets if ordered. No smoking. **Light suppers** if ordered.
1 Sitting-room. With TV. No smoking.
Small garden

High in the Derbyshire Peaks lies the village of Crich. The name derives from an old English word meaning mound or hill; and Crich Stand, a memorial dedicated to the men of the Sherwood Foresters Regiment who died in the Great War, can be seen for miles around. In the centre of the village is Mount Tabor House, a former Methodist chapel which served the community for more than a hundred years. Converted several years ago, this fine Victorian building, with its exposed stone walls and Gothic-style windows, most retaining their original stained glass, is now owned by Fay and Steve Whitehead.

Bedrooms are downstairs in what was once the schoolroom. One in terracotta and cream features a king-size antique pine bed.

Candlelit dinners are served in the large living/dining-area upstairs. The atmosphere is peaceful and the views of the Amber Valley are stunning. Fay uses local and organic produce for meals such as Mediterranean pâté with sesame toast, trout with watercress, and chocolate roulade.

Trout fishing and hot-air ballooning are amongst the many things you can do in this lovely area.

V

OLD ORCHARD

Stoney Lane, Thorpe, Derbyshire, DE6 2AW   Tel/Fax: 01335 350410
North-west of Ashbourne. Nearest main road: A515 from Ashbourne to Buxton.

4 Bedrooms. £17.50–£20 (less for 7 nights or more). Some have own shower/toilet.
1 Sitting-room. With open fire, TV. No smoking.
Small garden
Closed from December to February.

Dovedale is one of the loveliest parts of the Peak District; and in this area there are particularly fine views of it where the Manifold Valley runs down into the dale (at the foot of Thorpe Cloud – one of several 1000-foot hills here).

On the edge of Thorpe village is a very prettily sited stone house in traditional style, which stands where once an orchard of damson trees grew. This is the comfortable home of Barbara Challinor and her husband; keen gardeners, as is obvious from the herbaceous beds, stone terraces, rock garden and stream with waterfalls in their sloping, landscaped grounds.

This part of the National Park is known as 'the White Peak' because the underlying rock is limestone (further north, in 'the Dark Peak', the geology changes). There is a network of paths around here by which to explore Milldale, Wolfscote Dale and Beresford Dale.

But scenery is not the only attraction of the area. There are the stately homes of Chatsworth and Haddon Hall to visit, the old towns of Matlock and Bakewell, and busy Ashbourne with a splendid church and antique salerooms.

Readers' comments: Ideal hostess. Excellent: went out of her way to make us welcome. Excellent accommodation, homely and friendly people. Excellent. Most satisfying accommodation with friendly atmosphere.

ROCK HOUSE

Alport, Derbyshire, DE45 1LG   Tel: 01629 636736
South of Bakewell. Nearest main road: A6 from Bakewell to Matlock.

3 Bedrooms. £20. All have some or all of the following: own bath/shower/toilet. No smoking.
Light suppers if ordered.
1 Sitting-room. With gas fire, TV. No smoking.
Small garden

The rock for which this house is named is a great crag of tufa, formed 300 million years ago, rearing up alongside it. Only a few yards from the 18th-century house two rivers join, splashing over weirs constructed long ago to contain trout downstream. Lathkill Dale is a National Nature Reserve: Tony and Jan Statham are first-rate sources of information about the history of this most beautiful of valleys.

The front door opens straight into the stone-flagged sitting-room, its walls now painted mushroom, with buttoned velvet armchairs, where you will be served tea on arrival. Glass doors lead through to the breakfast-room.

By pre-arrangement, Jan may serve supper platters, beautifully presented (but most visitors go to the nearby Druid Inn or other pubs). Breakfast possibilities include muffins, poached fruit, home-made jams and some vegetarian dishes. All bedrooms are well furnished.

Readers' comments: One of our favourites, lovely house; thoughtful and friendly people. A charming house with lovely walks all round, and delicious breakfasts. Very friendly, couldn't do enough for us. One of the best. Nothing too much trouble.

SHIRLEY HALL

C(6) X

Derby Lane, Shirley, Derbyshire, DE6 3AS Tel: 01335 360346
South-east of Ashbourne. Nearest main road: A52 from Derby to Ashbourne.

3 Bedrooms. £17–£20 (less for 2 nights or more). Some have own bath/shower/toilet; TV.
Light suppers if ordered. No smoking.
1 Sitting-room. With open fire, TV. No smoking.
Large garden

William the Conqueror gave land near Ashbourne to the Shirley family, who still own much of it (they forfeited the rest as a result of siding with Charles I in the Civil War). It includes the pretty village of Shirley and Shirley Hall where the Fosters now farm.

In a richly oak-panelled Tudor sitting-room, the Shirley family's elaborate coat-of-arms has survived the centuries. Books scattered around give a homely feel. Some bedrooms (two are en suite) have huge mahogany furniture, exposed timbers and board doors, and views of the sweeping lawns, beyond which lie the remains of a moat, and further afield a pond with tench and carp (coarse fishing available).

The green-carpeted dining-room, where Sylvia Foster serves light suppers, has views over the gardens.

The house is close to Edmaston Manor, built by Lutyens, with a notable garden to visit. Kedleston Hall, six miles away, is a magnificent Adam house. Also within easy reach are the Derbyshire Dales and the Peak District. The traffic of Derby is worth braving to visit the cathedral and museums.

V

SHOTTLE HALL

C D M P T S

Shottle, Derbyshire, DE56 2EB Tel/Fax: 01773 550276
North-west of Belper. Nearest main road: A517 from Ashbourne to Belper (and M1, junction 28).

8 Bedrooms. £20–£33 (less for 7 nights or more). Some have some or all of the following: own bath/shower/toilet; TV. No smoking.
Dinner (by arrangement). £13 for 4 courses and coffee, at 7.30pm (not Sundays). Vegetarian or other special diets if ordered. Wine available. **Light suppers** if ordered.
2 Sitting-rooms. With TV. No smoking. **Bar.**
Large garden
Closed in November.

The guest-house is over a century old and has all the solid Victorian quality of that period: big rooms, fine ceilings and doors, dignity in every detail. Not only the bedrooms but even the bathrooms are large and close-carpeted, with everything in pristine condition. As well as a sizeable sitting-room, there are two dining-rooms – one is used for breakfasts because it gets the morning sun. From both, the huge windows have views of hills and of the fertile valley stretching below the house. Two bedrooms are on the ground floor; and there is a self-contained suite, which is suitable for ... ially disabled people.

Guests enjoy Phyllis Matthews's straightforward home cooking. A typical meal: mushrooms in cream and garlic; chicken with brandy and cream sauce; hazelnut meringue.

Readers' comments: Superb cook. Thoroughly enjoyed our stay, charming and friendly people. Very impressed; could not have been more helpful. Very good hosts. An idyllic country house. The best! Warm welcome, delicious food, comfortable room. Excellent.

WAYSIDE COTTAGE

D PT X

106 Padfield Main Road, Padfield, Derbyshire, SK14 7ET   Tel: 01457 866495
North of Glossop. Nearest main road: A57 from Manchester to Glossop (and M67, junction 4).

3 Bedrooms. £15–£20 (less for 7 nights or more). Some have some or all of the following: own bath/shower/toilet; TV. No smoking.
Dinner (by arrangement). £10.50 for 3 courses, wine and coffee, at 7pm. Vegetarian or other special diets if ordered. No smoking. **Light suppers** if ordered.
1 Sitting-room. With woodstove, TV. No smoking.
Small garden

Only the dilapidated shell of this 17th-century farm building remained when the Galvins bought it. With Terry's skill as a stonemason and woodworker and Denise's imaginative decor, it is now a lovely home with oak beams, inglenook fireplaces and hand-made doors. One bedroom has a canopied, Cromwellian, oak four-poster bed and an 18th-century seaman's chest. There are fresh flowers in every room and crisp cotton sheets on the beds.

In summer, guests can enjoy the delights of the pretty cottage-garden with its stream trickling under a little bridge. In winter, they can relax around the wood-burning stove in the comfortable sitting-room. Meals are served at individual tables in the small dining-room. Dinner might consist of liver and duck pâté, fresh salmon with hollandaise sauce and vegetables, followed by home-made apple pie.

From here you may explore the Peak District National Park and beyond. The old mill towns of Glossop and Stalybridge are nearby; and Manchester, with its science museum, exhibition centre and Granada Studios, is a half-hour drive away. For a small charge, the Galvins will collect guests from Manchester Airport.

Reader's comments: Best equipped room we've found, excellent breakfast.

WELLHEAD FARM

C D S

Wormhill, Derbyshire, SK17 8SL   Tel: 01298 871023
East of Buxton. Nearest main road: A6 from Buxton to Bakewell.

4 Bedrooms. £20–£22 (less for 2 nights or more). All have some or all of the following: own bath/shower/toilet. No smoking.
Dinner. £12.50 for 4 courses and coffee, at 6–8pm. Vegetarian or other special diets if ordered. **Light suppers** if ordered.
2 Sitting-rooms. With woodstove, TV. No smoking in one.

When Yvonne and Barry Peirson moved to this 400-year-old limestone farmhouse with stone-slabbed roof, there was no running water – it had to be pumped up from the well in the cellar. Here the original slabs of stone on which animals were cut up (to be sold on the black market during the war) are still to be found.

Today, this characterful, oak-beamed house (and adjoining tea-room) is filled with a homely mixture of antiques and personal memorabilia. Stairs lead up from the main sitting-room to pretty, cottage-style bedrooms (some have four-posters, and one is a family room).

Yvonne serves such dinners as devilled mushrooms; chicken breasts with white sauce, nuts and grapes; pavlova; and cheese. In summer, you can take the footpath along the river to the Angler's Rest pub in Miller's Dale (the Peirsons will collect you), just one of several excellent walks in the area.

Readers' comments: Very friendly and informal atmosphere, quiet and comfortable, good food, a highlight of the trip. Outgoing, friendly people, willing to put themselves to any amount of trouble.

V

WOLFSCOTE GRANGE

C S

Hartington, Derbyshire, SK17 0AX   Tel: 01298 84342
North-west of Ashbourne. Nearest main road: A515 from Ashbourne to Buxton.

3 Bedrooms. £17–£21 (less for 7 nights or more). Bargain breaks. One has own shower/toilet. No smoking.
Light suppers if ordered. Vegetarian or other special diets if ordered.
1 Sitting-room. With open fire/stove, TV.
Large garden
Closed in December and January.

Truly remote, Wolfscote Grange is an isolated beef and sheep farm, parts of the ancient building dating back to the 13th century. Just outside, the land drops down 200 feet to the River Dove. Jane Gibbs keeps her rooms as traditional as is compatible with modern comfort: in keeping with the narrow, mullioned windows and low rafters, her armchairs are cretonne-covered and antique sporting-guns hang on the walls. Frequently, television companies seek out this authentic setting for costume dramas. Twists and steps lead you to bed: for the best view, ask for the pink room.

Hartington is a pretty village, its busy past as market and lead-mining town now long gone. Arbor Low, nearby, is a place of mystery – a circle of white stones erected on a windswept site 4000 years ago and with burial mounds nearby. Beyond it lies possibly the most perfect mediaeval stately home in this country: turreted Haddon Hall, with terraced gardens descending to a sparkling river. Across high heather moors lies Matlock – there is a mining museum worth visiting here.

Some proprietors stipulate a minimum stay of two nights at weekends or peak seasons; or they will accept one-nighters only at short notice (that is, only if no lengthier booking has yet been made).

Facts (prices, etc.) at the top of entries are supplied by the proprietors themselves. While every effort is made to ensure that these are correct at the time of going to press, they may alter thereafter: please check when you book.

To find the right accommodation in the right area at the right price, use an up-to-date edition of this book – revised every year. For an order form for the next edition (published in November), send a stamped addressed envelope with 'SOTBT 1999' in the top left-hand corner, to Explore Britain, Alston, Cumbria, CA9 3SL.

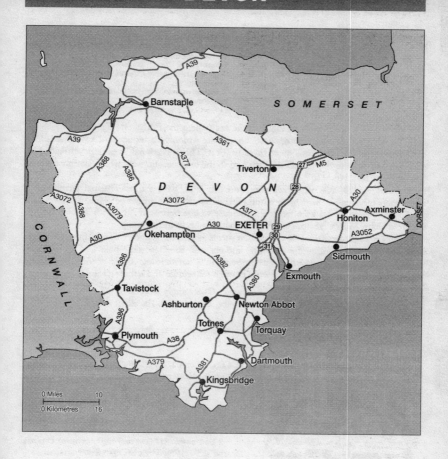

APPLYING FOR INCLUSION IN SOTBT   Many proprietors ask for their houses to be included in this book, and – although few can be accepted – such applications are welcomed, particularly from areas not already well covered; *provided that* the b & b price is within the book's limits (see page ix). Ideally, either dinner or light snacks should be available in the evening. There is no charge for an entry but, compiling the book being expensive, nearly all proprietors make a contribution at the end of each year (no bills are issued). Every house has to be visited first and it may be some time before this takes place. Brochures, prices, menus, etc. should be posted to: **Walter Gundrey (SOTBT)**, c/o Arrow Books, 20 Vauxhall Bridge Road, London SW1V 2SA. No phone calls please.

Devon

AYRMER HOUSE

S

Ringmore, Devon, TQ7 4HL   Tel: 01548 810391
West of Kingsbridge. Nearest main road: A379 from Kingsbridge to Plymouth.

4 Bedrooms. £18–£20. Some have some or all of the following: own bath/shower/toilet; TV; views of sea; balcony. No smoking.
Dinner. £12 for 3 courses and coffee, at 7pm. Vegetarian or other special diets if ordered. No smoking.
2 Sitting-rooms. With open fire, TV. No smoking.
Garden

The superb view down a broad valley to the sea (where the Eddystone lighthouse flashes at night) is what brings many visitors here: big picture-windows, a terrace and a wide verandah outside three of the bedrooms make the most of it. This is National Trust land, threaded by a stream and path to the secluded beach and to the long coastal walk which can take you to Salcombe or to Plymouth.

Jim and Ella Dodds, who keep sheep on this land, have a most unusual farmhouse – completely modern and with such natural features as walls of timber or stone, polished slate for floors or hearth, and an open-tread staircase to one bedroom suite with its own sitting-room. William Morris fabrics contrast with white walls in most rooms.

Except in high summer, Ella offers such meals as salmon, a choice of puddings (pavlova, tarts and chocolate pudding for example) and cheeses. Bread is home-baked.

Around the attractive resort of Salcombe there is outstanding coastal scenery (especially at the National Trust's Bolt Head), mild enough for orange and lemon trees.

Readers' comments: Delightful house and view. Charmingly decorated. Warmly welcomed, home-from-home atmosphere, excellent service, most restful. Excellent meals.

V

Devon

THE BEEHIVE

C(13)

Steep Hill, Maidencombe, Devon, TQ1 4TS   Tel: 01803 314647
North of Torquay. Nearest main road: A380 from Exeter towards Paignton.

2 Bedrooms. £17 (less for 7 nights or more). One has own bath/shower/toilet; TV; views of sea.
Large garden

On a hill with virtually no traffic, The Beehive has stunning views across Lyme Bay which is at the foot of the hill. This modern house was designed by its owner Norman Sibthorp to handsome standards and is furnished immaculately. Comfort within is complemented by a beautifully tended garden, reached via a terrace of red sandstone outside the sliding glass doors of the dining-room. A few yards downhill is the Thatched Tavern for excellent meals at reasonable prices; just beyond this, a sandy cove and the coastal footpath to Teignmouth.

All the coast along here (from Dawlish south to Brixham) has a Mediterranean air – luxuriant flowers, golden sands, blue seas with elegant yachts, and luxury hotels among the palm trees of its major resort, Torquay. It is probably the most popular part of Devon – though Maidencombe is well tucked away from the crowds – and so there is ample provision for such diversions as golf, boating, watersports and so forth.

Readers' comments: Beautifully decorated. Never met hosts who were kinder and more anxious to please. Thoroughly enjoyed our stay. Superb quality, exceptional hospitality.

V

BICKLEIGH COTTAGE HOTEL

PT S

Bickleigh, Devon, EX16 8RJ   Tel: 01884 855230
South of Tiverton. On A396 from Exeter to Tiverton (near M5, junction 27).

9 Bedrooms. £19.50–£23.50 (less for 7 nights or more). All have some or all of the following: own bath/shower/toilet; views of river. No smoking.
Dinner. £11.50 for 3 courses and coffee, at 7pm. Vegetarian dishes if ordered. Wine available. No smoking.
2 Sitting-rooms. With TV. No smoking in one. **Bar.**
Large garden
Closed from November to March.

Built about 1640 and later extended, this very picturesque thatched cottage has been run as a small hotel by the same family for over 60 years. It stands on a busy road by the River Exe, with a foaming weir a few yards downstream: a typically Devonian beauty-spot.

The rooms downstairs are full of antiques such as old chests and carved oak chairs, as well as a collection of blue glass and other interesting trifles including articles of Honiton lace made by Mrs Cochrane, which are for sale. The bedrooms are more simply furnished, though one has a four-poster bed. For total quiet, ask for a river-facing room (there are several). Outside is a pretty riverside garden and a glasshouse containing a collection of cacti and succulents.

Meals are of plain home cooking, a typical menu being smoked mackerel, roast lamb, and pineapple meringue.

Readers' comments: Delightful. A favourite place. Beautiful position, good meals. Delightful cottage and scenery. Lovely setting, lots of history and charm. Very friendly. Excellent.

BROOKSIDE

C D S X

Lustleigh, Bovey Tracey, Devon, TQ13 9TJ   Tel: 01647 277310
North-west of Newton Abbot. Nearest main road: A382 from Bovey Tracey to Moretonhampstead.

3 Bedrooms. £19 (less for 4 nights or more). All have views of river. No smoking.
Light suppers if ordered.
1 Sitting-room. With woodstove, TV. No smoking.
Small garden

rear view

A show village of the Dartmoor National Park, Lustleigh is sometimes crowded with sightseers – but even then Brookside, well tucked away, is peaceful. The landscaped garden is raised up on what was once a railway embankment. Round it winds the River Wrey, and one can sit above its waters on the little bridge across which trains once puffed their way.

One enters the Halseys' old house through a combined sitting/breakfast-room, which has a great granite hearth (with woodstove) at one end. A twisting stair rises to bedrooms furnished in simple cottage style. The house was originally a thatched cottage belonging to a 15th-century farm, now the Cleave Inn, which serves good dinners.

An excellent area for birdwatching; mountain bikes and guided walks available.

Readers' comments: Excellent hospitality, tranquil surroundings. Beautiful views, excellent food.   **V**

BUCKYETTE

C

Littlehempston, Devon, TQ9 6ND   Tel: 01803 762638
North of Totnes. Nearest main road: A381 from Newton Abbot to Totnes.

6 Bedrooms. £18 (less for 7 nights or more). All have some or all of the following: own bath/shower/toilet.
Light suppers if ordered. Vegetarian or other special diets if ordered. Wine available.
1 Sitting-room. With open fire, TV, piano.
Large garden
Closed from November to February.

The curious name of this house appears in the Domesday Book and is believed to be a Saxon word meaning 'head of spring': the spring is still there, and in use. The present building, made from stone quarried on the farm, dates from 1871. It is on a commanding site with far views, and is furnished with Edwardian pieces suited to the scale of the lofty rooms. In the sitting-room is a log fire for chilly days, and for sunny ones tall French doors open onto a wisteria-hung verandah. The peppermint-pink dining-room has particularly handsome tables, which Roger Miller himself made from timber from the estate, and pictures of theatrical costumes. Bedrooms are not elegant but comfortable. Everything about the house is solid, comfortable, unpretentious, and very English. Children are particularly welcome. There are four good pubs for meals, two of them within a mile.

Littlehempston is well placed for a family holiday because the safe sands of Torbay are so near – as are Paignton's zoo, miniature gardens, a scenic steam railway and river trips.

Readers' comments: Amazingly good welcome. Beautifully served food. Very charming lady.

CORBYNS BRIMLEY

C(12) M

Higher Brimley, Bovey Tracey, Devon, TQ13 9JT   Tel: 01626 833332
North-west of Newton Abbot. Nearest main road: A38 from Exeter to Plymouth.

2 Bedrooms. £20–£21 (less for 4 nights or more). One has own shower/toilet. No smoking.
Light suppers if ordered. Vegetarian or other special diets if ordered. No smoking.
1 Sitting-room. With open fire/stove. No smoking.
Large garden
Closed from mid-December to mid-January.

In the Dartmoor National Park is this exceptionally pretty, 450-year-old cottage of white walls and thatch. It has been attractively furnished by Hazel White in a style that is in keeping with its age. Snack suppers, or visitors may eat at the Toby Jug, Bickington; the Rock Inn, Haytor Vale; or at the Rumbling Tum.

Wild and rugged, Dartmoor is the south's largest stretch of open land, preserved now as a National Park. There are tors and solitary moorland contrasting with valleys and woods among which villages and little market towns lie hidden (prehistoric remains too). Picturesque North Bovey has thatched stone houses around a green. Near it is Grimspound ('Grim' is Saxon for the god Woden) where the remains of over 20 Bronze Age huts can be seen. In the market town of Moretonhampstead, old buildings include 17th-century granite almshouses, while Ashburton is more Regency in style.

Readers' comments: Superb views, splendid accommodation, caring proprietors; shall return again and again.

GOLDCOMBE FARMHOUSE

Gittisham, Devon, EX14 0AB   Tel: 01404 42559
South-west of Honiton. Nearest main road: A30 from Honiton to Exeter.

3 Bedrooms. £17.50–£20. All have some or all of the following: own bath/shower/toilet. No smoking.
Dinner (by arrangement). £11 for 3 courses and coffee, at 7.30pm. Vegetarian or other special diets if ordered. No smoking. **Light suppers** if ordered.
1 Sitting-room. With open fire, TV. Piano.
Large garden

At old and picturesque Goldcombe Farmhouse (near pretty Gittisham), renovations have revealed a rare feature – a screen wall of oak planks dividing rooms downstairs. The house has beautiful views across the Otter Valley and towards far Dartmoor. A sun-room and one ground-floor bedroom open onto the garden with its lavender bushes and old apple-trees. There are a grass tennis court and a games barn. One breakfasts in the hall, with a view into the kitchen where Ann Stansell, a trained cook, also produces cordon bleu meals (but only by arrangement), such as eggs dijonnaise, trout with hollandaise sauce and spinach timbales, and lemon soufflé.

Northward, the Blackdown Hills are an Area of Outstanding Natural Beauty, and in the opposite direction is a lovely coastline dotted with such old-fashioned resorts as Sidmouth, Branscombe and Beer. Visitors also enjoy the nearby donkey sanctuary, Bicton Park and the old Seaton–Colyton tramway.

Readers' comments: Comfortable, breakfast generous, hosts discreet and friendly. Very good. An unalloyed pleasure.

V

GOODMANS HOUSE

C D S X

Furley, Devon, EX13 7TU   Tel: 01404 881690
North-west of Axminster. Nearest main road: A30 from Honiton to Chard (and M5, junction 25).

8 Bedrooms. £19–£23 (less for 2 nights or more). Bargain breaks. All have own bath/toilet; TV. No smoking (some).
Dinner (by arrangement). £19 for aperitif, 3 courses and coffee, at 7pm. Vegetarian or other special diets if ordered. Wine available. No smoking. **Light suppers** sometimes.
1 Sitting-room. With stove. No smoking.
Large garden
Closed from mid-November to mid-February, except Christmas and New Year.

This mostly 18th-century house has well-chosen furnishings which create an ambience that is elegant without being formal. Complimentary aperitifs are served in the Georgian garden room, before a candlelit dinner in an arched dining-room with inglenooks at each end. The bedrooms are some of the most attractive in this book, with handsome bathrooms.

Alternatively, some families (and smokers) prefer to have accommodation in garden cottages, which cost less. Robert and Pat Spencer, who were hoteliers, use much organic produce for such meals as seafood and mango platter, pork with apricot and orange stuffing (imaginatively prepared vegetables), hazelnut meringues with raspberries.

Readers' comments: Breathtaking scenery, very caring hosts, delicious food. A super place, standards as high as ever. I can't think of anywhere nicer to spend a few days. A unique and very special place. Cottage most comfortable. Cannot speak too highly of it. Food superb.

V

GREENCOTT

C S

Landscove, Devon, TQ13 7LZ   Tel: 01803 762649
South-east of Ashburton. Nearest main road: A38 from Plymouth to Exeter.

2 Bedrooms. £17 (less for 7 nights or more). Bargain breaks. Both have own bath/shower/toilet.
Dinner. £8 for 4 courses and coffee, at 7pm. Vegetarian or other special diets if ordered. **Light suppers** if ordered.
1 Sitting-room. With TV.
Small garden

From Sue Townsend's immaculate tile-hung 1970s house you can see Haytor Rocks. There are two attractive en suite bedrooms; and from the quarry-tiled kitchen (with Aga) one steps through glass patio doors straight into the colourful garden. Rooms are compact and restfully furnished. After a starter such as melon or pâté, dinner will probably include a roast, or steak pie, perhaps followed by fruit pie with Devonshire cream, then cheese and coffee. The nationally renowned Hillside garden centre is close, and for steam enthusiasts the South Devon Railway in the Dart Valley.

Also in the vicinity are plenty of inns, theatres and concerts including those at Dartington's celebrated arts and crafts centres. Totnes, a centre for complementary medicine, has its castle and streets of ancient buildings.

V

Readers' comments: Sue is one of the best cooks; food beautifully presented. Warm welcome, good food. Sensational cook. Caring hostess. Superb food.

HINES HILL

East Prawle, Devon, TQ7 2BZ   Tel/Fax: 01548 511263
South-east of Kingsbridge. Nearest main road: A379 from Kingsbridge to Dartmouth.

3 Bedrooms. £20–£29 (less for 3 nights or more). All have some or all of the following: own bath/shower/toilet; TV; views of sea. No smoking.
Dinner (by arrangement). £17.50 for 4 courses and coffee, at 7.30pm. Vegetarian or other special diets if ordered. Wine available. No smoking. **Light suppers** if ordered.
1 Sitting-room. With open fire, TV. No smoking.
Large garden
Closed from November to mid-March.

This luxuriously furnished modern house has big windows to make the most of spectacular sea views from the 400-foot promontory, and a terrace overlooking the tiny sandy beach below. Many oriental pieces are among the antiques, and the elegant soft furnishings were made by Sylvia Morris herself.

A typical dinner: ratatouille with feta cheese and smoked chicken as a starter, fillet of lamb with plum and ginger sauce, lemon sorbet layered with meringue and lime cream, and cheeses (an aperitif and wine ad lib are included in the price). When Sylvia ran a restaurant previously, she received Michelin's coveted commendation.

Nearby is Salcombe, Devon's southernmost resort, and arguably its most beautiful one. Even orange and lemon trees grow here which, together with palms, remind one of parts of the Mediterranean. The estuary is very popular for sailing, garden-lovers come to see Sharpitor (NT), walkers make for the viewpoints of Bolberry Down and Bolt Head. All along the coast from here to Plymouth are picturesque waterfront villages.

Readers' comments: Wonderful views, peaceful, furnished to a high standard, attentive and helpful. Imaginative and ample cooking.

HOLE MILL

Branscombe, Devon, EX12 3BX   Tel: 01297 680314
East of Sidmouth. Nearest main road: A3052 from Lyme Regis to Sidmouth.

3 Bedrooms. £17–£19 (less for 3 nights or more). All have views of river. No smoking.
Light suppers if ordered, or guests can use kitchen.
1 Sitting-room. With open fire, TV. Piano. No smoking.
Large garden

A scenic lane winds up then very sharply down – one hears rushing water and clucking hens before the former cornmill comes into sight below. Within the thick and crooked stone walls are beamy rooms reached by steps up or down, which Rod and Amanda Hart have furnished in antique style, with a collection of clocks (they aren't allowed to chime upstairs!), Victorian bric-a-brac, and a cage with young Adrian's family of enchanting, bushy-tailed Chinchillas. In one bedroom is a particularly high iron bedstead from which you can watch the bubbling stream and the comings and goings of deer.

If you want more than a snack supper, the village has a choice of pubs and restaurants; a lift can usually be arranged. The Harts are infinitely flexible, even willing to serve breakfast at any hour: 2.20pm is the record!

Readers' comments: Most welcoming, house done up beautifully, peaceful. Goose eggs for breakfast! Charming couple.

V

HOWARDS GORHUISH

Northlew, Devon, EX20 3BT   Tel/Fax: 01837 53301
North-west of Okehampton. Nearest main road: A30 from Okehampton to Launceston.

4 Bedrooms. £20–£23. Bargain breaks. Some have own shower/toilet; TV. No smoking.
Dinner (by arrangement). £10 for 3 courses and coffee, at 7pm (not Sundays, Tuesdays or Thursdays). Vegetarian or other special diets if ordered. No smoking. **Light suppers** if ordered.
1 Sitting-room. With open fire, TV. No smoking.
Large garden

Not long ago, this 'long-house' was still being used as its 16th-century builders intended: cattle at one end, living quarters in the centre, and storage at the other.

Rugged stone walls, inglenook, low doorways and many steps are a reminder of its past. The contrasting decor, of oriental furnishings and English antiques, marries surprisingly well with this background. All around the remote, pink-walled house are acres of garden and orchard and beyond these spectacular views of Dartmoor's tors. And in an outbuilding is an excellent games room with table tennis, sofas and books.

On four evenings a week, Heather serves dinner – with such dishes as prawn-and-lobster bisque, lemon chicken, and a brandy sponge into which also go chocolate and cream.

She is an accomplished quilter: every room has examples of her work and such sparkling colour schemes as peppermint and white or coral and white. A particularly good bathroom has pretty tiles complementing the pine fitments.

Readers' comments: Superb. A very charming couple, delightfully attentive. Wonderful location, fine accommodation.

V

HUXTABLE FARM

West Buckland, Devon, EX32 0SR   Tel: 01598 760254
East of Barnstaple. Nearest main road: A361 from South Molton to Barnstaple.

C M

6 Bedrooms. £20–£24 (less for 3 nights or more). Bargain breaks. All have own bath/shower/toilet; TV.
Dinner. £14 for 4 courses, home-made wine and coffee, at 7.30pm. Vegetarian or other special diets if ordered. No smoking. **Light suppers** if ordered.
1 Sitting-room. With open fire.
Large garden, farmland and woodland.

Oak beams and screen panelling, open fireplaces with bread-ovens, flagstones for the floors – all are still to be seen in this house, built in 1520. Today it is the comfortable home of Antony and Jackie Payne who farm the land and manage the accommodation.

On the farm are sheep, goats, chickens, and a kitchen garden. There is a stream to paddle in, a tennis court – and a fitness room and sauna.

The Paynes really do welcome even the smallest children, and provide a baby alarm and nightlight in the big family room; and high-teas specially for them.

Bedrooms in the farmhouse, up stairs which some may find tricky, are cottagey in style. Those in the barns are on the ground floor and are spacious.

A typical 4-course candlelit dinner, using much local produce: wild mushroom soup; lamb chops with lemon, garlic and mint; a pudding with clotted cream; and Devon cheese.

Readers' comments: Very relaxed atmosphere. Excellent treatment, wonderful surroundings. Enjoyed our stay; excellent meals. Accommodation excellent, food superb, atmosphere very congenial.

For explanation of code letters and **V** symbol, see inside front cover.

When writing to the authors, if you want a reply please enclose a stamped addressed envelope.

'Bargain breaks' are usually out-of-season reductions for half-board stays of several nights.

Addresses shown are to enable you to locate a house on a map. They are not necessarily complete postal addresses (though the essential post-code is included), and detailed directions for finding a house should be obtained from the owner.

JUBILEE COTTAGE

75 Chapel Street, Sidbury, Devon, EX10 0RQ   Tel: 01395 597295
North of Sidmouth. Nearest main road: A375 from Sidmouth to Honiton.

3 Bedrooms. £15–£18. Bargain breaks. All have some or all of the following: own bath/shower/toilet; TV. No smoking.
Dinner (by arrangement). £10 for 4 courses and coffee, at 7pm. Vegetarian or other special diets if ordered. Wine available. No smoking. **Light suppers** if ordered.
1 Sitting-room. With stove, TV. No smoking.
Garden

16th-century, thatched Jubilee Cottage at Sidbury overlooks the lovely Sid Valley. All bedrooms are neat and pleasant – two spacious back rooms have a good view of Buckley Hill. Front rooms, overlooking Chapel Street, are double-glazed. There is a snug sitting-room, and all walls are of very thick, white-painted cob (solid clay, built up lump by lump). Major Coles and his German-born wife Marianne are adventurous cooks, and dinner might include such German and Italian specialities as apfelstrudel or tiramisu. Breakfast is sometimes served on the sunny patio which overlooks a pond and waterfall in the secluded garden.

This, the more accessible part of Devon, is exceptionally fertile and most of the cream for which Devon is famous comes from here. Birdwatchers and others who appreciate quiet prefer this part to the so-called 'riviera' coast further along. The area is full of historical associations (ancestral homes of Raleigh and Drake, Marlborough and Coleridge, for instance). Sidmouth is a particularly charming old resort.

Readers' comments: Enjoyable time, good accommodation. Meals carefully prepared.

V

LANSCOMBE HOUSE

Cockington Lane, Cockington, Devon, TQ2 6XA   Tel: 01803 606938
West of Torquay. Nearest main road: A379 from Torquay to Paignton.

7 Bedrooms. £20–£23 (less for 5 nights or more). All have some or all of the following: own bath/shower/toilet; TV. No smoking.
2 Sitting-rooms. With open fires. No smoking in one.
Bar.
Large garden

Closed in November.

An ideal spot for anyone who wants that 'off the beaten track' feel while being close to all the amenities of a major seaside resort. Picturesque and secluded, Cockington village has just survived being swallowed up by the spread of Torquay's palms and promenades.

The life of the thatched village used to be dominated by a great house set in a park, Cockington Court (now a Rural Skills Centre, where you can watch traditional crafts being taught). Pink-walled Lanscombe was its dower house. It was built in the early 18th century and has the features of that very fine architectural period – for instance, the floor-to-ceiling sash windows in the tea-room, where the Perrymans serve an all-day snack menu including Devon cream teas during the summer season. This and other rooms overlook the secluded garden with pools fed by a stream that flows to the sea some 300 yards away.

Bedrooms are spacious, decorated in soft pastel colours and with flowery fabrics. Several of the beds have prettily draped coronas or pelmets, and one is a four-poster.

Those who want more than a snack supper in the tea-room can stroll to the thatched Drum Inn nearby, almost the only inn to have been designed by Lutyens.

OVERCOMBE HOTEL

C D M S X

Old Station Road, Horrabridge, Devon, PL20 7RA   Tel/Fax: 01822 853501
South-east of Tavistock. Off A386 from Plymouth to Tavistock.

11 Bedrooms. £20–£27 (less for 2 nights or more). Prices go up from June **except to readers of this book.** Bargain breaks. All have some or all of the following: own bath/shower/toilet; TV. No smoking.
Dinner. £14 for 4 courses and coffee, at 7.30pm. Vegetarian or other special diets if ordered. Wine available. No smoking.
2 Sitting-rooms. With open fire, TV. **Bar.**
Small garden

Conveniently placed for one to explore Dartmoor and the coast, the Overcombe Hotel (now run by Brenda and Maurice Durnell) consists of two houses joined in one to make a very comfortable small hotel. You can relax in either of the sitting-rooms, according to what you want – a bar in one, TV in another, log fires, pleasant views. From the bay window of the dining-room, one looks across to the moors. Bedrooms are pretty (two on the ground floor) and one has a four-poster.

There is always a selection of dishes on the menu with such choices as pear and parsnip soup, salmon in filo pastry, traditional puddings and cheeses.

The Dartmoor National Park attracts people touring by car, anglers, riders, golfers and – above all – walkers (for them, Maurice organizes special bargain breaks, with experienced guides accompanying visitors on walks of eight miles or more, and illustrated after-dinner talks about the moors).

Readers' comments: Delightful hosts. We will go again. A relaxed, easy atmosphere; we could recommend this hotel to any of our friends. Quite perfect in every way. Wonderfully imaginative cooking. Most comfortable. Probably the best so far for welcome, food, organization.

PRESTON FARMHOUSE

C(4) S

Harberton, Devon, TQ9 7SW   Tel: 01803 862235
South of Totnes. Nearest main road: A381 from Totnes to Kingsbridge.

3 Bedrooms. £18–£19. All have some or all of the following: own bath/shower/toilet; TV. No smoking.
Dinner (on 4 nights a weeks). £12 for 4 courses and coffee, at 6.45pm. Vegetarian or other special diets if ordered. No smoking.
2 Sitting-rooms. With woodstove, TV. No smoking.
Small garden

The Steers' house, built in 1680, has been in the same farming family for generations: Isabelle was born in it. All the rooms are comfortable, and bedrooms have pretty co-ordinated fabrics. Next to the farmhouse kitchen is the dining-room, with beams and inglenook.

At the back is a sunny courtyard, and an unimaginably ancient iron-studded door.

There is good home cooking at dinner, with dishes as varied as fresh salmon from the River Dart, chicken Marengo, roasts, pies, baked Alaska, treacle pudding. The ingredients are mostly home-grown or local. Breakfast comes on 'help-yourself' platters – conventional bacon and eggs or more unusual things like hog's pudding or smoked haddock.

Harberton is a picturesque cluster of old cottages with colourful gardens, set in a valley. Preston Farm was once a manor house, which is why rooms are spacious.

Readers' comments: Quite simply the best b & b. Of the best we have encountered. Most comfortable and delightful four days. Truly a gem. Unusual combination of efficiency, courtesy and kindness; food excellent. Delightful place to stay.

V

SAMPSONS FARM RESTAURANT

Preston, Devon, TQ12 3PP   Tel/Fax: 01626 54913
North of Newton Abbot. Nearest main road: A380 from Newton Abbot towards Exeter (and M5, junction 31).

10 Bedrooms. £17.50–£25 (less for 2 nights or more). Bargain breaks. Some have some or all of the following: own bath/shower/toilet; TV. No smoking. **Dinner.** £12.50 for 3 courses and coffee, or à la carte, from 7pm. Vegetarian or other special diets if ordered. Wine available. No smoking. **Light suppers** if ordered. **1 Sitting-room.** With open fire. **Bar.**
Large garden

To this traditional Devon house, all whitewash and thatch, came a Cornish farming family who gave it a new way of life – as a renowned restaurant. Hazel Bell runs the bed and breakfast, and her son Nigel the restaurant. Chefs Kristin and Chris cook the gourmet-class lunches and dinners.

After scallops with garlic, one might have the house speciality – a half-duckling in orange sauce with vegetables cooked to perfection, and then a lemon ice cream with biscuity topping. (There is a good wine list too.) Dinner is served in a low, cosy dining-room, with candle-lamps. Beyond the small bar is a snug, timbered sitting-room with log fire in an inglenook.

The way to the bedrooms is all steps and twists (two of the rooms have a four-poster), for the house has grown in a higgledy-piggledy way since its probable beginnings in the 15th century. More bedrooms in an immacutely converted barn across the yard.

Readers' comments: Most welcoming, food excellent. Restaurant fabulous; very helpful. Hospitality outstanding, food exceptional.

V

SLOOP INN

Bantham, Devon, TQ7 3AJ   Tel: 01548 560489 (Fax: 01548 561940)
West of Kingsbridge. Nearest main road: A379 from Kingsbridge to Plymouth.

5 Bedrooms. £20 **(to readers of this book only)**–£29. Less for 7 nights or more. Bargain breaks. All have some or all of the following: own bath/shower/toilet; TV; views of sea/river.
Dinner. From £12 for 3 courses à la carte, at 7–10pm. Vegetarian or special diets if ordered. Wine available.
Light suppers.
Bars.
Closed in January.

It goes without saying that this 400-year-old inn by the sea has a history of smuggling. Owned by Neil Girling, the inn is unspoilt: everything one hopes that a village inn will be but rarely is, low-beamed, stone-flagged and snug. Some walls are of stone, some panelled. One of its several bars is made from old boat-timbers. Here you can take on the locals at a game of darts or table-skittles after enjoying an excellent bar meal; or stroll down to the sandy dunes to watch the sun set over the sea. Bathing, building sandcastles and exploring rock pools delight children; and there is surfing. Many of the plainly furnished bedrooms have a view of the sea or River Avon. (Sometimes the traffic noise is noticeable.)

Soups are home-made and ham home-cooked; smoked salmon, crabs and steaks are all local produce. Fish is, of course, particularly good and fresh. All portions are generous.

Readers' comments: Food very good. A most enjoyable stay. Quiet, peaceful, idyllic scenery. Excellently furnished. Food the best I've eaten lately. Really comfortable.

V

SPLATTHAYES

C M S

Buckerell, Devon, EX14 0ER   Tel: 01404 850464
West of Honiton. Nearest main road: A30 from Honiton to Exeter (and M5, junction 28).

5 Bedrooms. £18.50–£20 (less for 4 nights or more). Some have some or all of the following: own shower/toilet; TV. No smoking.
Dinner. £16 for 4 courses and coffee, at 7.30pm. Vegetarian or other special diets if ordered. No smoking. **Light suppers** if ordered.
1 Sitting-room. With open fire, piano. No smoking.
Large garden

This is a quintessential, picturesque Devon cottage: thatched roof and white cob walls; flagged floors, beams and brick hearth inside. It is 400 years old. In the pretty garden are 30 eucalyptus trees, a ginkgo and a sequoia (with fields of sheep beyond), a view you can enjoy from an L-shaped, ground-floor bedroom which has its own sitting-area.

It is Douglas Cowan who cooks the dinners, to a very high standard. A typical menu might include (among several choices) cannelloni filled with smoked mackerel and spinach as a starter, pork fillet with cherry sauce, blackberry and apple filo, then cheeses. He uses much home-grown and organic produce, makes his own bread and preserves, and has a repertoire of imaginative vegetarian dishes. Mandy has trained in aromatherapy, reflexology and electro-crystal therapy – treatments are available while you stay.

Honiton, celebrated for lace-making, is full of antique shops and has twice-weekly markets too. Historic Exeter is only 15 miles away.

Readers' comments: Delicious meal; nothing too much trouble. Dinner excellent; friendly and welcoming.

V

STOWFORD HOUSE

C

Stowford Lane, Stowford, Devon, EX20 4BZ   Tel: 01566 783415
South-west of Okehampton. Nearest main road: A30 from Okehampton to Launceston.

6 Bedrooms. £19.50–£22 (less for 2 nights; **further reductions for 3 nights mid-week to readers of this book only**). Bargain breaks. Most have some or all of the following: own bath/shower/toilet; TV. No smoking.
Dinner. £14.50 for 4 courses and coffee, at 7–8.30pm. Vegetarian or other special diets if ordered. Wine available. No smoking. **Light suppers** if ordered.
1 Sitting-room. With open fire, TV. **Bar.**
Large garden
Closed from late December to early March.

This former country rectory is now a comfortable hotel, dignified by its 18th-century features such as the fine windows, handsome front door, a graceful archway inside and impressive staircase. The large garden is at its best in May.

The hotel has a reputation for good food. With over 25 years' experience of running first a catering service and then a restaurant, Jenny Irwin has accumulated a wide repertoire of recipes. Typical dishes she may serve – in a dining-room with a fine Victorian fireplace – include Stilton and apricot mille-feuilles, casserole of venison, and pecan and date tart.

Bedrooms are large, light and airy. Everywhere is a profusion of pot-plants; and on some walls are delicate watercolours by David's father, Sydney Irwin.

Readers' comments: Really beautiful house. Exceptional food. Wonderful experience. Exceptionally warm and welcoming; devoted to making guests comfortable. The place we'd most like to visit again. Standard of meals cannot be too highly commended.

V

TAILRACE

Crowdy Mill, Bow Road, Harbertonford, Devon, TQ9 7HU Tel/Fax: 01803 732340
South of Totnes. Nearest main road: A381 from Totnes to Kingsbridge.

4 Bedrooms. £19.50–£24.50 (less for 5 nights or more). All have some or all of the following: own bath/shower/toilet; balcony; views of river.
Dinner (by arrangement). £15 for 4 courses and coffee, at 7.30pm. Vegetarian or other special diets if ordered. Wine available. No smoking.
2 Sitting-rooms. With open log stove (in one), TV, piano. No smoking.
Large garden

Don and Ann Barnes used to run the working watermill here, but they now live in one of two well-converted cottages. This cottage, called Tailrace, has two comfortable en suite double bedrooms. Guests have the use of the living-room with antique furniture, paintings, books, and sculpture by Ann's father, William Reid Dick. One window looks out directly onto the river where, in season, trout can be seen swimming upstream, wild ducks can be fed, kingfishers flash past and wagtails and the occasional dipper can be watched. The other large window opens onto a terrace where, in warm weather, breakfast can be enjoyed with a lovely view of the surrounding hills.

The other bedrooms are on the ground floor of the second cottage, just across the garden (which is also available for self-catering), where guests have the use of the whole cottage, including a single room for family or friend. Upstairs, there is a sitting-room with a south-west facing balcony, a kitchenette and dining-area. Breakfast and dinner are served in Tailrace.

Don Barnes is responsible for the free-range eggs and organic vegetables; Ann makes all the breads, jams, marmalades and chutneys. There is much use of organic local produce.

VALE HOUSE

C(10) **PT S**

Sands Road, Slapton, Devon, TQ7 2QT Tel: 01548 580669 (Fax: 01548 581180)
South-west of Dartmouth. Nearest main road: A379 from Dartmouth to Kingsbridge.

2 Bedrooms. £19. TV (in one). No smoking.
Light suppers if ordered. No smoking.
1 Sitting-room. With open fire, TV, piano.
Large garden

Along the scenic coast road lies the stone village of Slapton where Roberta and Tim Price's 400-year-old Vale House is tucked away within a walled garden. All around is an Area of Outstanding Natural Beauty. There's a white-panelled dining-room with a long mahogany table; a cream-and-blue sitting-room with log fire and big sash windows; marine paintings everywhere; and, up a pretty galleried staircase, very attractive bedrooms. From Slapton it is easy to reach the Dart (boat trips, and steam rail alongside) and Dartmoor.

This part of Devon is called the South Hams – meaning a sheltered place: it is Britain's mildest area, with flowers often blooming even in winter. Five rivers meander through the fertile fields, and past prosperity has left a legacy of fine mediaeval and Tudor houses, snug villages of thatched cottages, handsome churches. Behind the long sands at Slapton a lagoon is at the centre of a wildlife reserve. Dartmouth has a castle, its Naval College and picturesque byways.

Readers' comments: Delightful house, most enjoyable, lovely furnishings and beautiful china. Made most welcome.

V

WAVENDEN

C(10)

Compass, Dartmouth, Devon, TQ6 0JN   Tel: 01803 833979

Nearest main road: A379 from Dartmouth to Kingsbridge.

3 Bedrooms. £20–£22 (less for 6 nights or more). All have views of sea/river. No smoking.
Dinner (by arrangement). From £12.50 for 4 courses and coffee, at 7.30pm. Vegetarian or other special diets if ordered. Wine available. No smoking.
1 Sitting-room. With woodstove, TV. No smoking.
Large garden
Closed from late December to late January.

So beautiful is the coastal scenery beyond Dartmouth (owned by the National Trust) that today no-one is allowed to build on it: Wavenden is the only house there to enjoy the superb view of the River Dart's wide estuary. The large two-level dining- and sitting-room has huge glass doors through which to savour it; outside is a paved sundeck.

The grounds run down through woodland to the foreshore, where you can swim or fish and see the Gardners' lobster pots.

Ken (an award-winning journalist) and Lily both cook, and dinner often includes a local seafood platter, preceded perhaps by mixed hors d'oeuvres, and followed by apple pie, and cheese.

Readers' comments: The location, the welcome, the comfort, the decor – everything was superb value. Lovely views and atmosphere generated by the Gardners. Friendly and relaxed. Very well looked after. One of the most beautiful locations.

WELLPRITTON FARM

C D S X

Holne, Ashburton, Devon, TQ13 7RX   Tel: 01364 631273

West of Ashburton. Nearest main road: A38 from Exeter to Plymouth.

4 Bedrooms. £18 (less for 7 nights or more). Bargain breaks. Only weekly bookings in high season. All have some or all of the following: own bath/shower/toilet; TV. No smoking.
Dinner (by arrangement). £9 for 4 courses and coffee, at 7pm. Vegetarian or other special diets if ordered. No smoking.
1 Sitting-room. With stove, TV.
Small garden

Tucked away in a fold of the gentle hills south of Dartmoor is this small farm where sheep and hens are kept; horses and goats too. (Children's riding by arrangement.) From the farm, which has a small swimming-pool, there are views of the moors.

Sue and Colin Gifford have furnished the bedrooms prettily, and supply them with fruit-squash and biscuits as well as tea. There are two family units of two rooms and a shower, and a ground-floor suite. A comfortable sitting-room is available to guests, and there is also a games room with snooker and table tennis.

After a starter such as melon or pâté, dinner will probably include a roast, poultry or steak pie, perhaps followed by fruit pie or flan, always accompanied by Devonshire cream, then cheese and coffee. Bread is home-baked.

Readers' comments: Excellent in every way. Made welcome and comfortable. Extremely good food. A delightful break. Welcome, helpfulness and food are memorable.

WOODSIDE COTTAGE

Blackawton, Devon, TQ9 7BL   Tel: 01803 712375 (Fax: 01803 712605)
West of Dartmouth. Nearest main road: A3122 from Dartmouth towards Totnes.

3 Bedrooms. £18–£20 (less for 3 nights or more). Bargain breaks. All have own shower/toilet; TV. No smoking.
1 Sitting-room. No smoking.
Small garden
Closed from November to February.

Being perched on a high bank, 18th-century Woodside Cottage has wonderful valley views. A steep little garden of slabs, ferns and flowers brings you to the front door, inside which is a beamed breakfast-room, which Val and John Clark have furnished with antiques, a conservatory with bamboo chairs, and stone fireplaces. Bedrooms are very pretty (pine and delicate fabrics predominate) and en suite shower-rooms too.

Once a gamekeeper lived here, and the woods are still full of pheasants (in the stream, herons pursue the trout). This is a great area for wildflowers. For meals, village pubs are close. Discounts are available for local golf, swimming-pool, etc.

The surrounding countryside is superb, with marvellous walks along the coast and over the moors. Dartington with its gardens, sculpture and craft shops is only a few miles away, and the newly opened High Cross House (a mini St Ives Tate) is also there. The trip down the River Dart from Totnes to Dartmouth should not be missed.

Readers' comments: Peaceful and pretty. Hospitable.

Prices are per person sharing a room at the beginning of the year.

Book well ahead: many of these houses have few rooms. Do not expect dinner if you have not booked it or if you arrive late.

Houses which accept the discount vouchers on page ii are marked with a **V** symbol next to the relevant entries.

Where wine is not available (meaning it is on sale or can be fetched for you), you are nearly always welcome to bring in your own drinks.

DORSET

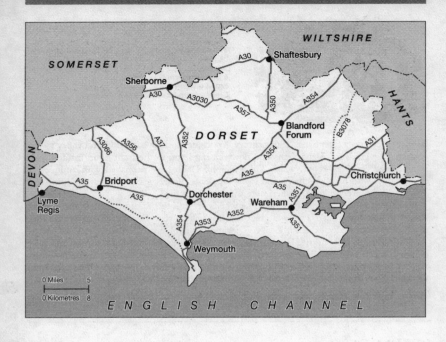

THANK YOU . . . to those who send details of their own finds, for possible future inclusion in the book. Do not be disappointed if your candidate does not appear in the very next edition. We never publish recommendations from unknown members of the public without verification, and it takes time to get round each part of England and Wales in turn. Please, however, do not send details of houses already featured in many other guides, nor any that are more expensive than those in this book (see page ix).

THE BEEHIVE

Church Lane, Osmington, Dorset, DT3 6EL   Tel: 01305 834095

C(6) **D S X**

North-east of Weymouth. Nearest main road: A353 from Weymouth towards Wareham.

3 Bedrooms. £16–£18.50 (less for 3 nights or more). Bargain breaks. One has own shower/toilet. No smoking.
Light suppers if ordered. Vegetarian or other special diets if ordered.
1 Sitting-room. With stove, TV. No smoking.
Small garden
Closed in January and February.

Mary Kempe's father was Lord of the Manor at Osmington; and this little thatched stone cottage was the holiday home of her childhood. While the manorial lands passed into other hands, she was pursuing an academic career at the universities of Nairobi and London: the former accounts for the presence of African crafts in the old cottage, which is now her permanent home. It is tucked away – in a pocket-handkerchief garden – down a lane leading to countryside of great beauty, with lovely walks; fine coast is only a mile away.

The friendly sitting-room is a place of books and watercolours, lead-paned windows and comfortable sofas or chairs. Meals are served in the big, cork-floored kitchen. You can eat well at the nearby Smugglers' Inn.

Readers' comments: Superb; delightful haven of peace; a marvellous hostess. One of the best meals we have ever sampled. A lovely welcome. Breakfast was excellent. A wonderful person. So comfy; Mary so full of helpful info.

V

BRADLE FARM

Church Knowle, Dorset, BH20 5NU   Tel: 01929 480712 (Fax: 01929 481144)

S

South of Wareham. Nearest main road: A351 from Wareham to Swanage.

3 Bedrooms. £19–£20 (less for 7 nights or more). Bargain breaks. All have own bath/shower/toilet; TV.
Light suppers if ordered.
1 Sitting-room. With stove.
Large garden

From this handsome Victorian house of local Purbeck stone there are beautiful views – across the duckpond – of the so-called Isle of Purbeck and of the gaunt ruins of Corfe Castle looming over all. Window-seats at the shuttered casements help you to make the most of these, with unlimited help-yourself tea and home-made cake in hand. Upstairs, low corridors lead to bedrooms (one is particularly spacious) with similar views.

Holes have lived here for generations, with what is now 1400 acres of their mixed farm (cows, sheep, corn) stretching right down to the sea and up to high Swyre Head. The long coastal footpath goes through their land: you can watch milking and lambing or help feed the chickens . . . or just laze by the log stove.

Although Gillian sometimes provides guests with snack suppers, she has an arrangement with the thatched New Inn to give her visitors a discount on their good Dorset meals – it has a skittle alley too.

The coast is only 1½ miles from the house, with beautiful walks there and inland too.

Readers' comments: Superb. Welcoming hospitality.

V

BROADSTONE BARN

D S

Lower Walditch Lane, Walditch, Dorset, DT6 4LA   Tel: 01308 427430
East of Bridport. Nearest main road: A35 from Bridport to Dorchester.

3 Bedrooms. £18.50–£21 (less for 5 nights or more). Some have some or all of the following: own bath/ shower/toilet. No smoking.
1 Sitting-room. With log stove, TV. No smoking.
Closed from mid-December to mid-February.

A fine old barn of golden stone was most handsomely converted, with its original character carefully retained, to make this beautiful house. Rugged stone walls and slate floors contrast with a splendid open-tread spiral staircase with a rope handrail. Val and Guy Barnes have grouped sofas round the stove in the sitting-room, with glass doors on both sides. In the dining-room, a particularly impressive pine table and fiddleback chairs stand under old rafters still exposed to view and a new gallery where there are wicker armchairs. Adjoining this gallery are attractive bedrooms (one has windows on three sides); one of the bathrooms is particularly elegant, its tiles patterned with cornstalks. Outdoors is a conservatory; an area chequered with cobbles and paving around a raised, circular lily-pool; a lawn with seats; and a vegetable garden frequented by badgers.

At breakfast, not only marmalade and bread are home-made but yogurt too; and black pudding is among the choices on offer. There is unlimited tea and coffee available in the sitting-room at all times.

Dorset is a wonderful county for walkers, particularly along the nearby coast, while those who want to explore it on wheels can hire mountain bicycles at the house.

BUCKNOWLE HOUSE

C D

Bucknowle, Dorset, BH20 5PQ   Tel: 01929 480352 (Fax: 01929 481275)
South of Wareham. Nearest main road: A351 from Wareham to Swanage.

3 Bedrooms. £20–£25 (less for 3 nights or more). All have some or all of the following: own bath/shower/ toilet; TV.
Light suppers if ordered.
1 Sitting-room. With open fire.
Large garden

At this imposing Victorian dwelling of Purbeck 'marble', a black-and-white tiled hallway leads one up a broad staircase, with intricately carved balustrade and galleried landing, to spacious bedrooms decorated in bold colours. One double, in bottle green with modern tartan curtains, has a lovely view of Corfe Castle. Another, in pale terracotta, has an attractive carved bedhead. Sara Harvey serves meals in the elegant blue-and-gold dining-room, walls hung with old prints, and, at one end, a grand overmantel mirror. Afterwards guests can relax by the fire in the sitting-room, where family portraits and mirrored wall-sconces decorate the walls. There is a tennis court sometimes available to guests.

All around this area are marvellous places to visit – the following is merely a selection: Poole Harbour, the second largest and loveliest natural harbour in the world; the Blue Pool beauty-spot; Durlston Head – cliffs, birds, country park, lighthouse; the army Tank Museum at Bovington; and the resort of Bournemouth is only a half-hour drive away.

CERNE RIVER COTTAGE

8 The Folly, Cerne Abbas, Dorset, DT2 7JR   Tel: 01300 341355
North of Dorchester. Nearest main road: A352 from Dorchester to Sherborne.

2 Bedrooms. £19 (less for 4 nights or more). Bargain breaks. Both have some or all of the following: own bath/shower/toilet. No smoking.
1 Sitting-room. With open fire, TV. No smoking.
Small garden

A good view of the Cerne Abbas giant, an enormous pagan chalk-cut figure, is afforded from the twin room of this pretty 18th-century cottage. At one time a tannery and then a school, it is now the home of Ginny Williams-Ellis, her husband Nick, a landscape gardener, and their children. Not surprisingly, their garden (where guests can have breakfast in summer) is particularly pleasant, with the River Cerne meandering through it.

They have worked hard to restore their home. In the dining-room guests can enjoy home-made apple juice with their breakfast and jam made from the many fruit trees in the garden. Eggs are free-range and milk is organic. Bedrooms are simply furnished in pastel shades; the double has a good brass bedstead and view of the garden. Good evening meals can be had at any of Cerne's inns.

Readers' comments: Thoroughly recommended. Made very comfortable.

THE CREEK

Ringstead, Dorchester, Dorset, DT2 8NG   Tel: 01305 852251
East of Weymouth. Nearest main road: A353 from Weymouth towards Wareham.

2 Bedrooms. £17.50. Bargain breaks. Both have some or all of the following: own shower/toilet; TV; views of sea. No smoking.
Dinner (by arrangement). £9.50 for 3 courses and coffee, at 7pm. Vegetarian or other special diets if ordered. Wine available. No smoking. **Light suppers** if ordered.
1 Sitting-room. With stove, TV. No smoking.
Large garden
Closed in January.

By the seashore is this rambling house, built in the 1920s and later extended. It is the home of Michael and Freda Fisher, retired headmaster and headmistress. Portraits of their ancestors line the walls of this elegantly furnished house, which has quite stunning views across open sea. In summer you can swim in the heated pool, or walk through the garden and down onto the beach for a dip, or take a coastal walk as far as Swanage. Bedrooms are small and neat; one has attractive flower studies on its walls. Freda was a professional cook, so expect interesting dinner menus. (The Creek is reached by a toll road but guests do not pay.)

Birdwatchers go out from here to spend days at Radipole Lake, the Fleet or Studland nature reserve. Others tour the Thomas Hardy sites. Further afield, one can visit such beauty-spots as Lulworth Cove and the Purbeck Hills; T.E. Lawrence's cottage at Clouds Hill; and picturesque villages like Wool which has *Tess of the D'Urbervilles* associations.

Readers' comments: Delightful. A natural hostess. Will return again. Friendly and interesting people. Cooking most excellent.

DOWER HOUSE

C(8) **PT S**

Bradford Peverell, Dorset, DT2 9SF   Tel: 01305 266125
North-west of Dorchester. Nearest main road: A37 from Dorchester to Yeovil.

3 Bedrooms. £17.50 (less for 4 nights or more). All have own bath/toilet. No smoking.
Light suppers if ordered.
1 Sitting-room. With open fire, TV, piano. No smoking.
Large garden
Closed from December to February.

One steps straight into the dining-hall of this 1830s house, with oriental rugs on a floor of polished boards, Chippendale-style chairs and interesting heirloom paintings. From the coral-walled sitting-room, bookshelves surrounding its log fire, is a pretty village view.

Upstairs, past more books and a doll's house on the landing, are attractive bedrooms with sprigged wallpaper, pine or flower-painted bedsteads, and real cotton or linen sheets and old spreads which Kips Eaton regularly tracks down in Dorchester market. Old-fashioned bathrooms are another pleasure in keeping with the style of the house – as are the large walled garden (providing fruit and vegetables), the home-made cakes at teatime, and Michael's home-baked bread at breakfast. Jam, too, is home-made and honey comes from the Eatons' hives.

When Kips provides a light supper it is likely to comprise something like fennel and prawn pasta followed by raspberries with meringues and cream.

Readers' comments: Very pleasant. Particularly welcoming and a beautiful home. Wonderful: we felt welcome and at home. Whimsical collections. Warm, happy, gracious hosts. Very friendly. Breakfasts generous and delicious. Could hardly be bettered. Good advice on walks.

GARDEN COTTAGE

C D M P T S X

3 Bladen Valley, Briantspuddle, Dorset, DT2 7HP   Tel: 01929 471287
East of Dorchester. Nearest main road: A35 from Dorchester to Poole.

1 Bedroom. £16.50 (less for 3 nights or more). Bargain breaks. Has own shower/toilet. No smoking.
Light suppers if ordered. Vegetarian or other special diets if ordered.
1 Sitting-room. With TV.
Large garden

Sir Ernest Debenham's plans for a picturesque model village outside Briantspuddle were halted by war in 1914, so its wide grass-verged main avenue, called Bladen Valley, leads nowhere. Among the thatched houses flanking the avenue is Beverley Stirling's Garden Cottage. In the big garden (where chickens roam at the end, and goat Hebe too), visitors have their own private annexe, prettily decorated. In the comfortable sitting/dining-room, its dresser laden with old china finds, Beverley serves breakfasts and snack suppers.

One is in the midst of 'Hardy country' here with his so-called Casterbridge (Dorchester) quite near, together with his birthplace at Bockhampton. Weymouth, Bere Regis and Puddletown all feature in his novels along with the scenic heaths and hills of the county. Hardy exhibits are in Dorchester's museum, which also has Roman remains (south of the town was an amphitheatre to seat 10,000 spectators!). Australian visitors head for Tolpuddle, village of the famous 'martyrs' (would-be trade unionists) transported in 1834. Near Moreton is the simple cottage where T.E. Lawrence lived at the end of his life (his striking memorial is in Wareham). To get fine views, try the Purbeck Hills.

HOLEBROOK FARM

Lydlinch, Sturminster Newton, Dorset, DT10 2JB Tel/Fax: 01258 817348

C M

South-west of Shaftesbury. Nearest main road: A357 from Sturminster Newton to Stalbridge.

9 Bedrooms. £18–£23 (less for 3 nights or more). Bargain breaks. All have some or all of the following: own bath/shower/toilet; TV.
Dinner (by arrangement). £13.50 for 3 courses and coffee, at 7pm. Vegetarian or other special diets if ordered. Wine available. No smoking. **Light suppers** if ordered.
1 Sitting-room. With open fire, TV.
Large garden

A long track brings one into the yard behind this large farm; on one side are stables handsomely converted into bedrooms and on the other, a new wing where there are more bedrooms. In the big old kitchen, with its original flagged floor and stone ovens carefully preserved, Charles Wingate-Saul serves dinner. (The main course may be anything from lasagne to pheasant; puddings include chocolate roulade; and there are prize-winning local cheeses too.)

From a gracious sitting-room (apricot walls, damask chairs, log fire) deep-set, pine-shuttered windows overlook the lawn at the front of the house beyond which are apple-trees.

The stable rooms include some that are enormous, each with sitting-room and bathroom. Small concealed kitchens are useful for visitors who want to prepare any meals themselves. There are also a games room, a swimming-pool and clay-pigeon shooting.

Readers' comments: Relaxed and helpful. Excellent accommodation, helpfully equipped. Meal delicious and outdoor pool a boon. Very good value. Had a wonderful stay. Like part of the family. Very happy and comfortable place, friendly atmosphere. Food excellent.

V

MELBURY MILL

Melbury Abbas, Dorset, SP7 0DB Tel: 01747 852163

South of Shaftesbury. Nearest main road: A350 from Shaftesbury to Blandford Forum.

3 Bedrooms. £20–£25. All have own bath/shower/toilet. No smoking.
Dinner (by arrangement). £15 for 3 courses and coffee, at 7.30pm. Vegetarian or other special diets if ordered. No smoking.
1 Sitting-room. With woodstove, TV. No smoking.
Large garden

By lovely Cranborne Chase, a watermill at Melbury Abbas was mentioned in Domesday Book. On its Saxon foundations the present Melbury Mill was built in the 18th century (its historic wheel still turns). Trained as an architect, Richard Bradley-Watson has done a beautiful conversion of beamed outbuildings to provide two exceptionally good bedrooms with en suite facilities overlooking the millpond. In the house itself there is a third, large bedroom, sitting-room with woodstove, and a stone-flagged dining-room where Tavy (cordon bleu trained) serves such meals as marinated mushrooms, pheasant, and meringue gâteau. The Mill is linked by footpath to Melbury Beacon and Fontmell Down, both owned by the National Trust.

There are plenty of good drives around here. For instance, one might go via Mere to visit the world-famous landscaped gardens and lake of Stourhead and the 18th-century mansion itself (full of art treasures). Alternatively, one could drive to Tollard Royal on a road of hairpin bends that is an outstanding scenic route with superb views when you get to the top.

OLD GRANARY

C PT

The Quay, Wareham, Dorset, BH20 4LP   Tel: 01929 552010 (Fax: 01929 552482)
Nearest main road: A351 from Poole to Swanage.

5 Bedrooms. £20–£40. **20% discount in winter to readers of this book (2 days, excluding Fri and Sat).** All have some or all of the following: own bath/shower/toilet; TV; views of river. No smoking.
Dinner. £15.95 for 3 courses and coffee, at 6–9pm. Vegetarian dishes or other special diets if ordered in advance. Wine available.
Bar. With open fire.

Standing right on the quay (where cars park) by the River Frome, this 18th-century brick building was once a warehouse for grain that went by barge to Poole, and it still has much of its old character.

Derek and Rosemarie Sturton run a restaurant here, furnished with cane chairs and attractive colours. A typical dinner might comprise, for instance, fresh mussels, sea bass, and banoffee pie. There is a riverside conservatory for cream teas and drinks, and a bar with open fire. Upstairs are three floors with pretty, beamed bedrooms, their windows giving a view of the river, swans, and the Purbeck Hills beyond. The local landscapes on their walls are for sale.

Wareham is an interesting old town, a great mixture of history and of architectural styles.

Readers' comments: Absolutely professional but very personal; spotlessly clean, excellent food. Lovely situation, a personal touch. Food superb. Pretty bedrooms, high quality food. Unique place, very comfortable. Wonderful! Exceptionally friendly and welcoming.

> **Months when houses are shown as closed are inclusive.**

> **Private bathrooms are not necessarily en suite.**

> **Complaints about matters which could not have been settled on the spot will be forwarded to proprietors. Please enclose a stamped addressed envelope if you want the authors to acknowledge receipt of your complaint.**

> **Addresses shown are to enable you to locate a house on a map. They are not necessarily complete postal addresses (though the essential postcode is included), and detailed directions for finding a house should be obtained from the owner.**

OLD MANOR COTTAGE

Winterbourne Steepleton, Dorset, DT2 9LG   Tel: 01305 889512
West of Dorchester. Nearest main road: A35 from Dorchester to Bridport.

C(8) **PT S X**

3 Bedrooms. £20 (less for 3 nights or more). Bargain breaks. Some have some or all of the following: own bath/shower/toilet; TV; views of river.
Dinner (by arrangement). £10 for 3 courses and coffee, at times to suit guests. Vegetarian or other special diets if ordered. Wine available. **Light suppers** if ordered.
1 Sitting-room. With open fire, TV.
Small garden

Thatched roof, latched doors, low beams and flagged floors are as you would expect in 1586, the year when Old Manor Cottage was built. In the thick walls, little leaded casements are stone-mullioned; and floors slope with age.

Charmian Goodenough-Bayly has furnished the rooms in simple cottage style, white walls complemented by pine furniture. Her husband made model ships when in the Navy: these, his collection of shells, and his mementoes of years in the Middle East give the house individuality. Outside, a brilliant japonica is a feature of the flint-walled garden. Charmian's dinners (which include a glass of wine) may comprise such courses as home-made chicken liver pâté, pork casserole or pigeon pie, and treacle tart.

Historic Dorchester has many Hardy associations, as well as a lively dinosaur museum.

Readers' comments. Very nicely furnished. Friendly and interesting hosts.

V

OLD VICARAGE

Affpuddle, Dorset, DT2 7HH   Tel/Fax: 01305 848315
East of Dorchester. Nearest main road: A35 from Dorchester to Poole.

C(10) **PT S**

3 Bedrooms. £17.50–£22.50. All have own bath/shower/toilet; TV.
Light suppers if ordered, in winter.
Large garden

Before Anthea and Michael Hipwell moved here, it was an ambassador's country home: a handsome Georgian house with fine doorways, windows and fireplaces – surrounded by smooth lawns (with croquet) and rosebeds within tall hedges of clipped yew, the old church alongside.

Anthea has a flair for interior decoration. Even the corridors are elegant, with portraits and flower-prints on walls of apple-blossom pink.

Breakfast is served in the prettiest dining-room in this book. Taking as the starting-point her collection of aquamarine glass (housed in two alcoves) and a series of modern lithographs in vivid turquoise, Anthea decorated the walls to match, and chose a dramatic turquoise curtain fabric reproduced from a Regency design. As no evening meal is provided, many visitors go to the Brace of Pheasants at Plush or Perry's Restaurant in Weymouth.

Readers' comments: Delightful decor. Tea on the porch especially nice. Delightful house, charming hostess. Excellent in every way. Elegant and beautiful rooms. Surroundings superb.

POWERSTOCK MILL FARM

CDS

Powerstock, Dorset DT6 3SL   Tel: 01308 485213
North-east of Bridport. Nearest main road: A3066 from Bridport to Beaminster.

2 Bedrooms. £17.50 (less for 3 nights or more).
Dinner (by arrangement). £12 for 3 courses and coffee, at times to suit guests. Vegetarian or other special diets if ordered. **Light suppers** if ordered.
1 Sitting-room. With open fire, TV.
Large garden
Closed from mid-December to mid-January.

The great iron waterwheel at this farm ceased to turn long ago but the wandering stream still goes by the old farmhouse in its secluded valley, so sheltered that palms grow there. It can be reached by a dramatic drive over Eggardon Hill (the 'Egdon Heath' of Hardy and Holst) and along lanes where celandines and bluebells throng the banks. The sea is only five miles away.

This is a truly traditional farm: board ceilings, tiled floors, dresser with blue-and-white china, coal fire and the slow tick of a grandfather clock – with the landowner's ducal coat-of-arms on one wall. There are cows, chickens and ducks around; and for dinner Elaine Marsh serves a proper farm meal – soup, a roast, fruit salad, and cheeses.

There are Iron Age hill forts, and many literary associations in this lovely area.

Readers' comments: A lovely farm. Pretty and spotless bedrooms. Warm welcome, delicious breakfast, hope to go back.

RED HOUSE

C(8) PT

Sidmouth Road, Lyme Regis, Dorset, DT7 3ES   Tel/Fax: 01297 442055
Nearest main road: A3052 from Lyme Regis to Exeter.

3 Bedrooms. £18 **(to readers of this book)**–£25 (less for 4 nights or more). Bargain breaks. All have some or all of the following: own bath/toilet; TV; views of sea. No smoking.
Light suppers if ordered.
Garden
Closed from December to February.

This dignified 'twenties house was built for Aldis (inventor of the famous signal-lamps which bear his name) on a superb site with a 40-mile sea view south-east as far as Portland Bill. It is a house with handsome features – iron-studded oak doors, leaded casements and window-seats, for example. On sunny mornings (occasionally even in late autumn), you can take breakfast on the wide verandah and enjoy sea breezes while you eat; at your feet, sloping lawns with colourful rhododendrons, camellias, fuchsias and wisteria. On chilly mornings, breakfast is served in an attractive room with a fire.

Each bedroom is equipped with armchairs, TV, a refrigerator, and fresh flowers – the aim being to provide individual bedsitters for guests, as there is no full-size sitting-room.

The house is full of pictures and objects from the Normans' overseas postings (Anthony was in the Navy) and in the garden is a timber cabin where Vicky makes exceptionally pretty cloth dolls: she also teaches this skill.

V   *Readers' comments:* Splendid views and pleasant gardens. Rooms perfectly equipped. Top rate.

SOUND O' WATER

16 Duck Street, Cerne Abbas, Dorset, DT2 7LA   Tel: 01300 341435
North of Dorchester. Off A352 from Dorchester to Sherborne.

6 Bedrooms. £16.50–£18 (less for 7 nights). Some have some or all of the following: own bath/shower/toilet. No smoking.
Light suppers if ordered. Vegetarian or other special diets if ordered. No smoking.
1 Sitting-room. With open fire, TV. No smoking.
Small garden
Closed from mid-December to mid-January.

In a side street of the ancient little town is a former inn which Jean and Doug Simmonds have modernized to provide a comfortable guest-house. Some rooms are in an annexe opening onto a pretty garden that wanders down to the winding River Cerne. Light suppers offered, but all Cerne's inns do good food.

Cerne Abbas is a lovely village which grew up around a now ruined 10th-century Benedictine abbey. A useful 'town trail' guides you through the village. St Mary's Church is well worth a visit. Its fine east window has 15th-century glass thought to have come from the abbey. The famous prehistoric giant is cut into the chalk on the hillside above the village. Southward are the strange Isle of Portland (source of stone exported worldwide), Abbotsbury (great swannery) and pebbly Chesil Bank (a geological curiosity); northward lies lovely Sherborne (outstanding church, two castles).

Reader's comment: Very comfortable and friendly.

STOURCASTLE LODGE   X

Gough's Close, Sturminster Newton, Dorset, DT10 1BU   Tel: 01258 472320
(Fax: 01258 473381)
South-west of Shaftesbury. Nearest main road: A357 from Blandford Forum to Wincanton.

5 Bedrooms. £20–£33 **(less 10% for 3 nights half board to readers showing the current edition of this book on arrival).** Bargain breaks. All have some or all of the following: own bath/shower/toilet; TV. No smoking.
Dinner. £16 for 4 courses and coffee, at 7.30pm. Vegetarian or other special diets if ordered. No smoking.
1 Sitting-room. With open fire, TV.
Large garden

Gourmets seek out this secluded town house, for peace as well as good food. Although just off the market place, Gough's Close is traffic-free and quiet: a narrow lane opening out into a green and pleasant place, with the River Stour beyond. The 17th-century Lodge has been agreeably furnished by Jill Hookham-Bassett, with soft greens and pinks predominating. Everything is spick-and-span, the bedrooms cottagey in style, and all have garden views.

Ken and Jill, who achieved a gold star for cooking when she trained at Ealing Technical College, provide food well above average. A typical dinner might be: kedgeree, chicken cooked in tarragon and mushroom sauce, and charlotte Malakoff (made with cream and almonds). An unassuming house with a lot to offer in the way of hospitality.

Readers' comments: Jill's cooking was superb. Delightful. Made to feel welcome and at home. Room charming. Enjoyed our visit so much. Delicious food. Evening meal was highlight of my stay; breakfast faultless with vast array of choice.

Dorset

STRAWBERRY COTTAGE

C(8) **S**

Packers Hill, Holwell, Dorset, DT9 5LN   Tel: 01963 23629

South-east of Sherborne. Nearest main road: A3030 from Sherborne to Sturminster Newton.

3 Bedrooms. £18.50–£20 (less for 4 nights or more). One has own shower. No smoking.
Light suppers if ordered. Vegetarian or other special diets if ordered. Wine available. No smoking.
1 Sitting-room. With TV. No smoking.
Garden

Partly 16th, partly 18th century, this former agricultural workers' cottage is built of thatch, stone and brick, with furnishings of high standard. There is a comfortable TV room which is well supplied with tourist literature. The cottage is situated in quiet countryside near Sherborne. Ornamental strawberries are grown here by Vivienne Powell – hence the name.

Mediaeval Sherborne's superb 15th-century abbey of golden stone deserves a lingering visit because of its remarkable fan-vaulting, colourful roof-bosses and other outstanding carvings. There are two castles: one, the ruins of a 12th-century fortified castle destroyed by Cromwell in the Civil War; the other, built for Sir Walter Raleigh in 1594 and home of the Digby family since 1617. It is surrounded by gardens and parkland designed by Capability Brown and contains a series of very fine rooms and art treasures.

Readers' comments: What a find! I want to go back! Kindness and hospitality, cottage beautiful, breakfast delicious. Gentle friendliness.

V

VARTREES HOUSE

C(10) **D PT S**

Moreton, Dorset, DT2 8BE Tel: 01305 852704

East of Dorchester. Nearest main road: A35 from Dorchester to Poole.

3 Bedrooms. £18–£23. One has own shower. No smoking.
1 Sitting-room. With TV, piano.
Large garden
Closed in December and January.

When Thomas Hardy's most trusted friend, the inspired eccentric Hermann Lea (whose interests ranged from humane rabbit-traps to Goethe), built himself this handsome house, Hardy helped to name it Vartrees, after the nearby River Frome – once Var. It is in Arts and Crafts style, with much use of Japanese oak, maple, exposed brickwork, iron-latched doors, and big windows overlooking grounds brilliant with colour at azalea time.

Lea photographed and wrote about Hardy, 30 years his senior, and the sites in Dorset which figure in his books: Doris Haggett can show you Lea's publications. A small, bearded countryman, he cared passionately about animals (not only was he a vegetarian but he refused to wear leather shoes). He kept 20 dogs, did water-divining and was a pioneer motorist, often driving Hardy to the high viewpoints that he loved. The secretive Hardy confided many private matters to Lea rather than to more highbrow friends, and his trust was never betrayed.

This is the valley ('green trough of sappiness') where Tess was a dairymaid; the sea is only 10 minutes away. Moreton's unique church is full of Laurence Whistler windows. Lawrence of Arabia is buried in the graveyard.

WILLOW COTTAGE

Ware Lane, Lyme Regis, Dorset, DT7 3EL   Tel: 01297 443199

C(8) PT

Nearest main road: A3052 from Lyme Regis to Sidmouth.

1–2 Bedrooms. £18–£23 **(to readers of this book).**
One has own shower/toilet; TV; views of sea; balcony.
Light suppers if ordered.
Small garden
Closed from mid-December to mid-January.

In a flowery hollow down Lyme's pretty Ware Lane is Willow Cottage, where now the Griffins (formerly of Red House) welcome guests, who not only have their own bedsitting-room (with balcony overlooking the sea, which is reached by footpath) plus single room if required, but also a private breakfast-room below: here Liz also serves snack suppers out of season by arrangement.

This is a perfect base from which to explore the locality. Sandy beaches with their shrimp-pools are ideal for children. There are excellent walks (in Marshwood Vale or along the coast) including nature trails; National Trust houses; drives along lanes of primroses, bluebells and subtropical wildflowers in the downs.

Delightful old Lyme has many claims to fame – Jane Austen; fossils (including dinosaur bones) found along its beaches; the landing of the Duke of Monmouth in 1685 to start his abortive rebellion; and, in more recent times, *The French Lieutenant's Woman*, the author of which, John Fowles, lives locally.

Readers' comments: Kindness itself, so caring. Gracious hosts. Griffins delightful.

YOAH COTTAGE

West Knighton, Dorset, DT2 8PE   Tel: 01305 852087

C(7) D S

South-east of Dorchester. Nearest main road: A352 from Dorchester to Wareham.

2 Bedrooms. £16.50–£18.50 (less for 7 nights or more). No smoking.
Dinner (by arrangement). £12.50 for 3 courses and coffee, at 7.30pm. Vegetarian or other special diets if ordered. No smoking. **Light suppers** if ordered.
1 Sitting-room. With open fire, TV. No smoking.
Large garden
Closed from mid-December to early January.

In every room of this picturesque cottage, all whitewash and thatch, are ceramic sheep, pigs, Noah's Arks or Gardens of Eden – which both Furse and Rosemary Swann make in their studio at the back. The great beam over one of the inglenook fireplaces carries the date 1622. Rooms are low and white-walled, the staircases narrow and steep, floors stone-flagged, windows small and deep-set.

The Swanns have filled the house with an immensely varied collection of treasures. Bedrooms are attractive (the pretty bathrooms are on the ground floor).

Rosemary produces not only imaginative dishes of her own (for instance, pork tenderloin with mushrooms in a green pepper and cream sauce) but also specialities from Sweden, where she lived for many years. Furse prepares breakfasts; and he makes all the jams.

Readers' comments: Most beautiful and characterful. Delightful atmosphere. Idyllic. A memorable place to stay. Truly outstanding. Cottage and food wonderful, hosts extremely welcoming.

County DURHAM

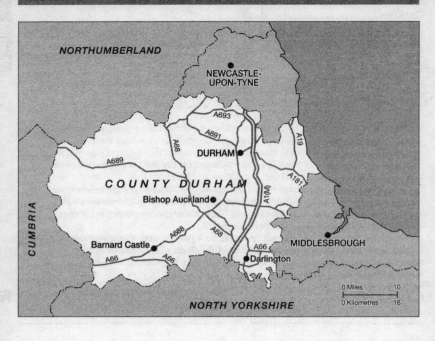

You stand a better chance of finding the right accommodation at the right price in the right area if you are using an up-to-date edition of this book, which is revised every year. Obtain an order form for the next edition (published in November) by sending a stamped addressed envelope, with 'SOTBT 1999' in the top left-hand corner, to Explore Britain, Alston, Cumbria, CA9 3SL.

CLOUD HIGH

C(10)

Eggleston, County Durham, DL12 0AU   Tel/Fax: 01833 650644
North-west of Barnard Castle. Nearest main road: A688 from Barnard Castle to
Staindrop.

3 Bedrooms. £18. All have some or all of the following: own bath/shower/toilet; TV; balcony. No smoking.
Dinner. £12.50 for 3 courses and coffee, at 7.30pm. Vegetarian diets if ordered. Wine available. No smoking. **Light suppers** if ordered.
1 Sitting-room. With TV. No smoking.
Garden

With views almost to the coast from the garden and from the balcony of one of the bedrooms, Cloud High is a pre-war house with many extensions (and a 'folly' the Bells have built in the garden). One recent addition is the conservatory, where Frank and Eileen sometimes serve meals – usually prepared by Frank, who enjoys making such dishes as smoked salmon with prawns, peppered steak, and a choice of desserts. Breakfasts are well out of the ordinary, usually with an assortment of garnished fresh fruit on offer.

The balcony room is particularly spacious, with an extra-large bed and two settees. It is off a first-floor sitting-room with comfortable armchairs and plenty of books about this little-known area.

Close by are bare Stanhope Moor and dense Hamsterley Forest. The nearest sights are Eggleston Hall Gardens – beautiful, and with an excellent nursery – and spectacular High Force (England's highest waterfall).

DEMESNES MILL

C(5) **PT S**

Barnard Castle, County Durham, DL12 8PE   Tel/Fax: 01833 637929
Nearest main road: A66 from Scotch Corner towards Brough.

4 Bedrooms. £17.50–£20 (less for 3 nights or more). Some have some or all of the following: own bath/shower/toilet; TV; views of river; balcony. No smoking.
1 Sitting-room. With open fire, TV. No smoking.
Small garden
Closed from November to March.

After 25 years in Canada, Joan and Bob Young returned to their native county and fell for a near-derelict mill on the River Tees. Years of hard and patient work have transformed it.

Where four pairs of millstones once ground flour is now a long sitting-room furnished in antique style. Windows overlook the rushing river immediately below and a new conservatory at one end gives a splendid downriver view of a natural weir, where herons, dippers and king-fishers are often seen. Under the beamed ceiling supported by cast-iron columns, some of the mill mechanism survives, including one of the millstones. Off the sitting-room is the breakfast-area where Joan's visitors help themselves from an extensive buffet with fresh-baked bread.

The big bedrooms upstairs, which overlook the weir, are decorated elaborately and have bathrooms equipped to high Canadian standards. The single room is generous.

The mill is approached across the Demesnes, a big public open space almost in the centre of Barnard Castle, where numerous eating-places are within walking distance for dinner.

Reader's comments: Wonderful house, everything about it marvellous, dramatic surroundings; made so welcome.

GROVE HOUSE

C(8) S

Hamsterley Forest, County Durham, DL13 3NL   Tel: 01388 488203
(Fax: 01207 520336)
West of Bishop Auckland. Nearest main road: A68 from Darlington to Corbridge.

3 Bedrooms. £19.50–£24 (less for 7 nights or more). All have some or all of the following: own bath/shower/toilet. No smoking.
Dinner. £14.50 for 4 courses and coffee, at 7.30pm. Vegetarian or other special diets if ordered. No smoking. **Light suppers** if ordered.
2 Sitting-rooms. With open fire, TV. No smoking.
Large garden
Closed from mid-December to mid-January.

Amid a 5000-acre Forestry Commision holding, a few houses are buried in the original forest. Among them is Grove House, once an aristocrat's shooting-box, surrounded by its own big gardens. The windows of the prettily furnished guest-rooms look across the garden or into the forest. Birdsong is the loudest sound you will hear.

The downstairs rooms have a touch of aristocratic grandeur and some unusual fittings from Germany (notice the art deco doorhandles). Helene Close prepares all the food from fresh ingredients. A typical dinner: warm smoked-haddock creams, pork tenderloin stuffed with celery and onion fondue, Normandy apple tart, and cheese. She discusses guests' preferences beforehand. Bicycle hire and pony trekking are available.

Readers' comments: Fairytale house in beautiful setting. A wonderful 'find'; it was perfect. Idyllic. Exceptionally varied menus, beautifully cooked. Marvellous situation, food and welcome. A trip to paradise! Of a very high standard in every way.

LANE HEAD FARM

D X

Hutton Magna, County Durham, DL11 7HF   Tel: 01833 627378
South-east of Barnard Castle. Nearest main road: A66 from Scotch Corner to Brough.

3 Bedrooms. £15. One has own shower/toilet; TV (in two). No smoking.
Light suppers if ordered.
1 Sitting-room. With open fire, TV.
Large garden

You could bring your horse on holiday here (or your dogs), to stay in the range of loose-boxes which were built when this farm was used to train racehorses. Its current total of 600 acres is now mostly arable, with wide views across the Vale of York. There are Roman remains in the area and since their time there has been a highway in the gap in the Pennines through which the busy A66 now runs.

Sue Ormston's bedrooms are tucked under the sloping roof of this wide, creeper-clad house, which was built two or three centuries ago. There is a cosy sitting-room for guests, who have their own entrance, and also a kitchen for them to use if they want hot drinks and so on. Sue offers no evening meal because numerous pubs offering outstandingly good meals are a feature of North Yorkshire – the farm is just on the county boundary.

As well as being close to the Yorkshire Dales, the house is near beautiful Teesdale, which is much less well known. Nearby are Palladian Rokeby House and, by the Tees, the ruins of Eggleston Abbey.

Reader's comments: Excellent for accommodation, value, homeliness and location.

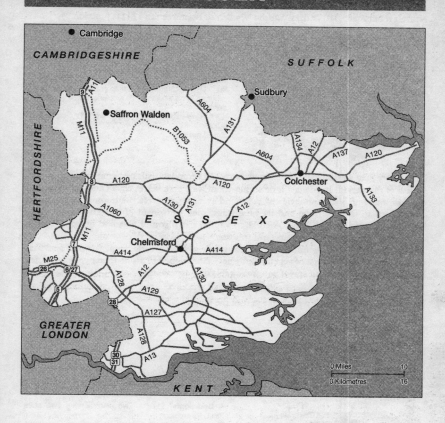

Facts (prices, etc.) at the top of entries are supplied by the proprietors themselves. While every effort is made to ensure that these are correct at the time of going to press, they may alter thereafter: please check when you book.

BEECH VILLA

CDPTSX

1 Borough Lane, Saffron Walden, Essex, CB11 4AF   Tel: 01799 516891
(Fax: 01799 521390)
Nearest main road: B1053 from Saffron Walden to Braintree (and M11, junction 9).

3 Bedrooms. £17–£19 (less for 3 nights or more). One has own shower/toilet. No smoking.
Dinner (by arrangement). £11 for 3 courses and coffee, at 6.30–7.30pm. Vegetarian or other special diets if ordered. Wine available. No smoking. **Light suppers** if ordered.
1 Sitting-room. With open fire, TV, piano. No smoking.
Small garden

This pretty villa was built in 1820: its glass-roofed verandah with cast-iron columns is very typical of the period. Inside is a little sitting-room with pink velvet chairs and a pink-walled dining-room with Victorian-style chairs around a mahogany table. Bedrooms are pleasantly furnished: e.g. stripped pine and ice-blue walls, blue bedspread of fringed brocade from Portugal, blue-and-white china. A children's room has plentiful toys and books. There is also a cellar games room with darts and snooker.

Marilyn Butler will produce such simple meals as home-made soup, lasagne, and fruit salad (she has a wide range of vegetarian dishes). She trained in aromatherapy, and you can book a session during your stay if you want a relaxing experience.

Readers' comments: Made to feel so welcome and relaxed. Very friendly and knowledgeable. Haphazard family home – we felt like part of the family.

V

BULMER TYE HOUSE

CDSX

Bulmer Tye, Essex, CO10 7ED   Tel/Fax: 01787 269315
South-west of Sudbury. Nearest main road: A131 from Halstead to Sudbury.

4 Bedrooms. £17.50. Two singles have own bath/toilet. No smoking.
Dinner (by arrangement). £10 for 2 or 3 courses and coffee, at times to suit guests. Vegetarian or other special diets if ordered. No smoking. **Light suppers** if ordered.
3 Sitting-rooms. With open fires, TV, piano. No smoking in one.
Large garden

One of Gainsborough's most famous paintings is of the Andrews family and it was one of their sons, a parson, who in the 18th century 'modernized' this house, most of which dates back to the reign of Elizabeth I. Today its old timbers resonate to the sound of music (played by family or guests), for Peter Owen is a maker of very fine clavichords – and of much of the interesting furniture seen in the rooms. His wife Noël is an authority on antiques, so not surprisingly there are some unusual period pieces in the house. The Owens have contrasted the antiques with strong modern patterns.

Guests eat with the family in the quarry-tiled kitchen. Garden produce goes into soups and puddings; wine is home-made and Peter bakes the bread. Popular dishes include: beef-and-lentil flan, fish pie, a cheesy bread-and-butter pudding with stir-fried vegetables. For breakfast, you will be offered home-made muesli, bread and marmalade, as well as free-range eggs (no fry-ups).

Readers' comments: Characterful house, beautiful garden, very informal and friendly. Very interesting house, superb garden.

GREYS

Margaret Roding, Essex, CM6 1QR   Tel: 01245 231509

C(10) S

North-west of Chelmsford. Nearest main road: A1060 from Bishop's Stortford to Chelmsford.

3 Bedrooms. £18–£19 (less for 3 nights mid-week). No smoking.
Light suppers if ordered..
1 Sitting-room. With TV. No smoking.
Large garden

Once a pair of farmworkers' cottages, Greys became the Matthews' home when they moved out of their large farmhouse to let their son take over management of the farm. They painted the exterior apricot – in typical East Anglian style – and furnished the rooms simply (a mixture of Habitat and antiques) and with light, clear colours. The beamed breakfast-room has pine furniture and rhododendron-patterned curtains.

'It's lovely when guests book in for one night and then stay for several,' says Joyce. This often happens because so many people think Essex consists of Dagenham's motorworks, Southend's trippers and little else – then, when they come here, find a revelation.

The eight Roding villages include some of England's prettiest, in an area of winding streams and lanes. Many visitors base themselves here to visit London (45 minutes by train from Epping), Cambridge, Roman Colchester and the rest of East Anglia. Every night you could dine at a different, excellent local inn.

Reader's comment: Warmth and good food.

---

1 GUNTER'S COTTAGES

Thaxted Road, Saffron Walden, Essex, CB10 2UT   Tel: 01799 522091

South-east of Saffron Walden. Nearest main road: A1301 from Cambridge to Saffron Walden (and M11, junction 9).

1 Bedroom. £17.50. Has own bath/toilet; TV. No smoking.
Light suppers if ordered. Vegetarian diets if ordered. No smoking.
Small garden

Originally built in 1840 as homes for farmworkers' families, these cottages have now been combined and modernized. The special attraction of staying at No. 1 is a heated, indoor swimming-pool built onto the back. This is directly accessible from the guests' self-contained suite of bedroom and bathroom.

In the spacious dining-room, with its blue Wedgwood collection, Pat Goddard serves sandwiches if you do not want to go into the town for a meal. An interesting feature of Gunter's is the pargeting: decorative exterior plasterwork, usually found only on the historic houses of Essex and Suffolk but here a modern artist-craftsman has created some outstanding work – particularly the owl and the huntsman on, of all things, garage walls. To the rear of the house are cornfields, and the Goddards can recommend several pleasant walks locally.

Reader's comment: Welcoming and helpful.

V

OLLIVER'S FARMHOUSE
Toppesfield, Halstead, Essex, CO9 4LS   Tel: 01787 237642 (Fax: 01787 237602)
North-west of Colchester. Nearest main road: A1307 from Colchester towards
Cambridge.

2 Bedrooms. £18.50–£25 (less for 3 nights or more). One has own shower/toilet; TV (on request). No smoking.
Light suppers if ordered. No smoking.
1 Sitting-room. With open fire, piano. No smoking.
Large garden

To the attraction of a historic (16th-century) house is added that of a particularly interesting garden created only a few years ago by Sue Blackie, a qualified landscape gardener. Her award-winning architect husband James makes wine from the small vineyard adjoining the garden: Domesday Book records a vineyard here.

In the huge sitting-room, with an equally huge brick fireplace and chamfered ceiling beams, hang some of the modern paintings which James collects. His paintings also fill the terracotta walls of the landing, where latched board doors open into bedrooms with old china, garden flowers, and pleasant colour schemes.

As to the garden (at its best in spring, or in June when it is occasionally open to the public), this consists of a whole series of experiences as one area opens into another, each with a different theme – something for each season, and each with its own colour scheme. Up a mossy-roofed barn Sue has trained jasmine and a grapevine. A deep iron vat is now a lily-pool, frequented by birds.

YARDLEYS   C S
Orchard Pightle, Hadstock, Essex, CB1 6PQ   Tel: 01223 891822
South-east of Cambridge. Nearest main road: A1307 from Cambridge to Haverhill
(and M11, junctions 9/10).

3 Bedrooms. £19–£22 (less for 3 nights or more). Bargain breaks. All have some or all of the following: own bath/shower/toilet. No smoking.
Dinner (by arrangement). £10.50 for 3 courses and coffee, at 7pm. Vegetarian or other special diets if ordered. No smoking. **Light suppers** if ordered.
2 Sitting-rooms. With open fire, TV. No smoking.
Small garden
Closed in January and February.

In picturesque Hadstock, almost in Cambridgeshire, is a flowery close called Orchard Pightle ('pightle' is an old word for an enclosure) within which is Gillian Ludgate's home. Above one of the sitting-rooms are well-equipped bedrooms in pale colours, neat and airy, with private bathrooms; and at the back a conservatory brimming with flowers, where meals are sometimes served. Gillian is a keen cook, serving suppers or such meals as salmon mousse, pork fillet with apricots, and pavlova. Breakfast may include garden fruit, local sausages, her own jam, and dry-cured bacon.

Cambridge and the attractive town of Saffron Walden are within easy reach. The Imperial War Museum's collection of historic aircraft (at Duxford) is also close by.

Readers' comments: Like home from home, one of the nicest. Vegetarian breakfasts substantial and imaginative. All sorts of generous little extras, excellent evening meals. Lovely place; the most pleasant of hosts; food second to none. Made to feel like family friends.

GLOUCESTERSHIRE
(including South Gloucestershire)

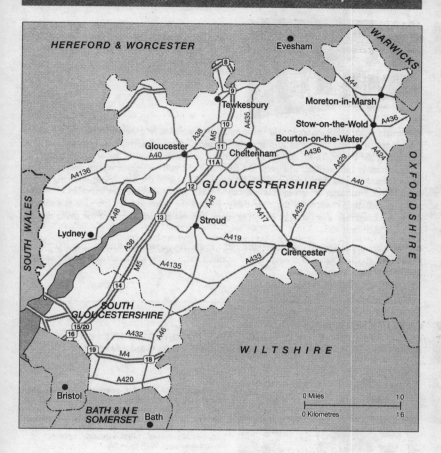

'Bargain breaks' are usually out-of-season reductions for half-board stays of several nights.

BOUCHERS FARMHOUSE
C(5) S

Bentham, Gloucestershire, GL51 5TZ Tel: 01452 862373
South-west of Cheltenham. Nearest main road: A46 from Cheltenham to Stroud (and M5, junction 11a).

2 Bedrooms. £14.50. No smoking.
1 Sitting-room. With open fire, TV. No smoking.
Large garden
Closed from mid-December to mid-January.

Previously a farm, Bouchers is still surrounded by hayfields just beyond the garden, where rock doves fly across the lawns to a graceful weeping willow. A sundial on one wall declares the date of the house, 1661, and of the old cider-house which is now Bruce's workshop.

Inside all is immaculate and very comfortable, and you will get a warm welcome from Anne Daniels as you step through the front door straight into the big U-shaped living-room. Here velvet armchairs are grouped round the hearth where an open fire crackles in winter, and a grandfather clock ticks the time away. Round the other side of the U is the dining-room, for breakfast only (visitors eat other meals at local inns or at one of the many restaurants in Cheltenham).

Readers' comments: Service excellent – the sort for which you would expect to pay double the price. Will go there again. Very satisfied. Excellent value. Wonderful hosts, fantastic setting. Did everything possible for us.

COLLEGE HOUSE
PT

Chapel Street, Broadwell, Gloucestershire, GL56 0TW Tel: 01451 832351
North of Stow-on-the-Wold. Nearest main road: A429 from Stow to Moreton-in-Marsh.

3 Bedrooms. £20 **(to readers of this book only)**–£31. All have some or all of the following: own bath/shower/toilet; TV. No smoking.
Dinner (by arrangement). £16.50 for 3 courses and coffee, at 7.30pm. Vegetarian or other special diets if ordered. No smoking. **Light suppers** if ordered.
1 Sitting-room. With open fire.
Small garden

Broadwell is a charming and unspoilt little village, once the home of the Knights Templar, with lovely Cotswold stone houses of which 17th-century College House is a fine example.

Stylishly furnished by Sybil and Robert Gisby, bedrooms (including the least expensive) are spacious and comfortable, all with big double beds and large bathrooms too. One in lemon and white has an unusual Victorian 'slipper' bathtub, another an elegant sleigh-bed.

Sybil is a former restaurateur and produces imaginative menus. You might start with Stilton and mushroom crêpes, to be followed by lamb and rosemary casserole in winter, or pesto salmon and salad in summer, with a fresh fruit meringue to finish. There is a stone-flagged and shuttered sitting-room to relax in. Plenty of colourful guidebooks help you plan the next day of your holiday. You may sleep safely in this house, secure in the knowledge that Cotswold stone lions guard the perimeter, warding off any evil spirits!

Reader's comment: Very comfortable.

DAMSELLS LODGE

The Park, Painswick, Gloucestershire, GL6 6SR   Tel: 01452 813777
North of Stroud. Nearest main road: A46 from Stroud to Cheltenham (and M5, junction 11a).

C D M P T S

3 Bedrooms. £20–£21.50. Bargain breaks. One has own shower/toilet; TV (in all).
Light suppers if ordered.
1 Sitting-room. With log stove, TV, piano.
Small garden

This very comfortable house was originally the lodge to the nearby mansion. It is in a peaceful rural lane and has truly spectacular views from every window across a small garden of lawns, stone terrace and flowering shrubs.

Judy Cooke is a welcoming hostess who soon makes friends with her visitors. The huge sitting-room has windows on three sides, and a big log stove. Everywhere there are thick carpets and good furniture (even the bathroom is pretty luxurious). Perhaps the best bedroom is one separate from the house: it is in a one-floor garden cottage, with huge sliding windows through which to step straight onto the lawn or to view the distant hills while still in bed, and ideal for anyone who finds stairs difficult.

Readers' comments: Immaculate; lovely setting, gorgeous view. Absolutely marvellous. Delightful hosts. Wonderful, homely place. Perfect setting. First-class accommodation. Helpful, and very warm welcome. Impeccably kept house, quiet. Great place to stay.

DORNDEN

C D

Church Lane, Old Sodbury, South Gloucestershire, BS17 6NB   Tel: 01454 313325
(Fax: 01454 312263)
North-east of Bristol. Nearest main road: A432 from Bristol to Old Sodbury (and M4, junction 18).

9 Bedrooms. £20–£25 (less for 2 nights at weekends or 4 mid-week). Some have some or all of the following: own bath/shower/toilet; TV.
Dinner (by arrangement). £10 for 3 courses and coffee, at 6.45pm. Vegetarian or other special diets if ordered. No smoking.
1 Sitting-room. With piano.
Large garden
Closed from mid-September to mid-October.

An immaculate garden surrounds the big guest-house – flowerbeds and box-hedges in trim and neat array, with a large vegetable and fruit garden to supply the kitchen. From its lawns and grass tennis court, set high up, there are splendid views.

This is the place for a quiet stay, well placed for exploring the scenic counties around it. All the rooms are sedate and comfortable in a style appropriate to what it was: in mid-Victorian days, a vicarage and with features of the period still retained – from the beautifully polished tiles of the hall to the terrace onto which the sitting-room opens.

Daphne Paz serves traditional favourites at dinner – such as roasts, steak-and-kidney pie, sticky-toffee pudding, pies or crumbles: very moderately priced.

Readers' comments: Strongly recommended. Cooking of high standard. Excellent value. Very friendly. Always excellent, delightful hosts. Friendly attitude, always ready for a laugh.

V

EDALE HOUSE

C(12) M

Folly Road, Parkend, Gloucestershire, GL15 4JF   Tel: 01594 562835
(Fax: 01594 564488)
North of Lydney. Nearest main road: A48 from Chepstow to Gloucester.

5 Bedrooms. £20–£25. Bargain breaks. All have some or all of the following: own bath/shower/toilet; TV. No smoking.
Dinner (by arrangement). £15.50 for 3 courses and coffee, at 7pm. Vegetarian or other special diets if ordered. Wine available. No smoking.
2 Sitting-rooms. Bar.
Garden
Closed in December and January.

Parkend is in the middle of the Forest of Dean and here, facing the cricket green, is Edale House. The five en suite bedrooms are luxurious – decorated in soft blues and cream, with pretty fabrics and furniture of polished pine. Village cricket can be watched from the rooms, two of which are on the ground floor. There is a lobby designed for walkers' wet shoes and coats.

In the comfy sitting-room is Sheila Reid's growing collection of unusual honeypots. The dining-room overlooks the garden, with its numerous feathered visitors from the Nagshead RSPB reserve at the rear of the house. Ex-restaurateurs James and Sheila serve such meals as seafood chowder, suprême of chicken with Madeira and green peppercorns, and chocolate brandy mousse.

An area of great beauty and wildlife interest, the Forest of Dean also has remains of Roman iron mines, strange rock formations, caves, rivers, gardens . . .

FAIRVIEW FARMHOUSE

C(8) S

Bledington Road, Stow-on-the-Wold, Gloucestershire, GL54 1AN
Tel: 01451 830279
East of Stow-on-the-Wold. Nearest main road: A436 from Stow-on-the-Wold towards Chipping Norton.

3 Bedrooms. £20–£22 (less for 3 nights or more). Bargain breaks. All have some or all of the following: own bath/shower/toilet; TV. No smoking.
Dinner (by arrangement). £15 for 3 courses and coffee, at 7pm. Vegetarian or other special diets if ordered. No smoking. **Light suppers** if ordered.
1 Sitting-room. With open fire.
Large garden
Closed from mid-December to February.

In the more peaceful south of the Cotswolds, Fairview Farmhouse is the home of Susan and Andrew Davis. Sue, a fitness instructor, is also an accomplished cook. An evening meal might comprise home-made soup, then chicken in mushroom and wine sauce, and a sunken chocolate soufflé with Amaretto prunes to finish. Bedrooms, all with their own bathrooms, are decorated in burgundies and pinks with draped canopies above the beds. Fair views indeed – of rolling countryside to Icomb Hill.

A main attraction of the region is the Cotswold Farm Park, home to the Rare Breeds Survival Trust, which exists to preserve historic breeds of farm animals that might otherwise die out; and here you can spend a day among, for instance, little Soay sheep first domesticated by Stone Age man and piglets of a prehistoric strain.

Reader's comment: Wonderful hosts.

GRANCHEN

PT S

Church Road, Bitton, South Gloucestershire, BS15 6LJ   Tel: 0117 9322423
North-west of Bath. Nearest main road: A431 from Bristol to Bath (and M4, junction 18).

3 Bedrooms. £15–£17 (less for 3 nights or more). No smoking.
Dinner (by arrangement). £10 for 4 courses and coffee, at times to suit guests (not Thursdays). No smoking. **Light suppers** if ordered.
1 Sitting-room. With open fire, TV, piano. No smoking.
Small garden
Closed from December to February.

Once the kitchen of a Norman manor house, Granchen was altered by John Wood, the celebrated 18th-century architect of Bath (which is close) who gave it the distinctive round windows and triple arches which make its façade unique.

The stone-flagged sitting-room is dominated by an enormous arched, stone inglenook. Liberty curtains in glowing colours contrast with almond-green walls, Valerie Atkins's patchwork cushions match the russet tones of the oriental rugs, and to one side of the hearth are her elegant appliqué pictures of farm gates and hedgerows.

Valerie prepares such meals as chicken-and-lentil soup, baked gammon with cauliflower cheese, and redcurrant fool. Meals are served in a coral dining-room (with unusual, carved stickback chairs from Canada) which looks through a pilastered archway into her kitchen.

Readers' comments: Perfect. Lovely house, made very welcome. Charming atmosphere. Beautiful house. A lovely time.

V

GUITING GUEST-HOUSE

C D PT S

Post Office Lane, Guiting Power, Gloucestershire, GL54 5TZ   Tel: 01451 850470
(Fax: 01451 850034)
West of Stow-on-the-Wold. Nearest main road: A436 from Andoversford towards Stow-on-the-Wold.

5 Bedrooms. £19–£23.50. All have some or all of the following: own bath/shower/toilet; TV. No smoking.
Dinner (by arrangement). £17 for 4 courses and coffee, at 7pm. Vegetarian or other special diets if ordered. Wine available. No smoking. **Light suppers** if ordered.
2 Sitting-rooms. With open fire, TV. No smoking.
Small garden

This is a quintessential Cotswold village with stone cross on a green and wisteria clambering up mellow walls. Changes to the 450-year-old guest-house have been done with sensitivity. New pine doors have wood latches; the dining-room floor is made of solid elm; logs blaze in a stone fireplace; and in the snug sitting-room are flagstones with oriental rugs. Bedrooms are pleasantly decorated, with such touches as beribboned cushions or an old cane-backed rocking-chair, and four-posters.

Yvonne Sylvester will cook whatever you want, but a favourite menu is trout from a nearby fish farm, chicken in lime and ginger sauce, strawberry baskets with cream, and cheeses.

Readers' comments: Marvellous hosts. Made us so welcome. Beautiful house. One of the happiest breaks I've had. Nothing too much trouble. Charming, faultless, relaxing, ideal. Very relaxed atmosphere. Our favourite, will definitely return. Marvellous cook, tasteful rooms.

HONEYBROOK COTTAGE
C(8) S

Main Street, Adlestrop, Gloucestershire, GL56 0YN   Tel/Fax: 01608 658884
East of Stow-on-the-Wold. Nearest main road: A436 from Stow-on-the-Wold towards
Chipping Norton.

2 Bedrooms. £18.50–£20 (less for 2 nights or more). Both have some or all of the following: own bath/shower/toilet. No smoking.
Dinner (by arrangement). £10.50 for 2 courses and coffee, at 7.30pm. Vegetarian or other special diets if ordered. No smoking. **Light suppers** if ordered.
1 Sitting-room. With open fire, TV. No smoking.
Small garden
Closed from December to March.

Adlestrop is a small village yet at one time had its own railway station, celebrated in an Edward Thomas poem. The old station sign now marks your arrival in the village. Honeybrook Cottage is a new house of local stone which Margaret and Bob Warrick designed and built themselves, with evident skill. There are two bedrooms, both en suite; the smaller double in peach and blue also has its own excellent walk-in shower-room downstairs. Visitors can relax in a small conservatory, off the sitting-room, in summer. Breakfast includes home-baked rolls and honey from the Warricks' own hives. Dinner is sometimes available, or transport can be arranged to the nearby Fox for good food.

Stow-on-the-Wold merits unhurried exploration: it's a little town of antique and craft shops, restaurants and byways.

Readers' comments: Breakfast was wonderful. Every consideration. Most accommodating hosts. Very good value. Made us most welcome. Hospitable and helpful.

LAMB INN
D

Great Rissington, Gloucestershire, GL54 2LP   Tel: 01451 820388
(Fax: 01451 820724)
East of Cheltenham. Nearest main road: A40 from Oxford to Cheltenham.

14 Bedrooms. £20 **(for 2 rooms to readers of this book, January to April)**–£42.50. Sunday nights free to over-60s. Bargain breaks. All have some or all of the following: own bath/shower/toilet; TV. No smoking.
Dinner. A la carte, from 7–9pm. Vegetarian or other special diets if ordered. Wine available. **Bar meals** available.
1 Sitting-room. With open fire, TV. **Bar.**
Large garden

This is exactly what one asks of a typical old Cotswold inn! It is a place of little windows, zigzag corridors and stairs, quaint oak doors, thick stone walls; outside are magnificent views of the Cotswold countryside. Kate and Richard Cleverly have furnished the bedrooms with care – restful colours, everything neat, a pretty tulip wallpaper in one room, and in the dining-room pine chairs at polished tables with candle-lamps lit at night. The menu includes such dishes as Stilton-topped fillet steaks, veal-and-sweetcorn pies, salmon-and-prawn mousse, lamb with apricots. Outside is a landscaped garden from which to enjoy the summer view with a glass of 'real ale' in hand; and a summer-house. In cold weather, there is a log fire in the bar, and in the attractive residents' sitting-room. There is a choice of suites – four-poster and king-size beds – including a luxurious honeymoon suite and two in the garden. In former stables are two double bedrooms, with en suite showers.

Readers' comments: Excellent. Clean, friendly and comfortable. The food varied, well-cooked and plentiful. Superb accommodation, very friendly. Good atmosphere.

V

LOWER GREEN FARMHOUSE

Haresfield, Gloucestershire, GL10 3DS   Tel/Fax: 01452 728264

South of Gloucester. Nearest main road: A38 from Gloucester to Bristol (and M5, junction 12).

C D

3 Bedrooms. £16–£17.50 (less for 2 nights or more). One has own bath/toilet; TV (in two). No smoking.
Light suppers if ordered.
1 Sitting-room. With woodstove, TV. No smoking.
Large garden

This attractive house of stone walls and mullioned windows sits at the foot of a National Trust hill (Haresfield Beacon) on the western edge of the Cotswolds; the light and airy family bedroom has views in the other direction across the Severn to the Forest of Dean (superb sunsets); yet with all this Lower Green Farmhouse is still within easy reach of the motorway. All the bedrooms are spacious, with board-and-latch doors and beamed ceilings; downstairs, the sitting-room has a stone fireplace with ogee arch, the dining-room a huge inglenook. In the garden is a stone barbecue, a pool with bulrushes and yellow flag irises, and a 40-foot well, and all around is lovely countryside with countless picturesque villages to explore.

Margaret Reed will provide light suppers by arrangement, but the local pub (within easy walking distance) does good food at very reasonable prices.

Readers' comments: Can't recommend too highly. Excellent cook and hostess.

MANOR BARN

Cowley, Gloucestershire, GL53 9NN   Tel: 01242 870229

South of Cheltenham. Nearest main road: A435 from Cheltenham to Cirencester.

C(11) PT S

3 Bedrooms. £17–£20. All have own shower/toilet. No smoking.
Light suppers if ordered. Vegetarian or other special diets if ordered. No smoking.
1 Sitting-room. With open fire, TV. No smoking.
Small garden

South of Cheltenham (still a very fine spa town) is 19th-century Manor Barn, cleverly converted into a home by Linda and Andrew Roff. Bedrooms, in white and pink with pine doors and some brass bedsteads, are light and airy. The sitting-room, with open fire, and dining-room are on a split level, with a charming gallery above from which to watch the sun setting in the valley below.

The Cotswolds are on the route south to Bath. Gloucester with its cathedral, historic Cirencester (don't miss the Roman museum), Tewkesbury and the Forest of Dean are all within easy reach, as are Prinknash Abbey and the Wye Valley. Also in the area are Slimbridge Wildfowl Trust, Westonbirt Arboretum and Badminton House (a Palladian mansion, where the Queen is often seen at the spring horse trials).

Within the vicinity of the house, you will find such lesser-known gems as High Bisley (fountains, old lock-up, Saxon cross and Bear Inn with secret passages), North Cerney (Norman churches and old waterside houses), and Sapperton, overlooking 'the Golden Valley' (ancient Daneway House and historic canal nearby).

V

MANOR FARMHOUSE

D S X

Wormington, Gloucestershire, WR12 7NL   Tel: 01386 584302 (Fax: 01386 584649)
South-east of Evesham. Nearest main road: A46 from Broadway to Cheltenham
(and M5, junction 9).

3 Bedrooms. £17–£20 (less for 4 nights or more).
Bargain breaks. All have own shower/toilet. No smoking.
Light suppers if ordered.
1 Sitting-room. With open fire, TV.
Small garden

Once this house was known as Charity Farm because 'dole' was dispensed to wayfarers.
There are leaded casements in the comfortable sitting-room, a stone inglenook in the hall,
slabs of Welsh slate on the floor, steps and turns everywhere on one's way up to beamy all-
white bedrooms well furnished with mahogany pieces. There's still a cheese-room dating
from the time when this was a dairy-farm.

What was once a cattle-yard is now a very attractive court with lawn, fountain and stone
sinks planted with flowers. To one side is an old granary of brick and timber which dates,
like the house itself, from the 15th century. From the stable door five small ponies watch
visitors' comings and goings. On the farm are shooting and trout fishing.

Pauline Russell usually serves only breakfast, recommending for other meals Goblets
wine bar in Broadway – best known of all the picturesque villages hereabouts.

V *Readers' comments:* Lovely farmhouse; looked after us so well. Friendly, good value.

MARKET HOUSE

C(12) PT

The Square, Northleach, Gloucestershire, GL54 3EJ   Tel: 01451 860557
South-east of Cheltenham. Nearest main road: A40 from Cheltenham to Burford.

4 Bedrooms. £19 (less for 3 nights or more). Bargain
breaks. One has own shower/toilet. No smoking.
1 Sitting-room. With open fire, TV. No smoking.
Large garden

In the central square of Northleach is Market House – so called because fleeces were
marketed here in the time of Elizabeth I. Next to an old inn, it still retains ancient beams
and rugged stone walls (even in the cottage-style bedrooms at the top of a steep stair) as a
background to the immaculate modern comforts provided by Theresa Eastman. There is a
walled garden at the back. In the breakfast/sitting-room, logs blaze in an inglenook when
the weather is chilly.

The principal attractions of Northleach itself are the splendid 15th-century church, an
old wool-merchant's house now housing the 'World of Mechanical Music' (its owner is a
restorer of clocks, musical boxes and automata), and the Cotswold Countryside Collection
(with reconstructed rooms showing rural life, as well as agricultural waggons and equipment). Chedworth's fine Roman villa is nearby, and the Cotswold Farm Park, with its
V collection of rare breeds, only a few miles away.

ORCHARD COTTAGE

C(5) **D S**

Back Lane, Upper Oddington, Gloucestershire, GL56 0XL Tel: 01451 830785
East of Stow-on-the-Wold. Nearest main road: A436 from Stow-on-the-Wold towards
Chipping Norton.

rear view

2 Bedrooms. £18.50–£20 (less for 2 nights or more).
Bargain breaks. Both have own bath/shower/toilet. No
smoking.
Dinner (by arrangement). £14.50 for 3 courses and
coffee, at 7–8pm. Vegetarian or other special diets if
ordered. No smoking. **Light suppers** if ordered.
1 Sitting-room. With open fire, TV. No smoking.
Small garden
Closed from December to February.

A few ancient apple-trees are all that remain of the great orchard which gave this 18th-century cottage its name. Originally two tiny dwellings, the house has been repeatedly modernized over the last two hundred years, most recently by its present owner, Jane Beynon. She has used soft colours in the rooms – for instance, creams and pinks in a bedroom with lace bedspread; rush-seated and spindle-backed chairs in the small dining-hall. The garden is her pride and joy.

A typical dinner might comprise spicy avocado; chicken in a creamy piquant sauce; local fruits or tangy lemon Dutch flummery. As an alternative to a cooked breakfast, she can provide cold meats and cheeses in continental style. Jane drives a community minibus around the Cotswolds once a week and gladly takes visitors along.

Readers' comments: Cooking, comfort, hospitality all first class. Outstanding meal and cheerful warmth. Accommodation and facilities excellent. Superb cooking. Very high standard. Kind and helpful. Delightful. A lovely place. Perfect in every way.

PARKVIEW

C(1) **D PT S X**

4 Pittville Crescent, Cheltenham, Gloucestershire, GL52 2QZ Tel: 01242 575567
Nearest main road: A435 from Evesham to Cheltenham.

3 Bedrooms. £18 (less for 3 nights or more). Bargain
breaks. All have TV. No smoking.
1 Sitting-room. With TV, piano. No smoking.
Small garden

In springtime a cherry tree in bloom marks Parkview. Overlooking Pittville Park, this elegant Georgian house in a quiet residential area is a useful base for exploring the town, or for travelling further into the Cotswolds. The stairway of the house is lined with Sandra and John Sparrey's interesting finds from local auctions: old playbills, sepia-toned photographs and a land deed with George IV's royal seal. Bedrooms are pleasantly furnished; one has a lovely art deco dressing-suite. Guests share a bathroom, but there are washbasins in all rooms.

Cheltenham's Regency houses date from its heyday as a fashionable spa: the Duke of Wellington regularly came here whenever rheumatism or affairs of state got him down. The town needs repeated visits to see everything: the birthplace of composer Gustav Holst, the Pump Room (where you can still 'take the waters'), the elegant Promenade and Montpellier area, distinguished art gallery, and lovely gardens. Racegoers throng here at Gold Cup time; others come for various arts festivals.

V

POSTLIP HALL FARM

D

Winchcombe, Cheltenham, Gloucestershire, GL54 5AQ   Tel: 01242 603351
North-east of Cheltenham. Nearest main road: A435 from Cheltenham to Evesham.

3 Bedrooms. £19–£20 (less for 4 nights or more). All have some or all of the following: own bath/shower/toilet; TV. No smoking.
Light suppers if ordered. Vegetarian or other special diets if ordered. Wine available.
1 Sitting-room. With stove, TV. No smoking.
Large garden

This livestock farm, situated at the end of a sweeping and tree-lined drive in the hamlet of Postlip, was at one time part of the local Broadway family estate. Fine views of 15th-century Postlip Hall, with its magnificent gabled frontage, are to be had from this modern farmhouse of Cotswold stone.

Valerie and Joe Albutt have created a comfortable atmosphere for their guests. The large sitting-room, with panoramic views, has brocade sofas and armchairs and two recliners gathered around a wood-burning stove. Bedrooms are of a good size. One in beige and peach has unusual antique headboards; another, with double aspect, has views of open farmland and the old Hall beyond.

The farm adjoins Cleeve Common, at 1800 acres the largest area of common land in the county, so there are attractive cross-country walks, one of which takes you to nearby Winchcombe, a picturesque village that was the capital of the ancient kingdom of Mercia. Sudeley Castle, too, is a short walk away.

Readers' comments: Immaculate. Breakfast the best ever.

THE RIDGE

C(6) PT

Whiteshoots Hill, Bourton-on-the-Water, Gloucestershire, GL54 2LE
Tel: 01451 820660
East of Cheltenham. On A429 from Cirencester to Stow-on-the-Wold.

4 Bedrooms. £18–£20. Bargain breaks. All have own bath/shower/toilet; TV. No smoking.
Large garden

Nearby Bourton-on-the-Water is too picturesque for its own good (it is thronged in summer) but this guest-house is well away from all that. A gabled Edwardian house, it is surrounded by lawns and fine trees, with hill views. Breakfast-tables are in a new conservatory overlooking a sunken garden.

Pamela Minchin has several comfortable bedrooms, two on the ground floor (one with its own entrance). Good pubs are close for meals.

Walking or motoring in the Cotswolds is a pleasure in itself, but there are many other things to do – horseracing, shopping for antiques or country clothes, visiting gardens or the many stately homes and even statelier churches for which this county is famous. Moreton-in-Marsh on the Fosse Way is well worth a morning's exploration; there are lots of old inns and antique shops, with a busy general market on Tuesdays and a collectors' fair later in the week.

Readers' comments: Superb. Delightfully furnished, hospitable hostess. Have stayed three times.

ROOSTERS

Todenham, Gloucestershire, GL56 9PA   Tel: 01608 650645

C D S

North-east of Moreton-in-Marsh. Nearest main road: A429 from Moreton-in-Marsh to Warwick.

3 Bedrooms. £20–£22 (less for 3 nights or more). Bargain breaks. All have some or all of the following: own bath/shower/toilet; TV. No smoking.
Dinner (by arrangement). £14 for 3 courses and coffee, at 7.30pm. Vegetarian or other special diets if ordered. Wine available. **Light suppers** if ordered.
1 Sitting-room. With open fire. No smoking.
Large garden

Situated near the old 'four shires' stone, this 17th-century cottage provides an ideal base for touring not only the Cotswold villages but also Stratford-upon-Avon (only 20 minutes away) and, further afield, Cheltenham to the west or Warwick and Leamington Spa to the north.

Returning after a busy day sightseeing, and having been greeted by Rosie the golden retriever, you can relax by the inglenook fireplace with its gleaming copper cowl and admire Chris Longmore's eclectic collection of china, before she serves dinner. Chris and her husband Paul, a former golf professional, lived for some time in Sweden, so after perhaps broccoli-and-cheese soup you might be served Scandinavian pork, followed by a more traditional summer pudding or strawberry cheesecake.

Bedrooms are all individual, comfortable and furnished with imagination. One in yellow and blue has unusual pale pine and leather scrolled headboards, and a striking golden pine and green bathroom. Another has pretty rose-stencilled walls and white lace bedspreads. Some of Paul's grandfather's watercolour landscapes adorn the walls in the low-beamed hallways.

V

STEPPING STONE

Rectory Lane, Great Rissington, Gloucestershire, GL54 2LL   Tel: 01451 821385

C P T

East of Cheltenham. Nearest main road: A40 from Oxford to Cheltenham.

5 Bedrooms. £20. Bargain breaks. Some have some or all of the following: own shower/toilet; TV; balcony. No smoking.
1 Sitting-room. No smoking.
Large garden

Well placed to explore the Cotswolds is Stepping Stone, home of Jane and Allan Peates – a modern house yet blending beautifully with its surroundings. The Peates chose the plot for the breathtaking views it affords of the Windrush Valley. Bedrooms in the house are in celadon and pink chintzes, and outside are two stylish and well-equipped self-contained suites, both facing down the valley. One at first-floor level has its own balcony and another is on the ground floor. Visit the Lamb Inn close by for evening meals.

The house is midway between two famous Cotswold villages – Bourton-on-the-Water and Burford. Most people come here simply for the scenery, but also in the vicinity are the Cotswold Wildlife Park, Folly Farm (160 breeds of waterfowl and rare poultry), and Sudeley Castle, once the home of Catherine Parr. Only a little further are Oxford, Stratford-upon-Avon, Warwick and Woodstock (with Blenheim Palace). For gardens, go to Sezincote, Hidcote or Batsford (the last has a Japanese-style arboretum). There are antique shops in nearly every village.

TILED HOUSE FARM

C(10) M S

Oxlynch Lane, Oxlynch, Gloucestershire, GL10 3DF   Tel: 01453 822363
North-west of Stroud. Nearest main road: A4173 from Stroud to Gloucester (and M5, junction 13).

3 Bedrooms. £17–£19 (less for 3 nights or more). Some have some or all of the following: own bath/shower/toilet. No smoking.
Light suppers if ordered. Vegetarian or other special diets if ordered. No smoking.
1 Sitting-room. With open fire, TV, piano. No smoking.
Large garden
Closed in December.

Four-hundred-year-old Tiled House Farm was the first house in the area to have the innovation of tiles to replace thatch on its roof, hence its name. In the big sitting-room, with huge stone fireplace, the original bacon-hooks in the beams and gun-racks above the hearth still remain. Steep stairs go up from the dining-room (which overlooks the farmyard) to some of the bedrooms, the largest of which has timber-framed walls; there is also a self-contained ground-floor suite with good bathroom; here a strange little 'gothick' window was uncovered in a thick stone wall when renovations were being done.

For visitors not wanting to go out, Diane Jeffery will make an inexpensive meal of, say, tuna mousse with salad, baked potato and garlic bread, or chicken casserole, followed by apricot gâteau with cream.

The Rococo Garden at nearby Painswick is a popular draw for visitors.

Readers' comments: First-class accommodation and superb breakfast. Delightful.

UPPER VINEY FARMHOUSE

C D

Viney Hill, Lydney, Gloucestershire, GL15 4LT   Tel: 01594 516672
South-west of Gloucester. Nearest main road: A48 from Gloucester to Chepstow (and M48, junction 2).

3 Bedrooms. £18–£20 (less for 3 nights or more). Bargain breaks. All have own bath/shower/toilet; TV. No smoking.
Dinner. £15 for 4 courses and coffee, at 7pm. Vegetarian or other special diets if ordered. Wine available. No smoking. **Light suppers** if ordered.
1 Sitting-room. With open fire, TV. No smoking.
Small garden

Occasionally the Littens lay on two-day breaks of forest walks with an expert guide. Often, participants are shown such things as salmon-net making, or a cider-press in a private house: not typical tourist 'sights'. The house is on the southern edge of the historic Forest of Dean, a royal hunting forest since before the Norman Conquest.

Upper Viney is a 16th-century house of stone walls and floors, exposed timbers and ancient, twisting staircase. The sitting/dining-room has an inglenook with bread oven, and in an alcove are finds that have turned up in the garden (clay pipes, hand-forged nails), as well as a small iron-studded child's boot which has been dated at 1835.

There is a particularly big family room and very nice shower/bathrooms.

Mary Litten cooks straightforward meals like sardines on toast, chicken chasseur, and apple charlotte (always with two choices of starter and pudding).

V   *Reader's comment:* Very welcoming and friendly.

WINDRUSH HOUSE

Hazleton, Gloucestershire, GL54 4EB   Tel: 01451 860364
South-east of Cheltenham. Nearest main road: A40 from Cheltenham to Oxford.

S.

4 Bedrooms. £18.95–£25. Bargain breaks. Some have some or all of the following: own bath/shower/toilet; TV. No smoking.
Dinner. £19.50 for 4 courses and coffee, at 7.30pm. Vegetarian diets if ordered. Wine available. **Light suppers** if ordered.
2 Sitting-rooms. With open fire, TV, piano. No smoking.
Large garden
Closed from mid-December to mid-February.

The greatest attraction of this small guest-house built of Cotswold stone is Sydney Harrison's outstanding cooking. Not only is everything impeccably prepared – vegetables delicately sliced and lightly cooked, bread home-baked, breakfast orange juice freshly squeezed – but she has a repertoire of imaginative dishes that puts many an expensive restaurant in the shade.

Sydney's friendly welcome is manifest the moment you arrive, and a free glass of sherry awaits you in your room. As to the house itself, this is furnished with much attention to comfort, and in tranquil colours. All the rooms are immaculate, the furnishings traditional.

The house stands in a quiet spot some 800 feet up in the Cotswold hills, where the air is bracing and the views are of far fields and grazing sheep. It is on the outskirts of a rambling village of old stone farmhouses and close to beautiful Northleach.

Readers' comments: First-rate; inventive menu. Excellent food. Food outstanding; what a find! Superb cooking. Excellent in every way, especially food and wine. The best cook we've found in England. Delightful, scenic and peaceful location.

WYCK HILL LODGE

Wyck Hill, Stow-on-the-Wold, Gloucestershire, GL54 1HT   Tel: 01451 830141
On A424 from Stow-on-the-Wold to Burford.

M

3 Bedrooms. £20–£23 (less for 4 nights or more). All have own bath/shower/toilet; TV. No smoking.
Light suppers if ordered.
2 Sitting-rooms. With open fire. No smoking.
Garden
Closed from December to February.

This picturesque house, now the home of Eddie and Gloria Holbrook, was built around 1800 as the lodge to a nearby mansion. It is surrounded by very lovely gardens, where guests can have afternoon tea in summer and enjoy far views across Bourton Vale. There are good walks straight from the door.

In the L-shaped sitting-room are comfortable sofas, and, in winter, a crackling fire. A small reading-room is particularly attractive: like some other rooms, it has windows set in pointed arches with stained-glass panes at the top. There is a view of the terraced garden (with pond) and far hills.

Two of the bedrooms (one opening onto the garden) are on the ground floor, and there is another upstairs – this is a big, two-level room with easy chairs.

At breakfast, Gloria offers plenty of choices – smoked haddock, for instance.

Readers' comments: Excellent! Warm, friendly welcome. Room very pleasant and comfortable. Breakfast very good indeed. Beautiful house with magnificent views.

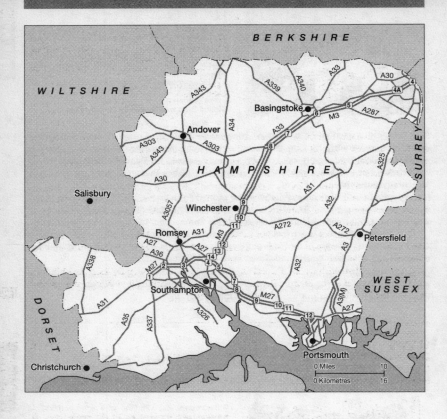

BROADWATER

Amport, Hampshire, SP11 8AY Tel/Fax: 01264 772240
West of Andover. Nearest main road: A303 from Andover to Amesbury.

C X

2 Bedrooms. £20. Both have some or all of the following: own bath/shower/toilet. No smoking.
Light suppers only. Vegetarian or other special diets if ordered.
1 Sitting-room. With open fire, TV.
Small garden

Stonehenge, that great megalithic monument on Salisbury Plain, is only a few miles from the quiet and unspoilt village of Amport. Indeed, discoveries such as flint instruments and burial mounds have been made in the area, suggesting that man has lived here for 5000 years.

Broadwater was built near Pill Hill Brook, a clear chalk stream, in the 1600s. The cottage is attractively furnished by Carolyn Mallam and, with its pretty garden (full of roses, lavender, herbs and fruit trees), is a peaceful place. In the beamed sitting/dining-room are watercolours painted by a relative who served in Nelson's fleet. Bedrooms are cosy, with views of the garden and surrounding countryside.

Cots and high chairs are provided as well as books and board games for children. Carolyn serves light suppers (including home-made bread), recommending local inns for more substantial meals.

In the immediate vicinity are the Hawk Conservancy, the Danebury Iron Age hill fort, and the Museum of Army Flying. The cathedral towns of Salisbury and Winchester are also near and the New Forest is only a 30-minute drive away.

V

CAMS

Hambledon, Waterlooville, Hampshire, PO7 4SP Tel: 01705 632865
(Fax: 01705 632691)
North of Portsmouth. Nearest main road: A3 from Portsmouth to Petersfield.

C D S

3 Bedrooms. £17–£19 (less for 3 nights or more). Bargain breaks. Some have some or all of the following: own bath/shower/toilet. No smoking.
Dinner (by arrangement). £8.50 for 3 courses and coffee, at 7pm. Wine available. No smoking. **Light suppers** if ordered.
1 Sitting-room. With open fire, TV. No smoking.
Large garden

Hampshire is rich in historic houses: this is one. Its 17th-century pine-panelled dining-room is impressive, with marble fireplace and shuttered glass doors opening onto the garden; beyond a haha sheep graze (beside a tennis court). Spindle-backed rush chairs surround a great circular table of polished yew, where Valerie Fawcett may serve such meals as pâté, chicken breasts in lemon and coriander, and apple pie. In the sitting-room, chinoiserie curtains and pink walls make a pleasing background to antique furniture. Up the impressive staircase are pretty bedrooms: the oldest, in pink and white, has beamy walls and leaded windows.

Northward lies Alresford with its millstream and dam built in the 12th century; and also a lovely footpath through watercress beds and past a black-and-white thatched mill spanning the river. Other villages worth seeking out include Tichborne – famous for a *cause célèbre* in 1871 when an Australian imposter laid claim to the estate here; and for the Tichborne Dole, flour given to villagers since 1150.

V

COTTAGE CREST
C

Castle Hill, Woodgreen, Hampshire, SP6 2AX   Tel: 01725 512009
South of Salisbury. Nearest main road: A338 from Ringwood to Salisbury.

3 Bedrooms. £19–£20 (less for 4 nights or more). All have some or all of the following: own shower/toilet; TV; views of river. No smoking.
Light suppers if ordered.
Large garden

Bedrooms in the Cadmans' home are some of the most beautiful and well-equipped in this book. A great brass bed with pink-and-white lacy linen is in one; it is in an L-shaped room with windows on two sides from which to enjoy superb views of sunsets over the River Avon in the valley below. There is no guests' sitting-room, but there is a garden suite with private sitting-room facing this view.

One can sit on a paved terrace with a little pool, or take a zigzag path down to a lower garden, or walk straight into the New Forest.

Particularly picturesque villages nearby include Breamore (with 16th-century Breamore House open to the public, and a mediaeval maze), Rockbourne (Roman villa close to it), and the hamlets of Moyles Court and Burley.

Readers' comments: Delightful, made so welcome, very comfortable. Most charming and friendly. Very warm welcome. Made most comfortable. Garden suite beautifully furnished, and with fresh flowers. Charming hostess, friendly and interesting too.

FOREST GATE
C(10) **PT**

Hambledon Road, Denmead, Hampshire, PO7 6EX   Tel: 01705 255901
North of Portsmouth. Nearest main road: A3 from Petersfield to Portsmouth.

2 Bedrooms. £18–£20 (less for 5 nights or more). Both have some or all of the following: own bath/shower/toilet; TV. No smoking.
Dinner (by arrangement). £10 for 2 courses and coffee, at 7.45pm. Vegetarian or other special diets if ordered. No smoking. **Light suppers** if ordered.
1 Sitting-room. With open fire. No smoking.
Large garden
Closed at Easter.

Small villages dot the one-time Forest of Bere, to which the name of the house alludes. It is the graceful 18th-century home of Torfrida Cox and her husband, with a large garden, and is on the 70-mile Wayfarers' Walk. This is an informal home furnished with antiques. Meals (which have to be ordered in advance) include such dishes as Armenian lamb pilaff or moussaka, mousses or lemon meringue pie.

Handy as a stopover for people using Portsmouth's port, Forest Gate deserves a longer stay, for Portsmouth (and its adjoining Victorian resort, Southsea) have so much to offer: HMS *Victory*, the *Mary Rose*, HMS *Warrior*, the Royal Navy's Museum and that of the Marines, cathedral and historic church, Henry VIII's Southsea Castle, the D-Day Museum, Hayling Island and the wild places of Chichester Harbour.

Readers' comments: Like staying with friends. Bedroom comfortable, dining-room elegant.

FORTITUDE COTTAGE

PT

51 Broad Street, Old Portsmouth, Hampshire, PO1 2JD   Tel/Fax: 01705 823748
Nearest main road: A3 from London to Portsmouth.

3 Bedrooms. £20–£22 to readers of this book. Less for 3 nights or more. Bargain breaks. All have some or all of the following: own bath/shower/toilet; TV; views of the sea; balcony. No smoking.
Light suppers if ordered.

Carol Harbeck's little cottage – one room piled on top of another – backs onto her mother's (also a guest-house), with a flowery little courtyard and fountain between the two: its appearance has won it awards. It is named for the Fortitude Inn, once next door; itself named for HMS *Fortitude*, a ship-of-war which ended as a prison hulk – overlooked by the big bay window of Carol's first-floor sitting-room. This is Portsmouth's most historic area. It's a place of ramparts and bastions, quaint buildings and byways, much coming-and-going of ships and little boats. The waterbus leaves from the quay just outside.

All the rooms in the cottage are prettily furnished. One can dine well at The Seagull.

Readers' comments: Excellent accommodation, spotless. Absolutely excellent, high standard. Delightfully unusual. What a find! Particularly enjoyable. Such an interesting old house.

V

GREEN PATCH

D

Furze Hill, Fordingbridge, Hampshire, SP6 2PS   Tel: 01425 652387
(Fax: 01425 656594)
West of Southampton. Nearest main road: A31 from Southampton to Ringwood.

3 Bedrooms. £20–£23. All have some or all of the following: own bath/shower/toilet; TV. No smoking.
Light suppers only. Vegetarian or other special diets if ordered. No smoking.
1 Sitting-room. No smoking.
Large garden

Nestling in a hillside with the New Forest as a backdrop, this 1920s house offers total peace and seclusion.

Eating breakfast in the oak-panelled dining-room is a treat, not least because of the wide and interesting choice of dishes which Meg Mulcahy is happy to prepare. Porridge with whisky and maple syrup might be on the menu, and kippers, sautéed kidneys and mushrooms in Madeira sauce, soft cod roes on toast or scrambled eggs with smoked trout on a toasted muffin; and, of course, the more usual fare.

All year round, guests can relax in the plant-filled conservatory. There is a fridge here, and on summer days you are welcome to barbecue your own food on the adjoining patio, whilst enjoying lovely views of the forest.

Meg offers light suppers only, but there are several eating-places nearby.

Flower-painting is a hobby which she particularly enjoys, and examples of her work and that of the celebrated botanical artist Marianne North are displayed in the spotless bedrooms, some of which have very good views.

V

LAND OF NOD
Headley, Bordon, Hampshire, GU35 8SJ   Tel: 01428 713609 (Fax: 01428 717698)
North-east of Petersfield. Nearest main road: A3 from Guildford to Petersfield.

3 Bedrooms. £20–£25 (less for 7 nights or more). Bargain breaks. All have some or all of the following: own bath/toilet; TV; balcony. No smoking.
Light suppers if ordered. Vegetarian or other special diets if ordered. No smoking.
1 Sitting-room. With open fire, piano.
Large garden

'And Cain went out from the presence of the Lord and dwelt in the land of Nod' (Genesis). They say that in the 16th century a man called Cain was excommunicated by the local vicar for some misdemeanour and came to live in a house on this site. The name has remained but this is the third house to be built here amid 100 acres of private estate. It was built in 1939 by Jeremy Whitaker's father: Whitakers have lived here since 1884.

The elegant red-brick house is surrounded by beautiful gardens with some formal areas and much informal woodland (tennis and croquet too) and, from the square bay window in the sitting-room, you can enjoy lovely views. There are good views too from the spacious bedrooms.

The dining-room takes the Orient as its theme, having been inspired by a piece of antique Japanese needlework which hangs here. Hand-painted chinoiserie panels adorn the walls and the circular resin dining-table is surrounded by specially made Chinese-style chairs in rosewood. Jeremy and Philippa Whitaker are interesting people, having travelled widely.

MALT COTTAGE
Upper Clatford, Hampshire, SP11 7QL   Tel: 01264 323469 (Fax: 01264 334100)
South of Andover. Nearest main road: A303 from Andover to Amesbury.

3 Bedrooms. £20–£25. All have some or all of the following: own bath/shower/toilet; TV. No smoking.
Light suppers if ordered.
1 Sitting-room. With log stove, TV.
Large garden

Such was his interest in gardens that Richard Mason gave up a career in industry in order to design them for a living. His wife Patsy has always been a keen gardener too, so it's hardly surprising that the six acres of land which they have gradually acquired is now an area of great beauty which guests can enjoy at their leisure. There is a formal garden containing a variety of shrubs and trees, including Liquidambar with its stunning autumnal colour. There are ponds and a rose arbour and, beyond all this, a chalk stream with trout and meadowland where wildlife flourishes. You might spot a kingfisher on one of its visits or the swans who come to nest every year.

The cottage itself, once a malting barn, is elegant and spacious. The entrance hall leads to a beamed dining-area where guests eat at an Edwardian refectory table. The sitting-room, in pastel shades, features a large inglenook fireplace and log-burning stove. Bedrooms are comfortable and some have garden views.

Light suppers only, but guests can eat at the Mayfly, a short drive away, with its attractive waterside setting.

MAYS FARMHOUSE

Longwood Dean, Hampshire, SO21 1JR   Tel: 01962 777486 (Fax: 01962 777747)
South-east of Winchester. Nearest main road: A272 from Winchester to Petersfield (and M3, junction 9).

3 Bedrooms. £20 (less for 3 nights or more). All have some or all of the following: own bath/shower/toilet; TV. No smoking.
Dinner (by arrangement). £12.50 for 4 courses and coffee, at 7pm. Vegetarian or other special diets if ordered. Wine available. No smoking. **Light suppers** if ordered.
1 Sitting-room. With open fire, TV, piano. No smoking.
Large garden

Twelve-foot trees grew in the kitchen and the 16th-century house had no roof. Undeterred, James Ashby (expert in renovations) bought and transformed it to the highest standards – unvarnished oak beams in the dining-room are now complemented by a woodblock floor, and a handsome log stove stands in the old inglenook, for instance.

Rosalie has painted bedroom furniture decoratively – she runs classes on how to do this (on Mondays). All the rooms have views of the Ashbys' white goats, and of a pretty garden and the woods beyond. One has a Jacuzzi. A stair-lift is available for those who need it. Dinner (with fresh garden produce) might include pheasant pâté, pork in orange and cider sauce, and a raspberry flan.

Nearby Winchester was England's capital in the days of King Alfred (indeed, it had been a considerable town long before that, during the long Roman occupation). The Norman cathedral dominates all, its most famous bishop – William of Wykeham – being the founder of one of England's great public schools, Winchester College (which can be visited).

V

MICHELMERSH HOUSE

Michelmersh, Hampshire, SO51 0NS   Tel: 01794 368644
North of Romsey. Nearest main road: A3057 from Romsey to Stockbridge.

3 Bedrooms. £19–£20 (less for 3 nights or more). Bargain breaks. All have own bath/toilet. No smoking.
Dinner. £15 for 3 courses and coffee, at 8pm. (Sunday to Thursday only). Vegetarian or other special diets if ordered. No smoking. **Light suppers** if ordered.
1 Sitting-room. With open fire, TV, piano. No smoking.
Large garden
Closed from mid-December to mid-January.

Where this largely 18th-century house now stands, Henry V assembled his army before departing from Portsmouth for France and the Battle of Agincourt. The adjacent church goes back even further: its tower is Saxon.

All this contrasts with 20th-century comforts within the house, and tennis court without.

Through the high sash windows of the primrose sitting-room is a view over the valley of the River Test towards Salisbury. Ancestral portraits line the walls of the dining-room where Jennifer Lalonde serves such meals as fish pâté, roast beef, and Mississippi mud pie.

Bedrooms are attractive, in particular the spacious blue and yellow one with large bathroom adjoining and lovely views beyond. Many old features remain to give the house character, from the elegant staircase to bacon-racks and a coal stove for flat-irons in the former kitchen.

Readers' comments: Very tastefully decorated, most comfortable. Beautifully cooked meal. Made most welcome. Superb home, charming bedroom. Warm welcome. Faultless breakfast. Delightful hostess. Beautiful house.

V

MORESTEAD GROVE
CPTS

Morestead, Hampshire, SO21 1LZ   Tel: 01962 777238
South-east of Winchester. Nearest main road: A272 from Winchester to Petersfield (and M3, junction 11).

1 Bedroom. £18–£20 (less for 3 nights or more). Has own bath/shower/toilet; TV. No smoking.
Dinner (by arrangement). £12 for 4 courses and coffee, at 8pm. Vegetarian or other special diets if ordered. Wine available. No smoking. **Light suppers** if ordered.
1 Sitting-room. With open fire. No smoking.
Large garden

At hives beyond the badminton court, a swarm of two dozen veiled bee-keepers were holding a 'meet' when we arrived at Morestead Grove, a late Georgian rectory with handsome rooms. Katharine Sellon serves such dinners (if ordered in advance) as smoked haddock mousse, chicken in wine and mushroom sauce, and candied oranges, using her own vegetables and eggs.

The clear chalk streams, with occasional watermills, have made this lovely area well known for its watercress and its trout: the River Itchen is famous among anglers, and its valley is outstandingly beautiful – to drive or walk it from Itchen Stoke is an unforgettable experience, pausing at Ovington's mediaeval inn on the way. Old and New Alresford are on opposite banks of the River Alre: in the latter, colourful Broad Street is worth visiting.

Readers' comments: Hospitable and helpful; house charming, comfortable and stylish. Very pleasant rooms, attractive garden.

MORNINGTON HOUSE
CD

Hambledon, Waterlooville, Hampshire, PO7 4RU   Tel/Fax: 01705 632704
North of Portsmouth. Nearest main road: A3 from Portsmouth to Petersfield.

2 Bedrooms. £16. No smoking.
Light suppers if ordered.
1 Sitting-room. With open fire, TV, piano.
Large garden

In 1760, the year when Mornington House was built, Hambledon produced the first cricket club of all (still going strong) and laid down today's complicated rules.

Charles Lutyens, for many years chairman of the club, is a great-nephew of Sir Edwin Lutyens and may show his Delhi plans to interested visitors as they relax in the bay-windowed sitting-room or the adjoining conservatory with grapevine overhead. There are splendid views over brimming herbaceous flowerbeds, beech hedges, rooftops and church. In the garden is a swimming-pool (unheated).

Everywhere are interesting antiques – an inlaid escritoire from Holland, Edwardian chairs painted with garlands. In the dining-room, 'spitting images' of Disraeli and Gladstone preside over the breakfast-table, and an unusual rocking horse is a magnet to little children.

One bedroom, with lace spread and bamboo bedheads, leads to a bathroom with another bedroom, in blue and white, adjoining it.

Readers' comments: Delightful. Lovely welcome and attention. Look forward to returning. Delightful house, charming hosts. Excellent supper. So comfortable. Shall return. My vote for the b & b of the year. Very pleasant, every kindness. A warm, inviting welcome.

OLD STATION

Mottisfont, Hampshire, SO51 0LN   Tel: 01794 368609
North of Romsey. Nearest main road: A3057 from Romsey to Stockbridge.

2 Bedrooms. £17.50. One has own bath/shower; TV; views of river. No smoking.
Large garden
Closed from Christmas to March.

Mottisfont is famous for the rose gardens of its 13th-century abbey (NT), converted into a stately home in the 18th century and decorated in trompe l'oeil by Rex Whistler in the 20th. The village used also to have a lesser claim to fame: the 'sprat and winkle' railway line along which were once carried not only villagers but loads of chalk for export to Canada. The Victorian Old Station beside the disused track (now part of the River Test Way – a long and lovely walk from Andover to Totton) is today the home of Helen Hall. Her visitors' bedrooms (and the sun-room) overlook the River Test, frequented by herons and swans. They are simply furnished, but the bathroom is quite splendid!

You do not need to drive far for outings. Northward is 18th-century Houghton Lodge, recently used in the filming of *Pride and Prejudice*; and in the other direction are Broadlands (Lord Mountbatten's home), palatial Beaulieu Abbey (home of the Montagu family since 1538) where the National Motor Museum is to be found, and the great city of Southampton, with an excellent art gallery, mediaeval gates and walls, and historic buildings which still survive around the High Street. A little further are the waterside village of Bucklers Hard with its maritime museum and lovely Exbury gardens.

PILLMEAD HOUSE

North Lane, Buriton, Hampshire, GU31 5RS   Tel: 01730 266795
(Fax: 01730 264042)
South of Petersfield. Nearest main road: A3 from Petersfield to Portsmouth.

C D S

2 Bedrooms. £20–£25 (less for 3 nights or more). Bargain breaks. Both have own bath/shower/toilet; TV. No smoking.
Dinner. £15 for 4 courses and coffee, at 7pm (not Sundays). Vegetarian or other special diets if ordered. No smoking. **Light suppers** if ordered.
1 Sitting-room. With open fire. No smoking.
Large garden

The lozenge-paned windows and brick-and-flint walls are typical of many houses in this area, but the Tudor chimneys – very elaborate, and 8 feet high – came from a mansion. The house overlooks a valley, its lawn and rock garden descending steeply among terraced beds of roses and lavender. Visitors can enjoy a view of the Queen Elizabeth Country Park and Butser Hill while drinking their after-dinner coffee in the garden.

The dining-room's bow windows, too, make the most of the view. This is a pretty room, with pink wildflower curtains and Victorian mahogany furniture. Upstairs, white walls contrast with moss-green carpets. One bedroom, cottage-style, has pink fabrics and patchwork cushions; in another primrose predominates, with a patchwork bedspread.

Sarah Moss serves such meals as soufflé, free-range chicken, and fresh fruit compote, using much produce from her large kitchen garden.

Readers' comments: Excellent: our second visit. Magnificent dinners, an inspired cook. A lovely cook, always makes us most welcome.

V

RIDGE COTTAGE
C PT X

164 Burley Road, Bransgore, Hampshire, BH23 8DE   Tel: 01425 672504
North of Christchurch. Nearest main road: A35 from Christchurch to Southampton.

3 Bedrooms. £16 (less for 4 nights or more). One has own balcony. No smoking.
Dinner (by arrangement). £9 for 2 courses and coffee, at 7–8pm. Vegetarian or other special diets if ordered. No smoking. **Light suppers** if ordered.
1 Sitting-room. With open fire, TV, piano. No smoking.
Large garden

From a gardener's cottage in 1913, this has gradually been extended to become a quite large house in the New Forest, handsomely modernized and with an attractively landscaped and walled garden all round it – sloping upwards to a polygonal, glass-walled summer-house. Big windows give clear views of this and of the terrace where barbecues are sometimes organized. The sitting-room, dark green and white, is full of small antiques and other finds the Blythes have collected over the years. There are excellent carpets, a piano and open fire, hanging pot-plants and a rocking-chair. The dining-hall is furnished with oak chairs made for them by a Cornish craftsman, with seats of needlepoint stitched by Janet – who is also a good cook, serving such meals as roast lamb or Dover sole followed by profiteroles or traditional puddings.

There's a pretty bathroom (with bidet); a family suite; and a games room for table tennis and darts. Books galore – rag dolls, too.

Readers' comments: Made very welcome, delicious meals, convivial company.

SOUTH FARM

East Meon, Hampshire, GU32 1EZ   Tel: 01730 823261 (Fax: 01730 823614)
West of Petersfield. Nearest main road: A272 from Winchester to Petersfield.

3 Bedrooms. £20–£22 (less for 3 nights or more). Bargain breaks. Some have some or all of the following: own bath/toilet; views of river. No smoking.
Light suppers if ordered. Vegetarian or other special diets if ordered. Wine available.
1 Sitting-room. With open fire, TV. No smoking.
Large garden
Closed from mid-December to Easter.

The approach to the farm is delightful. There are specimen trees on a lawn (ash, chestnut), an old granary and a grapevine under glass. In the 500-year-old house is a brick-floored dining-room with huge inglenook, rush ladderback chairs and a big oak table. The very large sitting-room has antique furniture and chinoiserie curtains in gold and blue. Bedrooms have been very agreeably furnished by Jane Atkinson: one with poppy fabrics, for instance; in another are exposed beams and a lace bedspread. An oak-panelled room has peony fabric. All are outstanding.

The house is full of flowers because Jane, an accomplished flower-arranger, regularly has large deliveries from Covent Garden market. You can dine at the George or Izaak Walton inns in East Meon if you want more than a light supper.

The Meon Valley amid the South Downs has churches that go back to Saxon times, flint-walled houses, and prehistoric burial mounds. To the south are woodlands, remnants of the once-great Forest of Bere, and then comes Portsmouth Harbour.

SPURSHOLT HOUSE

Salisbury Road, Romsey, Hampshire, SO51 6DJ   Tel: 01794 512229
(Fax: 01794 523142)
Nearest main road: A27 from Romsey to Salisbury.

3 Bedrooms. £18–£24 (less for 4 nights or more). Bargain breaks. All have own bath/shower/toilet; TV. No smoking.
Dinner (by arrangement). £14 for 4 courses and coffee, at 7.30–8.30pm (not weekends). Vegetarian or other special diets if ordered. **Light suppers** if ordered.
1 Sitting-room. With open fire, TV. No smoking.
Large garden

In the 1830s this was the home of Lady Cowper, one of Lord Palmerston's many mistresses.

There are paved terraces with urns of geraniums, overlooking a lawn, impressive topiary, and a view of Romsey Abbey. Beyond flowerbeds, yew hedges enclose a succession of further pleasures – a parterre with lily-pool, and a dovecote with fantails.

Rooms have been furnished by Anthea Hughes in keeping with the character of the house. The spectacular sitting-room has stained glass originally in the Palace of Westminster. One bedroom is oak-panelled, and all contain antiques and extra-large beds.

Dinner, served in a dining-room handsomely furnished in Victorian style, may consist of such dishes as potted shrimps, marinated lamb kebabs, lemon meringue pie, and cheeses.

Readers' comments: Thoroughly enjoyed staying. Made most welcome. Lovely house with beautiful gardens. Most comfortable. Couldn't have been kinder. A joy to stay in, keynote seems to be quality; atmosphere most welcoming.

STREET FARMHOUSE

Alton Road, South Warnborough, Hampshire, RG29 1RS   Tel/Fax: 01256 862225
South-east of Basingstoke. Nearest main road: A287 from Odiham to Farnham
(and M3, junction 5).

3 Bedrooms. £16–£20 (less for 3 nights or more). Some have some or all of the following: own bath/shower/toilet; TV. No smoking.
Dinner (by arrangement). £15 for 4 courses and coffee, at 7.30pm. Vegetarian or other special diets if ordered. No smoking. **Light suppers** if ordered.
1 Sitting-room. With log stove, TV.
Large garden

Two 16th-century cottages were combined into one to make this attractive house, beamed and with inglenook fireplace, in an ancient village through which a stream runs. Wendy Turner's choice of furnishings admirably complements the old house. There are prettily carved chairs in the pale green dining-room; pine doors have been stripped and brick walls exposed; buttoned chairs in rust-colour covers are gathered around a log stove in the sitting-room. Bedrooms are very pleasant – for instance, furnished with chest-of-drawers of woven cane, with very good armchairs and colour schemes. One bathroom has an oval bath in peach, and a bidet. Standards throughout are high and in the garden there is a heated swimming-pool. Dinner might include pork in cider with apricots, and raspberry pavlova.

Readers' comments: An outstanding experience. A place of great character; seldom have we met such friendly people. Excellent in all respects. Our third visit, excellent value. Beautifully kept. Made most welcome; warm and comfortable.

TOAD'S ALLEY

C(7) PT

South Lane, Buriton, Hampshire, GU31 5RU   Tel: 01730 263880
South of Petersfield. Nearest main road: A3 from Petersfield to Portsmouth.

2 Bedrooms. £16.50–£17.50 (less for 4 nights or more). Bargain breaks. Both have TV. No smoking.
Dinner (by arrangement). £12 for 3 courses and coffee, at 7.30pm. Vegetarian or other special diets if ordered. Wine available. **Light suppers** if ordered.
1 Sitting-room. With open fire, TV.
Small garden

There really are toads at Toad's Alley, home of interior designer Patricia Bushall. They can sometimes be seen heading to the stream which lies between the garden and the crest along which walkers follow the South Downs Way. The secluded house comprises three tiny farmworkers' cottages built in the 15th century, with brick-floored hall and low-sloping ceilings upstairs. Both bedrooms have splendid views of sheep grazing on the hillside. A sitting-room for guests is attractively furnished, like the other rooms, with pale colours. Meals are taken at a handsome, oval table of oak. A typical dinner menu might include stuffed tomatoes, lemon and lime pork, and pancakes.

In Buriton, a picturesque downland village, are a Norman church and a pond. All around are pleasant walks. At Queen Elizabeth Country Park, there are forest trails and rides, and at Chalton a re-created Iron Age farm with animals, crafts and demonstrations. Uppark (just over the county boundary in West Sussex) is a glorious 17th-century house that has been meticulously restored by the National Trust after a fire reduced it to a shell in 1989.

VINE FARMHOUSE

Bentley, Alton, Hampshire, GU34 4PW   Tel/Fax: 01420 23262
South-east of Basingstoke. Nearest main road: A31 from Farnham to Alton (and M3, junction 5).

2 Bedrooms. £15–£20 (less for 7 nights or more). Bargain breaks. One has own bath/toilet; views of river. No smoking.
Large garden

The River Wey runs within a few yards of this turn-of-the-century farmhouse and, with an acre or so of informal garden and farmland beyond, this is indeed a secluded spot.

The circular entrance hall is just one of the many additions made by the present owners, Gail and David Sinclair. The red-and-cream striped fabric covering the walls in the dining-room gives it a cosy feel, and guests can enjoy fine views of the river and fields beyond while eating breakfast around a circular table. For other meals, you could try the Hen and Chicken or the Anchor in nearby Froyle.

Hunting prints and family photos line the staircase and landing. One small bedroom in blue and yellow has a shared bathroom; the other has windows with good views at each end.

Barn owls breed in a box at the side of the house and, about three miles away, in 20 acres of parkland, is Birdworld with its numerous species of birds. Jane Austen's house is at nearby Chawton. Ten minutes away you can board the Watercress Line, a steam railway which passes through beautiful countryside between Alton and Alresford.

V

WALNUT COTTAGE

Old Romsey Road, Cadnam, Hampshire, SO40 2NP   Tel/Fax: 01703 812275
West of Southampton. Nearest main road: A31 from Ringwood towards Winchester (and M27, junction1).

C(14) M PT

2 Bedrooms. £20–£22 (less for 2 nights or more). Both have some or all of the following: own bath/shower/toilet; TV. No smoking.
2 Sitting-rooms. With open fire (in one), TV. No smoking.
Small garden

Old Romsey Road no longer leads anywhere (its days ended when a nearby motorway replaced it). Little, white Walnut Cottage stands in a pretty garden (with an old well) which traps the sun. One bedroom opens onto this.

All the rooms have been attractively furnished by Charlotte and Eric Osgood, who did much of the work themselves. There are two sitting-rooms, one with windows on three sides. For meals other than breakfast, Charlotte recommends the White Hart inn nearby.

The cottage is on the edge of the New Forest (it was originally occupied by foresters) and is a good choice for an October break, when the forest colours are superb.

Readers' comments: Beautifully located, most helpful people. Delightful couple, charming rooms, comfortable; superb breakfasts. Faultless accommodation and welcome. Splendid. Brilliant hosts. Made most welcome; situation ideal. Have returned 9 times.

WEIR COTTAGE

Bickton, Hampshire, SP6 2HA   Tel: 01425 655813
South of Salisbury. Nearest main road: A338 from Ringwood to Salisbury.

C (5)

2 Bedrooms. £19–£22. Both have some or all of the following: own bath/shower/toilet; views of river. No smoking.
Dinner. £12.50 for 3 courses and coffee, at 8pm. Vegetarian or other special diets if ordered. Wine available. No smoking. **Light suppers** if ordered.
2 Sitting-rooms. With open fire, TV, piano. No smoking.
Large garden

Near Fordingbridge, Weir Cottage was once the flour store for the nearby watermill (now converted). Seated on the sofa in a turquoise and white ground-floor bedroom, one has a view of the tranquil watermeadows. On the sunny upper floor is another bedroom, and a vast room with rafters above a long chestnut table and armchairs grouped around the open log fire. A breakfast-table is placed to make the most of the mill-race view. From another sash window one can see the garden – winding herbaceous beds and a paved terrace with swing-seat.

Philippa Duckworth serves such meals as cucumber mousse, local pheasant with vegetables from the garden, and rhubarb fool.

There are two pianos in the house, played not only by Geoffrey but by guests too. A retired brigadier, he also catches the trout which often appear on the dinner-table. His father, and the Duckworths' daughter, painted the watercolours seen on the walls.

To the north lies Salisbury and its cathedral, but most people stay here to enjoy the New Forest – William the Conqueror's hunting reserve nearly a thousand years ago.

HEREFORD & WORCESTER

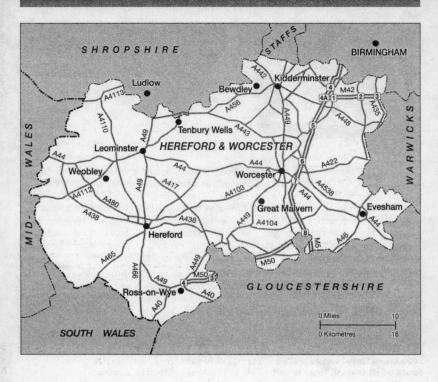

Addresses shown are to enable you to locate a house on a map. They are not necessarily complete postal addresses (though the essential postcode is included), and detailed directions for finding a house should be obtained from the owner.

APPLETREE COTTAGE

Mansell Lacy, Hereford & Worcester, HR4 7HH   Tel: 01981 590688
North-west of Hereford. Nearest main road: A480 from Hereford to Kington.

C(8) PT S

3 Bedrooms. £15–£18 (less for 2 nights or more). Bargain breaks. One has own shower/toilet. No smoking.
Dinner (by arrangement). £12 for 3 courses and coffee, at 8.30pm. Vegetarian or other special diets if ordered Wine available. No smoking.
1 Sitting-room. With stove, TV. No smoking.
Large garden

Because Monica Barker previously lived in India, Appletree Cottage, built of half-timbering and brick in the reign of Henry VI, is full of exotic touches such as Kashmiri crewel bedspreads and curtains. These nevertheless assort well with pretty fabrics, antique oak furniture, and chairs covered in traditional tapestry or velvet. Previously two cottages, then a ciderhouse, the building still has many of its original features, such as low beams and small, deepset windows; and when Monica had to put in a new, twisting staircase, she had it woodpegged in the traditional way. By arrangement, she will cook such meals as cucumber and yogurt soup, steak pie, and meringues – using wholefood ingredients. The cottage stands at the foot of a hill popular with walkers and birdwatchers alike.

Ancient Hereford, its turbulent military history behind it, is still a market town with a mediaeval network of streets. The cathedral is full of treasures, including the famous *Mappa Mundi*, the largest surviving mediaeval map of the world. The Norman nave is exceptionally impressive, some bishops' tombs particularly ornate, the cloisters tranquil. The town is also the home of Bulmers, whose cider museum is well worth a visit.

COWLEIGH PARK FARMHOUSE

Cowleigh Road, Great Malvern, Hereford & Worcester, WR13 5HJ
Tel/Fax: 01684 566750
Nearest main road: A449 from Worcester to Ross-on-Wye (and the junction of the M5 with M50).

C(7) D PT

3 Bedrooms. £20–£23 (less for 4 nights or more). All have some or all of the following: own bath/shower/toilet; TV. No smoking.
Dinner. £14 for 3 courses and coffee, at 7pm (Monday–Friday only). Vegetarian or other special diets if ordered. Wine available. No smoking. **Light suppers** if ordered.
1 Sitting-room. With open fire, piano. No smoking.
Large garden

The half-timbered house is 350 years old, and some of its beams are even older. On driving up to the door, there is a tranquil scene – snowy alyssum spreading over old stone walls, an ancient cider-press on the brick terrace. (The Worcestershire Way starts here.)

Beyond the slate-flagged hall, Sue Stringer has furnished the low-beamed rooms attractively – comfortable antique chairs are placed around a large inglenook in the main sitting-room. In the dining-room there is a yew refectory table with 18th-century rush-seated chairs. Bedrooms have deep-pile carpets, stripped pine, board-and-latch doors, and soft colours. One has a particularly pretty view, of lily-pool and rock garden.

A typical meal: Stilton-and-apple soup, goulash, and blackcurrant gâteau.

The house has its own piped Malvern water.

Readers' comments: Warm, hospitable and friendly. Wished we could have stayed longer. Very relaxing and comfortable home. Pretty rooms. Charming home. Made very welcome. Food excellent and plentiful. Really nice welcome. Very comfortable. Delicious breakfasts.

V

CWM CRAIG FARM

C S X

Bolston Road, Little Dewchurch, Hereford & Worcester, HR2 6PS
Tel: 01432 840250
North-west of Ross-on-Wye. Nearest main road: A49 from Ross-on-Wye to Hereford
(and M50, junction 4).

3 Bedrooms. £16–£18 (less for 7 nights or more). Two have some of the following: own bath/shower/ toilet; TV.
Light suppers if ordered.
2 Sitting-rooms. With open fire, TV. No smoking in one.
Large garden

This 18th-century farm in the Wye Valley would be a good choice for a family. Children can watch cattle being fed, and use the games room, which has a snooker table and dartboard. A good family room (with figured walnut suite and shapely bevelled mirrors) has books, television and games; also a particularly good bath- and shower-room. There is a second dining-room (with kitchen) reserved for those who want to bring in their own food, a utility room, and an attractive garden.

All rooms are high and light, kept in immaculate condition by Gladys Lee, with far views through their large sash windows. Fine architectural details, including marble fireplaces, are complemented by pink velvet wing chairs or others in William Morris covers.

Readers' comments: Lovely, friendly people. Amazing attention to detail – three kinds of marmalade, and even the shower is computerized! Quite entranced: I defy anyone to better it. Bright and cheerful (a lot like the hostess); extremely good value.

V

GRAFTON VILLA FARM

C(5) PT

Grafton, Hereford & Worcester, HR2 8ED   Tel: 01432 268689
South of Hereford. On A49 from Hereford to Ross-on-Wye.

3 Bedrooms. £19–£20 (less for 3 nights or more). Bargain breaks. All have some or all of the following: own bath/shower/toilet; TV. No smoking.
Dinner (by arrangement). £15 for 4 courses and coffee, at 7pm. Vegetarian or other special diets if ordered. No smoking. **Light suppers** if ordered.
1 Sitting-room. With open fire, TV. No smoking.
Large garden
Closed from December to mid-February.

The 18th-century farmhouse, set well back from the road, is furnished with antiques and well-chosen fabrics. Each bedroom is named after the woodland of which it has a view (Aconbury, Dinedor, Haywood), for the panoramic scenery in every direction is one of the attractions of staying here. The pretty family room also overlooks the farmyard with its free-ranging chickens and ducks – sometimes foals too. Bath- and shower-rooms are good; the little sitting-room snug, its velvet chairs grouped around the fire. The sunny dining-room looks onto patio and garden from which come vegetables for the table.

When she is able to serve dinner, Jennie Layton's portions are generous. Meals often feature cider soup, chicken breasts in tarragon sauce, and a hazelnut meringue gâteau with hot apricot sauce. Her vegetables are imaginatively prepared. As well as conventional breakfast choices, she may offer you fruit compote, poached haddock and croissants.

The house is close to the cathedral city of Hereford and within a few miles there are other historic towns such as Ledbury, Ross-on-Wye and Hay-on-Wye ('book city').

THE HAVEN

CDMPTS

Hardwicke, Hereford & Worcester, HR3 5TA   Tel/Fax: 01497 831254
West of Hereford. Nearest main road: A438 from Hereford to Brecon.

6 Bedrooms. £20 **to readers of this book**–£26.50 (less for 4 nights or more). All have some or all of the following: own bath/shower/toilet; TV. No smoking.
Dinner (by arrangement). £13 for 3 courses and coffee, at 7.30pm. Vegetarian or other special diets if ordered. Wine available. No smoking. **Light suppers** if ordered.
2 Sitting-rooms. With open fire, piano. No smoking in one. Bar.
Large garden
Closed from December to February.

Kilvert, a frequent visitor here when it was a vicarage, wrote in his now famous diary that paintings done by the vicar's wife were auctioned – but her flowers and birds still adorn one of the doors.

There is a ground-floor bedroom (with bathroom) equipped to suit disabled people – even a wheelchair for use under the shower. Janet Robinson has stencilled the walls with a waterlily pattern to match the Liberty fabrics used in the furnishings.

In every room her flair for decoration is evident. One bathroom (raspberry and gold, with sunken bath, bidet and two basins) is not so much a bathroom as an event.

Meals are unusually imaginative: scrambled eggs with rosemary and sesame toast might be followed by chicken with pink grapefruit, and then red fruit mallows.

Readers' comments: Exceptional, have booked to go again. Kind and genuine hospitality. Very comfortable; food lovely. Very thoughtful, cooking outstanding. First-class room, food excellent. Friendly and stimulating company.

V

HERMITAGE MANOR

C(12) PT

Canon Pyon, Hereford & Worcester, HR4 8NR   Tel/Fax: 01432 760317
North-west of Hereford. Nearest main road: A4110 from Hereford towards Knighton.

3 Bedrooms. £20–£25. All have own bath/shower/toilet; TV. No smoking.
2 Sitting-rooms. With open fire/stove, piano. No smoking.
Large garden
Closed from December to February.

An *escalier d'honneur* sweeps grandly up to the front door which opens into a room of baronial splendour, its ceiling decorated with Tudor roses and strapwork, motifs which are repeated on the oak-panelled walls. Through stone-mullioned bay windows are some of the finest views from any house in this book. There is also a very lovely music room (damask walls and velvet chairs are in soft blue; the limewood fireplace has carved garlands).

The bedrooms, and their bathrooms, are of the highest standard and very large. No. 4 has a view of a hillside spring flowing through stepped pools of pinkish limestone (from a quarry in the area) which Shirley Hickling created when she was converting this exceptional house. She and her partner Bert Morgan serve bed-and-breakfast only – but there are good inns nearby, and Hereford is only 10 minutes away. (Croquet and bowls in the garden.)

Readers' comments: Magnificent view, magnificent bedrooms. So outstanding that we stayed several times this year and last. So pleased by house and view we stayed longer. Fantastic, delightful host and hostess. The equal of 4-star hotels. Probably the best b & b.

HIGHFIELD

PT S

Ivington Road, Leominster, Hereford & Worcester, HR6 8QD   Tel: 01568 613216

Nearest main road: A44 from Worcester to Leominster.

3 Bedrooms. £17.50–£19 (less for 5 nights or more). All have some or all of the following: own bath/shower/toilet. No smoking.

Dinner. £12 for 3 courses and coffee, at 7–7.30pm or when requested. Vegetarian or other special diets if ordered. Wine available. No smoking. **Light suppers** if ordered.

2 Sitting-rooms. With open fire, TV. No smoking in one.

Large garden

The big comfortable house, built in Edwardian times, stands among fields just outside the old market town of Leominster. Twin sisters Catherine and Marguerite Fothergill have furnished it handsomely – Chippendale-style chairs in the dining-room, for instance, scalloped pink tablemats and napkins, William Morris armchairs.

Not only are dinners very special but breakfasts too can be memorable – with such options as home-made brioches, fishcakes, kedgeree, home-cooked ham.

For other meals, residents can take the house menu or (after their first night) can choose a gourmet one which might include Marsala chicken-liver puffs; cider-baked gammon with orange sauce; profiteroles or pear pie with brandy cream to finish.

Readers' comments: Cooking, service and friendliness made my stay seem like a house party. Excellent food and attention. Ideal. Everything perfect. Evening meal splendid.

HUNTHOUSE FARM

C(8) D

Frith Common, Tenbury Wells, Hereford & Worcester, WR15 8JY

Tel/ Fax: 01299 832277

West of Bewdley. Nearest main road: A456 from Tenbury Wells to Bewdley.

3 Bedrooms. £18. Bargain breaks. All have some or all of the following: own bath/shower/toilet. No smoking.

1 Sitting-room. With stove, TV.

Large garden

Closed from mid-December to end of January.

In this part of England, very fine, old timbered houses are a characteristic sight – evidence of agricultural wealth in centuries past. This 16th-century house is typical: inside, antiques complement the oak beams and big fireplaces (in front of which Jane Keel will offer you tea and home-made cake when you arrive); and outside is rural peace with fine views on all sides – the Clee Hills in one direction, the Teme Valley in the other. There are horses and sheep on the farm lands. Bedrooms are trim and freshly decorated, the dining-room spacious. It's said that Elizabeth I once stayed here on her way to Wales.

There are innumerable good walks in this hilly northern part of Worcestershire, particularly in Wyre Forest, and plenty of 'sights' to visit – such as Witley Court (with its exceptional baroque church), the Elgar Museum (his house is at Lower Brockhampton), the gardens of Burford House and several National Trust properties.

Readers' comments: Splendid establishment, breakfasts superb, stunning views.

LINDEN HOUSE

C(8) PT X

14 Church Street, Ross-on-Wye, Hereford & Worcester, HR9 5HN
Tel/Fax: 01989 565373
Nearest main road: A40 from Gloucester to Monmouth (and M50, junction 4).

6 Bedrooms. £20–£24. Some have all of the following: own shower/toilet; TV. No smoking.
Small garden

Although close to the central market square of this historic town, the guest-house is in a quiet street opposite the church. It was built in 1680 but its façade was altered in the 18th century. At every sash window there is a window-box ablaze with flowers during summer.

Indoors, Clare O'Reilly has stencilled the bedroom walls. Some of the rooms are small (and there is no sitting-room) but all are pretty, and there are four with an attractive view of the old churchyard. Most rooms have period beds.

Much is home-made, such as the marmalades and jams at breakfast. A vegetarian cooked breakfast is also available.

The old market town of Ross is ideally placed for touring some of the best parts of England and Wales, midway in a scenic corridor between Hereford and Chepstow.

MELLINGTON HOUSE

C PT

Broad Street, Weobley, Hereford & Worcester, HR4 8SA   Tel: 01544 318537
North-west of Hereford. Nearest main road: A4112.

3 Bedrooms. £18–£22 (less for 4 nights or more). Bargain breaks. All have some or all of the following: own bath/shower/toilet; TV. No smoking.
Dinner (by arrangement). £12 for 3 courses and coffee, at 7.30pm (not weekends). Vegetarian or other special diets if ordered. **Light suppers** if ordered.
1 Sitting-room. With open fire, TV, piano. No smoking.
Large garden

Although Mellington House has a front in Queen Anne style, its real age is revealed at the back where the original mediaeval half-timbering is still exposed.

Ann Saunders has furnished the house very pleasantly (for instance, brass beds and wild-flower duvets), the sitting-room is large and comfortable, and there is a downstairs bedroom which Ann (a physiotherapist) provides for people who have mobility problems. The dining-room opens onto a large, old, walled garden where, on sunny mornings, she serves breakfast.

A typical meal: melon, roast beef with garden vegetables, home-made cheesecake.

Readers' comments: Beautiful surroundings. Delicious dinners. Could not have been made more welcome. Spacious accommodation. Warm and friendly. Everything done to make us comfortable. Such good service. Outstanding.

V

OLD MILL

CDMPTSX

Hoarwithy, Hereford & Worcester, HR2 6QH   Tel: 01432 840602
North-west of Ross-on-Wye. Nearest main road: A49 from Hereford to Ross-on-Wye
(and M50, junction 4).

7 Bedrooms. £16–£19 (less for 6 nights or more). Bargain breaks. Some have some or all of the following: own bath/shower/toilet. No smoking.
Dinner. £10 for 3 courses and coffee, at 7pm. Vegetarian or other special diets if ordered. No smoking. **Light suppers** if ordered.
1 Sitting-room. With open fire, TV. No smoking.
Large garden

Picturesque Hoarwithy, on the River Wye, has not only an exceptional Italianate church, with much use of marble, porphyry and other exotic materials, but also a good guest-house in this 18th-century building. The mill-race flows through the garden, clematis and roses grow up the front of the cream-painted house. Beyond a tiled and stone-walled hall is a beamed sitting-room with woodstove and a dining-room of scarlet-clothed tables (a typical meal: melon-and-prawn cocktail, chicken casserole, chocolate roulade). Carol Probert has furnished the bedrooms in cottage style.

Visitors come to this area not only for the surrounding scenery but to go antique-hunting in Ross-on-Wye and to see the 'lost streets' museum (old shops preserved and re-erected). A trip to Symonds Yat is a 'must': around the foot of this rock, 500 feet high, the great River Wye makes a loop that almost turns it into an island and in every direction are superb views of river, wooded slopes and fields.

Readers' comments: Hospitable and helpful. Excellent accommodation. Made to feel very much at home, food excellent. Friendly welcome, picturesque building, pleasant outlook, dinners imaginative. A lovely room; friendly hospitality.

OLD PARSONAGE FARMHOUSE

D

Hanley Castle, Hereford & Worcester, WR8 0BU   Tel: 01684 310124
South-east of Great Malvern. Nearest main road: A38 from Worcester to Tewkesbury
(also M5, junctions 7/8; and M50, junction 1).

rear view

3 Bedrooms. £20–£24.50 (less for 7 nights or 3 nights mid-week **to readers of this book only**). All have own bath/toilet. No smoking.
Dinner. £15.40 for 4 courses and coffee, at 7.30pm. Vegetarian or other special diets if ordered. Wine available. No smoking. **Light suppers.**
2 Sitting-rooms. With open fire, TV. No smoking in one.
Large garden

It is not just the surrounding views of the Malvern Hills or the handsome 18th-century house of mellow brick which makes this worth seeking out: Ann Addison has a flair for both cookery and interior decoration, while Tony is a wine expert.

You enter the house via a vaulted entrance hall, then through double doors into the sandalwood sitting-room. On the right is the pale sea-green drawing-room with its arched Georgian windows and marble Adam fireplace. The sunflower-yellow dining-room has the original brick hearth and bread oven. Upstairs are elegant bedrooms.

A typical meal: mushrooms and herbs in puff pastry; chicken breasts with prawns in cream and brandy; bramble mousse; cheeses.

Readers' comments: Extremely comfortable. High standard of imaginative food. Superb standards and unrivalled personal service. Lovely, large bedroom. Very friendly. Most welcoming and comfortable. Skills in every department quite exceptional.

OLD RECTORY

C PT

Byford, Hereford & Worcester, HR4 7LD   Tel: 01981 590218 (Fax: 01981 590499)
West of Hereford. Nearest main road: A438 from Hereford to Brecon.

3 Bedrooms. £20 (less for 3 nights or more). All have own bath/shower/toilet; TV. No smoking.
Dinner (by arrangement). £13 for 3 courses and coffee, at 7pm. Vegetarian or other special diets if ordered. No smoking. **Light suppers** if ordered.
1 Sitting-room. No smoking.
Large garden
Closed from December to February.

An enormous cedar of Lebanon dominates the garden outside the Rectory, a handsome brick house which, though built in 1830, is Georgian in style – having big, well-proportioned rooms and great sash windows which make the most of the very fine views of hills and church. Audrey Mayson and her husband have put a great deal of loving care not only into the restoration of the big house (recently adding Victorian-style bathrooms) but also the landscaping of the formerly neglected garden. The house is run in an informal, caring way.

The sitting/dining-room has pale green walls, deep pine-shuttered windows, pine-panelled doors, and their collection of unusual Escher pictures.

For dinner Audrey serves such dishes as caesar salad, almond chicken, and hazelnut meringue. Local crafts are on display.

Readers' comments: Very friendly, relaxed and roomy. Good food. Outstanding.

OLD RECTORY

D PT S

Ewyas Harold, Hereford & Worcester, HR2 0EY   Tel/Fax: 01981 240498
South-west of Hereford. Nearest main road: A465 from Hereford to Abergavenny.

2 Bedrooms. £18–£20 (less for 2 nights or more). Bargain breaks. Both have some or all of the following: own bath/toilet; TV. No smoking.
Dinner (by arrangement). £11 for 3 courses and coffee, at 7pm. Vegetarian or other special diets if ordered. No smoking. **Light suppers** if ordered.
1 Sitting-room. With open fire, piano. No smoking.
Large garden

Close to the Welsh border, Ewyas Harold tells of its early history in its name. Once this whole region was part of the Welsh province of Ewyas. Before the Normans came, however, Harold – Earl of Hereford and Edward the Confessor's successor – made a foray into this area and seized much of its territory. The present inhabitants of the Georgian Old Rectory can trace their roots to that period, for there were Juckes who came over with William the Conqueror.

Jenny and Chrix, previously Cotswold farmers, have an elegantly furnished home, sporting prints hanging alongside portraits of Jenny's Royalist ancestors. Bedrooms are stylish and neat. The dining-room, with antique furniture, has French doors leading onto the secluded garden where there is a small summer-house on rotating runners to follow the sun's course, and common land beyond. Guests may relax in the shuttered sitting-room after an evening meal which might comprise leek and potato soup, gammon with ratatouille and potatoes dauphinoise, and apple and apricot tart.

Equidistant from Hereford, Hay-on-Wye and Abergavenny, this is an area with ample country pursuits, as well as arts festivals in the late spring and summer months.

V

ORCHARD FARMHOUSE

D PT S

Mordiford, Hereford & Worcester, HR1 4EJ   Tel: 01432 870253
South-east of Hereford. Nearest main road: A438 from Hereford to Ledbury.

3 Bedrooms. £16.50–£18 (less for 4 nights or more). Bargain breaks. One has own bath/toilet; views of river (two). No smoking.
Dinner (by arrangement). £11.50 for 3 courses and coffee, at 7pm. Vegetarian or other special diets if ordered. Wine available. No smoking. **Light suppers** if ordered.
2 Sitting-rooms. With open fire, TV. No smoking. Bar.
Large garden

Country antiques and Victorian china decorate this 17th-century house of reddish stone walls, inglenooks, flagged floors and beams. An old Norwegian stove (decorated with reindeer) warms the sitting-room. Pink and pine bedrooms with wicker armchairs have high ceilings and nice bathrooms; the dining-room has rush chairs and a dresser with more china dishes. Beyond woods at the back, the Black Mountains rise high. You may spot deer, foxes and even badgers; kestrels and buzzards; cowslips and violets – for the house is in an Area of Special Scientific Interest within the Wye Valley, itself an Area of Outstanding Natural Beauty.

Fishing can be arranged on the Wye, the Lugg or the Frome (all within a mile); guided walking holidays are available, and Ken James also runs driving courses.

Angela specializes in good farmhouse cooking. Dinner might comprise home-made leek and potato soup, lamb cooked in cider, honey and rosemary, and home-made apple pie, for example. Bread rolls are home-made; most produce is local.

V

ST ELISABETH'S COTTAGE

D S X

Woodman Lane, Clent, Hereford & Worcester, DY9 9PX   Tel: 01562 883883
East of Kidderminster. Nearest main road: A456 from Kidderminster to Birmingham (and M5, junctions 3/4).

3 Bedrooms. £20–£23 (less for 3 nights or more.) Bargain breaks. All have some or all of the following: own bath/shower/toilet; TV. No smoking.
Dinner (by arrangement). £12 for 3 courses and coffee, at variable times. Wine available. No smoking.
Light suppers if ordered.
1 Sitting-room. With open fire, TV. No smoking.
Large garden

The 18th-century cottage has been much extended over the years and is now quite a large house, surrounded by a particularly beautiful garden. There is a willow-fringed pool which attracts herons, shrubs, a big sloping lawn, summer-house and swimming-pool.

Sheila Blankstone has furnished her home elegantly with, for instance, pink chintz and a fine inlaid walnut table and cabinet in one of the bedrooms. Huge picture-windows make the most of garden views. In addition to the large sitting-room there is a sun-room and a small 'snug'. Some visitors will appreciate having their own entrance to their bedroom, and the choice of continental breakfast in their room or a cooked breakfast in the dining-room. Everywhere are Sheila's lovely flower arrangements. She will sometimes do dinners, such as melon, roast lamb, cheese and fruit – or visitors may use her kitchen. Vegetables are grown in the garden. Central Birmingham is only 20 minutes away.

Readers' comments: Bedroom was the largest and most elegant we have ever stayed in. Made most welcome.

V

STONE HOUSE FARM

Tillington, Hereford & Worcester, HR4 8LF Tel: 01432 760631
North-west of Hereford. Nearest main road: A4110 from Hereford towards Leominster.

C D PT S X

3 Bedrooms. £16–£16.50 (less for 3 nights or more). Bargain breaks. One has own bath/shower/toilet. No smoking.
Dinner. £11.50 for 4 courses and coffee, at times to suit guests. Vegetarian or other special diets if ordered. Wine available. No smoking. **Light suppers** if ordered.
2 Sitting-rooms. With open fire/stove, TV, piano. No smoking in one.
Garden

Judy Seaborne's very good home cooking is the main attraction of Stone House Farm. The setting is very peaceful, with fine views, and children in particular enjoy spring visits when there are lambs, calves and foals to be seen. A typical meal: home-made soup, a roast, fruit pie – served from Royal Worcester dishes, in a dining-room with log stove. (Sunday lunch is also available by arrangement.) Made of solid stone, the house is well away from any road, and has fine greenery beyond its small orchard. There is an old pump in the front garden.

Nearby are Hereford and its cathedral; Hay-on-Wye for secondhand bookshops; the lovely River Wye with footpaths alongside. Many visitors, with 'The Black-and-White Village Trail' in hand, motor from one picturesque village to the next.

Readers' comments: Well fed and received with great friendliness. Food of high quality and ample. Most welcoming; excellent cook. A real farmhouse experience.

V

TARN

Long Bank, Bewdley, Hereford & Worcester, DY12 2QT Tel: 01299 402243
West of Kidderminster. Off A456 from Kidderminster to Tenbury Wells.

D PT

4 Bedrooms. £19–£22 (less for 3 nights or more). No smoking.
1 Sitting-room. With TV, piano. No smoking.
Large garden
Closed in December and January.

Until 1923, two adjacent workers' cottages stood on this site close to the Georgian town of Bewdley; then they were knocked into one and built around, and some 50 years later Topsy Beves and her family completed the transformation into the gracious red-brick house Tarn is today. It takes quite a leap of the imagination to realize that a century ago two families of six children grew up in an area the size of the present kitchen.

Having approached the house down a long winding drive, one enters through the slate-floored hall, off which lies a magnificent split-level library, complete with a Pleyel grand and a square piano. Cork-tiled floors are spread with fine old rugs; Liberty fabrics cover comfortable chairs from which to look out at Topsy's magnificent garden. Glass doors from the dining-room (with very pretty chandelier) open onto a terrace with fig tree and rambling vine – a summer breakfast here is a memorable event. Upstairs are four bedrooms (two are singles) furnished in a light, practical style; and a number of bath- and shower-rooms.

UPPER BUCKTON

C X

Leintwardine, Hereford & Worcester, SY7 0JU Tel: 01547 540634
West of Ludlow. Nearest main road: A4113 from Knighton towards Ludlow.

3 Bedrooms. £20–£25 **to readers of this book** (less for 3 nights or more). Bargain breaks. All have own bath/shower/toilet; views of river. No smoking.
Dinner. £16 for 4 courses and coffee, at 7pm. Vegetarian or other special diets if ordered. Wine available. No smoking. **Light suppers** if ordered (for late arrivals).
1 Sitting-room. With open fire, TV. No smoking.
Large garden

Yvonne Lloyd is an accomplished cook, serving such starters as bananas and bacon with curry sauce or stuffed mushrooms; then roasts, salmon, or chicken with orange and almonds; vacherins or chocolate roulade. It is largely her reputation for good food which brings visitors here – that, and the peace and quiet of this 18th-century house (the heart of a 300-acre sheep and cereal farm) in which antiques furnish the comfortable rooms.

Yvonne has a decorative touch, with a taste for ribbon-and-posy fabrics in one room, poppies in another, for instance. All the frilled or pleated valances are made by her.

Outside is a verandah on which to sit with pre-dinner drink or after-dinner coffee to enjoy the view towards the high ridge of the Wigmore Rolls. A granary has been equipped with table tennis, darts and snooker; there are also a croquet lawn and other games.

Readers' comments: Outstanding location. Marvellous hosts, lovely house, food excellent. Warm, attractive rooms, we felt completely at home. Could not have been more warmly and sensitively welcomed. Super retreat for jaded townies. Bedrooms delightful; most welcoming.

UPPER ELMORES END FARM

C(7)

Linley Green Road, Whitbourne, Hereford & Worcester, WR6 5RE Tel: 01886 821245
West of Worcester. Nearest main road: A44 from Worcester to Leominster.

3 Bedrooms. £16.50–£18. Bargain breaks. One has own shower/toilet. No smoking.
Dinner (by arrangement). £11.50 for 4 courses and coffee, at 6.30pm. Vegetarian or other special diets if ordered. No smoking.
1 Sitting-room. With stove, TV. No smoking.
50 acres of farmland

The foundations of Margaret and George Simpson's handsome black-and-white farmhouse date back to the 13th century, but most of the present house was rebuilt in the 16th, with beamed ceilings (unusually high for the period), uneven floors and, in the dining-room, a particularly wide board-and-latch door to allow ingress of hefty furnishings. The sitting-room boasts a magnificent japanned fire-surround brought from Pembridge Court; lavish sofas and chairs are upholstered in gorgeous fabrics. Bedrooms are roomy and comfortable, with views of the farm (where sheep and cattle are reared) and countryside; one has a fine walnut bedhead, another a beamed shower-room. There is much to see: stone sinks colourfully planted up around the old pump in the yard; and an area of ancient woodland (best seen at bluebell-time) to which guests can walk over the farm's land.

For dinner, everything is home-made: soup or salmon mousse, perhaps, followed by steak-and-kidney pie or a roast, and apple pie.

Readers' comments: Rooms are spacious, meals excellent, and the whole atmosphere is one of relaxation. A delightful family; extremely comfortable; very enjoyable home cooking and a most friendly and welcoming atmosphere.

VAULD FARMHOUSE

Vauld, Hereford & Worcester, HR1 3HA   Tel: 01568 797898
North of Hereford. Nearest main road: A49 from Hereford to Leominster.

C(12) **PT X**

4 Bedrooms. £20–£27.50 (less for 3 nights or more). Bargain breaks. All have some or all of the following: own bath/shower/toilet; TV.
Dinner (by arrangement). £16.50 for 4 courses and coffee, at 7.30pm (not Sundays). No smoking. **Light suppers** if ordered.
Sitting-rooms: see text.
Large garden

'Sleepy hollow', the locals call this area where the ancient farmhouse lies hidden, its creamy, black-timbered walls lopsided with age (it was built in 1510). One steps through the front door into a great room with stone-slabbed floor, half-timbered walls, log fire and colossal beams overhead.

Those who book the granary suite (which has its own stone staircase from outside) have a private sitting-room, with deep velvet armchairs, bathroom and a choice of bedrooms (one a gallery). Other visitors may prefer the ground-floor oak room with four-poster (this, too, has its own entrance and shower-room). The house is well-endowed with private sitting-areas.

Jean Bengry will prepare dinners using much local produce, for this is an area of fruit-farms. A typical menu: stuffed mushrooms, duck breasts, and apple and hazelnut tart.

Readers' comments: None of us wanted to leave. Nothing was too much trouble. Made us completely at home. A superb break. What a wonderful place! The food was a treat. Enchanting. Our fourth visit, always excellent. Wonderful hostess; attractively decorated.

WINDRUSH

Little Comberton, Hereford & Worcester, WR10 3EG   Tel: 01386 710284
West of Evesham. Nearest main road: A44 from Evesham toWorcester.

C(2) **S**

2 Bedrooms. £13 (less for 5 nights or more). No smoking.
1 Sitting-room. With TV. No smoking.
Small garden
Closed in December and January.

At Windrush, two thatched 17th-century cottages have been combined as one, with a particularly pretty garden created around them. Rooms are low-beamed, and the inexpensive little bedrooms furnished in appropriately cottagey style. Altogether, a really 'old world' effect. Bed-and-breakfast only, but there is good food to be had at the Mill (Elmley Castle) or the Fox & Hounds (Bredon).

From here one can drive to the fruitful Vale of Evesham (loveliest in spring), high Bredon Hill ringed by pretty villages, Tewkesbury to see the abbey, historic Evesham for boat trips on the Avon, Pershore (abbey church and 18th-century houses), or little Ripple with old houses and quaint carvings in the church.

Westward lie the Malvern Hills, with stupendous views from the Herefordshire Beacon (over 1100 feet high). Worcester has its cathedral, Charles II's headquarters in the Civil War (the Commandery), Royal Worcester porcelain (museum, factory and shop) and various good shops.

Readers' comments: Beautifully preserved; garden a joy. A gem of a find. Mrs Lewis is charming and friendly. Warm welcome and hospitality.

HERTFORDSHIRE

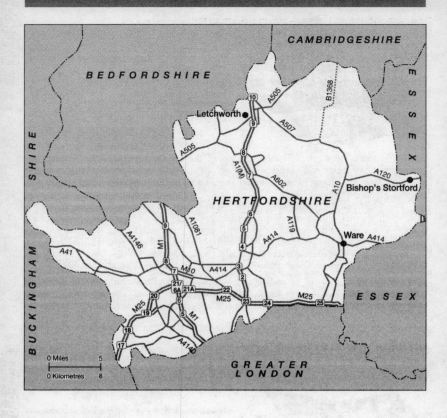

MILLER'S COTTAGE

D PT S

Pig Lane, Bishop's Stortford, Hertfordshire, CM22 7PA Tel: 01279 503487
(Fax: 01279 465378)
Nearest main road: A1184 from Bishop's Stortford towards Ware.

2 Bedrooms. £19.50 (less for 2 nights or more). Both have own shower/toilet; TV.
Dinner (by arrangement). £12 for 3 courses and coffee, at times to suit guests. Vegetarian meals if ordered. No smoking. **Light suppers** if ordered.
Large garden

Just past a lock where colourful narrow-boats cluster and a once-active watermill still stands, a narrow track leads to this picturesque thatched cottage, 450 years old. Outside it are an old pump, a fig tree, and a paved terrace brimming with petunias and sweet peas around its sundial. Chickens wander the lawns, beyond which lie fields.

The bedrooms, simply furnished, are in an annexe with its own entrance.

Catherine Cook provides meals (such as soup, casserole, and home-made ice cream or pudding) only sometimes, but can recommend local inns and restaurants.

Bishop's Stortford, an old town of pargeted (decoratively plastered) and half-timbered houses, is on the River Stort, which is flanked by attractive gardens. London is within easy reach and there are an exceptional number of mansions to visit in the vicinity.

The house is very convenient for Stansted Airport.

SCHOOL HOUSE

Newnham, Hertfordshire, SG7 5LA Tel: 01462 742815
North-east of Letchworth. Nearest main road: A1 from Baldock to Biggleswade.

2 Bedrooms. £20 (less for 4 nights or more). Bargain breaks. Both have some or all of the following: own bath/shower/toilet; TV. No smoking.
Dinner. £10 for 3 courses and coffee, at 7–8.30pm. Vegetarian or other special diets if ordered. Wine available. No smoking. **Light suppers** if ordered.
1 Sitting-room. With open fire, TV. No smoking.
Large garden
Closed from early December to mid-January.

Farrs have farmed here for generations; but this house had different beginnings, being first a village school – hence the bell high up on the peach-coloured façade, above a porch now covered in roses – and then a shooting-lodge. All around are fields and deep peace.

Trish Farr has an eye for striking colours, and every room seems to sing – with walls of brilliant viridian or coral, raspberry or mint. There are such distinctive touches as butterfly tiles in a fireplace, a budgerigar-patterned bedspread, and unusual antiques or junk-shop finds.

As she has four young children, she serves only simple meals (like chicken Kiev and fruit fool) and breakfast, sometimes eaten on the terrace; but there are lots of inns with good food, particularly in nearby Ashwell – famous for its church, music festivals (every Christmas) and old houses. (The high-towered church has mediaeval graffiti – old sayings, a record of the Black Death in 1350, and even an important picture of St Paul's Cathedral before the Great Fire.)

Newnham's own church is 10th-century, with frescoes of St Christopher and a moat alongside, where trout are caught.

TIMBER HALL

D

Cold Christmas, Wadesmill, Hertfordshire, SG12 7SN   Tel: 01920 466086
(Fax: 01920 462739)
North of Ware. Nearest main road: A10 from Ware to Cambridge.

5 Bedrooms. £17.50–£20. Bargain breaks. Some have all of the following: own bath/toilet; TV. No smoking.
Dinner (by arrangement). £13.50 for 4 courses and coffee, at 8pm. Vegetarian or other special diets if ordered. No smoking. **Light suppers** if ordered.
1 Sitting-room. With open fire. No smoking.
Large garden

One steps straight into the raftered, mediaeval hall which gives this house its name. Beyond is a gracious sitting-room added much later, its many windows and French doors opening onto an attractive garden. The carpet and walls of soft green are a good background to interesting pictures and to the huge, oak court cupboard which has been in Angela Shand's family since it was made in 1604 (she is distantly related to the earls of Verulam, whose stately home nearby – Gorhambury House – is occasionally open to the public). All around the house are wide fields and complete tranquillity (even though London is half an hour away), a scene that can be enjoyed from any of the pleasant bedrooms.

Angela is a good cook of such candlelit meals as leek and prawn gratin, roast chicken (with a sauce of pine nuts and raisins), summer pudding and cheeses; fruit and vegetables come from the garden.

From here one can visit historic Stansted Mountfichet, the old market towns of Ware and Hertford, the Lea Valley (country park, boat trips), Hatfield House, St Albans and Cambridge. Golf courses abound, and Stansted Airport is handy.

For explanation of code letters and **V** symbol, see inside front cover.

Prices are per person sharing a room at the beginning of the year.

When writing to the authors, if you want a reply please enclose a stamped addressed envelope.

Major tourist attractions, such as Stratford-upon-Avon and Cambridge, can often be easily reached from houses in adjacent counties.

KENT

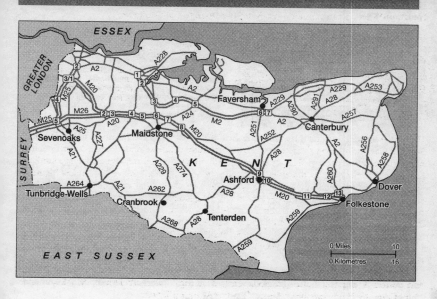

BARNFIELD FARM

Kent

C S

near Charing, Kent, TN27 0BN   Tel/Fax: 01233 712421
North-west of Ashford. Nearest main road: A20 from Maidstone to Ashford (and M20, junctions 8/9).

5 Bedrooms. £19–£21 (less for 7 nights or more). Some have views of river. No smoking.
Dinner. £12.50 for 3 courses and coffee, at 7pm. Vegetarian or special diets if ordered. Wine available. No smoking. **Light suppers** if ordered.
2 Sitting-rooms. With open fires, TV. No smoking.
Large garden with tennis court.

This historic farmhouse was built about the time of the Battle of Agincourt (1415). One steps into a large hall, where the oak framework of the house is exposed to view (draped with hop bines) and a cask holding shepherds' crooks stands in one corner – for outside are sheep pastures, with arable fields beyond. The dining-room has an exceptionally large inglenook, and an especially fine door made from a church chest.

Bedrooms are fresh and unpretentious, and some overlook the River Stour.

Phillada Pym serves such meals as egg mayonnaise, casseroled lamb cutlets, and chocolate mousse – loading a hot-tray on the sideboard for second helpings.

Readers' comments: Enjoyed our stay very much; a warm welcome. Unobtrusive but charming hostess. Delightful house and garden. Excellent meal. Nicely secluded position. A house full of treasures and perfectly beautiful. Delightful.

V

BETTMAN'S OAST *(illustrated on front cover)*

Kent

C M S

Hareplain Road, Biddenden, Kent, TN27 8LJ   Tel: 01580 291463
South-west of Ashford. Nearest main road: A262 from Biddenden towards Tunbridge Wells.

3 Bedrooms. £20–£24 (less for 3 nights or more). One has own shower/toilet; TV. No smoking.
Dinner (by arrangement). £15 for 3 courses and coffee, at 7–8pm. Vegetarian or other special diets if ordered. No smoking. **Light suppers** if ordered.
1 Sitting-room. With open fire, TV. No smoking.
Large garden

Just outside the beautiful village of Biddenden, is the 500-year-old Bettman's Oast, a converted black-and-white timbered oast house and barn where Janet and Roy Pickup live. Exposed beams and modern pine furniture characterize this clever conversion. The guests' sitting-room, where breakfast is taken, has a large inglenook fireplace. There are log fires in winter, when evening meals may be ordered (such as soup, beef chasseur, and fresh fruit salad); also a large selection of videos. Off the sitting-room, the family room, with cottage-style furnishings and domed ceiling, has an en suite shower-room. Other rooms are decorated in pastel shades – one has a picture-window with views overlooking the lane and fields beyond.

Sissinghurst Castle and its world-famous gardens are close by, and in the picturesque market town of Cranbrook (with cathedral-like church) is the biggest working windmill in the country, built before the Battle of Waterloo.

V

Readers' comments: Well-cooked and plentiful breakfast. Best ever shower.

BOWER FARMHOUSE

Bossingham Road, Stelling Minnis, Kent, CT4 6BB   Tel: 01227 709430
South of Canterbury. Nearest main road: A2 from Dover towards Canterbury.

CDPTS

2 Bedrooms. £19.50. (less for 7 nights or more). Both have own bath/shower/toilet.
1 Sitting-room. With open fire, TV, piano.
Small garden

This 300-year-old house with exposed oak beams and central staircase was in Victorian times a small school. It is now the home of Nick Hunt, a secondary school head, his wife Anne, a part-time teacher in a special-needs school, and their teenage daughters. There is a cosy sitting-room with old and modern watercolours, wing chairs and a chesterfield in warm reds, and a piano. The double bedroom has pastel striped and sprigged wallpaper and pretty patchwork bedspreads; the other twin room (also with its own bathroom) has peach curtains, fine walnut veneered furniture and headboards, and a gently sloping floor encouraging one bedwards! Home-made bread and eggs from the Hunts' own chickens are served at breakfast.

The Minnis or common land of 125 acres lies opposite the house; two nature reserves and a rural heritage centre are close by. Canterbury, the Shuttle terminal, Dover and Folkestone are only short drives away.

Reader's comments: Delightful house, charming hosts.

BRATTLE HOUSE

Watermill Bridges, Tenterden, Kent, TN30 6UL   Tel: 01580 763565
Nearest main road: A28 from Ashford to Hastings.

PTS

side view

4 Bedrooms. £19.50–£29 (less for 4 nights or more). Bargain breaks. All have some or all of the following: own bath/shower/toilet. No smoking.
Dinner. £18.50 for 4 courses and coffee, at 7.45pm. Vegetarian diets if ordered. No smoking. **Light suppers** if ordered.
1 Sitting-room. No smoking.
Large garden
Closed from late December to mid-January.

The tile-hung house where Nelson's daughter lived (parts of which date back to the 17th century) has great dignity – white marble fireplace from the 18th century; wide, panelled doors with handsome brass fittings; bay windows with leaded casements. The Rawlinsons are a painter and calligrapher, and their work hangs on the walls.

Bedrooms are equally handsome. There are two very large rooms at the front with window-seats, brick hearths and draped bedheads. Another is all roses and cream.

Breakfast and tea are served in a conservatory off the sitting-room. Maureen cooks such evening meals as sweet-sour cucumber, lamb with apricots and almonds, and chocolate roulade. The Rawlinsons usually dine with their guests.

Readers' comments: Elegant house in beautiful countryside. Delightful couple. Enjoyed every minute. Dinner up to Michelin-star standard. Absolutely beautiful. No amenity they do not extend. Gourmet food. Outstanding accommodation and service. Our best of all.

CATHEDRAL GATE HOTEL

36 Burgate, Canterbury, Kent, CT1 2HA   Tel: 01227 464381 (Fax: 01227 462800)
(M2, junction 7, is near.)

C D PT X

24 Bedrooms. £20–£36. Full breakfast extra from March. Bargain breaks. Some have some or all of the following: own bath/shower/toilet; TV; telephone; views of cathedral.
Dinner. £13 for 3 courses, at 7–9pm. Vegetarian or other special diets if ordered. Wine available. No smoking. **Light suppers.**
2 Sitting-rooms. With piano. Bar.

The cathedral has a great, sculpted, mediaeval gateway. Tucked beside it is a row of shops and restaurants, above part of which is this upstairs guest-house (which has direct access to the cathedral precincts), not luxurious but characterful. Bedrooms are reached via a maze of narrow corridors and creaking stairways. All are quiet; and some at the top have superlative views of the cathedral – floodlit at night (during summer).

When the small hotel was taken over by Caroline Jubber and her husband, they greatly improved most bedrooms while retaining ancient beams, leaded casements and bow windows. Breakfast (continental in summer, unless you pay extra) is brought to you in the small dining-room or in your bedroom. The hotel's locked carpark (for which there is a charge) is several minutes' walk away.

Readers' comments: Incredible situation. Very nice people. Location superb. Delicious breakfasts. We can't wait to return.

V

> **Months when houses are shown as closed are inclusive.**

> **'Bargain breaks' are usually out-of-season reductions for half-board stays of several nights.**

> **Some proprietors stipulate a minimum stay of two nights at weekends or peak seasons; or they will accept one-nighters only at short notice (that is, only if no lengthier booking has yet been made).**

> **To find the right accommodation in the right area at the right price, use an up-to-date edition of this book – revised every year. For an order form for the next edition (published in November), send a stamped addressed envelope with 'SOTBT 1999' in the top left-hand corner, to Explore Britain, Alston, Cumbria, CA9 3SL.**

DEAN COURT FARM

Challock Lane, Westwell, Kent, TN25 4NH   Tel: 01233 712924

North-west of Ashford. Nearest main road: A20 from Maidstone to Ashford (and M20, junction 9).

2 Bedrooms. £16–£18. One has own bath.
Dinner (by arrangement). £10 for 3 courses and coffee, at times to suit guests. Vegetarian or other special diets if ordered. Wine available. **Light suppers** if ordered.
1 Sitting-room. With open fire, TV.
Large garden

Among rolling hills with fine views is Dean Court Farm, a 200-acre sheep farm close to the Pilgrims' Way. The house's name is listed in Domesday Book, but the present building is 200 years old, with some early 20th-century additions – for example, the garden room, which has comfortable cane furniture and views over Eastwell Park, which the farm borders. Tony Lister, a chartered surveyor, and his wife Susan encourage an informal family atmosphere. They both have a good eye for pictures, which cover the walls. Accommodation is simple, with good-sized rooms. One has pink-striped walls, another exposed beams covered with rosettes from family successes in three-day eventing. There is a good walk around the farm perimeter and interesting wildlife. An evening meal may comprise chicken casserole, a fruity pudding, cheese, and a glass of wine.

For a scenic drive, go across the North Downs to the valley of the River Stour, taking in the Tudor village of Chilham and then on to Hastingleigh.

DRAYCOTT

Green Lane, Temple Ewell, Kent CT16 3AR   Tel: 01304 823060

North-west of Dover. Nearest main road: A2 from Dover towards Canterbury.

2 Bedrooms. £17.50 (less for 3 nights or more). Bargain breaks. One has own balcony. No smoking.
Dinner (by arrangement). £11.50 for 4 courses and coffee, at 6.30–7.30pm. Vegetarian or other special diets if ordered. Wine available. No smoking. **Light suppers.**
1 Sitting-room. With open fire, TV. No smoking.
Large garden
Closed from December to Easter.

After many years in the RAF, John Drover, and his wife Rosemary became hoteliers in Dover before they both retired to Draycott in Temple Ewell, a small village just outside the port. The Drovers have decorated this Victorian house with Laura Ashley prints and borders in keeping with the period, retaining original picture-rails and fireplaces. There is a small study area where guests may sit and read and also a sitting-room with television, both shared with the proprietors, as is the bathroom. One daughter is a paper conservator and has produced a beautifully leather-bound visitors' book for the house. Simple home cooking is provided, by arrangement, with fresh ingredients and home-made puddings. Guests may also relax in good weather in the pretty (but vertiginous!) terraced garden at the rear of the house.

This is a useful place to stay before or after a ferry-crossing to the continent – or as a base from which to explore the historic south Kent coast.

FISHPONDS FARMHOUSE

Brook, Kent, TN25 5PP   Tel: 01233 812398
East of Ashford. Nearest main road: A20 from Ashford to Folkestone (and M20, junction 10).

C D

2 Bedrooms. £16. Both have some or all of the following: own bath/shower/toilet; TV.
Large garden

Trust the map that Di Owen sends her guests when they book and, down winding country lanes, some three miles from Wye, you will eventually reach Fishponds Farmhouse: a 19th-century tile-hung and whitewashed building, originally two labourers' cottages. Standing in the Wye Downs Nature Reserve, the house has a large garden with banks down to a small spring-fed lake with waterfall – in previous times a sheep-dip. The grounds are home to a variety of wildlife including deer, foxes and badgers, and in the downstairs toilet you will find a constantly growing list (compiled by John, a much-travelled retired diplomat) of the numerous different birds seen here.

Two large bedrooms are prettily furnished, each with its bath- or shower-room: the twin in pink with quilted bedspreads, the double with dark pine bed and prints of 18th-century Jamaican scenes. Breakfast is taken in a beamed dining-room decorated with African artefacts reflecting the Owens' time spent in that continent.

At nearby Charing are remains of the archbishop's palace where Henry VIII stayed en route to the Field of the Cloth of Gold (1520), and from Charing Hill are views across the Weald.

FRITH FARM HOUSE

Otterden, Kent, ME13 0DD   Tel: 01795 890701 (Fax: 01795 890009)
South-west of Faversham. Nearest main road: A20 from Maidstone to Charing (and M2, junction 6).

3 Bedrooms. £19–£24 (less for 3 nights or more). **5% reduction for readers of this book.** All have some or all of the following: own shower/toilet; TV. No smoking.
Dinner (by arrangement). £18.50 for 4 courses and coffee, from 7pm. Vegetarian or other special diets if ordered. No smoking. **Light suppers** if ordered.
1 Sitting-room. With open fire. No smoking.
Large garden

Once, there were cherry orchards as far as the eye could see: now Frith has only six acres. (From their fruit Susan Chesterfield makes sorbets for her gourmet dinners.)

Those cherry trees also financed the building in 1820 of this very fine house. Maroon damask wallpapers and sofas are in keeping with its style. The bedrooms are beautifully decorated and very well equipped (one has a four-poster).

In a very lovely dining-room, fiddleback chairs and a collection of antique plates contrast with a bold geometrical Kazak print (Liberty's) used for the curtains, and with the white dishes of German bone china on which Susan serves such meals as avocado with taramasalata, sorbet, lamb steaks with capers, meringues glacés, and cheeses. Breakfast is served in the polygonal conservatory.

The house is so high up on the North Downs that its views across orchards and woods extend – in the case of one of the pretty bedrooms – as far as the Isle of Sheppey.

V   *Readers' comments:* Extremely helpful, beautiful home, delicious dinner.

THE GRANARY

Plumford Lane, Faversham, Kent, ME13 0DS   Tel: 01795 538416
South of Faversham. Nearest main road: A2 from Sittingbourne to Canterbury
(and M2, junction 6).

3 Bedrooms. £19.50–£21 (less for 4 nights or more).
All have some or all of the following: own
bath/shower/toilet; TV; balcony. No smoking.
Light suppers if ordered. No smoking.
1 Sitting-room. With TV. No smoking.
Large garden

Having taken early retirement, Alan Brightman, with his wife Annette, moved to this
converted oasthouse in a quiet byway in the midst of apple-orchard country. A comfortable
sitting-room, with exposed beams and richly coloured stripped pine floors, opens onto a
large balcony running the length of the house, where guests can sit in warm weather.
Rooms (all with own bathrooms) are boldly decorated in simple blues and whites. The
family room has a particularly spacious bathroom. The Brightmans are keen golfers and can
arrange for guests to play at the local Belmont course. Supper trays by arrangement, but
there is good local eating too.

Historic Faversham has a fine church and particularly interesting Heritage Centre
among its old houses.

Readers' comments: A delightful home. Everything we could hope for. The warmest welcome. Superb, ideal hosts.

HEATH HOUSE

Scords Lane, Toys Hill, Westerham, Kent, TN16 1QE   Tel: 01732 750631
South-west of Sevenoaks. Nearest main road: A25 from Sevenoaks to Reigate (and M25,
junction 6).

2 Bedrooms. £18.50–£20 (less for 4 nights or more).
Bargain breaks. One has own bath/shower/toilet. TV (in
both). No smoking.
Large garden

Octavia Hill, co-founder of the National Trust, lived near here – gardening, mapping the
innumerable footpaths needing preservation, and ultimately presenting to the Trust the top
of Toys Hill, which commands a superb view over the Weald of Kent.

It is over the scenery which she preserved that Heath House looks out, and from close by
is one of the footpaths to Ide Hill which she mapped – a very pretty walk.

Two hundred years ago, it was just a cottage for workers at Scords Farm but it has been
extended by Mike and Patricia Murkin's own hard work to make the lovely home it is
today. The original walls were built of Sevenoaks greenstone quarried in the garden and,
there being no more of this, they bought part of a demolished house made from it so that
the new wing should be indistinguishable from the old, with clematis and honeysuckle
climbing up both. Bedrooms have fresh, pale colour schemes. The sunny breakfast-room
opens onto a paved terrace, a lawn with seats, and a view across a pond towards Ashdown
Forest.

HEAVERS

C D

Chapel Street, Ryarsh, West Malling, Kent, ME19 5JU Tel/Fax: 01732 842074
West of Maidstone. Nearest main road: A228 from Tonbridge to Rochester (and M20, junction 4).

2 Bedrooms. £16–£18 (less for 7 nights or more). Bargain breaks. No smoking.
Dinner (by arrangement). £14 for 4 courses and coffee, at 7.30pm. Vegetarian or other special diets if ordered. Wine available. No smoking. **Light suppers** if ordered.
1 Sitting-room. With open fire, TV, piano. No smoking.
Large garden

Perched on a hilltop, this 17th-century red brick farmhouse with dormer windows in the roof and clematis around the porch is at the heart of a smallholding.

The cosy sitting-room has very comfortable armchairs grouped around the brick hearth (stacked with logs), which still has the old bread oven alongside.

Jean Edwards enjoys cooking a wide repertoire of dishes. She bakes her own bread; honey, eggs and lamb are home-produced.

Beamed bedrooms are small but prettily furnished. Through the windows are views of the Downs or of the garden which, even in winter, is colourful.

Readers' comments: Very good indeed. As charming as could be; convivial hosts; mouth-watering and plentiful food. Charming house, food delicious. Well informed, witty and helpful hosts. Gourmet dinners.

HILLBROOK HOUSE

C D M P T X

North Elham, near Canterbury, Kent, CT4 6UX Tel: 01303 840220
North-west of Folkestone. Nearest main road: M20, junction 12.

3 Bedrooms. £18–£20 (less for 3 nights or more). Bargain breaks. One has own bath/shower/toilet; TV. No smoking.
Dinner (by arrangement). £12 for 2 courses, wine and coffee, at 7.30pm. Vegetarian or other special diets if ordered. No smoking. **Light suppers** if ordered.
1 Sitting-room. With open fire, TV. No smoking.
Large garden

Families with young children are especially welcome at this large detached Victorian house. It is the home of Charlotte and Jeremy Sisk, she a BSc in home economics and former restaurateur, he an estate agent with an interest in a wine business. The house was almost a shell when they bought it, but they have worked hard to restore it, putting in old stripped-pine doors and a rather splendid Victorian fireplace and oak surround in the ground-floor family room, which has a very pretty bath/shower-room.

Breakfast is served in a dining-room with peach and blue fleur-de-lys patterned walls and Edwardian-style curtains, at a solid table of Mvule wood, brought back from Kenya. Evening meals are also eaten here, and, as you might expect, Charlotte is an accomplished cook with a wide repertoire; her recipes include Folkestone fish pie, Indonesian-style chicken with spices and coconut, and many French-based dishes.

HOATH HOUSE

Penshurst Road, Chiddingstone Hoath, Kent, TN8 7DB   Tel: 01342 850362
North-west of Tunbridge Wells. Nearest main road: A264 from Tunbridge Wells to
East Grinstead.

3 Bedrooms. £20–£25 (less for 2 nights or more). One has own bath/toilet; TV (in all). No smoking.
Dinner (by arrangement). £15 for 3 courses and coffee, at 8pm. Vegetarian dishes if ordered. No smoking. **Light suppers** if ordered.
1 Sitting-room. With stove, piano. No smoking.
Large garden
Closed from December to February.

Hoath House is a building of exceptional mediaeval interest which, starting as a simple hall house, has had wings and other additions built on through the centuries. The massive, chamfered beams of the sitting-room, its lattice-paned windows and the plastered walls where the hand-prints of the Tudor builders can still be seen, are impressive.

To reach the bedrooms one passes through passages with 18th-century ancestral portraits and other family heirlooms. A vast family bedroom has a sofa in the bay window. There is an enormous bathroom in 'thirties style. (The en suite bedroom is in a ground-floor annexe.)

Jane Streatfeild provides straightforward dinners: home-made soup or pâté; devilled chicken; fruit fool or pie. Fruit and vegetables come from the garden.

Readers' comments: Fascinating house. Helpful and welcoming. Wonderful, interesting house. Like stepping back into the first Elizabethan age. Stunning views. Could not have been kinder. Charming, very interesting. Quite an experience to stay here.

JESSOPS

Tonbridge Road, Bough Beech, Kent, TN8 7AU   Tel: 01892 870428
North-west of Tunbridge Wells. Nearest main road: A21 from Sevenoaks to Tonbridge
(and M25, junction 5).

3 Bedrooms. £18–£19.50 (less for 3 nights or more). Bargain breaks. Some have some or all of the following: own shower/toilet; TV. No smoking.
Light suppers if ordered. Vegetarian or other special diets if ordered. No smoking.
1 Sitting-room. With open fire, TV, piano. No smoking.
Large garden

In the scenic and fertile Kentish Weald is 15th-century Jessops, home of artist Frank Stark, whose landscapes line the walls. Every room has unusual antiques and other interesting finds from afar. There are beams and lattice windows, pot-plants and bouquets of dried flowers, a buttoned leather sofa and grand piano. Outside are a flowery garden and the Starks' hens, geese, ducks and dogs. Judith's excellent breakfasts include varied home-made breads, croissants and her own marmalade.

Lanes meander through the Wealden hills, among orchards and hop fields. This is one of the most fertile places in Europe, yet with no prairie-sized fields to spoil the scene: small is beautiful. Only the stately homes are of great size – and magnificence: Penshurst, Hever Castle, Knole and Ightham Mote, in particular. Villages and half-timbered farmhouses are picturesque. There's no fast traffic in the winding lanes; a delight to explore at blossom time (May). Westerham has Churchill's Tudor home.

V

MAPLEHURST MILL

M PT

Mill Lane, Frittenden, Kent, TN17 2DT   Tel/Fax: 01580 852203
North-east of Cranbrook. Nearest main road: A229 from Maidstone towards Hastings.

3 Bedrooms. £20–£35. All have some or all of the following: own bath/shower/toilet; TV; views of river. No smoking.
Dinner (by arrangement). £19 for 4 courses and coffee, at 7.45pm. Vegetarian or other special diets if ordered. Wine available. No smoking. **Light suppers** if ordered.
1 Sitting-room. With woodstove, piano. No smoking.
Large garden

'It was like the Marie Celeste,' said Kenneth Parker, describing this 18th-century mill when they took it over, with the miller's tools lying as he left them. It now has every up-to-date comfort, yet the ambience of the past has been vividly preserved. Through the entrance hall, one comes to a pleasant bedroom with a window right by the waterwheel and the mill-race flows under its floor. Everywhere are exposed beams, low doorways, white or pine-boarded walls, a tree-trunk that forms part of the structure, iron pillars or mechanisms and brick or cast-iron fireplaces. Each bedroom has different soft furnishings. In the grounds are a small vineyard, a heated swimming-pool, and a nature trail with over 70 species of birds.

Heather's meals are imaginative. For example: Sussex smokies (haddock) in a cheese and wine sauce followed by chicken breasts with a sauce made from avocados, sherry and cream, and then a home-made ice cream. Afterwards, one can relax either on the waterside terrace or in the huge and gracious sitting-room.

V   *Reader's comment:* Outstanding.

NUMBER TEN

C D M PT S X

Modest Corner, Southborough, Kent, TN4 0LS   Tel: 01892 522450
North of Tunbridge Wells. Nearest main road: A21 from Sevenoaks to Hastings.

3 Bedrooms. £18–£20 (less for 3 nights or more). Bargain breaks. All have TV.
Dinner. £10 for 3 courses and coffee, at 8pm. Vegetarian or other special diets if ordered. Wine available. No smoking. **Light suppers** if ordered.
Small garden

On a wooded hillside close to Tunbridge Wells is a hidden hamlet, well called Modest Corner. Here is the equally modest home of Dutch-born picture-framer Anneke Leemhuis. The ground-floor bedrooms are simple, furnished with pine and Laura Ashley wallpapers and fabrics; the bathroom is good. Meals (such as lamb with ratatouille, followed by trifle) are eaten in Anneke's kitchen. Visitors can explore the many footpaths in the surrounding countryside. The house is only five minutes from a station with fast trains to London.

Elegant Tunbridge Wells is all you expect of an 18th-century spa that once rivalled Bath. The famous 'Pantiles' is a colonnaded pedestrian precinct among attractive shops (you can taste the waters from the spring there) and close by is a fine 17th-century church dedicated to the martyr king, Charles I.

V   *Readers' comments:* Homely atmosphere, wonderful walks. Unequalled hospitality and helpfulness. I have stayed four times and am continually impressed.

OLD POST HOUSE

Fairseat, Kent, TN15 7LU   Tel: 01732 822444   C S

West of Maidstone. Nearest main road: A227 from Tonbridge to Gravesend (and M20, junction 2).

3 Bedrooms. £17.50. All have TV. No smoking.
Dinner (by arrangement). £12 for 3 courses and coffee, at times to suit guests. Vegetarian or other special diets if ordered. No smoking. **Light suppers** if ordered.
1 Sitting-room. With open fire/stove, TV. No smoking.
Small garden

'Stella Henden, postmistress/telephonist, lived here over 50 years . . . loved by all who knew her'. So runs the rather touching inscription on a plaque at the Old Post House, an 18th-century cottage, its walls hung with climbing clematis Montana. It is the home of Nevill Acheson-Gray, a solicitor and part-time antique dealer, and his wife Elizabeth. Breakfast as well as evening meals, to be ordered in advance, are taken in a light and airy double-aspect dining-room. (A typical meal: avocado, salmon mousse, and chocolate roulade.) Windows are hung with tapestry curtains and splendid antique tie-backs. Small bedrooms are decorated in cottage style. Guests may sit in the hallway-cum-sitting-room or on the small patio overlooking the pond.

Kent is a county rich in castles and mansions, its position between the capital and the Continent giving it a crucial place in historical events. In the immediate vicinity are Allington Castle, Aylesford Priory, Leeds Castle and Brands Hatch.

Readers' comments: Made very welcome. Excellent cooking.

PARKFIELD HOUSE

Hogben's Hill, Selling, Kent, ME13 9QU   Tel: 01227 752898   C S

South of Faversham. Nearest main road: A251 from Faversham to Ashford (and M2, junctions 6/7).

5 Bedrooms. £17.50 (less for 2 nights or more). No smoking.
Light suppers if ordered.
1 Sitting-room. With open fire, TV. No smoking.
Large garden

There were Hogbens on this hill in 1086 (they are named in the Domesday Book) and there still are! It is Mr and Mrs Hogben who own Parkfield, a largely modern house with a pretty garden, as well as the small joinery works alongside – John Hogben's principal activity. It is worth staying at Parkfield House simply to listen to him talk about Kentish ways and history (especially his stories of past Hogbens).

The house, built in 1820, had become run down until about 40 years ago when Mr Hogben renovated and extended it. Now it is immaculate and very comfortable. In the sitting-room are big, velvet armchairs in which to relax by a log fire. And if you want something special for breakfast, Mrs Hogben will get it.

Selling is in a very beautiful and tranquil part of Kent, well situated for touring.

Readers' comments: Excellent in all respects, exceptional hospitality. Excellent service, well cared for. Warm welcome. Spotless. Attractive bedroom.

RIPPLE FARM

C S

Crundale, Kent, CT4 7EB   Tel: 01227 730748

North-east of Ashford. Nearest main road: A28 from Ashford to Canterbury (and M20, junction 9).

rear view

2 Bedrooms. £17.50–£18.50 (less for 3 nights or more).
Light suppers if ordered. Vegetarian or other special diets if ordered. Wine available. No smoking.
1 Sitting-room. With log stove, TV, piano. No smoking.
Large garden
Closed from Christmas to end of January.

There is no formality at 15th-century Ripple Farm, where the Baurs grow organic produce. They are an artistic family: their own pictures grace the walls of the house. Hop bines or bunches of dried flowers hang from ceilings, floors are of polished boards, and there is much use of stripped pine. In each of the bedrooms there is a platform (plus ladder) for children's beds above their parents'. The bathroom is on the ground floor, along with the sitting/dining-room for guests. This is a simple room with shuttered windows, pyjama-stripe wallpaper and log stove. Outside are an 18th-century barn and three oast houses. Swimming-pool by arrangement.

It is, of course, the great cathedral which brings most visitors to nearby Canterbury. The ancient walled city still has many surviving mediaeval and Tudor buildings, old churches and inns, Roman remains, two theatres, and lovely shops in its small lanes. Popular Howlett's Zoo is also close by.

Book well ahead: many of these houses have few rooms. Do not expect dinner if you have not booked it or if you arrive late.

SISSINGHURST CASTLE FARM

Sissinghurst, Kent, TN17 2AB   Tel: 01580 712885 (Fax: 01580 712601)
East of Tunbridge Wells. Nearest main road: A262 from High Halden towards
Tunbridge Wells.

6 Bedrooms. £20–£26 (less for 3 nights or more).
Bargain breaks in winter to readers of this book.
Some have some or all of the following: own
bath/shower/toilet; TV. No smoking.
Light suppers by arrangement.
1 Sitting-room. With open fire, TV. No smoking.
Large garden

'Hydrangea petiolaris will grow under trees and ramble over an old stump', wrote Vita
Sackville-West to her tenant at the Castle Farm. James Stearns (grandson of that tenant,
who still farms here) treasures this note from one of England's most famous gardening
ladies, creator of the adjacent gardens at Sissinghurst Castle (now NT).

The farmhouse, which dates from 1855, was once a mansion inhabited by a substantial
family – hence the row of servants' bells which still survives, along with such period features
as panelled sash windows, fretted woodwork and the galleried staircase. Here hang two fine
paintings lent by Nigel Nicolson (son of Vita and Harold Nicolson) who still lives in a wing
of the castle. Furniture is a homely, pleasant mixture of old pieces; and one bedroom, with
windows on two sides, has a good view of the castle. (B & B only, but Pat Stearns will
provide light suppers if specially requested.)

Reader's comment: We enjoy the very homely atmosphere and friendliness.

SUNSHINE COTTAGE

The Green, Shepherdswell, Kent, CT15 7LQ   Tel: 01304 831359 or 831218
North-west of Dover. Nearest main road: A2 from Dover towards Canterbury
(also M2, junction 7; and M20, junction 13).

6 Bedrooms. £19–£21. All have some or all of the
following: own bath/shower/toilet. No smoking.
Dinner. £14 for 3 courses and coffee, at 7pm.
Vegetarian or other special diets if ordered. No smoking. **Light suppers** if ordered.
2 Sitting-rooms. With open fire, TV. No smoking.
Small garden

Neither shepherd nor well gave this pretty village its name: the Saxons knew it as Sibert's
Wold. Sunshine Cottage, built in 1635, is now the home of Barry and Lyn Popple.

One steps into a cosy sitting-room with shaggy, cocoa-coloured carpet and low beams, a
velvet sofa facing a brick inglenook that has logs piled high and hop bines draped across it.
In a kitchen that is open to view, Lyn cooks such meals as home-made soups, chops or
chicken, fruit salad or spotted dick. These are served in a dining-room where antique pine
is complemented by coir matting, dressers display antique plates, old pews and stickback
chairs surround tables laid with pretty china.

There is one ground-floor bedroom (with shower), decorated with Liberty fabrics.
Those upstairs vary in size and style; several have antique iron bedsteads and views of
village rooftops. Barry is an artist and some of his pictures are on the walls.

Readers' comments: Full of treasures. A relaxed cottage atmosphere. Made us very welcome.
Quite delightful.

VINE FARM   M

Waterman Quarter, Headcorn, Kent, TN27 9JJ   Tel: 01622 890203
(Fax: 01622 891819)
North-west of Tenterden. Nearest main road: A274 from Maidstone towards Tenterden
(and M20, junctions 8/9).

3 Bedrooms. £19–£26 (less for 7 nights or more). Bargain breaks. All have some of the following: own bath/shower/toilet; TV. No smoking.
Dinner (by arrangement). £17 for 4 courses and coffee, at 7pm. Vegetarian or other special diets if ordered. No smoking. **Light suppers** if ordered.
1 Sitting-room. With woodstove, TV. No smoking.
Large garden
Closed in late December.

Nothing could be more typical of Kent than this white weatherboarded farmhouse, originally the home of a Tudor yeoman. It stands in 50 acres of its own land, with ponds and flowerbeds (the Harmans are keen gardeners).

One enters through what was the big brick-floored kitchen, its ceiling low and beamed. This is now the guests' sitting-room, with Victorian armchairs of buttoned velvet and book-lined walls. Next door is the dining-room which has a huge inglenook with log stove and is similarly furnished with fine antiques and pretty chintz curtains. Here Jane Harman serves dinners such as pancakes stuffed with shrimps in a cream sauce, fillet of lamb with home-grown vegetables, chocolate roulade, and cheeses.

Bedrooms have antiques, chintz fabrics, and bedheads of brass curlicues or ladderback mahogany. There is one ground-floor room (with en suite bathroom).

Readers' comments: Absolutely delighted. Lovely house, super food, most charming hostess. Can't wait to go again.

WOODGATE   D PT S

Birling Road, Leybourne, West Malling, Kent, ME19 5HT   Tel: 01732 843201
West of Maidstone. Nearest main road: A228 from West Malling to Rochester
(and M20, junction 4).

3 Bedrooms. £20–£22. Bargain breaks. All have some or all of the following: own shower/toilet; TV. No smoking.
Dinner (by arrangement). £15 for 4 courses and coffee, up to 9pm. Vegetarian or other special diets if ordered. Wine available. No smoking. **Light suppers** if ordered.
2 Sitting-rooms. With open fire, TV. No smoking.
Large garden
Closed in January.

This old brick and tile-hung house – originally two woodcutters' cottages – is now the unusual home of Judy and Ken Ludlow, and the fascinating artefacts about the house testify to their many years of travel in Egypt and the Middle East.

Guest bedrooms are small but well decorated in a bold style. The main sitting-room (in gold) has scroll-ended and Knole sofas, Egyptian and Chinese *objets d'art*, and an intricately carved dark wood shutter from Bosnia. The large conservatory, where guests dine, has a big, beautifully polished table made from South African railway sleepers.

Judy's cooking is eclectic and inventive in style: sometimes with Middle-Eastern influences, at others traditionally English, with some Delia Smith recipes. The result might be roasted red peppers, Thai chicken, and bread-and-butter pudding.

Readers' comments: Never stayed in a more interesting house. Magnificent dining. More than value for money.

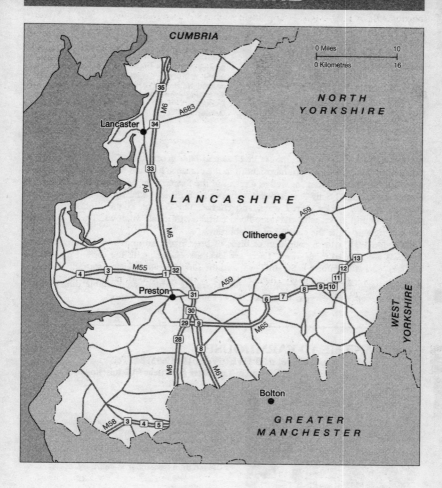

THE BOWER

C(12) **D PT X**

Yealand Conyers, Lancashire, LA5 9SF   Tel: 01524 734585
North of Lancaster. Nearest main road: A6 from Lancaster to Kendal (and M6, junction 35).

2 Bedrooms. £19.95–£30 (less for 3 nights or more). Both have own bath/shower/toilet; TV. No smoking.
Dinner (by arrangement). £18 for 4 courses and coffee, at 7.30pm. Vegetarian or other special diets if ordered. No smoking. **Light suppers** if ordered.
1 Sitting-room. With open fire, TV, Piano. No smoking.
Garden

The Bower was built as a farmhouse in 1745 and later gentrified. (The cast-iron porch is handsome.) There is a modern harpsichord in the entrance hall and hi-fi in both the sitting-room and the dining-room (as well as a piano in the former), for Michael Rothwell teaches music (also bridge). Sally-Ann serves for dinner such dishes as individual Stilton soufflés, chicken chasseur, pears in red wine, and cheese. The colours in the rooms are mostly muted greys and pinks, with elaborate floral curtains at the tall windows. These give views across a big garden, to the summit of Ingleborough.

Leighton Hall, with a collection of birds of prey in the grounds and Gillow furniture inside, is a couple of miles away. There are local associations with the earliest days of the Quakers, and at Carnforth is Steam Town and the *Brief Encounter* railway station.

Readers' comments: Charming young couple, charming garden, comfortable dining-room, superb bedroom with every convenience. Most enjoyable in every respect.

CLAY LANE HEAD FARMHOUSE

C PT

Cabus, Garstang, Lancashire, PR3 1WL   Tel: 01995 603132
North of Preston. On A6 from Preston to Lancaster (and near M6, junctions 32/33).

3 Bedrooms. £15–£18 (less for 5 nights or more). Bargain breaks. Some have some or all of the following: own bath/shower/toilet; TV. No smoking.
1 Sitting-room. With open fire, TV.
Small garden
Closed from December to February.

Though hardly off the beaten track, both Clay Lane Head Farmhouse and its surroundings have much to offer visitors who like an easy-going atmosphere.

The stone house, which is more characterful than it appears to be from the outside, is basically 16th century, and some of the internal walls are of plastered reeds. It is a rambling, beamy old place, full of family antiques and Victoriana, with a book-lined sitting-room to sprawl in (it has a log fire); and it has not been modernized. The rooms face away from the main road. Although this is no longer a working dairy-farm, there are cattle, goats and sheep.

Joan Higginson, a pharmacist, provides bed and breakfast only.

Start by visiting the Garstang Discovery Centre before you investigate the hinterland – notably the Trough of Bowland, which is like a miniature Lake District without the lakes.

Readers' comments: Very enjoyable. Attentive service. Concerned for our every comfort, spotless rooms. Interesting place. Very satisfactory. Friendly and bright. Very comfortable. Stands out for warm and friendly welcome.

HERON LODGE
Edgworth, Lancashire, BL7 0DS   Tel/Fax: 01204 852262
North of Bolton. Nearest main road: A676 from Bolton to Ramsbottom.

D PT S X

3 Bedrooms. £20–£25 (less for 7 nights or more). All have some or all of the following: own bath/shower/toilet; TV. No smoking.
Light suppers if ordered. No smoking.
1 Sitting-room. With open fire, TV. No smoking.
Large garden

Moorside villages like Edgworth should serve as a reminder that in this part of England you are never far from spectacularly beautiful countryside.

There had been a building on this site for as long as anyone could remember when the Miltons bought the single-storey property in the late 1980s and set about converting it into an immaculate, traditionally styled family house. The dining-room incorporates a massive old beam from a derelict barn, and local stone has been used in the construction.

Bedrooms have generous floral curtains, and lacy covers on Victorian brass bedsteads (one king-size) in two of them. Edwardian-style fittings in the excellent shower-rooms enhance the period atmosphere. Another bedroom at the back of the house is a very pretty L-shaped twin with patchwork quilts and has an attractive adjoining bathroom.

Guests tend to converge on the comfortable quarry-tiled kitchen, especially on baking days; for Roland Milton, who has lived in the village all his life, is renowned for his boiled fruit cake and rhubarb pies. There is a variety of good, reasonably priced eating-places within easy reach.

V

Prices are per person sharing a room at the beginning of the year.

Private bathrooms are not necessarily en suite.

Facts (prices, etc.) at the top of entries are supplied by the proprietors themselves. While every effort is made to ensure that these are correct at the time of going to press, they may alter thereafter: please check when you book.

Complaints about matters which could not have been settled on the spot will be forwarded to proprietors. Please enclose a stamped addressed envelope if you want the authors to acknowledge receipt of your complaint.

THE LIMES
CPTX

23 Stankelt Road, Silverdale, Lancashire, LA5 0TF   Tel/Fax: 01524 701454
North of Lancaster. Nearest main road: A6 from Carnforth to Kendal
(and M6, junction 35).

3 Bedrooms. £19.50 (less for 3 nights or more). All have own bath/shower/toilet; TV. No smoking.
Dinner. £12.50 for 5 courses, dessert wine and coffee, at 7 or 7.30pm. Vegetarian or other special diets if ordered. No smoking. **Light suppers** at 6pm.
1 Sitting-room (conservatory). No smoking.
Large garden

Near Carnforth is an Area of Outstanding Natural Beauty, quite different from the Lake District National Park, whose boundary it meets. Almost at sea level, this is wooded countryside rich in wildlife, most of it protected in nature reserves.

The Limes is a Victorian house run by Noel and Andrée Livesey. From the tented conservatory with its basketwork chairs to the one attic bedroom, with its sunken bathroom, they have decorated the rooms with flair. The dining-room reflects their travels and their interest in art and antiques. A typical dinner might be hot brandied grapefruit; chestnut and broad-bean soup; lamb blanquette; baked apple stuffed with vine fruits; and cheese.

Readers' comments: Imaginative dinners, delicious and meticulously prepared. Couldn't do enough for us. Comfortable, spotless, what a delight! Recommend it unreservedly. Hospitality unbeatable, meals out of this world. Surrounding area delightful.

PETER BARN
C(5)

Cross Lane, Waddington, Lancashire, BB7 3JH   Tel: 01200 28585
(Messages: 01200 22381)
North-west of Clitheroe. Nearest main road: A59 from Preston to Clitheroe.

3 Bedrooms. £18.50–£20 (less for 3 nights or more). Bargain breaks. All have some or all of the following: own bath/shower/toilet; TV. No smoking.
Light suppers if ordered.
1 Sitting-room. With open fire, TV. No smoking.
Large garden

On a single-track road that runs through a tunnel of trees, Peter Barn was indeed a barn. The upper floor is exclusively for guests. The large, airy sitting-room is reached by an open-tread staircase and has a roof made of old church rafters. By a stone fireplace are leather-covered settees and armchairs, near the head of the staircase is the breakfast-table, and off the other end of this well-proportioned space are the bedrooms and bathroom. (The arrangement is such that a large family would have the use of a virtually self-contained flat.) Much of the furniture consists of antiques, and there is some interesting bric-a-brac.

Jean Smith has the greenest of fingers, for the one-acre garden is a remarkable achievement, having been a field when the house was converted 15 years ago. Now it is beautifully landscaped and lovingly tended. There is no shortage of places for an evening meal, not least in Clitheroe, the lively market town a couple of miles away.

Readers' comments: Hope to visit again – a wonderful experience. A superb stay. Highlight of our holiday. Like being entertained by good friends. A visit is pure pleasure; can't wait to return. Garden a sheer delight. 'Readers' comments' all exceeded.

LEICESTERSHIRE
(including Rutland)

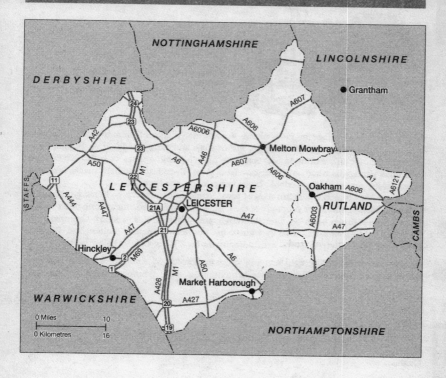

Addresses shown are to enable you to locate a house on a map. They are not necessarily complete postal addresses (though the essential postcode is included), and detailed directions for finding a house should be obtained from the owner.

CHURCH COTTAGE

C(1) **PT S X**

The Green, Holwell, Leicestershire, LE14 4SZ   Tel: 01664 444255
North-west of Melton Mowbray. Nearest main road: A606 from Melton Mowbray to Nottingham.

2 Bedrooms. £17.50 (less for 4 nights or more). One has own bath/shower/toilet. No smoking.
Light suppers if ordered. Vegetarian or other special diets if ordered. No smoking.
1 Sitting-room. With TV. No smoking.
Garden

The conservation village of Holwell has a particularly ancient church (1200) alongside which is 18th-century Church Cottage, full of steps and turns inside. Here Brenda Bailey gives visitors not only a beamed bedroom with brass bed and a spacious bathroom but their own small sitting-room too, and their own front door. Breakfasts and light snacks are served in her dining-room, which overlooks the sloping, landscaped garden.

Melton Mowbray is a pleasant market town (from which you can go home laden with its famous pork pies and other products of the pig), and is well placed for visiting other historic Leicestershire towns such as Loughborough and Oakham (as well as Grantham and Stamford in Lincolnshire). Stately homes in the vicinity include Belton and Burghley Houses, and great Belvoir Castle which dominates the Vale of Belvoir below it.

Readers' comments: Delightful, beautiful. Superb hospitality. Amazing breakfast on silver salver, with newspaper. A delightful weekend; impressed by attention to detail.

V

THE GRANGE

C M **PT X**

New Road, Burton Lazars, Leicestershire, LE14 2UU   Tel: 01664 560775
South-east of Melton Mowbray. Nearest main road: A606 from Melton Mowbray to Oakham.

4 Bedrooms. £18.50 (£22–£25 after April, **less £1 to readers of this book**). All have some or all of the following: own bath/shower/toilet; TV; balcony. No smoking.
Dinner. £14 for 4 courses and coffee, from 7pm. Vegetarian or other special diets if ordered. Wine available. **Light suppers** if ordered.
1 Sitting-room. With open fire.
Large garden

Until recently this was the home of the McAlpine family – a creeper-covered country mansion in 18th-century style with such features as leaded window-panes, arches, prettily plastered ceiling and barley-sugar banisters on the oak staircase.

Pam Holden has decorated the rooms with imagination, and hung the walls with good paintings. In the spacious aquamarine sitting-room are shell-pink armchairs. There is one rosy ground-floor bedroom with a large bathroom; a yellow bedroom upstairs has its own balcony. The four-poster room has a particularly good bathroom (and every guest is provided with an outsize bath-sheet). There is a small kitchen for guests' use.

Landscaped grounds include a sunken garden, orchard and paved terrace with chairs from which to enjoy the view across terraced lawns to the Vale of Stapleford.

Pam, a trained cook, enjoys preparing such dinners as melon with strawberries, chicken tarragon, pecan pie, and cheeses.

HOME FARM

Church Lane, Old Dalby, Leicestershire, LE14 3LB   Tel: 01664 822622
(Fax: 01664 823155)
North-west of Melton Mowbray. Nearest main road: A46 from Leicester to
Newark-on-Trent.

5 Bedrooms. £20–£22.50 (less for 5 nights or more).
All have some or all of the following: own bath/
shower/toilet; TV. No smoking.
Light suppers if ordered.
1 Sitting-room. With piano. No smoking.
Small garden

Set in an idyllic garden and facing the church, this 18th-century house has great charm and
an atmosphere of peace. Clematis and quinces grow up its walls, and lawns extend beyond
herbaceous beds. (It is no longer a farm.) Two single rooms are in a barn.

Indoors, every room has old furniture, pot-plants and white walls. Country-style dining-
chairs surround the long table where breakfast is served, a fire crackling on chilly mornings.
Val Anderson's collection of 'twenties and 'thirties photographs of local hunting personalities hangs here. Normally, Val serves only breakfast as the award-winning Crown Inn nearby is popular for other meals. Home-grown fruit is served at breakfast.

Readers' comments: Recommend the welcome, the breakfasts and the pub. The home, the
area, and most importantly the proprietors are delightful. Friendly and helpful owners,
beautiful house and garden. Very comfortable room, outstandingly good breakfasts.

V

MEDBOURNE GRANGE

Medbourne, Leicestershire, LE16 8EF   Tel: 01858 565249 (Fax: 01858 565257)
North-east of Market Harborough. Nearest main road: A427 from Market Harborough
to Corby.

3 Bedrooms. £16–£17 (less for 5 nights or more).
Light suppers if ordered.
1 Sitting-room. With open fire, TV. No smoking.
Large garden

At Nevill Holt's great 17th-century Hall (now a school) Emerald Cunard held her salons,
attended by the leading political and literary lions of the Edwardian era. Medbourne
Grange was a principal farm on its large estate, a dignified house standing at the heart of
500 acres of dairy pastures and arable fields.

Sally Beaty has furnished it attractively: the capacious, cut-velvet armchairs are of the
same soft blue as the sitting-room carpet; one rosy bedroom (with far view) has a carved
walnut suite, another (overlooking the dairy-yard) is paisley-patterned – this, though a
single bedroom, has a sofa-bed too.

Outside are stone troughs of flowers and, sheltered by old walls, a heated swimming-
pool; while beyond lies the valley of the River Welland which flows all the way to The Wash.

Reader's comments: An excellent stay, fully recommended.

V

OLD FORGE
Main Street, Medbourne, Leicestershire, LE16 8DT   Tel: 01858 565859
North-east of Market Harborough. Nearest main road: A427 from Market Harborough to Corby.

C S X

3 Bedrooms. £17–£18 (less for 3 nights or more). One has own bath/toilet. No smoking.
Light suppers if ordered. Vegetarian or other special diets if ordered. Wine available. No smoking.
1 Sitting-room. With TV, piano.
Large garden

Built of reddish sandstone and with panoramic views, Old Forge is now the very attractive home of Margaret Locke – every room decorated in carefully chosen colours and with good pictures. Her snack suppers, well presented, comprise home-made soup and hot rolls, cheeses and fruit. Some visitors enjoy the grand piano, others relax on the patio in her sunny garden with tea and home-made cakes.

Medbourne village has handsome buildings and a particularly pretty stream frequented by kingfishers and herons. In East Carlton Park are not only woods and ponds but a heritage centre that features the history of iron-making. Market Harborough has a great many 18th-century houses and a school of 1614 on wooden pillars.

Readers' comments: Lovely house, very comfortable, have stayed three times, strongly recommended.

OLD MANSE
Swingbridge Street, Foxton, Leicestershire, LE16 7RH   Tel: 01858 545456
North-west of Market Harborough. Nearest main road: A6 from Market Harborough to Leicester.

C PT

3 Bedrooms. £20. Bargain breaks. All have some or all of the following: own bath/shower/toilet; TV. No smoking.
Light suppers if ordered.
1 Sitting-room. With open fire. No smoking.
Large garden

Ancient and tiny Foxton, its 13th-century church restored by John of Gaunt and preached in by Wycliffe, is famous for its 'staircase' of 10 locks on the Grand Union Canal, which raises boats 75 feet uphill (there are a canal museum and horse-drawn barge trips). It played a part in the Civil Wars (Naseby is near); and the little booklet called *The Foxton Story* is well worth reading.

The Old Manse was built in the 17th century, just beyond a swing-bridge over the canal; and in it the Baptist minister later ran a school. Now it is home to the Pickerings and their collection of classic cars.

Rooms are elegant and immaculate, and there is a fine garden – open to the public at times – with an array of fuchsias. Some of the light and flowery bedrooms have a good view of this. Downstairs, an attractive sitting-room houses a grand piano and pink velvet furnishings, alcoves are full of books, and there is a big collection of saucy china fairings. Altogether, a characterful house in a little-known spot of considerable interest; and surrounded by such sights as Boughton House, Canons Ashby and Rockingham Castle.

V

PEACOCK FARMHOUSE

C D M PT X

Redmile, Leicestershire, NG13 0GQ   Tel: 01949 842475 (Fax: 01949 843127)
West of Grantham. Nearest main road: A52 from Nottingham to Grantham.

10 Bedrooms. £20–£24 (less for 7 nights or more).
Bargain breaks. All have some or all of the following:
own bath/shower/toilet; TV.
Dinner. £14.50 for 3 courses and coffee, at 7.15pm.
Vegetarian or other special diets if ordered. Wine available. No smoking. **Light suppers** if ordered.
2 Sitting-rooms. With TV, piano. No smoking in one.
Bar.
Large garden

This guest-house with restaurant (built as a farm in the 18th century) is ideal for a break when doing a long north-south journey on the nearby A1, particularly with children.

It is in the outstandingly beautiful Vale of Belvoir, with the Duke of Rutland's Belvoir Castle (full of art treasures) rearing its battlemented walls high above a nearby hilltop.

The Needs have created a happy family atmosphere here. Most bedrooms have views of Belvoir Castle, while others on the ground floor include a self-contained pine cabin and a coach house outside the main building. Children can safely play in the garden which has a large lawn, hammock, swings, small covered swimming-pool, playroom, pool-room, bicycles, barbecue, and farm pets. Indoors are snooker and table tennis.

Food is above average, with home-made bread and soups, herbs from the garden and much local produce. A typical meal: trout and cream cheese terrine; beef and venison carbonnade; 'tipsy' bread-and-butter pudding.

Readers' comments: Good food, delightful hosts. Room attractively furnished, meal excellent.   **V**

RUTLAND COTTAGES

C M S X

5 Cedar Street, Braunston-in-Rutland, Rutland, LE15 8QS   Tel: 01572 722049
South-west of Oakham. Nearest main road: A6003 from Oakham to Kettering.

4 Bedrooms. £19 (less for 5 nights or more). Bargain
breaks. All have own bath/shower/toilet; TV. No
smoking.
2 Sitting-rooms. With open fire, TV, piano. No
smoking.
Small garden

A 17th-century bakehouse is the home of John and Connie Beadman (she taught music); and in addition they own nearby cottages let on a bed-and-breakfast basis. All guests take breakfast together in the beamed dining-room of the house (on Sundays, cooked breakfasts are available only between 7.30 and 8.30am). Visitors can eat at two inns in this pretty conservation village of golden stone.

Guests have the use of the Beadmans' huge and beautifully furnished sitting-room (it has a see-through stone fireplace in the middle, and a 'curfew window' through which the village watchman could check that the baker's fires had been properly extinguished for the night). Its windows open onto a heather garden.

Readers' comments: Most friendly. Cottage excellent. B & b at its best. Nothing is too much trouble. The accommodation is first class. Very pleasant welcome, excellent. Good breakfast. Warm welcome. Most helpful and friendly. B & b at its very best in every way.   **V**

WATER MEADOWS FARMHOUSE

C D X

Billington Road East, Elmesthorpe, Leicestershire, LE9 7SB Tel: 01455 843417
North-east of Hinckley. Nearest main road: A47 from Hinckley to Leicester
(also M69, junction 1; and M1, junction 21).

3 Bedrooms. £15 (less for 3 nights or more). Some have some or all of the following: own toilet; TV. No smoking.
Dinner. £8 for 3 courses and coffee, at 7pm. Vegetarian or other special diets if ordered. **Light suppers** if ordered.
1 Sitting-room. With open fire, TV.
Large garden

In the depression of the 1930s, smallholdings with houses were provided through the Land Settlement Association, a 'self-sufficiency' scheme eventually abandoned. Peter Robinson bought two of these plots (which are on the site of a lost mediaeval village and Roman remains) and has gradually turned them into his own private conservation area.

Bedrooms are good: for instance, a huge family room with sofa and large TV (concealed in a fitment) has fine inlaid Edwardian furniture and windows on three sides from which to enjoy the garden – floodlit at night.

June is an accomplished cook. You might be offered a Chinese or Mexican meal, or something less exotic like lettuce soup, fish Wellington, and home-made ice cream served with chocolate-fudge sauce. Most vegetables come from the garden. And every day breakfast is different, with such unusual choices as kidneys or cheese-and-potato pancakes.

V

Houses which accept the discount vouchers on page ii are marked with a
V symbol next to the relevant entries.

'Bargain breaks' are usually out-of-season reductions for half-board stays
of several nights.

Where wine is not available (meaning it is on sale or can be fetched for
you), you are nearly always welcome to bring in your own drinks.

Major tourist attractions, such as Stratford-upon-Avon and Cambridge,
can often be easily reached from houses in adjacent counties.

LINCOLNSHIRE
(including North Lincolnshire)

You stand a better chance of finding the right accommodation at the right price in the right area if you are using an up-to-date edition of this book, which is revised every year. Obtain an order form for the next edition (published in November) by sending a stamped addressed envelope, with 'SOTBT 1999' in the top left-hand corner, to Explore Britain, Alston, Cumbria, CA9 3SL.

BODKIN LODGE

C(8) M

Torrington Lane, East Barkwith, Lincolnshire, LN8 5RY Tel: 01673 858249
North-east of Lincoln. Nearest main road: A157 from Wragby to Louth.

2 Bedrooms. £20–£22.50 (less for 3 nights or more). Both have some or all of the following: own bath/shower/toilet; TV; balcony. No smoking.
Dinner (by arrangement). £13 for 4 courses and coffee, at 7.30pm. Vegetarian or other special diets if ordered. No smoking. **Light suppers** if ordered.
1 Sitting-room. With open fire/stove,TV, piano, No smoking.
Large garden
Closed from mid-December to January.

Anne and Richard Stamp have furnished Bodkin Lodge with great care, adding much character to this stylish home. From the entrance hall, doors open onto a light, airy sitting-room with floor-to-ceiling windows and far-reaching views. Paintings and ornate mirrors hang on the walls, and French windows lead onto a terrace, where breakfast may be served in the summer. One bedroom has direct access to the garden.

Anne (who occasionally writes short stories for women's magazines) serves meals such as smoked haddock and chive creams; lamb with apricot stuffing; and almond and pear flan.

Tealby, nearby, is a particularly beautiful Wolds village by the River Rase from which Tennyson often walked to Hainton where there is a park that was landscaped by Capability Brown. Kingerby has outstanding church monuments and woodlands full of wildflowers.

Lincolnshire is the county to choose if you want to unwind in the peace of a remote and solitary countryside, where the skies are open wide and the pace is slow-changing.

Readers' comments: The standard of food, presentation, etc. could not have been bettered. Welcomed as friends; excellent food. Wonderful ambience, perfect hosts. Exceptionally comfortable. Never found such de luxe facilities, gracious hospitality and delicious meals.

COACH HOUSE

PT S

Belton-by-Grantham, Lincolnshire, NG32 2LS Tel: 01476 573636
North of Grantham. Nearest main road: A607 from Grantham to Lincoln.

4 Bedrooms. £18–£20 (less for 4 nights or more). Bargain breaks. All have own bath/shower/toilet; TV. No smoking.
Dinner (by arrangement). £14 for 3 courses and coffee, at about 7pm. Vegetarian or other special diets if ordered. Wine available. No smoking. **Light suppers** if ordered.
1 Sitting-room. With TV. No smoking.
Large garden
Closed in January.

For an overnight stop on the long haul from Cambridge to York, the coaches once paused here at an inn, next door to which the buildings of Ancaster stone that are now the Nortons' home were stables surrounding a coach yard.

Bernard Norton has created such attractive features as a second, sun-trapping courtyard with a fountain in the centre of a circle of blue-brick paving: an attractive view to enjoy while dining. The guests' sitting-room has French windows which open onto the garden. There are ground-floor bedrooms (one with courtyard view, one with none) and others upstairs – be prepared for rafters and steps – which have roof-lights. Sue has made ruffled pelmets and, on one bed, a prettily draped corona, using silky pink or rose-patterned fabrics.

For dinner she may offer you minestrone, lemon chicken, and strawberries.

All around the conservation village is National Trust land with good walks.

Readers' comments: Delightfully situated, very attractively furnished. Meals cooked to perfection. Very friendly and helpful. A lovely stay, food good.

THE GRANGE

C(12) **X**

Torrington Lane, East Barkwith, Lincolnshire, LN8 5RY   Tel: 01673 858670
North-east of Lincoln. Nearest main road: A157 from Wragby to Louth.

2 Bedrooms. £20–£25. Bargain breaks. Both have some or all of the following: own bath/shower/toilet; TV. No smoking.
Dinner (by arrangement). £13 for 4 courses, sherry and coffee, at 7pm. Vegetarian or other special diets if ordered. No smoking. **Light suppers** if ordered.
1 Sitting-room. With open fire. No smoking.
Large garden
Closed in December.

Set in acres of farmland (mainly arable) which adjoin a conservation area, this late-Georgian house is on a working farm. Until recently, it was the home of Anne and Richard Stamp (see **Bodkin Lodge**). Now son Jonathan has taken over the farm business.

Built in 1820, the house has sash windows deep-set in shuttered embrasures. The hall has a stained-glass door, black-and-white floor tiles, and a graceful staircase leading up to attractive bedrooms.

Outside is a lawn with topiary, swing-settee, croquet and tennis. Children, too, will enjoy the large garden (the Stamps have two young ones of their own).

Sarah Stamp (a trained home economist and accomplished cook) serves, for example, watercress and salmon roulade; chicken in white wine and tarragon sauce; chocolate brownie gâteau.

The Grange has won three conservation awards, and has a private trout lake (where guests can fish or relax with a picnic), as well as direct access to nature trails. It is ideally situated for visiting Lincoln and the Wolds.

GUY WELLS

C(10) **D**

Eastgate (road), Whaplode, Lincolnshire, PE12 6TZ   Tel: 01406 422239
East of Spalding. Nearest main road: A151 from Spalding to King's Lynn.

3 Bedrooms. £18–£21. One has own shower/toilet; TV (on request). No smoking.
Dinner. £10 for 2 courses and coffee, at 7pm. Vegetarian or other special diets if ordered. No smoking. **Light suppers** if ordered.
1 Sitting-room. With log stove, TV. No smoking.
Large garden

Springs in the land around this Queen Anne house are what gave it its name. It is in a lovely and secluded position, surrounded by a traditional garden, trees, and beyond that the Fens.

The interior of the house is full of imaginative touches. Hall and staircase are pretty (with sprigged wallpaper, an old cedar chest, prints and bouquets of flowerheads dried by Anne) leading to the bedrooms – one of which is huge, with en suite shower-room, and windows on two sides. Another has a half-tester bed with antique bedhead.

Using their own vegetables, honey and eggs, Anne's wholefood meals may consist of a traditional roast and puddings like raspberry pavlova or a crème brûlée in which yogurt combines with cream as a topping to brandied grapes. Pâtés, soups and quiches are home-made.

Readers' comments: Lovely place, superb food, nice lady. Very warm welcome, happy atmosphere, glorious food. Interesting part of the country, have visited twice. Welcoming couple, pleasant place. Great hospitality, food good, accommodation excellent.

HOE HILL

C(5) **S X**

Swinhope, Binbrook, Lincolnshire, LN8 6HX   Tel: 01472 398206
North-west of Louth. Nearest main road: A16 from Louth to Grimsby (and M180, junction 5).

4 Bedrooms. £18–£25 (less for 3 nights or more). Bargain breaks. One has own bath/shower/toilet. No smoking.
Dinner (by arrangement). £14 for 4 courses and coffee, at 7.30pm. Less for 2 courses. Vegetarian or other special diets if ordered. Wine available. No smoking.
Light suppers if ordered.
1 Sitting-room. With open fire, TV.
Large garden
Closed in January.

One enters the white house, built in 1780, through a porch filled with geraniums. Off a poppy-papered hall is the large and attractive sitting-room. Antiques and a marble fireplace contrast with modern furniture of bamboo. One particularly attractive bedroom overlooks the walled garden and has an extra-large bed (which can be made into twin beds if required) and a spacious en suite bathroom with a spa bath.

As to the meals which have won Erica Curd so much local renown, you might be offered cheese-stuffed mushrooms before, for instance, roast duck (or fish straight from Grimsby). The choice of puddings might be a home-made sorbet or a traditional favourite such as bread-and-butter pudding. Breakfasts, too, are impressive, with such options as Lincolnshire sausages, kippers, kidneys in bacon, kedgeree and occasionally Arbroath smokies.

Readers' comments: We have made this a regular venue for family get-togethers. Excellent room. Outstandingly friendly welcome. High quality food. Couldn't praise too highly, perfect hosts, nothing lacking, super value. Excellent cook; made very welcome.

OLD MILL

C D **S X**

Mill Lane, Tallington, Lincolnshire, PE9 4RR   Tel: 01780 740815
(Fax: 01780 740280)
East of Stamford. Nearest main road: A16 from Stamford to Market Deeping.

6 Bedrooms. £20–£27.50. Bargain breaks. All have some or all of the following: own bath/shower/toilet; TV; views of river. No smoking.
Light suppers if ordered. Vegetarian or other special diets if ordered. Wine available. No smoking.
Garden

Tourists 'discovered' mediaeval Stamford when it was used for filming *Middlemarch*. It is a jewel of a stone town, rich in old inns and churches, on the River Welland.

As the river flows eastward, it passes by Tallington village and here stands the 18th-century watermill where the Olvers now welcome guests. Much of the conversion was done by John himself, a task that would daunt most men, but he is a PE teacher and once played rugby for England. Though the mill ceased to grind corn long ago, its gears, shafts, winches and mill-stones still survive; and he retained them all in their proper place. This means that the low, beamed breakfast-room and even bedrooms have such curious features incorporated in the decor. Some rooms look out over the river as it flows beneath.

Susan has chosen pretty fabrics to complement pine furniture that is in keeping with the old timbers of the mill. There are some particularly spacious bedrooms at the top; and every room has its own neat and elegant bathroom.

The Mill is likely to be full every September when there are horse trials at great Burghley House nearby, or in spring when Spalding's bulb-fields are a big attraction.

OLIVER'S

Church Street, Scawby, North Lincolnshire, DN20 9AH Tel: 01652 650446   C(10) **PT S X**
South-east of Scunthorpe. Nearest main road: A15 from Lincoln to Brigg
(and M180, junction 4).

3 Bedrooms. £18–£20 (less for 7 nights or more).
Bargain breaks. All have own shower/toilet; TV.
No smoking.
Dinner. £12.50 for 3 courses and coffee, at 7pm.
Vegetarian or other special diets if ordered. Wine
available. No smoking.
1 Sitting-room. With TV.
Garden

This 17th-century house in the village centre was once the post office. Within is a cosy
guests' lounge leading to the dining-room, traditionally furnished. Here Hazel Oliver serves
such meals as spiced hot grapefruit, chicken in white wine, and raspberry-and-apple crumb-
ble. Derek Oliver, who practised as a surveyor until recently, is an able watercolourist, and
his framed pictures of the area are on sale.

Bedrooms are sizeable; the largest has lemon walls, a flowered border and velvet bedheads; another pale green walls with white furniture. There is a large and pleasant garden.

The nearest town is Brigg, whose fair, at which gypsy horse-dealers used to gather, has
been commemorated in music by Delius. Cleethorpes is a traditional seaside resort, with
sandy beaches and one of the few remaining piers. Near it is Grimsby, with a reconstruction
of an Iron Age village and the new National Fishing Heritage Centre. Westward of Scawby
is the 'Isle' of Axholme, where John Wesley's Epworth birthplace is open to the public. Bog
oak is often ploughed up in fields round here. Look out for the area's many windmills.

v

SPROXTON LODGE

Skillington, Lincolnshire, NG33 5HJ Tel: 01476 860307   C S
South of Grantham. Nearest main road: A1 from Grantham to Stamford.

3 Bedrooms. £15 (less for 3 nights or more). All have
TV. No smoking.
Dinner (by arrangement). £7 for 2 courses and coffee,
at 6pm. Vegetarian or other special diets if ordered. No
smoking. **Light suppers** if ordered.
1 Sitting-room. With open fire, TV. No smoking.
Large garden

18th-century Sproxton Lodge is popular with walkers because the long Viking Way borders
its fields. This is a homely, working farm – with silver ploughing-trophies won by Ted on
display to prove it. He still has his very first tractor of 40 years ago, now almost a museum
piece. Unpretentious comfort (and an enormous, carpeted bathroom) are what hospitable
Eileen Whatton provides here, with dinners or snacks by arrangement.

There are many popular sights in this region: Belvoir Castle, Belton House, Stapleford
Park, Rutland Water and Wollaton Hall in its park; also Holme Pierrepont Hall,
Doddington Hall, and Newstead Abbey (Byron's home). Eastwood has D.H. Lawrence's
birthplace. Lincoln (cathedral), Southwell (minster), Sherwood Forest (Robin Hood display) and Nottingham are also near – the last a much underrated city. There is an arts
museum in the castle and others at its foot (the lace museum is fascinating), river trips and
walks through the Georgian quarter. The historic market towns of Stamford (in particular)
and Newark are of great interest. One can shop for local Stilton, crafts and Nottingham lace
to take home – Melton Mowbray is famous for pies and other pork delicacies.

LONDON

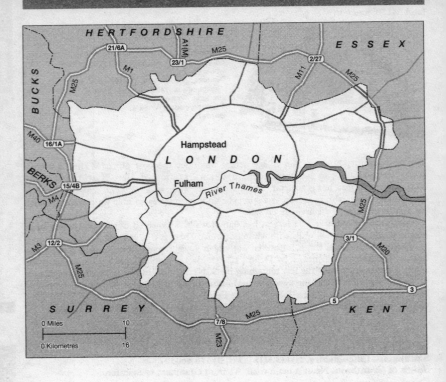

IOLANTHE

86 Wildwood Road, Hampstead, London, NW11 6UJ   Tel: 0181-455 1417
(M1, junction 1, is near.)

2 Bedrooms. £20–£26.50. One has own shower/toilet; TV (in both). No smoking.
Light suppers if ordered.
Small garden

For country quiet while in London, this is the place to be. The Hampstead Garden Suburb was founded by the philanthropist Henrietta Barnett in 1907 when, appalled at the housing conditions of London's poor, she determined that as the Underground spread northward a new all-classes community should be built there – green and leafy, with cottages and manor houses in 16th- and 17th-century styles. Alas for Dame Henrietta's idealism: today only the well-to-do can buy even the smallest cottage.

Situated right by Hampstead Heath, Iolanthe is a Lutyens-designed house. Here, Rosy Gill provides breakfast and snack suppers either in visitors' rooms or downstairs – overlooking or even on the terrace of the garden. Bedrooms are light and airy, with cottage-style furnishings and fresh white walls. Central London is 20 minutes away by Underground.

Readers' comments: Excellent; very good value. Super location for visiting London; Gills are some of the nicest people we met.

LANGORF HOTEL

20 Frognal, Hampstead, London, NW3 6AG Tel: 0171-794 4483
(Fax: 0171-435 9055) Toll-free from USA on: 1-800-925-4731
Nearest main road: A41 (Finchley Road) from London to Aylesbury
(M1, junction 1, is near).

31 Bedrooms. £31 (with continental breakfast) **to readers of this book only.** Less for 7 nights. All have own bath/shower/toilet; TV; washing/cleaning service.
Light snacks etc. (24 hours). **Bar.**
Small garden

For readers visiting London, we have negotiated a very special price at a small but luxurious hotel in a quiet residential road (with good access into central London).

The bedrooms are elegant: modern furniture is complemented by excellent soft furnishings, and all bathroom fitments are of the highest quality. There are remote-control TV sets in each room, direct-dial telephones, hair-dryers, etc. Some bedrooms are on the ground floor, others are served by a lift. Twenty-four-hour room service for snacks and drinks.

Downstairs, an attractive coral reception/sitting-area leads into the airy breakfast-room, which overlooks a leafy garden. Here one helps oneself from a buffet of some two dozen items that include assorted fruits, ham, cheeses, croissants and much else. Individual dietary requirements can be catered for, if the hotel is forewarned. The manager is Caroline Bright.

Readers' comments: Very nice and helpful staff. Wonderful gem, everything superb. Each guest very special. The best value we have found in London. Excellent value for the city.

91 LANGTHORNE STREET

PT X

Fulham, London, SW6 6JS Tel/Fax: 0171-381 0198
Nearest main road: A219 from Hammersmith to Putney.

3 Bedrooms. £25 (with continental breakfast). Less for 3 nights. TV (on request). No smoking.
Light suppers if ordered. No smoking.
Garden

In a quiet residential street between Fulham Palace Road and the River Thames is this turn-of-the-century terraced house where Brigid Richardson offers bed and breakfast only. Guests, however, can prepare light meals in the comfortable kitchen, which has glass doors leading to the long, south-facing garden – ideal for relaxing in on summer evenings.

On the ground floor is a charming blue-and-white bedroom (the bedhead is an intricately carved panel from a 15th-century chest) and delightful bathroom: huge, free-standing, old-fashioned bath as well as roomy shower. Upstairs are two more attractive bedrooms, both overlooking the garden, and another spacious bathroom. Brigid restores works of art on paper and she is also training to be a tourist guide.

Three minutes away, frequent buses (or a stiffish walk) will take you to Hammersmith Broadway (tube trains to Heathrow or central London; buses in all directions too).

Readers' comments: A very charming typical English house, very well equipped. Each room has its own character; beautiful old furniture; warm-hearted host. Have stayed 10 times. Very helpful and kind. Elegantly decorated. Wonderful host, decor fascinating.

For explanation of code letters and **V** symbol, see inside front cover.

Prices are per person sharing a room at the beginning of the year.

Some proprietors stipulate a minimum stay of two nights at weekends or peak seasons; or they will accept one-nighters only at short notice (that is, only if no lengthier booking has yet been made).

Facts (prices, etc.) at the top of entries are supplied by the proprietors themselves. While every effort is made to ensure that these are correct at the time of going to press, they may alter thereafter: please check when you book.

NORFOLK

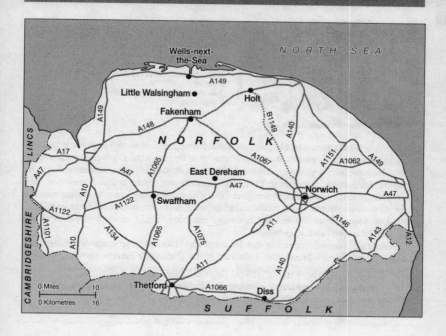

BERRY HALL

Norfolk

C(10) S

Great Walsingham, Norfolk, NR22 6DZ Tel: 01328 820267
North of Fakenham. Nearest main road: A149 from Sheringham to Wells-next-the-Sea.

5 Bedrooms. £17.50. Some have own bath/shower/toilet. No smoking.
Dinner. £10 for 3 courses and coffee, at 6.45pm. Vegetarian or other special diets if ordered. No smoking.
1 Sitting-room. With open fire, TV. No smoking.
Large garden

This is a fine Tudor house in big grounds named after the merchant who built it in 1532. Once, Rupert Brooke's family lived here. Now it is the home of Doris Wilson and Joan Sheaf. Many rooms, all very big, have fine panelling; in the hall are a flagstone floor and impressive oak ceiling; Portuguese Delft tiles decorate the dining-room. There is a great balustraded staircase and unusual antiques. The sitting-room overlooks the large, pleasant garden with rosebeds and a magnificent copper beech tree, beyond which lies a moat with ducks. For dinner Doris cooks such dishes as watercress soup, lamb noisettes in sherry sauce, and meringues with strawberries.

Less than an hour away are many stately homes and National Trust properties – Blickling, Felbrigg, Houghton, Holkham and Oxburgh Halls, and Sandringham House, the royal Christmas residence. Nearby Thursford has a steam museum and an organ collection.

Readers' comments: Most attractive, comfortable and spacious. Food cooked to perfection. Charming and characterful. Lovely home; spacious room.

BURGH PARVA HALL

Norfolk

C D S X

Melton Constable, Norfolk, NR24 2PU Tel: 01263 860797
South of Holt. Nearest main road: A148 from Fakenham to Cromer.

2 Bedrooms. £17 (less for 7 nights or more).
Dinner (by arrangement). £10 for 3 courses and coffee, at 7.30pm. Vegetarian or other special diets if ordered. **Light suppers** if ordered.
Small garden

Burgh Parva Hall was a farm in the 16th century; in the 1840s an imposing wing was added. It is the only house left at Burgh (pronounced 'borough') Parva, for the village was destroyed after the Great Plague of 1665.

One enters through the dining-hall where logs crackle under the ogee arch of the fireplace. Furniture is old in style, rooms huge; your bedroom will have a sofa or armchairs from which to enjoy the view through sash windows – fine sunsets, and even a distant glimpse of the sea. William Heal will either give you a lift to and from a local inn for dinner, or by arrangement you may dine at the house.

Nearby Holt is a picturesque market town; and the very beautiful heritage coastline is only a few miles away. The bird sanctuary and seal colony at Blakeney are worth a visit.

V *Readers' comments:* Impressive house, excellent breakfasts. Very helpful.

182

COLLEGE FARMHOUSE

Thompson, Norfolk, IP24 1QG   Tel: 01953 483318
North of Thetford. Nearest main road: A1075 from Thetford to East Dereham.

C(7) **S X**

3 Bedrooms. £18–£19. All have some or all of the following: own bath/shower/toilet; TV.
Large garden

Priests used to live in College Farmhouse until Henry VIII disbanded them. Later owners added oak panelling, a coat-of-arms and other features. There are Gothic windows; walls (some three feet thick) have odd curves. Lavender Garnier has collected interesting furniture, family portraits (it was an ancestor who selected dark blue as Oxford's boat-race colour), and attractive fabrics for bedrooms that have armchairs and TV (no sitting-room). A lovely garden slopes down to eel-ponds. Bicycles for hire. Inn food one mile away.

Thompson is in an attractive, leafy part of Norfolk, where the landscape undulates and villages are pretty. Thetford was the birthplace of Thomas Paine and there is a statue of him in the town.

Readers' comments: Warm hospitality. Magical peace in a beautiful house. Very comfortable, warm and friendly. Breakfasts a joy. Excellent. As near perfect as makes no difference; excellent value. Quite wonderful. Perfection?

V

CORFIELD HOUSE

Sporle, Norfolk, PE32 2EA   Tel: 01760 723636
North-east of Swaffham. Nearest main road: A47 from King's Lynn to Norwich.

C M S

5 Bedrooms. £18.50–£21.50 (less for 7 nights, half-board). All have some or all of the following: own bath/shower/toilet; TV. No smoking.
Dinner. £12.50 for 4 courses and coffee, at 7pm. Vegetarian or other special diets if ordered. Wine available. No smoking. **Light suppers** if ordered.
1 Sitting-room. No smoking.
Garden
Closed from Christmas to mid-March.

Much hard work went into adapting this early Victorian farmhouse and creating a particularly pretty garden. Inside, Linda Hickey has used delicately patterned wallpapers, much pine and rattan furniture, soft blues and pinks. There is a ground-floor room with bathroom that would suit any disabled person.

A typical dinner might comprise crab and avocado salad, boeuf bourguignonne, raspberry clafouti (a type of pancake) and some unusual cheeses.

Martin runs the Tourist Information Centre at nearby Swaffham and both he and Linda are mines of information about the area. Swaffham has a huge market square and many 18th-century buildings (Nelson used to stay at Montpellier House). The hammerbeam roof of the church is impressive, and the local history museum is worth a visit.

Readers' comments: Strongly recommended. Excellent value. Superb breakfast. First class. Outstanding dinners. Helpful and considerate hosts. The loveliest house we have stayed in, food superb, delightful people.

THE GRANGE

CDPTS

Northwold, Norfolk, IP26 5NF   Tel: 01366 728240 (Fax: 01366 728005)
North-west of Thetford. Nearest main road: A134 from Thetford to King's Lynn.

5 Bedrooms. £18–£22. Bargain breaks. All have some or all of the following: own bath/shower/toilet; TV. No smoking.
Dinner. £13 for 4 courses and coffee, at 7pm. Vegetarian or other special diets if ordered. Wine available. No smoking. **Light suppers** if ordered.
1 Sitting-room. With open fire, TV. No smoking.
Large garden

Behind Northwold's church, its 18th-century rector not only built himself a very fine house but laid out a 12-acre garden with rare trees to which has been added a heated swimming-pool.

In the dining-room, there is a plan of the original house. The coral walls in here match chinoiserie curtains patterned with pheasants, and there is a fireplace handsomely carved. Pretty Villeroy & Boch china complements such meals as mushroom pots, salmon parcels with watercress sauce, almond meringue with apricot coulis, and cheeses.

Not only is Sue Whittley an accomplished cook but, with a colleague, she runs weekend cookery courses – demonstrations plus practical work. And she is an expert needlewoman, hence all the attractive cushions in every room. Her husband's excellent watercolours (of local scenery and wildlife) fill the walls, and many are for sale.

A galleried staircase leads to bedrooms furnished with, for instance, William Morris fabrics and lace bedspreads. Some of the deep-set, shuttered sash windows overlook the flint and stone tower of the 13th-century church.

V   *Readers' comments:* Superb grounds, exceptionally nice hostess, very good food.

GREENACRES FARM

CDS

Wood Green, Long Stratton, Norfolk, NR15 2RR   Tel: 01508 530261
South of Norwich. Nearest main road: A140 from Norwich towards Diss.

3 Bedrooms. £20–£22 (less for 2 nights or more). Bargain breaks. All have some or all of the following: own bath/shower/toilet; TV. No smoking.
Dinner. £12 for 2 courses and coffee, at 7pm. Vegetarian or other special diets if ordered. No smoking. **Light suppers** if ordered.
1 Sitting-room. With wood-burner, TV, piano.
Large garden

17th-century Greenacres Farm is right on the edge of a 30-acre common with ponds and ancient woods. Bedrooms are spacious and comfortable, with own shower or bath. In the huge snooker room you can peer into the floodlit depths of a 60-foot well as old as the house itself. Joanna Douglas's dinners are homely two-course meals, such as meatballs in tomato sauce and cheesecake. There is a tennis court.

Norwich is one of the most beautiful of mediaeval cities, complete with castle and cathedral, full of craft and antique shops in cobbled byways. The Sainsbury Art Centre outside Norwich is exceptional.

This is an excellent spot from which to explore in all directions. Bressingham Hall has fine gardens and steam engines. The Broads are near and, a little further afield, the re-created 19th-century village at Burgh St Margaret, with fairground rides, craft-making areas and a miniature railway, is a popular attraction for families.

V   *Reader's comment:* Very friendly, and quiet.

GREY GABLES

Norwich Road, Cawston, Norfolk, NR10 4EY   Tel: 01603 871259
North-west of Norwich. Nearest main road: B1149 from Norwich to Holt.

8 Bedrooms. £20–£30 (less for 2 nights or more). Bargain breaks. All have some or all of the following: own bath/shower/toilet; TV.
Dinner. From £16 for 3 courses and coffee, from 7pm. Vegetarian or other special diets if ordered. Wine available. No smoking. **Light suppers** if ordered.
1 Sitting-room. With open fire. **Bar.**
Large garden

Every year, James and Rosalind Snaith travel in Europe looking for new wines and recipes to add to their repertoire. At this former rectory, their dinner may include mushroom filo parcel with gazpacho sauce; mussels in a cream sauce; roast lamb; a choice of desserts (home-made ice cream or sticky-toffee pudding, for example); and cheese. There is a long wine list. Dinner is eaten at mahogany tables with velvet-upholstered chairs; silver, rosy Royal Albert china and candles make it an elegant occasion.

They have rung the changes on blue and beige colour schemes in nearly every room from the Victorian-style sitting-room and up the handsome mahogany staircase to the bedrooms. On the walls hang oil paintings and watercolours, many of them by Rosalind and her daughter.

Beyond the grass tennis court is a vineyard and an orchard with many specimen trees.

Readers' comments: Excellent; marvellous food. Very friendly, good food. Very comfortable and friendly. Remarkable service. Very professional. Dinners delicious, with exotic choices.

V

HIDEAWAY

D S

Red Lion Yard, Wells-next-the-Sea, Norfolk, NR23 1AX   Tel: 01328 710524
Nearest main road: A149 from Cromer to Hunstanton.

3 Bedrooms. £17–£19.50 (less for 7 nights or more). Bargain breaks. All have some or all of the following: own bath/shower/toilet; TV.
Dinner. £9.50 for 3 courses, at 6–7.30pm. Vegetarian or other special diets if ordered. Wine available. No smoking. **Light suppers** if ordered.
1 Sitting-room. With TV. No smoking. Bar.
Small garden
Closed from mid-December to mid-January.

Aptly named, these converted stables are – although only 200 yards from the harbour – so tucked away that they take some finding! Beyond a secluded courtyard garden (the nicest of the bedrooms is actually in this), a door opens into a small sitting-area. Beyond this lie further bedrooms, compact in size and neat rather than characterful in style – all on the ground floor. You can use the sauna or spa bath for a small charge.

From the tables in the dining-room is a view through sliding glass doors of a little paved patio. And, a considerable asset in the town centre, Hideaway has its own parking space.

Ex-teacher Madeline Higgs and her helpers run the guest-house on very well-organized lines. There is a wide range of choices for dinner: you are asked to select what you want at breakfast-time, so everything is freshly prepared. A typical choice might be a mousse of Stilton, avocado and prawns; lamb in red wine; lemon pudding.

Readers' comments: We have returned many times. Most hospitable. A perfect cook, delicious meals. Winter weekends are very, very good value. Pleasantly informal, food superb.

KIMBERLEY HOME FARM

CS

Wymondham, Norfolk, NR18 0RW   Tel: 01953 603137 (Fax: 01953 604836)
South-west of Norwich. Nearest main road: A11 from Norwich to Thetford.

4 Bedrooms. £18–£22.50. Some have own bath/shower/toilet; TV.
Dinner. £15 for 3 courses and coffee, at times to suit guests. Wine available. **Light suppers** if ordered.
1 Sitting-room. With open fire, TV.
Large garden
Closed from December to March.

This is a beautifully furnished farmhouse with stables at the front and a large garden at the back, onto which the glass doors of the large sitting-room open. There is a pond with ducks, and a hard tennis court. Apart from the hundreds of acres of crops, the main activity at Kimberley is training and racing horses.

The bedrooms are particularly pretty, the bathroom excellent, and the dining-room has a long Regency table. Jenny Bloom is not only a superb cook but a generous one, leaving pheasants or joints of meat on a hot-tray from which guests may help themselves. Starters are imaginative (avocado mousse, for instance), and puddings delicious.

You can have the exclusive use of rooms if you wish, or get more involved with the family and the farm. There is a very good attic family-suite.

Readers' comments: Total peace, comfortable rooms, delicious food. Comfortable, and very good food. Excellent. Very warm welcome. Lovely people. Delicious supper. Nothing was too much trouble: very highly rated. Fun, very welcoming.

LODGE FARM

C(8) D S

Fersfield, Bressingham, Norfolk, IP22 2BQ   Tel: 01379 687629
West of Diss. Nearest main road: A1066 from Thetford to Diss.

3 Bedrooms. £17–£19.
Light suppers if ordered. Vegetarian or other special diets if ordered. Wine available.
1 Sitting-room. With open fire.
Large garden

Henry VIII had a 'palace' for hunting near here and at the boundaries of his great estate were lodges, of which this was one. Its windows and pink walls give little hint that the house goes back so far, but inside are chamfered beams, low ceilings, odd steps and angles.

David and Pat Bateson have furniture that is very much in keeping – for instance, a wedding-chest dated 1682; a big refectory table; and an iron fireback of 1582 which furnishes the great inglenook where logs blaze on chilly nights. Bedrooms are cottagey in style, one lime-and-white, one (with brass bed) pink-and-white. This is a marvellous place for a family holiday, with plenty of sightseeing outings likely to appeal to older children. Outside is a garden and the Batesons' smallholding (they keep sheep, ducks and horses). There is also accommodation in a converted coach house which can be booked on a b & b or self-catering basis.

For a full dinner, most visitors drive to the White Horse at South Lopham (two miles).

V   *Readers' comments:* Made so welcome. Delightful weekend. Reasonable bill.

MILL HOUSE

CPTSX

Millgate, Bracondale, Norwich, Norfolk, NR1 2EQ   Tel: 01603 621151
Nearest main road: A47 from Swaffham to Great Yarmouth.

2 Bedrooms. £17–£20 (less for 3 nights or more). Both have own bath/shower/toilet; views of river. No smoking.
Light suppers if ordered. Vegetarian or other special diets if ordered. Wine available. No smoking.
1 Sitting-room. With open fire, TV, piano. No smoking.
Large garden

It is a surprise to find this quiet backwater so near the city centre. Facing the placid River Yare, its waters a haven for coots and kingfishers, stands a handsome 18th-century house built of flint and brick. Behind the walled garden run the trains from Norwich to London, but all is silent at night. You can borrow Gillian Evans's rowing boat and take a picnic out onto the marshes; or the strenuous might even get as far as Norwich Cathedral.

Inside the house is a higgledy-piggledy mixture of good antiques and old leather armchairs, interesting pictures (many by Gillian's husband) and pot-plants, log fire in the sitting-room, stone flags on the hall floor. There are handsome architectural details and an elegant staircase to bedrooms that include a good family suite. (Light suppers only, which are from organic wholefood produce whenever possible.) Bicycles on loan.

Readers' comments: Lovely peaceful retreat; wonderful to row down the river in the family boat. Highly recommended.

V

OLD BAKEHOUSE

C

33–35 High Street, Little Walsingham, Norfolk, NR22 6BZ   Tel/Fax: 01328 820454
North of Fakenham. Nearest main road: A148 from King's Lynn to Cromer.

3 Bedrooms. £18.50–£21.50 (less for 7 nights or more). One has own shower/toilet. TV (in all).
Dinner. £13.50 for 3 courses and coffee, at 7pm. Vegetarian or other special diets if ordered. Wine available. No smoking.
1 Bar/lounge
Closed from January to February.

Over a restaurant, renowned for good food, are excellent bedrooms, double-glazed to reduce street noise and comfortably furnished with settees and armchairs.

From 1550 until recent times, part of this house was a bakery and the old brick ovens are still to be seen. Above an ancient cellar bar is a large, lofty dining-room – in the 18th century it was a corn exchange. There is a great brick fireplace at one end, and a huge iron-hinged door. Chris and Helen Padley serve such delectable table d'hôte meals as fresh peaches baked with cheese and herbs; banana-stuffed chicken with a mild curry-and-almond sauce; and ice-cream coffee-cake; there is a wider à la carte choice too.

A pilgrimage centre since the Middle Ages, the village has a museum charting the history of the pilgrims.

Readers' comments: Gourmet food; friendly and efficient. Loving attention to detail; food superb. Food wonderful. Comfortable rooms, friendly and accommodating hosts. Food first class. Took real pains to make us welcome.

V

OLD PUMP HOUSE

C D S

Holman Road, Aylsham, Norfolk, NR11 6BY   Tel: 01263 733789
North of Norwich. Nearest main road: A140 from Norwich to Cromer.

5 Bedrooms. £18–£22 (less for 7 nights or more). Bargain breaks. Some have some or all of the following: own bath/shower/toilet; TV. No smoking.
Dinner (by arrangement). £10 for 2 courses and coffee, at 6.30–7.30pm. Vegetarian or other special diets if ordered. No smoking. **Light suppers** if ordered.
1 Sitting-room. With open fire, TV. No smoking.
Small garden

There is peace as well as beauty inside this house, which is a surprise as it is on a junction of roads. But the old walls are thick and the view from the back (originally it was the front) is of a secluded garden: ask for a bedroom that overlooks this. Those at the front look onto the quaint, thatch-roofed pump which gives the former farmhouse its name.

It is a house of twists and turns, extended many times since it was built about 1750, with innumerable steps. To this characterful background Hazel Stringer's decorative flair has contributed strong colours like raspberry and turquoise, complemented by bamboo or pine furniture and jungly-patterned duvets. The apricot walls of the staircase contrast with a traditional floor of terracotta slabs; and, in the dining-room, scarlet walls with a very dark board floor and pale pine shutters. There is a small sitting-area on the landing.

Very English dishes are served at dinner, such as steak and kidney pie or salmon mayonnaise, and bread-and-butter pudding.

Within a short stroll are Aylsham's historic church and the market place.

PEACOCK HOUSE

C D S X

Peacock Lane, Old Beetley, Norfolk, NR20 4DG   Tel: 01362 860371/01760 24172
North of East Dereham. Nearest main road: A47 from East Dereham to Norwich.

rear view

3 Bedrooms. £18–£20. All have some or all of the following: own bath/shower/toilet. No smoking.
Light suppers if ordered. Vegetarian or other special diets if ordered. Wine available. No smoking.
2 Sitting-rooms. With open fire/stove, TV, piano. No smoking.
Large garden

Once a farm, the tranquil house hides its Elizabethan beams behind a façade added in Victorian times. On arrival, guests are taken by Jenny Bell into their own little sitting-room with cretonne chairs facing a log stove and given home-made flapjacks or scones with tea. In another, larger sitting-room an open fire blazes on cold days – or when it is sunny you may prefer to wander out to the large lawn, with old apple-trees and a pond, surrounded by fields with the Bells' sheep and chickens (lambs among the daffodils in spring).

Upstairs are rooms with impressively handsome brass beds, sprigged wallpaper matching the curtains, exposed timbers, and a really huge bathroom.

Breakfasts are both generous and varied (home-produced eggs and local sausages are very popular with guests); and as to dinner, there is a good local inn or, by arrangement, Jenny will serve you supper.

Readers' comments: Truly rural. Wonderful welcome. Spared no efforts in caring for our comfort. Tastefully furnished; lovely room.

REGENCY HOUSE

Neatishead, Norfolk, NR12 8AD   Tel: 01692 630233
North-east of Norwich. Nearest main road: A1151 from Norwich to Stalham.

3 Bedrooms. £18–£23 **(less for 2 nights or more to readers of this book).** Bargain breaks. Some have some of the following: own bath/shower/toilet; TV (in all).
Light suppers if ordered.
1 Sitting-room. With stove.
Small garden
Closed in November.

In the Norfolk Broads, former Manchester bank-manager Alan Wrigley and his wife Sue run this 18th-century guest-house to an immaculate standard.

The breakfasts are outstanding: standard issue is 2 sausages, 4 rashers of bacon, 6 mushrooms, 2 whole tomatoes, 2 slices of fried bread and as many eggs as you request! But if you prefer it, Sue will produce a vegetarian breakfast instead. This is served in an oak-panelled room on tables that were specially made by a local craftsman. Bedrooms have Laura Ashley fabrics (two have king-size beds). The sitting-room has leather armchairs and a beamed ceiling. For dinner, there is a choice of eating-places within yards of the guest-house.

Readers' comments: Welcoming, friendly. Large rooms, lovely furnishings. Amazing breakfasts, generous hospitality. The best b & b we've stayed in. Very neat, well-appointed rooms. Excellent in every way. Highly recommended.

V

STODY HALL

Stody, Norfolk, NR24 2ED   Tel/Fax: 01263 860549
North-east of Fakenham. Nearest main road: A148 from Cromer to Fakenham.

3 Bedrooms. £20–£25 (less for 7 nights or more). Some have own bath/toilet; TV. No smoking.
Dinner. £18 for 3 courses and coffee, at 7.30pm (not Sundays). Vegetarian or other special diets if ordered. No smoking. **Light suppers** if ordered.
1 Sitting-room. With open fire, TV, piano.
Large garden

This handsome, 400-year-old house has the flint walls typical of the area. Inside, there are comfortable sofas in a sitting-room with silky coral walls and marble fireplace, log fire, watercolours of local scenes on the walls. There are mementoes of Khartoum (where a family forebear served with General Gordon); and 'Spy' cartoons in another sitting-room. In the garden are a hard tennis court and a croquet lawn. (Carriage drives available.)

The dining-room is particularly dramatic, the colour of its Turkey carpet repeated in the scarlet walls that are the background to a great Regency table and chairs. Miriam Rawlinson serves such dinners as haddock mousse, beef Stroganoff (with garden vegetables), and crème brûlée.

Upstairs are attractive bedrooms with, for example, a tufted white spread contrasting with the rosy satin of bedhead and curtains, lacy cushions (made by Miriam), a wardrobe of figured mahogany, and draped dressing-tables. One room has a four-poster bed.

Readers' comments: Wonderful food, ambience and hosts. Elegant house in charming village; cooking imaginative and excellent.

TOLL BARN

C(12) **D M**

off the Norwich Road, North Walsham, Norfolk, NR28 0JB   Tel: 01692 403063
(Fax: 01692 406582)

North of Norwich. Nearest main road: A149 from Great Yarmouth to Cromer.

6 Bedrooms. £19–£25 (less for 2 nights or more).
Bargain breaks. All have some or all of the following:
own bath/shower/toilet; TV. No smoking.
Light suppers if ordered. Vegetarian or other special
diets if ordered. No smoking.
Small courtyard gardens

In the 14th century, the nearby market town of North Walsham became a centre for the wool trade, and standing right on the famous footpath known as 'The Weavers Way' is the huge, 18th-century Toll Barn, now immaculately converted and handsomely furnished. Beyond two courtyard gardens with fountains are six spacious, ground-floor bedrooms. All have en suite facilities and pretty colour schemes; and are very well equipped, including fridges. Annette Tofts provides good suppers which guests have in their rooms (each has its own sitting-area). Breakfast is served in bedrooms or the large, brick-and-beamed dining-room in the main house.

Readers' comments: Delightful home, superb conversion. Spacious, comfortable. Ideal hosts, professional but warm and relaxed. Could have stayed for ever! Food outstanding. Owners absolutely charming, rooms and facilities first class. The best we have stayed in. Second to none.

WHITE HALL

C

Carbrooke, Norfolk, IP25 6SG   Tel/Fax: 01953 885950
North-east of Thetford. Nearest main road: A1075 from Thetford to East Dereham.

3 Bedrooms. £19–£22 (less for 4 nights or more).
One has own bath/toilet. No smoking.
Light suppers if ordered.
1 Sitting-room. With open fire, TV, piano.
Large garden

The hamlet was already an ancient settlement when the Romans came here. In the mediaeval church, the hammerbeam roof and rood-screen are particularly fine. White Hall is, by contrast, quite a recent addition to the scene – little more than two centuries old. An elegant Georgian house, it is surrounded by grounds where you may encounter guinea-fowl and bantams.

Inside, Shirley Carr has furnished the sitting-room with peony sofas facing the marble fireplace, and the light bedrooms with pink roses or green-sprigged fabrics complementing white or shell-pink walls. The dining-room has a big log stove and, like other rooms, large sash windows through which to enjoy tranquil views.

For active visitors, there are available croquet, bicycles, badminton.

Readers' comments: I felt like a very privileged guest. Delightful couple, easy-going attitude. Staying there was a real pleasure. Nothing too much trouble. Beautifully decorated. Friendly and welcoming. Excellent decor. Best one yet, helpful and charming owners.

NORTHAMPTONSHIRE

Major tourist attractions, such as Stratford-upon-Avon and Cambridge, can often be easily reached from houses in adjacent counties.

CASTLE FARM

C

Fotheringhay, Northamptonshire, PE8 5HZ   Tel: 01832 226200
South-west of Peterborough. Nearest main road: A605 from Peterborough to Oundle.

6 Bedrooms. £17.50–£25 (less for 5 nights or more). All have some or all of the following: own bath/shower/toilet; TV; views of river.
Dinner (by arrangement). £11 for 2 courses and coffee, at 7pm. Vegetarian or other special diets if ordered. No smoking. **Light suppers** if ordered.
1 Sitting-room. With open fire, TV.
Large garden

In the castle that was once here, Richard III was born. Later, Mary Queen of Scots' heart was secretly buried in the mound on which the keep stood: part of the land belonging to Castle Farm today. The thistles that grow here are called Queen Mary's Tears.

At the Victorian farm, one steps straight into Stephanie Gould's huge quarry-tiled kitchen where a pine staircase rises to spacious bedrooms that are spick-and-span, all with nice views. There are very good bath- or shower-rooms, and much stripped pine. The big, comfortable sitting-room, too, has a view to enjoy – of the swift River Nene beyond the lawn, and a picturesque bridge. The Goulds have converted outbuildings to make more bedrooms.

Stephanie produces traditional meals of two courses (such as lamb navarin, followed by sticky pear-gingerbread) or one can eat well at the nearby Falcon Inn.

Readers' comments: Very relaxed. Good breakfast. Lovely view. Beautifully furnished. Excellent room. Friendly young hostess. Could not have been more hospitable. Rooms excellent and very up-market. Excellent facilities.

DAIRY FARM

C D M S

St Andrews Lane, Cranford, Northamptonshire, NN14 4AQ   Tel: 01536 330273
East of Kettering. Nearest main road: A14 from Kettering towards Cambridge.

3 Bedrooms. £20–£28 (less for 4 nights or more). All have some or all of the following: own bath/shower/toilet; TV. No smoking.
Dinner (by arrangement). £12.50 for 3 courses and coffee, at 7pm. Vegetarian or other special diets if ordered. No smoking. **Light suppers** if ordered.
1 Sitting-room. With open fire, TV. No smoking.
Garden

This is not in fact a dairy-farm but arable and sheep. Its name derives from the old dairy around which the manor house was built, in 1610. It is a fine building with mullioned lattice windows in limestone walls and a thatched roof. Its noble chimney-stacks, finials on the gables, dormer windows and dignified porch give it great character. In the grounds stands a circular stone dovecote (mediaeval) with unique rotating ladder inside.

Audrey and John Clarke have hung old family portraits in the sitting-room, and furnished the house with things like oak chests and ladderback chairs that are in keeping with it. Some bedrooms, one with four-poster, overlook church and mansion nearby.

Meals consist of straightforward home cooking – soups, roasts, fruit pies – using fruit and vegetables from the garden. Mrs Clarke also does a cordon bleu menu, which costs a little more and has to be ordered ahead. Visitors enjoy croquet, good walks and cycling.

Readers' comments: Very special, will return. Delicious food; peaceful; attentive hosts. Very kind, food plentiful, peaceful. Delightful house and setting. Good, friendly reception. Good food, relaxed atmosphere.

V

DINGLEY LODGE

CD

Harborough Road, Dingley, Northamptonshire, LE16 8PJ   Tel: 01858 535365
East of Market Harborough. Nearest main road: A427 from Market Harborough to
Corby.

7 Bedrooms. £20–£26 (less for 7 nights or more). All
have some or all of the following: own bath/shower/
toilet; TV. No smoking.
Dinner (by arrangement). £10 for 3 courses and
coffee, at 7.30pm. Vegetarian or other special diets if
ordered. Wine available. No smoking. **Light suppers**
if ordered.
2 Sitting-rooms. With open fire. **Bar.**
Large garden

Victorian Dingley Lodge, overlooking the Welland Valley, has been converted by two young
teachers, Bruce and Christine Kirkman, into a comfortable hotel. Most of the en suite bedrooms, spacious and with their original little iron fireplaces, enjoy the far view – as does the
bay window of the dining-room, which opens onto a brick terrace where sometimes there is
a barbecue. Meals usually comprise a menu such as local Brixworth pâté with Cumberland
sauce, coq au vin, and bananas in brandy sauce. The sitting-areas have a bar, Victorian-
style wallpaper and church pews.

Georgian Market Harborough is at the centre of rich grazing country – a tranquil region
threaded by waterways with, at Foxton, 10 locks stacked in a tier to raise boats up a 75-foot
incline. The many stately homes of this prosperous county include Althorp (childhood
home of the late Diana, Princess of Wales) and Boughton House (modelled on Versailles).
There are Saxon churches at Brixworth and Earls Barton.

V

MURCOTT MILL

CDPTSX

Long Buckby, Northamptonshire, NN6 7QR   Tel/Fax: 01327 842236
North-west of Northampton. Nearest main road: A428 from Northampton to Rugby
(and M1, junction 17).

3 Bedrooms. £18–£20. All have own bath/shower/
toilet; TV.
Dinner (by arrangement). £7.50 for 2 courses and
coffee, at 7.30pm. Vegetarian or other special diets if
ordered. No smoking. **Light suppers** if ordered.
1 Sitting-room. With open fire, TV.
Small garden

This 18th-century house, approached via a long, private drive, is a mill no longer but a
farm. Carrie, descendant of the original owner, married Australian Brian Hart who (revers-
ing the usual order of things!) immigrated here to keep sheep and raise a young family. The
house – no ordinary mill – has big bay windows, marble fireplaces, handsome doors, alcoves
and pretty plasterwork, all of which Carrie has complemented with pretty colour schemes
such as coral and pale turquoise in the en suite bedrooms, with wisteria-patterned chintz
downstairs. She serves snacks or such traditional meals as chops and apple pie.

The mill is well placed for seeking out not only the pretty and unspoilt villages hidden in
Northamptonshire's unappreciated lanes but also such masterpieces as the stately homes of
Althorp, Canons Ashby and Castle Ashby, Cottesbrooke (inspiration for Jane Austen's
Mansfield Park), mediaeval Deene Park, Kirby and Lamport Halls, and Sulgrave Manor,
which Henry VIII sold to an ancestor of George Washington.

Northamptonshire

OLD VICARAGE

C D X

Laxton, Northamptonshire, NN17 3AT   Tel: 01780 450248 (Fax: 01780 450398)
North-east of Corby. Nearest main road: A43 from Kettering to Stamford.

4 Bedrooms. £16.50. All have TV.
1 Sitting-room. With open fire, TV. Piano.
Large garden

Humphry Repton, famous as a landscape gardener, designed the whole village of Laxton in 1804; which is why this house is so attractive, in 'gothick' style. Susan Hill-Brookes and her husband have filled every room with Victorian landscapes and still-lifes, portraits of dogs and other treasures. The guests' elegant sitting-room is light and airy and overlooks the garden. A twisting stair at the back leads to old-fashioned bedrooms furnished with antiques. There is a small, unheated swimming-pool; also a croquet lawn.

This is a good area for walking or cycling (bikes for hire) and other country pursuits, and for sightseeing too: the historic schools at Uppingham and Oundle, the mediaeval town of Stamford, castles at Rockingham and Belvoir as well as the stately homes of Burghley and Belton – at the former, horse trials take place every September. Rutland Water is a particularly fine man-made reservoir where fishing and sailing are available.

V

Northamptonshire

RECTORY FARM

C D

Sulgrave, Northamptonshire, OX17 2SG   Tel: 01295 760261 (Fax: 01295 760089)
North-east of Banbury. Nearest main road: A43 from Northampton towards Oxford (and M40, junction 11).

3 Bedrooms. £17.50 (less for 5 nights or more). No smoking.
Dinner (by arrangement). £14 for 3 courses and coffee, at 7.30–9pm. Vegetarian or other special diets if ordered. Wine available. No smoking.
1 Sitting-room. With open fire, piano. No smoking.
Small garden

George Washington's ancestors lived at Sulgrave Manor, which remained in the Washington family for 120 years and is now a museum. Overlooking the manor house is 17th-century Rectory Farm, thatched without and stone-flagged within. Generously proportioned rooms have wide, panelled doors and deep-set windows with white shutters behind cream curtains that contrast with rust-red rugs on the floor and the peonies on the capacious armchairs. Bedrooms are in pleasant country-house style; and from the window of the upstairs landing you can see the Stars and Stripes and Union Jack flags flying over Sulgrave Manor.

Joanna Smyth-Osbourne, despite bringing up a young family, finds time to produce such beautifully cooked dinners as parsnip soup flavoured with ginger and orange, pork-and-apple ragoût, and a delicious kiwi fruit ice cream. Outside are sheep, ponies, featherylegged bantams and pheasants strutting the autumn fields. Joanna can recommend several lovely walks nearby. Winding lanes go up and down, passing picturesque villages like Moreton Pinkney and ancient churches.

V

194

SHUCKBURGH ARMS

Stoke Doyle, Northamptonshire, PE8 5TG Tel: 01832 272339
South-west of Oundle. Nearest main road: A605 from Peterborough to Oundle.

5 Bedrooms. £20 **to readers of this book.** All have own shower/toilet; TV.
Dinner. £10 for 2 courses and coffee, from 7–9.30pm. Vegetarian or other special diets if ordered. Wine available. No smoking.
1 Bar. With open fire.
Small garden

The quintessential English pub is something of a rarity these days, but the character of this 17th-century inn remains unspoiled. Paul Kirkby has added the comfort of cherry velvet chesterfields and panelled walls in the bar, where logs blaze in a stone inglenook. Food (in bar or restaurant) is excellent. Casseroles are a speciality of the house and there are real ales to sample. The mulberry-and-white en suite bedrooms are not only of the highest standard but well segregated from the inn by a garden, which has a children's play area.

Oundle is as attractive as many Cotswold towns, for the local stone is the same, but much less frequented by tourists. The buildings of its famous public school are like an Oxford college. One can take boat trips on the River Nene, visit watermills, and (at Kettering) Wicksteed Park is an ideal place to take children. Fotheringhay, where Mary Queen of Scots was executed, has a particularly fine church with interesting tombs. Cromwell defeated Charles I's army at Naseby in 1645 (good bar food at the Fitzgerald Arms, and a museum of the battle).

UPTON MILL

Upton, Northamptonshire, NN5 6UY Tel/Fax: 01604 753277
West of Northampton. Nearest main road: A45 from Northampton to Daventry (and M1, junctions 15a/16).

3 Bedrooms. £17.50–£25. One has own bath/toilet; TV (two); views of river (two). No smoking.
Dinner (by arrangement). £10 for 4 courses and coffee, at times to suit guests. Vegetarian or other special diets if ordered. **Light suppers** if ordered.
1 Sitting-room. With piano.
Large garden
Closed from Christmas to Easter.

It's hard to believe there is such a peaceful haven for wildlife just off the busy A45. Built right across the bubbling River Nene, Upton Mill (mentioned in the Domesday Book), now a farmhouse, is the focal point of many lovely footpaths: they were first trodden by farmers carrying grain to the mill. From the dining-room (with high-back, French-style chairs and a Jacobean-style carved wooden sideboard) and a sun-room, one steps into a wildlife garden on the river bank, with pond for moorhens beyond and over 1000 acres for sheep and cows.

Jane Spokes cooks such dinners as apple and curry soup, chicken, and lemon soufflé, and in warm weather meals may be served outside in the garden.

The area is excellent for birdwatching; fishing is available in the millpond, and just a short walk away are two large lakes with ducks.

WALLTREE HOUSE FARM

C M

Steane, Northamptonshire, NN13 5NS   Tel: 01295 811235 (Fax: 01235 811147)
North-west of Brackley. Nearest main road: A422 from Banbury to Brackley
(and M40, junctions 10/11).

6 Bedrooms. £20–£40 (less for 3 nights or more). Bargain breaks. All have some or all of the following: own bath/shower/toilet; TV. No smoking.
Dinner (by arrangement). £12–£15 for 3 courses and coffee, at 7pm. Vegetarian or other special diets if ordered. Wine available. No smoking. **Light suppers** if ordered.
2 Sitting-rooms. With open fire, TV, piano. No smoking in one.
Large garden
Closed from mid-December to end of January.

Quite a surprise to find, at the end of a long farm lane, a park-like setting in which this handsome Victorian farmhouse stands.

Pauline and Richard Harrison have transformed the house and its outbuildings. Bedrooms in the adjacent courtyard, which look out onto specimen trees, are modern in style: Stag furniture in some, rosy fabrics, much pine, very good bathrooms. You can be sure of ample warmth at any time of the year, for Richard installed a special straw-burner which means all his central heating costs him nothing but the labour of gathering straw from his fields after each harvest. There is a lovely sitting-room with adjoining conservatory.

Dinner (ordered in advance) may be anything from a farm supper to a gourmet menu.

It was at Brackley that the barons negotiated Magna Carta before its sealing at Runnymede later in 1215. The attractive town has some fine historic buildings.

V   *Reader's comment:* Delighted by the facilities and the great welcome.

WOLD FARM

C D P T S X

Old, Northamptonshire, NN6 9RJ   Tel: 01604 781258
North of Northampton. Nearest main road: A508 from Northampton to Market Harborough (also M1, junction 15; and M1–A1 link).

6 Bedrooms. £19–£24 (less for 3 nights or more). Some have some or all of the following: own bath/shower/toilet; TV. No smoking.
Dinner (by arrangement). £15 for 4 courses, wine and coffee, at 7pm. Vegetarian or other special diets if ordered. No smoking. **Light suppers** if ordered.
2 Sitting-rooms. With open fire, TV. No smoking in one. Billiards.
Garden

This 18th-century house has particularly attractive and spacious rooms, and two delightful gardens with rose pergola, golden pheasants and swing-seat. A garden-cottage has been converted to provide more bedrooms (en suite), one of which is on the ground floor. Throughout the house are attractive fabrics and wallpapers. In the sitting-room are alcoves of Hummel figures, in the dining-room a carved 17th-century sideboard, and in the breakfast-room a dresser with the exhortation: 'Nourish thyself with lively vivacity'.

For dinner, in the oak-beamed dining-room with inglenook fireplace, Anne Engler (once a 'Tiller girl') serves such meals as home-made soup followed by a roast and then perhaps fruit salad or Bakewell tart, and cheeses – with a sherry, wine or beer included.

Readers' comments: Cooking outstanding. Very thoughtful attention. Harmony and friendliness. Exactingly high standard. Kind and generous. It excels. Attractive garden. Pretty and **V**   very comfortable room. Food a delight; table-settings superb.

NORTHUMBERLAND

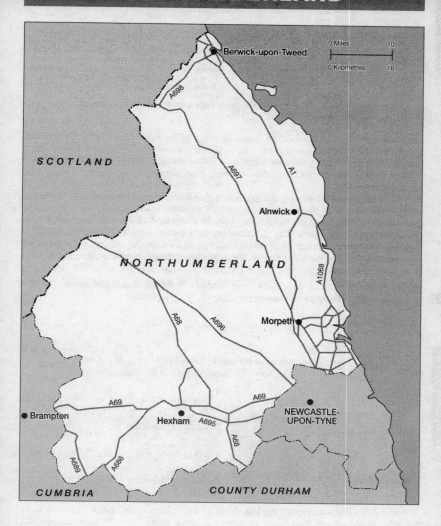

To find the right accommodation in the right area at the right price, use an up-to-date edition of this book – revised every year. For an order form for the next edition (published in November), send a stamped addressed envelope with 'SOTBT 1999' in the top left-hand corner, to Explore Britain, Alston, Cumbria, CA9 3SL.

Northumberland

BILTON BARNS   C

Bilton, Alnmouth, Northumberland, NE66 2TB   Tel: 01665 830427
(Fax: 01665 830063)
South-east of Alnwick. Nearest main road: A1 from Newcastle to Berwick-upon-Tweed.

3 Bedrooms. £19. Bargain breaks. All have own shower/toilet; TV; views of sea. No smoking.
Dinner (by arrangement). £12 for 3 courses and coffee, at 6.30pm. Vegetarian diets if ordered.
2 Sitting-rooms. With open fire. Piano.
Garden
Closed from mid-October to Easter.

On a 400-acre mixed farm is Bilton Barns, an early 18th-century house with very spacious rooms, which – like the sun lounge – all overlook the sweep of Alnmouth Bay across a croquet lawn. For dinner, Dorothy Jackson offers for instance, smoked trout from Craster, a roast, and sticky-toffee pudding, or something more elaborate on occasion. A farm walk can be arranged.

From here you could explore the grand coastline with its sandy beaches, and numerous castles. The nearest of these is at picturesque Warkworth (galleries here for craft and art too), which was the home of Hotspur. In *Henry IV Part 1* he called it 'this worm eaten hold of ragged stone', but parts were progressively refurbished over the centuries. Inland is Cragside, the mansion which Norman Shaw designed for Lord Armstrong, the armaments king. One of the most complete late-Victorian houses there are, it was the first in the world to be lit by electricity.

Readers' comments: Most hospitable and helpful. Spacious and comfortable. Dinner delicious. I would heartily recommend it.

BRUNTON HOUSE   C S

Brunton, near Embleton, Northumberland, NE66 3HQ   Tel: 01665 589238
North of Alnwick. Nearest main road: A1 from Alnwick to Berwick-upon-Tweed.

7 Bedrooms. £17–£20 (less for 7 nights or more). Some have some or all of the following: own bath/shower/toilet. No smoking.
Dinner (by arrangement). £12 for 4 courses and coffee, at 7pm. Vegetarian or other special diets if ordered. No smoking.
2 Sitting-rooms. With open fire, TV. No smoking in one.
Large garden
Closed from November to March.

At the end of a tiny hamlet near the sea, this is an 1850s house surrounded by woods and a big, well-tended garden. The rooms are large – even the singles, one of which is, unusually, en suite – and one twin room has its own dressing-room. Simple decoration, as in the blue-painted sitting-room, and old furniture bring out the character of the interior.

Brenda Robson often caters for private dinner parties in the big hall at the foot of the staircase, and so people staying here can take their choice (in advance) from a particularly long menu of over a dozen first and main courses and a loaded sweet trolley.

Close by are not only the Cheviots inland but the big sweep of unspoiled Druridge Bay, massy Dunstanburgh Castle, Holy Island, and Seahouses for boat trips to the Farne Islands to see seals and puffins at close quarters.

Readers' comments: A charming country house; kindness itself.

COACH HOUSE AT CROOKHAM

Cornhill-on-Tweed, Northumberland, TD12 4TD   Tel: 01890 820293
(Fax: 01890 820284)

South-west of Berwick-upon-Tweed. On A697 from Wooler to Coldstream.

C D M S

11 Bedrooms. £20–£36 (less for 7 nights or more). All have some or all of the following: own bath/shower/ toilet; TV.
Dinner. £16.50 for 4 courses and coffee, at 7.30pm. Vegetarian or other special diets if ordered. Wine available. No smoking.
1 Sitting-room. With open fire.
Large garden
Closed from November to Easter.

Close to the site of Flodden Field, this is a group of several old farm buildings forming a square. What was the coach house itself is now the sitting-room, with lofty beamed ceiling and great arched windows and an enormous brick fireplace.

The highly individual bedrooms have interesting paintings, and fridges. Lynne Anderson used to travel a great deal and so has a lot of practical ideas about what travellers need.

Breakfasts are excellent; and for dinner there is a choice of 6 starters; a roast or casserole; puddings or one of 15 home-made ice creams. Organic produce is used increasingly.

Readers' comments: So much room, the very best breakfast, and Lynne is exceptionally good at making guests at ease with one another. Outstanding. Charm, friendliness, service; cannot be too highly praised, meals difficult to better at any price. Everything a guest might want.

V

HOLMHEAD

Greenhead, Northumberland, CA6 7HY   Tel/Fax: 016977 47402
East of Brampton. Nearest main road: A69 from Carlisle to Hexham.

C M P T S X

4 Bedrooms. £20–£23.50 (less for 3 nights or more). Bargain breaks. All have own shower/toilet. No smoking.
Dinner. £16.95 for 4 courses and coffee, at 7.30pm. Vegetarian or other special diets if ordered. Wine available. No smoking. **Light snacks.**
1 Sitting-room. With open fire, TV, organ. No smoking.
Large garden
Closed from mid-December to mid-January.

Beside a salmon river, just where the walkers' Pennine Way crosses Hadrian's Wall, this remote house has the ruins of Thirlwall Castle looming overhead, within view through the windows of the guests' large and comfortable upstairs sitting-room.

Although some of the bedrooms are small, there are all kinds of unexpected 'extras': a foot-massager for weary walkers; pure spring water; table tennis; snacks at any hour. Pauline Staff makes all the preserves, chutneys, cakes, bread and scones. A typical dinner: melon with kiwi fruit; trout in hollandaise sauce; almond meringue with wild raspberries. Out of season, a ground-floor flat is available for b & b, and groups can be accommodated over Christmas. Breakfast choices include haggis, black pudding, kedgeree, muffins and crumpets.

Pauline has a diploma in archaeology and local history and is a qualified guide.

Readers' comments: Excellent accommodation; highlight was the food. Delightful place, superb meals. Situation beautiful, food excellent. Mealtime a joy. Kindness and hospitality terrific. Food memorably good. Comfortable; very knowledgeable hostess.

V

MANTLE HILL

C(3) S

Hesleyside, Bellingham, Northumberland, NE48 2LB Tel: 01434 220428
(Fax: 01434 220113)
North-west of Hexham. Nearest main road: A68 from Corbridge to Jedburgh.

3 Bedrooms. £20–£25. Bargain breaks. All have some or all of the following: own bath/shower/toilet; views of river.
Dinner (by arrangement). £15 for 3 courses and coffee, at 8pm. Wine available. **Light suppers** if ordered.
1 Sitting-room. With open fire, TV.
Large garden

Mantle Hill is a 17th-century farmhouse with well-proportioned rooms and two acres of fine gardens. These provide most of the fruit and vegetables which Charlotte Loyd uses for the dinners she provides by arrangement; and the farm, run by her husband, provides the lamb and beef. As he is also in the wine business, the short wine list is well chosen. Charlotte's marmalade won a *Daily Mail* 'taste test'. Close by, the River North Tyne (in which fishing is often possible) runs through peaceful, well-wooded country – at its most beautiful in May. In the nearby mansion, a reiver family (bandits, now reformed!) has lived for 650 years. Views from all rooms are magnificent.

Further into the Northumberland National Park is Kielder Water for sailing, etc.

Readers' comments: Jewel in the crown of this area. A feeling of warmth and friendship. Most attractive house, wonderful setting. Never felt more at home. Made very welcome, food delicious.

V

PHEASANT INN

C D M P T S

Stannersburn, Northumberland, NE48 1DD Tel/Fax: 01434 240382
North-west of Hexham. Nearest main road: A68 from Corbridge to Jedburgh.

8 Bedrooms. £20–£28 (less for 2 nights or more from October to May). Bargain breaks. All have own shower/toilet; TV. No smoking.
Dinner. £15 for 4 courses and coffee, at 7–9pm. Vegetarian or other special diets if ordered. Wine available. No smoking. **Light suppers.**
2 Lounge bars. With open fires.
Small garden

Close to Kielder Water, this is everything one wants a country inn to be – nearly four centuries old, stone-walled and low-beamed and in particularly lovely countryside. The Kershaws are determined to keep it unspoilt. The bedrooms, however, are modern, in a former hemel (farm implements store) and barn; many of them are on the ground floor.

The main bar (where very good snacks are served) is big and beamy, with a stone fireplace and some agricultural bygones, such as hay-knives and peat-spades; and a stuffed pheasant appropriately sits on the window-sill.

The dining-room is light and airy, with raspberry-coloured walls and pine furniture. Food is freshly prepared – one interesting starter is avocado with grapefruit and Stilton; trout comes with a sauce of yogurt and herbs.

Readers' comments: Delightful country inn. Mr Kershaw and his family could not have been more friendly and courteous, our room was spotlessly clean, the food truly delicious – we look forward to a return. A real pub, very good food, friendly and helpful staff.

V

SHIELDHALL

Cambo, Northumberland, NE61 4AQ Tel/Fax: 01830 540387
West of Morpeth. Nearest main road: A696 from Newcastle to Otterburn.

6 Bedrooms. £17–£25 (less for 3 nights or more). All have own bath/shower/toilet. No smoking.
Dinner (by arrangement). £14.75 for 4 courses and coffee, at 7pm. Vegetarian or other special diets if ordered. Wine available. No smoking. **Light suppers** if ordered.
2 Sitting-rooms. With open fire, TV. No smoking.
Bar.
Large garden
Closed from December to February.

Eighteenth-century stone buildings enclose a courtyard where white fantails strut, the former barns to left and right providing very well-equipped ground-floor bedrooms for visitors – each with its own entrance. Meals are taken in a beamed dining-room in the centre, furnished with antiques and an inglenook fireplace (a typical dinner might be home-made soup, a roast or coq au vin, blackcurrant tart, and local cheeses – with produce from the garden and orchard); and to one side are two sitting-rooms (one with library) for visitors.

Stephen Robinson-Gay is an accomplished cabinet-maker, happy to show visitors the workshop where he makes or restores furniture. Most of the work in all the rooms is his. For instance, beyond the arched doorway of the mahogany room is a colonial-style bed with very fine inlay, and in the oak room a Flemish-style four-poster with carved canopy.

Celia is a fount of information on local history and what to see.

Readers' comments: Super place. Fantastic holiday; everything you said and much more; lovely couple, food delicious.

STOTSFOLD HALL

Steel, Northumberland, NE47 0HP Tel: 01434 673270
South of Hexham. Nearest main road: A695 from Hexham to Corbridge.

4 Bedrooms. £19.50.
1 Sitting-room. With open fire, TV. **Bar.**
Large garden

Off a quiet road which leads to nowhere in particular is Stotsfold Hall.

Once the heart of a big estate now broken up, the present house stands at the end of a long drive in a 15-acre park. There are big lawns, flowerbeds, a rose garden, and a large greenhouse. Even though the house is at 800 feet, the lie of the land is such that everything seems to flourish. Particularly impressive are the trees which are a feature of the grounds.

The house was built in 1900 and is full of the monumental joinery characteristic of the time. The scale is large, ceilings high, windows big. Furnishings are conventional and comfortable. On the walls hang old deeds and mortgages.

As the Woottons do not provide an evening meal, guests go to Hexham or Slaley to eat. On their return, visitors can make use of the house bar.

Readers' comments: Difficult to conceive of a better place to stay. Brilliant! Very warm welcome. Idyllic. A splendid country house. What a delight to walk in the garden and woodland. So many comforts and extras. Incredible value. Excellent hosts.

THORNBROUGH HIGH HOUSE

C D

Corbridge, Northumberland, NE45 5PR Tel: 01434 633080
East of Hexham. Nearest main road: A69 from Newcastle towards Hexham.

3 Bedrooms. £20–£25 (less for 4 nights or more). All have own bath/toilet. No smoking.
Dinner (by arrangement). £15 for 3 courses and coffee, at 8pm. No smoking. **Light suppers** if ordered.
1 Sitting-room. With open fire, TV, piano. No smoking.
Large garden
Closed from mid-December to Easter.

Not only the house but the outbuildings are 'listed' here, some of the latter housing Ailsa Speke's horses (including hunters and thoroughbreds). The spacious Regency house has impressive views, across a haha, of the rolling fields of the Tyne Valley, some of them belonging to the farm. It is pleasantly furnished: in the dining-room, for example, are old oak ladderback chairs round a big table, carpets are plain, and fabrics are well chosen. Ailsa, who is cordon-bleu trained, might serve a dinner of pâté, pheasant, and home-made ice cream and meringues. Outside are a tennis court and plenty of play equipment for children, including a big trampoline.

Both sides of the family have deep roots in the area, and Ben Speke is descended from the famous explorer.

With a history that goes back to the Romans, picturesque Corbridge, a couple of miles away, is a large village where there are good pubs and superior shops. A big attraction here is Hadrian's Wall, some of the best sites being close. Not far away are the birthplaces of George Stephenson, the railway pioneer, and of the wood-engraver Thomas Bewick.

Readers' comments: Stunning views and tranquillity; made extremely welcome; meals delicious; a fantastic place.

THORNLEY HOUSE

D S X

Allendale, Northumberland, NE47 9NH Tel: 01434 683255
South-west of Hexham. Nearest main road: A69 from Newcastle towards Hexham.

3 Bedrooms. £18.50 (less for 4 nights or more). Bargain breaks. All have some or all of the following: own bath/shower/toilet.
Dinner. £11 for 3 courses and coffee, at about 7pm. Vegetarian or other special diets if ordered. No smoking.
2 Sitting-rooms. With TV, piano. No smoking.
Large garden

Allendale Town is a large village in a sheltered valley amid some of the most open scenery in England – deserted grouse moors and breezy sheep pastures which stretch for uninterrupted miles, punctuated only by isolated farmhouses. On the outskirts of the village is this large and solid inter-war house in a big garden with woods and fields around it.

Eileen Finn is a keen cook, and though guests are offered conventional fare (vichyssoise soup, breaded chicken, salad, and chocolate mousse, for example), she needs only a little encouragement to cook a dish from Mexico, where she lived for eight years, or from another of the many countries to which she has paid long visits. Mementoes of her journeys abound in the house. A fine Steinway grand piano attracts musicians, who sometimes play duets with Eileen. Rooms are spacious and light.

Readers' comments: Delightful venue. Nice house, excellent room. Superbly quiet and comfortable. Wonderful food. Outstanding. Most welcoming. Piano duets a real bonus.

WEST CLOSE HOUSE

C(10) **PT S X**

Hextol Terrace, Hexham, Northumberland, NE46 2AD   Tel: 01434 603307
Nearest main road: A69 from Newcastle to Carlisle.

4 Bedrooms. £17.50–£23.50 (less for 4 nights or more). One has own shower/toilet. No smoking.
Light suppers only. Vegetarian or other special diets if ordered. No smoking.
2 Sitting-rooms. With TV. No smoking.
Small garden

Only 10 minutes' walk from the centre of characterful Hexham, West Close House is in a quiet cul-de-sac. Designed by an architect for himself about 70 years ago, it is a red-brick villa comfortably furnished in an uncluttered style. The prize-winning gardens, enclosed by tall, clipped beech hedges, are beautifully tended, with a revolving summer-house at the back. Patricia Graham-Tomlinson provides varied breakfasts; also simple snacks.

There are excellent Italian, Indian and Chinese restaurants among others in Hexham. The abbey here was founded in the 7th century. The crypt survived the depredations of the Danes, and you can see Roman inscriptions on some of the stones: it was built of material taken from Hadrian's Wall, some of the best sites on which are close.

Readers' comments: The best so far: a winner. Made to feel at home. Breakfast and accommodation excellent.

V

WESTLEA

C(2) **M PT**

29 Riverside Road, Alnmouth, Northumberland, NE66 2SD   Tel: 01665 830730
South-east of Alnwick. Nearest main road: A1068 from Newcastle to Alnwick.

6 Bedrooms. £19–£24 (less for 2 nights or more). Bargain breaks. All have some or all of the following: own bath/shower/toilet; TV; views of estuary. No smoking.
Dinner (by arrangement). From £12 for 4 courses and coffee, at 6.30–7pm. No smoking.
1 Sitting-room. With TV.
Small garden

This is a very comfortable modern guest-house facing the Aln estuary, immaculately kept by Janice Edwards. One attractive bedroom (wildflower fabrics and cane bedheads) opens onto the sunny front garden; others vary in size and style but all are well equipped. The upstairs sitting-room has a balcony from which to enjoy the river view.

Breakfasts are imaginative; and for dinner there may be such dishes as beef, salmon, Cheviot lamb (with Northumbrian baked suet-puddings) or game pie. For the way she runs Westlea, Janice has received many awards. As many visitors come repeatedly for long holidays, booking well ahead is essential.

Readers' comments: A most enjoyable week. Nothing was too much trouble. Excellent food and an amazing choice for breakfast. Excellent value for money. Very impressed with warmth of welcome and unrivalled concern for guests. Overall excellence. Very comfortable.

NOTTINGHAMSHIRE

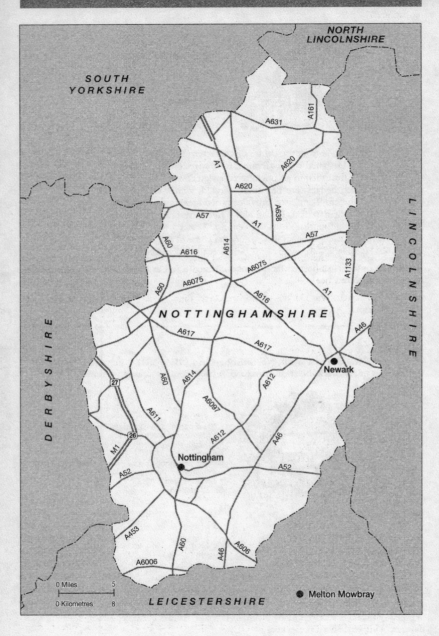

For explanation of code letters and **V** symbol, see inside front cover.

ARCHWAY HOUSE

C(10) D S

Kirklington, Nottinghamshire, NG22 8NX   Tel: 01636 812070 (Fax: 01636 812200)
West of Newark. Nearest main road: A617 from Newark to Mansfield (and M1, junction 27).

3 Bedrooms. £17.50–£19.50 (less for 3 nights or more). All have some or all of the following: own bath/shower/toilet; TV. No smoking.
Dinner (by arrangement). £12.50 for 3 courses and coffee, at 7–9pm. Vegetarian or other special diets if ordered. Wine available. No smoking. **Light suppers** if ordered.
2 Sitting-rooms. With open fire, TV. No smoking (in one).
Large garden
Closed from mid-December to mid-January.

Early this century, the wealthy owner of a coalmine built himself this spacious mansion, its big bay windows overlooking croquet or tennis lawns, with chestnut trees now grown to a great height. As the grounds are bounded by a haha, there is an uninterrupted view of the surrounding fields and parklands. Snowdrops and wood anemones abound early in the year.

Erica McGarrigle has furnished the rooms appropriately with antiques, Victorian paintings, big sofas, and mahogany and silver in the dining-room where a cherry carpet complements walls of billiard-table green. Trained at the celebrated Tante Marie cookery school, she serves such meals as mackerel pâté, boeuf bourguignonne, and lemon meringue pie.

Another of her skills is furniture decoration, examples of which are to be seen around the house. She has used her artistic skills to good effect in bedrooms that have, for instance, garlanded quilts, beribboned curtains or pintucked spreads. There are a snooker table for guests' use and practice golf greens.

Readers' comments: Warmly welcomed, excellent dinner, tastefully furnished. Excellent. Such civilization!

V

HALL FARM HOUSE

C PT

Gonalston, Nottinghamshire, NG14 7JA   Tel: 01159 663112 (Fax: 01159 664844)
North-east of Nottingham. Nearest main road: A612 from Nottingham to Southwell.

3 Bedrooms. £20–£25 (less for 3 nights or more). Bargain breaks. One has own bath/shower/toilet; TV (on request).
Dinner (by arrangement). £15 for 4 courses, drinks and coffee, at 7–8.45pm. Vegetarian or other special diets if ordered. Wine available. **Light suppers** for children.
2 Sitting-rooms. With open fires, TV, piano.
Large garden

To the attractions of the house itself, which was built early in the 18th century, are added the varied pleasures of a pretty garden which include rosebeds, a large heated swimming-pool, tennis court, fish-pond and vegetable garden from which come fruit and other produce for the dinner-table. Stables have been converted to provide a games room (with table tennis).

Rosemary Smith's visitors eat either in the beamed and quarry-tiled dining-room (its French doors open onto the garden) or in the big kitchen. She uses a lot of Prue Leith and Delia Smith recipes. (A typical dinner: tomato vinaigrette, chicken Florida with rice and salad, applecake with clotted cream, and cheeses – wine included.)

The sitting-rooms, also beamed and with oak floors, have antiques and, in one, mallard-patterned sofas around the brick fireplace. Bedrooms are attractive.

Visitors come for a variety of reasons – to enjoy the National Watersports Centre, browse through the many antique shops, follow riverside walks, or visit stately homes.

V

HOLLY LODGE
C M PT X

Ricket Lane, Blidworth, Nottinghamshire, NG21 0NQ Tel: 01623 793853
(Fax: 01623 490977)

North of Nottingham. Nearest main road: A60 from Nottingham to Mansfield (and M1, junction 28).

4 Bedrooms. £20–£22 (less for 5 nights or more). All have some or all of the following: own bath/shower/toilet; TV. No smoking.
Dinner (by arrangement). £15 for 3 courses and coffee, at 7.30pm. Vegetarian or other special diets if ordered. No smoking. **Light suppers** if ordered.
1 Sitting-room. With open fire, TV, piano. No smoking.
Large garden

What remains of great Sherwood Forest lies to the north of Nottingham, and here you will find this Victorian hunting-lodge. It is near the estate of ancient Newstead Abbey which became Byron's home: it and its grounds are open to the public. Most of the visitors' bedrooms at the Lodge are in converted stables opening onto a grassy court with chairs. A Laura Ashley suite with mahogany-fitted bathroom is particularly attractive. Dinners are eaten in the house, sometimes in the big kitchen with its dresser and copper pans: by arrangement, Ann Shipside produces such meals as stuffed tomatoes, salmon, apple-and-sultana custard crumble. Afterwards, one can sit under the grapevine and fuchsias of the conservatory to enjoy a view of old roses and woodland, or by a log fire in the sitting-room.

The Robin Hood Centre is close by, and the historic towns of Southwell, Newark and Nottingham are all within easy reach. There are boat trips on the River Trent.

Readers' comments: The most congenial accommodation we have found. Everything was done with a smile. Superb meal. Rooms beautifully appointed.

OLD FORGE
C D PT X

Burgage Lane, Southwell, Nottinghamshire, NG25 0ER Tel: 01636 812809
(Fax: 01636 816302)

North-east of Nottingham. Nearest main road: A612 from Nottingham to Southwell.

5 Bedrooms. £20–£24 (less for 4 nights or more). Bargain breaks. All have some or all of the following: own bath/shower/toilet; TV. No smoking.
Light suppers if ordered. Vegetarian or other special diets if ordered. Wine available. No smoking.
1 Sitting-room. No smoking.
Small garden

Flower-baskets hang on the pale pink house where once a blacksmith lived and worked. The forge itself, at the back, is now two bedrooms, clematis growing over its roof; and the great stone rim round which iron for wheels was hammered now lies idle by the lily-pool in the little garden. This is overlooked by a small quarry-tiled conservatory from which there is a view of historic Southwell Minster nearby.

Hilary Marston has filled the 200-year-old rooms with treasures such as a very old 'log cabin' quilt from Boston (now used as a wall-hanging), Staffordshire figures, a tapestry chair stitched by a great-aunt, and a brass bed with lace spread.

Each bedroom has its own character. One has a trellis-effect bedhead built in, and tulip-bud wallpaper; another has a good view of the minster floodlit at night. Because there are 10 eating-places within 5 minutes' walk, full evening meals are not provided.

Readers' comments: Nothing too much trouble. Well-decorated, comfortably furnished, each room very individual. Warm welcome. Well-appointed rooms. Outstanding breakfast. First class. Excellent rooms. Superb breakfast, altogether a pleasant experience.

SULNEY FIELDS

CDS

Colonel's Lane, Upper Broughton, Nottinghamshire, LE14 3BD
Tel: 01664 822204 (Fax: 01664 822087)
North-west of Melton Mowbray. Nearest main road: A606 from Melton Mowbray to Nottingham.

5 Bedrooms. £17.50–£22.50 (less for 3 nights or more). Some have some or all of the following: own bath/shower/toilet; TV. No smoking.
Dinner (by arrangement). £15 for 3 courses and coffee, at times to suit guests. Vegetarian or other special diets if ordered. Wine available. No smoking.
Light suppers if ordered.
1 Sitting-room. With open fire, TV.
Large garden
Closed in late December.

Panoramic views over the Vale of Belvoir stretch in front of this handsome 18th-century house, entered through a pretty 'gothick' porch filled with flowering plants. A big sitting-room has a wall of tall windows making the most of this scene. Its silky coral walls are matched by the armchairs.

Hilary Dowson's bedrooms are equally handsome. A big blue one, with fine mahogany furniture and good paintings, has a shower-room and an adjoining room, which makes it ideal for families; the pink room has a bay window for enjoying those views. Outside is a sheltered swimming-pool.

Melton Mowbray is famous for pies (visit Ye Olde Pork Pie Shoppe) and Stilton cheese, made in Colston Bassett village where you can buy it direct; there are riverside parks and an ancient church. Other churches (and villages) well worth a visit include those of Waltham-on-the-Wolds (carved monks) and Bottesford (monuments, and witchcraft associations).

V

Prices are per person sharing a room at the beginning of the year.

Houses which accept the discount vouchers on page ii are marked with a **V** symbol next to the relevant entries.

APPLYING FOR INCLUSION IN SOTBT Many proprietors ask for their houses to be included in this book, and – although few can be accepted – such applications are welcomed, particularly from areas not already well covered; *provided that* the b & b price is within the book's limits (see page ix). Ideally, either dinner or light snacks should be available in the evening. There is no charge for an entry but, compiling the book being expensive, nearly all proprietors make a contribution at the end of each year (no bills are issued). Every house has to be visited first and it may be some time before this takes place. Brochures, prices, menus, etc. should be posted to: Walter Gundrey (SOTBT), c/o Arrow Books, 20 Vauxhall Bridge Road, London SW1V 2SA. No phone calls please.

OXFORDSHIRE

Addresses shown are to enable you to locate a house on a map. They are not necessarily complete postal addresses (though the essential post-code is included), and detailed directions for finding a house should be obtained from the owner.

ASHEN COPSE

Coleshill, Oxfordshire, SN6 7PU Tel/Fax: 01367 240175
North-east of Swindon. Nearest main road: A420 from Swindon to Oxford (and M4, junction 15).

3 Bedrooms. £19–£21. One has own shower/toilet. No smoking.
1 Sitting-room. With open fire, TV. No smoking.
Large garden

A long drive leads past pheasant woods to this 300-year-old house built of stone and brick; and around lie the 600 acres of the Hoddinotts' farm, near Highworth.

It is an ideal house to bring children for a country holiday as there is a particularly good family room separate from the rest. By the staircase to another room are row upon row of colourful rosettes won at pony shows by the Hoddinotts' daughter every year since she was eight. From this bedroom you can look beyond the small swimming-pool (unheated) to the famous Uffington White Horse and the prehistoric Ridgeway.

This is good walking country. From Ashen Copse there is a footpath all the way to Great Coxwell Barn, built by monks in the 13th century. Another goes all round Badbury Clump (site of an Iron Age fort), which is prettiest at bluebell time and from which there are fine views. Also in the vicinity are attractive villages such as Lechlade, Buscot with a National Trust mansion, and Kelmscot (Tudor manor house where William Morris lived).

Readers' comments: Attractive house, pleasant welcome and attention. A tremendously positive experience.

V

BURLEIGH FARM

Bladon Road, Cassington, Oxfordshire, OX8 1EA Tel: 01865 881352
North-west of Oxford. Nearest main road: A4095 from Bicester to Witney.

2 Bedrooms. £20–£22 (less for 2 nights or more). Bargain breaks. Both have own bath/shower/toilet; TV. No smoking.
Light suppers if ordered.
1 Sitting-room. With open fire, TV. No smoking.
Large garden

In the 18th century, the farming scene was drastically changed by the Enclosure Acts. Hedges were planted to enclose fields, and farmhouses were built in remote spots among them, into which villagers moved as tenants of the lord. Burleigh was one such 'enclosure farm' on the great Blenheim estate. It is still owned by the Duke of Marlborough, and farmed by the Cooks, who keep a herd of pedigree Friesian cows.

The stone house combines historic character (stone floors, log fires) with modern comfort. From some rooms there are distant glimpses of Oxford's spires and from others of Blenheim Palace, a romantic prospect when the setting sun glints on the far windows. Visitors are welcome to look round the farm and to follow footpaths through its fields to Bladon church, where Churchill is buried. Little Cassington is even more historic – Bronze and Iron Age relics have recently been found, and the church is Norman.

Readers' comments: Very efficient and well furnished. Warm welcome. Most friendly, welcoming, and extremely helpful and knowledgeable about local amenities.

V

THE CRAVEN

Fernham Road, Uffington, Oxfordshire, SN7 7RD   Tel: 01367 820449
South-west of Oxford. Nearest main road: A420 from Oxford to Swindon (and M4, junction 14).

8 Bedrooms. £18–£28 (less for 7 nights or more). Bargain breaks. Some have some of the following: own bath/shower/toilet; views of river. No smoking.
Dinner (by arrangement). From £14.50 for 3 courses and coffee, at 7pm. Vegetarian or other special diets if ordered. Wine available. No smoking. **Light suppers** if ordered.
1 Sitting-room. With open fire, TV, piano.
Large garden

Three hundred years ago, this cream-walled and thatched house was a hostelry – later described in *Tom Brown's Schooldays*. One of the best bedrooms is on the ground floor – its four-poster hung with cabbage-rose chintz, its pillows in embroidered Victorian pillowslips; in the pretty bathroom is an antique weighing-machine. Upstairs, where passages and steps turn this way and that, are other beamed rooms, equally attractive. The single rooms are as good as the double ones, and bathrooms too.

The beamed sitting-room, with a log fire in its inglenook, has among other antiques a particularly splendid grandfather clock made in Lincolnshire.

Carol Wadsworth serves dinners at a big pine table in her huge L-shaped kitchen or occasionally in the brick-paved courtyard among tubs of plants. A typical dinner: watercress soup; lamb with herb crust; summer pudding with cream. Sunday lunches too.

Readers' comments: Charming place and proprietor. Friendly. Special and enjoyable. Nothing too much trouble, house most attractive, dinner delicious.

---

22 EAST ST HELEN STREET

Abingdon, Oxfordshire, OX14 5EB   Tel/Fax: 01235 533278
Nearest main road: A34 from Oxford to Newbury (and M4, junction 13).

4 Bedrooms. £18–£25 (less for 2 nights or more). One has own bath/shower/toilet; TV (in all); views of river. No smoking.
Dinner (by arrangement). £10 for 3 courses and coffee, at 7.30pm. Vegetarian or other special diets if ordered. No smoking. **Light suppers** if ordered.
1 Sitting-room. With open fire, TV, piano. No smoking.
Small garden

In an ancient side street of old Abingdon, Susie Howard welcomes visitors to her early 18th-century house (near St Helen's, the town's handsome church, five aisles wide). Once the home of an estate bailiff, it is notable for the pine panelling in two rooms and a pilastered doorway on the narrow and twisty staircase. From the attic room is a river view; first-floor rooms overlook an old roofscape; others have views of a very pretty garden. Antiques, attractive fabrics and a stone-flagged dining-room all add to the character of the building. A typical dinner may comprise home-made soup, vegetarian lasagne, and lemon tart. Book well ahead here!

Close by is a house where William III stayed during 'the glorious revolution' of 1688, one of the town's many historic houses; and round the corner you can board a pleasure-boat to go to Oxford (frequent buses nearby, too).

GORSELANDS FARMHOUSE

C D PT X

Boddington Lane, near Long Hanborough, Oxfordshire, OX8 6PU
Tel: 01993 881895 (Fax: 01993 882799)
North-east of Witney. Nearest main road: A4095 from Woodstock to Witney.

5 Bedrooms. £20 **to readers of this book** – £25 **(less for 4 nights to readers of this book).** Bargain breaks. All have some or all of the following: own bath/shower/toilet; TV. No smoking.
Dinner (by arrangement). £14.95 for 3 courses and coffee, from 7–9pm. Vegetarian or other special diets if ordered. Wine available. No smoking. **Light suppers** if ordered.
1 Sitting-room. With open fire, piano. No smoking.
Large garden
Closed from mid-March to mid-April.

Within a short stroll of North Leigh's Roman villa is this comfortable home of Cotswold stone, the oldest part originally a barn. Today it is run as an 'auberge' by Barbara Newcombe-Jones. Beyond the stone-flagged hall is a sitting-room with log fire, a games room with full-size billiard table, and a conservatory where Barbara's staff serve such meals as melon with Parma ham, coq au vin, chocolate mousse, and French cheeses.

Bedrooms, simply furnished but comfortable, are spacious and in the bathroom of one is an oval bathtub. Well-behaved children are welcome; and there is a tennis court.

Gorselands is close to both Oxford and historic Woodstock; spectacular Blenheim Palace (in baroque style, set in grounds landscaped by Capability Brown and now with a huge new maze, as well as boats on its lake); the Cotswold Wildlife Park where exotic animals roam in the gardens and park of an old manor house; and Churchill's grave at Bladon (Blenheim, his birthplace, has a Churchill exhibition).

V

THE GRANARY

M S

Main Street, Clanfield, Oxfordshire, OX18 2SH   Tel: 01367 810266
South-west of Witney. Nearest main road: A4095 from Witney to Faringdon.

3 Bedrooms. £17–£18 **(less for 7 nights to readers of this book).** Bargain breaks. One has own bath/toilet. No smoking.
1 Sitting-room. With TV. No smoking.
Small garden

A willow-fringed stream runs alongside the village road as it pursues its course to the Thames. On the other side are an 18th-century cottage, Victorian shop and old granary that have been turned into a guest-house. There is a beamed dining-room, and guests have their own sitting-room. The best and quietest bedroom is on the ground floor (with its own bathroom); the others are above. Throughout, Rosina Payne's house is spotless, airy and decorated in light and pretty colours. (Good bar meals are available at the Clanfield Tavern.)

This part of the Cotswolds is full of interest. The lanes lead one to such famous sights as Bourton-on-the-Water, Stow-on-the-Wold, Bibury watermill, Burford (and its wildlife park), Witney's farm museum or old Minster Lovell Hall. Just along the road is Radcot and the oldest bridge over the Thames, from which (in summer) narrow-boat trips set out for 18th-century Lechlade. And William Morris's Kelmscott Manor is close.

Readers' comments: Warm and friendly. Accommodation excellent, breakfast delicious. We couldn't praise enough.

V

THE KNOLL

C D PT S

Little Bridge Road, Bloxham, Oxfordshire, OX15 4PU   Tel: 01295 720843
South-west of Banbury. Nearest main road: A361 from Banbury to Chipping Norton.

4 Bedrooms. £18–£22 (less for 3 nights or more). Some have some or all of the following: own bath/shower/toilet; TV. No smoking.
Light suppers if ordered. Vegetarian or other special diets if ordered. No smoking.
Small garden

Bloxham village is a web of steep and twisting lanes, greens, a stream, thatch, flowers, old pumps and richly golden stone walls. The Knoll is an 18th-century guest-house in a pretty walled garden, and near the Oxfordshire cycleway. One room is particularly pretty, with its mulberry Laura Ashley decor; and there is a single room. Wendy Woodward serves only light snacks, but two inns are near.

The Knoll is midway between those twin tourist honeypots, Oxford and Stratford-upon-Avon, and in a very attractive part of the north Oxfordshire Cotswolds. You can still buy Banbury cakes at nearby Banbury and see the cross (reconstructed in 1859) to which the lady of the nursery rhyme rode her 'white horse'. She is said to have been one of the Fiennes family who still live at moated Broughton Castle (open to the public). Gentle hills and streams, villages of golden stone, superb churches and mansions, make the local scene quintessentially English: don't miss Great Tew or Chastleton, for example, or (except at peak periods, when there are too many visitors) Chipping Norton.

V

Months when houses are shown as closed are inclusive.

Private bathrooms are not necessarily en suite.

Book well ahead: many of these houses have few rooms. Do not expect dinner if you have not booked it or if you arrive late.

Complaints about matters which could not have been settled on the spot will be forwarded to proprietors. Please enclose a stamped addressed envelope if you want the authors to acknowledge receipt of your complaint.

MAYFIELD COTTAGE

West End, Combe, Oxfordshire, OX8 8NP   Tel: 01993 898298
North-west of Oxford. Nearest main road: A4095 from Witney to Bicester.

C(12) **PT**

3 Bedrooms. £17–£19 (less for 2 nights or more). No smoking.
1 Sitting-room. With woodstove. No smoking.
Small garden
Closed from November to March.

The blacksmith from the Blenheim estate once lived in 18th-century Mayfield Cottage, now the home of Rosemary and Stan Fox. They discovered a little inglenook hidden in a wall, a feature of which is the salt ledge – to keep that precious commodity dry in times when homes were incurably damp. Breakfasts are served at one end of this room, chinoiserie sofas furnish the other. Doorways are low and ceilings beamed.

At nearby Combe Mill (the Duke of Marlborough's estate workshop) there is a restored working beam engine of 1852, as well as a waterwheel and a blacksmith's forge – open to the public on 'steaming days' when exhibitions are arranged.

St Laurence's, the local church, was built by the monks of Eynsham and parts date back the 12th century. It has some fine 15th-century wall paintings, rediscovered during the Victorian era. There are plenty of good walks hereabouts – the Oxfordshire Way is only 10 minutes away.

V

MORAR FARM

Weald Street, Bampton, Oxfordshire, OX18 2HL   Tel: 01993 850162
(Fax: 01993 851738)
South-west of Witney. Nearest main road: A4095 from Witney to Faringdon.

C(6) **PT S**

3 Bedrooms. £19–£21. Bargain breaks. All have some or all of the following: own bath/shower/toilet; TV. No smoking.
Dinner (by arrangement). £13 for 3 courses and coffee, at 7pm. Vegetarian or other special diets if ordered. Wine available. No smoking. **Light suppers** if ordered.
1 Sitting-room. With open fire, TV. No smoking.
Large garden
Closed from mid-December to mid-March.

This modern stone house, comfortable and trim, stands in an attractive garden. Janet and Terry Rouse, a lively couple, take exceptional care of their guests – whether it is by involving them in their many activities (Morris-dancing and bell-ringing, for example) or by their close attention to detail (two fresh towels provided daily, unlimited fruit juice at breakfast, filling vacuum flasks free of charge, etc.). During winter, Janet may serve a meal comprising home-made soup, their own lamb and six vegetables, Bakewell pudding and fruit to follow.

Bampton, a pretty village, is famous for its spring festival of Morris dancers when the village children all make wildflower garlands. It is well placed to visit Oxford, the Cotswold villages, Cheltenham and Cirencester.

Readers' comments: Excellent! Janet is a delight. Sunday bell-ringing was a highlight of our trip.

V

OLD FARMHOUSE
Station Hill, Long Hanborough, Oxfordshire, OX8 8JZ Tel: 01993 882097
North-east of Witney. Nearest main road: A4095 from Woodstock to Witney.

C(12) **PT**

2 Bedrooms. £19–£20 (less for 3 nights or more). Bargain breaks. One has own shower/toilet; TV. No smoking.
Light suppers if ordered. Vegetarian or other special diets if ordered. No smoking.
1 Sitting-room. With open fire, TV. No smoking.
Garden

At 17th-century Old Farmhouse, Vanessa Maundrell serves meals (vegetables come from the garden) in a stone-flagged dining-room with a dresser full of blue Spode china. One of the sitting-rooms has her collection of some 40 pot-lids over the inglenook. Beams, rugged stone walls and deep-set windows with far views are complemented by flowery fabrics and family treasures. Breakfast, which includes home-made bread and preserves, is sometimes served in the new conservatory. Outside is a pretty cottage-garden with old iron pump among the foxgloves.

There is ample parking space here and guests are welcome to leave their cars while sight-seeing in Oxford (only 10 minutes away by train). Oxford's colleges, churches and museums need no description, but there is always something new to be seen for those who stay several days. At the 'Oxford Story' you ride (literally) back through 800 years of history; Curioxity is a 'hands-on' science gallery. At Magdalen College is a version of Leonardo's 'Last Supper', even better – some say – than the one in Milan.

Readers' comments: Made very welcome. Most comfortable room, excellent breakfast.

OLD INN
Burford Road, Black Bourton, Oxfordshire, OX18 2PF Tel: 01993 841828
West of Oxford. Nearest main road: A40 from Oxford to Burford.

C D S

2 Bedrooms. £17. Both have TV. No smoking.
Dinner. £11 for 4 courses and coffee, at 7.30pm. Vegetarian or other special diets if ordered. No smoking preferred. **Light suppers** if ordered.
1 Sitting-room. With open fire, TV. No smoking preferred.
Small garden

No longer an inn, this 17th-century house is now the elegant home of Pat and John Baxter. It has thick stone walls, low beams in the sitting/dining-room and views of the village, with the mediaeval church close by.

The bedrooms are very attractive: one is all-white (a crisp and light effect); the other is a beamy room with nice old furniture. Even the bathroom has been furnished with style. Only one family (or group of friends) is taken at a time.

Mrs Baxter provides the best of typically English food, asking her guests beforehand what they would like. Melon with port might be followed by a joint or fish, and then perhaps brandy-chocolate cake. Afterwards, when guests relax on the sofas and armchairs in front of the log stove, the Baxters may join them for coffee.

Readers' comments: Extremely comfortable; delicious dinner. Extremely good value, very hospitable. Delightful, charming – just like staying with friends. Warm, welcoming, a very high standard. Lovely place, good meal, very helpful. Very convivial hosts.

RECTORY FARM

Northmoor, Oxfordshire, OX8 1SX   Tel: 01865 300207 (Fax: 01865 300559)
South-west of Oxford. Nearest main road: A415 from Witney to Abingdon.

2 Bedrooms. £20–£22 (less for 3 nights or more). Both have own shower/toilet. No smoking.
1 Sitting-room. With woodstove, TV, piano. No smoking.
Large garden
Closed from mid-December to end of January.

Until a generation ago, this ancient stone farmhouse (the ogee arches of its fireplaces have been dated to the 15th century) was owned by St John's College, Oxford.

The deep-set windows are stone-mullioned, with views of fields and a great slate-roofed dovecote that was built in the 18th century. The Floreys' 400 acres are used for sheep, cattle and crops. In the house are Mary Anne's beautiful arrangements of dried flowers.

Having a growing family to look after, she provides breakfasts only, but there are many restaurants nearby. The breakfast/sitting-room has chamfered beams overhead, red Turkey rugs on the floor, tapestry armchairs, and a sideboard laden with Victorian silver-plate.

The bedrooms are particularly spacious, light and attractively decorated, their shower-rooms immaculate (outsize bath-towels much appreciated!); and their windows have farm or garden views. On the farm are Thames-side walks (fishing too).

V

ROOKS ORCHARD

C D X

Little Wittenham, Oxfordshire, OX14 4QY   Tel: 01865 407765
South-east of Abingdon. Nearest main road: A4074 from Oxford to Wallingford (and M40, junction 7).

2 Bedrooms. £19–£21 (less for 3 nights or more). Both have some or all of the following: own bath/shower/toilet; TV. No smoking.
Light suppers if ordered.
1 Sitting-room. With open fire, TV, piano.
Large garden

'Mother Dunch's buttocks', they rudely called the twin hills dominating the nature reserve that surrounds Rooks Orchard – the lady in question, who once owned this village, was Cromwell's aunt, now buried in the church. In snowy winters skiers speed down the slopes, while summer brings out wild orchids. Waterfowl frequent the ponds below, and at twilight you may spot badgers at play.

The 17th-century house has not only the beams and inglenooks you might expect but a fascinating collection of family heirlooms – from a rocking-horse used by generations of young Welfares to embroideries done by Jonathan's great-grandfather to while away long hours aboard HMS *Challenger* on her voyage charting the oceans for the British government.

Deborah Welfare has complemented antique furniture with restful colours, chinoiserie or beribboned fabrics, and pretty flower arrangements.

TRIGGER POND COTTAGE

C S

33 Bicester Road, Bucknell, Oxfordshire, OX6 9LP   Tel/Fax: 01869 245560
North-west of Bicester. Nearest main road: A34 from Oxford to Bicester
(and M40, junction 10).

2 Bedrooms. £19–£20. Both have TV. No smoking.
Small garden

Each side of the sign outside the Trigger Pond Inn (notable for its food) tells a different story as to the pond's name: its trigger shape is on one side; the 'twiggers' who collected basket-making twigs from its banks on the other. The cottage itself, nearly four centuries old, once belonged to the local thatcher (though today its roof is tiled). Roses clamber up its thick walls of golden stone.

The low, beamed rooms have been attractively decorated by Joan Hemsley. A fresh and pretty bedroom has sprigged white fabrics that go well with the cane furniture, for instance; a cocoa-coloured bathroom is full of pot-plants. As there is no sitting-room for guests, they are welcome to relax in the small conservatory where breakfast is served; wisteria climbs overhead and there is a view of a little waterfall and fields beyond.

In an outbuilding, a surprise awaits – an array of dolls' houses, correct in every period detail, hand-made by Jim Hemsley, who started doing them as a second career in mid-life.

Peaceful little Bucknell is only an hour from London (and even less from Birmingham).

UPPER GREEN FARM

M

Manor Road, Towersey, Oxfordshire, OX9 3QR   Tel: 01844 212496
(Fax: 01844 260399)
East of Thame. Nearest main road: A4129 from Thame to Princes Risborough
(and M40, junctions 6/8).

10 Bedrooms. £20–£30 (less for 4 nights or more). All
have some or all of the following: own bath/shower/
toilet; TV. No smoking.
2 Sitting-rooms. With TV. No smoking.
Large garden

A building of whitewash and thatch overlooking a duck-pond at the front, Marjorie and Euan Aitken's house is one of the prettiest in this book. They uncovered 15th-century beams with the original carpenters' identification marks; came across Elizabethan coins; restored the wood shutters which (window-glass having yet to be invented) were all that kept out wintry blasts five centuries ago; found a secret priest-hole where, in the days of religious persecution, a Catholic priest might have to hide for days when the search was on. Across the lawned farmyard is Paradise Barn, dated 1790, with six bedrooms. Breakfast is served in the barn which has the original hayrack, a beamed ceiling and brick floors. Marjorie, who used to be an antique dealer, has filled every room with fascinating trifles.

Bed-and-breakfast only; there is excellent pub food within a short walking distance.

Readers' comments: Charming home, warm hospitality: we arrived as guests and left as friends. Much impressed by warm welcome, delightful house and excellent breakfast. Wonderful couple – it always feels like going home! Superb breakfast. Absolutely excellent.

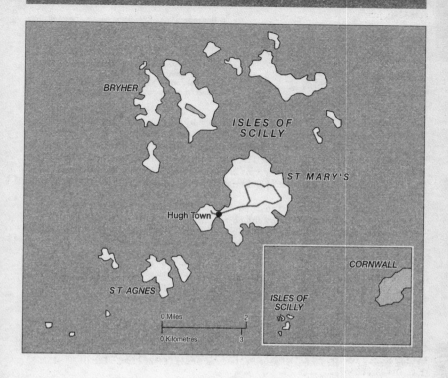

BANK COTTAGE

C(8) S

Bryher, Isles of Scilly, TR23 0PR   Tel/Fax: 01720 422612

5 Bedrooms. £20–£24. Some have some or all of the following: own shower/toilet; TV; views of sea; balcony. No smoking (some).
Dinner. £15 for 4 courses and coffee, at 7pm. Vegetarian or other special diets if ordered. Wine available. No smoking. **Light snacks** available.
1 Sitting-room.
Small garden
Closed from November to March.

Visitors here have a superb sandy beach (right outside) virtually all to themselves; beyond it is one of England's most beautiful seascapes, dotted with 22 islets.

Mac Mace works as a diver: sometimes diving for lobsters and crabs, sometimes for archaeological finds. He and his wife Tracy have a cottage built at least 300 years ago, but with later additions. The attractive rooms have low ceilings and thick walls to keep winter's gales at bay. Bedrooms are cheerful and bright. One en suite bedroom has its own balcony with sea view.

Many visitors are content just to sit all day in the colourful garden to enjoy the view of the bay; or they can use a small boat and go out fishing. Sunsets are outstanding.

Vegetables and loganberries are home-grown, rolls home-baked, eggs from the Maces' hens. A typical meal: fish pâté, a roast or casserole, and sherry trifle.

Visitors arriving by boat from St Mary's are met and their baggage taken up for them.

Readers' comments: Felt completely at home; happy and relaxed atmosphere. Comfortable room, excellent food. Simply delighted, a marvellous time. Nothing is too much trouble. Excellent food and accommodation, good hosts. Now a regular and much-loved destination.

THE BOATHOUSE

D S

Town Beach, Hugh Town, St Mary's, Isles of Scilly, TR21 0LN   Tel: 01720 422688

5 Bedrooms. £20–£29. Most have views of sea.
Dinner. £13 for 4 courses and coffee, at 6.45pm. Vegetarian or other special diets if ordered. No smoking.
1 Sitting-room.
Closed from November to Easter.

With its feet in the sea (or the golden sands at low tide), this little house is down a quiet byway – yet only yards from the few shops and inns that constitute the town centre. Most of its neat pine-furnished bedrooms look over the sea and the stone jetty from which small boats regularly depart to other islands or on trips to see a lighthouse, seals or seabird colonies. The first-floor sitting-room (where unlimited tea or coffee can be had) opens onto a sun-trapping roof-terrace with seats and pots of plants. The dining-room has pretty table-cloths, white walls and cork floor. Here, hospitable Maureen Stuttaford and her sister Joan serve such meals as mushroom tartlets, baked gammon (with ratatouille and pink fir-apple potatoes), Danish apple pudding and cheeses – using vegetables they have grown themselves.

St Mary's, the principal island of Scilly, is only three miles long. Even its centre of action, Hugh Town, can hardly be called busy by mainland standards (though it does receive tides of day-visitors during high summer), and so it is easy to find any number of unfrequented coves or beaches close by.

V

CARNWETHERS

Green Lane, Pelistry Bay, St Mary's, Isles of Scilly, TR21 0NX
Tel/Fax: 01720 422415

rear view

9 Bedrooms. £35–£45 **including dinner** (less for 7 nights). All have own bath/shower/toilet; TV; views of sea (three). No smoking.
Dinner. 4 courses and coffee, at 6.30pm. Vegetarian or other special diets if ordered. Wine available. No smoking.
2 Sitting-rooms. With open fire, TV. **Bar.** No smoking.
Large garden
Closed from October to April.

Carnwethers is more than an ordinary guest-house (and a very good one, at that). Its owner is Roy Graham, well known as an underwater explorer, photographer and marine archaeologist. Even non-experts appreciate his library of books on maritime subjects and his immense knowledge of Scillonian history and ecology.

Every room is as neat as a new pin. There is a bar and lengthy wine list, a heated swimming-pool, sauna, games room and croquet lawn.

Meal times fit in with the times of the buses that take visitors into Hugh Town for slide shows which are usually packed out, concerts and the pubs. Local produce is much used by the chef. A typical meal: soup, roast turkey, and roly-poly pudding. Breakfast options include haddock and kippers. Bedrooms are agreeably decorated; some spacious ones open onto the very lovely garden. In the sitting-room, there are pictures of ships and seascapes. Diving, boating and fishing can be arranged.

Readers' comments: Happy, friendly atmosphere. Could not ask for more. Nothing is too much trouble. Complete satisfaction.

COASTGUARDS

St Agnes, Isles of Scilly, TR22 0PL   Tel: 01720 422373

3 Bedrooms. £16–£18 **(less to readers of this book between Easter and Spring Bank Holiday).** All have some or all of the following: own bath/shower/toilet; views of sea. No smoking.
Dinner. £11 for 4 courses and coffee, at 7pm. Less for fewer courses. Vegetarian or other special diets if ordered. No smoking. **Light suppers** if ordered.
1 Sitting-room. With open fire. No smoking.
Large garden
Closed from November to March.

A group of former coastguard cottages stands on a high point of St Agnes, a little island so unspoilt that there are no cars and no hotel. It is a paradise for those who want nothing more than sunshine early or late in the year, wildflowers, walks, birdwatching and peace.

Wendy Hick provides accommodation for guests in two adjacent cottages. She has furnished the rooms simply but attractively, with interesting objects around. The sitting-room has a William Morris suite and views out to the sea, polished board floors, and an open fire for chilly evenings. The food is all of a very good, homely style.

Visitors reach St Agnes via St Mary's, from which boats take them in 15 minutes to the little quay at St Agnes. (Wendy will supply all the times etc. for getting to Scilly.) Luggage is conveyed for them up the steep track that leads to the few cottages.

Readers' comments: Excellent in every respect. Good food, lovely scenery, such nice people. Warmly welcomed, well looked after, delicious food, excellent value; beautiful and peaceful place. Superb food and hospitality.

V

SHROPSHIRE

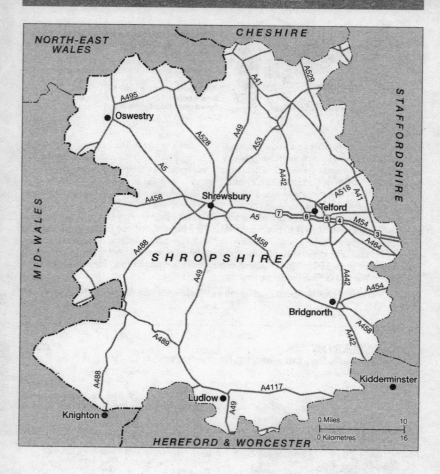

ALBYNES
Nordley, Shropshire, WV16 4SX Tel: 01746 762261
North of Bridgnorth. Nearest main road: A442 from Kidderminster to Telford.

3 Bedrooms. £18–£20 (less for 5 nights or more). Bargain breaks. All have own bath/shower/toilet; TV. No smoking.
Dinner (by arrangement). £12.50 for 4 courses and coffee, at times to suit guests. Vegetarian or other special diets if ordered. No smoking. **Light suppers** if ordered.
2 Sitting-rooms. With open fire/stove, TV. No smoking.
Large garden

Older readers may have grown up with the nature books of Frances Pitt: this is the house where she lived and wrote them. It was orginally built in 1823 for the Burgher of Bridgnorth, who named it after his son Albinius. The dining-room was designed to accommodate fine carved panelling removed from a nearby Tudor house, and there is an elegant oak staircase that spirals its way up to the bedrooms. Several of these overlook the lake (or far hills), as does the sitting-room – furnished with antiques and gold brocade chairs. Twisting passages and steps, unusual curved doors and round-arched alcoves add to the character of the house.

Cynthia Woolley's husband farms the adjoining land – a mixture of arable fields and pasture. A typical dinner may comprise curried parsnip soup, grilled lamb chops with fresh herbs, and lemon-cream pudding.

Readers' comments: Wonderful cook; generous and friendly hostess. Wonderful hosts, lovely home.

V

BROWNHILL HOUSE

C P T S X

Ruyton XI Towns, Shropshire, SY4 1LR Tel/Fax: 01939 260626
South-east of Oswestry. Nearest main road: A5 from Shrewsbury to Oswestry.

3 Bedrooms. £16–£19 (**less to readers of this book** and for 3 nights or more). All have own bath/shower/toilet.
Dinner (by arrangement). £10 for 4 courses and coffee, at 6.30pm. Vegetarian or other special diets if ordered. Wine available. No smoking. **Light suppers** if ordered.
1 Sitting-room. With open fire, TV.
Large garden

It is the garden which brings most visitors here. Although when they moved in Roger and Yoland Brown had not the slightest interest in gardening, within a few years the potential of the large, steep site had converted them into enthusiasts and then experts. They have provided a variety of experiences for the visitor – here a grotto, there a Thai spirit house, 500 different shrubs, 20 kinds of fruit or nut, a vegetable garden with glasshouses.

As to the house itself, the bedrooms are comfortable and homely. Bathrooms are good. The beamed sitting-room has a huge stone fireplace. Meals are served in the large farmhouse-style kitchen, and may comprise such things as soup made from the garden's vegetables, stuffed pork with a crisp crumb coating, and a compote of garden fruit. Breakfasts are exceptional. Fruit juice will be freshly squeezed (from the Browns' own berries or peaches, for example), bread is baked in the village and jams are home-made by Yoland (who is an authority on the village, with its strange name).

Readers' comments: Most generous hosts, excellent hospitality. Very warm welcome and a really delicious meal. Wished we could have stayed longer.

BUCKNELL HOUSE

C(12) **D PT**

Bucknell, Shropshire, SY7 0AD   Tel: 01547 530248
West of Ludlow. Nearest main road: A4113 from Ludlow to Knighton.

3 Bedrooms. £18.50 (less for 2 nights or more). All have own TV.
Light suppers if ordered. Vegetarian or other special diets if ordered.
1 Sitting-room. With open fire, TV, piano.
Large garden
Closed in December and January.

In the early 18th century, the clergy lived well: this huge and handsome house, honeysuckle and wisteria clambering up its walls, was a vicarage then. The vicar would have approved of the equally handsome way in which locally born Brenda Davies has furnished it – the dining-room with Sheraton chairs and fine wallpaper; the sitting-room with big velvet armchairs, curtains of pale green silk; flowers everywhere. Bedrooms are just as good, with lovely country views. All are spacious; one has antique furniture, floral fabrics and wicker armchairs. Breakfasts here are substantial (the honey is home-produced, marmalade home-made).

The grounds (garden and watermeadows) are secluded, looking across the valley of the River Teme to Wales. There are rosebeds, croquet lawn, a hard tennis court, shooting, and fishing in the river. The surrounding woodlands and hills are full of wildlife.

Readers' comments: Wonderfully comfortable bed, breakfast an ample repast, some of the most beautiful countryside in England. Outstanding amenities; marvellous people. Delightful couple; nothing was too much trouble. Looked after us splendidly.

CHURCH HOUSE

C M S

Aston Eyre, Shropshire, WV16 6XD   Tel/Fax: 01746 714248
West of Bridgnorth. Nearest main road: A458 from Bridgnorth to Shrewsbury.

2 Bedrooms. £17.50–£18.50 (less for 4 nights or more). Both have own shower/toilet. No smoking.
Dinner (by arrangement). £12 for 3 courses and coffee, at 7pm. Vegetarian or other special diets if ordered. No smoking. **Light suppers** if ordered.
1 Sitting-room. With open fire, TV. No smoking.
Large garden
Closed from November to March.

At Aston Eyre is a little Norman church with some exceptional stone carving. Next to it is Church House which was originally a wheelwright's cottage with a workshop. Now Margaret Cosh's home, it has some quarry-tiled floors, low beams and a brick inglenook in the sitting-room. Up a narrow staircase is a neat, cottage-style bedroom; another is on the ground floor and has French doors opening onto a terrace, garden with summer-house and Margaret's smallholding. The breakfast-room, too, has French doors with a view of the beautiful Shropshire countryside. A typical dinner: home-made vegetable soup; a casserole or roast lamb; fresh fruit salad or rhubarb crumble.

The nearby market town of Bridgnorth is unusual – part is high up (here are half-timbered houses and the remains of a castle) and the rest so far below that a steep cliff-railway links the two. You can see traces of cave dwellings in the cliff.

The Severn Valley Railway, which steams 16 miles from Bridgnorth to Kidderminster, goes up and down through lovely riverside country. In a car you can deviate to visit not only the vintage cars of Stanmore Hall and its park but also the hilltop village of Claverley.

FITZ MANOR

Fitz, Bomere Heath, Shropshire, SY4 3AS Tel: 01743 850295 (Fax: 01743 850146)
North-west of Shrewsbury. Nearest main road: A5 from Shrewsbury to Llangollen.

3 Bedrooms. £16–£25 (less for 7 nights or more). No smoking.
Dinner (by arrangement). £12.50 for 4 courses and coffee, at times to suit guests. Vegetarian or other special diets if ordered. Wine available. No smoking.
Light suppers if ordered.
2 Sitting-rooms. With open fire, TV. No smoking in one.
Large garden

This outstanding manor house was built about 1450 in traditional Shropshire style – black timbers and white walls. It is at the heart of a large arable farm.

The interior is one of the most impressive in this book. A vast, blue dining-room with parquet floor and Persian carpet overlooks rosebeds, pergolas and yew hedges. It is furnished with antiques, paintings by John Piper and a collection of Crown Derby. In the oak-panelled sitting-room there are damask and pink velvet armchairs around the log fire.

Bedrooms differ in size. For instance, adjoining one huge room with armchairs is a white cottage-style bedroom – a useful combination for a family.

Dawn Baly's candlelit dinners may include home-made pâté, casseroled pheasant with home-grown vegetables, chocolate mousse, and cheeses.

In the grounds are a heated swimming-pool and croquet lawn.

Readers' comments: Lovely place – quite magical. Dinner was extremely well cooked, abundant and well presented. No attention to detail spared.

V

FOXLEIGH HOUSE

Foxleigh Drive, Wem, Shropshire, SY4 5BP Tel/Fax: 01939 233528
North of Shrewsbury. Nearest main road: A49 from Shrewsbury to Whitchurch.

3 Bedrooms. £19.50 (less for 4 nights or more). Bargain breaks. All have some or all of the following: own bath/toilet; TV. No smoking.
Dinner (by arrangement). £11.50 for 4 courses and coffee, at 7pm. No smoking. **Light suppers** if ordered.
1 Sitting-room. With open fire. No smoking.
Small garden

Well tucked away in this little market town is handsome Foxleigh House, the most memorable feature of which is the fine sitting-room. Its cocoa walls, coffee ceiling and Chinese carpet are an excellent setting for antiques that include inlaid tables and a series of Hogarth prints. Bay windows open onto the croquet lawn and its towering Wellingtonia.

In the dining-room, Barbara Barnes serves such meals as avocado, roast lamb, trifle, and local cheeses. The bedrooms have art deco suites of figured maple, and the hall a gallery of ancestral portraits.

Wem still has many historic buildings, and Shrewsbury itself is near. So are meres frequented by wildfowl.

Readers' comments: Evening meal excellent. A very pleasant experience. Can't praise too warmly. Made us feel so cared for. Particularly kind and helpful. Very, very comfortable and roomy; meals delicious. Thoroughly satisfied. Very tasty meals. Very comfortable.

HOPE BOWDLER HALL

C(12) PT S

Hope Bowdler, Church Stretton, Shropshire, SY6 7DD   Tel: 01694 722041
North of Ludlow. Nearest main road: A49 from Shrewsbury to Ludlow.

2 Bedrooms. £18–£20. No smoking.
1 Sitting-room. With open fire, TV. No smoking.
Large garden
Closed from December to February.

The ancient, stone manor house was 'Georgianized' in the 18th century – hence the handsome sash windows and graceful staircase, though older features such as stone-flagged floors still remain. Rosaleen Inglis has decorated the sitting-room in apricot, furnished the dining-room with a fine mahogany table and damask wallpaper, and for one of the bathrooms found tiles with Shropshire views.

The big engraving of officers at the Siege of Lucknow (1857–8) and the impressive ceremonial sword were possessions of John's great-grandfather, who commanded the garrison during the siege of Lucknow, one of the major events in the Indian Mutiny. Among his other ancestors was the first Bishop of Nova Scotia. Outside is a large garden with pool frequented by mallard, and a hard tennis court. Scenery and good walking are big attractions here.

Readers' comments: Accommodation charming, proprietress most hospitable. Enjoyed an excellent week.

MONAUGHTY POETH

C(12) D

Llanfair-Waterdine, Shropshire, LD7 1TT   Tel: 01547 528348
North-west of Knighton (Powys, Wales). Nearest main road: A488 from Knighton to Shrewsbury.

2 Bedrooms. £18.50 (less for 2 nights or more). Bargain breaks. One has own toilet; TV (in the other).
Light suppers by arrangement. Vegetarian or other special diets if ordered.
1 Sitting-room. With open fire, TV, piano.
Small garden
Closed in December and January.

Here, where the border between Wales and Shropshire runs, two sisters grew up in the 1940s: Brenda (now of **Bucknell House**) and Jocelyn. Later they wrote a nostalgic history of their parish, tiny though it is, and Jocelyn has also written a book for young children about birds. Monaughty Poeth itself has an 800-year-old history, for it once belonged to the Cistercians of Abbey Cwmhir: Monaughty means 'monastery grange' and Poeth 'burnt' – the house burnt down and was rebuilt in the 19th century. This is where Jocelyn, now married to farmer Jim Williams, lives and welcomes visitors.

The accommodation at Monaughty is in traditional farmhouse style, with comfort the keynote, and in every room Jocelyn's pretty flower arrangements. For dinner, most visitors go to the picturesque old Red Lion nearby for steaks, duck, etc.

Readers' comments: Treated like royalty! Enjoyed every comfort. Warmest of welcomes. Large, pretty bedroom and lovely view. Wonderful concern for her guests. Extremely friendly. Idyllic location. Charming and unassuming people. Lovely farmhouse.

OLD CIDER HOUSE

M PT S

1 Lion Lane, Cleobury Mortimer, Shropshire, DY14 8BT Tel: 01299 270304
West of Kidderminster. Nearest main road: A4117 from Cleobury Mortimer to Ludlow.

2 Bedrooms. £19.50. Both have some or all of the following: own bath/shower/toilet. No smoking.
1 Sitting-room. With woodstove, TV. No smoking.
Small garden

Within sight of Cleobury Mortimer's crooked church-spire, down a narrow lane which was once the major route into this attractive market town, lies the Old Cider House – a welcome sight for weary drovers approaching journey's end with a serious thirst to quench. One steps straight into the low-ceilinged dining-room, where the oak beams have been dated to the 16th century and there is an unusual Orkney chair with oatstraw back. Through an alcove to one side lies the book-filled sitting-room (a wood-burning stove has been fitted in the stone wall between the rooms, providing comfort to both); on the other lies a bedroom with an excellent shower-room adjoining. Upstairs is another attractive bedroom, with a Lloyd Loom chair, pine furniture and bright fabrics; like the pretty tiled bathroom, it has a beamed ceiling.

Stroma Lennox does not serve dinner, since the various eating-places of Cleobury Mortimer are within a few minutes' walk. The town lies between the Wyre Forest and the Shropshire Hills; Wenlock Edge is not far away.

OLD FARMHOUSE

C D

Woodside, Clun, Shropshire, SY7 0JB Tel: 01588 640695
North of Knighton (Powys, Wales). Nearest main road: A488 from Knighton to Bishop's Castle.

2 Bedrooms. £17–£20 (less for 2 nights or more).
Dinner. £8.50 for 3 courses and coffee, at 7pm. Vegetarian or other special diets if ordered. No smoking. **Light suppers** if ordered.
1 Sitting-room. With stove, TV. No smoking.
Large garden
Closed from November to February.

The house shelters on the side of a valley outside the unspoilt little town of Clun that A. E. Housman called 'one of the quietest places under the sun'. There are fine views and much wildlife. Trout inhabit a pool of pink waterlilies fringed with kingcups. The house is at the foot of a sloping lawn with a willow tree, its old stone walls made colourful by baskets of busy Lizzies. Thick walls and a wood-burning stove help to create a cosy sitting-room, off which is a sunny conservatory, and in the dining-room beams still carry old bacon-hooks. Cottage-style bedrooms are light and bright.

For dinner Margaret Wall may offer you leek and potato soup; chicken and broccoli; and a compote made from the garden's summer fruit.

Readers' comments: Accommodation and cuisine superb. Lovely house in beautiful surroundings.

V

225

OLD VICARAGE

C D PT X

Leaton, Shropshire, SY4 3AP   Tel: 01939 290989
North of Shrewsbury. Nearest main road: A5 from Shrewsbury to Oswestry.

3 Bedrooms. £16. All have some or all of the following: own bath/shower/toilet; TV. No smoking.
Light suppers if ordered. Vegetarian or other special diets if ordered. No smoking.
1 Sitting-room. With open fire, TV.
Large garden

Leaton's Old Vicarage was built in 1859 for an archdeacon: hence the many pointed or trefoil-arched windows, the arcading in the sitting-room, handsome floor-tiles and doors of ecclesiastical design. One very big bedroom has a bay window and another an oriel from which to enjoy views of the garden. One Victorian bathroom is particularly attractive. Joan Mansell-Jones serves snack suppers; much is home-grown or home-made.

Almost islanded within a loop of the River Severn, Shrewsbury is a treasury of superb black-and-white buildings with several fine churches, gardens (Darwin, born here, is commemorated in a statue) and museums. It deserves repeated visits to explore twisting lanes (with such curious names as Dogpole, Shoplatch or Coffeehouse Passage), the castle, and the main square with flower-baskets hung around an open-pillared market hall. A market has been taking place here on Wednesdays for over 700 years.

Readers' comments: Beautiful house and garden, kind friendly welcome, delicious dinner. We were really spoilt.

RECTORY FARM

C(12)

Woolstaston, Shropshire, ST6 6NN   Tel: 01694 751306
South of Shrewsbury. Nearest main road: A49 from Shrewsbury to Ludlow.

3 Bedrooms. £20. All have own bath/toilet; TV. No smoking.
3 Sitting-rooms. With open fire/stove, TV, piano. No smoking.
Large garden
Closed from mid-December to early January.

In the foothills of the Long Mynd, this fine half-timbered house is surrounded by big clipped yews that may be 400 years old. Inside is panelling elaborately carved with pomegranates and roses. Three sitting-rooms open into one another, and all the en suite bedrooms are spacious, immaculate and with fine views – particularly one from which you can see the Wrekin beyond the lawns, rosebeds and lead nymphs of the garden. There is a long oak table in the dining-room used for breakfast; Jeanette Davies serves no other meals, so visitors go to the restaurants of Church Stretton.

Rectory Farm is very well placed for walkers, being so close to those famous Shropshire hills, the Long Mynd and Wenlock Edge. Offa's Dyke is also within easy reach. Both Shrewsbury and Ludlow are near, as well as Stokesay Castle (a litle gem, with fruit trees in its moat now but old features retained within), the Acton Scott farm museum, Ironbridge (with the Coalport china museum) and great Powis Castle.

Reader's comment: A delightful home.

SEVERN TROW

Church Road, Jackfield, Ironbridge, Shropshire, TF8 7ND Tel: 01952 883551
South of Telford. Nearest main road: A442 from Telford to Bridgnorth
(and M54, junctions 4/5).

3 Bedrooms. £20–£24 (less for 3 nights or more). All have some or all of the following: own bath/shower/toilet; TV; views of river. No smoking.
2 Sitting-rooms. With open fire, TV. No smoking.
Small garden
Closed in November and December.

Through the Ironbridge gorge, scenic birthplace of the Industrial Revolution, sailing-barges called trows bore goods downriver to Bristol. The Severn Trow provided the men with beer, dormitory lodgings and brothel. Then it became a church hall.

There are carpets on floors of red and black quarry-tiles, an old pine dresser serves as a bar, and there is an outstanding mosaic floor. The brew-house is now another sitting-room.

Upstairs are excellent bedrooms with light colour schemes and interesting furnishings. One bedroom, with good bathroom and small kitchen area, is accessible from street level.

Very substantial breakfasts are provided by Jim and Pauline Hannigan but no evening meal. However, there are over two dozen eating-places within a mile radius.

Readers' comments: Most comfortable, wonderful welcome. Has to be seen to be believed. Friendly couple, superb breakfasts, extremely helpful. The best we have visited. Breakfast fruits a work of art! Friendly hosts. Enormous breakfast. Four-poster a delight. Excellent.

UPPER HOUSE FARM

Hopton Castle, Shropshire, SY7 0QF Tel: 01547 530319
West of Ludlow. Nearest main road: A4113 from Knighton towards Ludlow.

3 Bedrooms. £18–£20. All have own bath/shower/toilet; TV. No smoking.
Dinner (by arrangement). £14 for 4 courses and coffee, at 7pm. Vegetarian or other special diets if ordered. Wine available. No smoking.
1 Sitting-room. With open fire. No smoking.
Large garden
Closed in December.

A very beautiful garden surrounds this 18th-century house, and indoors everything is of an equally high standard: from the good carpets and the velvet armchairs grouped around the fireplace to the cut-glass and silver on the dining-table, the antiques and the excellent bathrooms. You can enjoy a huge and sunny bedroom, a game at the pool table, or a stroll on the farm to look at cattle or Clun forest sheep. There's trout fishing to be had, free, in the river.

But above all it is Sue Williams's rich and imaginative cooking that brings visitors back. (Typically, vol-au-vent, pheasant casseroled in red wine, blueberry tart, and cheeses.)

The picturesque ruins of Hopton Castle are on the farm's grounds (it was built by the Normans; and in 1642 thirty Roundheads held it against 300 Royalists for three weeks).

Readers' comments: Cannot praise highly enough. Glorious countryside. Meals an absolute delight. Most charming and a wonderful cook. Lovely old house, splendid meals. Food with flair and imagination. Perfect in every way. Outstanding.

SOMERSET
(including Bath & North-East Somerset)

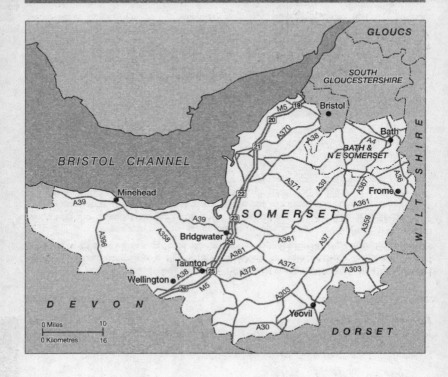

ALFOXTON COTTAGE

Holford, Somerset, TA5 1SG Tel/Fax: 01278 741418

West of Bridgwater. Nearest main road: A39 from Bridgwater to Minehead (and M5, junction 23).

3 Bedrooms. £20 (less for 4 nights or more). No smoking.
Dinner. £16 for 4 courses and coffee, at 7pm. Vegetarian or other special diets if ordered. Wine available. No smoking.
1 Sitting-room. With open fire. Piano. No smoking.
Small garden
Closed from December to February.

The cottage is truly remote, up in the Quantock Hills with their views across the Bristol Channel to Wales. You may believe you are never coming to it as you follow twists and turns up the small wooded lane to the top of the hill.

This little house is now the home of Richard and Angela Delderfield. Rooms are small and low but pleasantly furnished – for instance, bamboo or velvet bedheads; and a grandfather clock and flounced armchairs are by the log fire in the sitting-room, from which a door leads to the garden, woods, a trickling stream, donkeys and chickens.

Angela's cooking is one of the main attractions of staying here. A typical meal: prawns in a creamy sauce containing whisky, or lettuce soup; chicken breasts with coriander seeds; rhubarb and lemon flan.

Readers' comments: A wonderful establishment. A lovely home in a beautiful area. Very hospitable, food and service excellent. Friendly and genuine people. Truly gifted cook. Delightful hostess. Very enjoyable stay. Very friendly. Delightful.

ASTOR HOUSE

14 Oldfield Road, Bath, Bath & North-East Somerset, BA2 3ND
Tel/Fax: 01225 429134
Nearest main road: A367 from Bath to Shepton Mallet.

6 Bedrooms. £18–£22 (less for 2 nights or more). Most have some or all of the following: own bath/shower/toilet; TV. No smoking.
Light suppers only. No smoking.
1 Sitting-room. With TV. No smoking.
Garden
Closed from Christmas to February.

Among the bewildering variety of guest-houses in Bath, Astor House is quite a find: in a relatively quiet residential street, yet only minutes from buses and, to the more energetic, within walking distance of the abbey. Kathy and Rick Beech have furnished their bow-fronted Victorian house with inspired purchases from Bath's many auction-rooms: cast-iron fireplaces in several bedrooms, a fine oak fire-surround in the cosy sitting-room, a matching wardrobe and table with oriental embossed and lacquered panels. Four bedrooms are on the second floor, with sloping ceilings; one – no. 6 – has a splendid view down over the garden (complete with enormous walnut tree and nuts in season) and across the city to the heights of Lansdown beyond.

No dinner, but many guests have enjoyed the home-cooked food at a pleasant town pub less than 10 minutes' walk away. Rick's and Kathy's cooking skills are displayed instead in their range of imaginative breakfasts, which might include a cheese-filled Staffordshire oatcake, Spanish scrambled egg or a Roquefort omelette, and home-made cheese scones. The beautiful Russian paintings on the dining-room walls reflect Kathy's interest in languages and travel.

BRIDGE COTTAGE

C D M PT X

Ashley Road, Bathford, Bath & North-East Somerset, BA1 7TT
Tel: 01225 852399
East of Bath. Nearest main road: A4 Chippenham to Bath (and M4, junction 18).

3 Bedrooms. £18–£25 (less for 3 nights or more). Bargain breaks. Some have some or all of the following: own bath/shower/toilet; TV. No smoking.
Light suppers if ordered. Vegetarian or other special diets if ordered. No smoking.
Small garden

A two-bedroom suite occupies the ground floor in beautifully converted Bridge Cottage. There is a little dining-room for light suppers; a particularly pretty bathroom, with flowery fitments; and a spacious, fitted bedroom in Laura Ashley style with windows at each end. Across the courtyard is another, equally attractive suite, with its own patio garden. Tubs of begonias and petunias fill every corner: Ros Bright is a very keen gardener, and for the last two years her garden has been judged 'the best garden not seen from the road' in the Bath in Bloom competition.

All the pleasures of Bath are within about 10 minutes by car (or bus), yet this little village perched on a hillside seems deep in the country. At nearby Bradford-on-Avon, steep roads converge at the mediaeval bridge with domed chapel-turned-lockup on it. It takes time to discover all Bradford's handsome houses, Saxon church, vast tithe barn and old inns. A few miles away are such lovely spots as Corsham, Lacock and the Chippenham–Calne area.

V

CEDAR LODGE

C PT

13 Lambridge, Bath, Bath & North-East Somerset, BA1 6BJ   Tel: 01225 423468
On A4 from Bath to Chippenham.

3 Bedrooms. £20–£29.50 (less for 3 nights or more). Bargain breaks. All have some or all of the following: own bath/shower/toilet; TV. No smoking.
Dinner (by arrangement). £20 for 4 courses and coffee, at times to suit guests. Vegetarian or other special diets if ordered. No smoking. **Light suppers** if ordered.
1 Sitting-room. With open fire, TV. No smoking.
Garden

The 18th-century merchant who first owned this fine house celebrated peace when the American War of Independence ended by installing a window etched and painted with the American eagle bearing an olive branch. This is on a curved landing of the elegant staircase. At back and front are walled gardens, the latter with ample trees (as well as frog pools) to screen the verandahed house from the road into Bath: bus stop outside.

Derek and Hungarian-born Maria Beckett have furnished the house with 18th- and 19th-century antiques, an abundance of pictures and books, needlepoint cushions, and an alcove full of dolls and toys for visiting children. There is a small conservatory in which to take coffee and petits fours after one of Maria's cordon bleu dinners.

Upstairs are bedrooms with bay windows and handsomely panelled doors. One has a pine half-tester bed with lace drapery; another, a very wide four-poster and quilted spread.

Readers' comments: The home was warm with friendship, hosts more than gracious, very restful.

CLAYBATCH FARMHOUSE

Blatchbridge, Somerset, BA11 5EF   Tel: 01373 461193
South of Frome. Nearest main road: A361 from Frome to Shepton Mallet.

rear view

2 Bedrooms. £19. Both have own bath/shower/toilet. No smoking.
Dinner (by arrangement). £14 for 3 courses, and coffee, at 7.30pm. No smoking. **Light suppers** if ordered.
1 Sitting-room. With open fire, piano. No smoking.
Large garden
Closed from mid-December to mid-January.

Jacqueline and Ryan George's early 18th-century home used to be part of the estate of nearby Longleat House. The big sitting-room is memorable. Duck-egg blue walls and the mellow patina of walnut furniture contrast with the brilliance of apricot chairs grouped round a stone fireplace. Big casement doors open onto a sloping lawn and watergarden. The dining-room has Chippendale-style chairs (Prince of Wales feathers decorate their backs) with tapestry seats made by an aunt; and on the Etruscan red walls hang oil paintings. Here Jackie serves such dinners (on your night of arrival only) as smoked fish pâté; pork fillet with juniper berries and garden vegetables; and chocolate roulade (pre-dinner drinks are included). On other nights, guests can eat well in Frome, or at local pubs.

Bedrooms, too, are charming with little rosebuds on one bedspread, Chinese pavilions on another, for example.

Readers' comments: Made most welcome, delicious meals, beautiful home. Such a welcoming house and relaxing atmosphere, food plentiful and delicious.

CUTTHORNE

Luckwell Bridge, Wheddon Cross, Somerset, TA24 7EW   Tel/Fax: 01643 831255
South-west of Minehead. Nearest main road: A396 from Exeter to Minehead.

3 Bedrooms. £18.50–£25 (less for 5 nights or more). Bargain breaks. All have own bath/shower/toilet; TV. No smoking.
Dinner. £12.50 for 4 courses and coffee, at 7.30pm. Vegetarian or other special diets if ordered. No smoking. **Light suppers** if ordered.
1 Sitting-room. With log stove, TV. No smoking.
Large garden

There has been a farm on this spot since the 1300s; the present house is 18th-century, with a slate-flagged porch and apricot walls, and here Ann Durbin produces candlelit dinners with much home produce (meat and game). Bedrooms in the house are excellently furnished, with exceptionally pretty embossed wallpapers and lovely Exmoor views; one has a carved and tapestry-hung four-poster, another an unusual carved French bed. In the sitting- and dining-rooms are antique rugs, log fires and brass-rubbings.

There is a courtyard where chickens roam, and a pond with exotic species of ducks and geese. Trout fishing and shooting available. (Two immaculate cottages have their own kitchens and dining facilities for either b & b or self-catering: guests can dine in the main house.)

In the heart of Exmoor, the house is also near the sands and sea.

Readers' comments: Excellent food, kind hosts, quiet setting. Attractive rooms, comprehensively equipped. The Durbins were most helpful. Good food, well presented.

V

EDGCOTT HOUSE

D PT S X

Porlock Road, Exford, Somerset, TA24 7QG   Tel: 01643 831495
South-west of Minehead. Nearest main road: A396 from Exeter to Minehead.

4 Bedrooms. £19–£22 **(less for 3 nights or more to readers of this book only).** Bargain breaks. Some have some or all of the following: own bath/shower/toilet; views of river.
Dinner. £12 for 4 courses and coffee, at 7.30pm. Vegetarian or other special diets if ordered. No smoking.
1 Sitting-room. With open fire, TV, piano.
Large garden

Trompe l'oeil murals, in 'Strawberry Hill gothick' style, cover the walls of the long dining/sitting-room. They were painted in the 1940s by George Oakes, who became a director of the distinguished interior decorating firm of Colefax & Fowler. The tall bay windows of this room open onto a tiled terrace from which there is a fine hill view beyond the old, rambling garden where yellow Welsh poppies grow in profusion. In the long entrance hall are Persian rugs and unusual clocks. Bedrooms are homely; throughout there is a mix of antique and merely old furniture, with more trompe l'oeil alcoves or doors.

Gillian Lamble's style of cooking is traditionally English and she serves such meals as mackerel pâté, roast lamb, lemon meringue pie, and cheeses.

Readers' comments: Mrs Lamble is kindness itself. A house of character. She went out of her way to be helpful. Food excellent. Will definitely return. A lovely house. A favourite. One of the best. Absolute find; food excellent.

GREEN LANE HOUSE

C PT X

Green Lane, Hinton Charterhouse, Bath & North-East Somerset, BA3 6BL
Tel: 01225 723631 (Fax: 01225 723773)
South of Bath. Nearest main road: A36 from Bath to Warminster.

4 Bedrooms. £20–£27 (less for 3 nights or more). Some have own shower/toilet. No smoking.
Light suppers if ordered.
1 Sitting-room. With open fire, TV. No smoking.
Small garden

The house (originally three cottages) dates from 1725 and descendants of the family who inhabited it then still live in the village. Today it belongs to Christopher and Juliet Davies who spent nearly 30 years in hotel management overseas.

The restored house has such features as an old fireplace in one room and a massive stone inglenook in another, board doors and round-arched, wood-shuttered windows: these contrast with more modern furnishings and colour schemes – lyre-back dining-chairs, bamboo-patterned tiles in a very pretty bathroom, comfortable Parker Knoll chairs in the bedrooms. The Davieses have added mementoes from their years overseas, including alabaster from Oman, Makonde carvings from Africa and papyrus paintings from Egypt. There is a walled cottage-garden.

Two inns in the village serve meals, or snack suppers can be arranged.

Readers' comments: Service very friendly and helpful, accommodation excellent.

GREENHAM HALL

Greenham, Somerset, TA21 0JJ   Tel: 01823 672603 (Fax: 01823 672307)
West of Wellington. Nearest main road: A38 from Wellington towards Exeter (and M5, junctions 26/27).

6 Bedrooms. £17.50–£20 (less for 3 nights or more). Bargain breaks. Some have some or all of the following: own bath/shower/toilet.
Light suppers if ordered.
2 Sitting-rooms. With open fire, TV, piano.
Large garden

This great castellated pile with buttresses topped by barley-sugar finials stands on a commanding hilltop site. It was built at the height of the Gothic Revival period, but fell on hard times. Then the Ayre family came here and restored the mansion, including the west wing (to left of picture) where some bedrooms are available.

Rooms have impressive floor-to-ceiling windows, arched and stone-mullioned; solidly made, panelled doors; and ogee arches. From the huge galleried hall (with log stove, concert piano and the biggest dresser you are likely to see – carved and inlaid), a staircase with 'gothick' banisters and stained-glass windows rises to the bedrooms. The very large family room is especially impressive, with carved bedheads and a bay window-seat from which to enjoy the sight of terrace, lawn and stately trees.

Reader's comment: Very comfortable and pleasant.

V

THE HOLLIES

Hatfield Road, Bath, Bath & North-East Somerset, BA2 2BD   Tel: 01225 313366
Nearest main road: A367 from Bath to Shepton Mallet.

3 Bedrooms. £20–£24 (less for 3 nights or more). All have some or all of the following: own bath/shower/toilet; TV. No smoking.
Light snacks if ordered. Vegetarian or other special diets if ordered. No smoking.
1 Sitting-room. No smoking.
Small garden

Within minutes of the city centre, yet with off-street and garage parking, this early Victorian house (built in 1850 in a meadow beside the old Bath–Wells turnpike) has fooled even experts into believing its elegance and simplicity belong to the Georgian era. It faces across its pretty garden (where meadow flowers still bloom) onto the east window of the local church, and the views from the front bedrooms are correspondingly attractive. The back bedroom, too, is delightful; there's a lace-draped coronet at the bedhead, and sweet-pea wallpaper. Sanderson fabrics and pine furnishings enhance beautifully proportioned rooms. Downstairs, Nicky and David Stabbins have laid out the breakfast-room in such a way as to encourage guests to linger there in the evenings too, perhaps writing cards at the table under the south window, or reading beside the fireplace. Light snacks only, but there are good pub meals nearby, as well as Bath's enormous variety of restaurants.

The attractions of the city are legion, but not everyone finds the glass-blowing workshop (demonstrations on Saturdays) or the fascinating reclamation centre, both in Walcot Street.

LADY FARMHOUSE

S

Chelwood, Bath & North-East Somerset, BS18 4NN   Tel: 01761 490770
(Fax: 01761 490877)
South-east of Bristol. Off A368 from Bath to Weston-super-Mare.

3 Bedrooms. £17–£22 (less for 3 nights or more). All have some or all of the following: own bath/shower/toilet; TV; views of lake, river. No smoking.
Dinner (by arrangement). £15 for 3 courses and coffee, at 7.30pm. Wine available. No smoking. **Light suppers** if ordered.
1 Sitting-room. With open fire, TV. No smoking. Piano. Bar.
Large garden
Closed from mid-December to mid-January.

More than 25 years ago, Judy and Malcolm Pearce began the long process of transforming a rather ramshackle property into this gracious Georgian-fronted house of great beauty. It is set in six acres of landscaped grounds including two small lakes, a tennis court, and a garden which was recently accepted for the National Gardens Scheme.

Guests take breakfast in the conservatory, or in the big kitchen, homely with colourful fittings and old pine; dinner might be home-made soup, a casserole with vegetables from the garden, and fruit pie or home-made ice cream. The beamed dining-room is magnificent, with a vast open fireplace, impressive refectory table and fine paintings (the quarry-tiles in this room have been laid upside-down to produce a weathered effect). There is another huge open fire in the pale yellow sitting-room; and a grand piano in the hall. Bedrooms and bathrooms are lavish and lovely, furnished, like the rest of the house, with lots of antiques and richly decorative fabrics.

Located on the edge of the Chew Valley; Wells, Bath and Bristol are within easy reach.

Readers' comments: A lovely farmhouse with beautiful gardens. Most delightful stay.

MANOR HOUSE

C

Wellow, Bath & North-East Somerset, BA2 8QQ   Tel: 01225 832027
South of Bath. Nearest main road: A367 from Bath to Shepton Mallet.

3 Bedrooms. £17.50–£20 (less for 5 nights or more). Some have own bath/shower/toilet; TV. No smoking.
Large garden

This lovely old house began life in 1634 as Hungerford Manor, built by the local landowning family of that name whose coat-of-arms can still be seen above the fireplace in the panelled music room. Oak panelling, stone fireplaces, wide floorboards and mullioned windows testify to a long and relatively untroubled history.

Sarah Danny makes her own bread and yogurt for breakfast – home-mixed muesli and stewed fruit too; guests sit round a gateleg table in the panelled dining-room.

There are books everywhere, including the bedrooms: the double is huge, with a mullioned window in the en suite bathroom; the twin room next door is big enough to swallow a huge sofa and a desk without appearing crowded. There is a pretty single room.

Outside is a pleasing conglomeration of old outbuildings (cream teas in summer), courtyard and walled garden, and a paddock with tennis court, croquet and an ancient manorial dovecote.

V   *Reader's comment:* Very nice and good house.

MELON COTTAGE VINEYARD

Charlton, Radstock, Somerset, BA3 5TN   Tel: 01761 435090

South-west of Bath. Nearest main road: A367 from Radstock to Shepton Mallet.

2 Bedrooms. £16.
Light suppers if ordered. No smoking.
Large garden

Nestling in the Somerset hills, midway between Wells and Bath, is Melon Cottage Vineyard from the 200 vines of which come about a thousand bottles of dry white wine each year (go in October to see the harvest, and in spring for the bottling). It is known that the Romans, too, had vineyards in the area. The Pountneys' cottage has 39-inch stone walls, parts dating from mediaeval times. There are small stone-mullioned windows; one large bedroom is under the exposed rafters of the roof. (The Somerset Wagon in Chilcompton serves excellent meals.)

Somerset is a county of great beauty, its landscape punctuated by impressive church towers from the resplendent Perpendicular period of mediaeval architecture, big stone barns and little stone villages. Geology is what accounts for its great variety, with buildings made up of stone that ranges from lilac to gold (for every quarry is different), and a landscape of hills and levels contrasting with one another. Wells (glorious cathedral), mysterious Glastonbury, the myriad attractions of Bath, Cheddar Gorge and Longleat (Elizabethan mansion and safari park) are all within easy driving distance.

Readers' comments: Very comfortable. Excellent hospitality. Made very welcome.

OLD BOATHOUSE

Bath Boating Station, Forester Road, Bath, Bath & North-East Somerset, BA2 6QE
Tel: 01225 466407

Nearest main road: A36 from Bath to Warminster.

4 Bedrooms. £20–£25 (less for 3 nights or more). All have some or all of the following: own bath/shower/ toilet; TV; views of river; balcony. No smoking.
1 Sitting-room. With open fire, TV, piano. No smoking.
Large garden

The Old Boat House is a rare survival: an unspoilt Victorian boating-station with distinctive black-and-white verandah overlooking a quiet, willow-fringed reach of the River Avon, and with an open-topped launch available in season to take you (free) into the centre of Bath – unless you prefer to punt or row yourself. Four generations of Hardicks have built, repaired and hired out wooden skiffs and other craft here: you can still see these being clinker-built in the traditional way.

Some bedrooms face the rambling garden and trees; the best has windows on two sides and a verandah overlooking riverbank and geese (as does the sitting-room). A small cottage in the garden has two tiny bedrooms and its own spacious sitting-room. Separate from the house is a riverside restaurant, also with verandah.

Bath itself deserves at least a week-long stay and the surrounding countryside is full of interest. In the city centre there is much to see: the abbey, Roman temple and baths, the botanical gardens, the shopping arcades, several worthwhile museums and art galleries. On Saturdays there's a flea market with good bargains.

V

PARADISE HOUSE
88 Holloway, Bath, Bath & North-East Somerset, BA2 4PX   Tel: 01225 317723
(Fax: 01225 482005)
Nearest main road: A367 from Bath to Radstock.

C M P T

8 Bedrooms. £20 **to readers of this book**–£37 (less for 4 nights or more). Bargain breaks. All have own bath/shower/toilet; TV.
1 Sitting-room. With open fire.
Large garden
Closed in December.

Standing halfway up a steep, curving road, with panoramic views of the city, the house was built about 1720, with all the elegance which that implies: a classical pediment above the front door and well-proportioned sash windows with rounded tops in a façade of honey-coloured Bath stone.

David and Janet Cutting took it over many years ago and restored it impeccably throughout, revealing pretty plasterwork ceilings, for instance, and a lovely marble fireplace. They furnished to a very high standard indeed, with both antique and modern furniture, elegant fabrics and well-chosen colour schemes. The bedrooms vary in size and amenities. There is also a Jacuzzi. At the back is a walled garden with lawns, fish pool and pergola. The city centre is only 7 minutes' walk away – downhill. (Lock-up garages for a small fee; croquet and boules available.)

Readers' comments: Top class! Truly excellent. Ideal, with excellent facilities. Superbly equipped, very attractive. Outstanding hotel. Extremely comfortable. Beautiful home; made us very welcome. Lovely house and garden.

V

PICKFORD HOUSE
Bath Road, Beckington, Somerset, BA3 6SJ   Tel/Fax: 01373 830329
South of Bath. Nearest main road: A36 from Bath to Warminster.

C M P T S X

4 Bedrooms. £15–£17.50 (less for 4 nights or more). Some have some or all of the following: own bath/shower/toilet; TV; views of river; balcony. No smoking.
Dinner (by arrangement). £12 for 3 courses and coffee, from 7pm. Vegetarian or other special diets if ordered. Wine available. No smoking. **Light suppers** if ordered.
2 Sitting-rooms. With open fire, TV, piano. No smoking in one. **Bar.**
Large garden

Sometimes parties of friends take the whole of this hilltop house for a gourmet weekend together – for Angela Pritchard is a cordon bleu cook. On such weekends, the guests are invited to choose their menu for a candlelit dinner of 6 courses with appropriate wines. Traditional Sunday lunches too.

Even on everyday occasions Pickford House food is exceptional. Angela offers a 3-course dinner that might include: mushrooms in Dijon sauce in a filo basket, lamb with leeks and ginger, and a sweet with mulberries from the garden.

The house is one of a pair that were built from honey-coloured Bath stone in 1804. The furnishings are comfortable, with two modern bedrooms in the old school house (one with kitchen adjoining).

Readers' comments: Excellent: accommodation and dinner beyond praise. Welcome relaxed, warm and personal. Great care to make us comfortable. First class. Excellent; remarkable value, especially the evening meal. B & b at its best. Sheer delight; meals superb.

V

QUANTOCK HOUSE

C D

Holford, Somerset, TA5 1RY   Tel: 01278 741439
West of Bridgwater. Nearest main road: A39 from Bridgwater to Minehead (and M5, junction 23).

3 Bedrooms. £19–£25 (less for 7 nights or more). All have some or all of the following: own bath/shower/toilet; TV. No smoking.
Dinner (by arrangement). £12 for 3 courses and coffee, at 7pm. Vegetarian or other special diets if ordered. No smoking.
1 Sitting-room. With open fire. No smoking.
Small garden

At the foot of a hill nestles a picturesque, 17th-century cottage. Built of stone and thatch, it has beams and a huge inglenook inside, and outside a flowery garden. Attractively furnished, the house has samplers, embroidered cushions and patchwork spreads in the en suite bedrooms (one on the ground floor) which are all Pam Laidler's work. Except in high summer, Pam prepares such meals as sorrel soup, salmon with garden vegetables, or pork chop in celery and apple sauce, and summer pudding.

All round the cottage are the Quantock Hills and pretty hamlets in an Area of Outstanding Natural Beauty. Nearby Alfoxton House (now a hotel) was tenanted by Wordsworth and his sister and they used to walk along here to visit Coleridge (his cottage, now NT, is open).

Readers' comments: 'Soaking up the atmosphere' is a holiday on its own! Mouth-watering food. Cannot praise too highly: I could have stayed for ever. Incomparable food. Excellent cook; made very welcome. Excellent accommodation, gracious and attentive hostess.

V

SOMERSET HOUSE

C D P T S X

35 Bathwick Hill, Bath, Bath & North-East Somerset, BA2 6LD   Tel: 01225 466451
(Fax: 01225 317188)
Nearest main road: A36 from Bath to Warminster.

10 Bedrooms. £20–£32 (less for 3 nights or more). Bargain breaks. All have some or all of the following: own bath/shower/toilet; TV. No smoking.
Dinner. £19 for 4 courses and coffee, at 7pm (not Sundays). Vegetarian or other special diets if ordered. Wine available. No smoking. **Light suppers** on Sundays.
2 Sitting-rooms. With open fire, TV, piano. **Bar.** No smoking.
Large garden

The entrance hall of the Seymours' Georgian mansion leads to a sitting-room, with conservatory opening onto lawn. There are two bedrooms on the ground floor. The dining-room is below stairs (it has an open fire and pine dresser).

On the first floor is another sitting-room with a particularly pretty plasterwork ceiling and very old Venetian glass chandelier. The original panelled shutters flank the high sash windows; outside is a long verandah, with fine city views.

Bedrooms are large and pleasantly furnished, many with antique fireplaces.

A typical dinner: game soup; 'rolypoly, gammon and spinach' with home-grown vegetables; apples in cider served with home-made ice cream. On Saturdays, special gourmet dinners (at 7.30pm) are offered; Sunday lunch is also available except in summer.

Readers' comments: The best establishment I've stayed at; the cooking reinvigorates the taste buds. Superb comfort and food. Excellent accommodation. A favourite. Very relaxed ambience.

V

WATERCOMBE HOUSE

Huish Champflower, Wiveliscombe, Somerset, TA4 2EE Tel: 01984 623725
North-west of Taunton. Nearest main road: B3227 from Taunton towards Barnstaple
(and M5, junction 25).

C(10) **S**

3 Bedrooms. £19.50–£22.50 (less for 3 nights or more). Bargain breaks. All have some of the following: own shower/toilet; TV; views of river. No smoking.
Dinner (by arrangement). £15.50 for 4 courses and coffee, at 7.30pm. Vegetarian or other special diets if ordered. Wine available. No smoking. **Light suppers** if ordered.
1 Sitting-room. With open fire, TV. No smoking.
Garden
Closed from November to Easter.

It is the River Tone which gives this 18th-century house its name, for it flows through the valley garden – in and out of a trout pool. A glass sun-room overlooks the garden.

Moira Garner-Richards is a cordon bleu trained cook, and serves such dinners as pears with Roquefort, pork cooked in Somerset cider, baked cheesecake, and cheese; or two courses.

The Garner-Richardses have prepared a leaflet about the house, which originally dates from 1723 but has been extended since. For most of the 19th century it was a school, the children using water from the river to wash in, and only in 1984 did electricity come to the house.

Within easy driving distance are Exmoor National Park and Dunster Castle; picturesque villages such as Combe Florey and Bishop's Lydeard; and Taunton itself is only a few miles away.

Readers' comments: A place to unwind in. Simply furnished but with individual touches. Delicious breakfast (with fresh-picked raspberries!). Everything done for our comfort. Friendly and most helpful.

V

WENTWORTH HOUSE

106 Bloomfield Road, Bath, Bath & North-East Somerset, BA2 2AP
Tel: 01225 339193 (Fax: 01225 310460)
Nearest main road: A367 from Bath to Shepton Mallet.

C(5) **M PT**

17 Bedrooms. £20–£30 **(but to readers of the current edition of this book only, 5% less for 2 nights, 10% less for 3 nights).** Bargain breaks. Some have own shower/toilet; TV.
Light suppers if ordered.
Bar.
Small garden
Closed from mid-December to mid-January.

The big, four-storey house was built for a coal merchant a century ago. It is a fine building of creamy stone, now furnished and equipped to very good standards by Avril Kitching. The dining-room has a glass extension overlooking the swimming-pool and a lawn. Some of the nicest rooms are below this: they not only open onto the garden but in some cases are suites, each consisting of a small sun-room with armchairs and glass walls beyond the bedroom. At the other extreme, top-floor rooms have the finest views over the city far below.

With breakfast cereals come bowls of various seeds, nuts and fresh fruit. There is an ample carpark, and a bus stops just outside, saving you the steep walk up from the city after a day's sightseeing.

Readers' comments: A delightful stay. Owners kind and helpful. Charming, relaxing and home-like. Service excellent. The best to date. Exceptional breakfast choices. Lots of character and very comfortable. Beautifully appointed. The room was lovely. Food very good.

V

WHITTLES FARM

C(12) **S**

Beercrocombe, Somerset, TA3 6AH   Tel/Fax: 01823 480301
South-east of Taunton. Nearest main road: A358 from Ilminster to Taunton (and M5, junction 25).

3 Bedrooms. £18–£22. All have own bath/shower/ toilet; TV. No smoking.
Dinner (by arrangement). £15 for 4 courses and coffee, at 6.30pm. Wine available. No smoking.
2 Sitting-rooms. With open fire. No smoking in one. Bar.
Large garden
Closed from December to mid-February.

The excellence of the accommodation and Claire Mitchem's delightful personality make for an exceptional farmhouse holiday at Whittles Farm. At the end of a lane leading nowhere, part of the house dates back to the 16th century (hence the beams and inglenook of the sitting-room). Every bedroom is attractively decorated.

A typical menu: boeuf bourguignonne accompanied by four vegetables and a salad; queen of puddings with clotted cream; fresh fruit.

There are excellent woodland walks, and drives along lanes which vary at every turn. Within easy reach are the Palladian mansion of Hatch Court and the gardens at Hestercombe House; the coasts both north and south; and the county town of Taunton: the Vivary gardens here are well worth a visit, and also the castle (with exceptionally good museum) close to the River Tone.

Readers' comments: We liked it very much. Most pleasing. Cannot speak too highly of the care and attention.

V

WIGBOROUGH FARM

C D PT **S**

Lower Stratton, Somerset, TA13 5LP   Tel/Fax: 01460 240490
West of Yeovil. Nearest main road: A303 from Ilminster to Wincanton.

3 Bedrooms. £20–£23. Bargain breaks. Some have own bath/toilet. No smoking.
Light suppers if ordered. Vegetarian or other special diets if ordered. Wine available. No smoking.
1 Sitting-room. With open fire, TV, piano. No smoking.
Large garden
Closed from mid-December to March.

But for a fire in 1585, this mansion would doubtless have been one of England's oldest. Only one wing was rebuilt: even so, it remains among the most impressive of the houses in this book.

Outside are pinnacled gables, carved Tudor roses, handsome dripstones above mullioned windows – all in tawny Ham limestone. Inside are ogee arches, stone floors and iron-studded doors; there are still spit-racks above one of the huge fireplaces. One ground-floor room has a minstrels' gallery (now a bedroom) overlooking the great refectory table and its leather chairs.

Guests' bedrooms (varying in size and style) are on the second floor: the most outstanding has oak walls, its panels decoratively carved with arches and pilasters, and a four-poster bed.

From many windows are views of lawns with specimen trees, old stables and the walled vegetable garden. (Joan Vaux provides light suppers only.)

Readers' comments: As if out of a dream! Historic but comfortable; lovely gardens. Wonderful people. The best! Very loath to leave this most beautiful place and the relaxed generosity and the warmth of these charming people.

STAFFORDSHIRE

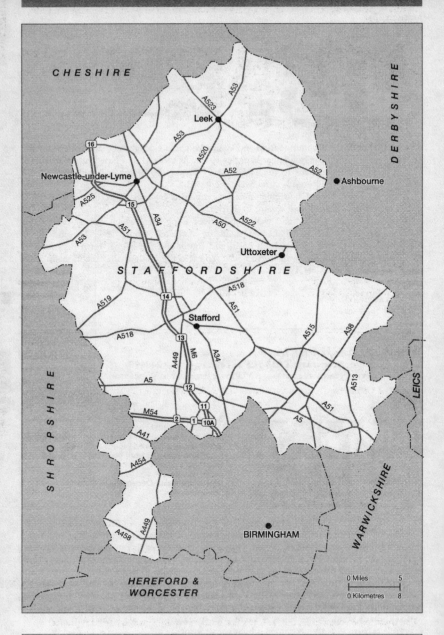

BICKFORD GRANGE

Bickford, Penkridge, Staffordshire, ST19 5QJ Tel: 01785 840257
South of Stafford. Nearest main road: A449 from Stafford to Wolverhampton (and M6, junction 12).

5 Bedrooms. £18. Some have some or all of the following: own bath/shower/toilet. No smoking.
Dinner (by arrangement). £10 for 3 courses and coffee, at times to suit guests. Vegetarian or other special diets if ordered. Wine available. No smoking.
Light suppers if ordered.
1 Sitting-room. With open fire, TV, piano.
Large garden

Once a farm (hence the huge bell to call fieldworkers in to dinner), this Georgian house, which was built in 1800, still has a stone-flagged hall but its architectural features are grander, from a prettily plastered ceiling to the balustraded terrace overlooking its lawns: glass doors open onto this from the handsome blue sitting-room. The long dining-room, with mahogany and silver, has views of the fields. On the second floor is a suite of two double rooms that would be ideal for a family. Even the single bedroom here is spacious. Gail Bryant enjoys cooking homely meals. Outside is a heated swimming-pool.

Lovely countryside surrounds the Grange, and there is much of interest to see – not only in this county but over the Shropshire border towards Telford and Ironbridge.

Readers' comments: Really superb. Beautifully furnished. Beautiful setting, room spacious and comfortable, food very good, most helpful.

MANOR HOUSE FARM

Prestwood, Denstone, Staffordshire, ST14 5DD Tel: 01889 590415 and 01335 343669 (Fax: 01335 342198)
North of Uttoxeter. Nearest main road: B5032 from Cheadle to Ashbourne.

3 Bedrooms. £18–£22 (less for 5 nights or more). Bargain breaks. All have some or all of the following: own bath/shower/toilet; TV. No smoking.
Light suppers if ordered.
1 Sitting-room. With open fire, TV.
Large garden

Once his family farmed here, but now Christopher Ball has turned to dealing in antiques; a fact reflected in the handsome furnishings of the 17th-century house. It was built of sandstone from nearby Hollington quarry.

High-backed settles flank the log fire in the sitting-room, which has stone-mullioned bay windows in its thick walls – with fine hill views. On the oak-panelled walls of the dining-room hang oil paintings. The bedrooms (with beams and exposed stone walls) have four-posters. The latest to be acquired by the Balls is a fine antique example with its original drapes.

The terraced garden is particularly attractive: weeping ash, pinnacled summer-house (it was once the cupola on a hospital roof), steps ascending between clipped yews, a tennis court and croquet lawn. You can barbecue your own meat if you wish.

Reader's comment: Excellent.

OLD HALL

C D

Poolside, Madeley, Staffordshire, CW3 9DX Tel/Fax: 01782 750209
West of Newcastle-under-Lyme. On A525 from Newcastle-under-Lyme to Whitchurch
(and near M6, junction 15).

3 Bedrooms. £20–£27.50 (less for 3 nights or more).
Bargain breaks. One has own shower/toilet; TV (in all).
No smoking.
Dinner (by arrangement). £14 for 3 courses and
coffee, at 7pm. Vegetarian or other special diets if
ordered. No smoking. **Light suppers** if ordered.
1 Sitting-room. With woodstove, TV, piano. No
smoking.
Large garden

Cheshire is famous for its black-and-white houses, and this – though just over the county
boundary – is a good example, with its beams and gables. In the sitting-room there is a
grand piano by the woodstove, and sometimes music-stands as well, for Mary Hugh is a
professional viola player. Through oak-boarded doors is the dining-room, where guests are
served with, for example, watercress soup or cheese soufflé, beef sirloin in mushroom and
pepper sauce, and chocolate roulade – cooked by Ann O'Leary, a professional caterer.

Bedrooms have low beams, antiques and handsome brass door-fittings. The tiled bathroom with its huge bath is almost unchanged since the 1920s, when it was one of the first
illustrated in *Ideal Home.*

Off the breakfast-room is a high-Victorian conservatory. In the two-acre garden, with
pond and pergola, are croquet and tennis lawns.

Readers' comments: Very good. Wonderful house. Serene atmosphere. First-class food.

PETHILLS BANK COTTAGE

C(5) M

Bottomhouse, Staffordshire, ST13 7PF Tel: 01538 304277 (Fax: 01538 304575)
South-east of Leek. Nearest main road: A523 from Leek towards Ashbourne.

3 Bedrooms. £19–£20.50 (less for 3 nights or more).
All have some or all of the following: own bath/
shower/toilet; TV. No smoking.
Dinner (by arrangement). £16.50 for 4 courses and
coffee, at 7.30pm. Vegetarian or other special diets if
ordered. No smoking. **Light suppers** if ordered.
1 Sitting-room. No smoking.
Small garden
Closed in January and February.

This 18th-century farmhouse, much modernized, stands in landscaped gardens on the crest
of a hill, at the edge of the Peak District. Thick and rugged stone walls are exposed in the
snug sitting-room which was once a cowshed – now soft lighting falls on pinky-beige
chesterfields, and from the big window there is a view of the Martins' rock garden. In the
dining-room are carved Dutch chairs and a log stove on a tiled hearth.

One particularly pretty bedroom, on the ground floor, has its own verandah overlooking
the hills, silky draperies and a private sitting-room. Up an open-tread stair are more bedrooms, one in a former hayloft. Each has its own style.

Yvonne's dinners (available on only some evenings) include such dishes as pasta, trout
en croûte, chocolate cheesecake, cheese with fruit.

Readers' comments: Warm and cheerful hostess. Excellent cook. Nothing was too much
trouble. Very attractive lounge, extremely attentive service. Warm and friendly, very helpful.
Excellent in every way and very good value. Breakfast here surpasses all others.

V

242

PORCH FARMHOUSE

Grindon, Staffordshire, ST13 7TP   Tel/Fax: 01538 304545
South-east of Leek. Nearest main road: A523 from Leek to Ashbourne.

3 Bedrooms. £19.50 **to readers of this book only.**
Bargain breaks. All have some or all of the following:
own bath/shower/toilet; TV. No smoking.
Dinner (by arrangement). £18 for 5 courses and coffee,
at 7pm. Vegetarian or other special diets if ordered. No
smoking. **Light suppers** if ordered.
1 Sitting-room. No smoking.
Garden

Grindon lies 1000 feet high, above the Peak District's lovely Manifold Valley. Sally Hulme and her husband Ron came upon the village on a walking tour and moved to this large 500-year-old limestone cottage some 15 years ago.

The beamed cottage is comfortable and smartly furnished. Meals are taken in the dining-room hung with Victorian 'lace' plates, and a lovely old oak dresser displays a collection of glass and silver. A typical menu: melon with smoked salmon; carrot and coriander soup; marinated breast of chicken; local cheeses; apricot and apple tart with home-made ice cream. Traditional breakfasts are complemented by a good choice of fresh and dried fruits.

Bedrooms, all with modern facilities, are decorated in cottage style.

Despite the village's isolated position, it lies only three miles from a National Express bus stop (with phone box nearby), and the Hulmes are able to collect visitors from there.

Readers' comments: Very welcoming. Perfect meals; very comfortable. First-class accommodation, cooking excellent. Wonderful – can't speak too highly. Entertained most royally. Lovely home, friendly personality. Cannot fault it.

V

For explanation of code letters and **V** symbol, see inside front cover.

'Bargain breaks' are usually out-of-season reductions for half-board stays of several nights.

Where wine is not available (meaning it is on sale or can be fetched for you), you are nearly always welcome to bring in your own drinks.

Major tourist attractions, such as Stratford-upon-Avon and Cambridge, can often be easily reached from houses in adjacent counties.

RED BARN

Hollington, Staffordshire, ST10 4HH   Tel: 01889 507221
North-west of Uttoxeter. Nearest main road: A522 from Uttoxeter to Cheadle.

C D M S

2 Bedrooms. £16.50 (less for 5 nights or more). Both have some or all of the following: own bath/shower/ toilet. No smoking.
Light suppers if ordered. Vegetarian or other special diets if ordered. No smoking.
1 Sitting-room. With stove, piano.
Small garden
Closed in December.

Conductor Howard Snell and his musical family used to live at 18th-century Hollington House. They have now moved 25 metres across the old farmyard into the Red Barn, which they have restored splendidly. Partly of stone and partly of red brick, their new home has a galleried sitting-room with exposed roof trusses, and a stone and tiled floor with a modern turquoise rug. This room has lovely views eastward across open country towards the distant Pennine foothills. The patchwork cushions were made – like the bedspreads – by Angela Snell herself (a former Hallé violinist).

Outside the village is the quarry from which came both pink and white stone for nearby Croxden Abbey, now a ruin, and for the modern cathedrals of Coventry and Liverpool.

Six towns make up the 'Ceramic City' of nearby Stoke-on-Trent containing Coalport, Spode, Wedgwood and other well-known potteries (visits available). Alton Towers leisure park is even closer.

Readers' comments: Treated like royalty; a haven of peace; Mrs Snell extremely thoughtful in her attention to detail.

STANSHOPE HALL

Stanshope, Staffordshire, DE6 2AD   Tel: 01335 310278 (Fax: 01335 310476)
North-west of Ashbourne. Nearest main road: A515 from Ashbourne to Buxton.

C

3 Bedrooms. £20–£32 (less for 3 nights or more). All have some or all of the following: own bath/toilet; TV. No smoking.
Dinner (by arrangement). £18 for 3 courses and coffee, at 7.30pm. Vegetarian or other special diets if ordered. Wine available. No smoking. **Light suppers** if ordered.
1 Sitting-room. With open fire, piano.
Large garden

Built in 1670 by Cromwell's quartermaster, Jackson, the Hall has seen many changes. It was greatly extended in the 1780s and when, at nearby Ilam, a great mansion burnt down in the 19th century, salvaged fireplaces were re-installed here. Later a theatrical designer made it his home, embellishing it with all sorts of trompe l'oeil effects. The murals with peacocks and trees in the sitting-room are in the manner of Rex Whistler, while in the entrance hall a stairway and arches of Hopton stone contrast with painted marbling.

Recently, local artists have repainted bedrooms with decorative murals (bathrooms too).

Not only the ambience but also the food provided by Naomi Chambers and Nick Lourie is out of the ordinary. A typical menu: carrot and ginger soup, followed by lamb in red wine and honey, then either gooseberry ice cream or Bakewell tart.

Readers' comments: A real home from home. Food excellent. Very relaxing and enjoyable break. Warm and comfortable with excellent views. Faultless; food exceptionally good. Charmed with the history and decor.

SUFFOLK

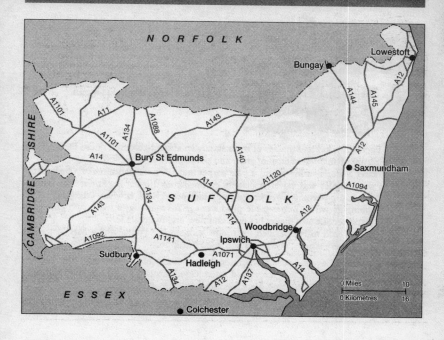

THANK YOU . . . to those who send details of their own finds, for possible future inclusion in the book. Do not be disappointed if your candidate does not appear in the very next edition. We never publish recommendations from unknown members of the public without verification, and it takes time to get round each part of England and Wales in turn. Please, however, do not send details of houses already featured in many other guides, nor any that are more expensive than those in this book (see page ix).

BUTTONS GREEN FARM

C(5) **D S**

Cockfield, Suffolk, IP30 0JF   Tel: 01284 828229
South of Bury St Edmunds. Nearest main road: A1141 from Lavenham towards Bury St Edmunds.

3 Bedrooms. £18–£19 (less for 2 nights or more).
Dinner (by arrangement). £10 for 3 courses and coffee, at 6.30pm. No smoking. **Light suppers** if ordered.
1 Sitting-room. With open fire, TV. No smoking.
Large garden
Closed from November to mid-March.

Behind a big duck-pond and masses of roses stands an apricot-coloured house built around 1400, the centre of an 80-acre farm of grain and beet fields.

In Margaret Slater's sitting-room, a pale carpet and silky wallpaper make a light background to the antiques and velvet armchairs grouped round a big log stove. The dining-room, too, has a log-burning stove in the brick inglenook. This is where Margaret serves meals with home-grown or home-made produce: egg mayonnaise, a roast, and chocolate soufflé, for instance. She also makes her own chutneys and marmalade.

Twisting stairs lead to big beamed bedrooms with sloping floors, which Mrs Slater has furnished with flowery fabrics, pot-plants and good furniture.

Readers' comments: Lovely house. Charming hosts. Good home cooking. Just perfect. Delightful, friendly, comfortable. Very good value. Good meals. Very nice people. Excellent all round. Simple but good cooking. Very friendly: excellent atmosphere.

EDGEHILL HOTEL

C D PT

2 High Street, Hadleigh, Suffolk, IP7 5AP   Tel: 01473 822458
West of Ipswich. Nearest main road: A1071 from Ipswich towards Sudbury.

8 Bedrooms. £20–£38 (less for 2 nights or more). Bargain breaks. All have own bath/shower/toilet; TV. No smoking (some).
Dinner. £18 for 3 courses and coffee, at 7pm. Vegetarian or other special diets if ordered. Wine available. No smoking. **Light suppers** if ordered.
1 Sitting-room. With open fire, piano.
Large garden

Hadleigh, once a rich wool town, went through bad times but is now prospering again. One of the High Street's many fine historic buildings to have been rejuvenated is a Tudor house with Georgian façade which is now this private hotel. Rodney Rolfe took over Edgehill Hotel in 1976 and began to convert it. The well-proportioned rooms have been furnished with style, and attractive wallpapers chosen for each one. In all the spacious bedrooms there are thick-pile carpets and good furniture. The sitting-room has glass doors opening onto the walled garden where an annexe has some bedrooms (for smokers).

Angela Rolfe, previously a teacher, and her mother do all the cooking and use home-grown raspberries, strawberries, vegetables and other produce from the kitchen garden. She serves soup, roasts, organic vegetables and desserts such as raspberry pavlova, ginger meringues, rhubarb and ginger fool (ordering ahead is always necessary).

V *Readers' comments:* Absolutely excellent. High standard. One of the very best.

GAVELCROFT

Holton, Suffolk, IP19 8LY   Tel: 01986 873117
South-west of Lowestoft. Nearest main road: A144 from Bungay to Halesworth.

2 Bedrooms. £18. Bargain winter breaks. Both have some or all of the following: own bath/shower/toilet; TV. No smoking.
Dinner (by arrangement). £8 for 2 courses and coffee, at 7pm. Vegetarian or other special diets if ordered.
Light suppers if ordered.
1 Sitting-room. With open fire/stove, TV. No smoking.
Large garden

Many refugees from 16th-century religious persecution on the Continent settled in Suffolk, often finding themselves employment in the local wool and silk-weaving trades. Gavelcroft was once home to such folk, its name deriving from the Dutch for 'gabled croft', and the Dutch gable-ends and dormers remain today. Now Sarah and Mike Hart live here. Sarah, a former speech therapist, looks after you, while Mike makes and restores double-basses in his workshop (which you may visit).

Accommodation here is cosy and private. One bedroom, decorated in celadon green and yellows, is on the ground floor and overlooks the apple orchard. The larger bedroom, in warm pinks and cream, with comfortable chairs, is in the eaves, converted from what was once an apple store. The low-beamed and stone-floored dining-room has antique and walnut furniture. Dinner might be chicken pie followed by chocolate mousse, or perhaps vegetable cannelloni and summer pudding.

It is only a few miles to picturesque Southwold or the wild Suffolk coast, or in fine weather you might take a peaceful riverside walk to the old market town of Halesworth.

Readers' comments: Homely and friendly atmosphere. The most perfect hosts.

V

GREEN FARM

Geldeston, Suffolk, NR34 0HG   Tel: 01508 518028
West of Lowestoft. Nearest main road: A146 from Norwich to Lowestoft.

rear view

3 Bedrooms. £17.50 (less for 2 nights or more). Some have some or all of the following: own bath/shower/ toilet. No smoking.
Light suppers if ordered. Vegetarian or other special diets if ordered. No smoking.
1 Sitting-room. With TV, organ.
Large garden

Both East Anglians in origin, Pam and John Meadows returned to the area after farming and offering bed and breakfast in Derbyshire. This farm in the Waveney Valley is where they settled, in a much modernized Victorian farmhouse. All is spick and span here. The sun-lounge, with enormous picture-windows, has wicker furniture where guests may relax and admire the views of the valley beyond. Guests sometimes join John for a walk on his evening rounds to check the cattle.

Bedrooms are simply but neatly furnished. One has a king-size bed, another in pink and grey has views of the pond and lovely garden where guests may sit in summer. Generous traditional breakfasts are served, while for evening meals there are restaurants in nearby Beccles.

This is an ideal spot for a quiet break. You might visit a cider farm at Ilketshall St Lawrence, a dried-flower farm at Weston, and in summer spend an evening at the repertory festival in Southwold. While there, take time to visit one of the finest churches in the county, St Edmund's, with its magnificent 100-foot flint-faced tower.

HIGH POPLARS
CDS

Hinton, Blythburgh, Suffolk, IP17 3RJ   Tel: 01502 478528
North-east of Saxmundham. Nearest main road: A12 from Ipswich to Lowestoft.

3 Bedrooms. £20–£22 (less for 7 nights or more). One has own bath/toilet. No smoking.
Dinner. £16 for 3 courses, wine and coffee, at 8pm. Vegetarian or other special diets if ordered. No smoking. **Light suppers** if ordered.
1 Sitting-room. With open fire, TV.
Small garden

For three centuries the same family, Blois, farmed here or nearby: there are memorials to them in Blythburgh church.

Now the half-timbered house is Mary Montague's home. She has furnished it with unusual antiques such as a Spanish dresser, a collector's cabinet from the 18th century, country dining-chairs and sofas upholstered in an art nouveau Liberty fabric. On the dining-room floor are heavy tiles of Spanish clay; and up winding stairs are big bedrooms with, for instance, pink patchwork spreads and cushions, and particularly good bathrooms.

Mary, who dines with her guests, might prepare such meals as Cromer crabs to start with; sole stuffed with mushrooms and prawns; then Belvoir pudding (a steamed lemon pudding with meringue and apple surrounding it); wine is included.

Hinton is in P. D. James country, an area where wildlife still flourishes. Mary's own pond is frequented by herons, kingfishers and ducks.

Readers' comments: One of the best. Charming and helpful. Delightful. Delicious dinner. Very warm and friendly. Lovely place. Made everyone feel welcome.

HILL FARMHOUSE
CDS

Bury Road, Hitcham, Suffolk, IP7 7PT   Tel: 01449 740651
North-west of Ipswich. Nearest main road: A1141 from Hadleigh towards Bury St Edmunds.

3 Bedrooms. £20 (less for 5 nights or more). All have some or all of the following: own bath/toilet; TV. No smoking.
Dinner. £11 for 3 courses and coffee, at times to suit guests. Vegetarian or other special diets if ordered. No smoking. **Light suppers** on Tuesdays and Thursdays.
3 Sitting-rooms. One with open fire.
Large garden
Closed from November to February.

Part Tudor, part early Victorian, this handsome house provides a choice between the spacious, traditional bedroom at the front of the house (with cornfield views); or the snug low-beamed ones at the back, with little oak-mullioned windows and rugs on brick floors. The brick oven and hearth of Tudor times are now a decorative feature which Pippa McLardy fills with arrangements of dried flowers. One enters the main house through a hall of powder-blue and white, with cherry-carpeted staircase. Pale pink sitting- and dining-rooms have mahogany antiques, a carved pine fireplace and views of countryside or garden (there are duck-ponds, a freestanding swimming-pool, croquet and badminton). Pippa is an imaginative cook: for dinner one might choose fennel Mornay or stuffed vineleaves; pork normande or Scotch salmon; raspberry-and-cream choux or lemon sorbet.

Readers' comments: House of character; relaxed atmosphere, good cooking. Warm welcome.

MANORHOUSE

The Green, Beyton, Suffolk, IP30 9AF   Tel: 01359 270960
East of Bury St Edmunds. Nearest main road: A14 from Bury to Stowmarket.

3 Bedrooms. £19–£22 (less for 7 nights or more). Bargain breaks. All have some or all of the following: own bath/shower/toilet; TV. No smoking.
Dinner (by arrangement). £13 for 3 courses and coffee, at 7pm. Vegetarian or other special diets if ordered. No smoking. **Light suppers** if ordered.
1 Sitting-room. No smoking.
Large garden

The beamed and panelled sitting/dining-room of this typical Suffolk long-house overlooks the village pond, and the geese resident there sometimes waddle past the window at breakfast time, as if pre-arranged by Kay and Mark Dewsbury, thus completing a picture of idyllic village life. Generous breakfasts here include home-made jams and eggs from the Dewsburys' own chickens. Dinners are well-planned affairs; for example, leek and potato soup, game casserole, and lemon mousse, all with fresh local ingredients. While dining you may admire Kay's collection of Staffordshire figures, and the rural landscapes painted by her mother.

The bedrooms, all with excellent bathrooms, are beautifully furnished. One, in pink, overlooks the village green and pond, and the yellow room, with a swagged voile hanging above the bed, has art deco-style lamps and pictures. Close by you might visit Blackthorp Barn with a summer music programme and a craft fair in November and December; or sample wine at Wyken Hall vineyard, with its good restaurant and attractive gardens.

Readers' comments: Delightful, tastefully restored and spotless. Breakfast excellent. Blissful bathroom.

MULBERRY HALL

Burstall, Suffolk, IP8 3DP   Tel: 01473 652348
West of Ipswich. Nearest main road: A1071 from Ipswich towards Sudbury.

3 Bedrooms. £18. No smoking.
Dinner. £15 for 4 courses and coffee, at 7.45pm (except in August). Vegetarian or other special diets if ordered. No smoking. **Light suppers** if ordered.
1 Sitting-room. With open fire, TV, piano. No smoking.
Large garden

Cardinal Wolsey owned this house in 1523 and it is Henry VIII's colourful coat-of-arms which embellishes the inglenook fireplace in the big sitting-room – pink, beamed and with a grand piano. From this a winding stair leads up to well-equipped bedrooms. There is a small dining-room where Penny Debenham serves such meals – to be ordered in advance – as trout mousse with watercress purée; pork au poivre accompanied by dauphinoise potatoes; and fruit tartlets with elderflower cream. Breakfasts, too, are good, with pleasant options in addition to the usual bacon and eggs.

Outside is an exceptional garden. Beyond a brick-paved terrace is a lawn with long lavender border, and a pergola leads past a rose garden to the tennis court.

Readers' comments: Beautiful house, outstanding food and service; will visit again. A lot of loving care. Bedrooms light and airy, extremely comfortable; excellent food, breakfast a highlight. Warm welcome, lovely house, superb breakfast. Very relaxed.

OLD VICARAGE

Higham, Suffolk, CO7 6JY   Tel: 01206 337248

North of Colchester. Nearest main road: A12 from Colchester to Ipswich.

C D S X

3 Bedrooms. £20–£28 (less for 3 nights or more). Bargain breaks. Some have some or all of the following: own bath/shower/toilet; TV; views of river.
Light suppers sometimes. Vegetarian or other special diets if ordered. Wine available. No smoking.
1 Sitting-room. With open fire, TV. No smoking.
Large garden

One of the most elegant houses in this book, the Old Vicarage stands near a tranquil village and is surrounded by superb views. Everything about it is exceptional, from the Tudor building itself to the pretty south-facing garden (with unheated swimming-pool).

Colonel and Mrs Parker have lived here for many years, and their taste is evident in every room. Lovely colours, pretty wallpapers and chintzes, antiques, flowers and log fires all combine to create a background of great style. In the breakfast-room, bamboo chairs surround a huge circular table (of mock-marble); bedrooms are equally attractive.

Most visitors dine at the Angel in Stoke-by-Nayland.

Readers' comments: Perfect! Delightful weekend; privileged to be there. Most beautiful house. Very friendly. Thoroughly enjoyed it, superb. Food of highest standard, attention to detail outstanding. Splendid home and hospitality. Very interesting, friendly hostess.

V

PIPPS FORD

Needham Market, Suffolk, IP6 8LJ   Tel: 01449 760208 (Fax: 01449 760561)

North of Ipswich. Nearest main road: A14 from Ipswich to Bury St Edmunds.

C(5) D M PT S

6 Bedrooms. £17–£32.50 (less for 4 nights or more). Bargain breaks. All have some or all of the following: own bath/shower/toilet; views of river. No smoking.
Dinner. £16.50 for 3 courses and coffee, at 7.15pm (£18.50, at 8pm, weekends). Vegetarian or other special diets if ordered. Wine available.
3 Sitting-rooms. With open fire, TV, piano.
Large garden
Closed from mid-December to mid-January.

On a stretch of the River Gipping that has been designated an Area of Outstanding Natural Beauty stands a large Tudor farmhouse once owned by Hakluyt. Raewyn Hackett-Jones has made patchwork quilts or cushion-covers for every room and searched out attractive fabrics for curtains or upholstery. Many of the beds are collectors' pieces; even the bathrooms are attractive. Some bedrooms are in converted stables, with sitting-room.

This is a house of inglenook fireplaces, sloping floors, low beams and historic associations. Meals may be served in a flowery conservatory, a vine overhead.

Breakfasts are exceptional. From an enormous choice, you could select exotic juices; home-made sausages; cinnamon toast or waffles; kidneys, mackerel, fishcakes. Popular dinner dishes include: avocado and smoked salmon baked with cheese; breast of duck with port; home-made ice creams and traditional puddings.

Readers' comments: Delightful house, beautifully furnished; food and service outstanding; one of the best holidays ever; friendly good humour. A fitting climax to our wonderful trip with your book. Charming and talented hostess, food beautifully garnished.

V

250

PRIORY COTTAGE

Low Corner, Butley, Suffolk, IP12 3QD Tel: 01394 450382
East of Woodbridge. Nearest main road: A12 from Ipswich to Lowestoft.

3 Bedrooms. £18–£25 (minimum 2 nights). All have some or all of the following: own bath/shower/toilet; TV; views of river. No smoking.
1 Sitting-room. With open fire, TV. No smoking.
Large garden

On arrival, visitors are greeted by Megan, the Newnhams' slightly daffy dog; all around is a prettily landscaped garden. The entrance hall has an unusual floor of polished 'pamment' tiles, sofas and arrangements of dried flowers. There are velvet chairs in the L-shaped sitting-room. For dinner, there are several inns and restaurants in the area: at one inn, Suffolk folk songs can be heard on Sundays.

Upstairs, rooms with clear bright colours, flowery wallpaper friezes, pine doors and beds, and louvred built-ins are neat and cheerful: some have views of Butley Creek. The blue-and-white one has a prettily draped bed.

The cottage is in a designated Area of Outstanding Natural Beauty, and completely unspoilt. It is on the Suffolk Coast Path (50 miles of footpath and bridleway).

Readers' comments: Beautiful location. Exceptionally well furnished. Friendly, hospitable and attentive. Wonderful, convivial evenings. Could not have had better accommodation and friendliness. Amusing hostess.

SHIP STORES

22 Callis Street, Clare, Suffolk, CO10 8PX Tel: 01787 277834 (Fax: 01787 277183)
North-west of Sudbury. Nearest main road: A1092 from Long Melford towards Saffron Walden.

5 Bedrooms. £18.50–£21 (less for 4 nights or more). Bargain breaks. All have some or all of the following: own bath/shower/toilet; TV. No smoking.
Dinner (by arrangement). £7.50 for 2 courses and coffee, at 7–8pm. Vegetarian or other special diets if ordered. Wine available. **Light suppers** if ordered.
1 Sitting-room. With TV.

Miles from the sea, this one-time inn was originally called the Sheep, not the Ship. Now it is a small shop run by Colin and Debra Bowles, with a few en suite bedrooms and an upstairs sitting-room for guests. It is a place of low beams, creaking floors, undulating roof and pink-plastered front: full of character. In the dining-room there is solid elm furniture locally made. There are two en suite rooms in a flint-walled annexe. For dinner, Debra serves such meals as vegetable soup, lamb chops, then fruit or a cream cake. Bread and croissants are home-baked.

Clare is a place to explore on foot, to enjoy all the details of its ancient houses – plaster-work decoration, exuberant inn signs, the old priory. It is close to Cavendish, Sudbury and other attractive places in Suffolk such as Kentwell Hall and gardens, Long Melford (good for antique-hunting), Clare country park, the Colne Valley steam railway, Gainsborough's house, Hedingham Castle and Melford Hall.

Reader's comments: A beautiful, charming and superbly run establishment.

V

SOUTH ELMHAM HALL

CX

St Cross, Suffolk, IP20 0PZ   Tel: 01986 782526 (Fax: 01986 782203)
South of Bungay. Nearest main road: A143 from Harleston to Bungay.

3 Bedrooms. £20 (less for 2 nights or more). All have some or all of the following: own bath/shower/toilet. No smoking.
Dinner (by arrangement). £12.50 for 2 courses or £15 for 3 courses and coffee, at 7.30pm. Vegetarian or other special diets if ordered. No smoking. **Light suppers** if ordered.
1 Sitting-room. With TV. No smoking.
Large garden

In mediaeval times, if members of the local ecclesiastical hierarchy felt like a weekend in the country, they might well have taken a short break at South Elmham Hall, for until the Dissolution it was a moated hunting-lodge belonging to the Bishops of Norwich. More sinister events included the trial here of a Lollard heretic, later burnt at the stake. Now anyone may safely stay and be guests of Jo and John Sanderson, who farm the surrounding land.

Bedrooms are of a good size, comfortably furnished and decorated in bold colours. One, with mulberry walls and aquamarine carpet, has a canopied bed and an excellent, colour-coordinated bathroom. Another has a brass bedstead and lovely views over the formal rose garden into the valley beyond. In the hallway, parts of the original 13th-century wall decoration remain. Winter evening meals could comprise a casserole, followed by apple pie or chocolate cheesecake. In summer there might be a barbecue, after which you could take an evening stroll following one of the farm walks the Sandersons have marked out.

V

SOUTH HILL HOUSE

C PT

43 Southgate Street, Bury St Edmunds, Suffolk, IP33 2AZ   Tel: 01284 755650
(Fax: 01284 752718)
Nearest main road: A134 from Sudbury to Bury St Edmunds (and A14).

3 Bedrooms. £17.50–£20. Bargain breaks. All have some or all of the following: own bath/shower/toilet; TV. No smoking.
Small garden

The simple Georgian exterior of South Hill House, described by Charles Dickens as 'a large, old, red-brick house, just outside the town', belies both its history and the generously sized, comfortable accommodation within. Reputedly the model for the school in *Pickwick Papers*, Dickens often read to the young ladies at Miss Amelia Hitchen's select establishment which occupied the building in the 1860s.

Sarah and Anthony Green (previously farmers), their family and dog Pernod now live here. All the bedrooms are spacious, with room to sit and relax. The largest (family) room has a luxurious bathroom with mocha-coloured suite and sunken bath. Extraordinarily, in times of Catholic repression this room was an oratory, the bedroom being its meeting-room. Breakfast, in the stone-slabbed and oak-furnished dining-room, includes local sausages, and kippers if you ask. There are plenty of restaurants a short walk away in the town, and much to see there too: lovely architecture, the beautiful Abbey Gardens, museums, an art gallery and the handsomely restored Theatre Royal.

V   *Reader's comments:* Absolutely sincere, heartwarming hospitality.

SPION KOP

Spring Lane, Ufford, Suffolk, IP13 6EF   Tel: 01394 460277
North of Woodbridge. Nearest main road: A12 from Ipswich to Lowestoft.

3 Bedrooms. £18–£22 (less for 7 nights or more). Bargain breaks. Some have some or all of the following: own bath/shower/toilet; TV.
Dinner (by arrangement). £15 for 3 courses and coffee, at 7pm. Vegetarian or other special diets if ordered. **Light suppers** if ordered.
1 Sitting-room. With open fire.
Large garden

When Colonel Walters returned from the Boer Wars he built himself a house reminiscent of his years on the veldt, with an almost conical roof of thatch and a wide-eaved verandah.

The Fergusons have added their own distinctive touches to what was already a very unusual house. Along the verandah (hung with brimming baskets of lobelias and begonias) are life-size marble nymphs, with more among the flowerbeds. Indoors, along with much other Victoriana are bronzes and paintings of turn-of-the-century beauties well displayed against the pale walls of sitting- and dining-rooms, through the lattice windows of which (or from the glass sun-room) there are wooded valley views.

Bedrooms are spacious and elegantly furnished; and Susan's meals are delicious. One example: a herby soup with croûtons; pork in a sauce of mushrooms, cream and wine (with vegetables cooked to perfection); raspberry meringues; and a glass of wine included.

Readers' comments: First-class. Food is of cordon bleu standard. Bedrooms very comfortably and stylishly furnished. Idyllic house and garden, warm and genuine welcome. Beautiful setting, friendly attitude, marvellous food. Probably the most interesting house we have stayed in.

Prices are per person sharing a room at the beginning of the year.

Months when houses are shown as closed are inclusive.

Book well ahead: many of these houses have few rooms. Do not expect dinner if you have not booked it or if you arrive late.

Some proprietors stipulate a minimum stay of two nights at weekends or peak seasons; or they will accept one-nighters only at short notice (that is, only if no lengthier booking has yet been made).

STREET FARM

S

Brent Eleigh, Suffolk, CO10 9NU   Tel: 01787 247271
South-east of Bury St Edmunds. Nearest main road: A1141 from Lavenham to Hadleigh.

3 Bedrooms. £20–£22 (less for 3 nights or more). Some have some or all of the following: own bath/shower/toilet; views of river. No smoking.
1 Sitting-room. With open fire, TV.
Large garden
Closed from November to mid-March.

Not far from Lavenham is Jean Gage's Street Farm, its apricot walls half-timbered, its garden well-groomed. Inside are beamed ceilings and fine furnishings – big velvet armchairs, and Hepplewhite-style chairs in the dining-room, for instance – and a comfortable sitting-room with a log fire. Bedrooms are spacious and immaculate, with good private bathrooms. There are pleasant country and river views.

Lavenham is one of the finest surviving examples of a small mediaeval town: lanes of half-timbered and lopsided weavers' cottages still intact, great guildhall (NT) housing a museum of wool history, and a resplendent church. Further south, in beautiful countryside threaded by rivers with old bridges and watermeadows, are such other historic villages as Bures (where St Edmund was crowned King of East Anglia in 855) and pretty Kersey, full of colourful half-timbered cottages.

Readers' comments: Very friendly. Comfortable. Beautifully maintained, very quiet. Best b & b we've had. Everything to make one feel welcome. Beautiful surroundings.

WESTERN HOUSE

C S X

High Street, Cavendish, Suffolk, CO10 8AR   Tel: 01787 280550
North-west of Sudbury. On A1092 between Long Melford and Clare.

3 Bedrooms. £15–£15.50 (less for 3 nights or more).
Large garden

Twice made redundant, industrialist Peter Marshall decided he would instead make a living from his best asset: his attractive 400-year-old house in the historic village of Cavendish.

He and his wife Jean (who teaches singing) are vegetarians, so at one end they started a wholefood shop, full of the smells of dried fruit and fresh herbs, and refurnished several bedrooms to take bed-and-breakfast guests. Options include all kinds of good things (such as their own muesli, eggs, mushrooms, tomatoes and home-made bread) but no bacon. They will recommend good restaurants of all kinds in the village, at Long Melford or in Sudbury.

Each beamed bedroom, reached via zigzag corridors, is very pretty, and spacious – well equipped with chairs, table, etc. One at the front (which looks onto the main road through the village) has a fresh white-and-green colour scheme extending even to the sheets. One of the nicest features is the large and informal garden.

Readers' comments: Excellent, with very good breakfasts. Much enjoyed it; and the shop is excellent. Extremely comfortable; warm welcome. Absolutely excellent, high standard. Charming and interesting people. Extremely attractive.

V

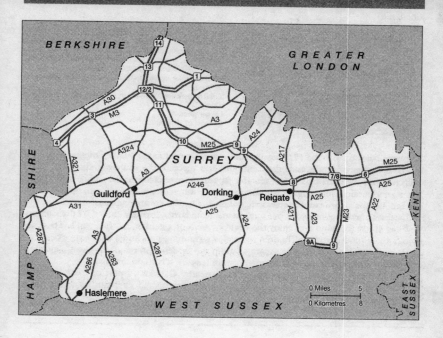

BARN COTTAGE

C D S

Church Road, Leigh, Surrey, RH2 8RF   Tel: 01306 611347
South-west of Reigate. Nearest main road: A25 from Reigate to Dorking (and M25, junction 8).

2 Bedrooms. £20–£25 (less for 3 nights or more). Bargain breaks. Both have TV.
Dinner (by arrangement). £15 for 4 courses and coffee, at 7–9.30pm. Vegetarian or other special diets if ordered. Wine available. No smoking. **Light suppers** if ordered.
1 Sitting-room. With open fire, TV. Piano in dining-room.
Large garden
Closed at Easter.

The barn dates back to the 17th century and was converted in the 1930s. Original beams are much in evidence, as are mahogany antiques and pieces of Copenhagen china, the latter collected over the years by Pat Comer. Her tapestries cover chairs in the sitting- and dining-rooms; and a talent for painting is displayed in her watercolours for children, on sale at the cottage. Bedrooms are comfortable, with wildflower bedcovers and curtains.

Lattice-paned windows look out onto immaculate lawns, lovingly tended by the Comers. One can sit on the patio and enjoy the beautiful view of a garden and fish pond. There are swings and a sandpit to keep children amused, a swimming-pool and a hard tennis court.

Evening meals might include asparagus from the garden, coronation chicken, chocolate-and-orange slice, and cheese. In summer, cream teas are served on the lawn.

The Comers will drive visitors to and from nearby Gatwick Airport or Redhill Station (regular trains into central London within half an hour); and cars can be left at Barn Cottage for a small daily charge.

V

BEEVERS FARM

C PT S

Chinthurst Lane, Bramley, Surrey, GU5 0DR   Tel: 01483 898764
South of Guildford. Nearest main road: A281 from Guildford to Horsham.

3 Bedrooms. £16–£18.50. One has own bath/shower/toilet; TV (in all). No smoking.
Light suppers if ordered. No smoking.
Large garden
Closed from December to January.

It is the genuine warmth and openness of Shelagh and Jim Cook's personalities that recommends a stay here. This plain, modern house just outside the village provides neat and simply furnished bedrooms decorated in pastel shades. The Cooks previously had plant nurseries on their surrounding land until these were destroyed in the great hurricane. Now the land is deliberately left wild, and hazel and elder trees tangle with willows. The result is that you may see rabbits, pheasants or even deer. There was probably a vineyard here in ancient times; Jim dug up old vines and a Roman quern stone when the house was being built.

The Cooks keep their own chickens and bees, the resultant produce being served at breakfast, together with home-made preserves from the garden's fruit. There is no sitting-room, but in fine weather guests may sit in the plant-packed conservatory. There are plenty of restaurants in the village and Shelagh will do packed lunches for walkers – the 30-mile Downs Link joining the North and South Downs is nearby. A disused railway route, it is now popular with walkers and cyclists.

V   *Reader's comments:* Very comfortable, exceptional hospitality.

BULMER FARM

Holmbury St Mary, Surrey, RH5 6LG   Tel: 01306 730210

C(12) **D M P T S X**

South-west of Dorking. Nearest main road: A25 from Dorking to Guildford (and M25, junction 9).

8 Bedrooms. £19–£21. Some have some or all of the following: own shower/toilet; TV; views of lake.
1 Sitting-room. With open fire, TV. No smoking.
Large garden

In the folds of Surrey's high North Downs a number of very picturesque villages lie hidden, and Holmbury is one. Near the centre stands Bulmer Farm, built about 1680. One steps straight into a large dining-room with gleaming furniture, and through this to an attractive sitting-room – a room of pink walls and old beams, logs crackling in the inglenook. It opens onto the large garden (with croquet).

Upstairs are pleasant, spacious bedrooms. Five additional and very comfortable rooms (with en suite showers) have been created in outbuildings for guests staying two nights or more. B & b only, but the area is full of inns offering good meals.

Outdoors, David Hill will show you the lake he created a few years ago, now a haven for herons, kingfishers, Canada geese, snipe and other wildfowl: it won a conservation award.

Readers' comments: Made so welcome, made to feel like one of the family. Picturesque, restful. Ultra quiet. Friendly, helpful owners. Good food. A great time. Very good accommodation and lovely area. Area wonderful, excellent place to stay to visit London.

V

CHERRY TREES

Gomshall Lane, Shere, Surrey, GU5 9HE   Tel: 01483 202288

C D M P T S

East of Guildford. Nearest main road: A25 from Guildford to Dorking (and M25, junction 9).

4 Bedrooms. £19. Bargain breaks. All have some or all of the following: own bath/shower/toilet; TV. No smoking.
1 Sitting-room. With open fire. No smoking.
Large garden
Closed from mid-December to mid-January.

Picturesque Shere with old cottages around a stream is one of Surrey's beauty-spots. Here is Cherry Trees, a traditional 'twenties brick and tile-hung house in a garden of winding flowerbeds and colourful shrubs (with seats in leafy nooks from which to enjoy hill views). One of the bedrooms is on the ground floor, in former stables overlooking the pretty garden. There is also a swimming-pool. Breakfast is served in a cream-walled room with oak dresser and leaded casements; for dinner, Olwen Warren recommends the White Horse inn a few yards away.

Dorking and Guildford (the latter with castle ruins, river trips and a good theatre) are each well worth a day's visit. Clandon Park and Polesden Lacey (stately homes) are close by, and so is Hatchlands (NT house with an interesting collection of musical instruments).

Reader's comment: Excellent location and perfect treatment.

V

CROSSWAYS FARM
C D PT

Raikes Lane, Abinger, Surrey, RH5 6PZ Tel: 01306 730173

South-west of Dorking. Nearest main road: A25 from Guildford to Dorking (and M25, junction 9).

3 Bedrooms. £17–£19 (less for 5 nights or more). Bargain breaks. Some have own bath/toilet. No smoking.
Light suppers if ordered.
1 Sitting-room. With open fire, TV, piano.
Small garden
Closed from mid-December to end of January.

Meredith's *Diana of the Crossways* (one of those books most people have heard of and few have read) took its title from this historic building of unusual architectural interest.

One steps through the arched door in a high wall to find a small, enclosed garden with a flagged path leading to the wide front door of the house. In its façade decorative brickwork combines with local sandstone, and Dutch-style arches curve over the small-paned windows. There is an immense chimney-stack towering above – 30 feet in circumference. But the most striking feature of all is the great oak staircase inside, its two flights leading up to large, beamed bedrooms, simply but comfortably furnished (there is a suite consisting of a double and a twin room with bathroom); the balusters and newels are handsomely carved.

The house has had many owners since it was built about 1620. For the last 30 years, the Hughes family have farmed here, producing beef and corn. By arrangement, Sheila Hughes serves homely farmhouse meals, or you can eat well at nearby Wootton Hatch.

Readers' comments: Warm welcome. Comfortable.

DEERFELL
C

Blackdown Park, Fernden Lane, Haslemere, Surrey, GU27 3LA Tel: 01428 653409 (Fax: 01428 656106)

South of Haslemere. Nearest main road: A286 from Haslemere to Midhurst.

2 Bedrooms. £19–£22. Both have own bath/shower/toilet; TV. No smoking.
Dinner (by arrangement). £9.50 for 2 courses and coffee, at 7pm (not Sundays). Vegetarian or other special diets if ordered. No smoking. **Light suppers** if ordered.
1 Sitting-room. With open fire. No smoking.
Large garden
Closed from mid-December to mid-January.

Originally the coach house to a neighbouring mansion, Deerfell stands near the summit of Black Down, a Stone Age stronghold 8000 years ago, which rises to almost 1000 feet.

Its conversion from coach house to home was well done, retaining such features as stone-mullioned windows and latched board doors, but with such modern additions as a glass sun-room and a fireplace of green marble. Elizabeth Carmichael has furnished it with antiques, old rugs and colour schemes which are predominantly soft brown and cream. Bedrooms are comfortable and spacious. Meals (which are usually served in the handsome dining-room with grandfather clock, piano and an ancestral portrait of William IV's physician) are well cooked, ample and unpretentious – for instance, moussaka and treacle tart or chocolate cheesecake. Breakfast sometimes includes wild mushrooms.

London is only 45 minutes away by train from Haslemere.

Readers' comments: Very comfortable and pleasant stay. Lovely home. Felt relaxed and rested. Everything very much to our liking. Total peace and quiet. Warm and friendly.

GADBROOK OLD FARM

C D PT S

Wellhouse Lane, Betchworth, Surrey, RH3 7HH   Tel: 01737 842183
West of Reigate. Nearest main road: A25 from Reigate to Dorking (and M25, junction 8).

2 Bedrooms. £17.50–£22. Bargain breaks. Both have own bath/shower/toilet; TV. No smoking.
Dinner (by arrangement). £12 for 3 courses and coffee, at 7pm. Vegetarian or other special diets if ordered. No smoking. **Light suppers** if ordered.
1 Sitting-room. With open fire, TV. No smoking.
Large garden

If you look into the pond at the front of this lovely 15th-century farmhouse, you will see an old christening stone, and in the garden, near a fallen yew tree, is an old water pump.

Nestling deep in the Surrey countryside, it is the home of Derek Bibby and his New Zealand-born wife, Jeanette. Although not a working farm, Gadbrook is not short of visitors of the feathered kind: ducks and hens wander about and the occasional pheasant comes to call.

Inside, oak beams are a feature of every room. In the low-ceilinged sitting-room, filled with antiques amassed over four decades, cretonne sofas are grouped round a large inglenook fireplace. Guests eat at a large oak dining-table, seated on Jacobean chairs.

The bedrooms, with their whitewashed walls and pale green carpets, have fine views. The Edwardian beds in the twin room are particularly handsome.

Derek's watercolour landscapes are displayed throughout the house. Having formerly worked in the toy industry (he invented the Sindy doll), he now spends much of his time painting. Jeanette will serve such dinners as asparagus and salmon mousse, chicken with apricot and ginger, and chocolate roulade.

HIGH EDSER

C D PT

Shere Road, Ewhurst, Surrey, GU6 7PQ   Tel: 01483 278214 (Fax: 01483 278200)
South-east of Guildford. Nearest main road: A25 from Guildford to Dorking.

3 Bedrooms. £20 (less for 5 nights or more). No smoking.
Dinner (by arrangement). £8.50 for 2 courses or £10 for 3 courses and coffee, at 7pm. Vegetarian or other special diets if ordered. No smoking. **Light suppers** if ordered.
1 Sitting-room. With TV. No smoking.
Large garden

Ewhurst means 'yew wood', and the great stump of an ancient yew stands like a monolith in the garden of this handsome 16th-century house where Carol and Patrick Franklin-Adams live. In the hall paved with York stone, where Carol has exposed some of the old wattle-and-daub construction, a winding staircase leads to smart bedrooms (with very low doorways). One bedroom has an oak floor, lovely yellow-and-blue tulip-patterned curtains and a pretty blue-and-white buttoned armchair, an example of Carol's upholstery skills. Another, with four-poster bed, is decorated in peach and terracotta, with a charming antique embroidery of a garden scene on one wall. From this room you look out over the garden, which is carpeted with daffodils in spring. There are croquet, a tennis court, and also a heated swimming-pool which guests may use by arrangement.

Meals are taken in the lattice-paned dining-room in front of an ancient, carved oak fire-surround. Evening meals may comprise simple soup and quiche or, more elaborately, Stilton and walnut pâté, pork with honey and chilli sauce, and lemon pudding. Afterwards, visitors can retire to the snug sitting-room to plan the next day's sightseeing.

V

NURSCOMBE FARMHOUSE

C(10) **PT S**

Snowdenham Lane, Bramley, Surrey, GU5 0DB   Tel: 01483 892242
South of Guildford. Nearest main road: A281 from Guildford to Horsham.

3 Bedrooms. £17.50–£20 (less for 4 nights or more). Some have some or all of the following: own bath/toilet; views of lake. No smoking.
Dinner (by arrangement). £10 for 2 courses and coffee, at 7.30pm. Vegetarian or other special diets if ordered. No smoking.
1 Sitting-room. With open fire, TV. No smoking.
Large garden

There are few houses in this book that have both their own tennis courts and private lake: Nurscombe Farmhouse, set in a quiet valley, is one. It is also exceptionally beautiful. A cream-walled, half-timbered house swathed in wisteria, it was built in the 14th century and added to in the 1600s. Bedrooms are prettily furnished, one with yellow-striped walls and views of the lake. The pale oak-panelled sitting-room is spacious and comfortable, some sofas grouped around the open fire and others at the far end of the room, which looks out onto old apple and nut orchards.

The high-ceilinged dining-room is the 17th-century addition made by a prosperous yeoman farmer. Here, among many family photos and paintings, Jane Fairbank serves breakfasts which include home-made jams and honey from her own bees. An evening meal might comprise fish pie or rabbit stew, followed by hot chocolate soufflé or bread-and-butter pudding. For excursions, perhaps take a boat trip on the Wey or, closer by, visit Winkworth Arboretum which has lovely autumnal colour or carpets of bluebells in spring.

For explanation of code letters and **V** symbol, see inside front cover.

When writing to the authors, if you want a reply please enclose a stamped addressed envelope.

Where wine is not available (meaning it is on sale or can be fetched for you), you are nearly always welcome to bring in your own drinks.

Facts (prices, etc.) at the top of entries are supplied by the proprietors themselves. While every effort is made to ensure that these are correct at the time of going to press, they may alter thereafter: please check when you book.

SIXPENNY BUCKLE

Gransden Close, Ewhurst, Surrey, GU6 7RL   Tel: 01483 273988

South-east of Guildford. Nearest main road: A281 from Guildford to Horsham.

C M PT S

2 Bedrooms. £18 (less for 5 nights or more). One has own shower; TV (in both). No smoking.
Dinner (by arrangement). £9 for 2 courses or £10 for 3 courses and coffee, at 7pm. Vegetarian or other special diets if ordered. No smoking. **Light suppers** if ordered.
Garden

Although only some 25 years old, this bungalow has very much its own character, thanks to pharmacist Derek Mortimore and his wife Pat. Their immaculate garden is full of variegated shrubs, with a lovely sward of healthy lawn. At one end are a heated swimming-pool and changing-room which guests may use. The Mortimores even have their own vine from which Derek makes his wine – with varying degrees of success, he says. Bedrooms, smart and spotless, are decorated in pastel shades. The family room has comfortable seating (there is no sitting-room).

In the cosy maroon-and-cream dining-room, Pat might offer you such evening meals as home-made minestrone, followed by roast lamb, and apple crumble in winter, or perhaps lasagne and green salad, followed by fruit pavlova in summer. They also serve afternoon tea on the lawn. The house is well placed for exploring Surrey or southward into Sussex; and close at hand are Wattlehurst Farm with friendly farm animals and the Hannah Pescha Sculpture Garden at Ockley, which has an exhibition of sculpture and ceramics in a dramatic watergarden setting.

V

STURTWOOD FARM

Partridge Lane, Newdigate, Surrey, RH5 5EE Tel: 01306 631308 (Fax: 01306 631908)

South-east of Dorking. Nearest main road: A24 from Dorking to Horsham (and M23, junctions 9/9a).

C D S X

rear view

3 Bedrooms. £17.50–£20. Some have some or all of the following: own shower/toilet; TV. No smoking.
Dinner (by arrangement). £8.50 for 2 courses or £10 for 3 courses and coffee, at 7.30pm. Vegetarian or other special diets if ordered. **Light suppers** if ordered.
Large garden

Honeysuckle twining with climbing roses bedecks the whitewashed walls of this attractive farmhouse, the oldest parts of which date back to 1777. Only some 20 years later a local curate thought the land so poor that Newdigate was 'the last place in the world I should choose to farm in'. Nevertheless Bridget and Roger Mackinnon have successfully farmed here for the last 20 years, also offering comfortable and homely accommodation. The best bedroom, with sofa to relax on (there is no sitting-room), has walnut headboards, antique furniture and an en suite shower-room.

By arrangement, Bridget might offer you vegetable soup followed by pheasant casserole, and rhubarb crumble. Meals are planned around what is fresh from the garden and in season. The dining-room, which looks out over the pond, has interesting antique furniture and old sporting prints on the walls. This house has the advantage of proximity to Gatwick Airport, yet is well away from flight-paths. Transport can be arranged to the airport for outward flights and you may also leave your car here for a small charge.

Reader's comment: Very comfortable indeed.

V

TANHOUSE FARM
C S

Rusper Road, Newdigate, Surrey, RH5 5BX   Tel/Fax: 01306 631334
South of Dorking. Nearest main road: A24 from Dorking to Horsham
(and M25, junction 9).

2 Bedrooms. £16–£18.50.
Light suppers if ordered.
1 Sitting-room. With open fire, TV. No smoking.
Large garden

A dozen shoes, at least two centuries old, are displayed in the kitchen of this 16th-century, half-timbered farmhouse. They were discovered at the back of chimneys when alterations were being done – inside several children's shoes were ears of corn (fertility symbols). The shoes came as no great surprise because, throughout this area, these are often found: putting them up chimneys was believed to bring good luck.

One can see through into the kitchen from the breakfast-room (low-beamed and with latched doors), which opens onto a terrace overlooking a small brook and a pond with an island frequented by 40 ducks, geese and coots. There's a 76-foot well and a lily-pool too.

All rooms have character. In a brick inglenook is an iron fireback dated 1644; around it are greeny-blue velvet armchairs and low oak tables, solid and heavy, which began life as wood-chopping or pig-slaughtering benches. Pastel walls and fabrics (complementing pale green or pink carpets) give the bedrooms a fresh, light look.

For dinner, Nina Fries recommends several of the many local inns.

THE WALTONS
C D PT X

5 Rose Hill, Dorking, Surrey, RH4 2EG   Tel/Fax: 01306 883127
Nearest main road: A24 from Leatherhead to Horsham (and M25, junction 9).

4 Bedrooms. £15–£20 (less for 3 nights or more).
Bargain breaks. All have TV. No smoking.
Dinner (by arrangement). £12 for 3 courses and
coffee, at 6.30–8pm. Vegetarian or other special diets if
ordered. Wine available. No smoking. **Light suppers** if
ordered.
Small garden

There's a hidden corner in Dorking: an oval green, high up, where horses graze (within minutes of the High Street). Around this conservation area pretty villas were built in 1830, one of which is now the home of Margaret Walton. She has chosen lovely fabrics and wallpapers while retaining such features as graceful cast-iron fireplaces and even rather splendid Victorian baths. The bedroom with the best view is on the second floor: beyond Dorking's mellow rooftops you can see Ranmore Common (NT) and Denbies' huge vineyard (open to visitors for tastings). In the handsome dining-room, she provides candlelit dinners (such as smoked salmon, chicken fricassée, pavlova), Sunday lunches and snacks. Breakfast is sometimes served on the sunny terrace overlooking a secluded garden.

The surrounding area of woodland and hills is one of the finest beauty-spots near the capital, truly rural, and dotted with footpaths to follow, historic churches and villages with craft and antique shops. The Royal Horticultural Society's gardens at Wisley are near, too.

V

SUSSEX
(East and West)

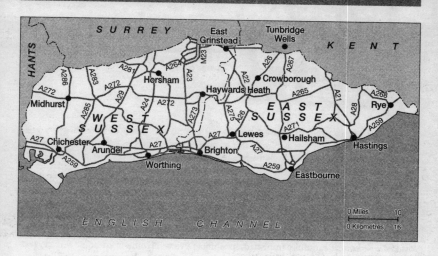

ASHLANDS COTTAGE

C(12) **PT S X**

Burwash, East Sussex, TN19 7HS   Tel: 01435 882207
North-west of Hastings. Nearest main road: A265 from Hurst Green to Heathfield.

2 Bedrooms. £17–£18. No smoking.
Light suppers if ordered.
1 Sitting-room. With TV.
Large garden

The garden of this pretty, lattice-paned cottage adjoins the estate of Batemans – a great 17th-century house that was Kipling's last home (it is now open to the public). Beyond its herbaceous beds and neat brick paths is a far view across the scenery that inspired 'Pook's Song' and you can glimpse Pook's Hill from the garden.

Trained as a singer, Nesta Harmer made her home here after many years spent in Bermuda; the pretty mahogany beds in one room came from there. Both rooms have wide views and a light, airy feel.

Beyond the garden is a wood in which Nesta has cleared a glade and planted woodland flowers. The inns and restaurants of Burwash are two minutes' walk away.

Readers' comments: Beautifully furnished, magnificent views. Home-from-home service, restful and delightfully furnished. Superb views, very comfortable. Very personal and gracious attention. View from our bedroom truly magnificent. Very generous and helpful.

BATES GREEN

Arlington, Polegate, East Sussex, BN26 6SH   Tel/Fax: 01323 482039
North-west of Eastbourne. Nearest main road: A22 from Eastbourne to East Grinstead.

3 Bedrooms. £20–£26. All have own bath/shower/toilet; TV. No smoking.
Dinner (in winter only). £14.50 for 3 courses and coffee, at 7.30pm. Vegetarian or other special diets if ordered. No smoking. **Light suppers** if ordered (all year).
1 Sitting-room. With log fire. No smoking.
Large garden

Goliath poppies mingling with tiny blue borage: that is the kind of unexpected juxtaposition of colour and scale which delights Carolyn McCutchan and makes her lovely garden so memorable. It is open to the public annually under the National Gardens Scheme, but visitors staying at the house can enjoy its colours all the year round. There are unusual plants everywhere, a tennis court, and a big bluebell wood which is a carpet of colour every May.

The house itself is tile-hung in traditional Sussex style. The sitting-room is beamed and panelled, with flowery cretonne armchairs around the log fire. The dining-room has leaded casements opening onto the garden. From the brick-floored hall, stairs rise to the pretty bedrooms and bathrooms. Dinner might consist of leek and cheese soufflé, fillet of lamb, and Sussex pond pudding.

Readers' comments: Lovely house and garden, sumptuous bedrooms, lovely food. Best we have been to. Beautiful house, excellent food, wonderful hosts.

BOLEBROKE WATERMILL

Edenbridge Road, Hartfield, East Sussex, TN7 4JP   Tel/Fax: 01892 770425
South-east of East Grinstead. Nearest main road: A264 from East Grinstead to
Tunbridge Wells.

5 Bedrooms. £19–£37 **(less 10% for 3 nights or
more to readers of this book only).** All have own
bath/shower/toilet; TV. No smoking.
Light suppers if ordered. Vegetarian or other special
diets. Wine available. No smoking.
2 Sitting-rooms. No smoking.
Large grounds
Closed in January.

Remember Pooh-sticks? The river that carried Pooh's sticks away is near the millstream
that powered the wheel of this ancient mill, first recorded in Domeday Book.

Visitors here have the choice of staying in either the white weatherboarded watermill or
the Elizabethan miller's barn. With just two bedrooms and a large sitting-room in each
building, guests are assured of seclusion in rustic surroundings. If you stay in the mill, however, you will need to be nimble, for when David Cooper restored it he was careful to retain
every original feature that he could – steep and narrow stairs to each bedroom, bathrooms
tucked into what were once the big corn-bins, for instance. The barn has a pretty ground-
floor bedroom and an upstairs 'hayloft' room with four-poster.

Readers' comments: Friendliest welcome, service excellent. Beautiful room.

CHURCHGATE

6 East Street, Billingshurst, West Sussex, RH14 9PY   Tel/Fax: 01403 782733
South-west of Horsham. On A272 from Haywards Heath to Petworth.

4 Bedrooms. £17.50. One has own TV. No smoking.
Dinner (by arrangement). £17.50 for 4 courses and
coffee, at times to suit guests. Vegetarian or other
special diets if ordered. **Light suppers** if ordered.
1 Sitting-room. With open fire, TV, piano.
Small garden

In pretty Billingshurst, right by the mediaeval church, is this beamy 17th-century house,
which Sheila Butcher has furnished in traditional country-house style. Views from its
windows (double-glazed in case light sleepers are disturbed by bell-ringing or passing
cars) are of a flowery little garden and the church. Dinner (to be ordered in advance) might
typically be pâté, coq au vin, home-made desserts and cheeses.

Sited on the main road the Romans called Stane Street (it ran from London to
Chichester), Billingshurst is well placed to visit the many beautiful gardens in the area
(Nymans, Leonardslee and Wakehurst Place, for example) and such stately homes as
Petworth and Uppark (both NT). Arundel (castle, cathedral and wildfowl reserve) is also
within easy reach.

Readers' comments: Excellent, personal service. Most delightful place. Superb atmosphere,
excellent food. Very comfortable, dinner superb, value for money.

CLEAVERS LYNG

D PT X

Church Road, Herstmonceux, East Sussex, BN27 1QJ   Tel: 01323 833131
(Fax: 01323 833617)
East of Hailsham. Nearest main road: A271 from Horsebridge towards Bexhill.

7 Bedrooms. £20–£25 (less for 7 nights or more). Bargain breaks. All have some or all of the following: own bath/shower/toilet; TV; balcony. No smoking.
Dinner (by arrangement). £12.50 for 3 courses and coffee, at 7pm. Vegetarian or other special diets if ordered. Wine available. No smoking. **Light suppers** if ordered.
2 Sitting-rooms. With open fire (in one), TV. No smoking (in one). Bar.
Large garden
Closed in January.

The unusual name means a woodcutter's (cleaver's) cottage by a marsh (lyng). Many centuries ago this was a yeoman's house, and its tile-hung exterior is typical of Sussex.

The bedrooms in this small hotel are prettily furnished, and some have views of the garden and its apple-trees, with the far distant hills beyond.

Sally Simpson serves such dinners (or Sunday lunches) as seafood cocktail, steak pie, and orange mousse.

Herstmonceux village is the centre of Sussex trug-making (trugs are traditional garden baskets made from slats of willow), one of many pretty Downland villages around here. Many craftsmen work locally and wrought iron is a speciality. Popular sights include Michelham Priory, Batemans (Kipling's last home), Battle Abbey, Pevensey Castle and picturesque Alfriston. The coast is near, with such resorts as Hastings (where there is a history of smuggling in the caves, a sea life centre, and the evocative ruins of Hastings Castle, high up on the cliffs) and Eastbourne.

V

EASTON HOUSE

C S

Chidham Lane, Chidham, West Sussex, PO18 8TF   Tel/Fax: 01243 572514
West of Chichester. Nearest main road: A259 from Chichester towards Portsmouth.

2 Bedrooms. £18–£20. Bargain breaks. One has own bath/toilet; views of sea. No smoking.
1 Sitting-room. With log stove, TV, piano. No smoking.
Small garden

Every corner of this Tudor house has been filled by Mary Hartley with unusual antiques and trifles. A modern white-and-red poppy wallpaper contrasts with old beams, oriental rugs with stone-flagged floor, scarlet folkweave curtains with antique furniture. All around is a fine collection of mirrors (Spanish, art deco, rococo) and pictures of cats; Mary is musical, and guests are welcome to play on the Bechstein or join in chamber music sessions. It's a free-and-easy atmosphere, a house full of character and cats. Bathrooms are pretty.

Although only breakfast is served, visitors are welcome to linger in the comfortable lime-green sitting-room with its log stove (where tea is served on arrival); or in the garden, under the shade of magnolia and walnut trees.

Readers' comments: Peaceful house with great character. A marvellous place. Mrs Hartley anticipates her guests' every need. Excellent. Most comfortable, helpful and friendly.

FAIRSEAT HOUSE

Station Road, Newick, East Sussex, BN8 4PJ Tel: 01825 722263
East of Haywards Heath. On A272 from Haywards Heath to Uckfield.

4 Bedrooms. £20 **to readers of this book**–£30 (less for 4 nights or more). All have some or all of the following: own bath/shower/toilet. No smoking.
Dinner (by arrangement). £25 for 4 courses, wine and coffee, at any convenient time. Vegetarian or other special diets if ordered. No smoking. **Light suppers** if ordered.
1 Sitting-room. With open fire, TV. Library with piano. No smoking.
Large garden

A big, yellow stucco Edwardian house – large and light – with a striking two-storey, arched window, Fairseat House stands in its own spacious grounds, which have a covered, heated swimming-pool. The library's big French windows open into the conservatory and the garden, and occasionally dinner is served on the terrace.

Visitors will enjoy Carol's decorative touches, the buttoned velvet chesterfields, Persian rugs, fiddleback chairs and a number of interesting 18th-century portraits. Everywhere handsome Edwardian fittings – from fireplaces to lamps – have been retained or installed. Up the wide staircase are attractive bedrooms (one with a four-poster bed) and good bathrooms – one has a Victorian rolltopped bath, another has a hip-bath with overhead shower.

Carol and Roy Pontifex have always enjoyed meeting people, and entertaining. A typical candlelit dinner may include salmon mousse, fillet of beef, a savoury, and lemon pie. Breakfast eggs come fresh from their own chickens. Also in the grounds is a flock of Gotland sheep. London is only 45 minutes away by train.

V

FELIX GALLERY

2 Sun Street, Lewes, East Sussex, BN7 2QB Tel: 01273 472668
Nearest main road: A27 from Brighton to Lewes.

2 Bedrooms. £18. Both have TV.
Small garden

In the centre of Lewes itself is this little gallery devoted entirely to cats – craft-made or antique, western or oriental, metal, china or wood. On the floor above are simple but pleasant bedrooms, well-equipped. The Whiteheads do not serve dinners but have no objection to food being brought in; however, many visitors eat at the White Hart's carvery. The small house, which dates from William IV's reign, is at the site of a Roman fort, long built over.

Lewes has some attractive old buildings and a Norman castle. Cosmopolitan Brighton, with its many antique and jewellery shops, restaurants and bars in The Lanes, and the Prince Regent's oriental Pavilion, is near. Opera-lovers head for Glyndebourne (festival between May and August) and families for Drusillas Zoo, on the outskirts of pretty Alfriston. Then there are all the great gardens for which Sussex is famous: Wakehurst, Sheffield Park, Borde Hill, Nymans, Leonardslee and Heaselands. Beachy Head, at the edge of the Downs, has spectacular views and a countryside centre with nature trails.

Reader's comment: Fresh, clean and charming, and everything a traveller could possibly need is supplied.

V

HOLLY HOUSE

C D M PT S X

Beaconsfield Road, Chelwood Gate, East Sussex, RH17 7LF   Tel: 01825 740484

South of East Grinstead. Nearest main road: A275 from East Grinstead to Lewes.

5 Bedrooms. £18–£20 (less for 7 nights or more). Bargain breaks. Some have some or all of the following: own shower/toilet; TV; balcony.
Dinner (by arrangement). £12 for 3 courses and coffee, at times to suit guests. Vegetarian or other special diets if ordered. No smoking. **Light suppers** if ordered.
1 Sitting-room.
Large garden

In the hamlet of Chelwood Gate (once literally a gate into Ashdown Forest) is Holly House where former teacher Dee Birchell welcomes guests to rooms given character by her flair for spotting 'finds' such as iron balustrades salvaged from a great house and old furniture she re-upholstered herself. Some bedrooms are on the ground floor, each with its own good shower-room; one upstairs has a balcony over the garden with its azaleas and magnolias, fish-pond and small, heated swimming-pool. Garden produce goes into such meals as leek soup, chicken in sherry and mushrooms, and gingernut gâteau.

In the area there is plenty to enjoy (in addition, the south coast is soon reached): Ashdown Forest (miles of footpaths); the beauty-spot of Ditchling Beacon; the 'Jack and Jill' pair of windmills; the Bluebell Line steam train; and such sights as Penshurst Place, Hever and Chiddingstone Castles, and a number of great gardens.

V

Readers' comments: Comfortable, pretty home; friendly service, well-equipped room.

Private bathrooms are not necessarily en suite.

Houses which accept the discount vouchers on page ii are marked with a **V** symbol next to the relevant entries.

Complaints about matters which could not have been settled on the spot will be forwarded to proprietors. Please enclose a stamped addressed envelope if you want the authors to acknowledge receipt of your complaint.

Addresses shown are to enable you to locate a house on a map. They are not necessarily complete postal addresses (though the essential postcode is included), and detailed directions for finding a house should be obtained from the owner.

LITTLE OREHAM FARM

off Horn Lane, Henfield, West Sussex, BN5 9SB   Tel: 01273 492931

North-west of Brighton. Nearest main road: A281 from Horsham towards Shoreham.

3 Bedrooms. £18–£20 (less for 5 nights or more). Bargain breaks. All have some or all of the following: own bath/shower/toilet; TV. No smoking.
Dinner (by arrangement). £15 for 3 courses and coffee, at about 6.30pm. Vegetarian or other special diets if ordered. No smoking. **Light suppers** if ordered.
2 Sitting-rooms. With open fire, TV. No smoking.
Large garden

Inside this brick and timbered house, 300 years old, rooms have beams and oak-mullioned or lattice-paned windows. There is a great inglenook fireplace with iron fireback as old as the house itself (a collection of big copper vessels is housed on its slate hearth), and red tiles cover the dining-room floor.

Some of the well-furnished bedrooms for visitors (pine furniture and sprigged fabrics) are in the converted outbuildings, but meals are taken in the house itself: typically Josie Forbes provides (if these are ordered in advance) such dinners as lettuce soup, salmon with watercress sauce, and strawberry tartlets.

Readers' comments: Beautiful surroundings; most charming lady and a marvellous cook; made me so welcome I am planning to return. Very friendly and warm. Peaceful. My best ever stay, ambience of house remarkable.

LYE GREEN HOUSE

Lye Green, East Sussex, TN6 1UU   Tel: 01892 652018

North of Crowborough. Nearest main road: A26 from Tunbridge Wells to Newhaven.

3 Bedrooms. £20–£27.50 (less for 4 nights or more). Bargain breaks. All have some or all of the following: own bath/shower/toilet; TV. No smoking.
Light suppers if ordered.
1 Sitting/dining-room. No smoking.
Large garden

Built in the tile-hung style that is a Sussex tradition and with wisteria on its red brick walls, the Edwardian house was dilapidated until the Hynes family restored it – and its grounds too. Part of these comprises formal gardens divided by yew hedges, part a chain of three ponds in woodland. There are a rose garden with pergola, and an avenue of pollarded limes. Most rooms have views from big windows, and sometimes breakfasts are served in the garden.

Soft blues, pinks and greens predominate in the rooms. In the dining-room, the long mahogany table is laid with good silver; there are prettily pleated curtains, big sofas, a marble fireplace with Britannia and tall ships, brass beds, flowery wallpapers, quilted patchwork spreads, cases of butterflies, antique mirrors and fans . . . every room is full of interest.

For full dinners, there is a choice of good inns locally.

Readers' comments: Delightful house and gardens, in charming, restful location; sumptuous room.

NEWBARN

Wards Lane, Wadhurst, East Sussex, TN5 6HP   Tel: 01892 782042
South-east of Tunbridge Wells. Nearest main road: A267 from Tunbridge Wells to
Heathfield.

3 Bedrooms. £20–£22 (less for 4 nights or more).
One has views of lake. No smoking.
Light suppers if ordered.
2 Sitting-rooms. With open fire, TV.
Large garden

In the 18th century this was a farmhouse, lattice-paned and tile-hung in traditional Sussex
style. Indoors, knotty pine floorboards gleam with polish, there are low beams, and wood-
latched doors. Christopher and Pauline Willis took great care, when renovating the house,
to ensure that every detail was in harmony. Bedrooms are light and flowery. The sitting-
room, which has an inglenook, is decorated in apricot and cream.

Usually only breakfast is served because the area is well supplied with good restaurants.
Visitors are welcome, however, to use the Aga cooker when it is convenient.

The landscaped garden descends right to the edge of Bewl Water reservoir, and there are
Shetland ponies in the surrounding fields.

Readers' comments: Views and peace superb. Outstanding. Exceptionally kind; a wonderful
peaceful haven. Wonderfully well appointed. The most accomplished host and hostess; a
delightful stay. High standard of comfort, very welcoming hostess, friendly atmosphere.

OLD RECTORY

Cot Lane, Chidham, West Sussex, PO18 8TA   Tel/Fax: 01243 572088
West of Chichester. Nearest main road: A259 from Chichester towards Portsmouth.

5 Bedrooms. £20–£25 (less for 4 mid-week nights).
Bargain breaks. Some have some or all of the following: own bath/shower/toilet; TV. No smoking.
1 Sitting-room. With open fire, TV, piano. No
smoking.
Large garden

Opposite the church in peaceful Chidham is the Old Rectory, built in 1830 and now well
furnished by Peter and Anna Blencowe in traditional country-house style (most rooms have
en suite bathrooms). The large garden has a swimming-pool (unheated) and the elegant
sitting-room a grand piano. Although only breakfast is served, one can dine well
in Chichester, at the Old House at Home in Chidham, or in nearby Emsworth.

Chidham looks across an inlet to ancient Bosham, one of the most picturesque sailing
villages on the winding shores of Chichester's lovely natural harbour (with boat trips): very
popular and crowded in summer. Chichester itself is near. It has a mediaeval cathedral,
Georgian houses and a theatre. Wherever you drive or walk there is fine scenery; and plenty
of interesting sights within a few miles – such as the huge Roman palace of Fishbourne and
splendid gardens at West Dean.

V   *Reader's comment:* Wonderful garden and furniture.

OLD VICARAGE

66 Church Square, Rye, East Sussex, TN31 7HF   Tel: 01797 222119
(Fax: 01797 227466)

C(10) PT

Nearest main road: A259 from Folkestone to Hastings.

6 Bedrooms. £20–£28.50 for a suite (less for 3 nights or more). **5% less to readers of this book staying 3 nights from April to October, excluding bank holidays.** Bargain breaks. All have some or all of the following: own bath/shower/toilet; TV. No smoking.
Light suppers if ordered. Vegetarian or other special diets. Wine available.
1 Sitting-room.
Small garden

This pink-and-white, largely 18th-century house is virtually in the churchyard, a peaceful spot since it is traffic-free and the only sound is the melodious chime of the ancient church clock. One steps straight into a very pretty sitting-room, yellow sofas complemented by Laura Ashley fabrics. Curved windows, antiques and pot-plants complete the scene.

The bedrooms are prettily decorated, mostly with pine furniture and flowery fabrics. Two have elegant four-posters. Those at the front have views of the church; others, of Rye's mediaeval roofscape. Henry James wrote *The Spoils of Poynton* while living here in 1896.

For dinner Julia Lampon recommends (after offering her guests sherry) one of Rye's many restaurants or she will do snack suppers.

Readers' comments: Outstanding. Charm and helpfulness of the owners gave us a perfect weekend. Very beautifully furnished and comfortable rooms. Friendly hosts. Fantastic – best breakfast I've ever had. Beautiful garden room. Huge and delicious breakfast.

PINDARS

Lyminster, West Sussex, BN17 7QF   Tel: 01903 882628
South of Arundel. On A284 from Littlehampton towards Arundel.

C(10) PT

3 Bedrooms. £16–£21 (less for 3 nights or more). Bargain breaks. Some have some or all of the following: own bath/shower/toilet; TV. No smoking.
Dinner. £11 for 3 courses and coffee, at 7pm (not Sundays). Vegetarian or other special diets if ordered. No smoking. **Light suppers** if ordered.
1 Sitting-room. With open fire, TV. No smoking.
Large garden

The Newmans themselves designed this attractive house on the road between Littlehampton and historic Arundel, with its castle and cathedral.

Some of the light, bright bedrooms overlook the beautiful garden at the back, where stonework contrasts with beds that brim with flowers and shrubs (there is a swimming-pool too); and the sitting-room – furnished with antiques – opens onto it. Garden produce goes into such meals as mushroom-and-spinach soup, chicken in a pimento sauce, and apple crumble with home-made ice cream: Jocelyne loves cooking. Breakfast may include kedgeree or fishcakes; preserves and scones are home-made.

Sunny rooms are furnished with Paisley sofas, Victorian miniatures and other characterful touches, and the Newmans have a variety of paintings collected when they ran an art gallery in Arundel.

Readers' comments: Warm welcome, delightful room. Artistically decorated, very comfortable, much care and attention to detail. Superior ambience, facilities and service. Made very welcome. Immaculate. Delicious food.

V

RACEHORSE COTTAGE

C(5) **D PT**

18 Nepcote, Findon, West Sussex, BN14 0SN Tel: 01903 873783
North of Worthing. Nearest main road: A24 from Dorking to Worthing.

2 Bedrooms. £16–£20.
Dinner (by arrangement). £13 for 3 courses and coffee, at 7.30pm. Wine available.
1 Sitting-room. With open fire, TV.
Small garden

The flint-walled hamlet of Nepcote is almost part of 18th-century Findon village, celebrated for its three racing stables (and very ancient church). This explains the name of the cottage, for which the previous owner chose a roadside position where he could watch strings of horses and their jockeys go by on their way to the surrounding South Downs for daily exercise. He built it in traditional Sussex style: upper storey weatherboarded, doors panelled.

It is a pleasant, unpretentious home with an L-shaped sitting/dining-room. Trim bedrooms have velvet bedheads and views of the Downs. There is a small garden and glasshouse from which come the fresh vegetables and fruit that Jean Lloyd uses for such meals (if ordered in advance) as ramekins of eggs with Stilton and cream or melon with kiwi fruit; gammon with Cumberland sauce; and loganberry flan. Bread, muesli and jams are home-made. The Lloyds dine with their guests.

V *Readers' comments:* Everything necessary for comfort. Evening meal delicious.

RIVER PARK FARM

C S

Lodsworth, Petworth, West Sussex, GU28 9DS Tel: 01798 861362
East of Midhurst. Nearest main road: A272 from Petworth to Midhurst.

3 Bedrooms. £18 (less for 5 nights or more). No smoking.
Light suppers if ordered.
1 Sitting-room. With stove, TV. No smoking.
Large garden
Closed from November to Easter.

The farm (of 340 acres of corn, bullocks, sheep and poultry) is in a secluded position among woods where, if you are up early enough, you may encounter deer. There is a 4½-acre lake with plentiful carp and ducks, and in front a pretty garden. The house itself, built in 1600, is old and beamy with comfortable bedrooms along twisting passageways. In the dining-room Pat Moss has a strikingly colourful collection of green leaf plates and wooden ducks.

Pat does not do full-scale dinners (available elsewhere locally) but has a list of homely dishes like meat pie or macaroni cheese, and for puddings like banana split she uses rich Jersey cream from the farm's own cows. Bread is home-baked and eggs free-range. Coarse fishing available. Many people come for the local walks and birdwatching.

Readers' comments: Enjoyed ourselves so much that we have twice visited for a week. Marvellous setting and house, kind hosts, good food. Outstanding. Warm, relaxed, friendly
V atmosphere, lovely farm. House charming, surroundings idyllic, rooms comfortable.

UPTON FARMHOUSE
Upper Brighton Road, Sompting, West Sussex, BN14 9JU   Tel: 01903 233706
East of Worthing. Nearest main road: A27 from Brighton to Worthing.

C(3) **D PT X**

3 Bedrooms. £17.50–£20 (less for 3 nights or more). Bargain breaks. All have some or all of the following: own bath/shower/toilet; TV. No smoking.
Light suppers if ordered. Vegetarian or other special diets if ordered. Wine available.
1 Sitting-room. With open fire, TV. No smoking.
Large garden

Close to Worthing is the old village of Sompting, with a Rhenish-style Saxon church. Behind the handsome 18th-century façade of this house are parts built in the 15th century. The bedrooms – which have soft colours, deep, velvety carpets, private bathrooms, and views over farmland – are all spacious, immaculate and well equipped. Breakfast is served on lace tablecloths, with locally smoked kippers offered as an option. The massive sitting/dining-room is very comfortably furnished – its walls lined with prints of old sailing ships. Penny Hall is a particularly caring hostess.

The area round here is not only scenic but full of gardens, stately homes, Roman remains and castles to visit. Walkers enjoy wending their way up to Cissbury Ring, a prehistoric hill fort. South coast resorts within easy reach include not only sedate Worthing but also Brighton, celebrated for its oriental-style Pavilion and sophisticated pleasures. At Shoreham, nearby, there is a museum of D-Day aviation.

Reader's comments: Warm welcome, excellent food.

WESTERN HOUSE
Winchelsea Road, Rye, East Sussex, TN31 7EL   Tel: 01797 223419
On A259 from Hastings to Folkestone.

PT

3 Bedrooms. £20–£22.50 (less for 3 nights or more). Bargain breaks. All have own shower/toilet; TV. No smoking.
Dinner. £12.50 for 3 courses and coffee, at 7pm. Vegetarian or other special diets if ordered. No smoking.
Large garden

The mediaeval port of Rye was perched high on a thumb of land (almost an island) projecting into the sea. But centuries ago the sea receded, leaving behind dry land, and here tile-hung Western House was built in the 18th century, commanding far views – you can even see Hastings in clear weather – from its paved terrace (with working pump), or from the huge lawn surrounded by brilliant flowerbeds set against mellow stone walls.

This is a house of character, as befits its long history. Among its visitors (in 1913) was the Impressionist artist Pissarro; and Ron Dellar has incorporated him in a mural featuring Rye church which he painted for one of the bedrooms. All these rooms are attractively decorated, with interesting wallpapers and fresh flowers, and some have good views of the marshes.

As to dinner, a typical meal may include home-made soup, baked trout with honey and almonds, and a whimwham, an 18th-century trifle.

Readers' comments: We were particularly delighted. View magnificent. Fabulous: great people, great room, great food. Comfortable. Very helpful.

273

WHYKE HOUSE   C P T X
13 Whyke Lane, Chichester, West Sussex, PO19 2JR   Tel: 01243 788767
Nearest main road: A27 from Worthing to Portsmouth.

rear view

3 Bedrooms. £19–£22.50 (less for 7 nights or more). All have some of the following: own bath/shower/toilet; TV. No smoking.
1 Sitting-room. With TV. No smoking.
Small garden

In a peaceful suburban cul-de-sac, very close to the historic centre of Chichester, is an unusual bed-and-breakfast house, ideal for families, with private parking. Here Tony and Lydia Hollis provide continental breakfasts, give advice on sightseeing, then depart to their own home next door. There is a fully equipped kitchen which guests are then welcome to use, if they do not wish to go to Chichester's many restaurants. It is almost like being at home, with complete freedom.

The furnishings throughout have great individuality. Family antiques mingle with Russian folk art, local paintings with soft furnishings made by Lydia. The baby's highchair is a century-old heirloom, so is the grandmother clock. For some older guests, the ground-floor bedroom and shower are particularly convenient.

Readers' comments: Comfortable, quiet, convenient; most welcoming. Pleasant weekend; a real treat to stay. Most kind. Most convenient. Home was an inspiration, welcome was heart-warming. Welcoming and helpful host.

V

WOODMANS GREEN FARM   C D S
Linch, West Sussex, GU30 7NF   Tel: 01428 741250
North of Midhurst. Nearest main road: A3 from Guildford to Petersfield.

3 Bedrooms. £20–£22.50 (less for 3 nights or more). One has own bath. No smoking.
Dinner (by arrangement). £12 for 3 courses and coffee, at 7.30pm. Less for 2 courses. Vegetarian or other special diets if ordered. No smoking. **Light suppers** if ordered.
2 Sitting-rooms. With open fire, TV, piano. No smoking.
Large garden
Closed from December to February.

This Tudor house has interesting features of the period, which include a particularly grand staircase, stone-mullioned windows in the gable, low doorways (on which Mary Spreckley drapes swags of dried flowers) and, in the farmyard, an unusual roofed and brick-walled midden. (There is a heated swimming-pool.)

Bedrooms are spacious and peaceful; under the beamed roof is a large and attractive family room. Adjoining the sitting-room is a bright garden-room.

By arrangement, Mary – who is a very good cook – will prepare either a full dinner (such as chilled lettuce, pea and mint soup; rosemary and honey roast lamb; and tarte tatin) or a light supper (such as pasta with broccoli, mushrooms and ham).

This very attractive area around Haslemere, Petersfield and Petworth is a good base from which to visit Chichester, Fishbourne Roman palace, Petworth House, and the open-air Weald and Downland Museum of ancient buildings. There are good walks, too.

Readers' comments: Friendly atmosphere, cooking imaginative and attractively served; very pleasant indeed. Delicious breakfast. Delightful hosts.

V

WARWICKSHIRE

STAFFORDSHIRE

LEICESTERSHIRE

10 A5

M42

9

8

4 M6

Nuneaton

A444

M69

3

2

M6

1

BIRMINGHAM

Coventry

Rugby

A428

3 M42 3A

16

Kenilworth A46

A445

A45

1 M45

M40

A4177

A423

NORTHAMPTONSHIRE

A4189

Royal Leamington Spa

A435

A3400

A46

15

14

13

Warwick

A425

A425

WARWICKSHIRE

A439

A429

A425

12 M40

HEREFORD & WORCESTER

Stratford-upon-Avon

A422

A422

A429 A3400

GLOUCESTERSHIRE

OXFORDSHIRE

0 Miles   5

0 Kilometres   8

Major tourist attractions, such as Stratford-upon-Avon and Cambridge, can often be easily reached from houses in adjacent counties.

BLACKWELL GRANGE

Blackwell, Warwickshire, CV36 4PF   Tel/Fax: 01608 682357

South of Stratford-upon-Avon. Nearest main road: A3400 from Stratford-upon-Avon towards Oxford (and M40, junctions 11/12).

C(10) **M S**

3 Bedrooms. £19–£26 **to readers of this book** (less for 5 nights or more). Bargain breaks. All have own bath/shower/toilet. No smoking.
Dinner (by arrangement). £15.50 for 3 courses and coffee, at times to suit guests. Vegetarian or other special diets if ordered. No smoking. **Light suppers** if ordered.
1 Sitting-room. With open fire, TV. No smoking.
Large garden

Stone-flagged floors and deep-set windows with chamfered mullions give this Cotswold house great character – but the Vernon-Millers had a tremendous task to give it modern comfort too. Liz has decorated the rooms with style – beribboned curtains in a shell-pink bedroom, for instance; very nice bathrooms. An en suite, ground-floor bedroom, overlooking the garden, has been specifically designed for disabled guests.

Many of the walls are decorated with old sporting prints, and an inglenook fireplace is the setting for a collection of country bygones and Victorian kitchen tools. Dinner, by candlelight, could consist of such dishes as home-made pâté, game, and damson ice cream.

Outside is a thatched barn, and among the staddlestones (rick-stones) of the garden strut the miniature Wyandottes which provide breakfast eggs.

Readers' comments: Outstanding accommodation and warmth of hospitality. Most charming hostess. Kind and attentive.

V

BROOKLAND

Peacock Lane, Middle Tysoe, Warwickshire, CV35 0SG Tel: 01295 680202

South-east of Stratford-upon-Avon. Nearest main road: A422 from Stratford-upon-Avon to Banbury.

C S

3 Bedrooms. £17.50 (less for 3 nights or more). No smoking.
Dinner (by arrangement). £11.50 for 3 courses and coffee, at 6.30pm. Vegetarian or other special diets if ordered. No smoking. **Light suppers** if ordered.
1 Sitting-room. With open fire, TV.
Small garden
Closed in January.

When one visits Brookland, one's first impression is of flowers everywhere, butterflies thronging the tall yellow spires of verbascum, stone troughs brimming with colourful blooms. There is a little sun-lounge where one can sit under a vine to enjoy the morning sunshine, while inside grandfather clocks tick peacefully. The old stone cottage still retains many of its original features, such as the tinderbox cupboard built into an inglenook fireplace; and Topsy Trought has furnished the dining-room with carved, cane chairs in William-and-Mary style.

Topsy makes wedding- and birthday-cakes for local families, but it is Tim who does the elaborate and colourful decorations of sugar fruit and vegetables. Topsy says her most popular meal is a peach-and-pineapple starter, lemon and thyme chicken, and loganberry mousse.

Readers' comments: Outstanding. Most beautiful and interesting. Lovely hosts. Fresh, attractive. Charming hosts. First class. Lovely enjoyable stay.

CRANDON HOUSE

Avon Dassett, Warwickshire, CV33 0AA   Tel/Fax: 01295 770652
South-east of Royal Leamington Spa. Nearest main road: A423 from Banbury to
Coventry (and M40, junctions 11/12).

5 Bedrooms. £19–£21 (less for 7 nights or more).
Bargain breaks. All have own bath/shower/toilet; TV.
No smoking.
Light suppers if ordered.
2 Sitting-rooms. With log stove, TV.
Large garden

A 'hostess of the year' award was once won by Deborah Lea – the most unassuming of people – who with her brother runs this guest-house on a smallholding where a few rare British
white cattle, sheep and poultry roam free. One can sit in the glass sun-room to watch the
geese and ducks enjoying life, with a view of hills beyond. There is a separate television
room with log stove, and a terrace outside. Everything about the house, built in the 1950s,
is solidly comfortable. The pink or blue bedrooms have nice pieces of furniture (a walnut
suite, for instance, and a shellback brocade chair) and large windows.

   There is a choice of pubs for evening meals within a mile. Breakfast options include
porridge, kippers and smoked haddock.

Readers' comments: We felt extremely welcome, no detail was overlooked. Splendid hosts,
house immaculate.

V

FORTH HOUSE

44 High Street, Warwick, CV34 4AX   Tel: 01926 401512 (Fax: 01926 490809)
(M40, junction 15, is near.)

2 Bedrooms. £20 (less for 3 nights or more). Bargain
breaks. Both have own bath/shower/toilet; TV. No
smoking.
Light suppers if ordered.
2 Sitting-rooms. With open fire, TV. No smoking.
Small garden

Past the antique and craft shops of the busy High Street is a terrace of trim Georgian
houses; overhead looms Warwick Castle. Not exactly 'off the beaten track'. But behind no.
44 lies a secret place: a long garden stretching far back. Stone steps and paths flank the
lawn; an ancient wisteria clambers high. Here is found an entire garden-suite for visitors:
virtually a flat with its own kitchen, and all on the ground floor. It is not only spacious but
very pretty – roses and ribbons on the bathroom curtains, the bath's sides made of pine.

   There's another bedroom at the back of the house, on the first floor. This has a pine
table and rush chairs for meals (if you want to take these in privacy), and a sofa. Elsewhere
are marble fireplaces and ruffled curtains in big bay windows.

   An extra bonus for many guests is often the sight of Labrador pups at play – Elizabeth
Draisey breeds them as guide dogs for the blind.

Readers' comments: Best equipped room we've had; large and quiet. Highly recommended.

V

GROVE FARM

C(10) D

Ettington, Warwickshire, CV37 7NX   Tel: 01789 740228
South-east of Stratford-upon-Avon. Nearest main road: A422 from Stratford to
Banbury.

3 Bedrooms. £18.50–£20 (less for 4 nights or more).
All have some or all of the following: own bath/
shower/toilet; TV. No smoking.
Light suppers if ordered. Vegetarian or other special
diets if ordered. No smoking.
1 Sitting-room. With open fire, TV. No smoking.
Small garden
Closed from mid-December to mid-March.

Grove Farm is found at the end of a brick path, with grapevine beside it and an old pump. It
is full of character, with unusual furniture and trifles Meg and Bob Morton have collected:
from a spectacular carved sideboard to an old imp's head built into one wall, an elm manger
to a collection of knobkerries. The chased silver pheasant-gun belonged to Bob's grandfather
and the old dough-chest to Meg's (he was a baker). Bedrooms, under the sloping eaves, have
own bathrooms, pretty fabrics, good carpets and old-fashioned furniture. Meg serves
only light suppers. (The bar food at the Houndshill Inn is very good.) Meg also cares for
elderly horses; they are to be seen grazing in the fields beyond which are deer woods and a
panoramic view of the Cotswolds.

It is easy to visit Stratford-upon-Avon, the Cotswolds and Royal Leamington Spa from
here. Warwick Castle, Charlecote and Hidcote (as well as other great gardens) make this
area a tourist honeypot.

Readers' comments: Warm, friendly welcome. Most impressed. The most friendly we
encountered, welcome fabulous.

HARDWICK HOUSE

C M PT S

1 Avenue Road, Stratford-upon-Avon, Warwickshire, CV37 6UY
Tel: 01789 204307 (Fax: 01789 296760)
Nearest main road: A439 from Stratford towards Warwick (and M40, junction 15).

14 Bedrooms. £19–£28. Bargain breaks. All have
some or all of the following: own bath/shower/toilet; TV.
No smoking.
Light snacks only.
1 Sitting-room

In a quiet residential part of the town, Hardwick House, built in 1887, is run to a high standard by Drenagh and Simon Wootton. Bedrooms vary, but most are spacious – particularly
those on the ground floor. In an airy dining-room, substantial snacks are served. There is
only a small sitting-reception room but, perhaps more important in Stratford, there is a
carpark. Furnishings are conventional and comfortable, everything is spick-and-span, and
Drenagh is a hospitable hostess.

The house is only a few minutes' walk from Shakespeare's birthplace, the Royal
Shakespeare Theatre, and the start of round-Stratford guided tours by open-top bus.

Other popular sights on the Shakespeare circuit include: mediaeval Holy Trinity church,
beside the river and its swans, where he was baptised and buried; New Place, where he finally
lived, and wrote *The Tempest* (a charming Tudor knot garden adjoins it); Hall's Croft, the
home of his daughter and son-in-law; and, in nearby Shottery, his wife's childhood home,
always known as 'Anne Hathaway's Cottage' even though it is a house of some size.

V

HILL HOUSE

off Mancetter Road, Caldecote, Warwickshire, CV10 0RS   Tel: 01203 396685
North-west of Nuneaton. Nearest main road: A5 from Atherstone to Hinckley (also M69, junction 1; and M42, junction 10).

4 Bedrooms. £16.50–£18. Some have some or all of the following: own bath/shower/toilet; TV; views of river; balcony. No smoking.
Dinner (by arrangement). £10 for 2 courses and coffee, at 7.30pm. Vegetarian diets if ordered. Wine available. No smoking. **Light suppers** if ordered.
1 Sitting-room. With open fire, TV. No smoking.
Large garden

A rough track leads to 18th-century Hill House – brimming with antiques and bric-a-brac collected by Jane Cox, from rococo mirrors to a naive portrait of the Queen. All contribute to the distinctive character of the house (where once Edward VII kept a mistress, it is said). Several bedrooms overlook arches where coaches used to be housed. There are a games room, canalside walks, panoramic views across the River Anker, and three goats and a donkey to divert visitors. Dinner comprises such traditional dishes as cottage pie and lemon meringue tart, often with vegetable soup before (vegetarian dishes are a speciality).

Nuneaton has the George Eliot museum, and all around are places associated with her (Arbury Hall, in particular) and the scenes she so vividly described. This lesser-known part of Warwickshire has attractions waiting to be discovered. The National Exhibition Centre and Coventry Cathedral are near; and close by, in Leicestershire, is historic Bosworth where the celebrated battle in which Richard III was defeated is re-enacted from time to time.

IRELANDS FARM

Irelands Lane, near Henley-in-Arden, Warwickshire, B95 5SA
Tel/Fax: 01564 792476
South-east of Birmingham. Nearest main road: A3400 from Birmingham to Stratford-upon-Avon.

3 Bedrooms. £17.50–£19 (less for 3 nights or more). Bargain breaks. All have own bath/shower/toilet; TV. No smoking.
Light suppers if ordered.
1 Sitting-room. With TV, piano. No smoking.
Large garden

In the middle of Shakespeare's Forest of Arden was built ancient Lapworth Hall, later re-named after the family who extended it. A copy of the first Ireland's will (1559) hangs in the house. Stone-flagged floors have survived the centuries, but much of the present house was built in 1820.

All around are the Shaws' fields (arable or pasture) and downhill lies the Tapster Brook: the whole area is one of undulating hills with small hidden valleys.

In the house, stairs twist up and down to bedrooms that are light, roomy and comfortable. One has a sofa and a pretty little Victorian fireplace. There are pleasant, farmhouse-style furnishings (much oak in the dining-room). Although picturesque Henley has a dozen eating-places as well as many antique and craft shops, notable church, etc., Pamela will prepare snacks for anybody who does not want to dine out.

V

LANSDOWNE HOUSE

C(5) **M PT**

Clarendon Street, Royal Leamington Spa, Warwickshire, CV32 4PF
Tel: 01926 450505 (Fax: 01926 421313)
Nearest main road: A425 from Warwick to Southam (and M40, junctions 13/14).

15 Bedrooms. £19.95–£24.95. **To readers mentioning this book when reserving:** £36.95–£42.50 (2 nights) for half board in a double or twin room. Bargain breaks. Some have some or all of the following: own bath/shower/toilet; TV.
Dinner (by arrangement). £17.95 for 3 courses and coffee, at 6.30–8.30pm. Less for 2 courses. Vegetarian or other special diets if ordered. Wine available. No smoking. **Light suppers** if ordered.
2 Sitting-rooms. With open fire, TV. **Bar.**
Small garden

A pretty creeper-covered house built in the 18th century, this small hotel cannot be described as truly 'off the beaten track' for it stands at a crossroads not far from the centre of Leamington. But bedroom windows are double-glazed to reduce any sound from traffic.

When David and Gillian Allen took it over they decided to furnish it to a very high standard and in keeping with its architecture. There is a particularly pretty sitting-room and every bedroom is attractively decorated in soft colours with well-chosen fabrics.

There are always several choices of good English dishes at dinner. Starters include particularly imaginative soups; main courses such things as liver and bacon with fresh sage. Connoisseurs will appreciate some little-known wines and the range of malt whiskies. There are discounts on tickets to Warwick castle.

Readers' comments: Excellent. Charming features, food excellent. The personal touch made such a difference.

LOXLEY FARMHOUSE

C D M

Stratford Road, Loxley, Warwickshire, CV35 9JN   Tel/Fax: 01789 840265
South-east of Stratford-upon-Avon. Nearest main road: A422 from Stratford to Banbury (and M40, junction 15).

2–3 Bedrooms. £20–£28 (less for 7 nights or more). Two have own bath/shower/toilet; TV.
Large garden

Loxley is a hilltop village with diminutive church. Just downhill from here Loxley Farm is tucked away: a picture-postcard house of half-timbering and thatch, parts dating back to the 13th century. There are Robin Hood connections.

Inside, everything is in keeping with the style of the ancient house: low ceilings with pewter pots hanging from the beams, flagged floors, small-paned windows, oak doors. In the dining-room, where Anne Horton serves breakfast, leather chairs surround a large oak table.

Two suites with sitting-rooms are in a separate, half-timbered, thatched barn conversion. In the main house a double room is sometimes available for guests.

Readers' comments: Idyllic surroundings. Much care and attention. Most welcoming and comfortable. Not a jarring note. The most delightful of all. Have enjoyed Mrs Horton's hospitality over the past ten years. Pleasant place and very pleasant people.

MINE HILL HOUSE

Lower Brailes, Warwickshire, OX15 5BJ   Tel: 01608 685594

South-east of Stratford-upon-Avon. Nearest main road: A3400 from Stratford towards Chipping Norton (and M40, junction 11).

C D S X

3 Bedrooms. £15.50–£22. Some have own bath/toilet; TV. No smoking.
Dinner. £17.50 for 3 courses and coffee, at 7.30–9pm. Vegetarian or other special diets if ordered. **Light suppers** if ordered.
2 Sitting-rooms. With open fire/stove, TV. No smoking in one.
Large garden

Standing alone at the top of a hill on the Cotswold borders, Mine Hill House has wonderful views across the patchwork fields of five counties. An 18th-century farmhouse surrounded by old outbuildings, the decor within is stylish and smart. The best bedroom, in blue with oakleaf-patterned walls, has its own bathroom in matching colours. Although very simply furnished, the family room under the eaves has the best views.

Hester Sale is a cordon bleu cook and might offer you warm goat's cheese salad with lardons as a starter, followed by chicken breasts stuffed with roast peppers in a red pepper and basil sauce, and frozen chocolate mousse with caramel oranges and mint as a pudding. While dining you can look at the Sales' collection of modern art. Many of the paintings throughout the house are by Hester's mother, an internationally exhibited artist. There is one snug sitting-room with a coal fire and another grander one with more paintings.

This is an area rich in Civil War history, and a short walk away are the ominously named Traitor's Ford and Gallows Hill. Stratford, Banbury and Oxford are within easy reach.

V

NORTHLEIGH HOUSE

Fiveways Road, Hatton, Warwickshire, CV35 7HZ   Tel: 01926 484203
(Fax: 01926 484006)

North-west of Warwick. Nearest main road: A4177 from Warwick to Solihull (also M40, junction 15; and M42, junction 5).

D M

7 Bedrooms. £19–£29. Bargain breaks. All have some or all of the following: own shower/toilet; TV. No smoking.
Dinner (by arrangement). £15 for 3 courses and coffee, at times to suit guests. Vegetarian or other special diets if ordered. No smoking. **Light suppers** if ordered.
1 Sitting-room. No smoking.
Small garden
Closed from mid-December to end of January.

A former dress designer, Sylvia Fenwick – a vivacious personality – has turned her creative talents to decorating every bedroom with elegance – each is different, each memorable, and many verge on the luxurious. They are all very well equipped and heated. For instance the L-shaped blue suite (with kitchenette in cupboard) has a sofa, bamboo tables and a carved bed in a silk-curtained alcove. On two sides of the big sitting-room are garden views.

Sylvia serves supper trays, or dinners (by arrangement) at which you might get something like avocado salad, chicken provençale, and tropical fruit pavlova. She used to farm here, and she maintains her interest in rare breeds (of sheep in particular).

Readers' comments: First class! Immaculate. We loved this place so much we spent an extra night there. A very warm and hospitable lady. Her scrambled eggs are heavenly! Warm welcome, comfortable stay. Sylvia is a real character. Well equipped and luxurious.

V

OLDWYCH HOUSE FARM

Oldwych Lane, Fen End, Warwickshire, CV8 1NR   Tel: 01676 533552
North-west of Kenilworth. Nearest main road: A4141 from Solihull towards Warwick
(and M42, junction 5).

3 Bedrooms. £20 (less for 5 nights or more). All have some or all of the following: own bath/shower/toilet; TV. No smoking.
Light suppers only.
1 Sitting-room. With TV. No smoking.
Large garden

Here is beautifully furnished accommodation in a spot well placed for visits to National Trust properties (such as Baddesley Clinton and Packwood House) as well as both Warwick and Birmingham. An ancestral home of the Shakespeare family, this 14th-century, timber-framed and red-brick farmhouse also has Knights Templar associations. From a crumbling shell, Ann and John Beaman have completely renovated and restored the house. The large, four-poster bedroom in blue and yellow is particularly attractive. Here and elsewhere, John's fine paintings hang on the walls. He is an artist and you may visit his gallery in the converted barn.

In the dining-room, where good and varied breakfasts are taken, antique china now occupies three niches above the fireplace where it is said ritual objects were placed during secret Catholic services held here in times of oppression. In the evening, one can relax in the cosy, oak-panelled sitting-room (ask John about its fascinating origins) or stroll around the farm to see sheep, Highland cattle and even peacocks. Plenty of restaurants nearby.

V   *Readers' comments:* Very welcoming. B & B with a difference.

PARK FARM
C(12) **X**

Spring Road, Barnacle, Warwickshire, CV7 9LG   Tel: 01203 612628
North of Coventry. Nearest main roads: M69 and M6 (junction 2).

2 Bedrooms. £19. Bargain breaks. Both have TV. No smoking.
Dinner (by arrangement). £13.50 for 3 courses and coffee, at 7pm. Vegetarian or other special diets if ordered. No smoking. **Light suppers** if ordered.
1 Sitting-room. With open fire. No smoking.
Large garden

The Roundheads burnt down the original house: several great Civil War battles took place in this region. This one was built about 1670. Outside it stand fine yews and within are such handsome features as the balustered staircase. All around is the 200-acre farm.

The house is immaculate, furnished with antiques and decorated in restful colours. In the green and cream sitting-room are flowery cretonnes and a small fireplace of pink marble. The big dining-room has windows at each end, and here Linda Grindal serves such meals as home-made pâté, chicken and broccoli casserole with dauphinoise potatoes, and blackcurrant shortcake. Upstairs are pleasant bedrooms – fine walnut beds in the yellow one, a prettily draped one in the pink room; and a very good bathroom.

Readers' comments: Extremely well cared for. Wonderful dinner, wicked breakfasts. The Grindals are delightful. Pleasurable experience. Comfortable, food excellent. Family charming, accommodation first class. Pretty home, gracious host. Made to feel most welcome.

PEAR TREE COTTAGE

Church Road, Wilmcote, Warwickshire, CV37 9UX   Tel: 01789 205889
(Fax: 01789 262862)

C(3) **PT**

North-west of Stratford-upon-Avon. Nearest main road: A3400 from Stratford to Birmingham (and M40, junction 15).

7 Bedrooms. £19–£23 (less for 7 nights or more). All have own bath/shower/toilet; TV. No smoking.
2 Sitting-rooms. With TV. No smoking.
Large garden

Mary Arden, Shakespeare's mother, grew up in the big half-timbered house which overlooks this cottage of much the same date. Pear Tree Cottage, too, is half-timbered. One steps into a hall with stone-flagged floor (of blue lias, once quarried at Wilmcote), oak settle, other antiques and bunches of dried flowers.

In the beamed dining-room, country Hepplewhite chairs and colourful Staffordshire pottery figures show well against rugged stone walls. There's a little television room and a pretty reading-room opening onto the gardens. Bedrooms (reached by steps and turns all the way) have very pleasant colour schemes. Some are in a new extension.

Outside are two gardens, a stream, stone paths and seats under old apple-trees. Although Margaret Mander does not serve evening meals, there are kitchens in which guests can prepare their own snack suppers, and two inns serving good food in the village.

Readers' comments: Ideal in all respects. Have always received most kind and courteous attention and a wonderful breakfast. Very friendly. Excellent. Exceptional.

V

POND COTTAGE

The Green, Warmington, Warwickshire, OX17 1BU   Tel: 01295 690682

C(13) **S**

South-east of Stratford-upon-Avon. Nearest main road: B4100 from Banbury to Warwick (and M40, junctions 11/12).

2 Bedrooms. £18.50. Both have some of the following: own bath/shower/toilet.
Dinner (by arrangement). £13.50 for 3 courses, and coffee, at 7pm. **Light suppers** if ordered.
1 Sitting-room. With open fire, TV.
Small garden
Closed from November to Easter.

The village of Warmington, near the M40, is so tucked away that few tourists find it. Around a sloping green with duck-pond are ranged rows of cottages built from local stone, and Pond Cottage is one of these. Vi Viljoen has furnished its rooms with great elegance – gleaming antique furniture and silver contrast with the rugged stones of the sitting-room walls. One pretty bedroom is all blue – from the silk bedspread to the birds-and-flowers wallpaper. Vi serves such meals as home-made soup, chicken with almond sauce, a tart of her own fruit or home-made ice cream.

The cottage is well placed for visiting not only Warwick Castle and Stratford but such stately homes as Upton House (wonderful collection of paintings; horse trials in autumn) and Blenheim Palace. The Heritage Motor Centre (with over 300 historic British cars) is six miles away.

Readers' comments: Delicious food, extremely good value. Like staying with a friend, every need anticipated.

V

283

SUGARSWELL FARM

X

Shenington, Warwickshire, OX15 6HW   Tel: 01295 680512 (Fax: 01295 688149)
South of Stratford-upon-Avon. Nearest main road: A422 from Stratford to Banbury.

3 Bedrooms. £19–£25. All have own bath/toilet; TV (on request). No smoking.
Dinner (by arrangement). £18 for 4 courses and coffee, at 6.30pm. Vegetarian or other special diets if ordered. No smoking. **Light suppers** if ordered.
1 Sitting-room. With open fire, TV. No smoking.
Large garden

Rosemary Nunnely is a cook of cordon bleu calibre – her greatest delight is preparing meals. Visitors who stay with her are likely to get something very different from ordinary 'farmhouse fare': for instance, seafood gratin followed by fillet steak (home-produced) in a sauce of port, cream and garlic, with crème brûlée to finish.

The house is modern but made from old stones taken from a demolished cottage. It has big picture-windows, and a striking staircase with 18th-century portraits. Sofas are grouped round a huge stone fireplace in the sage green sitting-room. Guests sit on Chippendale chairs to dine; and one side of the dining-room has a glass wall filled with Rosemary's collection of Crown Derby. Upstairs are elegant bedrooms – one with a sofa from which to enjoy woodland views, and a very large bathroom decorated in bright mulberry.

Readers' comments: Time capsule of the good life! Charming hostess, delightful accommodation. Superb welcome, superb cooking. An outstanding cook. First class. We have been back nine times. A truly beautiful house and excellent food. Wonderful holiday.

THORNTON MANOR

C(5)

Ettington, Warwickshire, CV37 7PN   Tel: 01789 740210
South-east of Stratford-upon-Avon. Nearest main road: A429 from Warwick to Stow-on-the-Wold (and M40, junction 15).

3 Bedrooms. £17.50–£19 (less for 4 nights or more). All have some or all of the following: own bath/shower/toilet; TV. No smoking.
Light suppers sometimes.
2 Sitting-rooms. With log stove, TV, piano.
Small garden
Closed from mid-December to February.

A stately home in miniature, this stone manor house, E-shaped in plan, declares its date, 1658, on a doorpost. Through an iron-studded oak door with decorative hinges, heavy bolts and locks, one enters a great hall dominated by a large stone fireplace with log stove. Overhead are massive chamfered beams.

Through the leaded panes of deep-set, mullioned windows in the breakfast-room (and in a bedroom above it) there are views of the garden, woods and fields. Little humps in the grass show where there was once a village in view until, in the 14th century, the Black Death killed off all its 60 inhabitants. Ancient outbuildings include an old pigeon-house.

Gill Hutsby (who occasionally sings at the Royal Shakespeare Theatre) has used old-fashioned furniture and rosy cretonnes in the bedrooms. There is a kitchen for guests' use, and also a tennis court.

V   *Readers' comments:* The place to get away from it all. Full of character.

TIBBIT FARM

Nethercote, Flecknoe, Warwickshire, CV23 8AS Tel: 01788 890239

C D X

South of Rugby. Nearest main road: A425 from Leamington to Daventry (and M45/M1, junction 17).

3 Bedrooms. £19–£22.50. Bargain breaks. All have some or all of the following: own bath/shower/toilet; TV. No smoking.
Light suppers if ordered.
2 Sitting-rooms. With open fire, TV, piano. No smoking.
Large garden

Very well tucked away near the banks of the River Leam (which gives Leamington its name) is a 17th-century farmhouse that once belonged to Baron Tibbit: in the nearby church you can see 13th-century monuments to his forebears. Alison Mills has decorated the beamed sitting-room (with inglenook) in pale green and pink to match the Chinese carpet; and has chosen a similar colour scheme for her bow-windowed dining-room. There are far views over fields of crops and across the humps which are traces of a village that had to be deserted in the 18th century, after the Enclosure Acts – the devastating effect of which inspired many poems of John Clare, the 'peasant poet'.

Bedrooms are large and airy. One has a silky quilt with bedhead painted to match; another (with lots of furry toys), white furniture painted with roses.

Alison does not provide dinners but gladly takes visitors to and from the nearby Olive Bush, where there is a cordon bleu cook.

WOODSIDE

C D M S

Langley Road, Claverdon, Warwickshire, CV35 8PJ Tel: 01926 842446
(Fax: 01926 842410).

West of Warwick. Nearest main road: A4189 from Warwick to Henley-in-Arden (and M40, junction 15).

5 Bedrooms. £18–£25 (less for 7 nights or more). Bargain breaks. One has own shower/toilet; TV (in all). No smoking.
Dinner (by arrangement). £12.50 for 3 courses, and coffee, at 7–8pm. Vegetarian or other special diets if ordered. Wine available. No smoking. **Light suppers** if ordered.
2 Sitting-rooms. With open fire, TV. No smoking in one.
Large garden

Woodside has its own wildlife reserve. Hillside woods, untouched since mediaeval times, have rare old trees and traces of ancient farming techniques. Furnished with antiques, the house has a good bedroom on the ground floor and a pretty family room. In the dining-room, Doreen Bromilow serves such meals as soup, a roast, and apple pie. There is a Bernese mountain dog.

Rural quiet surrounds the house – and yet it is only a few miles from Birmingham's National Exhibition Centre and international airport, Stratford-upon-Avon, Warwick and Coventry. Readers of Edith Holden's *Country Diary of an Edwardian Lady* will be familiar with a number of place-names around here such as Knowle, a historic village on a hill, with half-timbered houses; and Packwood House (NT) which has a lovely garden – Edith did many sketches here – and fine furniture inside.

Reader's comments: Very comfortable, food very well prepared.

V

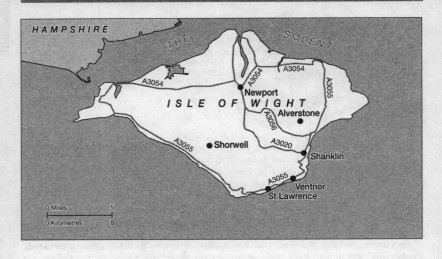

CAVENDISH HOUSE

Eastmount Road, Shanklin, Isle of Wight, PO37 6DN   Tel/Fax: 01983 862460
Nearest main road: A3055 from Shanklin to Sandown.

C(12) **PT S**

3 Bedrooms. £15.50–£17.50 (less for 7 nights or more). Bargain breaks. All have own bath/shower/toilet; TV.
Small garden
Closed from mid-December to mid-February.

This handsome town house, quietly situated, has particularly pretty rooms, Laura Ashley fabrics and well-chosen colours complementing antiques. Lesley Peters has emphasized the architectural features of the Victorian house by, for instance, painting the plasterwork vine of one ceiling blue, and filling an old tiled fireplace with pot-plants. Each bedroom has a table and chairs for breakfast as there is no dining-room. For other meals, guests go into Shanklin. A nearby cliff-lift takes you down to the sands, or you can walk through the famous scenic chine (a steep ravine). Buses go to all parts of the island. Outstanding sights are Osborne House and Carisbrooke Castle.

The island's coastline, its inland scenery and pretty villages appealed to the Victorians' love of the picturesque, and it was they who established Wight as an ideal holiday destination. Today there are over 70 man-made attractions if scenery and (usually) sunshine are not enough in themselves – such things as a whole 'village' of country craft studios at Arreton, tropical bird gardens and Robin Hill's exceptionally good adventure park for children.

Readers' comments: A real pleasure. Lovely house.

THE GRANGE

Alverstone, Isle of Wight, PO36 0EZ   Tel/Fax: 01983 403729
North of Shanklin. Nearest main road: A3055 from Ryde to Ventnor.

C **PT S**

7 Bedrooms. £19–£23 (less for 4 nights or more). All have own bath/shower/toilet. No smoking.
Dinner (by arrangement). £13.50 for 4 courses and coffee, at 6.30–7.30pm. Vegetarian or other special diets if ordered. No smoking. **Light suppers** if ordered.
1 Sitting-room. With open fire, TV, piano. No smoking.
Large garden
Closed from mid-November to January.

This immaculate guest-house, with light and modern rooms, was once the hunting-lodge of Lord Alverstone – MP for the island and Lord Chief Justice at the turn of the century. He built the whole village, the first in England to have water piped to each house because he banned strong drink in his village, which is why there is still no inn.

Geraldine Watling provides very good meals (she is a qualified cook) and husband David, who formerly worked in the space industry, is most helpful with books and maps for walkers: the island is threaded with scenic footpaths.

Meals usually comprise a soup such as carrot and barley, a roast or a dish such as filled pork medallions, and then a traditional pudding (like steamed apple and syrup pudding).

Readers' comments: Relaxed and happy atmosphere. Excellent accommodation, wonderful food. Extremely welcoming. Very good home cooking. Absolutely spotless, beautifully decorated. A real family welcome. Felt thoroughly at home.

V

LISLE COMBE

CPTS

Undercliff Drive, St Lawrence, Isle of Wight, PO38 1UW Tel: 01983 852582
West of Ventnor. Nearest main road: A3055 from Ventnor to Niton.

3 Bedrooms. £17.50–£19 (less for 3 nights or more). Bargain breaks. All have views of sea. No smoking.
Light suppers if ordered.
1 Sitting-room. With open fire, TV.
Large garden
Closed from mid-December to mid-January.

Surrounded by Hugh Noyes' rare breeds and waterfowl park to which guests have free access, Lisle Combe (previously home of poet Alfred Noyes) is an exceptional house. It was built in the early 19th century – but in Elizabethan style.

It has barley-sugar chimneys and lozenge-paned bay windows, many overlooking the English Channel; and a paved verandah with grapevine where breakfast is sometimes served. Hugh's mother brought to the house some very exceptional furniture and paintings that were salvaged when Lulworth Castle, her former home, was burnt down. One of the most attractive rooms is a small, pale-blue sitting-room with sea views. Through the garden and among palm trees, pools and streams a path leads down to the sandy beach.

No dinners: Judy recommends such nearby inns as the Crown at Shorwell.

Readers' comments: Beautiful house and setting. Warm, welcoming feeling. Helpful and courteous; interesting and delightful; friendly welcome. Memorably happy. A haven of interest, beauty and peace.

NORTH COURT

PT

Shorwell, Isle of Wight, PO30 3JG Tel: 01983 740415
South-west of Newport. Nearest main road: A3055 from Totland to Ventnor.

3 Bedrooms. £20–£22.50 (less for 3 nights or more). All have own bath/toilet; TV. No smoking.
Light suppers if ordered.
1 Sitting-room. With open fire, piano. No smoking.
Large garden

Swinburne and his girl cousin used to play the organ that stands in the hall of this 17th-century manor house – a big stone-flagged room with pale-blue walls, logs piled high around the stove.

The house is now the home of John and Christine Harrison, portraits of whose ancestors hang on the walls of the large dining-room with mahogany tables and marble fireplace. The great staircase was reputedly designed by Grinling Gibbons, and nearly every room has handsome detailing from that period – arched or scallop-framed doorways, egg-and-dart mouldings, shuttered windows in thick stone walls. All bedrooms are large, with armchairs.

Impressive though the house is, the really outstanding feature is the large and undulating garden with many plants of botanical interest. You can wander through woodlands or down terraces to a stream with water-plants, try to tell the time from a sundial in the knot garden, look down into the ancient bath-house, wander through arches of wisteria or lilac, play croquet . . . As only snacks are served, dinner for most people always involves a stroll through this lovely garden (opened to the public occasionally) to reach the nearby Crown Inn.

WILTSHIRE

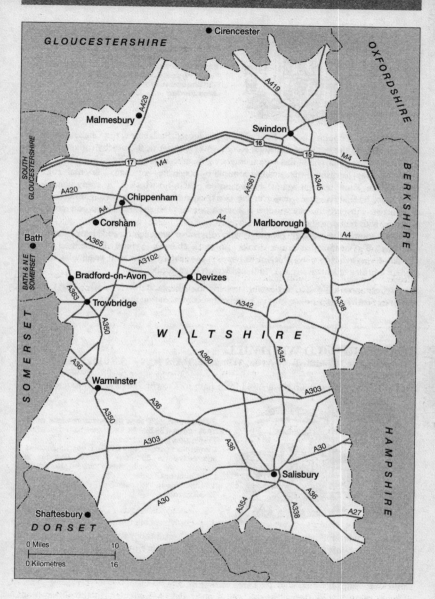

AVONSIDE

C(10) **PT S**

Winsley Hill, Limpley Stoke, Wiltshire, BA3 6EX Tel: 01225 722547
South of Bath. Nearest main road: A36 from Bath to Warminster.

2 Bedrooms. £18–£20 (less for 4 nights or more). Views of river. No smoking.
Dinner (by arrangement). £12 for 3 courses with aperitif and coffee, at 7.30pm. **Light suppers** if ordered.
1 Sitting-room. With open fire, piano.
Large garden

A typical English country house, built of honey-coloured Bath stone, the Challens' secluded home stands on the banks of the River Avon: walks along it or the nearby canal and fishing are among the attractions of this very scenic area. Bath itself is close by.

Ursula has furnished the sitting-room with tangerine armchairs, oriental rugs and antiques that show up well against walls painted peach, on which hang many paintings by Peter who, after serving as a major in the Gurkhas, turned to a completely different career as an artist. Through the bay window is a serene view of the well-kept lawn and landscaped grounds, with tennis and croquet.

Other rooms are equally pleasing, with attractive wallpapers and leafy views. The Challens offer visitors pre-dinner drinks (no extra charge). Typical of the kind of meal Ursula serves: avocado pâté; chicken in honey-and-mustard sauce with vegetables from the garden; a brûlée of brown sugar, cream and yogurt over raspberries.

Readers' comments: Wonderful people, very friendly. Elegant; lovely meals. The Challens make one feel like their house-guests. Excellent accommodation and food.

BRADFORD OLD WINDMILL

C(6) **PT**

4 Masons Lane, Bradford-on-Avon, Wiltshire, BA15 1QN Tel: 01225 866842
(Fax: 01225 866648)
East of Bath. Nearest main road: A363 from Bath to Trowbridge (and M4, junction 17).

3 Bedrooms. £20 **(one room for readers of this book only)**–£39.50. All have own bath/shower/toilet; TV. No smoking.
Dinner (by arrangement). £18 for 3 vegetarian courses and coffee, at 8pm (on Monday, Thursday and Saturday only). Special diets if ordered. No smoking.
Light suppers if ordered.
1 Sitting-room. With open fire, TV. No smoking.
Small garden

The original windmill here ceased to function in 1817, and today its stump is simply a very unusual stone house, perched on a hillside within picturesque Bradford-on-Avon.

It is now in the imaginative care of Peter and Priscilla Roberts, a much-travelled couple (engineer and teacher) who have brought back finds from the Far East, New Zealand, Tahiti and Australia which now decorate the rooms.

Every room has its own character and shape: some are circular. In the sitting-room, William Morris sofas and furniture of stripped pine face a log fire. One bedroom has a circular bed with a spread patterned with wildflowers and butterflies. In another, there is a water-bed covered with a patchwork bedspread.

Breakfasts are imaginative and suppers range from wholesome 'soup trays' to an occasional Thai meal. All evening meals must be booked in advance.

V *Readers' comments:* Everything you could want. Very friendly, I thoroughly enjoyed my visit.

BULLOCKS HORN COTTAGE

C(12)

Charlton, Wiltshire, SN16 9DZ   Tel: 01666 577600 (Fax: 01666 577905)
North-east of Malmesbury. Nearest main road: A429 from Cirencester to Chippenham (and M4, junction 17).

2 Bedrooms. £20–£25. Bargain breaks. Both have own bath/shower/toilet. No smoking.
Dinner (by arrangement). £14 for 3 courses and coffee, from 7–9pm. Vegetarian or other special diets if ordered. **Light suppers** if ordered.
1 Sitting-room. With open fire, TV.
Garden

For three centuries, cattle on their way from Malmesbury to Highworth Market would stop and water at the dew-pond in the peaceful hamlet of Bullocks Horn. The 150-year-old cottage here, surrounded by nearly an acre of garden with open farmland beyond, has been much extended by its present owners, Liz and Colin Legge. One enters the house via the light and airy conservatory filled with plants. Meals are sometimes taken here, or guests can eat in the big kitchen.

The sitting-room, with its plum-coloured walls and cream curtains, has a lovely Regency writing desk and an 18th-century square piano. French windows lead onto a pretty cottage garden and on summer days meals such as gazpacho, tarragon chicken with salad or vegetables from the Legges' kitchen garden, and summer pudding with home-made ginger ice cream are served in the rose-clad arbour.

Bedrooms are comfortable, with buttermilk walls, chintz fabrics and cotton sheets. Family portraits line the staircase.

The gardens at Prior Park and Barnsley House are just two of the many which you can explore. Bath, Bristol and Cheltenham are also within easy reach.

V

CHURCH HOUSE

C(12) X

Grittleton, Wiltshire, SN14 6AP   Tel: 01249 782562 (Fax: 01249 782546)
North-west of Chippenham. Nearest main road: M4 (junctions 17/18).

4 Bedrooms. £19.50–£27.50 (less for 3 nights or more). Bargain breaks. All have some or all of the following: own bath/shower/toilet; TV.
Dinner (by arrangement). £15.50 for 4 courses (with wine) and coffee, at 8pm. Vegetarian or other special diets if ordered. No smoking. **Light suppers** if ordered.
1 Sitting-room. With log fire. Piano.
Large garden

Church House began life in 1740 as a huge rectory. Around it are lawns with immense copper beeches (floodlit at night), an orchard, a covered swimming-pool, a croquet lawn, and a walled vegetable and fruit garden. Anna Moore produces imaginative meals if these are ordered in advance. A typical menu: quail-egg salad; chicken breasts in honey, lime and mustard; tarte tatin, British cheeses, fruit, and wine (included in the price).

The house has handsome and finely proportioned rooms. Guest-rooms are furnished with antiques; some have their bathroom facilities behind screens.

Anna and her family treat all visitors as house-guests and she often escorts overseas visitors on sightseeing tours.

Readers' comments: Anna Moore is an excellent cook. Bedrooms spacious and most comfortable. Peaceful. Lovely beds, charming house. Happy memories.

V

THE COTTAGE

C

Westbrook, Bromham, Wiltshire, SN15 2EE   Tel: 01380 850255
North-west of Devizes. Nearest main road: A3102 from Calne to Melksham (and M4, junction 17).

3 Bedrooms. £19. All have own shower/toilet; TV. **Large garden**

Converted stables, weatherboarded and pantiled, provide the accommodation in The Cottage. The quiet hamlet nearby was once the home of Thomas Moore, the Irish poet.

Inside, the roof beams are still visible. The bedrooms (on ground floor) have been furnished in keeping with the style of the building. Through the bedroom windows one can sometimes see deer and rabbits, with a distant landscape created by Capability Brown. At breakfast there will be local produce, muesli (home-made by Gloria Steed) and compotes of fruit. One can dine very well at the village pub 400 yards away.

There is an immense amount to see and do in the neighbourhood. Close by are such lovely spots as Corsham (with splendid Elizabethan mansion and the unusual Bath Stone Quarry Museum), Lacock (13th-century abbey, 18th-century houses and museum of photographic history) and Bowood House, with the gardens and parklands that were laid out by Capability Brown.

Readers' comments: Full of charm and character. We couldn't have asked for more.

---

2 COVE HOUSE

C D PT

Ashton Keynes, Wiltshire, SN6 6NS   Tel: 01285 861221
South of Cirencester. Nearest main road: A419 from Swindon to Cirencester (and M4, junctions 15/16).

4 Bedrooms. £20–£28 (less for 2 nights, or more). Discounts for repeat bookings. Bargain breaks. Some have all of the following: own bath/shower/toilet; TV. **Dinner.** £17.50 for 3 courses and coffee, at 7.30pm (not Sundays). Vegetarian or other special diets if ordered. No smoking. **Light suppers** if ordered. **1 Sitting-room.** With open fire, TV. **Large garden**

Peter and Elizabeth Hartland live in one half of this 17th-century manor house (with later alterations) which is surrounded by a particularly lovely and secluded garden.

Indoors is a large, friendly sitting-room; a dining-room that has antiques and huge heirloom paintings; and Elizabeth's lovely flower arrangements everywhere. In the small library is an alcove lined with a large-scale, illuminated map of the area.

Bedrooms have individuality – one green-and-white sprigged; another very flowery; a third (turquoise, with brass bedheads) has an unusual domed ceiling.

Elizabeth uses garden produce for meals, at which the Hartlands dine with their guests. A typical dinner: gazpacho, a roast or salmon mayonnaise, and fruit sorbet.

Readers' comments: Stayed several times. Excellent in all respects. Beautiful house, relaxed and friendly hosts. They could not have been kinder or more welcoming. The best breakfast I've ever had. Superb. Really lovely home and grounds. Delightful spot, extremely hospitable people.

V

EASTCOTT MANOR

Eastcott, Wiltshire, SN10 4PL   Tel: 01380 813313
South of Devizes. Nearest main road: A360 from Devizes to Salisbury.

4 Bedrooms. £19–£21 (less for 3 nights or more; and **15% reduction to readers of this book for 3 nights, December to February**). All have some or all of the following: own bath/shower/toilet; TV. No smoking.
Dinner (by arrangement). £15 for 4 courses, wine and coffee, at 7.30pm. Special diets if ordered. No smoking.
Light suppers if ordered.
1 Sitting-room. With open fire, TV, piano. No smoking.
Large garden

As early as 1150 there was a house on this spot. The present building has parts dating back to the 16th century, but every century since has added its contribution. Furnishings vary. Most are fine antiques – the refectory table in the dining-room (its walls hung with ancestral portraits) is 400 years old, for instance; and one alcove houses Crown Derby and other porcelain. Up the oak staircase with barley-sugar balusters are attractive bedrooms; the largest has peach-and-white panelled walls with big sash windows at each end and rural views. There is also a conservatory.

In outbuildings or paddocks are always some of the Firths' horses: they have trained many well-known 'trials' horses. Janet's other great interest is cookery, for which she has a number of diplomas. A typical meal, served on a generous help-yourself basis: fish soufflé, lamb provençale, caramelized fruit, and cheeses (vegetables and fruit are home-produced).

Readers' comments: Lovely house. Friendly and helpful. Delicious food. Very much enjoyed. Kind and welcoming. Delicious supper.

ELM FARMHOUSE

The Green, Biddestone, Wiltshire, SN14 7DG   Tel: 01249 713354
West of Chippenham. Nearest main road: A4 from Bath to Chippenham (and M4, junction 17).

3 Bedrooms. £17.50–£20 (less for 3 nights or more). Bargain breaks. All have some or all of the following: own bath/shower/toilet; TV. No smoking.
Light suppers if ordered. No smoking.
1 Sitting-room. With open fire, TV. No smoking.
Large garden

The 18th-century Cotswold stone farmhouse, with mullioned windows and pretty entrance porch, sits opposite the green and duck-pond in this tranquil Wiltshire village. Elaine Sexton was returning to her roots when she and husband Paul moved to Elm Farmhouse, where she has created a bed-and-breakfast house which is friendly, efficiently run and filled with interesting objects.

At one end of the spacious, beamed entrance hall is a walnut-cased Broadwood grand piano and framed above it are two extracts from an old copy of the *Bath Argus*, chronicling a small slice of Victorian daily life. The bedrooms overlook the pond, and the largest has a window-seat from which to enjoy the view.

In the dining-room, with its impressive stone fireplace, breakfast is served at a large Victorian mahogany table. For other meals, guests can stroll across the green to the local pubs.

Pride and Prejudice and *Moll Flanders* were filmed in nearby Lacock. Bath, Sheldon Manor, Bowood House and Corsham Court are also easily reached.

Readers' comments: Charmingly decorated. The welcome and help made a very personal experience.

V

ENFORD HOUSE

C D P T S

Enford, Wiltshire, SN9 6DJ   Tel: 01980 670414

South-east of Devizes. Nearest main road: A345 from Marlborough to Salisbury.

3 Bedrooms. £16–£18 (less for 3 nights or more). Bargain breaks. No smoking.
Dinner (by arrangement). £15 for 4 courses and coffee, at 7–8pm (must be ordered by lunchtime). Vegetarian or other special diets if ordered. **Light suppers** if ordered.
1 Sitting-room. With open fire, TV.
Garden

The 18th-century house (once a rectory) and its garden are enclosed by thatch-topped walls – a feature one finds in those parts of Wiltshire where, stone being non-existent, a mix of earth and dung with horsehair or else chalk blocks were used to build walls (which then needed protection from rain). The house has pointed 'gothick' windows on one side, doors to the garden on another. Antiques furnish the panelled sitting-room, which has a crackling fire on chilly nights. Bedrooms are simple, fresh and conventionally furnished.

Sarah Campbell serves, on pretty Watteau china, soups that she makes from garden vegetables, roasts, puddings such as gooseberry fool or lemon soufflé, then cheeses. The Campbells tell their guests a great deal about the area – not just its historic sights (Stonehenge is only a few miles away) for they are also knowledgeable about its wildlife.

Readers' comments: Everything quite delightful. A charming hostess and excellent food. Very comfortable. Pleasant and relaxed time.

V

FAIRFIELD HOUSE

C D M P T S

44 High Street, Corsham, Wiltshire, SN13 0HF   Tel/Fax: 01249 712992

South-west of Chippenham. Nearest main road: A4 from Bath to Chippenham (and M4, junction 17).

3 Bedrooms. £18–£20 (less for 7 nights or more). Bargain breaks. All have TV.
Small garden

Within a peacock's cry of Corsham Court (a palatial Elizabethan mansion with a famous collection of paintings) is a quiet and picturesque street, a backwater despite its name – which, in the 17th century, was lined with the cottages and workrooms of Flemish weavers.

At Fairfield House, one steps straight into a low, white breakfast-room with jade paintwork and curtains, beyond which lie two bedrooms and bathroom, with more upstairs. Christine Reid has furnished all of these with exceptional grace – using either silky cream duvets or pretty patchwork (made by her mother) on the beds, wallpapers patterned with sweet peas or with Chinese-style pheasants. White-shuttered windows are set in deep embrasures; fresh or dried flower arrangements are everywhere. This is altogether an exceptionally attractive house. Breakfast only; for dinner, visitors go to the Jaipur, Methuen Arms or other pubs in the little High Street.

V   *Readers' comments:* Delightful; great food; very welcoming. Excellent.

FARTHINGS

9 Swaynes Close, Salisbury, Wiltshire, SP1 3AE Tel: 01722 330749

4 Bedrooms. £18 (less for 3 nights or more). Some have the following: own shower/toilet. No smoking.
1 Sitting-room. With TV. No smoking.
Small garden

Farthings is very central (there's a view of the cathedral spire over rooftops) yet very quiet, and it has a garden with brimming flowerbeds. All rooms are immaculate, and pleasantly furnished. Gill Rodwell's breakfast choices include croissants and much else.

Salisbury is also known as New Sarum (new in 1220!) because the first town was else-where, on the hill now known as Old Sarum which began as an Iron Age fort – you can still see traces of a Norman cathedral up there. When it was decided to rebuild on a better site, the new cathedral, with the tallest spire in England, was surrounded by grass and big walls to keep the township that followed at a respectful distance. Within the precincts of the cathedral is Mompesson House, a beautiful Queen Anne building with a fine collection of paintings, china, glassware and period furnishings.

Readers' comments: Clean, quiet and excellent value for money. Gleamingly clean. Delighted. A treasure. Charming lady; accommodation and breakfast first rate.

FENWICKS

Lower Goatacre, Calne, Wiltshire, SN11 9HY Tel/Fax: 01249 760645
North-east of Chippenham. Nearest main road: A3102 from Calne to Wootton Bassett (and M4, junction 16).

3 Bedrooms. £20–£22 (less for 5 nights or more). All have some or all of the following: own bath/shower/toilet; TV. No smoking.
Dinner (by arrangement). £13.50 for 3 courses and coffee, from 6.30pm. Vegetarian or other special diets if ordered. No smoking. **Light suppers** if ordered.
1 Sitting-room. No smoking.
Large garden

'A small, sunny plot at the end of a lane or track': former teachers Fen and Margaret Fenwick decided to investigate when they saw this estate agent's description, and they fell in love with what they saw. Fenwicks was built on the two and a half acres of land which they bought in this peaceful valley, and lovely, formal gardens created.

The house itself is light and airy. The cream and peach-coloured sitting/dining-room overlooks a recently built ornamental fountain. Decorating one wall are framed reproduc-tions of costume designs by Korovin for the Bolshoi Ballet. In the pleasant atmosphere of this comfortable room, one may enjoy such meals as wild mushroom soup, chicken with mango and banana stuffing, wrapped in bacon and served with home-grown vegetables, followed by sticky-toffee pudding.

Reached by an open staircase, the bedrooms in pastel shades look out onto a field where sheep are often grazing. This secluded spot is within easy reach of many historic places, as well as an 18-hole golf course, riding, fishing and watersports.

Readers' comments: A real gem. Superb accommodation, extremely comfortable. Charming hosts, friendly and helpful.

FERN COTTAGE

C(12) **X**

74 Monkton Farleigh, Wiltshire, BA15 2QJ   Tel: 01225 859412 (Fax: 01225 859018)
South-east of Bath. Nearest main road: A363 from Bath to Trowbridge.

rear view

3 Bedrooms. £20–£25. All have own bath/shower/toilet; TV. No smoking.
Light suppers sometimes. No smoking.
Small garden

In one of the many pretty villages scattered over the lovely countryside around Bradford-on-Avon nestles Fern Cottage, home of Jenny and Christopher Valentine and now a haven for those who wish to visit the Bath area without staying in the city itself. Jenny does not serve dinner, but the nearby 17th-century coaching inn is excellent, and neither Bath nor Bradford-on-Avon is more than five miles away. Breakfast is served in the dining-room, where the colours of the pretty floral curtains are picked up by the Chinese rug, and an alcove has been filled with a black-leaded range. Portraits of Christopher's great-great-grandparents hang on the walls.

Bedrooms are immaculate, with board-and-latch doors and brass bedheads, and across the secluded guests' garden, with lily-pond and magnolias, is a separate suite. Best of all is the conservatory, where guests have lingered for hours in the comfortable, white-painted chairs under the passion flowers, reading, playing games or just dreaming the time away.

V   *Readers' comments:* Delightful, very warm welcome, very comfortable, excellent breakfast.

FLISTERIDGE COTTAGE

X

Flisteridge Road, Upper Minety, Wiltshire, SN16 9PS   Tel: 01666 860343
North-east of Malmesbury. Nearest main road: A429 from Cirencester towards Chippenham (and M4, junction 17).

3 Bedrooms. £16.75–£19 (less for 3 nights or more). One has own bath/shower/toilet. No smoking.
Light suppers if ordered. No smoking.
1 Sitting-room. With stove, TV.
Large garden

Ancient Flisteridge Woods, once owned by the Abbots of Malmesbury, border this old agricultural workers' cottage which, with its acre of garden, is a haven of peace. The exceptional garden is a labour of love for Fay Toop-Rose and her husband John. There is colour and interest here throughout the seasons – island beds full of evergreens and perennials and a variety of trees, flowering viburnums and winter jasmine.

The house itself is simply but comfortably furnished. It is filled with objects which Fay has collected over the years, such as an early 19th-century tea service on display in the small dining-room and Victorian pencil sketches in the sitting-room.

Two of the bedrooms have views of the garden, and another looks out onto the woods beyond.

The church at Upper Minety has 14th-century origins, and nearby Malmesbury, England's oldest borough, is rich in history. The remains of its Benedictine abbey, once one of the largest buildings in the country, now form the parish church and are worth a visit.

V

HEATHERLY COTTAGE

Ladbrook Lane, Gastard, Wiltshire, SN13 9PE   Tel: 01249 701402
(Fax: 01249 701412)

South-west of Chippenham. Nearest main road: A4 from Bath to Chippenham (and M4, junction 17).

3 Bedrooms. £19–£20 (less for 3 nights or more). Bargain breaks. All have some or all of the following: own bath/shower/toilet; TV. No smoking.
Light suppers if ordered. No smoking.
Large garden

You will indeed find heather growing in the garden of this much extended 17th-century cottage, lovingly tended by Jenny and Peter Daniel. There are fruit trees, too, whose produce provides home-made preserves for breakfast, and there are chickens providing fresh eggs.

Guests stay in the original part of the house, built of Bath stone. The beamed bedroom on the ground floor is spacious, with private corridor leading to a large white bathroom. The upstairs bedrooms, in pastel shades, with flowery duvets and matching curtains, have fine views towards Corsham, Lacock and the Westbury White Horse. In the entrance hall is a hand-carved sideboard known as a credence table. These were used in the past when testing food for poison before serving it.

As there is no sitting-room, guests are welcome to relax in the dining-room or in the garden in summer. For dinner, you could try The George in Lacock or the White Horse in Biddestone, both about two miles away. There is much to see and do in the area and, for golf enthusiasts, there is a one-hole golf course in the garden!

V

HERB COTTAGE

C S X

99 Bradford Leigh, Wiltshire, BA15 2RW   Tel: 01225 865554
East of Bath. Nearest main road: A363 from Bath to Trowbridge.

2 Bedrooms. £19. Both have some or all of the following: own bath/shower/toilet; TV.
Light suppers only. Vegetarian or other special diets if ordered. No smoking.
1 Sitting-room. With stove, TV, piano. No smoking.
Garden

Down a path bordered on one side by Suzanne Wise's organic fruit and herb bed and on the other by her daughter's dramatic wood totem symbols is a 200-year-old converted farmhouse filled with more good things: individually designed wooden furniture and glass sculptures (many for sale); rococo mirrors on bedroom walls; and books everywhere. One of the bedrooms is on the ground floor, with its own spacious shower-room and a lovely view northwards over countryside. Upstairs is another bedroom, with a fine Edwardian chest of drawers and carpeted bathroom, and a small room adjoining for accompanying child or relative.

Most guests dine at the Plough Inn at the end of the lane, but nearby Bradford-on-Avon has several pubs with good food, and Bath with its almost infinite variety of restaurants is only five miles away. Suzanne's interest in holistic health is reflected in her breakfasts: there is always a compote of home-grown fruit on the table, along with nuts, raisins, yogurt and good bread, and any dietary requirement can be catered for with notice.

MILTON FARM
East Knoyle, Wiltshire, SP3 6BG   Tel: 01747 830247
North of Shaftesbury. Nearest main road: A350 from Shaftesbury to Warminster.

C D

2 Bedrooms. £20 **to readers of this book only.** Bargain breaks. Both have some or all of the following: own bath/shower/toilet; TV. No smoking.
Dinner (by arrangement). £13.50 for 3 courses and coffee, at 7pm. Vegetarian or other special diets if ordered. Wine available. No smoking. **Light suppers** sometimes.
1 Sitting/dining-room. With open fire, TV.
Large garden
Closed from November to February.

This is a truly picturebook farmhouse – a stone-flagged floor in the entrance hall, glimpse of a kitchen with pine table and a gun-case beside the gleaming Aga. In the sitting-room, which has a boarded ceiling, logs hiss gently on the stone hearth.

The Hydes removed a lot of later accretions to reveal the original beams in this mainly Queen Anne house, and then added comfortable furniture and elegant fabrics. Janice Hyde serves candlelit dinners – she is a superb cook. One example: onion quiche, followed by a huge trout from the River Nadder (stuffed with almonds, mushrooms, lemon and I-know-not-what) and then the lightest of mousses. Clotted cream, milk and butter are from the farm's cows. (Heated swimming-pool *(see back cover)*; hand-painted Portuguese pottery for sale.)

Readers' comments: Janice Hyde is a delight; countryside and house are beautiful. Very welcoming; delicious dinner; very comfortable. Excellent service. Splendid bedroom.

V

OLD VICARAGE
Avebury, Wiltshire, SN8 1RF   Tel: 01672 539362
West of Marlborough. Nearest main road: A4361 from Swindon to Devizes (and A4 from Marlborough to Chippenham).

PT

3 Bedrooms. £19–£21 (less for 3 nights or more). Bargain breaks. One has own shower/toilet; TV (in all). No smoking.
Dinner. £15 for 3 courses and coffee, at 7.30pm. Vegetarian or other special diets if ordered. No smoking. **Light suppers** if ordered.
1 Sitting-room. With open fire, piano. No smoking.
Small garden
Closed in January.

Almost opposite the Norman church in picturesque Avebury village is the Old Vicarage, parts of which date back to the 17th century. Jane Fry has a flair for interior decoration, so each room has beautiful colour schemes. The front door opens into the canary dining-room with Chippendale chairs, window-seat in a bay, and Indian curtains embroidered with birds of paradise. The terracotta sitting-room, which has a handsome Broadwood concert grand piano, comfortable armchairs and window shutters of stripped pine, looks onto the walled garden with its begonia tubs and roses. All three double bedrooms are equally attractive.

Jane is an accomplished cook, serving such dinners as double cheese Swiss soufflé, salmon steaks with dill sauce, and chocolate mousse.

Reader's comment: Everything splendid.

298

STAG COTTAGE

Fantley Lane, Zeals, Wiltshire, BA12 6NX   Tel: 01747 840458
South-west of Warminster. Nearest main road: A303 from Wincanton to Amesbury.

C P T X

3 Bedrooms. £15–£18 (less for 7 nights or more). All have some or all of the following: own bath/shower/toilet; TV. No smoking.
Light suppers only. No smoking.
Small garden

In the 17th century, Stag Cottage, with its thatched roof and antlers above the front door, was the middle one of three farm labourers' cottages. Today, the thatch and the antlers remain, but the cottages now form one dwelling, combining a tea-room with bed-and-breakfast accommodation.

Marie and Peter Boxall serve hot snacks and cream teas all year round in the beamed dining-room, with its collection of cream jugs and old thatching-needles above the inglenook fireplace. For dinner, they recommend the White Lion, a five-minute walk away, or The Smithy in nearby Charlton Musgrove.

Bedrooms are small and cosy, with quilted headboards and matching curtains made by Marie. Framed examples of her talent for embroidery hang in one room while in another is a piece of artwork which the couple acquired whilst living in Rio de Janeiro. The whitewashed walls of the landing are filled with family photos, including some of children whom the Boxalls have fostered in the past.

Children are very welcome here and special china is provided for them as well as a supply of colouring books and pencils. Baby-changing facilities and a babysitting service are also available.

THE VINES

High Street, Marlborough, Wiltshire, SN8 1HJ   Tel: 01672 515333
(Fax: 01672 515338)
On A4 from Newbury to Bath (and near M4, junction 15).

C D PT S X

6 Bedrooms. £20 **(to readers who mention this book when making a reservation and show the current edition on arrival)**–£30. Also bargain breaks, available even at bank holidays. All have own bath/shower/toilet; TV and much else.
Dining- and sitting-rooms (see text).

From a modest guest-house, David Ball and Josephine Scott completely transformed the Ivy House Hotel at Marlborough into a large and elegant hotel with a restaurant that has won numerous accolades. They now also run the Vines opposite, an 18th-century terrace house converted and decorated to the same high standards as the hotel itself. Bedrooms overlooking the High Street are double-glazed.

Breakfast can be taken in the hotel, or will be brought to your room in the Vines. Other hotel amenities open to Vines visitors include a sitting-room, bar and sun-terrace.

Dinner is always a memorable occasion. You can choose from a three-course menu which may include such dishes as smoked fish terrine, stuffed breast of duck in orange sauce, and warm sticky-toffee pudding. There is also a simpler wholefood and fish restaurant, 'Options'. You need to book dinner.

Readers' comments: Delighted with the welcome and concern. Wonderful! The high point of our tour. Accommodation excellent, food exquisite.

299

WELAM HOUSE

C

Bratton Road, West Ashton, Wiltshire, BA14 6AZ   Tel: 01225 755908
East of Trowbridge. Nearest main road: A350 from Westbury to Chippenham.

3 Bedrooms. £16–£18. All have some or all of the following: own bath/shower/toilet. No smoking.
Light suppers if ordered. Vegetarian or other special diets if ordered. No smoking.
1 Sitting-room. With open fire, TV. No smoking.
Large garden
Closed from December to March.

This former vicarage was built from Bath stone in 1840 in the 'gothick' style so fashionable then – hence the pointed windows, arched fireplaces and stained glass in the hall (with the crest of Lord Long, a great local landowner at the time). There is exceptionally decorative plasterwork, particularly in the sitting-room added in 1865, which has pomegranates on the ceiling and massive Jacobean-style pendants. Outside is a lawn with lily-pool, bowling green and putting; alternatively, there is the shady canopy of a weeping cherry under which to recline in the Cronans' deckchairs on a sunny day.

Nearby Trowbridge is a town of handsome stone buildings that were built by rich cloth-merchants descended from Flemish weavers who fled here during times of religious persecution. Another weavers' town is Westbury, which is overlooked by the huge white horse cut into the chalky downs in the 18th century. The vast green undulations of Salisbury Plain have changed little over the centuries; its grandeur is as imposing as ever.

V *Readers' comments:* Very comfortable. Excellent value. Lovely, peaceful house.

For explanation of code letters and **V** symbol, see inside front cover.

'Bargain breaks' are usually out-of-season reductions for half-board stays of several nights.

Some proprietors stipulate a minimum stay of two nights at weekends or peak seasons; or they will accept one-nighters only at short notice (that is, only if no lengthier booking has yet been made).

To find the right accommodation in the right area at the right price, use an up-to-date edition of this book – revised every year. For an order form for the next edition (published in November), send a stamped addressed envelope with 'SOTBT 1999' in the top left-hand corner, to Explore Britain, Alston, Cumbria, CA9 3SL.

YORKSHIRE

(including East Riding of Yorkshire, North Yorkshire and West Yorkshire)

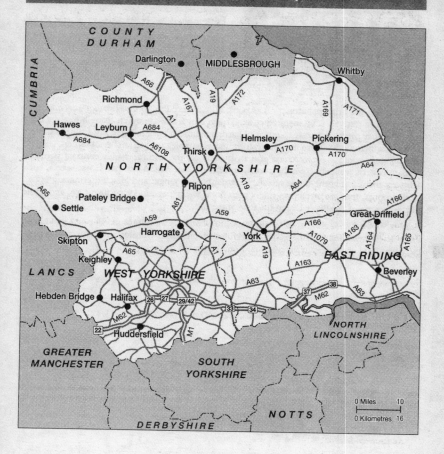

Facts (prices, etc.) at the top of entries are supplied by the proprietors themselves. While every effort is made to ensure that these are correct at the time of going to press, they may alter thereafter: please check when you book.

BANK VILLA

C(5) D

Masham, North Yorkshire, HG4 4DB   Tel: 01765 689605
North-west of Ripon. Nearest main road: A6108 from Ripon to Leyburn.

7 Bedrooms. £19. Bargain breaks. Some have own shower. No smoking.
Dinner (by arrangement). £17 for 3 courses, at 7.30pm. Vegetarian or other special diets if ordered. Wine available. No smoking.
2 Sitting-rooms. With TV. No smoking in one.
Large garden
Closed from November to February.

Good food is the principal attraction at Bank Villa, where Phillip Gill (former administrator of York's arts festival) is an inspired cook. The villa is a late-Georgian stone house set back from the busy road, with a steep terraced garden behind it (where there is a sunny summer-house in which to sit). Here are grown fruit and vegetables for the kitchen. Dinner is served in a pleasant room – pretty china and rush mats on the antique tables contrast with the William Morris wallpaper. Phillip cooks, and his partner Anton van der Horst serves, such delicious menus as home-made ravioli, duck confit, and ginger and kirsch meringue glacé.

Bedrooms, too, are attractive, many with floral wallpapers and pine furniture, and some with a glimpse of the River Ure at the foot of the hill.

Readers' comments: A great start to our stages to Scotland: we'll be back. Food as good as in the priciest restaurants. Energetic, cheerful and efficient. Comfortable and welcoming. Excellent food and pleasant proprietors. Food of superb quality.

BRAMWOOD

PT

19 Hallgarth, Pickering, North Yorkshire, YO18 7AW   Tel: 01751 474066
Off A170 from Thirsk to Scarborough.

5 Bedrooms. £20. Bargain breaks. All have own shower/toilet. No smoking.
Dinner (by arrangement). £10 for 3 courses and coffee, at 6.30pm. Vegetarian or other special diets if ordered. No smoking. **Light suppers** if ordered.
1 Sitting-room. With open fire. No smoking.
Small garden

The best approach to this 18th-century guest-house is from the back, through an old arch-way built for coaches – racks for the horses' tack and an old forge still survive, but beyond what was once the stable yard there is now a pretty and secluded garden, with clematis scrambling up old walls and an apple-tree.

The house was very popular with readers under its previous owners. It is now run by the Hacketts – Steve, who was connected with the construction industry, and Georgina, who is in the floristry business. They have improved the bedrooms, including Laura Ashley wall-papers, and Steve has taken to cooking with enthusiasm. He produces such meals as egg mayonnaise, salmon en croûte, and a choice of sweets. When, on occasion, he has done a curry, guests have asked for a repeat performance. In the dining-room, with rich red wall-paper, is old oak furniture which the Hacketts have collected, and an open fire.

Pickering is at one end of the North York Moors Railway (a good way of seeing this National Park) and also has the Beck Isle Museum of Rural Life and a castle.

302

BUCKLEY GREEN

Stanbury, West Yorkshire, BD22 0HL Tel: 01535 645095

C D PT S

South-west of Keighley. Nearest main road: A6033 from Hebden Bridge to Keighley.

2 Bedrooms. £15 (less for 3 nights or more). Bargain breaks. No smoking.
Dinner (by arrangement). £10 for 3 courses and coffee, at 7pm. Vegetarian or other special diets if ordered. Wine available. No smoking. **Light suppers** if ordered.
1 Sitting-room. With open fire/stove, TV.
Small garden
Closed in December and January.

In *Wuthering Heights* country high above the Worth Valley, this was formerly the home of Timmy Feather, the last handloom weaver in Yorkshire, and has been lovingly restored by the Archers. Whilst retaining many of the interesting original features, it is now a far cry from the dark and cluttered cottage of Timmy's time; there is a photo to prove it. Thanks to pale colours on the walls, natural unstained woodwork and interesting textiles, the whole feel is of freshness, light and comfort. Mrs Archer will provide an evening meal (such as egg mayonnaise, steak and mushroom pie, and a pavlova) if ordered in advance, but the local pub does excellent food.

A footpath (part of the Pennine Way) leads to Top Withens, supposed to be the original Wuthering Heights. The author's family home can be visited in Haworth, which makes the most of its Brontë connections. Another big draw is the Worth Valley Steam Railway, and there is scope for watersports nearby. A rewarding day trip might be to Ilkley, an old spa town which has retained much of its character, with the curious Cow and Calf Rocks on its outskirts.

V

CLOW BECK HOUSE

Monk End, Croft-on-Tees, North Yorkshire, DL2 2SW Tel: 01325 721075
(Fax: 01325 720419)

C M

South of Darlington. Nearest main road: A167 from Northallerton to Darlington.

11 Bedrooms. £20–£25. Bargain breaks. All have some or all of the following: own bath/shower/toilet; TV.
1 Sitting-room. With open fire, TV, piano.
Large garden

Heather Armstrong being a teacher of beauty therapy, it is not surprising that the rooms in Clow Beck House have been decorated and furnished with some flamboyance! The big sitting-room is in shades of the royal blue of the Chinese carpet, with white details such as Adam-style panels on walls and alcoves by the fireplace. Chandeliers hang over the armchairs and settee, which have carved wooden frames and blue velvet upholstery.

There is another chandelier in the marble-floored hall with its big gilt mirror. Up the oak staircase, one bedroom, in pink, has a tented fabric ceiling and a satin bedhead. The en suite double bedroom, in blue, has a canopied bed and Victorian mahogany furniture. More bedrooms (two with dressing-rooms) are in a separate converted stable block.

In the dining-room, the oak furniture is from one of the craftsmen for whom Yorkshire is well known.

Readers' comment: Additional accommodation to a very high standard.

COACHMAN'S COTTAGE

S

Hanlith, Malham, North Yorkshire, BD23 4BP Tel: 01729 830538
East of Settle. Nearest main road: A65 from Skipton to Settle.

3 Bedrooms. £19–£20 (less for 3 nights or more). Some have some or all of the following: own bath/shower/toilet; TV. No smoking.
2 Sitting-rooms. With open fire (in one), TV. No smoking.
Small garden
Closed in December.

Up a narrow road leading to only a few farms and a private mansion is this 17th-century cottage, which has been extended into its adjoining barn to create a rambling home where every bedroom has its own character.

There is a private sitting-room, with tea things, for the use of one bedroom (or two if a family is staying). Otherwise, guests can chat (in front of a log fire in cool weather) with the hospitable Monica and Glyn Jenkins. Monica runs the local history society, so she is knowledgeable about the area. The cottage being on the Pennine Way and both the Jenkinses being keen walkers, fellow enthusiasts are well catered for, with masses of books and leaflets and the Jenkinses' own recommendations for walks.

This is an area of fine scenery, most notably around Malham. Picturesque Settle is at one end of the spectacular railway line to Carlisle.

A few hundred yards down the road, the inn next to Kirkby Malham's mediaeval church is the nearest place for dinner, but within a short radius are many other excellent pub restaurants, including the nationally known Angel at Hetton.

CRIB FARM

C(7) S

Long Causeway, Luddenden Foot, West Yorkshire, HX2 6JJ Tel: 01422 883285
West of Halifax. Nearest main road: A58 from Rochdale to Halifax (and M62, junction 24).

4 Bedrooms. £16–£18 (less for 7 nights or more). Bargain breaks. Some have some or all of the following: own bath/shower/toilet; TV. No smoking.
Dinner (by arrangement). £8.50 for 3 courses and coffee, at 6.30pm. Vegetarian or other special diets if ordered. Wine available. No smoking. **Light suppers.**
2 Sitting-rooms. With open fire, piano. No smoking in one.
Small garden
Closed in November and December.

A necessary break to change horses on the long cross-Pennine journey from Lancashire to Yorkshire brought this 17th-century moorland house into being, for originally it was a coaching inn. Centuries later it became – and still is – a dairy-farm, though its role as a haven for travellers continues too. The Hitchen family have been here since 1815 and a framed auction notice on the wall proves it.

The old house has a warm and hospitable atmosphere, with rooms decorated in light and cheerful colours. Comfortable and unpretentious, it was first recommended because of Pauline's cooking. A typical menu: home-made asparagus soup, home-reared turkey with garden vegetables, and a choice of puddings, or cheeses.

Readers' comments: A welcoming family. Very comfortable and easy. A very happy week. Warmth of hospitality matched only by splendid breakfasts.

THE DAIRY

3 Scarcroft Road, York, YO2 1ND   Tel: 01904 639367

Nearest main road: A64 from Leeds to York.

CMPT

5 Bedrooms. £17–£21. Some have some of the following: own bath/shower/toilet; TV. No smoking.
Courtyard garden
Closed in December (part) and January.

In York, just outside the city walls, close to historic Clifford's Tower and the interesting Castle Museum, is The Dairy, which was just that until only some years ago: a milk churn now planted with flowers stands in the creeper-hung yard at the back. Rooms are cottagey in style, with original Victorian joinery, plasterwork and fireplaces, furnished with sprigged fabrics and stripped pine. One of the best, off the yard, is the room where Yorkshire curd was made; another has the use of a big Victorian bath. Breakfasts can be of wholefood. For dinner, there is an award-winning restaurant next door, or a big choice within walking distance.

York hardly needs description, with its carefully conserved streets, its city walls, the Minster and the railway museum. Tourist attractions, original or more recently created, abound, from the parish churches, with their notable stained glass, to Jorvik, the elaborate re-creation of the Viking settlement which was the first such attraction to use modern technology to reproduce the past.

EDEN HOUSE

120 Eastgate, Pickering, North Yorkshire, YO18 7DW   Tel: 01751 472289
(Fax: 01751 476066)

On A170 from Thirsk to Scarborough.

CDPTS

3 Bedrooms. £17–£19 (less for 3 nights or more). Bargain breaks. One has own bath/toilet; TV (in all). No smoking.
Dinner (by arrangement). £12.50 for 3 courses and coffee, at 6.30pm. Vegetarian or other special diets if ordered. Wine available. No smoking. **Light suppers** if ordered.
1 Sitting-room. With open fire.
Garden

With years of experience as hoteliers behind them, Adrian and Gaby Smith are food and wine enthusiasts who bake their own bread, make their own sausages and preserves, and grow their own vegetables. Visitors who can decide by 3pm have a choice of four to six fish and meat dishes for their first and main courses, and a choice of puddings.

The house is a pair of 250-year-old cottages in a terrace in the lively town of Pickering. Though it is on the main road, noise from traffic has never proved a problem. In any case, two of the bedrooms are at the back. They overlook the long garden, where the Smiths have made a pond; there is also private carparking.

Bedrooms are bright and neat, and very thoughtfully equipped, even down to shoe-polishing kits and dressing-gowns. Downstairs, the dining-room and cosy little sitting-room are furnished with country antiques and cretonne-covered chairs.

Readers' comments: Everything immaculate and cosy, delicious evening meal, wish we could have spent longer.

V

FAIRHAVEN HOTEL

CDPTS

The Common, Goathland, North Yorkshire, YO22 5AN   Tel: 01947 896361
South-west of Whitby. Nearest main road: A169 from Pickering to Whitby.

9 Bedrooms. £20–£25 (less for 7 nights or more). Some have some or all of the following: own bath/shower/toilet; TV. No smoking.
Dinner. £12 for 3 courses and coffee, at 7pm. Vegetarian or other special diets if ordered. Wine available. No smoking.
1 Sitting-room. With open fire, TV, piano. **Bar.**
Large garden

Goathland is one of the largest and prettiest of the villages in the North York Moors National Park, where sheep crop the grass right up to the front gates of the stone houses and the television series 'Heartbeat' is filmed. When the railway came in the last century, shipowners and the like built houses here and commuted to work in Whitby. Now many of their villas are hotels, one such being the Fairhaven Hotel, owned by Clare and Keith Laflin. As well as a large and comfortable lounge, there is a bar and snooker room. Bedrooms all have excellent views of the village and the moors. In the dining-room, where the wallpaper goes with plants and flowers, you might be served prawn fritters or soup, escalope of turkey, and a pudding or ice cream or cheese.

The railway is now run purely for pleasure, and its steam trains are an enjoyable way of seeing this spectacular countryside, perhaps dining while you do so. Alternatively, motoring across deserted heather moorland takes one from one attractive village to another.

V   *Readers' comments:* Excellent country hotel. Their standards are of the highest.

FOREST FARMHOUSE

CDPTS

Mount Road, Marsden, West Yorkshire, HD7 6NN   Tel: 01484 842687
South-west of Huddersfield. Nearest main road: A62 from Oldham to Huddersfield.

3 Bedrooms. £15 (less for 2 nights or more).
Dinner (by arrangement). £7 for 3 courses and coffee, at 7pm. Vegetarian or other special diets if ordered.
Light suppers if ordered.
1 Sitting-room. With open fire, TV, organ.
Small garden

Standing at 1000 feet, Forest Farmhouse is surrounded by a golf course (which visitors can often use) and moorland, much of it owned by the National Trust, at the top of the Peak District National Park. There was never a forest: the word is used in its sense of a hunting-ground and, at least according to the deeds of the house, the royal family still has the right to use it. This is a typical farmhouse of its kind, built of dark gritstone at least 200 years ago, with mullioned windows and stone-slated roof. Inside, the beamed wooden ceilings are low and the guests' sitting-room has a big stone fireplace. Seamus, the enormous and friendly Irish wolfhound, sometimes ambles about. Bedrooms, some with exposed masonry, have pine fittings.

Genial Ted and May Fussey run the place with walkers in mind (the open moors and the nearness of the Pennine Way attract them here). May provides, for example, home-made soup or grilled grapefruit, pork steak in breadcrumbs with fresh vegetables, and chocolate pudding with white sauce. All bread is home-made.

GRASSFIELDS

Wath Road, Pateley Bridge, North Yorkshire, HG3 5HL   Tel: 01423 711412

C D X

North of Harrogate. Nearest main road: A59 from Harrogate to Skipton.

9 Bedrooms. £20 **(to readers of this book only)**–£22.50. Less for 3 nights or more. Bargain breaks. All have own bath/shower/toilet; TV.
Dinner. £13 for 3 courses and coffee, at 7pm. Vegetarian or other special diets if ordered. Wine available. No smoking. **Light suppers** if ordered.
2 Sitting-rooms. With open fire. Bar.
Large garden

This country house is set back from the road, in its own gardens: it is a handsome Georgian building surrounded by lawns and trees. Most rooms are spacious and comfortably furnished. Barbara Garforth studies her visitors' interests and provides helpful information on local areas of interest, including many local walks.

Meals are prepared from local vegetables and produce wherever possible, including free-range eggs and Nidderdale lamb. A typical menu: pear and cream cheese salad, local beef, apple and mincemeat tart – all in generous quantities. There is a wide selection of wines.

Pateley Bridge is an interesting small town (in an Area of Outstanding Natural Beauty). In Nidderdale, there are crags, glens and How Stean gorge.

Readers' comments: Most helpful. Very fine food. Good food and plenty of it. Thoroughly enjoyed our stay. Wonderful. Very friendly atmosphere. Very comfortable, delightful atmosphere, splendid location. Lovely, peaceful location, kind hostess.

V

HIGH WINSLEY COTTAGE

Burnt Yates, North Yorkshire, HG3 3EP   Tel: 01423 770662

North-west of Harrogate. Nearest main road: A61 from Harrogate to Ripon.

4 Bedrooms. £18.50–£21.50 (less for 7 nights or more). Bargain breaks. All have some or all of the following: own bath/shower/toilet. No smoking.
Dinner (by arrangement). £12.50 for 3 courses and coffee, at 7pm. Vegetarian or other special diets if ordered. Wine available. No smoking. **Light suppers** if ordered.
2 Sitting-rooms. With open fire, TV. No smoking in one.
Large garden
Closed in January and February.

Off the road leading to Brimham Rocks is a one-time farm cottage now much extended, which has been modernized with care by Clive and Gill King. From the parquet-floored dining-room one steps down to a sitting-room where rosy sofas face a log fire and sliding glass doors open onto a terrace with views to the far hills. Lawn, flowers, orchard and bantams add to the charm.

Colour schemes have been well chosen. A blue-and-white bedroom has a matching bathroom; Laura Ashley briar-roses predominate in another, furnished with antiques; a large room has windows on two sides and comfortable armchairs from which to enjoy the views.

Gill puts as much care into making the simplest dishes as into a dinner such as lemons with a stuffing of smoked fish, pork in spiced orange sauce, and apple jalousie. Her own or local produce is used; bread is home-baked.

Readers' comments: Very beautiful and cosy. Charming host and hostess. The best cooking we ever had in the UK. A haven of peace, delightfully furnished rooms. A lovely stay, food good. Nothing but praise. First-rate b & b. Accommodation and food excellent.

HOLLY TREE

East Witton, North Yorkshire, DL8 4LS   Tel: 01969 622383
South-east of Leyburn. Nearest main road: A6108 from Masham to Leyburn.

C(10) S

4 Bedrooms. £20–£25 (less for 7 nights or more). Bargain breaks. All have some or all of the following: own bath/shower/toilet. No smoking.
Dinner (by arrangement). £14 for 5 courses and coffee, at 7.30pm. Vegetarian or other special diets if ordered. Wine available. No smoking. **Light suppers** if ordered.
2 Sitting-rooms. With open fire, TV. No smoking.
Small garden
Closed from November to February.

In the 12th century, part of this house provided stabling for the horses of monks travelling between the great Cistercian abbeys which are a feature of this area.

Beyond the sitting-room, which has a crackling fire and huge grandfather clock, are two small garden-rooms with glass doors opening onto terrace and lawn with seats from which to enjoy the far view. The formal dining-room has scarlet walls and antique furniture.

Bedrooms are particularly pretty. One, for instance, has a brass bed with cream, pink and green draperies. A garden bedroom has its own shower, basin, toilet and foyer.

Andrea Robson's greatest skill is cookery. Typically, one of her dinners might comprise salmon mousse, then her own recipe for chicken breast en croûte. Pudding might be pears – stuffed with walnuts and cherries, coated with chocolate and brandy, and served with cream.

Readers' comments: Freshly decorated and very comfortable. Fun to be with! Charming house, incredible food. Exceptionally comfortable, food superb. Some of the best value and comfort in the UK. They make the evening a special event.

HOLME HOUSE

Piercebridge, North Yorkshire, DL2 3SY   Tel/Fax: 01325 374280
West of Darlington. Nearest main road: A67 from Darlington to Barnard Castle (and A1 to Scotch Corner).

C D S X

2 Bedrooms. £18 (less for 3 nights or more). No smoking.
Light suppers only. Vegetarian or other special diets if ordered.
1 Sitting-room. With open fire, TV, piano.
Large garden

Piercebridge is a carefully conserved village and Holme House is just outside it, over the North Yorkshire border by a matter of yards. Down a tarmac farm road, it is a spacious Georgian house furnished with antiques and with many sporting prints and watercolours around. Guests breakfast at a long, stripped-pine farmhouse table. Anne Graham's family are animal-lovers, and there is a variety of livestock at the adjoining farm, which is managed by her husband. The two bedrooms have splendid views of open countryside. For dinner, visitors have a big choice of good food at the George Hotel.

Piercebridge was settled by the Romans, who have left many remains in the vicinity: by the village are a fort and a bridge – or was it a lock? The controversy about what is left is the subject of a book. Apart from Darlington, famous in railway history, the nearest town is Barnard Castle, with a picturesque market place and the remarkable collections in the château-style Bowes Museum, founded by an ancestor of the Queen Mother.

V *Readers' comments:* Wonderful welcome, warm and hospitable. Idyllic.

KELLEYTHORPE FARM

CDPTS

Great Driffield, East Riding of Yorkshire, YO25 9DW   Tel: 01377 252297
On A163 from Market Weighton to Great Driffield.

2 Bedrooms. £15–£18 (less for 7 nights or more). Both have some of the following: own bath/shower/toilet; views of lake.
Dinner (by arrangement). £10 for 3 courses and coffee, at 7pm. Vegetarian or other special diets if ordered. No smoking. **Light suppers** if ordered.
1 Sitting-room. With open fire, TV.
Large garden

This big 18th-century farmhouse, partly rebuilt after wartime bombing, has been in the Hopper family since the early 1800s. It takes its name from 'kell', the Anglo-Saxon word for spring, many of which rise in the small lake just at the back of the house. The bay window of the large sitting/dining-room overlooks the lake (as does one bedroom), and there is a terrace with chairs from which guests can watch the ducks and – with luck – kingfishers. This is the source of the River Hull, which gives the downstream city its name. There are lakeside and woodland walks on the 200-acre farm.

In spite of the size of the house, with its wide staircase hung with oil paintings, this is not a formal place, and family antiques – old furniture, pewter and silver – are scattered around almost casually.

Dinner here might consist of smoked trout or asparagus; pork fillet en croûte (much of which would have been produced on this or the family's other farm); and a fruit pudding.

V

LASKILL FARM

CDMPTSX

Hawnby, North Yorkshire, YO6 5NB   Tel: 01439 798268
North-west of Helmsley. Nearest main road: A170 from Thirsk to Helmsley.

rear view

8 Bedrooms. £18–£23.50 (less for 3 nights or more). Bargain breaks. Some have some or all of the following: own bath/shower/toilet; TV; views of lake, river.
Dinner. £11 for 4 courses and coffee, at 7pm (not Sundays or in winter). Vegetarian or other special diets if ordered. Wine available. No smoking. **Light suppers** if ordered.
1 Sitting-room. With open fire, TV. No smoking.
Large garden

This stone farmhouse lies in a hilly, wooded area of great scenic splendour ('Herriot country'), and close to famous Rievaulx Abbey. Its courtyard is made pretty with stone troughs, flowers and rocks; and around lie 600 acres with cattle and sheep.

In the sitting/dining-room is oak furniture hand-carved by local craftsmen. Here Sue Smith serves home-made soup or pâté before a main course which is likely to comprise meat and vegetables from the farm, followed by (for instance) lemon meringue pie or a fruit fool, and then an interesting selection of cheeses.

Two bedrooms are in a beamy outbuilding and open onto the lawn. Two others, more recently converted, are in another farm building. These rooms have their own bathrooms.

Readers' comments: Beautiful location. Comfort, good food and congenial company. Delightful room. Extremely comfortable. A welcoming hostess. Delighted with all aspects. Food quite superb. Friendly welcome. Wonderful place, surrounding countryside cannot be bettered.

V

LAUREL FARM

C D PT S

Brafferton-Helperby, North Yorkshire, YO6 2NZ Tel/Fax: 01423 360436
East of Ripon. Nearest main road: A1 from Wetherby to Catterick.

3 Bedrooms. £20–£25 (less for 3 nights or more). All have some or all of the following: own bath/shower/toilet; TV; views of river.
Dinner (by arrangement). £10–£16 for 2–4 courses and coffee, at 8pm. Vegetarian or other special diets if ordered. Wine available. **Light suppers** if ordered.
1 Sitting-room. With open fire.
Large garden
Closed from December to February.

The Keys have been Yorkshire landowners for 300 years (though not at Laurel Farm), so this house is rich with family portraits and antiques. Less venerable are the models and pictures of Spitfires and other aircraft, explained by Sam Key's many years in the RAF.

Standing on a knoll, this tall, 18th-century house has fine views – of the village church from two bedrooms and from the terrace. It is surrounded by the Keys' 28 acres – a hobby farm but enough land to provide lamb for the table and to support some rare breeds. There is also enough for a tennis court and a croquet lawn. There is angling, too.

Ann, who specialized in cookery at her finishing school, and Sam, who also cooks sometimes, join visitors at the old oak dining-table for such candlelit meals as prawns in garlic butter; roast lamb from the farm with home-grown vegetables; and summer pudding.

Families like the self-contained suite of double and single bedrooms (with bathroom).

Readers' comments: Rooms are delightful; pleasant, attentive but relaxed hosts.

LOW GREEN HOUSE

C D

Thoralby, Leyburn, North Yorkshire, DL8 3SZ Tel: 01969 663623
East of Hawes. Nearest main road: A684 from Leyburn to Hawes.

3 Bedrooms. £20. All have some or all of the following: own bath/shower/toilet; TV. No smoking.
Dinner (by arrangement). £13 for 4 courses and coffee, at 6.45pm (not Thursdays). Vegetarian or other special diets if ordered. No smoking.
1 Sitting-room. With open fire. No smoking.
Large garden

This stone house in a tiny hamlet is the home of Tony and Marilyn Philpott, who are founts of information on where to walk and what to see.

Within rugged walls are particularly comfortable and pretty rooms. There is a pink-and-white bedroom with deep brown carpet; and the bathroom is excellent. In the sitting/dining-room (which runs from front to back of the house, with a picture-window looking towards Wensleydale), soft colours, deep armchairs around a log fire and plentiful books provide a relaxed atmosphere. For dinner Marilyn may serve – with decorative flourishes – local smoked trout, pork cooked with cream and mushrooms, blue Wensleydale cheese, and raspberry torte. With the coffee comes a dish of chocolates. (All carefully prepared, and remarkably good value.)

Readers' comments: A Gundrey gem! A happy welcome. Friendly attention. Very comfortable, delicious meals. Good value. Exceptional hosts. A divine cook. A most special place. An absolute delight. Very welcoming and comfortable. One of our favourites.

V

THE MOHAIR FARM

York Road, Barmby Moor, East Riding of Yorkshire, YO4 5HU
Tel: 01759 380308 or 0385 916063 (Fax: 01759 388119)
East of York. On A1079 from York to Market Weighton.

C D S X

2 Bedrooms. £15. Bargain breaks. Both have own bath/toilet; TV.
Large garden

This would be a good choice for anyone who wants to see the city of York but prefers to stay in the country. And they will stay on an intrinsically interesting farm as a bonus. For this is the only farm in the country where the main enterprise is angora goats, whose long silky hair provides mohair. Lesley Scott formed her flock about 12 years ago, and visitors can buy, at surprisingly low prices, garments made from their hair.

In the farmhouse, which is decorated with some imagination, most rooms are rather small, and there is no sitting-room. However, the family room is spacious, with armchairs and a writing table. Ask to hear the story of Lesley's great-grandfather's will, which hangs on the breakfast-room wall. The farm, which is well away from the road, is on the site of a Roman settlement with a pottery.

Those who do not want to travel the 10 miles into York to dine have a fair choice in Pocklington, the nearest large village.

Readers' comments: Exactly as described; delightful.

V

MOULTON MANOR

Moulton, North Yorkshire, DL10 6QG Tel: 01325 377228
East of Richmond. Nearest main road: A1 to Scotch Corner.

C D P T S

3 Bedrooms. £16.50–£17.50 (less for 4 nights or more).
1 Sitting-room. With open fire, TV.
Large garden

Only a few miles from the A1, Moulton Manor in the village of that name is a tall Elizabethan house built on the site of a monastery to an unusual H-shaped plan. For most of its history it was in the family of the Dukes of Northumberland, and James I was entertained here. The house has been little altered since the 1670s. It was then that two great oak staircases were added (with a rare contemporary dog-gate); one leads to the guest-rooms under the roof, which overlook the orchard and large garden. Another 17th-century addition is the big carved-stone fireplace in the sitting-room. Gourmets walk to the Black Bull in the village to dine. Good but cheaper pub meals are a short drive away (as are the birthplace of George Baltimore and the Coast-to-Coast footpath); Sara Vaux will take you to them.

Midway between York and Durham, a stay here could include visits to two of our finest cathedrals. Closer are Richmond, a hilly riverside town with a big market place, a castle and a well-preserved Georgian theatre; and Northallerton, where there are some fine houses.

V

NUMBER ONE

C D P T S X

1 Woodlands, Beverley, East Riding of Yorkshire, HU17 8BT
Tel: 01482 862752
Nearest main road: A1079 from York to Beverley (and M62, junction 38).

3 Bedrooms. £17.50–£21.50 (less for 7 nights or more). Bargain breaks. One has own bath/shower/toilet. No smoking.
Dinner (by arrangement). £12 for 4 courses and coffee, at 7pm. Vegetarian or other special diets if ordered. No smoking. **Light suppers** if ordered.
1 Sitting-room. With open fire, TV. No smoking.
Small garden

Like York but on a smaller scale, Beverley consists of a minster rising from a warren of small streets within what was once a moated town. Number One is in a dignified and relatively quiet late-Victorian terrace.

The Kings have furnished the house with some brio, using wallpapers and bright colours to good effect. There is an abundance of house-plants, books and pictures. And some quirky decorative touches: a pair of antlers hung with assorted hats, for example. There is a grandfather clock on the landing, which leads to well-windowed bedrooms.

Sarah King provides for dinner a choice of several courses which might include grilled courgettes with walnuts and goat's cheese, a meat or fish main course, and a choice of out-of-the-ordinary puddings. Over coffee, which comes with chocolates, the Kings like to talk to their guests in front of the sitting-room fire.

V

OLD SUMMERHOUSE

C M P T

East End, Ampleforth, North Yorkshire, YO6 4DA   Tel: 01439 788722
North of York. Nearest main road: A170 from Thirsk to Pickering.

1 Bedroom. £17.50 (minimum 2 nights). Less for 3 nights or more. Has own shower/toilet; TV. No smoking.
Light suppers only if ordered. Vegetarian or other special diets if ordered. No smoking.
Small garden
Closed from November to Easter.

Tucked away behind Ampleforth village street, the Old Summerhouse contains not only a twin bedroom (and shower-room) but also its own breakfast-room. Linda Chambers brings breakfast across from her cottage, built on the site of the orchard which the summer-house once overlooked (it belonged to the old house just behind). She is a keen and able gardener, and guests can enjoy her work from a small crazy-paved patio by the stone and pantile summer-house. Ampleforth, best known for its Catholic public school, has the North York Moors to the north and York to the south.

A good outing from here would combine a visit to Nunnington Hall (NT), which has a display of miniature rooms within its 17th-century walls, and a meal at the old village inn. At Coxwold, Laurence Sterne's Shandy Hall is near another good pub for meals, as is ruined Byland Abbey. This part of North Yorkshire is home to many furniture-makers. The best-known workshop is at Kilburn, or you can see the varied work of a number of craftsmen at Balk, near Thirsk.

Readers' comments: Our second delightful stay. Highly recommended.

ORCHARD HOUSE

S X

Marton, North Yorkshire, YO6 6RD   Tel: 01751 432904
West of Pickering. Nearest main road: A170 from Kirkby Moorside to Pickering.

3 Bedrooms. £17–£20 (less for 3 nights or more). Bargain breaks. All have own bath/toilet. No smoking.
Dinner (by arrangement). £13 for 3 courses and coffee, at 7pm. Vegetarian or other special diets if ordered. Wine available. No smoking.
1 Sitting-room. With open stove, TV. No smoking.
Large garden
Closed in January.

Orchard House is one of the stone houses that face each other across the wide village street. It was built in 1784 as a farmhouse, and in the next century part was briefly a shop. Immediately inside the front door is the dining-room, with open fireplace. Walls are painted terracotta, except for one which consists of an expanse of stripped panelling. Paul Richardson is a wine connoisseur and a keen cook, producing such meals as grilled peppers with fennel; stuffed pork fillet; and spiced pears.

There is a large, light sitting-room with walls of pale yellow, carpeted like the rest of the ground floor with handsome woven sisal, and with well-filled bookshelves. Throughout the house, the interior design is particularly pleasant, which is not surprising since Alison Richardson is an architect. The long garden goes down to the River Seven, where fishing is possible. Sometimes breakfast (exceptional) is served on the terrace.

Readers' comments: Standard of accommodation very high; too good to be hidden from a wider audience. Quite exceptional; decorated with taste and style; excellent and enthusiastic hosts; cooking to a high standard.

V

POND COTTAGE

C PT S

Brandsby Road, Stillington, North Yorkshire, YO6 1NY   Tel: 01347 810796
North of York. Nearest main road: A19 from York to Thirsk.

2 Bedrooms. £15–£16. Bargain breaks. Both have own toilet. No smoking.
Light suppers if ordered. Vegetarian or other special diets if ordered. No smoking.
1 Sitting-room. With TV. No smoking.
Small garden
Closed in December.

In a barn adjoining this tiny primrose-yellow cottage is a treasure-trove of domestic bygones. For the Thurstans are antique dealers, specializing in 'kitchenalia' and pine furniture. The 18th-century house itself is furnished with antiques, and its shelves and nooks are filled with curios. There are collections of coronation mugs and Staffordshire dogs in the low-beamed sitting-room, where high-backed wing chairs are grouped around an inglenook fireplace. This is a house of twists and turns, unexpected steps and low windows. Its pleasant bedrooms overlook a terrace with stone troughs of flowers, a croquet lawn and a natural pond.

Dianne serves only breakfast and light suppers because the area is very well supplied with eating-places.

Stillington is almost equidistant from the city of York, the coast, the North York Moors and the Dales – each offering totally different holiday experiences needing many days to explore.

Readers' comments: A brilliant discovery. Fantastic treatment. Accommodation and catering excellent. Wonderful. Outstanding. Delightful and caring hostess. Nothing too much trouble.

V

PONDEN HALL

CDPTS

Stanbury, West Yorkshire, BD22 0HR Tel: 01535 644154
South-west of Keighley. Nearest main road: A6033 from Hebden Bridge to Keighley.

3 Bedrooms. £17.50–£18. One has own toilet. No smoking.
Dinner (by arrangement). £10 for 3 courses and coffee, at 7pm. Vegetarian or other special diets if ordered. Wine available. **Light suppers** if ordered.
1 Sitting-room. With open fire, piano.
Large garden

Emily Brontë knew Ponden Hall well: she is supposed to have based Thrushcross Grange in *Wuthering Heights* on the house. One of the objects of her visits was to use the library, now a guest bedroom. All the bedrooms are of interest, with mullioned and transomed windows, stone fireplaces, and beamed ceilings. A very large room, often used by parties of walkers or occasionally for courses, has a 'ceiling' consisting of woollen fabric draped from purlin to purlin.

The house has remained almost unchanged since an extension was built in 1801. The 'great chamber', in the Elizabethan part, is now the guests' sitting- and dining-room. At one end are a big fireplace, now with an iron stove where logs burn, and comfortable settees. At the other is a dining-table which can seat as many as 18 people: it was a cloth-cutter's table. Here Brenda Taylor and her helpers serve robust meals: soup with good bread; then, for instance, chicken roasted with tarragon and lemon, with a variety of vegetables, many of them fresh from the garden, followed by plum crumble with cream or Greek yogurt. The atmosphere is friendly and informal.

PROSPECT END

CMPTX

8 Prospect Terrace, Savile Road, Hebden Bridge, West Yorkshire, HX7 6NA
Tel/Fax: 01422 843586
West of Halifax. Nearest main road: A646 from Halifax to Burnley.

2 Bedrooms. £17 (less for 3 nights or more). Bargain breaks. Both have own shower/toilet; TV. No smoking.
Dinner (by arrangement). £8 for 3 courses and coffee, at 7pm. Vegetarian or other special diets if ordered. No smoking. **Light suppers** if ordered.
1 Sitting-room. With TV. No smoking.
Small garden

Terraced houses used to be built one on top of another to fit the steep slopes of Hebden Bridge. A pair of these have been united to form Prospect End, where the guest-rooms are approached through the garden, while the kitchen/breakfast-room above them is at street level and the sitting-room windows look onto treetops. The two en suite bedrooms, in pale pink, are neat and well equipped. Ann Anthon can provide dinners, but most guests go to the many restaurants in the town, which has become something of a cultural centre for the south Pennines and has some interesting shops. There is a museum devoted to beekeeping. The local beauty-spot is Hardcastle Crags (NT), with riverside walks.

In the nearby city of Halifax, the Piece Hall is an enormous Italianate building of the 18th century, where the handloom weavers of the area came to sell their pieces of cloth. As well as a museum devoted to that cottage industry, there are dozens of shops and galleries, and exhibitions and performances are held there. Also in Halifax is Eureka!, a purpose-built museum for children (aged 3 to 12) with lots of hands-on features.

V

ROGAN'S

Satron, Gunnerside, North Yorkshire, DL11 6JW Tel: 01748 886414
West of Richmond. Nearest main road: A684 from Leyburn to Sedbergh.

3 Bedrooms. £18–£21 (less for 7 nights or more). All have some or all of the following: own bath/shower/toilet; TV. No smoking.
1 Sitting-room. With open fire. No smoking.
Large garden
Closed in December.

When Maureen and Bill Trafford renovated Stable Cottage, they decided to call it after Rogan's Seat, the highest point in the hills that line Swaledale – though nobody seems to know who Rogan was. Visitors to this early 19th-century house have their own entrance to their sitting-room, where white-painted walls, bamboo furniture, and a colour scheme based on pink and green, together with vigorous house-plants, give a conservatory-like atmosphere. There is a large garden, from which footpaths lead directly into the countryside.

The bedrooms, also with white-painted textured walls, are fitted out in mahogany or pine; outlooks are leafy.

From near here, the Buttertubs Pass leads past Hardraw Force, one of the highest waterfalls in England. This is a way into Wensleydale, perhaps for a particularly good pub meal at the King's Arms in Askrigg. Simpler pub meals are closer at hand.

Readers' comments: Thoroughly enjoyed our stay. They take a lot of trouble to ensure one's comfort.

RYDERS CORNER

C D

Crambe, North Yorkshire, YO6 7JR Tel: 01653 618359 (Fax: 01653 618800)
East of York. Nearest main road: A64 from York to Malton.

2 Bedrooms. £17. Both have TV. No smoking.
Large garden

At Ryders Corner, Maureen Hewitt offers bed and breakfast only in her modernized 18th-century cottage, with a well-tended garden and a little land (with sheep and free-range hens). Maureen's husband, a professional leatherworker, makes such things as gun-cases in an outbuilding. There are smartly furnished bedrooms but only a small sitting-area (from which to admire the hilly view).

Castle Howard – the Vanbrugh masterpiece made even more famous by 'Brideshead Revisited' on television – is close. So are the fine grounds of another 17th-century mansion: Sheriff Hutton (where the house is the base of a theatre company). A fast road leads in one direction to York and all that it has to offer, and in the other direction to Malton, a pleasant market town where the museum has a particularly rich archaeological collection, well displayed. Wharram Percy is a deserted mediaeval village; Eden Camp is a museum of wartime life in Britain.

V

ST JAMES'S HOUSE

C M PT

The Green, Thirsk, North Yorkshire, YO7 1AQ   Tel: 01845 524120
Nearest main road: A19 from Middlesbrough to York.

4 Bedrooms. £17–£21 (less for 3 nights or more). Bargain breaks. Some have own shower/toilet; TV. No smoking.
1 Sitting-room. No smoking.
Small garden
Closed from mid-November to end of February.

Barry Ogleby being an antique dealer, it is not surprising that every part of this 18th-century house is well endowed with period pieces. You may sleep in a room with a bedstead of prettily turned spindles, for example, and in corridors as well as rooms there are such interesting pieces as inlaid blanket-boxes or unusual chairs. On the ground floor is a particularly convenient family room, looking onto flowerbeds, winding paths and lily-pool.

Only two minutes' walk from the quiet green, a conservation area, is Thirsk's busy market place and many restaurants – only breakfast is served by Liz Ogleby. This is where the world's most famous vet, writing under the name of James Herriot, had his surgery, which is now a museum. There are local guides who will accompany you on car tours, pointing out sites associated with Herriot, his books or the films.

Readers' comments: Beautifully furnished. Breakfasts are something special. One of the best b & bs we have encountered. Superb hospitality. Very warm welcome. Wonderful breakfasts. Every detail perfect. Make themselves feel like friends.

V

SANSBURY PLACE

C(5) PT S X

50 Duke Street, Settle, North Yorkshire, BD24 9AS   Tel: 01729 823840
North-west of Skipton. Nearest main road: A65 from Skipton to Kirkby Lonsdale.

3 Bedrooms. £20 (less for 3 nights or more). No smoking.
Dinner (by arrangement). £12 for 3 courses and coffee, at 7pm. Special diets if ordered. No smoking.
1 Sitting-room. With open fire, TV. No smoking.
Garden
Closed in late January.

Even carnivores enjoy the varied and interesting food at Sansbury Place, which is wholly vegetarian (almost vegan) and as 'green' as possible – down to the cleaning materials used. One of Sue Stark's dinners might be mushroom and walnut pâté, asparagus and peanut strudel, and hot prune cake with fromage frais. Breakfasts, different each day, could include, with home-made bread, home-made burgers or herby tomatoes, as well as muesli and fruit. What is not grown by the Starks themselves is wholefood and organic where possible.

Rooms are pleasantly furnished. There are a lot of Indian textile hangings and good pictures on the walls, a coal fire in the sitting-room, and a huge cast-iron bath.

The Victorian house is on a main exit from Settle, but the town is mercifully bypassed, and the rooms at the back have views of green hills.

The attractions of Settle – apart from the picturesque town itself, with its network of old streets and variety of shops – are the wealth of opportunities for walking and sightseeing around it and the chance it gives of using the famous and spectacular railway line to Carlisle or places in between. You could take one of Sue's packed lunches with you.

SEVENFORD HOUSE

Thorgill, Rosedale Abbey, North Yorkshire, YO18 8SE   Tel: 01751 417283
(Fax: 01751 417505)
North-west of Pickering. Nearest main road: A170 from Thirsk to Scarborough.

3 Bedrooms. £19.50 (less for 5 nights or more). All have some or all of the following: own bath/shower/toilet; TV. No smoking.
Light suppers only. Vegetarian or other special diets if ordered. No smoking.
1 Sitting-room. With open fire, piano.
Large garden

Rosedale Abbey now exists only in the name it gave this quiet village. It was something of an iron-mining Klondike in the late-Victorian era, when Sevenford House was built on its outskirts, and there was glassmaking here in the 16th century.

The house, with its spacious rooms, has been decorated and furnished in keeping with its period by Linda and Ian Sugars; on the walls are a lot of photoprints of local Victorian characters by Frank Meadows Sutcliffe of Whitby.

Visitors have a choice of two good restaurants in the village, or they can drive to one of the other villages which nestle in the wooded dales which score the airy grouse-moors, a National Park. England's best-preserved stretch of Roman road, prehistoric standing stones, and mediaeval crosses are to be found in the heather.

Readers' comments: Beautiful old house; very warm welcome; made most comfortable.

SPA HOUSE

Hovingham, North Yorkshire, YO6 4LP   Tel: 01653 628824
South of Helmsley. Nearest main road: A170 from Thirsk to Pickering.

2 Bedrooms. £20–£24.Both have some or all of the following: own bath/shower/toilet.
1 Sitting-room. With open fire, TV. No smoking.
Large garden
Closed from mid-December to New Year.

Carriages brought Victorians here from the Worsley Arms and the station in Hovingham to take the waters at these former pump-rooms until the British enthusiasm for spas waned. Though now unused, the waters still rise in the grounds, one filling a stone plunge-bath which Lynne and Jim Allen hope one day to rehabilitate. Unusually, the springs provide three different kinds of mineral water – chalybeate, sulphur and soda – and the bed of the stream which runs through the big garden is coloured with minerals.

The 1840s house is best approached from the hamlet of Cawton, up a drive nearly a mile long which, though not tarmaced, is well maintained. The house is hidden in trees and overlooks fields and the Howardian Hills across the lawns which Jim – now a professional gardener – tends. Lynne is a prize-winning bowler and amateur cabinet-maker, and both are keen walkers.

Guests breakfast at a sturdy arts-and-crafts oak table in a room with Jacobean-patterned wallpaper. For dinner there is a good choice of pub restaurants within a few miles. There is no shortage of sightseeing either, from Flamingo Land fun park and zoo to stately homes and National Trust properties.

SPROXTON HALL

S

Sproxton, North Yorkshire, YO6 5EQ Tel: 01439 770225 (Fax: 01439 771373)
South of Helmsley. Nearest main road: A170 from Thirsk to Helmsley.

3 Bedrooms. £20–£24 (less for 3 nights or more). Bargain breaks. Some have some or all of the following: own bath/shower/toilet; TV. No smoking.
Light suppers if ordered.
1 Sitting-room. With open fire, TV, piano. No smoking.
Large garden
Closed in late December and January.

Under a high-beamed ceiling, deep chintz-covered armchairs and a settee face a stone wall with an open fireplace in the large sitting-room, with plentiful antiques around. The bedrooms in this 17th-century house are just as prettily furnished, with flowery fabrics and sprigged wallpaper, and the double rooms have brass half-tester beds with crisp draperies. (The bathrooms too, whether private or shared, are pretty – Margaret Wainwright is understandably house-proud!) Views are of a trim garden with a bed of dwarf conifers, beyond which are the fields of this large mixed farm; or of a farmyard, with hills in the background.

Margaret Wainwright does not serve full dinners, for the area has excellent pub restaurants. It is also rich in 'sights' – castles, mansions, gardens, and the famous ruined abbeys of the Cistercian monks. One imposing castle is at nearby Helmsley, a picturesque market town with superior shops and galleries. Many of the villages in the area are very attractive, with their carefully conserved houses of honey-coloured stone and red pantiled roofs. Coxwold is an example: here is Laurence Sterne's house, Shandy Hall, and one of those good pubs.

V *Readers' comments:* Excellent value, a beautiful house, genuine Yorkshire hospitality.

WENNINGBER FARM

C D S

Hellifield, North Yorkshire, BD23 4JR Tel: 01729 850856
North-west of Skipton. Nearest main road: A65 from Skipton to Kirkby Lonsdale.

2 Bedrooms. £17.50–£19. Bargain breaks. No smoking.
Light suppers if ordered. Vegetarian or other special diets if ordered.
1 Sitting-room. With open fire, TV.
Large garden

A peaceful place hidden at the end of its own road, this house used to be a drover's cottage. It is surrounded by fields where Texel sheep and suckler cows (Blonde d'Aquitaine) are kept, overlooked by trim, cream-painted bedrooms. Downstairs, a green-and-gold suite faces a stone fireplace with polished iron pots and kettles around it. Behind, Windsor chairs surround the oak breakfast-table. Though snack suppers can be arranged with Barbara Phillip, most guests make use of the area's variety of good restaurants.

The house is well placed for outings in different directions. Northwards are the beauties of the Yorkshire Dales National Park, such as Malham Cove. The nearest main road takes one to Settle, perhaps for a scenic trip on the famous railway line to Carlisle; or in the other direction to Skipton, with its castle, or to Harrogate beyond. Not far away is the (almost

V treeless) Forest and Trough of Bowland.

WHASHTON SPRINGS FARM

Whashton, North Yorkshire, DL11 7JS Tel: 01748 822884 (Fax: 01748 826285)
North-west of Richmond. Nearest main road: A1 from Catterick to Scotch Corner.

C(5) S

8 Bedrooms. £19–£21 (less for 6 nights or more).
Bargain breaks. All have own bath/shower/toilet; TV.
No smoking in some.
1 Sitting-room. With open fire. No smoking. **Bar.**
Small garden
Closed from mid-December to end of January.

Far more handsome than the average farmhouse, 18th-century Whashton Springs has great bow windows and other detailing typical of this fine period in English architecture. Around it is a large, mixed farm run by two generations of Turnbulls. It is high among wooded hills, with superb views of the Dales and of a stream with mediaeval bridge below.

Fairlie Turnbull has decorated each bedroom differently. One, for instance, has flowery fabrics, broderie anglaise on the bedlinen, pretty Victorian antiques and a bow window; another, a four-poster with William Morris drapery and buttoned velvet chairs. Others in a converted stable-block are more modern in style (velvet bedheads, flowery duvets and pine furniture); most of these overlook a courtyard where tubs and stone troughs brim with pansies and petunias; one has a garden view.

Readers' comments: Very comfortable. Made very welcome. High praise. Lovely surroundings and easy access to many places. Charming proprietors, accommodation excellent. Exceptional value for comfort, amenities, atmosphere and personal welcome.

V

WOOD VIEW

The Green, Austwick, North Yorkshire, LA2 8BB Tel: 01524 251268
North-west of Settle. Nearest main road: A65 from Settle to Kirkby Lonsdale.

C D X

6 Bedrooms. £20 (less for 3 nights or more). Bargain
breaks. All have some or all of the following: own
bath/shower/toilet; TV. No smoking.
Dinner (by arrangement). £12.50 for 3 courses and
coffee, at 6–7.30pm. Vegetarian or other special diets if
ordered. No smoking. **Light suppers** if ordered.
1 Sitting-room. With open fire.
Large garden

The symmetrical front and small windows belie the size of this early 18th-century one-time farmhouse, for it is a capacious place. The biggest rooms are the attics, which are crossed by great wooden beams. Jenny Suri has furnished them and the other bedrooms with matching modern suites. Downstairs there is a snug sitting-room with a stone fireplace, and in the dining-room is a long oak table. Here Jenny serves straightforward meals, with a choice at each course: one might pick crab cocktail, chicken in white-wine sauce, and bread-and-butter pudding. In the summer, this room is open for teas (including home-made preserves), and Jenny can provide packed lunches.

Austwick is a village of stone houses and it stands in an area rich with spectacular geology. Hill-walking enthusiasts will know the Three Peaks (Ingleborough, Pen-y-Ghent and Whernside), but there is much to be seen by the less energetic: notably waterfalls, enormous caves, and the effects of glaciation many ages ago.

V

EXPLANATION OF CODE LETTERS

(These appear, where applicable, with each entry.)

C   Suitable for families with children. Sometimes a minimum age is stipulated, in which case this is indicated by a numeral; thus **C**(5) means children over 5 years old are accepted. In most cases, houses that accept children offer reduced rates and special meals. They may provide cots and high chairs; or games and sports for older children. Please enquire when booking. And do not expect young children to be lodged free, as babies are. Families which pick establishments with plenty of games, swimming-pool, animals, etc., or that are near free museums, parks and walks, can save a lot on keeping youngsters entertained. (Readers wanting total quiet may wish to avoid houses coded **C**.)

D   Dogs permitted. A charge is rarely made, but it is often a stipulation that you must ask before bringing one; the dog may have to sleep in your car, or be banned from certain rooms.

M   Suitable for those with mobility problems. Needs vary: whenever we have used the code letter **M**, this indicates that not only is there a ground-floor bedroom and bathroom, but these, and doorways, have sufficient width for a wheelchair, and steps are few. For precise details, ask when booking.

PT   Accessible by public transport. It is not necessary to have a car in order to get off the beaten track because public transport is widely available; houses indicated by the code **PT** have a railway station or coach stop within a reasonable distance, from which you can walk or take a taxi (quite a number of hosts will even pick you up, free, in their own car). The symbol **PT** further indicates that there are also some buses for sightseeing, but these may be few. Ask when booking.

S   Indicates those houses which charge single people no more, or only 10% more, than half the price of a double room (except, possibly, at peak periods).

X   Visitors are accepted at Christmas, though Christmas meals are not necessarily provided. Some hotels and farms offer special Christmas holidays; but, unless otherwise indicated (by the code letter **X** at top of entry), those in this book will then be closed. Even if a house is not shown as being open at Christmas, it may open immediately thereafter – please enquire.

V   Houses which accept the discount vouchers on page ii of this book.

REGIONAL DIRECTORY OF HOUSES AND HOTELS IN

WALES

Prices are per person sharing a double room, at the beginning of the year. You may be quoted more later or for single occupancy.

Prices and other facts quoted at the head of each entry are as supplied by the proprietors.

Sitting-room at Upper Trewalkin Farm, Powys (see page 347)

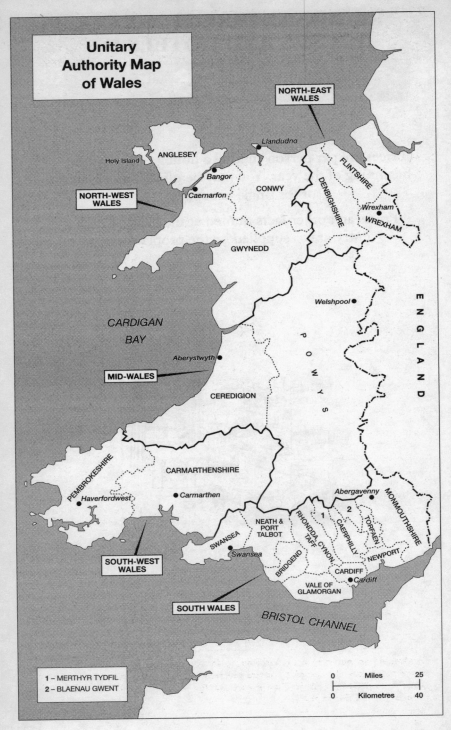

Unitary Authority Map of Wales

NORTH-EAST WALES

Llandudno

ANGLESEY

FLINTSHIRE

Holy Island

Bangor

CONWY

DENBIGHSHIRE

NORTH-WEST WALES

Caernarfon

Wrexham

WREXHAM

GWYNEDD

CARDIGAN BAY

Welshpool

E N G L A N D

P O W Y S

Aberystwyth

MID-WALES

CEREDIGION

PEMBROKESHIRE

CARMARTHENSHIRE

Abergavenny

MONMOUTHSHIRE

Haverfordwest

Carmarthen

1

2

Haverfordwest

NEATH & PORT TALBOT

RHONDDA, CYNON TAFF

CAERPHILLY

TORFAEN

SOUTH-WEST WALES

SWANSEA

Swansea

BRIDGEND

NEWPORT

CARDIFF

Cardiff

VALE OF GLAMORGAN

SOUTH WALES

BRISTOL CHANNEL

1 – MERTHYR TYDFIL
2 – BLAENAU GWENT

0   Miles   25

0   Kilometres   40

NORTH-WEST WALES
(including Anglesey, Conwy and Gwynedd)

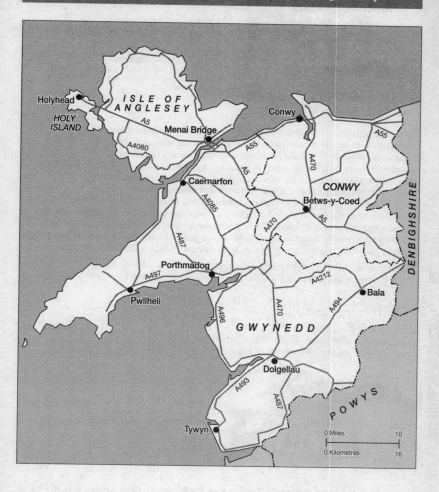

Addresses shown are to enable you to locate a house on a map. They are not necessarily complete postal addresses (though the essential postcode is included), and detailed directions for finding a house should be obtained from the owner.

ABERCELYN

C PT

Llanycil, Gwynedd, LL23 7YF Tel: 01678 521109 (Fax: 01678 520556)
South-west of Bala. Nearest main road: A494 from Bala to Dolgellau.

3 Bedrooms. £18–£20.50 (less for 4 nights or more). All have some or all of the following: own bath/shower/toilet; views of lake. No smoking.
Dinner (by arrangement). £12.50 for 3 courses and coffee, at 7.30pm. Vegetarian or other special diets if ordered. No smoking. **Light suppers** if ordered.
1 Sitting-room. With open fire, TV. No smoking.
Large garden

The Cunninghams were themselves regular users of *Staying Off the Beaten Track* (as are many proprietors with houses in the book) before they took to offering b & b in their 18th-century house close to the shore of Lake Bala (on some maps named Llyn Tegid). Once the home of a reclusive shipping magnate, it stands in landscaped grounds with a stream, a stone house with deep-set shuttered windows, log fires and its own mountain-spring water.

Judy has chosen attractive colour schemes: for instance, restful greys and greens in the sitting-room or, in one of the bedrooms, a particularly brilliant poppy wallpaper contrasting with all-white in the rest of the room. There are nice touches like embroidered pillowcases, antiques and interesting pictures. She is a very good cook, providing full dinners (such as a pâté with home-made bread, lamb, and chocolate pots de crème) only outside high season. However, her light suppers are at least as good as many people's dinners.

Readers' comments: Thoroughly recommended. Comfortable, lovely home. Most attentive without being intrusive. Nothing was too much trouble. Wonderful; friendly and hospitable.

V

BRONANT

C D PT S X

Bontnewydd, Gwynedd, LL54 7YF   Tel: 01286 830451
South of Caernarfon. Nearest main road: A487 from Caernarfon to Porthmadog.

3 Bedrooms. £16–£18 (less for 3 nights or more). Bargain breaks. Views of sea. No smoking.
Light suppers if ordered. Vegetarian or other special diets if ordered. No smoking.
2 Sitting-rooms. With TV, organ. No smoking.
Small garden

At the top of the Lleyn Peninsula (looking over the Menai Strait to Anglesey) is this handsome Victorian house, kept in immaculate order by Megan Williams and her nieces, who run a tea-room here. Their traditional Welsh teas are really authentic: the gingerbread, *bara brith* (speckled bread) and Welsh cakes regularly take first prizes at county shows.

Most rooms are spacious, with Welsh tapestry bedspreads in rich colours and views of sheep, pine trees and mountains. Some windows have stained glass depicting apples and pears, appropriate to a house where good, natural food excels. The light suppers are quite substantial.

Right at the end of the Lleyn is Mynydd Mawr, a National Trust headland with coastal views comparable to those of Cornwall's Land's End.

Readers' comments: Tasty, well-cooked meals. Spacious, comfortable bedroom. A great place with spectacular views. Very good value. Marvellous cakes. Beautiful and comfortable house; Megan Williams and her nieces charming.

V

CAE DU
Manod, Gwynedd, LL41 4BB Tel/Fax: 01766 830847
South-west of Betws-y-Coed. Nearest main road: A470 from Betws-y-Coed to
Dolgellau.

C(12) PT

5 Bedrooms. £20–£21 (less for 3 nights or more).
Bargain breaks. All have some or all of the following:
own bath/shower/toilet; views of sea/stream. No
smoking.
Dinner (by arrangement). £13 for 3 courses and
coffee, at 7.30pm. Vegetarian or other special diets if
ordered. No smoking.
2 Sitting-rooms. With open fire, TV. No smoking.
Large garden
Closed from December to February.

One crosses the track of a mountain railway and climbs to a breezy height where a small
stream chatters down through a pretty garden. Inside the 16th-century farmhouse, where
narrow passages twist and turn, are pretty rooms brimming with the Lethbridges' finds, collected from as far afield as West Africa (where they were relief workers) to local antique
shops. Colours and patterns (in bathrooms as well as bedrooms) are imaginative, books and
pictures abound, and each bedroom is named after a Welsh worthy – with biographical
details supplied. Decorative friezes adorn the walls. The needlepoint is Keith's as well as
Liz's. Liz cooks such meals as cream cheese and broccoli soup, local salmon or beef, and
bread-and-butter pudding.

Cae Du (pronounced *ky dee* and meaning 'dark meadows') is on a site inhabited for a
thousand years; and all around this area are historic remains such as castles, mines (some of
which go back for centuries), stately houses and gardens. There are mountain walks straight
from the garden, nature trails, pony-trek paths, waterfalls and lakes.

V

CAERLYR HALL
Conwy Old Road, Dwygyfylchi, Conwy, LL34 6SW Tel/Fax: 01492 623518
West of Conwy. Nearest main road: A55 from Conwy towards Bangor.

C D PT S

8 Bedrooms. £20–£30. All have some or all of the
following: own bath/shower/toilet; TV; views of sea. No
smoking.
1 Sitting-room. With open fire. No smoking. **Bar.**
Large garden
Closed from November to February.

In 1891, Leicester's MP, James Pickton, chose this superb position for his summer home,
perched high up for a view over what is now a golf course to the sea at Conwy Bay. The
best outlook is from the first floor, where there is a characterful bar. It has the original
stained glass and swallow-patterned fireplace, an old billiard table, tapestry chairs and lattice-paned skylights. Not only the breakfast-room but some bedrooms (big and comfortable) open onto verandahs. Ground-floor rooms are available for visitors who find stairs
difficult, but you have to go up if you want the one with a really splendid Victorian bathtub.

Michele Harpur and her partners run the place on thoroughly traditional lines – old-
fashioned, in the best sense of the word. Breakfast might include scrambled eggs with
smoked salmon, and home-made croissants.

Readers' comments: Heartily recommended. Pretty rooms, excellent hospitality. Beautifully
situated.

V

CWM HWYLFOD

C S

Cefn-ddwysarn, Gwynedd, LL23 7LN   Tel/Fax: 01678 530310
North-east of Bala. Nearest main road: A494 from Bala towards Corwen.

3 Bedrooms. £16–£18 (less for 7 nights or more). TV. No smoking.
Dinner (by arrangement). £10 for 3 courses and coffee, at 7pm. Vegetarian or other special diets if ordered. No smoking.
1 Sitting-room. With open fire, TV. No smoking.
Large garden

'Meeting of drovers' roads' is a rough translation of the name Cwm Hwylfod: a remote inn-turned-farm in the hills at Cefn-ddwysarn, still retaining its 400-year-old character. The Bests (civil engineer and teacher) bought it on impulse when holidaying in this spectacular area above the Dee Valley, falling in love with its odd-shaped walls, beams, deep-set windows, log fires, and screen wall of old timbers which once separated people from cows and hayloft. They keep 300 sheep as well as other livestock: children love the streams, sheepdogs, collecting eggs and exploring footpaths.

Bedrooms are simple, and Joan's food is good: a typical meal might be lettuce soup, a joint of lamb (one per family), and raspberry mousse.

Readers' comments: Received most warmly. Children in seventh heaven! Will certainly return.

DOLFFANOG FAWR

PT

Tal-y-llyn, Gwynedd, LL36 9AJ   Tel: 01654 761247
South of Dolgellau. Nearest main road: A487 from Dolgellau to Machynlleth.

4 Bedrooms. £20. Bargain breaks. All have some or all of the following: own shower/toilet; TV; views of lake. No smoking.
Dinner (by arrangement). £14.50 for 3 courses and coffee, at 7pm. Vegetarian or other special diets if ordered. Wine available. No smoking. **Light suppers** if ordered.
1 Sitting-room. With open fire. No smoking.
Large garden
Closed from November to February.

Rooms and food alike are exceptional in Pam Coulter's house, in a beauty-spot at the head of Lake Tal-y-llyn, over which looms great Cader Idris. (*Dolffanog* means a meadow of springs and *Fawr* a big house.)

There is a wall of rugged stone in the dining-room, appropriately furnished with oak sideboard and ladderback chairs, and another in the pretty pink and blue sitting-room with its log fire. Bedrooms are most attractively furnished (flowery duvets and well-chosen wallpapers, with much stripped pine); all have good lake or other views and particularly good showers.

Pam's meals are outstanding. On 'ordinary' occasions you might be served (after a complimentary sherry) parsnip and apple soup, pork in peach chutney, and cherry cobbler. (Vegetables too are imaginatively prepared – for instance, cabbage cooked with bacon and onion.) But if you stay several days, she produces at no extra cost a veritable banquet of 7–8 dishes, usually Chinese or Indian, presented with a flourish of flower decorations too.

Fortunately, there are plenty of scenic walks in the Snowdonia National Park all around to help burn up some of the calories!

HAFOTY

Rhostryfan, Gwynedd, LL54 7PH   Tel: 01286 830144 (Fax: 01286 830441)
South of Caernarfon. Nearest main road: A487 from Caernarfon to Porthmadog.

C

4 Bedrooms. £20–£24. Bargain breaks. Some have some or all of the following: own bath/shower/toilet; TV; views of sea. No smoking.
Dinner. £11.50 for 3 courses and coffee, at 7pm. Vegetarian or other special diets if ordered. Wine available.
1 Sitting-room. With open fire, TV, piano. No smoking.
Large garden
Closed in December and January.

The name means 'summer house', referring to the season when farmers would tend their livestock on the upper pastures of Snowdonia before bringing them down to their winter quarters. Perched up here, you get a view beyond Caernarfon Castle of the Menai Strait and the Isle of Anglesey, and towards the lovely Lleyn Peninsula: in every direction, tempting sights to explore. And many footpaths lead out from here, too.

In the 18th century, Hafoty comprised not only farmhouse and courtyard but an old mill and barns (since converted). Now there are attractively furnished rooms of high standard: some bedrooms, for instance, have lace draperies and soft colours to complement pine or bamboo furniture. The beamed dining-room has a large patio window to make the most of the spectacular castle view; and the sitting-room a big inglenook fireplace where logs crackle on chilly evenings.

Mari Davies serves straightforward meals such as egg mayonnaise, local trout, and fruit salad in ample quantity; and at breakfast you can even have Welsh rarebit if you choose.

V

HEN FICERDY

Abererch, Gwynedd, LL53 5YH   Tel: 01758 612162
East of Pwllheli. Nearest main road: A497 from Pwllheli to Porthmadog.

C(10) **PT**

3 Bedrooms. £17–£19 (less for 6 nights or more). All have some or all of the following: own bath/toilet; TV; views of sea. No smoking.
Light suppers if ordered. Vegetarian diets if ordered. No smoking.
1 Sitting-room. With open fire, TV. No smoking.
Large garden
Closed from November to March.

A Victorian vicarage with spacious grounds was built high enough up to provide outstanding views over Cardigan Bay in one direction and Snowdonia in the other: tall windows make the most of these, and one can step straight out into a garden with terrace, lawns and palms (for the Lleyn Peninsula has an exceptionally mild climate all year round).

Medi Lloyd Hughes has created a welcoming atmosphere with warm pinks and reds in a sitting-room of flowery sofas, shining brass and marble fireplace, and gently ticking grandfather clock. A Welsh dresser is laden with willow-pattern plates that contrast with coral walls in the dining-room. Bedrooms, too, are attractive: a green-and-white gingham room has pine and bamboo furniture, for instance; and one of the bathrooms is as luxurious as it is large.

The peninsula is one of the most Welsh parts of Wales, with the native language still very much alive. It has wild and dramatic scenery inland, sandy beaches along its shores. The Lleyn's most famous village is, of course, Portmeirion, an Italianate waterside fantasy designed by Sir Clough Williams-Ellis in 1925. Every architectural style, and every colour of the rainbow, seems to be represented here.

V

LAKESIDE

CDMX

Llanrug, Gwynedd, LL55 4ED   Tel: 01286 870065
East of Caernarfon. Nearest main road: A487 from Caernarfon to Porthmadog.

3 Bedrooms. £20 (less for 7 nights or more). Some have some of the following: own shower/toilet; TV; views of lake. No smoking.
Dinner (by arrangement). £13 for 4 courses and coffee, at any agreed time. Vegetarian or other special diets if ordered. No smoking. **Light suppers.**
1 Sitting-room. With open fire, TV. No smoking.
Large garden

In the foothills of Snowdonia, an early Victorian magnate built himself a turreted mock-castle, Bryn-Bras, surrounding it with spectacular gardens. A huge artificial lake was dug, beside which stood a lattice-paned gamekeeper's cottage – now the home of the Kanes, who can lend guests a two-seater canoe.

They have transformed the house (in its own woodland) and created a flowery garden, which is frequented by peacocks and pheasants; there is also a hide from which to watch barn owls.

The rooms are most attractive, with pretty colours and unusual finds from antique shops, oriental treasures, good carpets on tiled floors and modern leather chairs. In places there are walls of exposed granite, a log fire blazes in winter, and less mobile visitors will appreciate the elegant ground-floor bedroom with quite luxurious bathroom.

For dinner, Lyn may serve home-made vegetable soup with hot rolls, chicken cooked with pineapple and ginger, chocolate and pear mousses, and then cheeses.

Readers' comments: Felt so much at home. Tasty, varied and plentiful meals. Beautiful surroundings. Most comfortable, excellent cook. Have had several pleasant weekends here.

V

LLWYNDÛ FARMHOUSE

CDPTX

Llanaber, Barmouth, Gwynedd, LL42 1RR   Tel: 01341 280144 (Fax: 01341 281236)
West of Dolgellau. Nearest main road: A496 from Barmouth to Harlech.

7 Bedrooms. £20–£28 (less for 2 nights or more). Bargain breaks. All have some or all of the following: own bath/shower/toilet; TV; views of sea. No smoking.
Dinner (by arrangement). £16.45 for 3 courses and coffee, at 7.30pm. Vegetarian or other special diets if ordered. Wine available. No smoking. **Light suppers** if ordered.
1 Sitting-room. With open fire, TV. No smoking.
Large garden

In 1597, this handsomely built house was already of considerable consequence in the neighbourhood. The walls are immensely thick, and the living-room huge; one ceiling-beam is over two feet thick, and great blocks of granite form the fireplace. New discoveries continue to come to light – for instance, a 16th-century oak-mullioned window.

Most bedrooms have views (and sounds) of the sea waves, and two have four-poster beds – also excellent bathrooms. One room has a dressing-room, another its own stone stair to the garden; some are in a converted granary. Everywhere are attractive furnishings, and great pieces of driftwood from the beaches stand here and there like sculpture.

Peter and Paula Thompson are very keen cooks, preparing such meals as parsnip-and-apple soup, lamb in a mushroom and cinnamon sauce, rhubarb-and-banana pie.

Readers' comments: House has tremendous character. Lovely food, great value. Delightful situation, friendly welcome. Food superb. Excellent hostess and cook. Stunning views.

V

MELIN MELOCH

Llanfor, Bala, Gwynedd, LL23 7DP   Tel: 01678 520101
East of Bala. Nearest main road: A494 from Corwen to Bala.

C(5) **D S**

4 Bedrooms. £19.50–£22 (less for 6 nights or more). Bargain breaks. All have some or all of the following: own bath/shower/toilet; TV; views of river. No smoking.
Dinner (by arrangement). £12.50 for 3 courses and coffee, at 7pm. No smoking.
2 Sitting-rooms. With open fire, TV. No smoking.
Large garden
Closed in January.

This 13th-century watermill is a galleried house with pretty bedrooms. Through an arch by the big stone fireplace in the beamed sitting-room is a great table flanked by pews, where Beryl Fullard serves (by arrangement) such meals as melon with raspberry coulis, lamb, brandy-cake and cream.

The miller's cottage has a ground-floor bedroom and spacious family suite; other rooms are in a granary. Everywhere are paintings and 'finds' such as a milkchurn and a mangle. Richard has landscaped the large gardens, making the most of the stream, the waterfall and the ponds, and has annually received an award for his work.

The River Meloch feeds the mill-race (*melin* means mill), which drives a Pelton wheel, a Victorian form of waterwheel which Richard has restored.

Readers' comments: Spectacular. Food and location excellent. Lovely house. Perfection. Spoilt me with excellent cooking. The house is a beauty. Absolutely wonderful time. Never-to-be-forgotten, unique house. Garden is the heart and soul of this place. Perfect hosts.

PENTRE BACH

Llwyngwril, Gwynedd, LL37 2JU   Tel: 01341 250294 (Fax: 01341 250885)
South-west of Dolgellau. Nearest main road: A493 from Dolgellau to Machynlleth.

PT

3 Bedrooms. £20–£25 (less for 4 nights or more). All have own shower/toilet; TV. No smoking.
Dinner (by arrangement). £15.45 for 3 courses and coffee, at 6–8pm. Vegetarian or other special diets if ordered. No smoking. **Light suppers** if ordered.
Large garden

Close by the sea and with a backdrop of mountains, a tree-lined drive leads to 'little village' (as its name translates), a serene old farmhouse together with cottages now used for self-catering or b & b. The Smyths have made really sensitive use of this treasure, converting and furnishing to high standards without compromising the original character of the old stone buildings. Each bedroom enjoys a different view: panoramic seascape with spectacular sunsets, a vista of hills over which dawn rises, or looking to the picturesque village church.

Colours are tranquil, old fireplaces and window-shutters have been retained, and pictures are well chosen. (Alas, no sitting-room.)

Margaret Smyth won the title 'Mid-Wales Cook of the Year' in 1994 and a Radio 4 Food Programme award in 1996. She has a range of Welsh specialities, using a lot of Pentre Bach's own organic produce for her candlelit dinners, and you are invited to order in advance from a wide choice of such sophisticated dishes as mushroom pâté, venison escalopes with wine sauce, and mocha parfait with raspberry sauce.

PLAS GOWER

C S X

Llangower, Gwynedd, LL23 7BY   Tel/Fax: 01678 520431
South-west of Bala. Nearest main road: A494 from Dolgellau to Bala.

2 Bedrooms. £18.50–£20 (less for 4 nights or more). Bargain breaks. Both have own bath/shower/toilet; TV; views of lake. No smoking.
Dinner (by arrangement). £8.50 for 3 courses and coffee, at times to suit guests. Vegetarian diets if ordered. No smoking. **Light suppers** if ordered.
1 Sitting-room. With open fire, TV. No smoking.
Large garden

Above the less frequented side of Lake Bala is this 18th-century house, which has very fine views across lily-pond and lake to the mountains of Snowdonia. One enters past a cascade of begonias in the verandah to rooms furnished handsomely, with Victorian watercolours of Wales and such interesting features as an old spinet converted into a desk. There is a particularly elegant bathroom. A previous owner was the Welsh poet Euros Bowen who lived here until 1973, but the site has been inhabited since 1312 and Olwen Foreman has a sampler which lists all owners from then until now. She enjoys telling visitors about lesser-known routes to follow and cooking for them traditional meals such as leek soup, Welsh lamb, and blackberry-and-apple crumble. Her sister, too, takes b & b guests – at **Plas Penucha** in Flintshire.

Bala is Wales's largest lake, surrounded by wild hills offering scenic walks and drives among peaks nearly 3000 feet high. The loftiest road in Wales runs from Bala to Dinas Mawddwy, a very pretty village: footpaths lead to waterfalls.

V

PLAS TREFARTHEN

C

Brynsiencyn, Isle of Anglesey, Anglesey, LL61 6SZ   Tel: 01248 430379
South-west of Menai Bridge. Nearest main road: A4080 from Rhosneigr to Menai Bridge.

9 Bedrooms. £19–£21 (less for 7 nights or more). Bargain breaks. Some have some or all of the following: own bath/shower/toilet; TV; views of sea. No smoking.
Dinner (by arrangement). From £11 for 2 courses and coffee, at 6.30pm. Vegetarian or other special diets if ordered. No smoking.
1 Sitting-room. With open fire, piano. No smoking.
Large garden

This handsome 18th-century mansion stands at the heart of a 200-acre farm, and its water-front site is outstanding. In the sitting-room, a big picture-window makes the most of the view across the water to Caernarfon Castle. The green brocade walls and a big Welsh dresser display souvenirs of Marian Roberts' travels; musical mementoes are gathered in the dining-room. She has repeatedly won the highest accolades at the international *eisteddfod* and spent much time on concert tours.

Bedrooms are roomy – the pink one has an outsize bathroom and windows on two sides; the pine-fitted one has the best views of Snowdon. There are also attic rooms with large skylights. Marian serves such dinners as soup, Welsh lamb, and apple tart.

The house is in an Area of Outstanding Natural Beauty. Unlike the rest of Wales, Anglesey's 300 square miles are rocky but not mountainous: they have other charms.

Readers' comments: Warm welcome, good advice. Spectacular and excellent value. A very nice place.

ROYAL OAK FARMHOUSE & COTTAGE

Betws-y-Coed, Conwy, LL24 0AH Tel: 01690 710427 and 01690 710760

Nearest main road: A5 from Betws-y-Coed to Llangollen.

C(5) **PT S**

5 Bedrooms. £17–£18 (less for 6 nights or more). All have some or all of the following: own bath/shower/toilet; views of river. No smoking.
2 Sitting-rooms. With open fire, TV. No smoking.
Large garden

Royal Oak Farmhouse is a small, partly 13th-century watermill. Although so central, the mill is hidden in a little valley with a deep salmon pool close by. The lattice-paned windows, great stone fireplace, carved oak settle and very pretty bedrooms give this guest-house great character. Elsie Houghton serves only breakfast, but there are good eating-places in Betws.

Equally attractive (and with en suite bathrooms) is Royal Oak Farm Cottage, run by Elsie's daughter-in-law Kathleen.

Four wooded valleys meet at this village, with a high plateau looming above it. Walkers use it as a centre to explore in every direction, the serious ones making for Snowdon but most for the riverside paths, the Gwydyr Forest, any of several lakes or waterfalls, or the Fairy Glen, one of the area's finest beauty-spots.

Also in the vicinity are such sights as Dolwyddelan Castle, Ffestiniog power station (guided tours) and the cavernous slate mine at Llechwedd (you are conveyed by train through Victorian scenes underground).

TAN-Y-CYTIAU

South Stack, Anglesey, LL65 1YH   Tel: 01407 762763

West of Holyhead. Nearest main road: A5 from Holyhead to Bangor.

C D PT

7 Bedrooms. £18.50 (less for 2 nights or more). Most have views of sea. No smoking.
Dinner (by arrangement). £13 for 3 courses and coffee, at 7pm. Vegetarian or other special diets if ordered. No smoking. **Light suppers** if ordered.
1 Sitting-room. With TV.
Large garden
Closed from November to February.

On Holy Island (now linked by causeway to the Isle of Anglesey), St Cybi founded a monastery in the 6th century: hence the island's name. But the name of this house is even older, taken from that of the nearby prehistoric hut circles now being excavated. It is spectacularly placed, looking across the sea towards Ireland (day trips to Dublin by catamaran).

South Stack is a craggy promontory with lighthouse (1806, open to the public) presiding over a heritage coastline and some very nice beaches. It is a great place for birdwatching in early summer, sailing and golf; and on the island there are a permanent exhibition of Tunnicliffe's celebrated bird paintings, a sea zoo, and a big RSPB reserve.

The house itself was built in 1915 as a holiday home for Lady Antonia Williams of Bodelwyddan Castle. Now it is a guest-house run by the Keatings, who welcome visitors to share this unique site with them. Huge picture-windows make the most of the wonderful views (Snowdon is visible in one direction). A typical meal: mushroom soup, sweet-and-sour pork, home-made meringues (with choices of starters and desserts).

Readers' comments: Lovely setting. Nicely appointed rooms. Lovely place.

TY GWYN HOTEL

C D M P T S X

Betws-y-Coed, Conwy, LL24 0SG   Tel/Fax: 01690 710383 or 710787
On A5 from Betws-y-Coed to Llangollen.

13 Bedrooms. £17–£40 (less for 6 nights or more). Bargain breaks. Some have some or all of the following: own bath/shower/toilet; TV; views of river; balcony (one).
Dinner. £17.95 for 3 courses and coffee, at 7–9pm. Vegetarian or other special diets if ordered. Wine available. **Light suppers** if ordered.
1 Sitting-room. With TV. **Bar** with open fire.
Small garden

A former coaching inn, Ty Gwyn ('white house'), although on a road, has quiet bedrooms at the back. Sheila Ratcliffe has a flair for interior decoration, and every bedroom – small or large – is beautiful, many with en suite bathrooms (prices vary accordingly). The most impressive is an attic suite with four-poster and sitting-room; the most convenient for anyone with mobility problems, a pretty ground-floor room. There is an ancient, beamed bar (fire glowing in the old black range), a very comfortable sitting-room and another where Sheila sells antiques and old prints.

Cooking is done by chef Martin, the Ratcliffes' son, whose specialities include exotic dishes like pigeon with oyster mushrooms in Madeira, or Thai-style king prawns. These meals are served in a picturesque dining-room: antique furniture, crochet, crystal and silver on the tables. Even the bar snacks are interesting. Young children may stay free.

Readers' comments: Lovely setting, wonderful room. Good food. Very good, and a really beautiful attic suite. The highlight of the tour; have put real thought into vegetarian menu.

TY MAWR

C(12) D M S X

Llanegryn, Gwynedd, LL36 9SY   Tel/Fax: 01654 710507
North of Tywyn. Nearest main road: A493 from Tywyn to Dolgellau.

2 Bedrooms. £20 (less for 7 nights or more). Both have own shower/toilet; views of sea/river. No smoking.
Dinner (by arrangement). £12.50 for 3 courses and coffee, at 7pm. Vegetarian or other special diets if ordered. No smoking. **Light suppers** if ordered.
1 Sitting-room. With stove, TV, piano. No smoking.
Small garden

A little way inland, Ty Mawr ('big house') is perched among the hills at Llanegryn: stone-walled, slate-floored and oak-beamed but with a modern conservatory where you can sit to enjoy the view towards Aberystwyth 40 miles away. At your feet is the Dysynni Valley, world-famous for 'bird rock' where (uniquely) cormorants nest inland. What was once a milking-shed is now a sitting-room with coral walls and flowery frieze. Through its big glass doors you can step straight onto the terrace (ground-floor bedrooms, too, open onto this). Elizabeth Tregarthen is an accomplished cook of such meals as apple-and-parsnip soup, chicken-and-mushroom pie with a filo pastry crust, and baked peaches; and a hostess able to arrange for you to sea-fish, golf, ramble, or whatever takes your fancy.

All around are interesting villages and other sights. Derwenlas has attractive cottages on the Dyfi estuary; Ffwrnais (meaning 'furnace'), a watermill which once powered iron-making and a very beautiful waterfall; in the Dyfi National Nature Reserve is a mile-long nature trail; at Tre'r-ddol, a chapel with a museum of religion in Wales. Outside Machynlleth is the exceptionally interesting Centre for Alternative Technology.

Readers' comments: Made us so welcome. Lovely home.

TY MAWR FARM

Llanddeiniolen, Gwynedd, LL55 3AD   Tel/Fax: 01248 670147
North-east of Caernarfon. Nearest main road: A487 from Caernarfon to Bangor.

C D X

rear view

3 Bedrooms. £16–£22 (less for 3 nights or more). Bargain breaks. All have own bath/shower/toilet; TV.
Dinner (by arrangement). £12.50 for 3 courses and coffee, at 6–7pm. Vegetarian or other special diets if ordered. **Light suppers** if ordered.
2 Sitting-rooms. With open fire/stove, TV.
Large garden

Eighteenth-century Ty Mawr ('big house') is on a 150-acre farm where once-rare 'badger-faced' sheep are bred, now often bought as pets. Superb views of Snowdonia are one of the attractions of staying here; another is young Jane Pierce's cooking of such meals as prawns in puff pastry, lamb with baked leeks and other vegetables, and trifle. In two beamy sitting-rooms and elsewhere are a mixture of antiques and family possessions, pretty fabrics and colours, flowery armchairs grouped around a log stove.

One is in the heart of Snowdonia here, with Caernarfon in one direction and Bangor in the other. The rugged grandeur of the mountain passes is in complete contrast to the tranquil countryside around the farm, with wildflowers and birds in abundance. The island of Anglesey is soon reached; some of its sandy beaches sheltered and others open to Atlantic breakers, ideal for surfing. There are preserved railways – steam at Ffestiniog, rack-and-pinion up to Snowdon's summit; and, of course, some sensational castles – Caernarfon in particular, but also Beaumaris, Penrhyn and Conwy.

V

Y WERN

Llanfrothen, Gwynedd, LL48 6LX   Tel/Fax: 01766 770556
North-east of Porthmadog. Nearest main road: A4085 from Penrhyndeudraeth to Caernarfon.

C X

5 Bedrooms. £17–£20. Some have some or all of the following: own bath/shower/toilet. No smoking.
Dinner. £10 for 3 courses and coffee, at 7pm. Vegetarian or other special diets if ordered. No smoking.
1 Sitting-room. With stove, TV, piano. No smoking.
Large garden

Alder trees gave their name to Y Wern when it was built as a farm in the 17th century. It is a beamy house with homely furniture, deep-set windows, slate floors and stone inglenooks; the best hill views are to be had from the cottagey second-floor bedroom under the rafters. Paddy Bayley can tell you tales of the 18th-century *eisteddfod* bard Richard Jones, to whom there is a plaque over the front door, and of a local legal case which first made the reputation of a very young solicitor here – Lloyd George. Dinner is usually cooked by Tony (for instance, barbecued peppers, chicken in cider, and French pâtisserie) and is sometimes served on the terrace but usually in the dining-kitchen. Sheep, ducks and a rocky stream make a very special holiday for children.

The house is well placed for touring the beautiful Lleyn Peninsula and visiting such other sights as Portmeirion and Harlech Castle (splendid views of Snowdonia from the battlements).

Readers' comments: Memorable meals. Very peaceful and friendly. Shall certainly return.

V

NORTH-EAST WALES
(including Denbighshire, Flintshire and Wrexham)

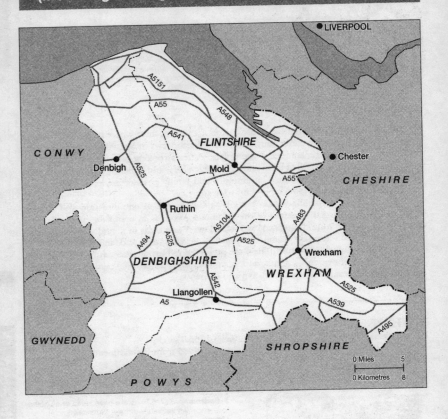

BUCK FARMHOUSE

C S

Hanmer, Wrexham, SY14 7LX   Tel: 01948 830339
South-east of Wrexham. On A525 from Wrexham to Whitchurch.

3 Bedrooms. £17–£18 (less for 3 nights or more). No smoking.
Dinner (by arrangement). £11.50 for 3 courses and coffee, at 7pm. Vegetarian or other special diets if ordered. Wine available. No smoking. **Light suppers** if ordered.
2 Sitting-rooms. With woodstove, TV. No smoking.
Small garden

In this 16th-century house a surprise awaits. For both Frances Williams-Lee and Cedric Sumner are much travelled and this is reflected in such meals as celery and almond soup; a pie of sweetcorn, leeks and red peppers (the range of vegetarian and vegan dishes is particularly wide) or perhaps pork with onions, tomatoes and garlic; and Nova Scotia bread-custard.

Meals are eaten in a low-beamed dining-room and prepared in a kitchen lined with jars of spices and other ingredients, through which visitors walk to reach the pretty little garden of herbs, rock plants, shrubs and lawn and the woodland (unless they prefer to sit after dinner in the snug sitting-room, well stocked with books).

Steep stairs lead to neat bedrooms furnished in cottage style: necessarily double-glazed as the house is, despite its rural surroundings, on a main road. (Bathrooms are downstairs.)

Readers' comments: Have returned 3 times. Fascinating house, interesting meals. Exceptional.

V

DEE FARMHOUSE

C D S

Rhewl, Denbighshire, LL20 7YT   Tel: 01978 861598
North-west of Llangollen. Nearest main road: A5 from Llangollen to Corwen.

2 Bedrooms. £18–£20 (less for 2 nights or more). Bargain breaks. Both have some of the following: own bath/shower/toilet; views of river. No smoking.
Light suppers if ordered. Vegetarian diets if ordered. No smoking.
2 Sitting-rooms. With open fire (in one). No smoking.
Small garden
Closed from November to March.

Perched high in the hamlet of Rhewl is Dee Farmhouse – so named because the River Dee lies just below its garden. Once this was a slate-miners' inn (hence the slate floor downstairs). From the garden come artichokes, spinach, herbs, etc. for the soups which form part of Mary Harman's light suppers (served in a huge dining-kitchen), as well as roses and lavender for her rooms. In the small and pretty sitting-room are antiques; cases of butterflies are in a beamy sitting-room upstairs which used to be a hayloft.

Nearby Llangollen is not only a walking centre but home of the international *eisteddfod* every July. National Trust properties in the area include Chirk Castle (best visited in May for the rhododendron display) and Erddig Hall. The abbey of Valle Crucis and horse-drawn boat trips on the historic canal are other local attractions.

Readers' comments: Fine old furniture, extremely comfortable. Concerned for one's comfort. Lovely view. Wonderful cook; pleasant, easy friendliness; house perfect; peaceful and restful.

V

EYARTH STATION

CDMX

Llanfair-Dyffryn-Clwyd, Denbighshire, LL15 2EE Tel: 01824 703643
(Fax: 01824 707464)
South of Ruthin. Nearest main road: A525 from Ruthin to Wrexham.

6 Bedrooms. £20 **to readers of this book**–£23 (less for 3 nights or more). Bargain breaks. All have some or all of the following: own bath/shower/toilet. No smoking. **Dinner.** £14.50 for 2 courses and coffee, at 7pm. Vegetarian or other special diets if ordered. Wine available. No smoking. **Light suppers** if ordered.
2 Sitting-rooms. With log stove, TV. No smoking in one. **Bar.**
Large garden

Ruthin is an attractive little town with half-timbered houses and a crafts centre. Just south of here, a disused railway station is now an unusual – and unusually excellent – guest-house. It has been imaginatively converted and furnished by Jen Spencer. Outside, all is white paint and flowers. Ground-floor bedrooms have such touches as festoon blinds and canopied bedheads; some (more simply furnished) are in what were the porters' rooms. Excellent bathrooms (even a bidet). What was once the waiting-room is now a very large sitting-room (one of two) with a balcony just above the fields: big sofas, log stove and thick carpet make this particularly comfortable. The conservatory/dining-room – once the platform – overlooks a small, well-heated swimming-pool which gets the afternoon sun. Jen offers meals with such dishes as Welsh lamb in apricot sauce followed by apple and bramble pie.

Readers' comments: Excellent accommodation, and welcoming. Delightful lounge and grounds. Meals superb. One of the best places. Exceptional food, wonderful hosts.

For explanation of code letters and **V** symbol, see inside front cover.

Prices are per person sharing a room at the beginning of the year.

Private bathrooms are not necessarily en suite.

Complaints about matters which could not have been settled on the spot will be forwarded to proprietors. Please enclose a stamped addressed envelope if you want the authors to acknowledge receipt of your complaint.

FRON HAUL

Bodfari, Denbighshire, LL16 4DY   Tel/Fax: 01745 710301
North-east of Denbigh. Nearest main road: A541 from Denbigh to Mold.

C D S X

3 Bedrooms. £17.50 (less for 3 nights or more). Bargain breaks. Some have some or all of the following: own bath/shower/toilet; TV; balcony. No smoking.
Dinner (by arrangement). £10.50 for 3 courses and coffee, at 8pm. Vegetarian or other special diets if ordered. No smoking. **Light suppers** if ordered.
1 Sitting-room. With open fire, TV, organ. No smoking.
Large garden

Fron Haul ('breast of the sun') guest-house is perched high on the edge of the lovely Vale of Clwyd. Originally the home of a Victorian surgeon, it has balconies from which to enjoy the wonderful view – or you can relax in the sitting-room, conservatory or tea gardens. Bedrooms are comfortable but homely, and the house is much used by long-distance walkers – it is on the Offa's Dyke path.

Gwladys Edwards provides an à la carte choice for dinner, with such dishes as salmon, steak or lamb from Fron Haul's farm. (Lunches too. Bread and cakes are home-made.)

Northward is St Asaph, with Britain's smallest cathedral; and at Dyserth, there is a spectacular waterfall and a stately home (Bodelwyddan Castle) with fine gardens – it is an out-station of London's National Portrait Gallery.

Readers' comments: Excellent food (super sweet trolley!). Made very welcome and nothing too much trouble. Stayed on numerous occasions. Unfailingly helpful. Comfort and food memorable.

V

THE MOUNT

Higher Kinnerton, Flintshire, CH4 9BQ   Tel/Fax: 01244 660275
South-west of Chester (England). Nearest main road: A55 from Chester to Conwy (and M56, junction 16).

C(12) D PT

3 Bedrooms. £19–£22 (less for 3 nights or more). All have own bath/toilet; TV. No smoking.
Dinner (by arrangement). £14 for 4 courses and coffee, at any agreed time. Vegetarian or other special diets if ordered. No smoking. **Light suppers** if ordered.
1 Sitting-room. With open fire, TV, piano. No smoking.
Large garden

Because of Rachel Major's enthusiasm for gardening, among the attractions of staying here are the fine grounds (sometimes open under the National Gardens Scheme) with herbaceous beds, flowering shrubs and cedar and other trees as mature as the early Victorian house itself. The garden also supplies fresh produce for the table.

Rooms are spacious, with (for instance) yellow panelling as the background to a Sheraton sideboard and ancestral portraits; and a prettily carved fireplace as the focal point in a very long, coral-walled sitting-room. Guest often relax among the plumbago in the conservatory or (more energetically) on the croquet lawn or tennis court, with views of the Peckforton Hills in Cheshire beyond.

For dinner, Rachel (a cordon bleu cook) often serves game, but her repertoire is large. Her other accomplishment is canvaswork, of which there are examples around the house.

V

PLAS PENUCHA

C S X

Caerwys, Flintshire, CH7 5BH   Tel: 01352 720210
North-west of Mold. Nearest main road: A55 from Chester to Conwy.

4 Bedrooms. £18.50 (less for 4 nights or more). Bargain breaks. Some have own shower/toilet. No smoking.
Dinner (by arrangement). £11 for 4 courses and coffee, at 7pm. Vegetarian or other special diets if ordered. No smoking. **Light suppers** if ordered.
2 Sitting-rooms. With open fire/stove, TV, piano. No smoking in one.
Large garden

Nêst Price is a harpist and violinist who used also to run the North Wales Music Festival; and this is her ancestral home. Spanish gold financed the original building (sited on top of a spring), home of one of Elizabeth I's buccaneers, but it has been much added to and altered by successive generations.

In the main room, there is a genial greeting, *Aelwyd a Gymhell*, carved on the oak beam across the fireplace: it means 'A welcoming hearth beckons'. Very appropriate in this hospitable house! There is another sitting-room (with built-in log stove), the blue in its oriental rugs on the polished wood-block floor matched by the blue damask sofas; books line one wall and Elizabethan panelling another. Bedrooms are attractive and comfortable; and Nêst is an excellent cook of such meals as soup; rack of Welsh lamb; syllabub; Welsh cheeses. Outside is a large garden, with a view towards the Clwydian Hills.

V *Readers' comments:* First-class atmosphere, facilities, food and comfort.

WYNN HALL

C(12) **PT S**

Penycae, Wrexham, LL14 1TW   Tel: 01978 822106
South-west of Wrexham. Nearest main road: A483 from Wrexham to Chirk.

3 Bedrooms. £17–£19 (less for 2 nights or more). One has own shower/toilet; TV (in all). No smoking.
Light suppers if ordered.
2 Sitting-rooms. With open fire, TV. No smoking.
Large garden

Construction of this historic house was completed – by a Roundhead officer – in the year that Charles I was beheaded (the date, 1649, is on the façade). The gables have decorative timbering, the front door great wrought-iron hinges. The Wynns were Nonconformists who, during the years of persecution, held secret religious meetings here.

The Hall remained in the same family's hands until Elian and Ian Forster came here in 1970 – by which time the ancient house was almost falling apart. Gradually they restored it, adding oak furniture to rooms that have exposed wall-timbers, stone inglenooks and low ceilings. Up the oak stair with its original finials are beamed bedrooms, one with a locally made patchwork duvet. The bathroom is excellent.

From the dining-room one can step straight into the garden with its winding lawn, badminton and croquet. Some guests enjoy the company of the dogs, others Ian's classic cars.

Readers' comments: All rooms delightful – large, beautifully decorated and furnished. Owners very friendly and go to great lengths. It really is something special.

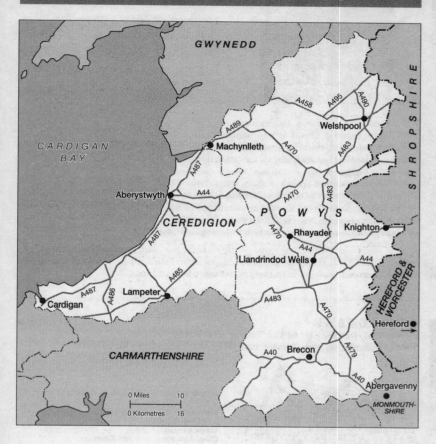

MID-WALES
(including Ceredigion and Powys)

Houses which accept the discount vouchers on page ii are marked with a
V symbol next to the relevant entries.

ABERYSCIR OLD RECTORY

C S

Aberyscir, Brecon, Powys, LD3 9NP   Tel: 01874 623457
West of Brecon. Nearest main road: A40 from Brecon to Sennybridge.

3 Bedrooms. £20 (less for 7 nights or more). Bargain breaks. All have some or all of the following: own bath/shower/toilet; TV. No smoking.
Dinner. £10 for 3 courses and coffee, at 7pm. Vegetarian or other special diets if ordered. No smoking.
1 Sitting-room. With piano. No smoking.
Large garden

Well tucked away in the hills, this Victorian stone house, standing in large grounds, has been furnished by Elizabeth Gould to high standards of comfort and solid quality. Bedrooms are particularly attractive, two with windows on two sides and very lovely views. Dinners include generous quantities of such dishes as smoked haddock ramekins, beef Stroganoff and Elizabeth's Malibu dessert – coconut liqueur combined with tropical fruits and whipped cream. Afterwards, there are velvet chairs and a chaise longue in the green sitting-room from which to enjoy the views or occasionally watch Elizabeth use her New Zealand spinning wheel.

The Brecon Beacons are the highest mountains in South Wales, with several peaks over 2000 feet. To the south, the underlying rock is limestone or millstone grit, producing different scenery and a multitude of cave systems, gorges and waterfalls.

Readers' comments: Outstanding value, lovely scenery, food and people. Wonderful accommodation and food. Exceptionally generous portions. Excellent. Most restful. Absolutely spotless, food delicious and attractively presented, warm welcome.

ARGOED FAWR

C(14) S

Llanwrthwl, Powys, LD1 6PD   Tel/Fax: 01597 860451
South of Rhayader. Nearest main road: A470 from Rhayader to Builth Wells.

4 Bedrooms. £16–£17 (less for 4 nights or more). No smoking.
Light suppers by arrangement.
1 Sitting-room. With TV. No smoking.
Large garden
Closed in November and February.

In the 18th century this house was owned by James Watt of steam-engine fame. Overlooking the River Wye, it is now the home of Maureen Maltby; and although old features have been retained – such as a ham-rack, slab floors and slate hearths – every room is comfortable and immaculate; the bathroom is excellent. Breakfast choices may include kidneys, black pudding or Ayr haddock. Supper is a help-yourself buffet of such things as chicken, salmon, quiches and pâtés. Water comes from a pure spring and there is an exceptional garden.

The region south of Rhayader has some spectacular areas. Take, for instance, a little road north of Llanwrthwl, high over the mountains. This began when Cistercian monks making their way from the distant abbey of Strata Florida to that of Cwmhir established a long footpath which became known as the Monks' Trod – a delight to walkers today because, ascending to open moorland at 1600 feet, it passes through an area of true wilderness with superb views as you go. Rare birds nest here (there is an RSPB sanctuary).

V *Readers' comments:* Delightful. Nicest ever visited. Breakfast fit for a king.

BRON HEULOG
Waterfall Road, Llanrhaeadr-ym-Mochnant, Powys, SY10 0JX
Tel: 01691 780521
North of Welshpool. Nearest main road: A483 from Welshpool to Oswestry.

C P T S X

3 Bedrooms. £19–£21. Bargain breaks. All have own shower/toilet; TV. No smoking.
Dinner (by arrangement). £12 for 3 courses and coffee, at 7pm. Vegetarian or other special diets if ordered. Wine available. No smoking. **Light suppers** if ordered.
1 Sitting-room. With open fire. No smoking.
Large garden

There is a very lovely drive through hills, moors and woods from Bala to the Tanat Valley. Here, on the way to the country's highest waterfall, is this handsome stone house of 1861 which, as its name (*bron*) suggests, is on a hillside.

Karon and Ken Raines have decorated the house to an immaculate standard. Period furniture, pine shutters and a fine Chinese carpet complement Ken's collection of militaria in the rosy sitting-room; original prints line the elegant curving staircase. Bedrooms are named after the flowers suggested by their colour schemes; one has a four-poster. The shower-rooms are excellent. A typical meal: Stilton soup, French lamb casserole, and flambé bananas.

Readers' comments: Food delicious, hosts friendly yet discreet. House beautiful, wonderful view, standard of decor the highest, meals excellent value. Superb food; lovely hosts, generous with their time. Pleasant room, quiet and comfortable. Absolutely delightful.

V

BRONIWAN
Rhydlewis, Llandysul, Ceredigion, SA44 5PF   Tel/Fax: 01239 851261
North-east of Cardigan. Nearest main road: A487 from Cardigan to Aberaeron.

C(8) D S X

3 Bedrooms. £18–£20 (less for 7 nights or more). All have some or all of the following: own bath/shower/ toilet. No smoking.
Dinner. £10 for 3 courses and coffee, at 7.30pm. Vegetarian or other special diets if ordered. No smoking. **Light suppers** if ordered.
1 Sitting-room. With log stove, TV. No smoking.
Large garden

Within easy reach of National Trust beaches, on a rocky hillside stands this ivy-clad, grey stone house, built in 1867, with much use of pitch-pine.

Carole and Allen Jacobs combine organic farming with teaching English as a foreign language. They have Aberdeen Angus beef-cattle, hens and a vegetable garden. The rooms are very attractive with, for instance, striped wallpaper, Welsh tapestry bedspreads, watercolours, books and old Staffordshire pottery figures.

A typical dinner: watercress soufflé, home-raised beef (with garden vegetables), pears in white wine.

Broniwan is well placed for a holiday full of varied interest. In one direction is the long sandy coastline around great Cardigan Bay, dotted with such pleasant little fishing villages as Aberaeron and Llangranog and with seals and dolphins to be seen; inland are hill walks among gorse and heather where butterflies and buzzards fly. There are old market towns along the bank of the River Teifi and coracle-fishing and the Welsh Wildlife Centre at Cenarth.

Mid-Wales

BRYNARTH
Lledrod, Ceredigion, SY23 4HX   Tel: 01974 261367
South-east of Aberystwyth. Nearest main road: A485 from Tregaron to Aberystwyth.

7 Bedrooms. £17–£20 (less for 3 nights or more). Most have some or all of the following: own bath/shower/toilet.
Dinner (by arrangement). £10 for 3 courses and coffee, at 7–7.30pm. Vegetarian or other special diets if ordered. Wine available. **Light suppers** if ordered.
1 Sitting-room. With open fire, TV. **Bar.**
Large garden

A very pretty group of white stone buildings, three centuries old, encloses a big courtyard with lily-pool, flowering shrubs and benches of stone and timber – inviting one to linger. Around are seven acres of grounds.

Inside the guest-house is a sitting/dining-area where the slate-tiled floor and stone walls are complemented by old pews and a chunky pine table. There is a small bar adjoining this; and an inglenook with a large, open log stove.

Brenda Ball serves such meals as ratatouille, lamb fricassée (with egg and lemon sauce), and plum or apple pies, often using home-produced fruit, vegetables and eggs.

Attractive bedrooms have king-size double, or twin, beds with panelled bedheads and wardrobes, flowers painted on their doors, and stone walls. There is also a games room.

Readers' comments: We give them the highest marks. Could not have been happier with food and accommodation. A delightful setting. Delightful. Glorious and remote setting.

V

Mid-Wales

BURNT HOUSE
C(12) **D S**
Trelydan, Powys, SY21 9HU   Tel: 01938 552827
North of Welshpool. Nearest main road: A490 from Welshpool to Guilsfield.

2 Bedrooms. £17. Bargain breaks. One has own bath/toilet.
Dinner. £10 for 3 courses and coffee, at 7pm. Vegetarian or other special diets if ordered. **Light suppers** if ordered.
1 Sitting-room. With open fire/stove, TV.
Large garden
Closed from December to February.

Not far from the Georgian market town of Welshpool is mediaeval Burnt House. Above a big, open-plan sitting/dining-room with ample sofas are two attractive bedrooms. One – in the oldest part of the house – has exposed timbers and pretty walnut beds. The other has a view of the Berwyn Mountains; its bathroom is outstanding – textured tiles around the built-in bath. Summer visitors see the garden at its best: Tricia Wykes won the 'Wales in Bloom' award for hotels, pubs and guest-houses throughout North Wales in 1994 and 1996 (runner-up in 1992). Tricia used to cook cakes professionally and so, after perhaps home-made pâté and pork fillet in a sauce of cream and sherry, one may be offered a gâteau or a tempting meringue confection.

Trelydan is very near to the English border, Offa's Dyke and the Shropshire towns of Oswestry and Shrewsbury. In the opposite direction lie lakes Vyrnwy and Bala.

Readers' comments: Lovely old house. Hospitality and cuisine excellent. Truly marvellous. Enjoyed every minute. Excellent value for money. Delightful place, peaceful and so comfortable. Cottage warm, welcome equally so; dinners delicious.

V

CWMLLECHWEDD FAWR

Llanbister, Powys, LD1 6UH Tel/Fax: 01597 840267
North of Llandrindod Wells. Nearest main road: A483 from Llandrindod Wells to Newton.

2 Bedrooms. £18. Bargain breaks. Both have own bath/shower/toilet; TV (on request). No smoking.
Dinner (by arrangement). £10 for 3 courses and coffee, at 8pm. Vegetarian or other special diets if ordered. No smoking. **Light suppers** if ordered.
1 Sitting-room. With open fire, piano. No smoking.
Large garden
Closed in March and April.

Negotiating a twisting track, you turn a corner and suddenly Cwmllechwedd Fawr comes into view in the distance, a 180-year-old farmhouse perched alone on the hillside in a rugged valley. This working farm is the peaceful and stylish home of John Underwood, a former antiquarian bookseller, and John Rath, a distinguished opera singer. Also in residence are numerous cats, two dogs, chickens and geese. Truly remote, so walking shoes and wellies are useful in bad weather.

Now completely refurbished, bedrooms, both with lovely country views, have teak floors with kilim rugs and modern lithographs on the walls. Afternoon tea is offered on the terrace in warm weather, where later you may be served such dinners as cold cucumber and yogurt soup, home-grown lamb, and delicious home-made ice cream to finish. In colder weather, dinners indoors are candlelit, in a dining-room with a great Welsh dragon painted above the hearth. The adjoining sitting-room, shared with the hosts, has pale lime-green sofas, contemporary paintings and plenty of local information to help plan your days out.

V

DYSSERTH HALL

by Powis Castle, Welshpool, Powys, SY21 8RQ Tel/Fax: 01938 552153
South of Welshpool. Nearest main road: A483 from Welshpool to Newtown.

4 Bedrooms. £19–£21 (less for 3 nights or more). Some have own bath/shower/toilet. No smoking.
Dinner (by arrangement). £15 for 3 courses and coffee, at 7.30–8pm. Vegetarian or other special diets if ordered. Wine available. No smoking. **Light suppers** if ordered.
1 Sitting-room. With open fire, TV, piano. No smoking.
Large garden
Closed from December to February.

A crag of red rock and a moat provided strong defences for 13th-century Powis Castle, from which the princes of Powis ruled much of Wales. The management of their descendants' estates was in the hands of Paul Marriott until he retired. His 18th-century manor house is close to the castle (now NT).

Paul and Maureen's elegant home is furnished with fine antiques, well-chosen wallpapers and fabrics – delicate clematis paper in one bedroom, blue brocade on the walls of the dining-room, for instance. There are good paintings everywhere. From a paved terrace with rosebeds one can enjoy the view across the Severn Valley to Long Mountain. (Tennis court in the grounds.)

Dinner may be a candlelit meal of avocado and prawns, Welsh lamb, meringues or, possibly, local cheeses. Vegetables come from the Victorian kitchen garden.

Readers' comments: Warm and welcoming, dinner very good. Wonderful comfort.

THE FFALDAU
D P T X

Llandegley, Powys, LD1 5UD   Tel/Fax: 01597 851421
East of Llandrindod Wells. Nearest main road: A44 from Kington to Rhayader.

4 Bedrooms. £20–£24. Bargain breaks. All have some or all of the following: own bath/shower/toilet; TV. No smoking.
Dinner. £15–£18 for 2–3 courses and coffee, at 7.30pm. Vegetarian or other special diets if ordered. Wine available. No smoking. **Light suppers** if ordered.
2 Sitting-rooms. With log fires, TV. No smoking in one. **Bar.**
Large garden

Roses climb up stone walls, rustic seats overlook beds of heather. Ffaldau ('sheepfold') began life around 1500 as a long-house. The Knotts transformed the house and gave it an ever-widening reputation for fine food.

Old features have been retained and restored, and upstairs one can see the cruck construction of the house. Mullioned windows are set into the stone walls, a log stove stands on an old inglenook hearth. In the 'Victorian' dining-room the tables might be spread with linen cloths exquisitely embroidered by Sylvia's grandmother.

For dinner one might choose langoustine packets with cucumber sauce or avocado and courgette soup; glazed poussins with pine kernels and grapes; apple shortcake with Calvados cream. Most menus include organic meat, and there is a wide list of wines.

Readers' comments: Family most welcoming and helpful. Food excellent and imaginative. Perfect hosts, food outstanding. A real jewel. Beautiful surroundings, meal superb. Epitomized our idea of a very well run, delightful country hotel. Superlative after superlative.

V

GLYNDWR
C S

Pen-y-Bont-Fawr, Powys, SY10 0NT   Tel: 01691 860430
North of Welshpool. Nearest main road: A483 from Oswestry to Welshpool.

3 Bedrooms. £16–£18 (less for 7 nights or more). All have some or all of the following: own bath/shower/toilet; TV (one). No smoking.
Dinner (by arrangement). £9.50 for 3 courses and coffee, at 7–7.30pm. Vegetarian or other special diets if ordered. No smoking. **Light suppers** if ordered.
2 Sitting-rooms. With open fire, TV. No smoking.
Small garden

In the beautiful and little-known Tanat Valley, Enid Henderson and her niece live at 17th-century Glyndwr, once the village inn. Behind is a pretty riverside garden with views of the Berwyn Mountains. Beams, low doorways and open fires give the house character. There is good home cooking – soup, Welsh lamb chops, and lemon pudding, for instance. One bedroom, with its own sitting-room, is in a self-contained annexe.

Lake Vyrnwy, nearby, is not only picturesque but surrounded by 5000 acres of woods. At the foot of grouse moors one finds Pistyll Rhaeadr, the country's highest waterfall. Small villages, inns and agricultural shows add to the interest of this very scenic area. Motoring is a traffic-free pleasure, alternating between roads that feel as if on top of the world – heather, gorse or bracken all around – and lanes that plunge deep into valleys.

Readers' comments: Superb meals, cosy and warm. Everything possible was done to make us feel at home.

V

TALBONTDRAIN

Uwychygarreg, Powys, SY20 8RR   Tel: 01654 702192

C D PT(limited) **S**

South of Machynlleth. Nearest main road: A489 from Machynlleth towards Newtown.

4 Bedrooms. £13–£20 (less for 6 nights or more). Bargain breaks. Some have own bath/shower/toilet. No smoking.
Dinner (by arrangement). £11 for 2 courses and coffee, at 7.30pm. Vegetarian or other special diets if ordered. No smoking. **Light suppers** if ordered.
1 Sitting-room. With open fire, pianola. No smoking.
Large garden

Hilary Matthews used to live in London before restoring this remote, slate-floored house, high in the hills, furnishing it very simply – for people who travel light – but with attractive colours and textures. No car is needed here: Hilary will book a taxi at Machynlleth station to drive you up her long, twisting lane; and she provides particularly well for children. She serves such two-course meals as bacon-and-leek flan with vegetables, followed by nectarines in a creamy sauce. Occasionally she does fungus identifying (and cooking) weekends or others on map-reading, singing, story-telling, etc. Her breakfasts feature Welsh specialities: for example, 'Glamorgan sausage', a type of cheese croquette. Some guests enjoy her excellent pianola as an after-dinner treat. Talbontdrain (its name means 'thorn tree at the end of the bridge') is in a varied area of woodland, waterfalls, moors and sheep pastures; utterly peaceful. Around the house are goats, wagtails and chickens; inside are warmth and comfort.

Readers' comments: Friendly; good food and company; extremely comfortable. Beautifully situated. Very friendly and interesting. Enriching atmosphere, beautiful environment.

TREWALTER HOUSE

Llangorse, Powys, LD3 0PS   Tel/Fax: 01874 658442

C

East of Brecon. Nearest main road: A40 from Abergavenny to Brecon.

3 Bedrooms. £18–£22 (less for 2 nights or more). Bargain breaks. All have some or all of the following: own bath/shower/toilet; TV. No smoking.
Dinner (by arrangement). £10 for 4 courses and coffee, at 7.30pm. Vegetarian or other special diets if ordered. Wine available. No smoking.
1 Sitting-room
Large garden
Closed from mid-December to mid-January.

Victorian Trewalter House is the stone-built home of Jean Abbott, who has renovated and decorated it to very high standards: everywhere is immaculate. You can wake to a panoramic view of the Brecon Beacons from some rooms, and of the Black Mountains (across the neighbouring farmyard) from others. Jean's ornamental 'bits and pieces' decorate every room. For dinner (by candlelight) she serves such straightforward meals as melon, roast lamb, raspberry charlotte russe, and Welsh cheeses. (Reflexology sessions are available.)

This is superb walking country, even if you do not want to tackle the mountain paths. Forest trails are well way-marked; and there are guided walks, too. In addition, there are plenty of castles to visit (Y Gaer, for instance, was the Romans' largest inland fort), Brecon has a Norman cathedral, and in many villages are churches with fine rood-screens. Steam trains, craft workshops, waterfalls and the Big Pit Museum of Mining at Blaenavon are other attractions of the area.

TY CROESO HOTEL

C D P T S X

The Dardy, Crickhowell, Powys, NP8 1PU   Tel/Fax: 01873 810573

North-west of Abergavenny. Nearest main road: A40 from Abergavenny to Brecon.

8 Bedrooms. £20–£32.50 (less for 2 nights or more). Bargain breaks. All have own bath/shower/toilet; TV; views of river.
Dinner. £15.95 for 4 courses and coffee, from 7–9pm. Also à la carte. Vegetarian or other special diets if ordered. Wine available. **Light suppers** if ordered.
1 Sitting-room. With open fire, piano. **Bar.**
Large garden

The name means 'house of welcome', a far cry from its early Victorian origins as a workhouse. It was used as such up to the Second World War. Now it is run very professionally by Mandy and Ian Moore as a small hotel of character.

Bedrooms vary in size. The majority have magnificent panoramic views, for the hotel is perched on a hillside in the Brecon Beacons, above the River Usk. Rooms are individually furnished. Bath- and shower-rooms are very good, and single rooms as attractive as doubles. One huge and particularly elegant bedroom has a four-poster and a sitting-area.

The restaurant has stencilled decorations on some walls (one is of rugged stone) and pretty arrangements of dried flowers. A typical meal: avocado and grapefruit with coriander dressing; chicken breast in a plum and brandy sauce; syllabub of honey and ginger (several choices at each course). A 'Taste of Wales' dinner is also available.

Readers' comments: Fresh home cooking. Cuisine almost as good as French. Ideal hosts; service, food and accommodation could not be better. Excellent menus and wine lists.

V

TYNLLYNE FARM

C(10)

Llanigon, Powys, HR3 5QF   Tel: 01497 847342

West of Hereford. Nearest main road: A438 from Hereford towards Brecon.

2 Bedrooms. £20. Both have own bath/shower/toilet; views of river. No smoking.
Dinner (by arrangement). £13 for 3 courses and coffee, at 7pm. Vegetarian diets if ordered. No smoking. **Light suppers** if ordered.
1 Sitting-room. With open fire, TV, piano. No smoking.
Large garden
Closed from mid-September to Easter.

Just within the Welsh border is this working dairy-farm with a big H-shaped house built in the year of the Spanish Armada: Tynllyne – 'house by the lake'. Low beams, three-foot-thick stone (or oak plank) walls and the turned balusters of the wide oak stair all date from that period. One bedroom has a high brass bed with broderie anglaise and a big carpeted bathroom. Outside is a terrace (with barbecue), an immaculate lawn, and a stream-and-woodland nature trail. For dinner, Lynda Price might serve (on local Black Mountain pottery) melon with port, venison, and chocolate mousse – always with many choices.

Three historic towns are equidistant from the farm: Brecon (ancient cathedral, antique and craft shops, museums and castle ruins), Hereford (mediaeval city at the heart of which is a very fine cathedral) and the former spa of Builth Wells in the lovely Wye Valley. Even nearer is 'book city', Hay-on-Wye. But for many the wide open spaces of the Black Mountains are a greater attraction.

Readers' comments: The best food I have tasted; beautiful bathroom.

UPPER TREWALKIN FARM

C(5) S

near Talgarth, Powys, LD3 0HA Tel/Fax: 01874 711349
East of Brecon. Nearest main road: A479 from Talgarth towards Crickhowell.

3 Bedrooms. £19.50 (less for 2 nights or more). Bargain breaks. All have own bath/toilet. No smoking.
Dinner (by arrangement). £12 for 4 courses and coffee, at 7pm (not Sundays). No smoking. **Light suppers** if ordered.
2 Sitting-rooms. With log-burner (in one), TV. No smoking.
Small garden
Closed from December to March.

The reputation of hospitable Meudwen Stephens has spread far and wide: she is often invited to do overseas tours promoting Wales and its food. So one thing of which you can be sure is a good dinner – such as courgette and tomato soup, lamb chops cooked in white wine and mushrooms (accompanied by garden vegetables), bread-and-butter pudding or spotted dick.

But there is more to Upper Trewalkin than this. In the 16th century it was a long-house (animals at one end, family at the other), built on a site previously owned by a Norman knight. It was updated in the 18th century, although many original features were retained.

From many rooms there are superb views of the Black Mountains. Some walls are of exposed stone, some attractively papered. At every turn are paintings by local artists.

The farm is in the Brecon Beacons National Park, an area of great interest to birdwatchers and walkers alike. Llangorse Lake is near and here, at the quieter end, grebes nest.

Readers' comments: Excellent home cooking, delightful hostess, comfortable accommodation. A gem.

SOME WELSH PLACE NAMES

Aber	River mouth	**Hafod**	Summer dwelling
Afon	River	**Hen**	Old
Bach/Fach	Little	**Hendre**	Winter dwelling
Bryn/Fryn	Hill	**Llan**	Parish
Cae/Gae	Field	**Llwyn**	Copse
Caer/Gaer	Fort	**Llyn**	Lake
Coed	Woods	**Mawr**	Big
Cwm/Gwm	Valley	**Mynydd**	Mountain
Dol	Bend	**Nant**	Valley
Dref/Tref	Town	**Pentre**	Village
Du	Black	**Plas**	Mansion
Dy/Ty	House	**Rhaeadr**	Waterfall
Eglwys	Church	**Rhos**	Moor
Gwyn/Wyn	White	**Ynys**	Island

SOUTH-WEST WALES
(including Carmarthenshire and Pembrokeshire)

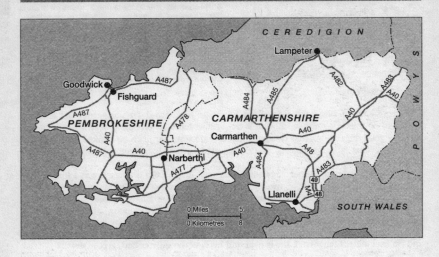

CAERNEWYDD FARM

CMPT

Pembrey Road, Kidwelly, Carmarthenshire, SA17 4TF Tel: 01554 890729
(Fax: 01554 891407)

North-west of Llanelli. Nearest main road: A484 from Llanelli to Carmarthen.

rear view

6 Bedrooms. £16–£17.50 (less for 3 nights or more). Bargain breaks. All have some or all of the following: own shower/toilet; TV. No smoking.
Light suppers if ordered. Vegetarian or other special diets if ordered. No smoking.
1 Sitting-room. With open fire, TV, piano. No smoking.
Large garden
Closed in December.

Despite its position on the road, all is peace once you are inside the house, for rooms are at the back. The huge sitting-room is where the stables used to be: its sliding glass doors open onto a sheltered, heated swimming-pool and it is furnished with handsome and ample modern sofas. There is much polished pine, bedspreads are of Paisley-patterned fabric (all are ground-floor rooms), and everything is neat as a new pin.

Margaret Beynon is willing to provide light suppers.

This would be a good choice for families wanting to enjoy the miles of clean, golden beaches along this coast, for walkers (who can follow footpaths on the cattle-farm's own land) or for birdwatchers who want to visit the nearby wildfowl reserve.

Readers' comments: Very good value. Enjoyed all and much more than promised in your book. Could not fault the accommodation and generous attention. Exceptionally high standard. Everything exceeded our expectations. A totally satisfying choice. Every comfort.

COACH HOUSE COTTAGE

CDPTS

The Square, Goodwick, Pembrokeshire, SA64 0DH Tel/Fax: 01348 873660
North-west of Fishguard. Nearest main road: A40 from Goodwick to Haverfordwest.

1 Bedroom. £13. Has own TV; views of sea. No smoking.
Dinner (by arrangement). £8.50 for 3 courses and coffee, at times to suit guests. Vegetarian or other special diets if ordered. No smoking. **Light suppers** if ordered.
1 Sitting-room. With stove, TV. Piano. No smoking.
Small garden
Closed in December.

Tucked away behind Goodwick's small square is Elizabeth Maxwell-Jones's home, where there is a multitude of pictures, books and interesting objects.

One reaches it up 20 steps beside a rushing mountain brook and enters through a stable-type door, straight into the dining-kitchen. From the pretty little bedroom, with its pine-panelled walls and sloping ceiling, are hill views and a glimpse of the sea; the long-distance Pembrokeshire Coastal Path runs close by.

Elizabeth is an accomplished cook who serves, for example, cauliflower soup, excellent chicken Marengo, and summer pudding – all made with organic ingredients. Guests are offered tea and home-made Welsh cakes on arrival.

The cottage is conveniently situated a mere stone's throw from Fishguard Harbour (ferries to Ireland). The footpath up the side of the cottage leads to the old Pilgrim's Way from Cardigan to St David's, which takes in many ancient religious sites.

Reader's comment: Extraordinarily kind and considerate.

CWMTWRCH

C D M X

Nantgaredig, Carmarthenshire, SA32 7NY   Tel: 01267 290238 (Fax: 01267 290808)
North-east of Carmarthen. Nearest main road: A40 from Carmarthen to Llandeilo (and M4, junction 49).

6 Bedrooms. £20–£26 (less for 7 nights or more). Bargain breaks. All have some or all of the following: own bath/shower/toilet; TV.
Dinner. £19.50 for 4 courses and coffee, from 7.30pm. Vegetarian or other special diets if ordered. Wine available. No smoking. **Light suppers** if ordered.
2 Sitting-rooms. With open fire, TV. No smoking in one. **Bar.**
Large garden

The name of this farmhouse-turned-hotel means 'valley of the wild boar'. Nothing so wild now disturbs the peace of this civilized spot where Jenny Willmott and her husband have transformed a group of old farm buildings with great sensitivity. The restaurant has stone walls painted white, slate floor and boarded roof above. At one side, the kitchen is open to view; on the other is a conservatory overlooking the courtyard. The food is exceptional, with such dishes as individual quiches, fresh salmon or boned Barbary duck, and a flan of grapes among the choices. Bread is baked daily. All rooms have interesting and lovely objects, paintings and pottery (for sale). Bedrooms (full of character) are in the house or in former stables. There is a heated indoor swimming-pool.

Readers' comments: Marvellous. Food excellent. Helpfulness and friendliness had to be seen to be believed. First class. Good food, friendly hosts, comfort and quiet. Delicious dinner. Professionally run; cosy and tastefully decorated. One of the very best.

ERW HEN

C D S X

Pumpsaint, Carmarthenshire, SA19 8YP   Tel: 01558 650495
South-east of Lampeter. Nearest main road: A482 from Lampeter towards Llandovery.

3 Bedrooms. £15. Some have own shower/toilet. No smoking.
Dinner. £10 for 3 courses and coffee, at 7–8pm. Vegetarian or other special diets if ordered. Wine available. No smoking. **Light suppers** if ordered.
1 Sitting-room. With open fire, TV.
Large garden

From Pumpsaint, a long, devious track leads up into the hills, past the Roman gold mine, to this remote house, whose name means 'old acre'. This valley is an Area of Special Scientific Interest for its wildlife (especially birds of prey), and Roman remains abound.

The 400-year-old house has been furnished by David and Brenda Vockings with individuality: plum-coloured tiles and wallpaper, a carved Burmese table, prints of hawks, salvaged black and red quarry-tiles.

Dinners comprise such things as peppered mackerel, chicken chasseur (with four vegetables), and mandarin flan. Riding holidays (week-long or shorter) can be arranged.

This area is one of vast moorlands – sweeping up some 2000 feet or descending into marshes. There are wonderful views to be had from the heights where the meadow pipits and the larks sing and rare red kites soar high. Birds are far more numerous than humans here. Wooded valleys stretch towards a coast of fine beaches, cliffs and coves.

Reader's comment: Exceptional.

350

FFERM-Y-FELIN

Llanpumsaint, Carmarthenshire, SA33 6DA Tel/Fax: 01267 253498
North of Carmarthen. Nearest main road: A485 from Carmarthen to Lampeter.

3 Bedrooms. £18–£19 (less for 3 nights or more). Bargain breaks. All have own bath/shower/toilet; TV; views of lake (from one). No smoking.
Dinner (by arrangement). £10 for 4 courses and coffee, at 7–8.30pm. Vegetarian or other special diets if ordered. No smoking. **Light suppers** if ordered.
1 Sitting-room. With open fire, TV, piano. No smoking.
Large garden

Fferm-y-Felin, or 'mill farm', is the 18th-century home of Anne Ryder-Owen: a place of particular interest to birdwatchers. You can be told where to spot pied flycatchers, buzzards and even the rare red kite. Beyond the dining-room is a sitting-room so large that it has a fireplace at each end; pink, buttoned velvet sofas and a walnut piano contrast with rugged stone walls. Anne serves snacks or such meals as corn-on-the-cob, wild trout, and apple crumble; breakfast options include laverbread and cockles.

This would be a good place for a family holiday: the farmhouse stands in 15 acres of countryside, with a large lake and interesting waterfowl; there is a pet donkey as well as other livestock. Self-catering accommodation too, with meals provided in the main house if wanted.

Readers' comments: Wonderfully looked after. Food excellent and plentiful. Kind, considerate, welcoming. Truly spectacular holiday; one of the best meals I have ever had.

V

MANOR HOUSE HOTEL

Main Street, Fishguard, Pembrokeshire, SA65 9HG Tel/Fax: 01348 873260
Nearest main road: A40 from Haverfordwest to Fishguard.

6 Bedrooms. £20–£24 (less for 3 nights or more). All have own bath/shower/toilet; TV; views of sea.
Dinner. £15 for 3 courses and coffee, at 7–8.30pm. Vegetarian or other special diets if ordered. Wine available. No smoking. **Light suppers** if ordered.
1 Sitting-room. With open fire. **Bar.**
Small garden

In the main street of Fishguard (but with quiet rooms overlooking the sea at the back) is Manor House Hotel, built in the 18th century. Most rooms are spacious, with a good deal of 'thirties furniture and interesting objects around. In a room on the ground floor, antiques are for sale.

Austrian-born Beatrix Davies has given the small hotel a reputation for its food. There is always a wide à la carte choice that includes such dishes as mussel pâté; chicken cooked in a purée of plums, garlic and parsley; a syllabub of blackcurrants and sherry. From the garden (where you can take breakfast) there are fine views across the sea to Dinas Head.

Fishguard, a picturesque port, is on a coastline so spectacular that it has been designated a National Park: windswept and dramatic cliffs alternate with sunny, sheltered coves. The harbour for ferries to Ireland is actually at Goodwick, a little further along the bay.

V

MOUNT PLEASANT FARM

C S X

Penffordd, Pembrokeshire, SA66 7HY   Tel: 01437 563447
North of Narberth. Nearest main road: A40 from Carmarthen to Haverfordwest.

2 Bedrooms. £16 (less for 3 nights or more). No smoking.
Dinner (by arrangement). £9 for 4 courses and coffee, at 7pm. Vegetarian or other special diets if ordered. Wine available. No smoking. **Light suppers** if ordered.
1 Sitting-room. With TV. No smoking.
Small garden

For anyone tracing their family history, a stay at inexpensive Mount Pleasant Farm is recommended because Pauline Bowen is an expert on the subject. A warm, hospitable person, her small, beamed farmhouse of rugged stone is immaculate and comfortable. Good home cooking, and then relaxation in big armchairs of pink velvet. A typical dinner: soup, Welsh lamb, mixed fruit tart, and a selection of cheeses.

Fine views of the Preseli Mountains – superb when heather is in bloom – which offer moorland drives northward to Cilgerran where dramatic Norman castle ruins tower high above the River Teifi as it runs through a woody ravine. One might return via the coast, visiting picturesque Nevern and the many curiosities of its church (including a 'bleeding' yew), and the old port of Fishguard, sited on a fine bay with high cliffs around. To learn more about the area, one can visit the county museum (inside castle ruins) at the market town of Haverfordwest.

V

Readers' comments: Exceptional value. Very hospitable. Charming holiday, very helpful.

TREGYNON

M X

Gwaun Valley, Pontfaen, Pembrokeshire, SA65 9TU   Tel: 01239 820531
(Fax: 01239 820808)
South-east of Fishguard. Nearest main road: B4313 from Fishguard to Narbeth.

8 Bedrooms. £20 **(to readers of this book only)** –£34. Less for 7 nights or more. Bargain breaks. All have some or all of the following: own bath/shower/toilet; TV. No smoking.
Dinner. £16.95 for 3 courses and coffee, at 7.30–8.30pm. Wine available. No smoking. **Light suppers** if ordered.
2 Sitting-rooms. With open fire, piano. **Bar.** Smoking discouraged.
Large grounds

In the heart of the Pembrokeshire Coast National Park is something quite exceptional. Of all the places one could stay in Wales, this remote, 16th-century country farmhouse hotel, restored by Peter Heard, has some of the most spectacular scenery around it. Not far away are some of the sunniest sandy beaches in the country, renowned for their pure air.

Jane Heard's meals are imaginative and additive-free, with vegetarian options a speciality; and the wine list is outstanding. Speciality breads, sausages, traditionally smoked ham, cheeses and Tregynon's own spring water contribute to the experience of eating here. You can relax afterwards by a log fire in the beamed sitting-room which has a massive stone inglenook and button-backed chesterfields, with a snug stone-walled bar adjoining it. Some bedrooms are in the house, others in converted stone outbuildings – spacious, pretty and well equipped.

Readers' comments: Excellent hosts. Varied and original menus of excellent quality (best ice cream we have tasted). Nothing too much trouble. Comfortable accommodation and superb food. Hosts went out of their way to make us feel welcome. Excellent value.

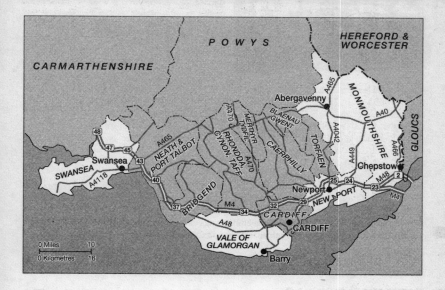

THANK YOU . . . to those who send details of their own finds, for possible future inclusion in the book. Do not be disappointed if your candidate does not appear in the very next edition. We never publish recommendations from unknown members of the public without verification, and it takes time to get round each part of England and Wales in turn. Please, however, do not send details of houses already featured in many other guides, nor any that are more expensive than those in this book (see page ix).

CROSSWAYS HOUSE

CDX

Cowbridge, Vale of Glamorgan, CF71 7LJ Tel/Fax: 01446 773171
North-west of Barry. Nearest main road: A48 from Bridgend to Cardiff (and M4, junctions 33, 34 or 35).

3 Bedrooms. £20 (less for 5 nights or more). All have some or all of the following: own bath/shower/toilet; TV. No smoking.
Dinner (by arrangement). £10 for 3 courses and coffee, at 8pm. Vegetarian or other special diets if ordered. **Light suppers** if ordered.
1 Sitting-room. With open fire.
Large garden

Crossways House is a rather grand place, built in 1921 by a local shipping magnate, who at the age of 55 married a 17-year-old girl (she promptly ran off with an Indian prince). This turreted country mansion of local stone is late Victorian Gothic in style – elaborate wood-carving and plasterwork abound, particularly in the sitting-room with its impressive barrel-vaulted ceiling and carved oak fire-surround. The present owner of the house, Anne Paterson, also has a seafaring connection – as a keen ocean racer, she twice crossed the Atlantic in a six-man crew.

Bedrooms are stylishly decorated in bold colours; one, looking out over six acres of woodland, has a jade, marble-effect wallpaper and frog-patterned tiles in the bathroom. There is a wide choice of Welsh specialities at breakfast, including such vegetarian options as home-made laverbread cakes and Glamorgan sausages (made with leeks and Caerphilly cheese). You may expect imaginative evening meals as Anne is cordon bleu trained.

Cowbridge is ideally placed for visiting historic Cardiff or further afield in Glamorgan.

FAIRFIELD COTTAGE

C(5) **PT S**

Knelston, Gower Peninsula, Swansea, SA3 1AR Tel: 01792 391013
West of Swansea. On A4118 from Swansea to Port Eynon (and M4, junction 47).

3 Bedrooms. £17 (less for 2 nights or more). TV (in one). No smoking.
Dinner. £12 for 4 courses and coffee, at 7pm. No smoking. **Light suppers** if ordered.
1 Sitting-room. With open fire, TV. No smoking.
Small garden
Closed in December.

The Gower peninsula is so scenic that there are few more attractive places. Knelston is roughly equidistant from north, west and south coasts.

Caryl Ashton's 18th-century home is a little white cottage made colourful by window-boxes, tubs and hanging-baskets of flowers. One steps straight into the sitting/dining-room from which a staircase rises between the joists to small but pretty, cottagey bedrooms. There is a very good bathroom.

One can take a complimentary aperitif by the inglenook fire or in the garden (it has a summer-house) before enjoying such a meal as gratin of haddock, roast beef, home-made lemon meringue pie, and a selection of cheeses. Fruit and vegetables come from local farms, and yogurt, Welsh cakes and scones are home-made.

Readers' comments: Very well kept and comfortable. Treated with particular care and love. Superb cook, wonderful hosts. All meals delicious; a most memorable experience. Friendly, helpful and very thoughtful. The best. House beautifully kept; extraordinarily kind.

HEATHFIELD

Nant-y-Derry, Monmouthshire, NP7 9DP   Tel: 01873 880675
South of Abergavenny. Nearest main road: A4042 from Abergavenny to Pontypool.

3 Bedrooms. £18–£20 (less for 4 nights or more). Some have some of the following: own bath/shower/toilet. No smoking.
Dinner. £12 for 3 courses and coffee, at 6.30–8.30pm. Vegetarian or other special diets if ordered. No smoking.
1 Sitting-room. With open fire, TV.
Large garden
Closed from December to February.

Midway between Abergavenny and the pretty town of Usk lies the hamlet of Nant-y-Derry and Heathfield, a Victorian house with great Wellingtonias standing tall in the garden. The comfortable accommodation in this house is well placed for exploring the Usk Valley and northwards into the Black Mountains.

Mary and John Pritchard are well travelled as John spent many years in the RAF, and they have plenty of ideas for local excursions. As well as walking and fishing, one can take a leisurely trip on the 'Mon and Brec' canal which hugs the mountainside above the valley of the River Usk, or perhaps explore the industrial heritage of the area at the Big Pit Mining Museum at Blaenavon.

Bedrooms in the house are pleasantly decorated and neatly furnished, and the dining-room (with countryside views) has a lovely old marble and tiled fireplace. Dinner might start with tomato and pepper soup, followed by Usk salmon and Mediterranean salad, and finish with lemon cheesecake.

Reader's comments: Excellent breakfast and delightful hosts, totally peaceful.

LAWNS FARM   C S

Grosmont, Monmouthshire, NP7 8ES   Tel: 01981 240298
North-east of Abergavenny. Nearest main road: A465 from Abergavenny to Hereford.

3 Bedrooms. £16–£21 (less for 4 nights or more). All have some or all of the following: own bath/shower/toilet; TV; views of river. No smoking.
Light suppers if ordered. No smoking.
1 Sitting-room. With stove, TV, piano. No smoking.
Large garden
Closed from December to February.

Standing at the summit of rolling terraced meadows which rise from the banks of the River Monnow, this rather splendid 17th-century manor house offers considerable comfort and breathtaking vistas. Ferneyhoughs have been here for over 100 years, and Edna and John have put much effort into creating a stylish and friendly atmosphere. Bedrooms are large and attractive. The double one, in duck-egg blue, has a fine old four-poster bedstead polished to a lustrous sheen, and views towards Grieg Hill and Grosmont Castle. Swagged chintz curtains in the sitting-room complement emerald-green sofas drawn around the fire. Breakfast seated in the bay window of the dining-room, looking out over unspoilt country-side, is the perfect way to start your day. Restaurant bookings and taxis can be arranged; and for a special meal, try the renowned Walnut Tree at Llanddewi Skerrid.

In an area rich in history, Grosmont Castle was once occupied by Henry III; and, with its two companions, Skenfrith and the White Castle, mounted guard in mediaeval times over the Golden Valley. There is now a lovely rural walk connecting the three.

V

OLD RECTORY

C(10) **D PT S X**

Reynoldston, Gower Peninsula, Swansea, SA3 1AD   Tel: 01792 390129
West of Swansea. Nearest main road: A4118 from Swansea to Port Eynon (and M4, junction 47).

3 Bedrooms. £18 (less for 2 nights or more). One has own shower.
Dinner (by arrangement). £10 for 3 courses and coffee, at times to suit guests. Vegetarian or other special diets if ordered. **Light suppers** if ordered.
1 Sitting-room. With open fire, TV, piano. No smoking.
Large garden

A short distance from Knelston, Reynoldston is a rather straggling village merging into the bracken-covered hills of Cefn Bryn ('ridge of hills'), a stretch of moorland where ponies roam free and yellow waterlilies brighten the pools. It is an area dotted with castle ruins, prehistoric burial chambers and other traces of a far-distant history. The Old Rectory is a handsome, grey, slate-roofed house, part 17th- and part 18th-century in origin, which Valerie Evans and her husband Michael have made into an elegant home, with guest bedrooms decorated in relaxing pastel shades.

The spacious and airy sitting-room has lovely old furniture and chintz-covered sofas and chairs grouped around the fireplace. French windows open onto the terrace where you may have breakfast in summer. Evening meals may start with lettuce soup, then tarragon-and-orange chicken, and gooseberry-and-elderflower soufflé to finish. The secluded garden is dominated by a magnificent Western Red Cedar, reminding one rather of an enormous and misshapen upturned umbrella-frame. Traditionally, it is the location for family wedding photos: bride, groom and guests perched among its branches.

V *Readers' comments:* Tastefully and comfortably furnished; nothing was too much trouble.

UPPER SEDBURY HOUSE

C D PT S X

Sedbury Lane, Sedbury, Monmouthshire, NP6 7HN   Tel: 01291 627173
East of Chepstow. Nearest main road: A48 from Chepstow towards Gloucester (and M48, junction 2).

6 Bedrooms. £16.50–£18.50 (less for 3 nights or more). Bargain breaks. Some have some of the following: own bath/shower/toilet; TV.
Dinner. £9.50 for 3 courses and coffee, at 7pm. Vegetarian or other special diets if ordered. **Light suppers** if ordered.
1 Sitting-room. With open fire, TV.
Large garden

Sedbury, not marked on all maps, is tucked between Chepstow and the Severn estuary – quite close to the Severn Bridge. In rural Sedbury Lane stands an old farm, Upper Sedbury House, with cottagey bedrooms; and also an attic flat, usually let for self-catering but Christine Potts is happy to do meals for those guests too. (A typical dinner, using garden produce: pears in tarragon mayonnaise, casserole of beef, fruit crumble.) There is a swimming-pool, unheated; badminton, etc.; and the Offa's Dyke footpath runs near the house.

In the immediate vicinity are Tintern Abbey's particularly beautiful ruins and the scenic splendour of both the Wye and the Usk valleys. Chepstow has an impressive Norman castle overlooking the harbour.

Also within easy driving distance are the Forest of Dean and historic Monmouth. Henry V was born in the castle, and Nelson stayed here – hence the naval temple on Kymin Hill, **V** commanding far views. Then there is Raglan, with spectacular castle remains nearby.

WENALLT FARM

Gilwern, Monmouthshire, NP7 0HP   Tel: 01873 830694

West of Abergavenny. Nearest main road: A465 from Abergavenny to Merthyr Tydfil.

8 Bedrooms. £16–£20. Bargain breaks. All have some of the following: own bath/shower/toilet; TV. No smoking.
Dinner (by arrangement). £11 for 4 courses and coffee, at 7.30pm. Vegetarian or other special diets if ordered. Wine available. No smoking. **Light suppers** if ordered.
2 Sitting-rooms. With open fire, TV. No smoking in one. **Bar.**
Large garden

The name, 'wooded hill', was given to this remote stone house when it was first built as a long-house: though most of it dates from about 1600, some parts are a good deal older. What is now a bar once housed cattle, and the bedroom above, hay to feed them; the sitting-room was a dairy. And from many windows in this hilltop house you can see for miles. Farmer Brian Harris made many improvements when he came here and in the new dining-room installed a stone fireplace from Tredegar House; he also converted a stone cow-byre to make more bedrooms.

There are scores of cups won at horse shows (Brian is now a judge at these), and other touches that give the house individuality – from a stuffed pheasant on a hearth to the beribboned fabrics in one of the bedrooms.

Meals are well above average – for example: stuffed courgette flowers (in season), a sorbet, turkey in walnut sauce, and the lightest of apple strudels.

Readers' comments: Friendly and helpful. Food excellent. Our spacious room was furnished with lovely antiques. Enjoyed so much that I extended my stay. Food and service excellent.

V

WEST USK LIGHTHOUSE

Lighthouse Road, St Brides Wentlooge, Newport, NP1 9SF   Tel: 01633 810126 or 815860 (Fax: 01663 815582)

South-west of Newport. Nearest main road: A48 from Cardiff to Newport (and M4, junction 28).

5 Bedrooms. £18–£34 (less for 4 nights or more). Some have some or all of the following: own shower/toilet; TV; views of sea/river. No smoking.
Dinner (by arrangement). £15 for 3 courses and coffee, at 7pm. Vegetarian diets if ordered. No smoking. **Light suppers** if ordered.
1 Sitting-room. With open fire, TV, piano. No smoking.
Large garden

The ex-lighthouse is not tall as most lighthouses are, and considerably bigger in circumference. In 1821, it was on an island where the Severn and Usk run into the sea (since then land has been reclaimed). On one side the loudest sound is of the sea when the tide comes racing in, on the other only the occasional mooing cow can be heard. The walls are over two feet thick, with wedge-shaped rooms. From the slate-paved hall a spiral stair rises to the bedrooms, pleasantly but simply furnished. In the sitting-room are unusual rococo armchairs from Italy. There is a flat roof with seats from which to watch ships go by and the spectacular sunsets.

The house is run in an informal way by Frank Sheahan, with relaxation classes and aromatherapy sessions available – even a flotation tank. For meals, a short conventional menu.

Readers' comments: Charmingly and artistically furnished and very unusual; peaceful. An inspired conversion. Friendly and open-minded host. Location excellent.

V

WYE BARN

PT(limited) **S**

The Quay, Tintern, Monmouthshire, NP6 6SZ   Tel: 01291 689456
North of Chepstow. Nearest main road: A466 from Chepstow to Monmouth.

3 Bedrooms. £20–£22 (less for 7 nights or more). All have some or all of the following: own shower/toilet (one); TV; views of river. No smoking.
Dinner. £13 for 4 courses and coffee, at 7pm. Vegetarian or other special diets if ordered. No smoking.
1 Sitting-room. With open fire, TV. No smoking.
Small garden

Perched right on the river bank, the house is occasionally islanded when the Wye's spring tides rise 20 feet (which is why the house itself is built up, with steps to the door).

From an exceptionally pretty garden, one steps through French doors into a pleasant sitting-room of soft blues and greys which complement the fireplace of grey stone quarried in the Forest of Dean. Because Judith Russill used to work for Britain's most celebrated furniture designer, John Makepeace, she has a number of very lovely and unusual pieces of furniture made by his students, to which she has added other finds of her own.

Bedrooms are just as attractive: one has floral curtains that match the pinkish carpet and Chinese silk pictures. From their windows are views of the River Wye.

Judith specializes in traditional Welsh cookery and you may be offered, for example, Anglesey eggs (they are cooked with leeks and cream en cocotte), Wye salmon with a herb sauce, and – the Welsh answer to cheesecake – a sour-cream and sultana tart.

V   *Reader's comment:* Excellent.

Houses which accept the discount vouchers on page ii are marked with a **V** symbol next to the relevant entries.

Facts (prices, etc.) at the top of entries are supplied by the proprietors themselves. While every effort is made to ensure that these are correct at the time of going to press, they may alter thereafter: please check when you book.

Addresses shown are to enable you to locate a house on a map. They are not necessarily complete postal addresses (though the essential post-code is included), and detailed directions for finding a house should be obtained from the owner.

To find the right accommodation in the right area at the right price, use an up-to-date edition of this book – revised every year. For an order form for the next edition (published in November), send a stamped addressed envelope with 'SOTBT 1999' in the top left-hand corner, to Explore Britain, Alston, Cumbria, CA9 3SL.